Praise for Joseph Califano's *Inside*

"*Inside* [is] Joseph A. Califano, Jr.'s vivid and frank memoir of his remarkable life. . . . The lesson of *Inside* is that power is neither inherently good, as some of Califano's contemporaries who felt they were doing God's work in Vietnam saw it, nor inherently evil, as the younger generation of liberals believed. It is a tool. Califano did far more good with it than bad.."
—Michael Tomasky, *The New York Times Book Review*

"This is the most revealing political memoir from a Washington insider since Katharine Graham's *Personal History* . . . a running theme of this frank autobiography is Califano's inner struggles to reconcile the demands of politics with the dictates of his Catholic upbringing. . . . In sum, this is a revealing self-portrait filled with vivid scenes from four decades near the center of American government."
—*Publishers Weekly* [starred review]

"Califano's book is a must-read for anyone interested in understanding American history in the latter part of the 20th century. It's full of golden tidbits. It's a terrific book."
—*The National Catholic Reporter*

"Califano, if not Yoda, is an Obi-Wan Kenobi among Democrats, his book filled with frank lessons about power, its dark pull as well as the good that can be done with it."
—Mike Danahey, *Chicago Sun-Times Red Streak Edition*

"This book is an extraordinary chronicle of recent times by someone truly on the inside. . . . It is a brilliantly personal account as well and perhaps that is why it resonates so strongly. This is an important book for lawyers to read. It is about success, challenge, disappointment, and resolve in the life of a fine human being."
—James D. Zirin, *The New York Law Journal*

"Engrossing. . . Faith and family are the cornerstones of Califano's life and the anchors of his book." —Steve Bennett, *San Antonio Express-News*

"This memoir is a testimonial to reflective, intelligent, courageous, Catholic living."
—*The Catholic News Service*

"Califano presents a fascinating memoir of his experiences inside high levels of government. . . . He also takes the reader inside his personal life. . . . Califano offers an engaging and often introspective firsthand account of the important events of post-World War II America. Highly recommended for most public libraries." —*Library Journal*

"Lyndon Johnson once told young Joe Califano that what he learned growing up in Brooklyn would help him navigate Washington better than a Harvard Law degree. It did. But Califano packed a lot of learning into a remarkable career, and in this engrossing memoir he shares the excitement and the heartache of the power he enjoyed. Califano has not written a this-is-what-I-did testimonial. With modesty and grace, he has crafted a rich, absorbing history of our times."   —Ken Auletta

"Califano's Inside gracefully juxtaposes tales of his public service (as a lawyer, a presidential adviser and a crusader against substance abuse) and private beliefs (an Italian American, Brooklyn-born boy who made good, he reveals how his Catholicism is central to all aspects of his life). Califano compellingly shares his views on politics, power and passion—he likens meeting his second wife Hilary to man's discovery of fire."
—the editors, *Town & Country*

"From Vatican II to Watergate, Califano makes his recollections intimate and interesting."   —*Booklist*

"Joseph Califano has lived many fascinating lives, and this important book takes you into each—growing up in hardscrabble Brooklyn, working alongside LBJ and Jimmy Carter, the experiences of a master Washington lawyer. Most inspiring of all is Califano's frank and sensitive account of how, after rising to the top of the American Establishment, he asked himself whether there was something missing in his life and decided to change it."   — Michael Beschloss

"In this richly documented and thoroughly engaging memoir . . . Califano writes about his struggle to understand and maintain his commitment to his family and his faith, an account that constitutes an important witness to the strength and challenges of contemporary Catholicism."   —Joseph O'Hare, S.J., *America Magazine*

"Joseph Califano's reflections upon this [his experience with abortion policy as HEW secretary] and his many other experiences, both public and private, are at once instructive and timely, especially in today's ecclesiastical and political environments."
—Fr. Richard McBrien, *National Catholic Reporter*

"In this memoir, it is the sensitive and frank writing that is most striking. Joe describes struggles between demanding public service and being a committed Catholic. His account of his courtship of the late William Paley's daughter, Hilary Byers (one of my favorite people), is moving, as are his revelations of his battles with cancer. This book reads like a novel. Give it a look."   —syndicated columnist Liz Smith

"The secrets keep spilling out . . . Califano names names."   —*The American Lawyer*

Inside

Joseph A. Califano, Jr.

INSIDE

A Public and Private Life

PublicAffairs

NEW YORK

BOOK DESIGN AND COMPOSITION BY JENNY DOSSIN. TEXT SET IN ADOBE MINION.

Library of Congress Cataloging-in-Publication Data
Inside: a public and private life / by Joseph A. Califano, Jr.
p. cm.
Includes index.
ISBN-13 978-1-58648-338-8
ISBN 1-58648-338-2 (pbk)
1. Califano, Joseph A., 1931– . 2. United States Dept. of Health, Education, and Welfare—Biog-
raphy. 3. Cabinet officers—United States—Biography. 4. United States—Politics and gov-
ernment—1945–1989. 5. Lawyers—United States—Biography. 6. Catholics—United States—
Biography. 7. Brooklyn (New York, N.Y.)—Biography.
I. Title.
E840.8.C35A3 2004
362.973'092—dc22
[B]
2003068977
10 9 8 7 6 5 4 3 2 1

For the Grandchildren:
Olivia and Nicky
Joe IV (Jack) and Pete
Brian, Russell, and Evan

For the parents who delivered them:
Mark and Margery
Joe and Beth
Brooke and Gene

And for the children who may deliver more:
Claudia
Frick

May you all believe in worthy causes
and have the courage to fight for them

Contents

Prologue

WHERE ELSE COULD a kid from Brooklyn—who played punch ball on the street in Crown Heights, who at age fourteen bought loosies at a penny a cigarette and sometimes stole cake from the back of a Dugan's Bakery truck on the same day he served Mass as an altar boy at St. Gregory's—walk the corridors of the Pentagon's E-Ring, the West Wing of the White House, and the secret tunnels of Capitol Hill, sit in the suites of Washington and Wall Street law firms and Fortune 500 corporate board rooms, and represent the *Washington Post* and the Democratic Party during Watergate?

Only in America.

There are moments when I still pinch myself to make sure I'm not dreaming the life I've led. Of course, there have been plenty of ups and downs: the high of being tapped by President Lyndon Johnson to be (as the *New York Times* put it) Deputy President for Domestic Affairs and the low of being fired by President Jimmy Carter as secretary of Health, Education, and Welfare.

Fortunately I was blessed with loving parents who brought me up American with a capital *A* and Catholic with a capital *C*—and instilled values that helped keep the peaks and valleys in perspective.

This is a memoir of growing up in Brooklyn and Washington, government and politics, medicine and the media, law and religion in a tumultuous era of political and social change so swift and sweeping as to be unthinkable when I graduated from law school in 1955. I write here of my role in the powerful currents that reshaped the contours of American life over the past half century and continue to do so to this day: the civil rights movement, the Great Society legislative explosion of the 1960s, the restructuring of the Democratic Party in the 1970s, the Watergate break-in, the miracles of medical science that revolutionized sexual conduct and blurred the line between Madame Curie and Dr. Frankenstein. These currents have swept over every American man, woman, and child, changing our culture, sparking hopes, ambitions, and fears, recasting the way we live and die.

When I went to Washington in 1961, I had no idea of the role I would play in shaping those changes, much less how the changes in my country, my church, my profession, and my party would change me.

Here is my story of life on the *Inside* during events that reshaped a nation.

Inside

CHAPTER 1

The Family

It was my first time on the South Lawn of the White House, 1 A.M. on Tuesday, July 13, 1965. We had just landed in President Lyndon Johnson's helicopter. I was returning from my first weekend at the LBJ ranch, where the President had asked me to be his special assistant for domestic affairs. As the President said goodbye, he smiled. "They tell me you're pretty smart, way up in your class at Harvard. Well, let me tell you something. What you learned on the streets of Brooklyn will be a damn sight more helpful to your president than anything you learned at Harvard."

THE BROOKLYN where I was born and grew up was less a borough of some 2.5 million people than a collection of lively parishes and neighborhoods nourished by Irish, Italian, and Jewish immigrants and first-generation parents. German-Americans, Polish-Americans, Spanish-Americans, White Anglo-Saxon Protestants, and African-Americans migrating from the south and Harlem lived there too. But in the early years of my life, two religions, Catholic and Jewish, and three ethnic heritages—Italian, Irish, Jewish—made up the world. Whatever their heritage, parents wanted their kids to be Americans with a capital *A*.

My father, Joseph Anthony, was born on November 6, 1899, in Brooklyn and baptized at the same church where his parents had married fourteen years earlier. He graduated from Commercial High on the border of Crown Heights and Bedford-Stuyvesant.

My mother, Katherine Eugenia Gill, was born on June 20, 1893, in Brooklyn. Fair skinned with blue eyes and blond hair, my mother graduated second in her class of eleven young Irish-American girls from St. Angela's Hall, a Brooklyn high school for Catholic girls. At her commencement on October 16, 1912, two essays received prizes: first prize went to "Emancipation of Woman," second to "Woman and Education." Eight years later, in 1920, the

Nineteenth Amendment to the Constitution would give women the right to the vote.

Mother and Dad met taking a night course in Italian at Fordham University with Professor Alexander Ausilli, pronounced "Oh Silly" to the amusement of the Irish girls in the class. Italians and Irish rarely mixed at that time. My parents laughed for years about Mother and one of her Irish girlfriends using the word "gondola" to describe a cannoli pastry the night they first dated.

When my father proposed, Mother's brothers and sisters, especially her older sister, May Gill Montague, were concerned that since Dad was a first-generation Italian-American, Mother would be marrying beneath herself. Mother's sister May, the matriarch of the family, nevertheless reluctantly approved the "mixed marriage" because Mother was already thirty-six. Five-foot-five Joe Califano and five-foot Kay Gill married late and for love on Thanksgiving Day, November 28, 1929, at St. Gregory's Church in Brooklyn.

I was born at 9:15 P.M. on May 15, 1931, at St. Mary's hospital in Brooklyn. Fifteen nights earlier, President Herbert Hoover had turned on the lights at the just-built Empire State Building, the world's tallest skyscraper. I was a blond, blue-eyed chubby baby, and though my hair was to turn to brown and my eyes hazel, that little fellow would never appear undernourished.

Despite trying, my parents were unable to have more children. Because of that and my mother's age—almost forty—at my birth, my father often said, "You are the only child God gave us and He gave us a good one." As far back as I remember, my parents and relatives treated me, as my cousin Jane Gill used to put it, like a "V.I.C."—very important child.

The first winter of my life was the worst of the Great Depression. Many people in Brooklyn slept with hot bricks at the end of their beds and stood on breadlines during the day. By the time I hit the terrible twos, Franklin Delano Roosevelt had succeeded Hoover as president and instituted the New Deal programs to combat the Depression, and Congress had repealed Prohibition, but my uncles continued to make their own red wine.

We lived in Crown Heights, just a few blocks from the border of Bedford-Stuyvesant, but we never thought of ourselves as living in Crown Heights.*

*Bedford, Stuyvesant, and Crown Heights were once three separate white, middle-class neighborhoods. After slavery was abolished in New York in 1827, blacks moved to the eastern part of Brooklyn, which was derisively called Crow Hill until years later when real estate salesmen changed the name to Crown

We thought of ourselves as living in St. Gregory's parish. My parents and relatives considered it a step above neighboring St. Teresa's parish, where, they said, the shanty Irish congregated.

Most of my aunts and uncles lived within walking distance of our apartment. Our building at 1030 Park Place, with the pretentious name "Brower Court" painted in Old English gold letters on the glass above the entrance doors, was six stories of red brick with several apartments on each floor. Our sixth-floor window looked out on Brower Park across the street, which housed the original Brooklyn Children's Museum in two converted mansions.[1] On early winter mornings, we were often awakened to the sounds of coal dropping into barrels from chutes on the side of trucks and of hot-water water radiators banging and whistling in our apartment. Other neighborhood noises included the ice truck, which came to fill each icebox, and the milkman, who delivered bottles of unhomogenized milk (with the cream floating on top) to each front stoop or apartment door.

We patronized the stores on Kingston Avenue: a pharmacist, small grocer (where butter and sugar were spooned out of tubs), butcher, and candy store with comic books and penny seltzers. On Nostrand Avenue, a few blocks away, we bought clothes and shoes and went to the tailor and shoemaker. All the merchants were either Italian or Jewish.

.   .   .

My mother told me many stories on those walks to the stores, in our small kitchen as she fixed dinner, and at night in my bedroom. She loved to tell of the four Gill brothers who came from England to the United States in the early 1800s. Three stayed in the Carolinas; the fourth, from whom Mother was descended, returned to England. Mother always considered it a mark of status that her family had some English roots and had lived in America for more than a hundred years.

As Mother recounted it, the four brothers were part of a staunchly Protestant family that lived in Devon during the mid-seventeenth-century

---

Heights to enhance property values. At the turn of the century, immigrants, primarily Italians and Jews from Europe, with a fair smattering of Irish, took over the area. By the 1930s, *Brooklyn Eagle* articles used the term Bedford-Stuyvesant to describe the area, which had growing "Negro" ghettos, slums, and racial tension.

reign of Oliver Cromwell, when virulent anti-Catholicism swept across England and Ireland. One evening during a violent storm, the family of the brother who had returned to England heard a terrible pounding on the door. Opening it, the Gills saw a huddled, soaking wet, shivering man. They took him in, stirred the fire to dry his clothing, and gave him food and drink.

The next day, the man said he was an Irish Catholic priest who had secretly entered England to provide sacraments to Catholics, but now there was a price on his head. He needed to reach France so he could flee to America. The Gills dressed the priest in a woman's clothing to hide him in their home for about a week, when they placed him on a boat to the safety of Normandy's coast.

The night the priest left, he profusely thanked the Gills and said, "I have nothing to give you except some books."

"And what books might they be?"

"These are books about my faith. They explain my beliefs. I want you to have them."

As he was leaving, the priest placed the books on the table over the protests of the Gills, who did not want to accept something so dangerous to them and precious to their visitor. Eventually curiosity took over, and surprisingly the family found the books to their liking. The Gills emigrated to the Galway region of Ireland, embraced the Catholic faith, and established themselves as businessmen, running hotels and operating ferries.

Grandfather Thomas Peter Gill was born in Brooklyn in 1845, one of seven children of Irish immigrants John Gill, a dry-goods merchant from Ballinalee in Longford, and Mary Fahey, who had emigrated from Eyrecourt in Galway. Grandfather Gill was christened in St. Peter's Church on Barclay Street in Manhattan, the same church that in 1805 baptized a converted Catholic named Elizabeth Ann Bayley Seton, a friend of the Gill family who would become the first American-born saint.

In 1862, at age fifteen, Grandfather Gill ran away and, claiming to be eighteen, joined the 47th Regiment of the New York State Militia to fight in the Civil War as a private in the Union Army. My Mother would show me Grandfather Gill's letters to his mother. "Dear Mother," he wrote on June 4, 1862, "I tend to my prayers as well as I can and am going to church every Sunday I can. Dear Mother do not send the *Metropolitan* here [the *Metropolitan*

Record was a New York diocesan paper that Archbishop John Hughes began in 1859]. It would be a laughing thing for the red-necked Protestants for I don't think there is a Catholic in the Company besides myself."

When the Civil War ended, in 1865, Grandfather Gill returned to Brooklyn, where he clerked in a law office, aspiring to be an attorney. Then doctors told him that he had tuberculosis and urged him to find work outdoors. He became a ship's carpenter and during the administration of President Grover Cleveland was chief clerk of the Brooklyn Navy Yard, responsible for handling mail, payroll, and invoices.

Grandfather Gill married Delia Veronica McQuade, also born in Brooklyn, and they had nine children, two of whom died in infancy. My Gill grandparents died before I was born, but my mother prayed for them every day.

For every one of those stories my mother told me about her English and Irish heritage and her father fighting in the civil war, she told me ten about "the Gill women."

My great aunt Marcella Gill at age eighteen entered the convent of the Sisters of St. Joseph and became Sister Mary Celestine Gill. Sister Celestine was committed to provide a first-class education to Catholic girls who, because of their religion and economic status, were denied admission to the finest private schools. In 1906 in Brooklyn, she founded St. Angela's Hall, an elementary and secondary school for women. In 1916, Sister Celestine started St. Joseph's College for Women in Brooklyn and served as its first dean.[2]

Mother was also proud of her father's cousins, Lucy and Elizabeth Gill, who were born in Galway, Ireland, and came to lower Manhattan in 1868. They entered the Ursuline convent, where Lucy became Mother Irene and Elizabeth became Mother Augustine. In 1886, they established "Board Classes" for women who wanted to become teachers, at the time the only Catholic teacher training for women in New York City. Mother Irene left New York City to start a college for Catholic girls in New Rochelle. Founded as the Ursuline Seminary for Girls in 1897 with ten boarders and sixty day students, it soon became the College of New Rochelle, the first Catholic college for women chartered by New York State. By 1929, with 157 graduates and 802 students, it was the largest Catholic women's college in the nation.[3]

·   ·   ·

For my mother—who wanted to be called "Mother," not "Mom" or any other colloquial appellation—the journey to Brooklyn began in Devon, England, and Galway, Ireland. For Dad—who preferred the warm informality of that name to either Father or Pop—the story began in Sorrento, Italy.

My grandparents, Giovanni Califano and Candida DeGennaro, met in Brooklyn, but both had emigrated from Sorrento, a town on the Italian peninsula. My paternal great grandparents, Antonio Califano and Mariarosalina Martino, lived in a house that still stands on Via Casa Nicca, a cobblestone street in Meta di Sorrento. At age twenty-four, Giovanni sailed from Naples to America on the *Caledonia* with his brother and 340 other Italians, arriving in New York on February 27, 1882. Like his father, Antonio, Giovanni had been a sailor who, as he told it, traveled to many nations around the world through many life-threatening storms, before settling in Brooklyn.

Grandpa Califano turned down an offer to head the grocery department at Abraham and Strauss, a premier Brooklyn department store, because he wanted to be his own boss. Instead, he opened a produce store and lived on the floor above it. Grandpa always had a pencil behind his ear to tally customers' bills on the back of their brown paper bags; he never had a cash register.

Grandpa Califano met my grandmother in a local bakery when the two of them were buying bread early one morning. The seventh of seven sons, he asked Candida DeGennarro to marry him on the seventh day after they met. He was twenty-eight; she was eighteen. She immediately accepted his proposal, over the objections of the Sessas, a banking family from Sorrento that had brought my grandmother to the United States to be their children's nanny. Giovanni and Candida were married in 1885, in Sacred Hearts and St. Stephen's, a small wooden Roman Catholic Church in South Brooklyn. They had nine children, three of whom died in infancy.

After Grandma Califano died in July 1939, Grandpa would sit alone in his Morris chair, talk little, and weep often. That December, Grandpa Califano died of a heart attack. I was only eight when he died, but he drew so many simple pictures of boats for me as he recounted his adventures that I can draw them exactly as he taught me to this day.

.   .   .

Dad went to work in 1925 as secretary to the advertising manager at International Business Machines Corporation (IBM) at 50 Broad Street in Manhattan, one of 2,633 employees then. He was promoted to working on the IBM newspaper and became the Administrative Assistant of the IBM World Trade Corporation in 1949. When IBM World Trade moved in 1954 to the United Nations Plaza at 46th Street and First Avenue, my father relished having an office facing the UN and meeting Secretary General Dag Hammarskjöld, whose book, *Markings,* he insisted I read.

Dad had a loyalty to IBM that is incomprehensible in the twenty-first century. He never entertained the thought that he might work somewhere else. Ten years after his retirement, Dad wrote to Thomas J. Watson, Jr., "As for myself, after spending 39 years with IBM, it will always be a part of me."

Dad meticulously obeyed the dress code of IBM founder Thomas J. Watson, Sr. For years he wore highly starched or stiff cardboard-collared white shirts, conservative neckties, and dark suits because "that's what TJ wants." My father even brought home and occasionally sang, as my mother played the piano, the IBM march, "March On With IBM," and the IBM rally song, "Ever Onward," which contained lyrics like:

March on with IBM. We lead the way!
Onward we'll ever go, in strong array;
Our thousands to the fore, nothing can stem
Our march forever more, with IBM.

And

Ever Onward—Ever Onward!
That's the spirit that has brought us fame!
We're big, but bigger we will be. . . .
For the Ever Onward IBM.

Mother, Dad, and I joked often about the IBM songs. But underlying the laughter, and giving it a nervous pitch, was the sense that our bread and butter—and my education—depended on Dad's unflagging loyalty to the company. We never let anyone outside the immediate family know that we sometimes made fun of the songs. Behind Dad's back my aunts and uncles joked about the songs, but never to his face; they too understood "the power of the Watsons." My father did not make millions on the company's stock. The stock market crash of 1929 had so shaken Grampa Califano and my father and his siblings that they feared investing in equities what little they could save.

Starting in 1917, my mother taught first and third grades at Public School 189 on East New York Avenue in Brooklyn. Mother loved teaching. She considered it a noble profession, an obligation of an educated Gill girl. She took a sabbatical shortly before I was born, but went back to teaching a year and a half later because our family needed the money.

In her early teaching years, the families were strong and the students were almost entirely Italian, Jewish, and Irish. As the neighborhood began to change, my father wanted her to retire because he feared for her safety. But my mother refused, insisting, "These poor Puerto Rican and Negro children need help." However, by the time she retired, in 1959, after teaching for forty-two years, she admitted that increasing violence and crime in the school's neighborhood terrified her.

·   ·   ·

As strong as Mother was, we spent more time with the Califanos than the Gills. The food at gatherings was usually Italian, but the talk wasn't. Though Dad had learned Italian from his parents and studied it in school, he never spoke it at home and never taught me. A first-generation Italian-American, my father made it a point of honor to be American. Dad's attitude was doubtless reinforced in May 1939, when Italy's Prime Minister Benito Mussolini signed the "Pact of Steel" with Adolf Hitler.

My father's sister Rosalie, my Aunt Rose, was the backbone of the Califano family, its indisputable matriarch and a second mother to me. For the first ten years of my life, Aunt Rose and her husband, Michael Scotto, lived five blocks from us in a brownstone with Grandpa and Grandma Califano. A year after I was born, Dad was stricken with what the doctors called a severe case of rheumatic fever (in those days a diagnosis doctors often gave when they couldn't determine the ailment). He was hospitalized for more than a year. During that time, since my mother had to work to support us, Aunt Rose taught me to walk while Uncle Mike worked at his family business, constructing and repairing boats. In 1939, Aunt Rose and Uncle Mike moved to a brick row house in a Flatbush development built by Fred Trump, Donald's father.

Aunt Rose and Uncle Mike had two sons, Louis Edward and John Ignatius (nicknamed Chub). These cousins were like brothers to me. They both fought in World War II, Louis in the infantry and Chub—who had graduated from St. John's College in Brooklyn, the first on my father's side of the family to go to college—in the Army Corps of Engineers. Chub fought in North Africa, Sicily, and Italy, but was never wounded. On three occasions, Louis was wounded and his entire company was wiped out—twice in France and just before the Battle of the Bulge in the Huertgen Forest in Germany. After a sniper's bullet shattered Louis's left wrist, he returned home with a permanent disability. He never fully recovered from his war experiences and suffered nightmares into his nineties.

Only eight blocks away from us, in a small one-bedroom apartment on Crown Street, lived my father's sister Constance, named in American idiom for her mother Candida. She married Anthony Martinez, and my father's brothers and sisters whispered out of Aunt Constance's hearing that their sister had married beneath herself, because Uncle Tony was of Spanish descent. Aunt Constance was a secretary at Singer Sewing Machine Company; Uncle Tony, a meter reader for Con Edison in Brooklyn.

My Aunt Jess, my father's sister Jasmine (named in the American idiom for Gelsomina), married my mother's brother Thomas Gill, a widower. Aunt Jess never had children, but Uncle Tom had two from his prior marriage, one of whom, his namesake, drew *The Lone Ranger, Bonanza,* and other cartoons for comic books and daily newspapers.

My father's older brother, my Uncle Gus, was a kind of Dale Carnegie for first- and second-generation immigrant families in New York. He conducted a course in private elocution and public speaking throughout New York City in the 1930s and 1940s. Uncle Gus taught thousands of immigrants and their children, ambitious to assimilate and succeed, how to speak, dress, interview for jobs, and make public presentations. His stationery advertised his business: "Augustus E. Califano—Effective Speaking, Personality Training, Human Relations." His motto was "He Conquers who Conquers Himself." Over the years as I traveled the country, many of those he taught told me how much they had learned from Augustus Califano and asked, "Are you related?"

My father had a sister, Anna, whom I never met. As a child I imagined all sorts of things about Anna because Mother and Dad refused to talk about her. I suspected she was on welfare—"the dole," which the family considered a shame and disgrace—or that she was in prison. It had to be something like that, I imagined, for my parents, aunts, and uncles to banish her. That would explain why they all ignored my questions. Years later, after my father died, I learned that the family was indeed ashamed of Anna—because she had married a Protestant. Over the years my father was the only one in the family who kept in touch with Anna. There was no mistake or sin Dad could not forgive. Indeed, if he hadn't met my mother, he would have become a priest and the line to his confessional would have been the longest in Brooklyn.

.   .   .

Though I saw far less of the Gill family growing up, they were loving, like my dad's relatives, and made it clear that family came first. My Aunt May and her husband, my Uncle Monty, who was in the coal business, were the formal relatives. When visiting their brownstone house on Sterling Place, two blocks from our apartment, I had to be scrubbed clean and dressed in freshly pressed shorts or clean corduroy knickers. Aunt May was the only relative who always served jellies, jams, and marmalades not out of the bottle but in cut-glass containers with fancy covers and tiny silver spoons.

My Uncle Joe Gill was the worldliest relative in the family. During World War I, he served in Europe as a lieutenant in the U.S. Army Corps of Engineers. After the war, he started his own leather business, travelling to Australia and becoming an expert in kangaroo hides. He was so successful that he drove a Chrysler and always gave me the most money (five or ten dollars) at Christmas. Uncle Joe had a mischievous and rakish sense of humor that he often displayed in teasing my mother. Once he stopped by our apartment just as one of Mother's monthly bridge games was ending and the prim ladies were having a drink. Uncle Joe had a rye Manhattan with the ladies and finished it without eating the fruit at the bottom of the glass. "May I have your cherry, Joe?" a friend of my mother's asked. "You're twenty years too late, dear," Uncle Joe replied. Mother didn't think it was funny; she let her brother have it when all her guests had left. I was twelve at the time and thought it was so hilarious and risqué that I couldn't wait to tell my class-mates at St. Gregory's elementary school.

Mother's brother George—unknown to me—was diagnosed as schizo-phrenic and spent his life at several institutions. Mother and her siblings shared the Irish penchant for secrecy about such family skeletons. No mat-ter how often I pestered, I was not told where she and her brothers would go each Christmastime when they visited their brother George. Years later I learned that she and my father wanted me never to have to put on any school or job application that I had a relative with a mental illness.

.   .   .

Christmastime was the happiest of the year. Dad would take me to help him pick out a tree on Kingston or Nostrand Avenue and the tree would remain until January 6, the Feast of the Epiphany.[4] When Grandma Califano was alive, she made struffoli, pieces of fried dough about the size of large marbles. I helped her dip each piece in honey and build little mounds to be given to each member of the family.* Christmas day I got to open presents and have a big Christmas dinner that Mother and Dad hosted for Uncle Joe Gill and some of Mother's cousins.

The signal family event of the season was on New Year's Day at Aunt Rose's. All the Califano aunts, uncles, and cousins would be there. The meal began around 1 P.M. and lasted until 7 P.M., with just enough space between courses to give the digestive tract a little rest: antipasto, steamed artichokes with garlic and oil, lasagna, sausages and meat balls, traditional turkey din-ner with all the trimmings, and for dessert, a mountain of cannoli, struffoli, bekenut, chewy macaroons with pignoli, and Italian grain pie. The wine with the meal had often been pressed by Uncle Mike and his brothers at the shipyard.

Throughout the year, on late Sunday afternoons at Aunt Rose's or Aunt Jess's, the family would gather for supper. We would listen to the radio—Jack Benny followed by Fred Allen. As a special treat some Sunday evenings we would board the St. John's Place trolley and go for pizza and calzone to South Brooklyn, one of the few places in those days where such delicacies

*At Eastertime, in coal- and wood-fired ovens, Grandma Califano baked the Italian Easter sweet bread that my cousins and I called "cozadil," our family's dialect for Columba Pasqual.

were available. I remember hearing—on a Sunday afternoon in December, at the age of ten—about the Japanese attack on Pearl Harbor, and the worry of the family about Louis and Chub, who had both been drafted. The next morning, the first map that the *Daily News* printed of the Pearl Harbor attack was drawn by my cousin Tom Gill, Uncle Tom's son.

CHAPTER 2

The Early Years

MOTHER WAS a stickler for discipline in everything—punctuality (especially for Mass), homework, elocution and grammar, general conduct and manners. She pounded the Brooklyn accent out of me, determined that I would say "never," not "nevuh;" "sewer," not "sewuh;" "soda," not "soder;" "idea," not "idear." When Aunt Jess pronounced oil "erl," Mother winced. She insisted on the correct usage of "I" and "me," and "we" and "us," and never hesitated to correct the moods of the verbs I used in conversation. She would not allow the tabloids—*Daily News* or *Daily Mirror*—in the house because she abhorred their slang phrases and misuse of the English language. She wanted me to read books, but on Saturday mornings when I went shopping for food with her, she let me buy one comic book—*Action Comics* with Superman, *Detective Comics* with Batman, or *Flash* or *Captain Marvel* comics.

Dad could ignore the language, but he ⦀⦀⦀⦀⦀⦀⦀⦀⦀⦀ pt me in knickers and out of long pants lon; PQN572744 l. I begged for months before I got Keds high-top sneakers, an ID bracelet, a key chain to hang from my belt loop to my right pants pocket, and a penknife. I pestered for permission to peg the bottoms of my pants around my ankles—to no avail.

I never heard either of my parents use a racial epithet. Because they both worked, we had a housekeeper named Mary Holly, a young black woman. I saw her every weekday around noon when I walked home for lunch, since there was no cafeteria in our elementary school. I loved her, and my parents stayed in touch with her for years after I left for college and she no longer worked for them.

I had to do my homework every night. When I got good marks, Mother and Dad allowed me, while doing homework, to tune the radio to *Captain Midnight, The Inner Sanctum, The Green Hornet* with his driver Kato, *The*

Lone Ranger, and later Martin Block's *Make-Believe Ballroom* playing Tommy Dorsey, Harry James, Benny Goodman, and Les Brown 78-rpm records.

Mother and Dad wanted me to learn everything. There were piano lessons—a disaster of struggling to practice with a metronome for two years. There were tap dancing lessons inspired by Gene Kelly and those Fred Astaire–Ginger Rogers movies—an even more pronounced calamity. Fortunately they kept building up my self-esteem as we discovered I was tone deaf and had no sense of rhythm. When I was in high school, Dad tried (in vain) to teach me shorthand, and he had someone at IBM give me lessons in how to use a keypunch machine. He told me often about computers, which then filled whole rooms. He said, "Someday everyone will have them in their homes, on their desks, maybe even in their pockets."

As much as I disliked piano and tap dancing lessons, I loved the games we played on the streets of Brooklyn. In my neighborhood, stickball took a distant second place to punchball. In spring and summer, in late afternoon and early evening, we played punchball in front of my apartment building. We turned asphalt streets into playing fields and manhole covers into bases. One sewer in the middle of the street would be home plate, the next, about eighty feet away, would be second base; first and third bases would be marked in chalk next to opposite curbs midway between the two sewers. There were usually five, sometimes six, players on each side. The hitter threw the spaldeen (a hollow, firm, high-bouncing pink ball made from the Spaulding Company's discarded tennis ball cores and sold in candy and five-and-dime stores) high in the air, and then punched it with his fist, in a motion similar to that of a tennis player serving. Some of the better players, like Rudy, could punch the ball in the air a distance of almost two sewers, about fifty yards (known as a two-sewer hit). Doug Keebles and I couldn't hit a distance of two sewers, but we became adept at punching the ball far enough to bounce off walls and windows so it couldn't be caught on a fly. The superintendent of our apartment and neighbors sat on park benches facing the street, watching our games, sometimes betting on them.

There was little traffic and cars rarely parked on the street. If someone tried to park on our asphalt field, we would shout at them to move down the street—and usually they did. If they didn't move far enough, however, they were likely to find their car aerials broken, their paint scratched, or chewing gum stuffed in their door locks. Our block—Park Place between Brooklyn and Kingston Avenues—was our turf and even the Good Humor man honored it; he didn't come ringing his bells until we had finished our punchball game.

Stoopball was played with one person on each side, sometimes two. The boy at bat would stand sideways and throw the spaldeen against the stoop. If the ball hit hard at just the right spot on the edge of the best step, it would take off over the head of the fielders and the batter would have a home run. If the ball, when thrown, hit the door or a window behind, that was an out— or a reason to run for cover from angry neighbors.

Territory involved jackknives. We traced a rectangle in dirt (near a tree) and divided it into one section for each player. A player would flip the jackknife into someone else's territory. He drew a line extending from the knife's blade. The player whose territory was hit had to choose a piece of land on either side of the line. The knife thrower got the other side. The knife thrower could keep throwing as long as his knife stuck in the territory of another player. Louis C. was the best knife thrower, and if he went first, the rest of us might never get a chance. Whoever ended up with the most territory within the rectangle won. Those of us who had switchblades—jackknives that opened with the press of a button—showed off by repeatedly closing the blades and snapping them open during the game.

In the winter, we played Johnny-on-the-pony. A few players would bend over, each one with his head between the legs of the guy on front of him. The player in front pressed his arms against the side of a building and protected his head. The first player on the other team would run, place both hands on the lower back on the player farthest from the wall, hoist himself kangaroo style as high as possible, and land on the back of a player closer to the wall, as though jumping on a horse. Each player would follow suit. To win, the jumping team had to force one of the bent-over guys to the ground.

One of my favorite games was ringolevio, a rough game of hide-and-go-seek with two sides and two jails. The first side to capture and jail, usually in a back alley with a gate, all the members of the other side won. Someone guarded the jail, because if a member of the opposite team got inside and shouted "Free All!" the prisoners were released in a jailbreak.

Knuckles was our favorite card game. It was blackjack with a harsh ending. The winner could take the wrist of the loser in one hand and, holding the deck of cards in the other, skin the four exposed knuckles of his closed fist. If the winner had blackjack—twenty-one on two cards—he could skin the knuckles of the loser twice. When blood was drawn from each of the four knuckles, the player dropped out of the game.

We played other street games, but not as often: hockey on roller skates, tag, and touch football. We never played soccer or basketball, and there were no fans of such sports in my neighborhood. We had no Little League teams, no coaches or parents on the sidelines—they only popped their heads out of the apartment windows around dinnertime.

What did Lyndon Johnson mean about what I learned "on the streets of Brooklyn" as key assets I brought to his White House staff? I'm confident they came from Johnny-on-the-pony, ringolevio, knuckles, and perhaps territory (though he probably never heard of those games).

.   .   .

We weren't always on the streets. Without air conditioning in the summer, many families rented bungalows at the beach or in the Catskill Mountains. My parents bought a small, brown-shingle bungalow at 41 New Hampshire Street in Long Beach, Long Island, where we went every summer until I was thirteen. As a public school teacher, my mother had the summer off; my father commuted to work in the city each weekday on the Long Island Railroad because my parents never owned a car. Between 1938 and 1942, I went to Jones Day Camp at Long Beach, where I learned to swim. On rainy days we did the usual arts and crafts and I learned I had about as much talent for these as for playing the piano or tap dancing.

On Saturday afternoons, we often went to the movies for twenty-five cents at Loews Kameo on Eastern Parkway and Nostrand Avenue or the Savoy on Bedford Avenue. For ten cents, the Lincoln on Bedford Avenue played old films and serials, which continued from week to week, of boat races and space hero Buck Rogers. World War II brought war movies, ration books, price controls, red tokens for coveted meat and dairy products, air raid drills, gas shortages, and V-mail from American soldiers. Gold star pennants hung in the windows of those families whose sons died in combat, and many Catholic windows were draped in black and purple. In December

1943, Brooklyn Union and Con Edison asked us to take cold baths to conserve gas.

But the one thing the war never changed was my, and my neighborhood's, commitment to the Brooklyn Dodgers. We all lived for—and often died over—"Dem Bums." We hung on every description of Red Barber's radio play-by-play in his southern accent. In the summer evenings when our punchball game was over, we went to the candy store on Kingston Avenue and Sterling Place to check the bulldog edition of the *Daily News* for the latest stats on our favorite players. There we also bought candy for a penny, egg creams (seltzer from the counter spigot with splashes of chocolate syrup and milk) if we had two cents, and "loosies," single cigarettes for a cent each.

One Sunday each summer, Uncle Tom Gill took me to a Brooklyn Dodgers double-header. The entrance to Ebbets field was a magnificent marble rotunda. There was a rickety wooden frame in right field with a scoreboard and billboards in the lower half advertising Schaefer beer ("The one beer to have when you're having more than one") and Abe Stark's clothing ("Hit Sign, Win Suit"). There were only 32,000 seats, fewer than at Yankee Stadium or the Polo Grounds, but this gave Ebbets Field a special intimacy. We dodged trolleys criss-crossing the street to reach the entrance and took our seats in the center field bleachers for fifty-five cents each. "This is where the real fans sit," Uncle Tom would tell me as he bought peanuts, orange soda, and hot dogs. Across the field we watched Hilda Chester harass visiting teams ringing her four-pound brass cowbell. Organist Gladys Goodding played "Three Blind Mice" when the umpires took the field; we all cheered and clapped. The Dodger Sym-Phony, a five-piece brass band, banged out "The Worm Crawls In" and the Dodger theme song:

There's a ball club in Brooklyn
The team they call "Dem Bums"
But keep your eyes right on them
And watch for hits and runs.

Uncle Tom and I sat in those bleachers for six or seven hours, watching and cheering Pee Wee Reese, Dolf Camilli, Preacher Roe, Billy Herman, Dixie Walker, Carl Furillo, Jackie Robinson, Duke Snider, Roy Campanella,

Ralph Branca, Don Newcombe,[1] and their teammates and booing the visiting team. We saw Jackie Robinson, in 1947 major league baseball's first black player, steal home. We marveled at Carl Furillo, with his uncanny ability to read the unpredictable caroms off the right field wall and his phenomenal arm, throwing out runners reckless enough to try to stretch doubles into triples or score from second base. We witnessed Pete Reiser smash into the concrete center field wall and hang on to the fly ball in his glove as he hit the ground.[2] We loved it when Eddie Stanky crouched to bamboozle pitchers into walking him at the start of an inning and Duke Snider hit home runs.

When I was a senior at Brooklyn Prep and there was a shortage of ushers at Ebbets Field, my classmates and I fought for the chance to fill in. The high school was nearby and Walter O'Malley (the Dodgers owner whom we would vilify for moving the team to Los Angeles in 1957) was an Irish Catholic whose daughter dated Prep students. There was no pay, but who needed it? We got to see the game and occasionally got tipped a nickel or dime for dusting off someone's seat.

CHAPTER 3

Born, Bred, and Branded Catholic

I REMEMBER THE first time I sensed the power of my mother's faith. I was ten years old. We were at our bungalow in Long Beach when a red-hot ash from her cigarette flew into her left eye. Her doctor feared she might lose sight in that eye. She prayed to God to save her eyesight, promising to sacrifice smoking and drinking forever in return. She kept her sight and never smoked or took another drink, even when doctors later urged her to sip red wine to "strengthen her blood," a remedy common among Italian families in those days.

Mother sometimes took me on her visits to the Carmelite nuns. In Brooklyn, the order lived cloistered from the world in a convent behind a twenty-foot-high wall at the corner of Bedford Avenue and St. John's Place. She regularly visited the nuns there and spoke to one through a screen that hid their faces from each other but unveiled a common faith. Mother would ask the nun to pray for her "intentions," such as "for the Good Lord to keep our family safe and healthy."[1]

Both Mother and Dad, and my aunts and uncles, went to Mass every Sunday and participated in novenas (a nine-day prayer routine for a special intention) and First Friday devotions (attending Mass and receiving communion on nine consecutive first Fridays of the month). They went to confession often, no less than monthly, though I doubt they had many sins to confess. They supported the parish church and numerous Catholic causes—missions in foreign lands, nuns working on Indian reservations, and the St. Vincent de Paul Society to help the poor.

Like most Brooklynites in the "city of churches" (as Brooklyn was often called), my parish was my neighborhood. St. Gregory's was founded in 1906 as a small building with a tin roof. By 1915, Irish immigrants had built a majestic church with a seven-story-high bell tower in Romanesque architecture inspired by the Basilica of Saint Laurence in Lucina, a neighborhood in Rome. It remains one of Brooklyn's treasures, among the finest examples of "fresco buono" in New York City because of its interior marble, religious tapestries, English stained glass, mosaic tiled floors, and Great Apse portraying Pope Gregory the Great in the company of the Fathers of the Church.

.   .   .

In 1936, my parents sent me to public school because the parochial school had no kindergarten. But in 1937, I was ready for first grade and there was never any doubt it would be at St. Gregory's.* Next door to the church, the school was three stories with sixteen classrooms, an assembly hall, and a basement. The hallway walls held crucifixes and paintings and statues of Mary and Joseph. Each classroom had large black chalkboards the length of a wall with a crucifix above.

The Sisters of Mercy taught our class of eighteen girls and seventeen boys. Over eight years, only one classmate moved away; only one entered after the first grade. The Sisters lived in a convent behind the school. With their long black habits, veils, and starched white coifs that covered everything except their hands and faces, they could have played supporting roles to Ingrid Bergman in the smash Hollywood movie of that day, *The Bells of St. Mary's.* The nuns wrapped oversized brown rosary beads around their waists, with five beads and a large crucifix hanging at their sides. Their faces, hands, and wrists—the only skin we could see—were always scrubbed clean. We never knew whether they had long or short hair or, as we sometimes imagined, shaved heads. Each was called Sister Mary before a different name.

Except for music and drawing classes conducted by lay Catholic women, every year a single nun taught us all our subjects: religion, English, reading, writing, spelling, arithmetic, history, civics, geography, nature study, elementary science, and hygiene.

Discipline was strict. We were expected to arrive at school properly dressed and washed. The nuns often examined our hands; they checked to see if our nails were clean and looked behind our ears. We had to raise our

*Children entered in September and February; eighth graders graduated in June and January.

hands to be recognized if we had a question or for permission to go to the bathroom. Our desks had to be neat. The homework we handed in could not have erasures. We were to learn our lessons, have perfect penmanship, and write the initials J.M.J. (Jesus, Mary, and Joseph) in the top right-hand corner of every written page. Three-, five-, or ten-question quizzes were frequent, and after the first two grades unannounced. If we were absent, we needed a note from our parents. If we were late, it cost us points on our grades. The nuns gave me my share of raps with a ruler on the knuckles for being rambunctious. It wasn't hard enough to hurt much, but, alert to the deterrent power of embarrassment, the Sisters always delivered the punishment in front of the entire class.

Our Bible was the Baltimore Catechism. The nuns hammered us with its first two questions and answers:

Who made you?
God made me.
Why did God make you?
God made me to know, love, and serve Him in this world and to be happy with Him forever in the next.

These questions and answers were our Catholic alphabet. We could recite them on demand and did. The Baltimore Catechism explained, in simple terms, the basic rituals, mysteries, and rules of our faith. In first through sixth grades, we memorized it. In the last two grades, we studied bible history, though we never read from the Bible itself. I was imbued with a dot-every-"i" and cross-every-"t" religion that left little room for the exercise of individual conscience.

We learned that God is perfect and omnipotent, while humans are imperfect and weak; that Jesus Christ is the Son of God, and that He was born of a virgin named Mary, before we knew what virgin meant. Mary, also called the Blessed Mother, was the only person conceived without the original sin that marked every other individual after Adam and Eve disobeyed God in the Garden of Eden. The lesson the nuns drove home was obedience to God.

In white chalk, the Sisters of Mercy outlined on the blackboard the mystery of the Holy Trinity: three beings—Father, Son, and Holy Ghost—in one Divine Being. They told us not to worry about being unable to under-stand the Trinity: it was a mystery that was a part of our faith.

We learned the seven sacraments. The first, Baptism, cleansed us of the original sin of Adam and Eve. Penance (confession) offered forgiveness for our sins and reconciliation with God. Holy Eucharist was receiving the body and blood of Jesus Christ at Mass in the form of a white, unleavened bread wafer the diameter of a quarter. Confirmation, which we received in eighth grade, strengthened our faith and reminded us that we might be called into battle as soldiers in Christ's army. Matrimony was an unbreakable covenant between a man and a woman for the purpose of producing a family and serving the church as lay people. Holy Orders was for those whose vocation was the priesthood. Extreme Unction, the last rites, cleansed us of our sins before death in order to open the gates to Purgatory and Heaven.

By fourth grade we could recite in our sleep the seven deadly sins (Pride, Covetousness, Lust, Anger, Gluttony, Envy, Sloth). We learned the seven cor-poral works of mercy (feed the hungry, give drink to the thirsty, clothe the naked, ransom the captive, harbor the harborless, visit the sick, bury the dead). We were taught to perform the seven spiritual works of mercy (admonish the sinner, instruct the ignorant, counsel the doubtful, comfort the sorrowful, bear wrongs patiently, forgive all injuries, pray for the living and the dead).

We had a lesson in religion every day, five days a week. Every Sunday, we went to nine o'clock Mass, where we sat with our classmates in the front pews while our parents sat in the back. Colorful tapestries and stained-glass windows depicting scenes from Jesus's life and the Stations of the Cross lined the front, back, and side walls of St. Gregory's, providing something to gaze at during long Masses. At Mass, boys always wore ties; girls, dresses; parents, suits and dresses. Women had to cover their heads, which made for colorful Easter bonnets but also required the nuns to tuck a handkerchief or two under their sleeves for girls who forgot a hat.

We regarded the Mass—the Consecration of the bread and wine into the Body and Blood of Christ—as the central miracle of Catholic worship. We learned that Jesus Christ is truly present in the sacred host given at Com-munion. We were taught that it was a mortal sin to miss Mass on Sunday or a Holy Day of Obligation.[2]

The nuns explained that we were all part of the mystical Body of Christ, the Communion of Saints, which was composed of three parts. The Church Militant was made up of the faithful on earth, who shared an apostolic mission to spread the gospel (literally "the good news") of Our Lord Jesus Christ throughout the world. The Church Suffering was the souls in Purgatory waiting to enter heaven. The Church Triumphant was the angels, saints, and all those in heaven. St. Joseph was my favorite saint, and on his feast day, March 19, my father bought brownies from Ebinger, Brooklyn's finest bakery, to celebrate.

If we followed the Baltimore Catechism's recipe for leading a good Catholic life, we would go to Heaven; if not, we were doomed to eternal damnation in the fires of Hell. In the early grades, the nuns described being in Heaven as a day full of wonderful surprises and boundless joy, a place where you could eat all the candy and ice cream you wanted and never get sick. (They might have added that we would never get fat, but getting fat was not considered a problem in the 1940s.) By eighth grade, the nuns cautioned us that Hell was the denial of ever being in God's presence, which was more painful than burning forever in a roaring fire. We didn't read Dante in St. Gregory's, but the Sisters of Mercy painted as vivid a picture of the underworld as the fiery author of *The Inferno*.

We never ate meat on Fridays. As a child, I remember being served pea soup at a friend's house. I asked if a ham bone had been used to flavor it. When told yes, I didn't eat it for fear of committing a serious sin.

The nuns hoped most of us would not commit a sin terrible enough to end up in Hell, but warned that we would be held in Purgatory to atone for our lesser transgressions (even if we went to confession and received forgiveness). The nuns never told us how long Purgatory would be, but they let us in on the world of partial and plenary indulgences to get time off for good behavior. A partial indulgence removed part of the time you spent in Purgatory for a certain sin; a plenary one removed all of it. Reciting prayers like the Hail Mary or Our Father, singing hymns, or reading scripture earned us partial indulgences. So did saying grace before and after meals, blessing ourselves with the Sign of the Cross, and using holy water. We could also shorten the time deceased souls suffered in Purgatory by giving our indulgences to them. The inside cover of our prayer books or Bibles often listed how much time we would gain for each good deed: "The faithful who spend at least a quarter of an hour in reading Holy Scripture . . . may gain an indulgence of 300 days." Three hundred days less in Purgatory! That made me wonder how many days more I'd have to work off for a taste of ham-flavored pea soup on a Friday. Five hundred?

Plenary indulgences were harder to obtain. If accompanied by confession, communion, and a prayer for the Pope, actions such as these earned a plenary indulgence: receiving a blessing by the Pope (even by radio), kissing the cross on Good Friday, attending the first Mass of a newly ordained priest, reciting the rosary in public. Visiting a church on All Souls Day (November 2) garnered a plenary indulgence for a soul in Purgatory. My parents and I performed many of these rituals and recited many of these prayers in the hope of gaining indulgences for ourselves and our deceased relatives.

The Sisters of Mercy reminded us repeatedly that we were fortunate to be members of The One True Church and that only those who were baptized could enter Heaven. The nuns did teach that most Protestant baptisms removed original sin. The Church accorded baptismal status in two other situations: baptism of blood for those who died in the service of God, which included those who gave their lives to save another human being, and baptism of desire for those who would have been baptized were they not victims of "invincible ignorance." This latter concept comforted me as a child. I had several Jewish friends in the neighborhood—they went to the synagogue a couple of blocks from our apartment—and there were other nice people on the block who never went to any church or synagogue. I thought they deserved to go to Heaven. The nuns taught that Jews and good individuals who did not believe in our God could be saved because their invincible ignorance was not their fault. Faith in The One True Church was a gift from God and since God was just, He would not deny Heaven to those invincibly ignorant individuals who lived good lives. Throughout the years at St. Gregory's, there was little, if any, sense of the ecumenical; indeed, we were prohibited from taking part in any non-Catholic religious service or contributing to any other church.

.   .   .

On Ash Wednesday, the first day of Lent, the priest rubbed ashes in the shape of a cross on our foreheads, visibly identifying the Catholic children in the neighborhood, who proudly sported them. Lent lasted forty days, not counting Sundays, in remembrance of the forty days and nights Jesus spent in solitude, prayer, and fasting before He was crucified for us. During Lent, in addition to the usual Friday abstention from meat, we ate meat no more than once a day on other days of the week and limited the food at breakfast and lunch to less than the amount consumed at dinner. During this season, like Mother and Dad, I usually gave up candy.

At St. Gregory's, the nuns gave each of us a Mite Box to take home.[3] We filled this small purple cardboard box with pennies and brought it to school at the end of the Lenten season. We believed money would help the "pagan [unbaptized] babies" in countries like China where Catholic missionaries worked. With every five dollars collected, the class could name a baby being baptized.

Mother took me to Mass on Holy Thursday to watch Monsignor Maurice Fitzgerald, our pastor, wash the feet of the parish priests as Christ washed the feet of His Apostles at the Last Supper. The next day, Good Friday, Mother took me to the Three Hours Agony from noon until three, where the priest would go through the Stations of the Cross and deliver several readings and homilies. The congregation would chant *Dies Irae* (Day of Wrath), a fifty-seven-line Latin poem often also recited at funeral Masses, to remember Jesus's death on the cross. Dad had to work on those days, but he went to St. Patrick's Cathedral in Manhattan during his lunch break.

On Holy Saturday at noon, Mother, Dad, and I opened a box of chocolate candy to mark the end of Lent. As a child, I was always given a new outfit to wear on Easter Sunday because it was the most holy day of the year.

.   .   .

On May 26, 1938, my classmates and I made our First Communion together during the first half of second grade. We rehearsed walking up to the altar with our palms together as if we were praying and sticking our tongues out so that the priest could place the Host on our tongue. We considered it a serious sin for anyone other than the priest—and he with only his thumb and forefinger—to touch the consecrated Host.

To be eligible to receive Communion at Mass, we had to fast from everything, including water, from midnight the evening before. That required being extremely careful in brushing your teeth in the morning to make certain not a drop of water went down your throat. Some parents with many children tied the faucets shut in case their kids got up for a drink of water in the middle of night. When we received Holy Communion, we were forbidden to chew it and had to allow it to become soft in our mouths so we could swallow it whole.

All parents of first communicants and all nuns in the school were at the children's nine o'clock Mass that Sunday. The girls dressed all in white— dresses, shoes, and socks. The boys dressed in blue blazers and shorts with a white shirt and a wide white ribbon bow where the tie would ordinarily be.

With my classmates, I walked up the aisle to the white marble altar rail, where we knelt. The priest came down from the altar, placed the Host on my tongue, and said, "Corpus Domini nostri Jesu Christi custodiat animam tuam in vitam aeternam, Amen" (May the body of our Lord Jesus Christ guard your soul into eternal life, Amen). I then rose and returned to my seat.

My parents and several uncles and aunts celebrated my First Communion more joyfully than any birthday I can remember. As presents, I received rosary beads and a prayer book with a white cover. First Communion marked a momentous change in my life as a Catholic. From that moment on, I assumed personal responsibility to observe the rules of the church.

My classmates and I also began going to confession, at least twice a month on Saturday afternoons, to seek forgiveness for our venial (not so bad) and mortal (very bad) sins, in order to be prepared to receive Communion at Mass on Sunday. During those elementary school years our confessions consisted of being unkind to a friend or classmate, lying, fighting, and by seventh and eighth grades, "taking the Lord's name in vain." The "impure thoughts and deeds" like kissing and petting didn't come until high school. I once walked around the outside of the church several times on a Saturday afternoon to muster the courage to tell the priest that I had hit a friend of mine over the head with a toy gun hard enough to make him bleed and cry. I was afraid that I had committed a mortal sin.

Confessions were so common that four priests would hear them for a couple of hours on a Saturday afternoon. Inside St. Gregory's, each dimly lit confessional box had three sections. The center housed the priest behind a closed door; on each side was a kneeler behind a heavy red-velvet curtain. You couldn't see which priest was behind the curtain, but you hoped that you had picked one of the more lenient ones. When I knelt behind the red curtain, I faced a small screen with a sliding panel that was closed while the priest listened to the confessor kneeling on the opposite side. We knew that the priest would die before revealing what he heard. The priest, acting in Christ's place, had the power to forgive our sins; all would be forgiven if we were genuinely repentant and tried not to sin again.

Once the priest slid open the panel, I made the sign of the cross and said, "Bless me father, for I have sinned. It has been two weeks since my last confession." Then I recited my sins. Sometimes the priest would ask questions, offer advice on how to avoid such sins, or underscore the importance of avoiding any "occasion of sin"—the Catholic concept of not putting oneself in situations where temptation would be almost impossible to resist. He would then impose some penance, usually to say a few Hail Marys and Our Fathers. Then I recited the Act of Contrition. While making the sign of the cross in the air with his right hand, the priest then offered the Latin absolution: "Ego te absolvo a peccatis tuis in nomine Patris et Filii et Spiritus Sancti, Amen." (I absolve thee of thy sins in the name of the Father, Son and Holy Spirit, Amen.) The panel closed; the priest turned to another penitent on the other side. I pushed back the red-velvet curtain to go to the altar rail or some pew in the church, kneel, say my penance, and go home or out to play.

In fourth grade, Mother and Dad gave me two choices: become either a choir boy or an altar boy. Since I couldn't keep a tune, I knew I'd never make the cut in the choir, so I became an altar boy. With Father Joseph Stapleton I went through three months of training, memorizing the Latin responses to the priest's Latin before I served my first Mass with an experienced altar boy, Robert Mattello.

Being an altar boy was a big deal. Girls couldn't do it. An altar boy led the way for the priest as he stepped into the sanctuary and knelt next to the priest, facing the altar, back to the congregation, as the priest began the Mass: "In nomine Patris et Filii et Spiritus Sancti, Amen. Introibo ad altare Dei."

I responded: "Ad Deum qui laetificat juventutem meam."*

Usually there were two altar boys at every Mass, one kneeling at the foot

*Priest: "In the name of the Father, Son, and Holy Ghost, Amen. I will go into the altar of God." Altar Boy: "To God who gives joy to my youth."

of the altar steps on the Gospel side (left facing the altar) and one on the Epistle side (right). They moved the Missal, red-leather bound with gold-edged pages, from the Epistle side to the Gospel side of the altar and delivered the wine and water to the priest. Different priests preferred different amounts of wine in their chalice to consecrate. The altar boy on the Epistle side rang the bells three times during the elevation of the Body of Christ and three during the elevation of the Blood of Christ.

As an altar boy, I walked alongside the priest as he dispensed communion to parishioners kneeling at the altar rail. I held the communion paten under the chin of each communicant as the priest placed the host on the communicant's tongue in order to provide maximum protection should the Host slip out of the priest's hand or the communicant's mouth.

There were half a dozen Masses on Sunday, the latest at 1 P.M. There were none on Saturday afternoon or Sunday evening. On weekdays and Saturdays, four Masses were said, every half-hour from 6:30 until 8:00 A.M. Each month, I was assigned a weekday Mass for at least one week and two Sunday Masses. My black cassock was kept in the sacristy, but I was given a white surplice, which Mother proudly washed, starched, and ironed to perfection. Father Harold Hanley would whip through Mass in less than twenty minutes. Monsignor Fitzgerald often ran over the allotted half-hour and the next Mass started a little late. Once a year, St. Gregory's had the forty hours' devotion to the Blessed Sacrament, during which the Consecrated Host was displayed atop a small altar in an alcove to the right of the main altar. Altar boys were assigned to hourly shifts to kneel in front of the Host. Seventh and eighth graders were given the hours between 11 P.M. and 6 A.M. As our neighborhood began to change and crime increased, Mother worried about my being out on the streets at such hours. I thought it was exciting.

To serve as altar boy at weddings and requiem Masses held the likelihood of a tip from the groom or the family of the deceased (a quarter or half-dollar was customary, a dollar a small fortune). A requiem Mass during the week meant that you were excused from school for the hour or so it took to prepare and serve. My crowning moment as an altar boy was in the eighth grade, when I was chosen to be one of the two main servers at the midnight Mass on December 25, 1944.

.   .   .

By eighth grade I was embarking on the first romance of my life, with Joan Hembrooke. Joan's mother was Italian-American and a first cousin of my father, but her father was a German-American, Emil Hemberger. Because of the intense antipathy toward Germans during World War II and the fact that so many people made fun of the name Hemberger ("hamburger" was an easy tease), her family changed its name to Hembrooke when Joan was in fifth grade. Joan and I would become high school sweethearts as she went to St. Saviour, a Catholic girls' school taught by Sisters of Notre Dame, and I went to the Jesuit high school, Brooklyn Prep.[4] For eighth grade confirmation names, I chose Robert, Joan chose Roberta.

That year, Joan delivered me my first academic setback. I was vying with her for first in the class. She ended up with the highest marks and took top honors. My publicly announced consolation at the graduation ceremony in St. Gregory's auditorium was that I had the highest marks among boys.

The nuns and priests of St. Gregory's anchored me in a Catholic religion circumscribed by rules of conduct as detailed as a tax code—but without loopholes. That structure provided me comfort and security as a thirteen-year-old graduating from elementary school. I had learned much of my religion by rote and did not question it. The lines were sharply drawn. Along with my parents and relatives, I followed the rules of our faith, and the rituals brought us together. I connected Sunday Mass with Sunday evening with the extended family and Lenten fasting with a love of chocolate I shared with my mother. The Sisters of Mercy made sure that the holy water Father Joseph Foley sprinkled on my head when he baptized me two weeks after I was born found its way into every pore of my childhood.

My parents reared me to be American and Catholic. America promised opportunity—and Catholicism salvation. Assured of both, I graduated from St. Gregory's elementary school with unlimited hope for the future.

CHAPTER 4

A Jesuit Education

I will never forget the night after I was accepted at Brooklyn Prep. Mother and Dad took me to see my first Broadway play, the hit musical "Oklahoma!" When we came home, Mother kept hinting to Dad to take me into the kitchen to talk. I went in to get a drink of water. Dad followed.

"You know a little about the facts of life don't you, Son?" he asked.

"Yes, Dad," I answered, even more nervous than he was.

"And what you don't know the Jesuits will teach you."

"Yes, Dad." I could sense his relief as he returned to the living room.

BROOKLYN PREP—or Schola Praeparatoria Brooklyniensis, by the Latin inscription circling the school seal—introduced me to the Jesuits. I entered The Prep—to us it was the only one—in January 1945 as the hot war was cooling off. I graduated three and a half years later, in June of 1948, as the cold war was heating up.

New York City public high schools were good at the time, but my parents scraped together $250 a year for me to have a Catholic education. "There is nothing like a Jesuit education," my father said, and I quickly learned what he meant.

I walked the dozen blocks to school each day except in the rain or snow, when I took the Nostrand Avenue trolley. The Prep was 100 percent white and, like St. Gregory's, dominated by the Irish, with some Italians on the side. Almost all the teachers were Jesuit priests or scholastics (young men teaching for a few years before they undertook final theological studies prior to ordination). Discipline was rigorous, second only to a military academy. The dress code prescribed jackets and ties; academic standards were demanding. Attendance was taken at every class; tardiness was punished; truancy was an unspeakable offense. Every Jesuit high school had a prefect of discipline. We dedicated our yearbook to ours, Francis Brock, S.J., whom we saluted as our "friend, counselor and priest" and praised for his "benevolent guidance." The fact is, he scared the hell out of us. We hoped this dedication would provide a little insurance that we wouldn't be in "jug" ("Justice Under God," Jesuit nomenclature for detention) during graduation week.

During my years at Brooklyn Prep, the United States was flush with the victory and power of winning World War II. I was thirteen years old when, on April 10, 1945, the Allies liberated Buchenwald, the first major concentration camp in Germany to fall. I remember pictures of skeletal bodies of children my age with hollow eyes wearing oversized black-and-white-striped pajama uniforms.

A few weeks later, on May 8, V-E Day, the *Daily News* headlined "It's over in Europe!" We prayed that my cousin Chub would soon come home from Italy. Half a million people jammed Times Square, stopping traffic for six hours. Ticker tape flew out of buildings, and ships in the harbor sounded their foghorns. The following night the Statue of Liberty, which had been dimmed since Pearl Harbor, was brightly lit. I listened to all of it on the radio.

In March 1946, as Winston Churchill cautioned in a speech at Westminster College in Fulton, Missouri, that "an iron curtain has descended across the Continent" of Europe, the nation's focus, and particularly that of Catholics, turned to the cold war against Godless communism in Soviet Russia, a clear and present enemy that was persecuting the Church in Eastern Europe. Across the nation, the biggest domestic problems were building the suburbs rapidly enough, shifting the nation's astonishing manufacturing capacity into civilian gear, and building schools for all those new babies that returning war heroes were producing.

For us at Brooklyn Prep, the Jesuits drew sharp lines between freedom and license, love and lust, selfishness and strength, right and wrong, normal and deviant behavior, passion and violence, good people and bad people, beauty and banality, skepticism and cynicism, healthy inquisitiveness and arrogant irreverence. We and our parents saw our social, moral, intellectual, and political lives painted in precise and vivid colors; we had little or no tolerance for pastels. In the dialogue between faith and family culture, the two spoke the same language. Most parents of Jesuit high school students were so proud that their sons had been admitted and so committed to their own faith that they reinforced each weeknight and weekend what the Jesuits taught us during the week.

The Jesuits at Brooklyn Prep were socially conscious—especially about excessive materialism in American society and the plight of the poor in our affluent society. But they toed the conservative theological line drawn by the Vatican. They were insistent that the Roman Catholic Church was the only true church—so much so that we trembled to enter a synagogue for a friend's bar mitzvah or sit in an Episcopal pew. The authority of the bishops was unquestioned. Sin was crisply defined. If any one of us had thoughts that the church should abandon celibacy for priests or ordain women— ideas then so inconceivable and heretical that they never entered my mind—he would never have expressed them, for fear of excommunication. If a student's parents separated, it was a major embarrassment and a big-league scandal for his classmates (and their parents) to whisper about. Divorce was so roundly condemned, and annulment seen as so narrowly reserved for the best connected and most well-to-do Catholics, that it just never happened to any of my classmates' parents or was hidden in the darkest corners of their family closets.

·   ·   ·

I had the most fun at Brooklyn Prep writing (often with classmate Jerry Siesfeld) the gossip column, "'Round The Prep," for the school newspaper, the *Blue Jug*. The column got me into trouble on more than one occasion as I tried, naïvely in a 1940s Catholic school environment, to exercise some First Amendment rights vis-à-vis school policies and the private partying of some classmates.

My father had warned me about how academically demanding the Jesuits were, so I studied hard my freshman year and received the silver medal for second-highest marks. In sophomore year, I received the gold for the highest. By junior and senior years, when I won no academic medals, I was a typical fun-loving, partying, cigarette-smoking, beer-drinking teenager. Somehow I managed to graduate twenty-third in a class of 239, the largest in the history of Brooklyn Prep. My lingering academic memories are of Latin—four full years of it, five days a week. By the time I left The Prep, I could read essays and poems in Latin and understand them.

Most of my friends and I got hooked on cigarettes early in our freshman year (there was a bathroom reserved for smoking at The Prep). We were allowed to eat breakfast off campus after the mandatory 8 A.M. Friday Mass, so we went to Cromas on Nostrand Avenue and smoked cigarettes with our buttered hard rolls and coffee.

Beer—Schaefer, Rheingold, and Piel's—was the drink of choice; by our junior year we drank it almost every weekend at parties. In New York, it was then legal to buy beer at age eighteen and liquor at age twenty-one, but enforcement was lax, so there was no problem being served beer by age sixteen. In our senior year we sometimes went late on Friday afternoon to Schneider's bar across Nostrand Avenue from The Prep for a beer to start the weekend. A favorite Saturday night hangout was Ma Hayes, on Ocean and Farragut Avenues in Flatbush, which served mayonnaise-sopped roast beef sandwiches, pickled eggs, and ten-cent beers. About fifty of us held our off-the-record stag graduation party there and shouted our order for one hundred beers. When Ma Hayes, the bar's short, slight, but tough Irish owner, who resembled the movie version of the 1930s outlaw Ma Barker, told us it was a first, we cheered.

.   .   .

At high school dances, we were told to "leave room for the Holy Ghost" if we slow danced too closely with the girls from St. Saviour or Bishop McDonnell. Petting or heavy necking was considered a serious sin; though a good number of us enjoyed it, virtually all of us who attended Jesuit high schools (and colleges) graduated as virgins.

The Catholic Church and our parents in those days were especially puritanical about sex in music, films, and personal conduct. My parents worried as swing music and bebop replaced "Let Me Call You Sweetheart" and the jitterbug scuttled the waltz. The sexiest song was Ezio Pinza singing "Some Enchanted Evening" to Mary Martin on a South Pacific island, both fully dressed, his hand gently resting high on her shoulder. The drug of choice for lyricists was "a cigarette that bears a lipstick's traces" in Holt Marvell's syrupy ballad, "These Foolish Things Remind Me of You."

Quick to recognize the power of films to influence culture and conduct, in 1933 American bishops formed an Episcopal Committee on Motion Pictures to study the cinema. A year later, the Legion of Decency was established to set a moral standard for Catholics regarding movies and to "condemn absolutely those salacious motion pictures" that were "corrupting public morals and promoting a sex mania in our land."[1] Catholics by the thousands in parishes across the country signed up to follow the Legion's guidance.

In Brooklyn, parents read the Legion's movie ratings on the second-to-last page of the *Tablet,* the paper sold for five cents every Saturday in the back of the church. The Legion gave each film a rating: A-I (Unobjectionable for General Patronage), A-II (Unobjectionable for Adults), B (Objectionable in part), down to C (Condemned, Catholics prohibited from viewing). Members of the Legion even put signs outside movie theaters advising Catholic patrons of condemned films such as *Lady of Burlesque, This Thing Called Love,* and *Two-Faced Woman. Miracle on 34th Street,* now a children's Christmas classic, only received a B rating, because Twentieth Century Fox refused to recast Maureen O'Hara's character from divorced mother to war widow. A condemned rating could deliver such a blow to the box office that Hollywood usually complied with the Legion's standards. Hollywood producer David Selznick endured a long battle with Legion forces to keep Rhett Butler's final words in *Gone With the Wind:* "Frankly, my dear, I don't give a damn." Long kisses, adultery, double beds, "damn," "hell," and many of Mae West's lines were taboo.[2]

When the Legion condemned Howard Hughes's film *The Outlaw,* parish pulpits shook with warnings of eternal damnation to anyone who bought a ticket to see this film about Billy the Kid. But like scores of rebellious teenagers, we trolleyed to downtown Brooklyn Fabian's Fox theatre on Fulton Street, where it was playing in 1943.[3] We were sorely disappointed to see only a little extra décolletage of a bosomy Jane Russell in the highly hyped scene where she kept a shivering Billy the Kid warm and alive by lying next to him in a haystack. The uproar had actually forced Hughes to replace Jane Russell's off-the shoulder blouse—portrayed in the film's advertisements and World War II pinups—with a marginally less revealing one.[4]

.   .   .

My lingering spiritual memory of those years at Brooklyn Prep is of our religious retreat on February 10 and 11, 1948, directed by Father Raymond

Kelly at Mount Manresa, the Jesuit retreat house on Staten Island, New York. Though laden with threats of the fires of hell, the retreat provided a remarkable interlude of meditation and prayer with one disturbing exception.

That exception was my sourest experience with any member of the Catholic clergy. During my retreat confession when I admitted to "impure acts" of heavy petting, the priest (whose name I can't remember) asked me to open my fly. I did and he took my penis in his hand and said, "See how ugly this is? This is not beautiful. It is too ugly to let any girl see or touch." I was shaken. Strangely, I did not feel sexually abused (though I was); I just thought something was wrong with this priest. I was too embarrassed about my own confession and the incident to tell my parents.

This incident came in my senior year, when I began to have doubts about the truth of the Catholic Church and its teachings. I continued to attend Mass each Sunday and occasionally went to confession, but the Church seemed old fashioned, out of touch with much that I was reading and feeling. Somehow, the Jesuits at The Prep sensed this adolescent crisis of faith. One suggested that I read Avery Dulles's book *A Testimonial to Grace*, about his conversion to the Catholic faith. At first, Dulles wrote, "the candles, the vestments, and the incense" repulsed him. But then, as he put it, "I came into the Church like one of those timid swimmers who closes his eyes as he jumps into the roaring sea. The waters of faith, I have since found, are marvelously buoyant. Indeed, when man is clothed with grace, the sea of faith is his natural element."[5] Dulles's book, doubtless along with my parents' prayers and those of the Jesuits at the Prep, brought me back to the Catholic Church. I realized how the Catholic faith had strengthened my parents and relatives with its secure traditions, sense of community, and clear moral compass.

Somehow, sometimes subliminally, the Jesuits at Brooklyn Prep charted a clear course for us. As the foreword to our graduating class yearbook recorded: we had "conquered many new fields of knowledge—spiritual, scholastic, physical," but the years at Prep would be of "no avail if we do not follow out these teachings in our daily, future lives." That meant "becoming active, militant Catholics; strong in our knowledge and appreciation of political and current events, strong in the courage of our convictions. . . . Only by such vigorous means," we wrote, "can we make use of the benefits Prep has given us, only by working always 'for the greater glory of God'"—

Ad Majorem Dei Gloriam (A.D.M.G.), as the Jesuit scholastics taught us to chant and write on the first page of all our exam blue books.*

Perhaps most important, the Jesuits at Brooklyn Prep imbued me with a sense that there was something special about being a Catholic, a uniqueness that carried both opportunity and obligation. My respect for them led me and my parents to choose The College of the Holy Cross.

.   .   .

Strict as it was, the discipline at Brooklyn Prep did not prepare me for Holy Cross. There classes were held five and a half days a week, including Saturday morning. Attendance was checked at each class. A Jesuit priest lived on every floor of every dormitory and conducted bed checks at seven and eleven each night. Specific permission was required to leave the campus from mid-day Saturday until the bed check at 7 P.M. Sunday. In addition to Sunday, we were required to go to Mass on four of the five week days—with assigned seats so that attendance could be taken. Smoking was permitted in the dormitories, but beer and women were prohibited; no one dared violate those rules—the punishment was expulsion.

At Holy Cross, I met for the first time people who were not from Brooklyn. Most were from New England, notably Massachusetts, but a number were from the South and Midwest. This opened my eyes and ears to new faces, dress, attitudes, and accents. My two roommates in my first year were both veterans on the GI bill. Though several years older, they were subjected to the same curfews and rules.

In my freshman year, I discovered college partying. At Dartmouth, where we went to watch a Holy Cross football game, I got so sick drinking gin that since I have never been able to stand its smell, much less its taste, and gin never again passed my lips.

In sophomore year, my rhetoric professor, Henry Bean, S.J.,† taught me how to think on my feet, write, and speak publicly. His was the only class that interested me. That year I flunked European history. At the time, I blamed my failing grade on the Irish priest who taught it, Patrick Higgins,

---

*My experience at Brooklyn Prep would lead me to send my two sons, Mark and Joe III, to Georgetown Prep, the Jesuit high school in Maryland just outside Washington, D.C.
†One of the two best teachers I ever had; the other was Paul Freund at Harvard Law School.

S.J., charging that he was prejudiced against Italian-Americans. My mother and father didn't buy that excuse. Instead, I studied during the summer, and when I returned to the Cross in September, I retook and passed the exam. I vowed never to fail a course again, an oath I kept.

For a bachelor of arts degree, I had to take two years of Latin and two years of either math or Greek. I chose math. We took no electives until junior and senior year—and then they were limited. I took most of mine in English literature. The Jesuits exposed me to the grace of English poetry, Shakespeare's tragedies and comedies, and carefully selected American literature. Nothing more recent or racy than Jack London, Bret Harte, and Ambrose Bierce's *The Devil's Dictionary*. I had to get a special dispensation to write my senior thesis on F. Scott Fitzgerald; my classmate Hugh Bradshaw had to mount a major campaign for permission to write his about William Faulkner, who had won the Nobel Prize for Literature in 1949.

These restrictions stemmed largely from the *Index Librorum Prohibitorum*—Index of Forbidden Books, first published in 1559 by Pope Paul IV. The Jesuits at Holy Cross followed it meticulously. The Index was intended to keep Catholics away from books that might lead them to lose their faith, be seduced by heretical positions on matters of doctrine, or engage in pagan rituals or sexual sins. Catholics who published, read, owned, sold, or translated books on the Index faced an array of penalties, including possible excommunication. The year I entered Holy Cross, the Index included books by the Marquis de Sade, Spinoza, Machiavelli, Adolf Hitler, Immanuel Kant, and Leon Trotsky, as well as Ernest Hemingway, John O'Hara, and Mark Twain.[6] During my years at Holy Cross, the Index did not stop me from reading—in the privacy of my room, often between brown-paper covers—just about everything by contemporary writers like Hemingway, O'Hara, and Truman Capote. By the time I graduated in 1952, the Index was irrelevant for me.[7]

I considered English my field of concentration, but in fact everyone those days graduated from Holy Cross as a philosophy major. In junior year, we were required to take half our academic load in philosophy courses (logic, epistemology, ontology, cosmology); in senior year, three-fourths (natural theology, fundamental psychology, advanced psychology, general ethics, and special ethics).

To teach philosophy, the Jesuits used syllogisms moving from a major and minor thesis to an airtight conclusion. To this day, I recall their basic example:

Major thesis: Lost articles should be returned to their rightful owners.
Minor thesis: The wallet I picked up is a lost article.
Conclusion: I should return this wallet to its rightful owner.[8]

In ethics, we debated—and concluded—that an individual has a right to a living wage, unions are "in se" (inherently) lawful, just strikes are appropriate exercises of union power, and the state has the duty to compel parents to educate their children. By modern standards, our ethics courses were conservative and dated. With hedges, they justified capital punishment and dismissed doubts about its effectiveness with this assertion: "The reason why capital punishment is often ineffectual [in deterring other crimes] is because it is frequently not carried out. The law's delays and sentimentality and clever lawyers so delay the proper enforcement of this penalty that it often has little effect on the criminal."[9]

Special ethics at Holy Cross kept women in their place ("barefoot in the summer and pregnant in the winter," as many joked at the time) with this proposition: "Marital and parental authority, at the first moment of the existence of conjugal and parental society, is conferred immediately by God upon the husband in the first case, upon the parents in the second case." The author, our professor Joseph Sullivan, S.J., continued in his book, "The authority necessary for conjugal society is conferred by God (through nature) upon that one of the two members who, generally speaking, is more fitted by nature to possess and exercise that authority. But generally speaking that one is the husband, as almost universal experience and conviction of mankind testifies."[10] With such high-powered women on my mother's side of the family, I had difficulty keeping a straight face as Fr. Sullivan elaborated on this proposition.

The Jesuits encouraged me to dive into the choppy waters of ethical debate, but they expected us all to swim back to the shore of Catholic doctrine. Socialism and communism were roundly condemned moral atrocities. Civil authority derived its validity from the consent of the governed. While private property was considered an inherent right and capitalism generally blessed, materialism, relativism, utilitarianism, and hedonism were rejected as immoral. Artificial birth control, abortion, eugenics, and euthanasia were viewed as serious sins.

The Jesuits at Holy Cross sent two clear messages: first, the need to repel communism and its Godless repression of the human spirit and the Catholic Church; second, the need to reject the excessive materialism of American society.

We took the first message to heart. In 1949, when the communists toppled American ally Chiang Kai-shek, we prayed that China would be freed of Mao Tse-tung and that Chinese Catholics would be free to practice religion. Our only complaint about Harry Truman's use of American forces to repel the North Korean invasion of South Korea was that it was not aggressive enough. When the Chinese Communists entered the war on the side of the North Koreans, we were frustrated at their ability to hold our troops at the 38th parallel, the border between the two Koreas. We condemned Truman for firing General Douglas MacArthur, cheered the imperious general when he addressed a joint session of Congress, and sang at all our parties "Old Soldiers Never Die," the hit song that came out of this incident.

At the time, we didn't pay much attention to the Jesuits' message about materialism. Many, perhaps most of us, were the first generation in our families to go to college. Our ambition, shared and encouraged by parents who had sacrificed to send us to Holy Cross (few scholarships were available except for returning GIs), was to be doctors, dentists, and lawyers or work for well-known corporations. Public service was not on the career list. My heart and mind, like those of most of my classmates, were focused on getting a piece of the materialism so many Jesuit professors warned us to reject. We wanted to make money. When my father said, "Someday you will make $50,000 a year," I thought that as a proud parent he was exaggerating the potential of his only child. But I was ready and willing to try.

.   .   .

Throughout high school and college I had to work during the summer. In the summer of 1945, at age fourteen, I got my working papers, a requirement of New York State law to stop abuse of child labor. A friend of my father gave me a job (and my father gave his son one). My first job was at *The New Yorker*, on West 43rd Street in Manhattan, where weekly deadlines for eccentric writers and cartoonists kept me and the other office boys running. The following summer I worked as a messenger for Hearst Publications in Manhattan. Of special interest for a fifteen-year-old was seeing so many beautiful, half-dressed models when I rushed coats, dresses, bathing suits, and lingerie to their dressing rooms for photo shoots.

In the summer of 1947 and on many Saturdays during the ensuing school year, I worked as a stockroom boy and wrapper at B. Altman, a prominent department store on Fifth Avenue and 34th Street. I needed the five dollars I made on a Saturday to take my high school sweetheart to the movies, including snacks and subway rides to and from downtown Brooklyn or Manhattan theaters, because boys always picked up the tab.

In the summer of 1948, I worked as a short-order cook at the Club at Breezy Point, a private summer neighborhood at the tip of the Rockaway peninsula. The community, accessible by permission only, with a guard post at the only entrance road, was almost 100 percent Irish Catholic. The Rockaway Point Company, which owned all the land, kept the area restricted from blacks, Jews, and probably Italian-Americans. My parents didn't favor Breezy Point, and I soon realized why. On the weekends, many men and a number of women drank to excess and needed help to get into their cars. (We never thought of stopping them from driving drunk back to their bungalows.)

In the summer of 1949, after my freshman year at Holy Cross, the economy was in such a recession—particularly in New York—that even with my father's help, I couldn't get a job. My parents insisted that I go to school instead. They were then urging me to be a doctor, noting that Holy Cross had a superb reputation for pre-med education. Since I hadn't taken any science courses, I enrolled at Fordham University and took two. At the end of that difficult and uninspiring summer, I knew I'd never be a physician.

In the summer of 1950, I worked as messenger for Brown Brothers Harriman on Wall Street, hand delivering, as firms did in those days, stock and bond certificates to clearing-house mailboxes in the financial district. Recounting stories of the power and wealth of the Harriman family, my parents filled me with awe for the firm. They admonished me to be especially respectful of everyone because "someday one of those powerful people might be able to help you—and if they don't like you, they could destroy your opportunities." Edward Harriman, a robber baron of the late nineteenth and early twentieth centuries, had amassed the family fortune through Union Pacific Railroad. Inconceivable to me that summer, his son, W. Averell, who became governor of New York in 1954 and served as undersecretary of state for political affairs in the Kennedy administration, would become a friend of mine. In November 1965, I would send him, on President Johnson's behalf, to Chile to help roll back an increase in the price of copper. When I at first suggested to the President that the journey to Chile on such short notice might be difficult for the seventy-four-year-old diplomat, Johnson chuckled and whispered, "You just call him and get a car over to his Georgetown house. Ol' Averell likes women. You just tell him what the President wants him to do. And tell him we'll put a couple of pretty nurses on the plane and they'll start working on him as soon as wheels are up and by the time he gets to Santiago he'll have it up!" In subsequent years I enjoyed many dinners at his art-filled house.

In the summers of 1951 and 1953, my Uncle Tom Gill, who was secretary treasurer of the Paper Handlers and Sheet Straighteners Union, got me a job as an apprentice. This Irish-American union controlled movement of the huge rolls of newsprint from the docks of Manhattan and Brooklyn into the city's newspaper presses and printing plants—after they were unloaded from boats to the docks by Italian-American stevedores. When we shaped up on the docks in the morning to see who would go to work each day, Irish union members wondered how, with a name like Califano, I ever got the job. My parents also encouraged me to travel: in the summers of 1950 and 1951, across the country; in the summer of 1952, as a graduation present, through Europe and the British Isles. The European trip, of almost three months, gave me my first brush with fascism.

My college roommate Ike Lancaster and I drove into Spain late at night inadvertently past a sleeping guard at a border post. When we got to a hotel in Zaragoza, the clerk looked at our passports and immediately called over an armed soldier standing in the lobby. Since our passports were not stamped for entry, the soldier took us to the police station, where they threatened to put us in jail as illegal entrants. Eventually, hours of questioning and waiting later, they believed our story and let us go. After that we noticed that there were soldiers everywhere. So that afternoon we went to a bullfight, à la Hemingway's *The Sun Also Rises,* and instead of going south to Madrid, drove out of Spain as fast as we could.

Our ship, the *Groote Beer*, encountered a hurricane on our return voyage that left half of the passengers seasick and terrified all of us. I stepped off onto the New York pier, still rattled by the experience, and headed to law school—with little appreciation of how appropriate a prelude that storm was to the churning of new people and experiences ahead.

CHAPTER 5

A Harvard Law School Education

"I F YOU ARE EVER going to be somebody," Mother and Dad chorused incessantly, "you've got to go to graduate school." Like most of my Holy Cross classmates, I wanted to go to work and earn some money. But in the 1950s, we did what our parents told us. Mine gave me four alternatives: medicine, business, education, or law.

I chose law as the least undesirable alternative. Fantasizing myself as a budding Perry Mason, I applied to three schools: Harvard, Columbia, and Fordham. Uncle Joe Gill, the most financially successful and experienced member of our family, pressed for Columbia because it was in New York ("where all the money is") and because my father had gotten IBM founder Thomas Watson to write a letter of recommendation for me there. But I decided on Harvard, not so much because I thought it was the best but because I liked Massachusetts. If I had to go to law school, I thought, it might as well be in a city like Boston or Cambridge with many other colleges and graduate schools offering plenty of parties and girls.

My father wouldn't let me take any scholarship or other aid from Harvard because, he said, "We pay our own way." Frightened about living on Park Place as crime increased in the neighborhood, my parents had moved into Uncle Joe's smaller rent-controlled Clinton Avenue apartment in Brooklyn. Mother and Dad sent a check each month to Uncle Joe, whose business had moved to Philadelphia but who kept the apartment under his name to maintain the controlled rent, which reduced the amount my parents had to borrow to pay for my tuition.

In September 1952, not one of us arriving as the Harvard Law School Class of 1955 was prepared for the world we were entering. Because of my trip to Europe, I missed the classic orientation lecture during which Dean Erwin Griswold asked all first-year students to look to their right and then to their left. As soon as they had, he remarked, "One of you will not be here at the end of three years."*

I didn't need to hear that speech to be intimidated. Phi Beta Kappa Keys dangled from chains. Almost everyone had graduated from college summa or magna cum laude in a day when those Latin accolades separated the top 1 or 2 percent from the rest of the class. Having received my diploma from Holy Cross without any such distinction, I felt like the only first-year law student without a fistful of academic medals.

While at The Law School, as we quickly learned to call it, *Time* magazine ran a cover story reporting that Harvard's medical school was the best in the nation, its business school had no peer, but "the law school is in a class by itself."[1] Dean Erwin Griswold and others quoted that reference ad nauseam. Giants in the law taught us: Warren Seavey, whose signature book on torts was used in just about every law school; Lon Fuller for contracts; Dick Field for civil procedure. Stanley Surrey, who in 1961 became the Kennedy administration's tax-policy guru, taught us taxation. We had A. James Casner for property and estates. Louis Loss taught us corporate and SEC law; Zechariah Chafee, Jr., unfair competition; Louis Jaffee, administrative law. Paul Freund was our professor of Constitutional law and conflicts of law.

The first year at Harvard Law was designed to be the most challenging intellectual experience of our lives, and it measured up. The sheer volume of cases and other materials that we were assigned to read overwhelmed us. Professors taught by the Socratic method, asking questions, forcing us to think hard, and trapping us into illogical extensions of legal principles. They rarely offered any answers, and had a knack for making us feel we deserved their ridicule and scorn. In Dick Field's procedure class, I began my answer to a question by saying, "I feel . . ." He snapped in his high-pitched voice, "At Harvard Law School we don't *feel*, Mr. Califano, we try to *think*." A few weeks later, I began my answer to his question about a case with "I think . . ." When I finished speaking he cracked, "I hardly call that *thinking*, Mr. Califano. I believe you're back to *feeling*."

Not one professor would have passed a political correctness test and every one of them would have seen that as an achievement. Only nine of our class were women, two less than in the class of 1953, which contained the first women to receive an L.L.B. from Harvard. An excerpt from the Casner and Leach Property I casebook captured the school's machismo world:

> *At common law* it was a man's world. There was no nonsense about equal rights, the single standard, or woman's suffrage. Husband and wife were

one, and the one was the husband. The married woman was not *sui juris*, in this respect being in the same class with infants and idiots. . . . However, before we burst into uncontrollable tears over the hard lot of the wife, let it be remembered that in the rough-and-tumble of feudal times the husband's function of protector involved something more than a hand under the elbow at street crossings and a scowl at too appreciative glances.[2]

There was only one exam—at the end of June—for each course, even those that had ended six months earlier, in January. Seventy-five or above was considered an A on the ground that correctly responding to three-fourths of what a Harvard Law professor asked was a monumental achievement. Grades were given in increments to the nearest tenth of a point. Every student was ranked from first to last and the list posted on bulletin boards for all to see. Thus, competition was instilled at Harvard Law School the way charity is in Catholic nuns who take the vow of poverty. It worked on me: at the end of my first year, I ranked forty-eighth of 501 and was determined to do better.

There were then only three academic societies at Harvard: the *Law Review,* by far the most prestigious student legal publication in the nation; the Board of Student Advisors, which conducted the Ames Moot Court appellate argument competition; and the first student-run Legal Aid Bureau in the nation, which serviced clients who could not afford lawyers. Selection was determined solely by academic standing. At the end of my first year, I was eligible for the Legal Aid Bureau.

My first client was a woman seeking to divorce her husband. She claimed that he was a drunk and abused her. I agonized over whether I could represent her; after all, I was Catholic and did not believe in divorce. Should I help someone violate God's law of the indissolubility of marriage? I tried to talk her into staying with her husband. She refused. I suggested we get a protective court order for her. She wanted out of the marriage. I then thought about passing her on to another member of the Bureau, but decided not to, because Harvard had already ingrained in me the conviction that in the American system of justice everyone is entitled to representation, and that lawyers need not share—and should not be tarred with—views or positions of their clients. The attorney's task was to present the client's case as persuasively as possible, not to judge the client. So I concluded that as this woman's lawyer my duty was to carry out her wishes if they were legal in Massachusetts. I was also motivated by my hunger to get into a courtroom (Massachusetts courts gave legal aid students special permission to do so). After more meetings with her, I drafted the papers to file for her divorce. She never kept future appointments to sign them.

As pleased as I was at making Legal Aid, I was disappointed not to make the *Law Review*. Because I had taken such a liberal arts education at Holy Cross, focusing on literature, philosophy, language, and math, I thought I could increase my chances by taking more practical courses that summer. In addition to my job as a paper handler, I took two courses, accounting principles and economic theory, at New York University Graduate School of Business Administration. The extra work paid off. At the end of my second year I ranked sixth out of 456 and made the *Law Review*.

.   .   .

Harvard Law School was my first non-Catholic educational experience. Most of the Jewish students were from the Northeast and very much like my Jewish friends in Brooklyn. However, I had never been exposed to White Anglo-Saxon Protestants—especially those with pedigree and affluence, who attended prep schools like Milton, Choate, Kent, Hotchkiss, and St. Paul's, and Ivy League colleges. These men carried themselves with a worldly swagger. They dressed in the WASP uniform, Brooks Brothers button-down. Classical music and art were familiar to them. They had traveled widely. At winter break they went to warm climates to sail or mountains to ski. Their fathers were lawyers, corporate executives, and physicians. Many became my friends, and in second and third year eight of us rented a house at 21 Sacramento Place, a few blocks from law school. It was quite a group: John McGillicuddy, a Princeton football star, eventually became chairman and chief executive officer of Chemical bank. David Maxwell, a Yalie, became chairman and chief executive office of the Federal National Mortgage Association (FannieMae) and was named by *Fortune* magazine as one of the ten greatest CEOs of all time. John Robson, another Yalie, became chairman of the Federal Aviation Administration and deregulated the airlines; he also served as undersecretary of the Treasury and head of the U.S. Export-Import Bank in a series of Republican administrations. Dick Button, a Harvard College graduate, was the first American Olympic figure-skating champion. John Steadman, a Yalie, from Hawaii, became a judge on the Court of Appeals for the District of Columbia. Dick Beresford, another Yalie who went on to medical school, became an outstanding academic with his law and medical degrees. Jim Bushby, a Yalie who practiced law for several years, became a New England innkeeper. These housemates opened my eyes to a far more sophisticated world than I had ever known—in the performing arts, foreign films, music, books, even in dress.

With such classmates, I found myself for the first time out of the cocoon of a nurturing Catholic family and institutions. Harvard Law School was a roiling secular sea of ambitious, pedigreed classmates from Ivy prep schools and colleges, and I was determined to prove myself at least their equal. I may not have gone to Exeter or Yale, but I was hellbent to surpass the graduates of such schools. Taking my cue from Irving Berlin's popular song of the day, anything they can do, I thought, I can do better. I added many of their social skills to my Brooklyn repertoire. I switched from burgundy corduroy to tweed in sport jackets and to the button-down shirts, striped ties, and cordovan shoes of the Ivy League. I studied harder than ever before. And I found I loved the law.

Most important, if Holy Cross had gotten me to think about the grand philosophical questions—God, life, ethics, truth—Harvard Law School started me thinking about public policy and politics and their relevance to the larger issues of maldistribution of wealth and individual rights.

My professors at Harvard were by and large far more liberal than any I had been exposed to before. The Jesuits had instilled a sense of social justice in terms of individually helping the poor and weak. But at Harvard, the professors were more attentive to broad issues of civil rights and freedom of expression. In my sixteen years of Catholic education and at home, the First Amendment had been celebrated for its protection of freedom of religion, not for its enshrinement of political and artistic expression.

In short order, I found myself completely comfortable with the human rights that the Supreme Court defined through our Constitution, because they snugly fit with what I had learned from my parents and the Jesuits at Brooklyn Prep and Holy Cross. If we are all made in the image of God our Creator, then we all deserve to be treated with dignity. If God has given us free will, then civil society should provide the freedom to exercise it. Not only was Harvard Law School adding to my life a dimension of social polish and intellectual sophistication, it was providing a powerful secular complement to the religious values instilled by my parents and the Jesuits.

My experiences at Harvard gave me greater respect and appreciation for my religion, my faith, and the values they had instilled in me. I engaged in conversations with very bright people who did not believe in God, who were agnostic, and who were skeptical, even scornful, of the Church. I was struck at how easily they ridiculed the Catholic Church and its doctrines—and how careful they were not to ridicule Jews or Negroes. It was my first inkling that among intellectuals anti-Catholicism might be the last permissible prejudice. Because I sensed that many of my classmates were troubled, some even tortured, by their agnosticism, I came to treasure the spiritual and ethical framework in which my life could be placed and my actions measured.

Steeped in concepts of natural law, I understood the differences between God's law and man's. It was, for example, a violation of God's law to commit adultery, but not a violation of the law in many states. It was a violation of state law to run a red light, but not of God's law. I was surprised to find that virtually none of my classmates thought this way.

Not quite everyone was liberal at Harvard. In first year, my property teacher was James Angell MacLachlan, nicknamed "Red" because of his (fading) shock of red hair. During parents' weekend, Mother and Dad came to Red MacLachlan's class. We were discussing a case involving landlord-tenant law and an eviction. During the course of the Socratic exchanges, a student asked, "What about tenants' rights?" MacLachlan reached in his pocket and pulled out a dollar bill. "I don't know what tenants' rights are. I can't feel them. I can't touch them." Then, waving the dollar bill high, he said, "Now, this is property. That's what we're talking about—property rights!"

I thought Mother would faint. She considered Harvard a hotbed of materialistic atheism and this incident stoked her concern about the Law School's potentially bad influence on me. The incident occurred soon after a young New Haven student, William F. Buckley, had published *God and Man at Yale,* his blistering book about Godlessness and agnosticism in the Ivy League. My mother had read the book, and she sent it to me after that weekend.

The summer of 1954 I worked as a clerk in the office of Dewey, Ballantine,

Bushby, Palmer & Wood, an old-line Wall Street law firm. Thomas Dewey, the former governor of New York, had been brought in to revitalize the institution, which had been started by Elihu Root, President William McKinley's secretary of war and President Theodore Roosevelt's secretary of state. Mother and Dad were delighted with the clerkship. To them, working in a Wall Street firm was evidence I had reached the top of the world. My recollection of that summer is hazy. I do remember, however, that when the partners learned I had made the *Harvard Law Review,* they took great notice of me and treated me to many lunches and dinners. I did think that they lived high on the hog, and I enjoyed the prospect of doing the same.

Harvard Law School turned me on intellectually and professionally—and stoked my ambition. As one of my professors, Zechariah Chafee, put it, "I envisage [in the lawyer] a thirst for exploration, a joy in life, the faith that effort can bring accomplishment, the dream that over the Alps lies Italy. Such a spirit . . . can turn law into more than an intellectual puzzle or a lucrative occupation. It is the quality which has turned many successful lawyers into great public servants."[3] The school's professors—and the examples of its successful graduates in private practice, politics, and government—blew open my horizon of opportunity. Graduates were cabinet members. They ran large law firms and giant corporations. They sat on the Supreme Court of the United States and hundreds of federal and state courts across the nation. I had fallen into the profession that was right for me. There was nothing I couldn't do, it seemed, after graduating from this law school.

CHAPTER 6

Landlubber in the Navy

FROM THE TOP of the heap at Harvard Law School, I went to the bottom of the heap in the U.S. Navy. The Korean War was raging when I entered law school. The Selective Service had classified me 1-A shortly after I arrived in Cambridge, but gave me a deferment for law school. That made it certain I would be drafted upon graduation in June 1955, even though the war ended in July 1953.

Well aware that many of us were draft bait, Rear Admiral Ira Nunn, judge advocate general of the Navy, came to the law school in December 1954 to recruit from our graduating class. I signed up.

I had been dating Trudy Zawacki while she was at the College of New Rochelle and I was at Harvard. Trudy was a delightful, intelligent, and pretty blonde from a wonderful Catholic family. Her father was a psychiatrist; her mother, a committed volunteer and member of St. Mary's choir in Taunton, Massachusetts. She was the eldest of four, with a sister and two brothers. I looked up to her and her family, a leading one in Taunton, where everyone seemed to know the Zawackis, a far cry from the anonymity of life in Brooklyn. I wanted to marry her as soon as I graduated from law school. It was a perfect fit: we were in love, both Catholic-educated for sixteen years; we went to Mass every Sunday and saw raising children as the central purpose of marriage. It was the model made by my parents and aunts and uncles.

Marriage wasn't feasible on an Army private's pay; a Navy officer's pay would give me enough money to support a wife. The last year of law school was hectic; being an editor of the *Review,* carrying a full course load, and writing an antitrust thesis was like holding down three full-time jobs. Exams ended in June. I rushed to New York to take a cram course for the state bar; took the bar exam on June 30 and July 1; went to Taunton the next day to get married on July 4; and was off to Navy Officer Candidate School in Newport, Rhode Island, a week later. There was no time for the pre-Cana preparation, which today precedes marriage in the Catholic Church.

At OCS, we rose at 5 A.M., shaved in two minutes, did calisthenics, ate sitting at attention, marched for hours choking on the summer dust rising from the dry naval base field, ran for a few miles with a pack on our back, and cleaned latrines. We learned to make beds so tightly that a quarter thrown flat on the sheets would bounce higher than the heads of the inspecting chief petty officer and lieutenant, j.g. Our boots had black hard rubber soles that marked the barracks floor, so we were endlessly scrubbing with steel wool to remove the dark streaks before waxing the floor to a brilliant shine. We fired .45 pistols until our wrists and palms ached. It took me so many shots to hit the torso outlined on the target paper the required number of times that my right hand resembled raw hamburger meat by the time I qualified. In my skivvies, I jumped into a pool from a frightening height holding my Navy jeans over my head, legs tied at the ends, to make sure I didn't hit the bottom and to fashion a life preserver. I was repeatedly dunked under water to simulate surviving in ocean swells if my ship were torpedoed and sunk. On two occasions I boarded a ship docked at the Newport pier. I never went to sea.

My academic record at OCS was mediocre. We had classes in engineering, navigation, operations, seamanship, and weapons. I did so poorly in mechanical aptitude that the officer in charge of training our unit said the Navy would never let me near a shipboard cannon or boiler room. I graduated in the bottom half of my class, with a well-below-average military aptitude score.

The Navy's need for lawyers was so pressing that we began an abbreviated session at the Naval Justice School two weeks before we completed Officer Candidate training and were commissioned. Back in my legal milieu, my grades soared. We graduated from the Naval Justice School on December 16, 1955.

Upon graduation, I was assigned to the Pay and Allowances Section, Fiscal and Taxation Branch, Administrative Law Division, Office of the Judge Advocate General in the Pentagon. Here I reviewed individual compensation claims of naval personnel. The legal work was as dreary as the title of the branch I worked in, so I soon began plotting to move to another assignment.

I decided to become the Navy's expert on issues related to the employment of retired naval officers. Most naval officers retired at relatively young ages—well before their fiftieth birthday. Many sought civilian jobs in government or with defense contractors. Those seeking federal jobs could be required to forfeit their retirement pay under the technically complex Dual Compensation Act; those seeking work with defense contractors faced restrictions from statutes prohibiting conflicts of interest. I wrote a guide describing how to negotiate these restrictions and (as I had hoped) it became a (free) bestseller that drew plaudits for Navy JAG.[1] When Admiral Chester Ward, then judge advocate general of the Navy, commended my work as "a fine example of excellent judgment, legal thought, and helpfulness to an individual," I asked for the reward of an assignment in appellate litigation.

I was detailed to the Appellate Defense Division in Navy JAG, which was responsible for briefing and arguing appeals of special and general courts martial convictions before Boards of Review and the Court of Military Appeals. I briefed more than two hundred cases and argued one hundred in just over a year, an invaluable experience for a young lawyer aspiring to be the new Clarence Darrow or William Fallon.

In all but one case, I felt justice was done, even when I lost, which was most of the time. The case involved a murder on an aircraft carrier. The defendant claimed that he was at a ship's movie at the time of the murder. Defense counsel at the court martial had put him on the stand, but did not question him in detail about various scenes in the movie and relate the times of those scenes to the time the coroner had set for the murder. I became convinced there was reasonable doubt about the defendant's guilt. I grew so concerned about the sloppy examination of the accused by his trial counsel that I obtained the ship's logs and other records and screened the film in an attempt to prove inadequate representation. Unfortunately, I failed to sway the court, which affirmed my client's conviction and sentence. At that moment, I had my first serious doubts about imposing the death penalty for any crime and about the support of such punishment in my Holy Cross ethics course.

While I appreciated the special situation that prompted creation of the system of military justice, I was often disturbed at what seemed like inadequate representation by counsel. This inadequacy was common in special courts martial, where the defendant could lose his freedom, be dishonorably discharged, and be fined—all without the benefit of trained counsel. In a parting letter to the judge advocate general when I returned to civilian life in November 1958, I urged a change in the system to require that defendants be given qualified attorneys at special courts martial, as well as in general courts martial. I also complained about the "various instructions of the Secretary of the Navy on larceny, homosexuality, and the like," which resulted in courts martial and dishonorable discharge, suggesting "if such persons are not desired in the Navy, they can easily be discharged administratively under some discharge of less than honorable stature [that would not impose such a serious stigma]." The Navy took no action on my recommendations.

I served in the Navy during early civil rights struggles. My sense of the immorality and savagery of discrimination was seeded in St. Gregory's religion class, where we learned how the Romans persecuted Christians and fed them to the lions for entertainment. My sense of the irrationality of discrimination came in college while reading Gordon Allport's book *The Nature of Prejudice*. There I learned that when the Nazi regime could no longer rely on visible characteristics to identify Jews they were made to wear yellow armbands. In America, I thought, white Christians and Jews could readily blend into society; blacks, however, no matter how well educated or dressed, remained easy-to-spot targets for discrimination. Trudy and I were appalled at the brutal murder of fourteen-year-old Emmett Till in Mississippi; we cheered Rosa Parks's refusal to relinquish her seat on a segregated bus in December 1955, which sparked the 381-day boycott of the Montgomery bus system led by Martin Luther King, Jr. We were proud of President Eisenhower when he sent the 101st Airborne Division to Little Rock, Arkansas, in 1957 to enforce the Supreme Court *Brown v. Board of Education* decision ordering desegregation of Central High School.

Trudy and I lived in Arlington, Virginia, where the Glebe movie theater (which screened popular films like *Around the World in 80 Days* and *The Bridge on the River Kwai*) was for whites only, as were most public restaurants and accommodations. We went to some civil rights meetings and picketed the theater on Glebe Road. My Navy commanding officer said it was against Navy regulations for those on active duty to take part in such demonstrations. "You could be reprimanded for such political activity, or worse," he warned. Thereafter I stayed home during public protests.

While I never served on a ship in the Navy, I did seek to make a few waves. The biggest swelled when I came across an obscure statute that provided that any reserve officer appointed "with a view to assignment . . . as . . . a . . . law specialist of the Naval Reserve . . . shall . . . be credited with a minimum amount of service in an active status of three years . . . ."[2] As soon as I read that provision, I thought I should have been commissioned a lieutenant j.g. and made a full lieutenant in eighteen months, with higher pay for the entire three years I was serving. I asked about it and was told the law did not apply, because all naval officers were commissioned with a view toward any kind of service the Navy ordered. That response so infuriated me that I got clippings from the *Harvard Law School Record* reporting Admiral Nunn's pitch for us to join the Navy and practice law there. I also pointed out that I was in Naval Justice School before being commissioned an ensign because of the Navy's need for lawyers. Clearly, I argued to the Office of Naval Personnel, I was commissioned "with a view to assignment" as a law specialist. I was summarily rebuffed. So on March 4, 1958, I sued the Navy to have my records corrected to reflect credit for the years in law school with an appropriate increase in rank and pay. I won the lawsuit and $1,700 in November 1958. Over the next years, several officers won similar claims citing my case. I had tasted legal combat and savored victory. Now I hungered for more.

CHAPTER 7

A Bite of the Big Apple

UPON RELEASE FROM the Navy, I returned to New York to Dewey, Ballantine, Bushby, Palmer & Wood. I was getting in line to become a partner in a Wall Street law firm, enjoying whiffs of the sweet smell of material success. However, based on my legal experience in the Navy, I thought I deserved more than my starting salary of $6,500. My parents thought the salary was excellent. (At the time I didn't know that the combined income of my Dad at IBM and Mother teaching in the New York public school system was not quite $15,000.)

In the beginning, the prospect of practicing big-time law at the firm headed by former prosecutor, New York governor, and Republican presidential candidate Thomas E. Dewey was exciting. One partner, John M. Harlan, had taken a seat on the Supreme Court in 1955, and Dewey was attracting new corporate clients and complex antitrust litigation.

The anticipation of being a Wall Street lawyer soon gave way to the reality that marks the life of fledgling associates. My first assignment was to review thousands of pages of old records in a dusty New Jersey warehouse in order to reconstruct the history of aureomycin. I spent weeks poring over wrinkled scientific papers and laboratory reports, largely incomprehensible to me. The goal: to protect American Cyanamid's patent on this profitable antibiotic.

I next worked for Charles MacLean, the patrician head of the tax department. He was representing American Can Company, which leased, but refused to sell, its can-closing machines. The courts had found that practice a violation of antitrust laws and ordered the company to offer the machines for sale. The company relented, but treated its profits from sales as capital gains. The Internal Revenue Service moved to subject those profits to significantly higher ordinary income tax rates, because the machines were "sold in the ordinary course of business."

MacLean told me the stakes were so high for the company that he wanted me to "read every decision ever written interpreting that phrase." Within the first few days of research, I concluded that the company would have to pay ordinary income tax on profits from sales of machines it had never leased. When I reported this to MacLean, he brushed me off with a brusque "Finish your assignment." In the pre-Lexis, pre-computer world, that patronizing command condemned me to ten weeks of summarizing several hundred decisions on three-by-five white index cards, and writing the longest memo ever composed on the meaning of the phrase. After a Tax Court hearing conducted in one morning's time, the judge decided the case exactly as I had predicted. If this was tax litigation, I wanted out of the tax department.

Such assignments made me wonder what I was doing at a Wall Street firm. I realized that when the stakes were high enough, no effort would be spared to win; several hundred thousand dollars in legal fees were a sound investment when the return might be many millions of dollars. I missed the freedom and responsibility of the Navy days, briefing and arguing cases with little or no supervision.

My next assignment added to my frustration. I helped prepare the Securities and Exchange Commission registration statement for what was then the biggest stock split in history. To comply with an antitrust decree, the Dupont family had been required to divest its controlling interest in General Motors. The family's GM shares were closely held in Christiana Securities stock, which was priced at about $16,000 a share. An 80-for-1 split would make the stock marketable by bringing the price down to $200 a share. As the lowest-level associate on this matter, I was a well-paid proofreader, years before the age of paralegals. After weeks preparing the papers, I filed them with the SEC in Washington late on a Friday afternoon.

The partner in charge, Stuart Scott, a pipe-smoking, rosy-cheeked, balding gentleman lawyer, included me in the team of five attorneys he took to a celebratory dinner at the Four Seasons restaurant on 52nd Street, the spectacular creation of the architect Philip Johnson. We had several drinks before a five-course meal, expensive wines with each course, and cognac after dessert. Raising his snifter, Scott turned to me and said, "Joe, you are the most fortunate young lawyer in the firm to be able to work on this matter."*

I merely nodded.

Then Scott added, "I've been practicing law for twenty-eight years, and this is the most exciting and significant matter I've ever handled."

*In old-line Wall Street firms in those days, all client work was on "a matter," not on "a deal" or "a lawsuit."

If that's the top, I thought, this life is not for me.

Some non-legal aspects of the Wall Street practice disturbed me as well. Many top partners appeared to get much of their satisfaction out of heavy drinking and extravagant partying. Late each January, the firm had a stag dinner. To me, the affairs seemed like Roman bacchanalias. Pre-dinner cocktails went on for two hours. Dinner consisted of several courses—the finest fish and steak, accompanied by fine wines. Between courses, associates staged skits satirizing the firm, capturing eccentricities of partners, and highlighting humorous incidents of the past year. After dinner, there were more drinks and gambling, largely poker and craps. Drunkenness was rampant. It was all capped off with a hearty breakfast around four in the morning before we went home. These dinners were always on Fridays to give everyone the weekend to recover. I joined in the merriment and wrote several lyrics for songs during the three annual dinners I attended, but I soon came to see in these events a desperate quest for fun by a number of senior partners who didn't have much else to celebrate.

At one of the annual spring dinner dances for attorneys and their wives my misgivings about this world increased. No girlfriends or significant others were allowed. At the 1960 dinner, I was seated next to the wife of a senior partner. She had been drinking and started to cry. She said, "I never see Charlie. It's like living alone. He works all the time. But we do have a beautiful home in Lloyd Harbor [Long Island] and Charlie is the local justice of the peace there." The remark struck home. My ambition to succeed, I thought as I looked over at my own wife, was prompting me to work more nights and weekends, leaving Trudy alone and putting a strain on our marriage.

The grinding life in a Wall Street firm, however financially rewarding, was not for me. I did not tell my parents; they were too proud of my being on the corporate-law fast track. But in November 1959, I visited my former Harvard Law professor Paul Freund, to inquire about a career teaching law. He was encouraging and offered to circulate my resumé. I also wrote Father Bean, my rhetoric professor at Holy Cross, who urged me to count to ten before making any decision:

> . . . you were all Outing Club when I knew you. Then I learned that you
> became a beaver at Harvard Law School; a new man, ever since. However
> I'm sure that you could not lose your sense of humor; with that and with

your Harvard background you could shine anywhere. So much for your capacity; as to how you would be reconciled to the academic calm: that's a horse of a different color. Think it out carefully.

As a result, when in early 1960 Columbus Law School of Catholic University in Washington, D.C., offered me a job, I turned it down and decided to stay in New York, at least for that time being. I wrote the dean:

> As a Catholic I believe that my contribution, however small, might be of more value in a secular academic community. More selfishly . . . I should prefer to teach in a law school with a larger faculty and student body. . . . I think that it would be better for me if I were—initially at least—subjected to intellectual stimulation from more sources, student and faculty.

. . . . .

Amidst this turmoil about my professional career, Trudy and I were growing anxious about having children as our efforts proved unsuccessful and our friends began to build families. For us, raising children was what marriage was about. We prayed hard, as did my parents. They made novenas, and my mother had a special devotion to the Blessed Mother, praying to her every day for us. I prayed especially to Saint Gerard Majella, the patron of childbirth.[1]

After many unanswered prayers, I had my first encounter with the mix of medical science and Catholic moral theology when Trudy and I sought help from a number of doctors. One medical expert concluded that our best hope for children lay in artificial insemination. Like most American Catholics in those days, I accepted the Vatican's prohibition of artificial insemination, set out in 1930 by Pius XI in *Casti Connubi*. But some moral theologians were questioning the Church's prohibition of the use of artificial insemination for purposes of procreation. As I read some of those theologians, I began to question this Church teaching. After all, we were trying to have children: Wasn't this the purpose of marriage according to the Church? How could a desire to enlist medical help to that end be immoral?

I shared my concerns with a few close Catholic friends, and through them contacted a Jesuit priest, Gerard Kelly, at St. Mary's College in Kansas.

Father Kelly had written a book, *Medico-Moral Problems*, and an article in the *University of Detroit Law Journal*, "Artificial Insemination—the Theological Natural Law Aspects." On September 28, 1959, I wrote him describing our situation, asking his help and noting that our physician considered artificial insemination our best hope of getting pregnant. I waited anxiously for a reply. Father Kelly penned a note at the bottom of my letter simply saying: "Let the doctor use this method [artificial insemination] if he feels it is the only chance."

We also went to the Rock Reproductive Study Center, which was named after John Rock, chief of gynecology and obstetrics at Harvard Medical School, a practicing Catholic and father of five children. In his research on hormones to cure female infertility, Rock teamed up with Gregory (Goody) Pincus and M. C. Chang of the Worcester Foundation, who were working with progesterone. As a team they had pioneered the chemistry of The Pill, which the Food and Drug Administration had approved in May 1960. We followed the advice of the doctors at the center, which included use of the pill for several months as a way to increase the likelihood we would get pregnant. At this point, though the Catholic hierarchy was condemning use of the pill in sweeping terms, I was comfortable in my own conscience, since our use was temporary and for the purpose of having children.

With no guarantee of success, we pursued the possibility of adoption through the Catholic Home Bureau for Dependent Children in New York, known as The Foundling. We underwent a series of interviews and home visits. In the fall of 1961 we received word we could expect a baby soon. Trudy was still not pregnant. Then in November she missed her period. In late December we got the greatest Christmas present of our lives when her doctor told Trudy that she was pregnant. As best I could determine, Trudy had become pregnant on October 15 or 16—on the eve of St. Gerard Majella's feast or on the day itself!

On July 14, 1962, we had a healthy baby boy. We named him Mark Gerard, in honor of the patron saint of childbirth, who had heard my prayers.

Non-Catholics, and indeed most young Catholics, perhaps including my own children, are likely to find the scrupulosity that I exhibited in the 1950s mystifying; some might find my conduct incomprehensible. But those who were immersed for sixteen years in the Catholic education and Catholic families of the 1940s and 1950s will remember how little space the Church then left for the exercise of individual conscience. It was a time of meticulous adherence to carefully crafted rules found in the questions and answers of the Baltimore Catechism. Catholic doctrine was articulated by nuns, priests, and bishops who spoke with one voice. In those pre–Vatican II days, the clergy wrote, in identical penmanship, directions for a laity whose obedience was taken for granted and unquestioning.

CHAPTER 8

Political Awakening

O N THE DAY Franklin Delano Roosevelt died, April 12, 1945, I got my first taste of the importance of politics. I had graduated from St. Gregory's elementary school that January and had begun my first semester at Brooklyn Prep. At school we heard that the President had suffered a cerebral hemorrhage. As soon as I got home late that afternoon, I turned on the radio to reactions of teary citizens and expressions of concern over Harry S Truman's ability to lead the nation to a successful conclusion of World War II. Mesmerized by reports of FDR's death and presidency, I lay on the living room floor and couch listening until my father came home from work.

At dinner that evening, Mother expressed her opinion that Roosevelt knew how sick he was in 1944 when he ran for reelection, but was "too power hungry" to retire from politics. Had Roosevelt stepped down, she said, Thomas Dewey, New York's Republican governor, would be president and we would not have to worry about "this haberdasher from the Midwest," Harry Truman. When I mentioned that radio commentators were praising Roosevelt for getting the nation out of the Great Depression, Mother said it was the war, not the New Deal, that had revived the economy.

Mother had often spoken of her distrust of FDR; she viewed Eleanor Roosevelt as a dangerous left-winger, soft on communism. Mother religiously read conservative columnist Westbrook Pegler in the *New York Journal-American,* sharing his suspicion that Roosevelt had known about the Japanese attack on Pearl Harbor in advance but kept it from our military. (My parents always read the *Journal-American*, the *Brooklyn Eagle*, and the Brooklyn Catholic weekly, the *Tablet;* they often bought the *World-Telegram,* the *Sun,* or the *Herald Tribune.*)

Dad teased Mother by saying nice things about Mrs. Roosevelt. But even in the bosom of our family he was always circumspect about politics. When Mother spoke at dinner about her concern that the United Nations would spawn a world government inimical to the United States and favorable to the communists, my father remained silent, because his employers, the Watsons and IBM, were strong supporters of this new international organization. Like most Catholics, Mother opposed "Godless communism" because it suppressed religious freedom and the Church.

To this day I can hear Mother at the dinner table railing against what she viewed as a Communist attempt to take over New York City through the system of proportional representation for electing city council members. Proponents saw proportional representation as a way to give voice to small parties and blacks and break Tammany Hall's hammerlock. When the Teacher's Union came out in favor of proportional representation, she resigned from it. Her concerns heightened when in 1941 a Communist, Peter Cacchione, was elected to the city council, and she knew they were justified when in 1943 Benjamin Davis of Harlem became the second Communist to take a council seat. In 1947, with anti-communism on the rise and my mother cheering over dinner, New Yorkers repealed proportional representation for city council elections.

As outspoken as Mother was at our dinner table, both she and my father repeatedly admonished me never to speak of politics outside our family. Like sex and religion, Mother and Dad repeatedly warned, politics was "never to be discussed in public." I always had a sense that my mother and father lived under a cloud of "knowing their place"—a limited one. They worried about jeopardizing their son's future by stepping out of their accustomed bounds. Political discussions were to be avoided especially by an Italian-American Catholic family whose chief breadwinner worked for the White Anglo-Saxon Protestant behemoth, IBM.

My Uncle Joe Gill, a conservative, and Uncle Tom Gill, a liberal, broke those rules. They discussed politics with me (and anyone else who would listen) all the time. Uncle Joe shared my mother's views; if anything, he was more vehemently anti-communist. As a young man, he not only had voted for Al Smith but had contributed $100 to the Democratic Party for Smith's campaign (a princely sum in 1928). That feisty Irishman was the last, and perhaps only, Democrat Uncle Joe ever voted for. Uncle Tom, a committed union leader, was liberal to the cusp of socialism. He was the only member of the family who voted for Harry Truman in 1948, confidently predicting Dewey's defeat. I thought Mother felt sorry for Uncle Tom; she believed that as secretary-treasurer of his union, he had to spout support for the union's favored political candidates.

During my early and young adult years I saw myself as a conservative Republican (when conservative largely meant staunchly anti-communist). I reflected the views of my parents and the milieu of most of my relatives, teachers, classmates at Holy Cross, and colleagues in the Navy. At Harvard Law School, I first recognized the limits of mere anti-communism as a political philosophy. Mother supported Catholic Wisconsin senator Joseph McCarthy's assault on the Truman administration for harboring communist spies in the State Department. In 1954, when McCarthy accused Army Secretary Robert Stevens of concealing evidence of espionage activities at Fort Monmouth, New Jersey, the Army fought back. It accused McCarthy of seeking preferential treatment for David Schine, an Army private who was one of his aides. The Senate Permanent Investigations Subcommittee held hearings on the charges and counter charges during my second year in Cambridge. Just about all my professors and most Harvard classmates opposed the Wisconsin senator. I tried to camouflage my McCarthyite leanings, but they emerged occasionally at our house on Sacramento Place, where we watched the hearings on a cheap, fuzzy black-and-white television set.

During this time, I was studying constitutional law under Paul Freund, and I began to appreciate the incompatibility of McCarthy's Red Scare tactics with constitutional values championed by justices like Benjamin Cardozo, Felix Frankfurter, Robert Jackson, and Hugo Black, whose positions Freund gently but firmly espoused. Under this extraordinary professor, I came to a new understanding of the values of free speech, freedom from unreasonable search and seizure, freedom of the press, rights of privacy, and equal protection under the law.

On May 17, 1954, as I was reviewing cases for my final exam in constitutional law, the Supreme Court decided *Brown v. Board of Education,* blowing away the separate-but-equal doctrine (established in *Plessy v. Ferguson)* that had kept southern schools segregated for fifty-eight years. The excitement at the law school was contagious. I remember going to Harkness Commons, where newspapers were sold and dining facilities located, and seeing the bold headlines in the evening papers. Like most of my classmates, and all of my professors, I was exhilarated. To me the Court's decision was as rooted in the Thomastic philosophy and Ignatian values of individual dignity I'd learned at Holy Cross as it was in the equal protection clause of the United States Constitution. I saw the decision as a perfect blending of the spiritual values propounded by the Jesuits and the legal rights propounded by the decidedly secular and predominantly liberal professors at Harvard Law School.

Despite such stirrings, as I left Harvard Law School my tropism to the left was tentative. I was tiptoeing from conservative Republicanism to a more moderate stance. The following years in the Navy I was amidst conservative military officers. This kept me solidly in the Republican camp and blunted any further inching toward the progressive side of the political street. Every officer and civilian I came in contact with in Navy JAG was an Eisenhower supporter; virtually all saw Democrats as soft on communism. I voted enthusiastically for Dwight Eisenhower when he ran against Adlai Stevenson in 1952 and 1956.

Indeed, the social highlight of my Navy years was going to the Inaugural parade and ball in January 1957. Uncle Joe Gill, now a generous Republican contributor, gave me his tickets for the parade and an inaugural ball. In the longest letter of my life, five single-spaced pages, I described the day to my parents as one in which "nothing, but nothing went wrong. . . . Even the toothpaste was a fresh and different brand and flavor that day." Trudy and I went to see the swearing-in on the Capitol steps. For the parade we had seats just to the left of the bank of TV cameras. I wrote with excitement of the ball at the National Guard Armory, where we glimpsed President Eisenhower and at one point were so close to Richard Nixon that "we could have clasped hands."

When I returned to New York at the end of 1958, I remained Republican. Though committed to the Republican Party and attending a few Young Republican meetings at the firm's offices, throughout 1959 and 1960 I was working such long hours at Dewey Ballantine that I had little interest or time for politics and no intention of becoming an active participant.

CHAPTER 9

Comfortable and Catholic in New York

T HE LATE FIFTIES and early sixties were full of action for a young Catholic in New York City. The Church as a whole had secured its place in American society with a surge in members, vocations, wealth, and political power. Catholics had provided services like orphanages and hospitals during the Great Depression, supported Roosevelt's social welfare programs, fought in the war, and gained influence in American culture.

Trudy and I and our friends in New York were all twenty-somethings, having fun and working hard, partying too much, arguing about the future of the Church too late into the night and sleeping too little, but talking endlessly about the materialism, secularization, racial discrimination, and poverty in American society. We weren't all Catholics, but the Catholics among us found in the Church useful ideals, guidelines, and inspiration. We debated its role in the modern world. We had high hopes for the ecumenical council, Vatican II, announced in January 1959 and scheduled for October 1962. At the time we scarcely grasped how Pope John XXIII would revolutionize the Church.

Pope Pius XII had already initiated some changes: He reduced the time of fasting for communion to three hours for solid food and one hour for non-alcoholic liquids; water no longer broke the fast. "Mindful of notable changes which have occurred in private and public working conditions as well as in all branches of social life,"[1] the Pope also allowed for the celebration of the Mass in early evening hours. That gave us the option to check off our Sunday obligation by attending late Saturday afternoon Mass. Pope John XXIII intended Vatican II to consider the "appropriate adaptation of Church discipline to the needs and conditions of our times."[2]

Open the windows, the Pope decreed, and the fresh breezes blew away the Latin Masses, the priest with his back turned to the congregation, ruler slaps, novenas, countless confessions, May processions, emphasis on indulgences, and insistence under pain of sacrilege that the Host be deposited on the tongue and never touched or chewed. New convents and chapels would have modern designs. Latin/English missals were packed away. Liturgical restrictions went out as lay readers and female lectors came in. Handshakes, hugs, and kisses of peace were exchanged in the pews. Fish on every Friday and the daily Lenten fasts were things of the past. Communion for us in the pews now included both bread and wine. Penance became the Sacrament of Reconciliation, and you could tell of your sins and be spiritually counseled with or without the anonymous screen. As the dress code relaxed, women went to church without hats. We all discovered that nuns had knees and didn't shave their heads.

To our excitement, Pope John XXIII called for increased participation by lay persons in the Church, missions, public life, social welfare, and the governance of their parishes. At our parish, the congregation now selected responsorial psalms, often the Gelineau chants developed by the French Jesuit Joseph Gelineau, to be sung between the Scripture readings. At home, we tapped our feet to the rhythms of the first long-playing record of an African Mass. Vatican II gave moral theologians an opportunity to write and explore alternatives to traditional Catholic thought that they had never before enjoyed. Within the Church, arguments about birth control became as common as disagreements about the new liturgy. In New York, being a Catholic, always comfortable, became exciting.

In Manhattan, Ed Rice, raised a Catholic, started *Jubilee*, "A Magazine of the Church and her People," with the help of his best college friends from Columbia University, two converts, Bob Lax and Thomas Merton. A brilliant writer and photographer, Rice had been layout editor for *Collier's*, a national magazine of reporting and photography. *Jubilee* focused on social issues, education, and civil rights. Its contributors included Richard Gilman (who later taught drama at Yale), François Mauriac, and Jack Kerouac, who became the dean of the Beat Generation with his 1957 book, *On the Road*. Thomas Merton, the Trappist monk who wrote *The Seven Storey Mountain*, sent articles from his retreat at Gethsemani Abbey in Kentucky. Wilfrid Sheed did movie reviews before he became a novelist and an editor of the *New York Review of Books*. Alice Mayhew, who would become famous as an editor at Simon and Schuster, wrote book reviews.

Jubilee, like the lay Catholic publication *Commonweal* and the Jesuit weekly *America,* pressed the Christian obligation to do more about the poor, the rights of workers to just wages and safe conditions, the need to renounce oppressive exploitation of the peoples of Latin America, the entitlement of the laity to full partnership in the Church, and the need to deal aggressively with racial discrimination. Trudy worked as a volunteer at *Jubilee.* I had high hopes that the magazine would be a Catholic version of *Life*: artistically and visually exciting, but grounded in socially conscious Christian theology. Despite my modest income, I gave a little money to help keep *Jubilee* afloat. In the February 1960 issue, I favorably reviewed Jacques Barzun's *The House of Intellect,* the Columbia University professor's brilliant and blistering assault on mediocrity, intellectual carelessness, and (though the term had not yet been coined) political correctness in academia.[3]

Through our Catholic network I met two sisters, Mary and Ellen Lukas, who like my wife had graduated from the College of New Rochelle. Ellen covered the United Nations for *Newsweek;* Mary worked for *Time.* They lived on the first floor of a brownstone on East 77th Street whose living room wall was lined with serious books, most with spines well worn from use. Concerned about poverty among the Puerto Rican community, the Lukas sisters recruited some of their friends, including Trudy and me, to rent a *cuartito* (little room) in Spanish Harlem. In this single room in a wooden tenement in Washington Heights, we created a community center where we helped Puerto Rican children with their schoolwork, offered adults legal assistance, and, for Catholic children who couldn't get into overcrowded parochial schools, taught catechism. Each of us spent at least one night a week there. Poverty and their limited English made Puerto Ricans easy targets for exploitation by unscrupulous landlords and shopkeepers. I was appalled at how little the police and prosecutors did to help—often nothing.

On most weekday nights I worked late at the law firm. Like many Wall Street lawyers, I spent more (of clients' money) on dinner at Delmonico's, the Wall Street culinary landmark on the corner of Beaver and South Williams streets, than most families in Spanish Harlem took home in a week. I grew increasingly conscious of the truth of F. Scott Fitzgerald's line: "The very rich are different from you and me."

.   .   .

I did a lot of reading to get beyond my world of work. In the morning on the bus to the office and late at night in bed, I devoured *The New Yorker* and Max Ascoli's *The Reporter*. Much of what I read questioned the prevailing values in our society and, like my experiences in Spanish Harlem, planted seeds of Catholic action and political consciousness.

I remained vehemently anti-communist. I admired books like Arthur Koestler's *Darkness at Noon*, Bertram Wolfe's *Three Who Made a Revolution*, and Whittaker Chambers's *Witness*. Reading *Witness*, I was struck by its image of Alger Hiss: a privileged man who held a winning hand of financial, social, and intellectual cards, including *Law Review* status at Harvard, but seemed to have no spiritual roots.

I worried about blending into the burgeoning suburban culture and becoming a cookie-cutout of corporate America, after reading David Reisman's *The Lonely Crowd*, William Whyte's *The Organization Man,* and Sloan Wilson's novel *The Man in the Gray Flannel Suit. The Lonely Crowd* and *The Organization Man* sketched for me the high cost of replacing inner direction (tradition, spiritual belief, self-esteem) with outer-directed conformity promoted by large, monolithic institutions like governments, outsized corporations, and unions, which were mass producing a middle class of individuals "who have left home, spiritually as well as physically, to take the vows of organization life. . . ."[4]

John Kenneth Galbraith's point in *The Affluent Society* that wealth was "the relentless enemy of understanding"[5] struck me. And C. Wright Mills's *The Power Elite* resonated with my experience in a Wall Street firm in its description of the "set of overlapping 'crowds' and intricately connected 'cliques.'"[6] Mills saw the power of corporate chief executives and the military as consolidating, while the middle class was adrift and the poor so "politically fragmented" that they were "increasingly powerless."[7] Already concerned about a certain aimlessness that I felt in my working life at Dewey Ballantine, I found that these books filled me with a sense of the danger of becoming an empty suit, neatly pressed and perpetually bored.

My doubts about the Wall Street law practice were reinforced by three Catholic authors. In *The Seven Storey Mountain*, Thomas Merton recorded his journey from hedonist to Roman Catholic monk at the Trappist monastery in Gethsemani, Kentucky. His most pointed question struck a thundering chord with me: "Is there any wonder that there can be no peace in a world where everything possible is done to guarantee that the youth of every nation will grow up absolutely without moral and religious discipline, and without the shadow of an interior life, or of that spirituality, charity and faith which alone can safeguard the treaties and agreements made by governments?"[8] In his book *We Hold These Truths: Catholic Reflections on the American Proposition,* the Jesuit theologian John Courtney Murray made the case for reconciling Catholic doctrine with American democracy and pluralism.[9] Teilhard de Chardin, a Jesuit priest and a paleontologist, rendered science and spirituality compatible in his exploration of evolutionary theory, religious values, and Catholic thought in *The Phenomenon of Man.*[10] As these authors reshaped my view of Catholicism in the modern world, I felt prodded to do more with my talent and education than prowl the narrow streets of lower Manhattan in service of the most powerful private interests in the nation.

The intersection of politics and religion came more sharply into focus when my fellow Holy Cross graduate Michael Harrington published *The Other America.* Harrington's book brought national attention to "the millions who are poor in the United States [who] tend to become increasingly invisible."[11] I began reading the *Catholic Worker.* The paper's philosophy, though a bit extreme for my political taste, seemed more attuned to that of Vatican II than the conservative Brooklyn *Tablet* my parents read. Trudy and I went to visit Dorothy Day and Peter Maurin at St. Joseph's House on East First Street on the Lower East Side, where all kinds of people, young and old, in suits and dirty work clothes, gathered for political and social discussions. Dorothy Day was by then a living legend. We drank her awful tea and listened to her theories: that capitalism imposed poverty on millions and that the only solution was a purified socialism, with government ownership of property and absolutely no private property, but without the repression that characterized Soviet communism. She genuinely believed there could be a world society in which everyone gave according to their abilities and received according to their needs. A committed pacifist, she did not need President Dwight Eisenhower to warn her about the dangers of the military-industrial complex; she was arrested often for her protests against militarism and war. She was too far left for me and I thought her naïve about communism, but I was deeply affected, nonetheless, by her special and powerful presence.

Among such engaged men and women, I felt we might be on the verge of some kind of golden age of Catholicism, led by American lay men and women like us. Educated lay Catholics were demanding a voice in their church and a greater recognition of the relevance of their individual consciences, and many moral theologians, especially Jesuits, were backing them up. Young priests became more vocal in expressing their views on current questions, especially poverty and race discrimination. We first- and second-generation American Catholics who had been educated at colleges and universities, both Catholic and non-Catholic, were not so quick to genuflect at every statement of a Francis Cardinal Spellman no matter how far afield from central matters of faith and doctrine. In some undefined yet powerful way, Vatican II seemed to open the door to greater engagement in politics for all of us.

.   .   .

Like many engaged young Catholics in New York, I had an early interest in Fidel Castro. On January 1, 1959, the dictator Fulgencio Batista fled Cuba and I cheered as Castro liberated (or so I thought at the time) Cuba on the following day. The *New York Times* rhapsodized:

Senor Castro is 31 years old, a big burly, low-voiced man with a fair command of English. He has a way of looking scholarly when wearing glasses. He likes rifles and cigars. "Above all," Senor Castro told one of his interviewers, "we are fighting for a democratic Cuba and an end to dictatorship." And he added: "You can be sure we have no animosity toward the United States and the American people."

Castro was seen as a "Great White Hope" for Cubans mired in poverty. Along with many church leaders, especially liberal American Jesuits, I believed that he would redistribute property and wealth and eradicate the gangsters running Havana's gambling casinos and prostitution. I took pretty much at face value C. Wright Mills's pro-Castro polemic, *Listen Yankee: The Revolution in Cuba*, in which he depicted Americans as imperialists, tourists in search of sex and gambling, greedy sugar monopolists, and supporters of the Batista regime. Mills described Castro as a committed graduate of Jesuit high school and Havana University, a reformer prepared to avoid the excesses of communism and capitalism by fairly distributing wealth without suppressing civil liberties and individual freedom.

Castro came to New York to address the United Nations in September 1960. When he left the Shelburne Hotel on Lexington Avenue and 37th Street and moved into the Theresa Hotel in Harlem, I viewed his act as a statement of solidarity with the poor Hispanics and blacks who lived where we had our *cuartito*. When Castro finally spoke at the United Nations on September 26, he attacked the United States for militarily supporting the Batista regime, and denied that he was a communist.

I fell off the Castro bandwagon over the next few months during the Cuban dictator's campaign to eliminate private property, install a totalitarian regime, jail political opponents, and suppress the Catholic Church. I got a sense of how Arthur Koestler and other mistaken true believers must have felt in the 1930s and 1940s.

CHAPTER 10

Ringing Doorbells for Kennedy

O N FEBRUARY 20TH, 1960, the Saturday of the long George Washington Birthday holiday weekend, I woke up with a muscle in my back so
knotted that I couldn't climb out of bed. Newspaper stories about John
Kennedy—the first Catholic to seek the presidency since Al Smith—had
interested me enough that I bought James MacGregor Burns's campaign
biography, *John F. Kennedy: A Political Profile.* I spent much of the weekend
reading the book.

I had first noticed Kennedy while watching the 1956 Democratic convention on television. Adlai Stevenson threw open the nomination for vice
president to the delegates and Kennedy mounted an effort against Estes
Kefauver, the Tennessee senator favored for the second spot on the ticket.
Kennedy did not have much going beyond the glamour of his family and his
socially prominent wife, Jacqueline Bouvier. Yet he came astonishingly
close, capturing 589 votes to Kefauver's 755 1/2. I watched, impressed as the
Massachusetts senator then made a politically adept and gracious appeal
that convention delegates unanimously nominate Kefauver.

I hadn't thought much about Kennedy after that. My parents and aunts
and uncles all felt that a Catholic would never be president of the United
States after Al Smith's defeat in 1928. Like anyone educated at Catholic
schools, I knew all about Smith's defeat, the Ku Klux Klan, and the anti-
Catholicism rampant in the South that made it impossible for a Catholic to
be nominated. One of the few jokes my mother ever told was about "a Negro
boy hitching a ride in Alabama during a fierce rainstorm. A car finally pulled
over being driven by a Catholic bishop, who threw open the door and
invited the shivering and soaked young boy to get in. 'No, thanks, Bishop,'
the boy said, 'I got enough trouble down here just being a Negro.'"

Nevertheless, that weekend Burns's book seized me. I identified with
Kennedy as a vehemently anti-communist Catholic, the kind of tried and

true cold warrior committed to battle the atheist world power of the Soviet Union. Kennedy expressed concern for the underprivileged, whether the poor in the United States or those abroad struggling for their independence. As Burns described it, Kennedy believed that man's inherent nature to be free would ultimately triumph over communism, a view I related to the philosophy I had learned at Holy Cross. Burns also stressed that Kennedy considered it essential to "track down the best talent" to lead the nation in such a "revolutionary time."[1] (As a former *Harvard Law Review* editor, I considered myself in that talent pool.)

I started to consider voting for a Democrat. I remembered my fascination with the administration of Franklin Delano Roosevelt. I had read Robert Sherwood's *Roosevelt and Hopkins: An Intimate History*, an account of the FDR years through the relationship of the President with his closest aide, Harry Hopkins, and Arthur Schlesinger Jr.'s first two volumes of *The Age of Roosevelt*. Schlesinger evoked the excitement of the New Deal years as he described platoons of idealistic and able young men (most of them lawyers) who believed that under FDR anything could be accomplished.[2] As Schlesinger put it, "By bringing to Washington a government determined to govern, Roosevelt unlocked new energies in a people who had lost faith, not just in government's ability to meet the economic crisis, but almost in the ability of anyone to do anything. The feeling of the movement was irresistible."[3]

Soon after that weekend, *Jubilee* asked me to review *Strategy of Peace*, a collection of Kennedy speeches on foreign policy. Kennedy's sensitivity to the plight of poor nations and his views on the revolution in Algeria and the situation in Indochina struck me. In 1957, years before Charles de Gaulle granted Algeria independence, Kennedy spoke of French colonialism there as an example of "Western imperialism," which he considered a great enemy of "the most powerful single force in the world today . . . man's eternal desire to be free and independent."[4]

About this time, Lewis Davis, who was on his way to becoming one of the nation's top architects, and his wife Lynn rang the doorbell of our apartment on East 23rd Street. They were soliciting, door-to-door, new members for the East Midtown Reform Democratic Club on Second Avenue between 27th and 28th Streets. Although I voted Republican, I was registered as a Democrat in New York City; since the Democratic nomination was tantamount to election, voting in that party's primaries was the only way to have any say about who would be elected mayor or to the city council or state legislature. The Davises talked about the importance of unseating New York political boss Carmine DeSapio and wresting control of the Democratic Party from Tammany Hall. I didn't much care about that, but I was interested in John Kennedy's bid for the Democratic presidential nomination. I agreed to go to a meeting with them.

The reform movement in New York was attracting young, college-educated professionals who were far more liberal than I. Most were well under forty and had been raised in Brooklyn or lower Manhattan, but had left for college and graduate school and were now living in more affluent Manhattan neighborhoods. By 1960, there were several reform clubs in Manhattan and one in the Bronx. The movement's eight thousand members included a far larger proportion of women than the regular organization clubs.[5] The reformers prided themselves on full membership and equal participation for women, whom regular clubs relegated to second-class status in "Auxiliaries."

At Midtown Reform Democratic Club meetings, I was impressed by the intelligence and commitment of members like Dick Ravitch and Arnold Fein.[6] I doubted DeSapio was the villain that reformers described, but I agreed with the reform mission to open up the Democratic Party and do more for the city's poor blacks and Puerto Ricans.

The ethnic dynamics of New York Democratic politics were striking. Members of the Midtown Reform Democratic Club—and indeed, leading members of the reform movement—were predominantly Jewish. The Regular Democrats (as they were then called) were predominately Irish- and Italian-American Catholics. Because of my Italian-American Catholic heritage the club considered me a valuable asset, although not one member shared my enthusiasm for Kennedy. All supported Adlai Stevenson, the Illinois governor twice defeated by Dwight Eisenhower. Since most had entered politics as "madly for Adlai" enthusiasts in the early 1950s, the club had originally been called the Stevensonian Democratic Club.

No one at the club had any lines to the Kennedy campaign, so I scratched around New York to find someone who did. Kennedy's Catholicism and outspoken anti-communism, his lack of liberal credentials, a sense that he was a rich socialite, and his father's suspected anti-Semitism—these all turned off the urban, self-made, liberal Jews who dominated the reform movement. I'd just about despaired of finding any link to Kennedy when I mentioned it to John Graham, a classmate at Harvard Law School. He suggested I write to John Stillman, a college friend of Kennedy's, who was chairman of the Orange County Democratic Party in Newburgh, a suburb sixty miles north of New York City. So unsophisticated was I in politics that I thought Stillman was a political powerhouse. Little did I realize at the time that Kennedy was having such difficulty getting any support in New York City that this outlier Democrat was his closest connection.

On March 23, 1960, I wrote Stillman, enclosing my resumé and telling him that I had heard that he was "interested in people who desire to work on behalf on Senator John F. Kennedy," and that "I am quite anxious to do anything that will further Senator Kennedy's candidacy." Providing additional evidence of Kennedy's lack of supporters in the New York area, Stillman wrote back only five days later, "awfully glad" to receive my letter, saying he had passed my "name and qualifications on to the Senator's staff in Washington," and inviting me to join him for lunch on "Wednesday, April 6 at 12:30 at the Au Canari D'Or," a trendy restaurant at Lexington Avenue and 61st Street.

April 6 was the day after the Wisconsin primary, which New York papers said would determine whether Kennedy had a credible shot at the nomination. He was running against Hubert Humphrey, the Democratic senator from neighboring Minnesota and the most popular politician in that part of the country. Against all odds, Kennedy defeated Humphrey by 478,901 to 372,034 votes and carried six of the ten congressional districts. Anonymous anti-Catholic ads in local newspapers served to energize the Catholic vote, including thousands of Republicans who crossed party lines to vote for Kennedy.

I was excited as I took the subway up from Wall Street to lunch with Stillman. I don't remember the meal, but I do remember Stillman as wealthy and well-born, with the social polish that came from family heritage, boarding prep schools, and Ivy League colleges. I was delighted to see someone so quintessentially aristocratic supporting an Irish Roman Catholic. We celebrated the Kennedy victory in Wisconsin and talked about the task ahead—defeating Hubert Humphrey in West Virginia, a proudly Protestant state with an anti-Catholic bent.[7]

Stillman was especially interested in my involvement in the reform Democratic movement in the city (little did I know then that Kennedy had no contacts there). By the end of the lunch, he promised to be in touch. I left on such a high I could have flown like Superman through the canyons of midtown back to my office at Dewey Ballantine. Stillman later sent me a lapel pin with a green background and the white letters FKBW (For Kennedy Before Wisconsin), which I wore with pride at meetings of the East Midtown Reform Democratic Club but not at the law firm.

Back at the firm the next morning, Governor Dewey called me into his office. I hoped that he was going to ask me to work on a case with him. He confided instead that he was assembling a few bright young lawyers to do "issue research for Richard Nixon, the certain Republican candidate." He invited me to join the group, saying the firm would accord hours spent on this endeavor the same value as those charged to paying clients. Translation: such time would not be relegated to the second-class status of pro bono hours.

My God, I thought, he thinks I'm a committed Republican. He must have heard I went to meetings of young Republicans here at the firm!

Hesitating and cautiously selecting my words as my palms dampened, I said, "I'm honored that you would consider me for the group." Then, fidgeting, I blurted out, "But I am committed to work as a volunteer for Kennedy."

So be it, I thought. I can no longer expect to make my career at this place; it's good that I've already started pursuing a career as a law school professor.

Without hesitation, this stuffy, hard-core Republican, who simply by example intimidated his partners into wearing fedora hats and who always had an elevator held to take him alone to his twenty-ninth floor office, responded, "Well, I must say I'm disappointed about your choice of candidate."

I coughed nervously.

Dewey continued, "But it is a good thing you are involved. It is important for our young attorneys to be involved in these affairs. Not enough associates here are."

With that, I thanked the governor and left his office, hoping his words were as genuine as they sounded.

Two days later, I received a letter: "I am very glad to know that you are in contact with our mutual friend John Stillman and you may be sure that I am most appreciative of your interest and support. I hope you will keep in close touch with John, as he will be aware of our plans in New York." It was signed *Jack Kennedy*.

The moment I read the letter I felt I was part of the campaign. I called my parents and read it to them. To my disappointment, though I think Mother and Dad were praying for Kennedy's success and safety (many Catholics of their generation feared Kennedy's life was in danger from an anti-Catholic assassin), they were cool to my "involvement in politics." As Mother admonished, "You keep up your hard work at the law firm. Politics is a dirty business."

Thank God I hadn't told Mother about my meeting with Governor Dewey, I thought.

So universal was the lack of support for John Kennedy in New York liberal circles that Stillman asked if I would debate on behalf of the Massachusetts senator in reform clubs around the city. I jumped at the opportunity. Kennedy's staff in Washington sent me material about his views. I tailored my presentation to address Kennedy's liberal positions—which were few compared with Humphrey's and Stevenson's—in order to appeal to reform audiences.

I debated for Kennedy at my own club, as well as at the Village Independent Democrats, and at the Lenox Hill, Lexington Democratic, and Yorkville Democratic Clubs, among others. Ed Koch, a leader of the Village Independent Democrats and the reform movement's most vocal opponent of DeSapio, presided over the debate there, which ended in a resounding endorsement of Stevenson (doubtless encouraged by Koch). Those who debated on Stevenson's behalf repeatedly invoked Eleanor Roosevelt's support. Though she didn't die until November 7, 1962, her name as a Stevenson supporter was intoned during these debates with the reverence usually reserved for dead saints. Stevenson won every club's endorsement; Humphrey got several votes and invariably placed second.

I don't recall either of the two other Democratic candidates, Lyndon Johnson and Stuart Symington, receiving a single vote at these debates. Johnson, the Texas senator and powerful Senate majority leader, was usually represented by Ed Weisl, Jr., whose father ran the law firm of Simpson, Thacher & Bartlett. Stuart Symington, elected to the U.S. Senate from Missouri in 1952 and secretary of the Air Force in the Truman administration, was so pro-defense that he rarely sent a representative or even answered the letters inviting him to these liberal club debates.

On May 10th, Kennedy defeated Hubert Humphrey in West Virginia.

There were ugly rumors about vote buying and dirty politics. Nevertheless, the Kennedy victory proved that despite being Catholic and despite the Democrats' experience with Al Smith in 1928, this Irish Catholic was a viable candidate who could beat Nixon in November. Humphrey, ever the decent party soldier, made no charges about irregularities. In a tearful withdrawal, he vowed to be a candidate for re-election to the Senate from Minnesota and congratulated Kennedy, his "friend and Senate colleague."

After West Virginia, my reform club debates in New York were one-on-one contests against a proponent of Adlai Stevenson. The last one was on May 24, where David Garth, chairman of the New York Stevenson for President Committee, and I debated at Pilgrim Hall on Grand Concourse in the Bronx before the Bronx Independents. I could not cool the reformers' ardor for Stevenson. If there were any Humphrey supporters in the audience, they shifted their allegiance to Stevenson. As I recall, Garth pulled out all the stops that evening: he asked how Eleanor Roosevelt would vote and conjured up fear that Kennedy's father, Joe, would involve himself in foreign policy matters, a special concern to Jewish voters, many of whom believed Joe Kennedy, while ambassador to England, had urged FDR and the British to placate Hitler. The Bronx Independents voted unanimously to support Stevenson. That clinched my perfect record. In all my debates, I was never able to capture a single vote for Kennedy.

.   .   .

To the surprise and disappointment of New York reform Democrats, Kennedy won the nomination at the Democratic Convention in Los Angeles. To their even greater dismay, he selected Lyndon Johnson as his running mate. Now a totally committed Kennedy supporter, I accepted his decision as essential to win the White House.

Robert Kennedy did not help his brother with true-believing Manhattan liberals. He opened the New York campaign at the Biltmore Hotel in August before 450 of us Democrats (including John Sweeney, who would decades later become president of the AFL-CIO). On his left sat reformers Herbert Lehman, Robert Wagner, and Eleanor Roosevelt; on his right, regulars Carmine DeSapio, Michael Prendergast, and former postmaster general Jim Farley. Pointing to each side, Kennedy said, "I don't care if you're with these guys or those guys. If you're not with my brother in November, you'll regret it." At a gathering of a couple of hundred reform Democrats in New York's Waldorf-Astoria, I remember Bobby Kennedy bellowing, "This ticket is Kennedy-Johnson. Stevenson is *not* a candidate; Johnson *is* the vice presidential candidate. Kennedy is going to be president and Johnson is going to be vice president, and anyone that doesn't work for them is never going to forget it while they are in office." On another occasion, when asked how he could ever hope to win over the minds and hearts of liberal and reform Democrats, exasperated with their skepticism and demands, Bobby Kennedy reputedly snapped, "Grab 'em by the balls. Their minds and hearts will follow." That story ricocheted off the walls of reform clubs for weeks and set back efforts to get them working for the ticket.

With John Kennedy's nomination, my commitment—and the fact that no one else wanted the job—led the East Midtown Reform Club to elect me to lead their efforts to support the Democratic ticket. That September and October, I spent every weekend and evening that I wasn't at work ringing doorbells and holding interminable meetings to persuade others to do the same. I avidly read the *New York Post*—then owned by Dorothy Schiff, who was making it the most liberal paper in the city—flipping first to Mary McGrory's well-written, invariably pro-Kennedy column. Teasing me, senior associates at Dewey Ballantine suggested that I read the *Post* folded inside the *New York Herald Tribune,* so Republican partners wouldn't see me with a "left wing, communist rag."

The Catholic issue lingered. I sensed that Kennedy's religion was a problem not only among evangelicals in the Deep South,* but among many liberal Jews and Protestants in the North. Responding to concerns, on September 27 Father Gustave Weigel, a Jesuit theologian, gave a lecture in Washington, D.C., that the *New York Times* reported on its front page. The *Times* led with Weigel's assertion that "the Roman Catholic Church would not attempt to interfere in the political activities of a Catholic President nor would a Catholic President be bound by Catholic morality in deciding public issues."

On the Saturday before the election, I stood in the rain at a Kennedy rally

---

*Donald Gill, a descendant of my mother's ancestors who had emigrated to the Carolinas from England, was a Baptist minister and executive director of the Citizens for Religious Freedom, a group spearheading anti-Catholic opposition to Kennedy's presidential bid.

held outside the Coliseum on West 59th Street just to get a glimpse of the candidate as he closed out his campaign in New York and headed to New England in a final, around-the-clock series of appearances in Connecticut, New Hampshire, and Massachusetts, before going to Hyannisport to vote and await the returns. The pouring rain intensified our excitement as Kennedy, getting soaked himself, spoke:

> The Republicans are home in bed and we [Lyndon Johnson, his wife Lady Bird, and daughters Lynda and Luci were alongside Kennedy] are standing out here in the rain. But the sun is going to shine on us next Tuesday. . . . Tom Dewey has just joined Dick Nixon out on the coast to give him some last minute strategy on how to win this election. You have seen these elephants in the circus. They have their heads of ivory, thick skins, no vision, long memory, and when they move around the ring in the circus, they grab the tail of the elephant in front of them. Well, Dick grabbed that tail in 1952 and 1956, but in 1960 he is running, not the President [Eisenhower].

I took election day off to help Kennedy voters get to the polls and take a turn at poll watching. That evening Trudy and I went to an election-night party at Lew Davis's in Greenwich Village. The Davises had one of those six-feet-long Italian heroes from Manganero's on Ninth Avenue. We all ate, drank beer and cheap wine, and watched the returns. As the race tightened, everyone left except Trudy and me. We sat with Lew and Lynn on their double bed, propped up on pillows awaiting a decision. Nixon almost conceded defeat in a speech around 3:20 A.M. New York time but held back. Exhausted, I went home to bed after 4 A.M. and slept through the alarm. I awoke around noon after Illinois returns gave Kennedy a majority of the electoral college vote, just in time to hear Kennedy's victory statement at Hyannisport.

.   .   .

With the election over, I returned to the practice of corporate law but it was less satisfying than ever. During the campaign, I had given no consideration to going to Washington as part of the administration. Now, as the tedium of Wall Street law practice closed in on me, I began thinking about it.

The law school of the University of Wisconsin in Madison had offered me a teaching position. But I feared it would be too passive a life, so I sought a job with Arnold, Fortas & Porter, a Democratic law firm headed by Thurman Arnold, antitrust division chief during the Roosevelt administration; Abe Fortas, undersecretary of the Interior during World War II; and Paul Porter, head of the Office of Price Administration under President Truman. Several Harvard classmates were there. In early 1961 I interviewed with a partner, but the firm wasn't hiring.

Then one of my law school roommates, John McGillicuddy, who had been working at Simpson, Thatcher & Bartlett, called me for an urgent lunch. Over sandwiches, he said that his firm had just told him that he was not likely to make partner, but had assured him they would get him a job at one of their clients, Manufacturer's Hanover bank. In those days, the Wall Street firms began trimming the ranks of associates near the end of each year, with the objective of having just a couple around in eight or nine years to make partners. McGillicuddy and I commiserated about "what bastards these guys are."

"You know, Joe," McGillicuddy said to me, "the best partner in our firm is going to Washington. Cyrus Vance. To be general counsel of the Department of Defense. You're interested in politics. You love Kennedy. You should get in touch with Vance."

I didn't know Vance, but that Wednesday afternoon as soon as I returned to my office I sent him a letter with my resumé, expressing interest in a job. On Friday, Vance called and asked me to come for an interview the next morning. I flew to Washington on the Eastern Shuttle (the only time I'd been on a plane except for my honeymoon trip to Bermuda) that Saturday. Vance subjected me to the longest interview of my life, some two hours, and then swept me in and out of another office for a ten-second handshake with Robert McNamara, Kennedy's secretary of defense. That Monday, Vance offered me a job as his special assistant. "You'll do a lot of different things," he said. "But Secretary McNamara intends to reorganize the Pentagon, and your primary responsibility will be to do the legal work for that effort."

Vance offered me a salary of $9,500, which was $1,500 less than I was making at Dewey Ballantine. When I mentioned that it was a big cut, he said,

"We all have to make sacrifices for the New Frontier." Anxious to be part of the new administration, I agreed. Vance conveniently failed to mention that his personal income sacrifice was cushioned by his wife Grace (Gay) Sloane, heiress of the W. J. Sloane carpet and furniture retailing family, which owned a highly profitable store on Park Avenue.

When I told partners in the law firm about the offer, they urged me to turn it down—with one exception. Governor Dewey called me to his office and asked me to describe the offer. "Take it," he said. "Go down there for a while. It will make you a better lawyer. The best, most interesting years of my life were spent in government and politics."

Is he as bored as I am, I wondered, practicing law here? Though I needed no other encouragement, I got some in the backhanded way other partners encouraged me to stay. The firm at the time was so solidly white Protestant that I sometimes thought tracing one's roots back to the *Mayflower* might be as important for success as first-rate legal work. More than one partner made it clear that I should stay because I would likely be the first Italian-American to make partner there. I decided to go.

Trudy was as enthusiastic as I about returning to Washington and joining the new administration, but my parents were concerned about my economic security. To allay their concerns and avoid burning my bridges, I followed Dewey's suggestion to view the Pentagon job as a leave of absence. What few conflict-of-interest laws then existed were largely ignored absent a political scandal.

Unstated in all my correspondence and conversations at Dewey Ballantine during this time was the fact that Kennedy was Catholic. I was so proud that a Catholic had won the presidency, and I wanted to contribute to the effort of the nation's first Catholic president to govern the nation. His hard-line anti-communism and pronounced commitment to helping the disadvantaged at home and around the world were exactly what most young Catholics of my circle believed. And when in his inauguration address, on that crisp cold, sunny day in Washington, President John F. Kennedy said, "The torch has been passed to a new generation of Americans," I knew he was talking about me.

I wrote on January 31, 1961, to George Young, then dean of the law school at the University of Wisconsin, that I was going to Washington, "largely because I hope my work will have some impact on society during my lifetime. . . . I cannot resist the temptation to be some small part of an administration that seems willing to tackle the problems of my generation. . . . I am not unmindful of my emotional involvement in the administration because of my enthusiastic work for Kennedy during the campaign. . . . Although my efforts in Washington will doubtless go unheralded in the press, I think that I should give in to my desire to go there for psychological reasons. It is one of those things on which I might later reflect with regret for not having done."

CHAPTER 11

A Whiz Kid in McNamara's Pentagon

Shortly before I left New York for the Pentagon, I talked to Vladimir Bogachev, a Russian Tass News Agency reporter, at the sendoff party Mary and Ellen Lukas gave at their East 77th Street apartment. One guest, who worked for Radio Free Europe, reported this to someone in the U.S. government. Suggesting that Tass reporters were assumed to be spies, military intelligence and FBI agents questioned me repeatedly about my "connection" to Bogachev before granting my security clearance. Their suspicions were my first exposure to how fired up the cold war was in Washington.*

O N April 10, 1961, I parked at a distant edge of the sixty-seven-acre, 9,500-car parking lot at the Pentagon and walked the few hundred yards to the River Entrance, with a spectacular view behind me of the Capitol, the White House, and the Washington Monument. An imposing five-sided, five-storied workplace of 25,000 military and civilian personnel, the building had been designed by George Edwin Bergstrom in 1941 so that employees or visitors could walk the slanted corridors from one point to any other in ten minutes—provided they didn't get lost.

There was no security check to enter at the building, so I sauntered in the River Entrance and bounded up to Cyrus Vance's office on the third floor, taking my first steps as a member of the New Frontier. I'd worked in the Pentagon before, in the bowels of Navy JAG, but this day I felt like part of the

---

*Years later, as secretary of Health, Education, and Welfare, I took action to protect citizens from similar suspicions. FBI reports on two of my top appointees contained allegations that as university students and young graduates they had participated in pro-communist demonstrations and organizations and talked with Russian spies. I went ahead with the appointments, and the two appointees served with distinction. I kept their files in my own desk drawer, not wanting them to be available to anyone who might use the information to hurt them. On my last day in office, I took those files with me. Shortly after becoming a private citizen, I destroyed them.

management and I proudly identified myself to Vance's secretary, Velma. To my dismay, she asked what I wanted.

"I'm reporting to work as special assistant for Department of Defense General Counsel Cyrus Vance."

Puzzled, she said, "Mr. Vance isn't here now. He's with the secretary."

"Should I wait for him here?"

"Just a minute," she said, as she got up and walked across the anteroom to the office of the deputy general counsel, Leonard Niederlehner. A balding, tall man with almost rosy cheeks and the cautious gait of a bureaucratic survivor, Niederlehner came out from his office and greeted me with a hesitant smile. "Mr. Vance didn't tell us that he had someone new coming to work today. Unfortunately, he's at a hearing on the Hill with Secretary McNamara."

Having moved all my belongings and my wife down to the Parkfairfax apartments in Alexandria, I was now unable to disguise my concern. I hadn't seen or spoken to Vance since he'd called two months earlier to offer me the job. Someone whose name I couldn't remember handled the security clearance and paperwork. Had I come on the wrong date?

"Do you want to come back after lunch? I'll tell him you were here this morning," Niederlehner offered. He volunteered that McNamara and Vance were appearing before the House Appropriations Committee on the Defense Department budget and should be back in the early afternoon.

Damn, I thought. Today could be the most embarrassing blunder of my life. But I wasn't going anywhere.

"Can I just wait somewhere?"

Niederlehner looked around awkwardly, and acquiesced. "Well, you can sit here," he said, pointing to one of the nondescript burgundy leather chairs with scarred but polished wooden arms found in high-level government offices.

"Thanks," I said.

I sat down and hung on to the seat. In early afternoon the tall, slender, youthful-looking Vance arrived, walking swiftly but unobtrusively into his office. Just as he crossed the threshold, he caught sight of me out of the corner of his eye, turned around, smiled, then gasped, "Oh, my God! Come on in."

Vance profusely apologized—he had either failed to let anyone know of my arrival or forgotten the date we had agreed upon. "Since there's no office for you yet," he said, "you can start by working at the conference table in mine."

I stayed there for a couple of days until I received a desk in room 3-E-985, a cluster of two offices inhabited by McNamara's reorganization team, led by Solis Horwitz, who had the imposing title director of organizational and management planning in the Office of the General Counsel. A short, chubby former staffer on Lyndon Johnson's Senate Preparedness Investigating Subcommittee, Horwitz supervised three young military officers: Army lieutenant colonel Jack Cushman, a brittle, brilliant, straight-backed, decorated West Point graduate; Abbott Greenleaf, a softer-spoken, equally brilliant Air Force major and West Point graduate; and David O. (Doc) Cooke, a Naval Reserve lieutenant commander and former Navy JAG officer who told me that my successful suit against the Navy had benefited him. As Vance's special assistant—a title I already reveled in—I would advise this group on legal issues.

Within days I felt as though I had stepped into a Pentagon version of the kind of revolution that Arthur Schlesinger had described in his books on the New Deal. Just as Roosevelt had attracted a small army of bright young lawyers and domestic policymakers in 1932, McNamara, who had insisted that Kennedy give him authority to make all appointments in the department, recruited an energetic young team to wrestle the Pentagon behemoth.* The press quickly dubbed the group of young civilians McNamara's "whiz kids." I was proud to be considered one of them, but to the top military brass "whiz kids" had already become a term of disdain.[1]

.   .   .

McNamara was full-speed-ahead reorganizing the military to deliver on Kennedy's inaugural address commitment to "pay any price, bear any burden, meet any hardship, support any friend, oppose any foe to assure the survival and success of liberty." He presided over a department that then spent more than half of every federal tax dollar and 10 percent of the

---

*Four of McNamara's appointees later became cabinet secretaries: in the Nixon administration, John Connally at Treasury; in the Carter administration, Vance at State, Harold Brown at Defense, and I at HEW.

nation's Gross National Product, with six hundred military installations in the United States and 3.5 million uniformed and one million civilian personnel deployed at home and across the world. He was acutely conscious of the ominous warning in Dwight Eisenhower's farewell address, which attracted more attention than any such presidential statement since George Washington's: "In the councils of government, we must guard against the acquisition of unwarranted influence, whether sought or unsought, by the military-industrial complex. . . ."

Eisenhower's concern sprang from the fact that civilian control of the military was becoming an oxymoron. No defense secretary had been able to get a handle on the military services and put an end to their high-stakes jockeying for more money for pet projects. At the urging of President Harry Truman, Congress passed the National Security Act of 1947 in an effort to unify the Army, Navy, Air Force, and Marine Corps under a new civilian cabinet officer, the secretary of defense. James Forrestal, the first to hold that post, found the task of unification so daunting that he fell into a profound depression and in 1949 dove to his death from a sixteenth-floor window of Bethesda Naval Hospital.

In 1958, thoughtful senators, led by Washington Democrat Henry (Scoop) Jackson, pushed through Congress amendments to the National Security Act in order to strengthen the defense secretary's hand to control the military. McNamara intended to push the envelope of power that those amendments gave him, and Vance told me, "Your job is to find the legal support to back him up."

When I arrived three months into the administration, McNamara had the Pentagon jumping as he moved to shatter the bureaucratic china of duplication and consolidate power in the secretary's office. He had already instituted a program planning and evaluation system and a five-year budgeting cycle, which revolutionized the way the services assessed their resource needs. I learned immediately that rapid action was typical of McNamara, who repeatedly warned, "Not deciding is a decision. Let's all remember that when we decide not to do something."

Within a week I was thrown into the turmoil and excitement of those days. McNamara asked our organization group to examine the savings to be reaped by creating a Defense Supply Agency to acquire common items that the services were buying separately, such as uniforms and other equipment.

The military brass opposed the idea. To present our findings to the defense secretary and the generals and admirals assembled in his huge conference room, we decorated enormous pegboards with common items that each service was purchasing on its own: scores of belt buckles, men's underwear and women's lingerie, shoes, butcher's smocks, caps and hats, insignia of rank, toilet seats, and the like. Each one was slightly different depending on the service that purchased it. When McNamara asked for an explanation of why such items could not be purchased commonly, the Marine Corps commandant responded that their belt buckle was the only one that could also be used as a bottle opener. After a few seconds of embarrassed silence, everyone in the room knew that the Defense Supply Agency would be established, and McNamara issued the necessary directive the next day.

.   .   .

During the campaign, Kennedy had repeatedly accused the Republican administration not only of losing the race to conquer space[2] but also of falling dangerously behind the Russians in developing long-range missiles. The "missile gap" became Kennedy's shorthand for charging that Republicans had weakened our defense posture vis-à-vis the Soviets. Once in office, however, McNamara learned that only Air Force Intelligence thought there was a missile gap, and upon analysis he concluded that none existed. His discovery led him to question the need for separate intelligence organizations in each of the military departments (in addition to those in the Central Intelligence Agency and the State Department). Vance asked me if I had any affiliation with Naval Intelligence while in the Navy. I had not. "Fine," he said. "Bob wants fresh minds to see whether we should create a Defense Intelligence Agency. You're on the team."

We set out three options—creating the agency, giving responsibility to one of the services, or parceling responsibilities among them—and asked for comments from the military departments within thirty days. We worked nights and weekends on alternatives and the military department responses. In less than two months, we sent McNamara a recommendation to create a Defense Intelligence Agency and attached a draft directive. A few days later, on August 2, after meeting with the Joint Chiefs to discuss it, McNamara astounded the military by establishing the Defense Intelligence

Agency. I was invigorated and amazed by our ability to reshape the Pentagon so rapidly.

.   .   .

The Defense Supply and Defense Intelligence agencies have stood the test of time, unlike our work on civil defense. Neither Truman nor Eisenhower paid much attention to civil defense, and Congress had slashed their modest funding requests. But early in the Kennedy administration, Soviet premier Nikita Khrushchev announced support for "wars of liberation" around the globe; communist insurgencies erupted in the Congo and Laos as Africa decolonized; South Vietnam came under increasing assault from the communist North. As the cold war heated up, nuclear war was seen as a clear and present danger, and civil defense to protect against a nuclear attack moved high on the Kennedy administration's agenda.

United States defense strategy under Kennedy and McNamara renounced use of nuclear weapons in a preemptive first strike. To support this policy of deterrence, McNamara was determined to amass a sufficient number of nuclear weapons to survive a first strike and be able to destroy an enemy that launched one. Central to this second-strike capability were nuclear missiles on the Navy's Polaris submarines and Air Force Minuteman intercontinental ballistic missiles (ICBMs) in indestructible silos.

Pursuing a second-strike strategy also required a major investment to provide the population as much protection as possible from a first strike by an enemy. McNamara asked our group to determine the feasibility of establishing a massive civil defense system. As usual, the defense secretary wanted a swift answer. We scrambled for experts and brought in Herman Kahn, a senior physicist at the Rand Corporation.[3] Kahn, who grew up in New York City, had served in the Army during World War II and graduated from the University of California at Los Angeles in 1945. He was author of *On Thermonuclear War,* a bestseller widely read in military circles and one that had impressed President Kennedy. Kahn concluded that nuclear war was not unthinkable, the "picture of total world annihilation" was false, and countries "should be able to restore a semblance of prewar conditions quite rapidly."[4] He saw the casualties of such a war as two to 20 million people, not the 50 to 100 million others estimated.

Kahn, all three hundred pounds of his six-foot frame, came to our cramped office to brief us and answer our questions. He stood at the blackboard drawing concentric circles with a piece of chalk in his thick fingers. Within the first small circle around the blast, he said all would be killed. Then he drew a larger one and said only a portion of those living there would be killed; then larger and larger circles until he reached a distance where no one would die. The number of people who would be killed or wounded beyond the first circle depended on how well prepared they were to stay underground and avoid radioactive fallout. Kahn proposed concrete-and-lead bunkers, filtered air systems, and plenty of protected food and water.

In retrospect, that day with Kahn seems surreal, but in 1961 the five of us sat there, asked questions, and for the most part accepted his analysis when we put together the civil defense program. Like most Americans, I had seen on film the devastation at Hiroshima and Nagasaki, but Kahn was convincing as he argued, "With a system of bunkers and supplies, many more Japanese would have survived the thermonuclear blasts." Kahn's analysis fit neatly into the Kennedy-McNamara no-first-strike doctrine.

Under the Jesuits, I had studied the three conditions for a just war: legitimate authority, a just cause, and just methods of waging it.[5] Our duly elected government was a legitimate authority and the battle against Godless communism was a just cause. If there was a moral use of nuclear weapons, I thought sitting there, the policy of using them only in self-defense in response to an enemy's first nuclear strike seemed to satisfy the requirement for a just method of waging war.

On May 25, 1961, Kennedy signaled his commitment to a civil defense program and gave McNamara responsibility for leading it. *Life* magazine wrote of the importance of the program. Republican governor Nelson Rockefeller became an outspoken proponent and spearheaded his own effort in New York.

On July 25, a shaken President Kennedy reported to the nation on his meetings in Vienna with Soviet leader Khrushchev: "His grim warnings about the future of the world, his aide memoire on Berlin [to end three-power (U.S., Britain, France) control and swallow West Berlin in Communist East Germany], his subsequent speeches and threats . . . and the increase in the Soviet military budget . . . have all prompted a series of decisions by the administration. . . ." Kennedy asked Congress for $3.25 billion to add more men for the armed forces, support the civil defense program, and construct fallout shelters: "In the event of an attack, the lives of those families which are not hit in a nuclear blast and fire can still be saved—*if* they can be warned to take shelter and *if* that shelter is available." McNamara assured Congress we could design a civil defense program "to produce many million shelter spaces at the lowest possible cost—a cost we estimate at $4 per person, including finding, marking, and stocking the shelter spaces with essentials for survival."[6]

When East Germany began construction of the Berlin Wall to stem the rising number of its people escaping to the West, President Kennedy questioned whether our civil defense efforts were sufficient. In a memorandum to McNamara dated August 20, 1961, the President asked, "Do you think it would be useful for me to write a letter to every home owner in the United States giving them instructions as to what can be done on their own to provide greater security for their family, or should we look into this at a later date after your organization of the civil defense programs has been completed?"[7] No such letter was ever sent—not because we didn't think individual households should prepare for a nuclear attack, but because we convinced the President that it might set off hoarding and panic among the American people.

As we prepared for civil defense in case of a nuclear attack, McNamara's whiz kids Charles Hitch and Alain Enthoven put flesh on the bones of a "flexible response" strategy to strengthen the military's ability to fight a non-nuclear war. Out of this effort came an increase in the number of Army divisions, creation of an air cavalry through the use of helicopters, and the building of the gigantic C5A transport plane to move at one time up to seven hundred troops along with supporting jeeps, tanks, and land vehicles. Driven in good measure by the insistence of Robert Kennedy, McNamara created the Special Forces with their green berets, who were trained for no-holds-barred warfare on military, health, social, and economic fronts in order to counter Khrushchev's support of wars of liberation. The attorney general and defense secretary saw these moves, especially the creation of the Special Forces, as ideal for Vietnam, where President Kennedy sent the first sixteen thousand U. S. troops in late 1961.[8]

There was an air of invincibility about the whiz kids and our leader McNamara in the early 1960s. We were imposing hands-on civilian control of the military. The top-to-bottom reorganization generated more than a dollar of value for each tax dollar invested in the Pentagon. We saw ourselves as giving the President and the secretary of state an unprecedented box of flexible military tools to aid in negotiations with the Soviets, counter wars of liberation, and respond to communist aggression anywhere in the world. Often over the objection of generals and admirals, with our Ivy League brains reshaping their military brawn, we were creating an invincible force that could fight any way, any time, anywhere. In our enthusiasm and from our perches on the Pentagon's E-Ring, we couldn't see any clouds on the horizon for the bright sunshine of the spanking new, uniquely powerful flexible military and civil defense capability we were assembling. I had no misgivings at the time, but in writing of the excitement in my job to Wilkie Bushby at the Dewey law firm in the summer of 1961, I noted that the most significant difference between private practice at a Wall Street law firm and working in McNamara's Pentagon was "the speed with which decisions have to be made. Rarely do we have enough time to consider all the possible ramifications of decisions."

.   .   .

McNamara's tight control over the military drew privately expressed, bitter resentment from a number of high-ranking officers in all three services. The angriest, Air Force Chief of Staff General Curtis LeMay, made no secret of his belief that the United States should maintain its first-strike option and was outraged that McNamara and his twenty- and thirty-something whiz kids, who lacked combat experience, were second-guessing uniformed officers about military strategy. Democratic senator Strom Thurmond of South Carolina and Republican senators Karl Mundt of South Dakota[9] and Barry Goldwater of Arizona[10] shared LeMay's concern that the new team at the Pentagon did not appreciate the gravity of the communist threat and that McNamara would use his newly created Defense Intelligence Agency to soft-pedal assessments of communist military threats.

This simmering resentment formed the backdrop for the most intense firestorm McNamara faced in his first years as defense secretary: the battle that became known as "muzzling the military." It was the most furious assault from the anticommunist right since Senator Joseph McCarthy's endeavors ten years earlier.

The controversy was rooted in the Korean War in the 1950s, when no American prisoner of war (POW) escaped and most provided their captors with information well beyond the "name, rank, serial number, and date of birth" restriction of military law. North Koreans paraded U.S. POWs before television cameras to condemn American aggression and praise the communists as freedom fighters. Several POWs signed false confessions that they had engaged in germ warfare.[11]

The Senate Permanent Subcommittee on Investigations and its counsel Robert Kennedy concluded that American servicemen were easily "brainwashed," because they were ignorant of Communism.[12] A Department of Defense Advisory Committee found "Many had never before heard of Karl Marx."[13] A 1958 National Security Council directive encouraged the military to educate its troops and the public about the dangers of communism and the threat of communist aggression, tasks many officers pursued with gusto.

In April 1961, the privately owned American magazine *Overseas Weekly* reported that Army major general Edwin Walker told troops stationed in Germany that most of the U.S. press was communist controlled, that Truman, Eleanor Roosevelt, former secretary of state Dean Acheson, Kennedy, and Lyndon Johnson were "pinkos," and that 60 percent of all Americans were communist influenced. Walker's source was the "Blue Book" (pro-blue as opposed to pro-pink), a publication of the John Birch Society, an extreme right-wing group founded in 1953 by Robert Welch, a Massachusetts candy manufacturer. General Walker, a member of the society, distributed to his troops the Americans for Conservative Action (ACA) Index, which ranked members of Congress based on how "American" their 1960 voting record was.

Army Secretary Elvis Stahr admonished Walker for his actions and statements. But that was not enough for Arkansas Democrat J. William Fulbright, chairman of the Senate Foreign Relations Committee. On June 28, 1961, he charged that the 1958 National Security Council directive was being misused by right-wing radicals in the military and demanded that Secretary McNamara stop uniformed officers from making anti-communist speeches contrary to U.S. foreign policy.[14] Two weeks later, McNamara ordered all military personnel to submit their public speeches to the Directorate of Security Review in the office of the assistant secretary of defense for public affairs in order to assure that they did not contain any classified information and comported with the administration's foreign and military policies.

McNamara also ordered a review of troop information and education programs.[15]

On August 31, the Senate Armed Services Committee announced an investigation to determine whether the administration was "gagging the military"—preventing it from expressing anti-communist views and conducting anti-communist seminars, actions South Carolina senator Strom Thurmond called "vital to the survival of the Nation."[16]

McNamara and Vance asked me to be the secretary's lawyer for the hearings. Just thirty years old and barely six years out of law school, I was determined to deliver for this demanding duo. I had no idea—nor did anyone in the Pentagon—that this investigation would be a long last gasp from the hard-line anti-communist right.

For the first time, I came in almost daily contact with Robert McNamara. Behind his rimless glasses and slicked-down hair was a brain of extraordinary power. McNamara started work around 6:30 A.M. and ended around eight in the evening. He worked all day Saturday, leaving around 6 P.M. Every lunch was a working lunch. He was meticulously on time, did not start meetings late, and ended them as scheduled. He socialized less than most of the cabinet and was extremely fit. He played squash several times a week, usually with his favorite adversary, Agriculture Secretary Orville Freeman, but never with anyone in the Pentagon. As I came to know McNamara and understand his management style, I realized that he did not want anyone in the Defense Department to beat him at anything.

For McNamara, who first shrugged Thurmond off as a pesky fly, the hearings festered into a serious distraction and threat to his power as secretary of defense. For me, the hearings were a crash course in Washington politics. We had a week to prepare. I read speeches that had been censored and listened to tapes of anti-communist seminars conducted by the military in order to find outrageous examples of attacks on national policies. I read months of *Overseas Weekly* and reviewed General Walker's activities. It was an eighteen-hour-a-day marathon to be ready for hearings set to begin two days after Labor Day.

On September 6, 1961, the Senate Committee on Armed Services opened hearings in the ornate Senate Caucus Room in the Old Senate Office Building.[17] As I walked behind Secretary McNamara and Vance underneath four crystal chandeliers lighting the room, I thought, I'm entering the site of the Army-McCarthy hearings; this is a place where history is made.[18]

Every committee member was present, seated behind tables covered with green felt. At the witness table, McNamara faced a microphone, with a pitcher of ice water on his left. Vance and I sat behind him. The room was wall-to-wall spectators and reporters. Television cameras were not permitted, but still photographers clicked away, sitting on the floor facing the secretary.

McNamara's opening statement was the first Congressional testimony I had drafted, and I was exhilarated as he read it. After recognizing the dangerous "drive of Soviet communist imperialism to colonize the world . . . without . . . the faintest trace of moral restraint," McNamara agreed that members of the military should be educated on communism and democracy. But he would not let partisan politics infiltrate such education programs:

> The military establishment is an instrument—not a shaper—of national policy. Its members—as free Americans—are entitled to their views on the issues of the day, and they have every right to try to make their views effective through the ballot. They do NOT have the right, however, to use the military establishment to advance partisan concepts or alter the decisions of the elected representatives of the people.

McNamara said he, like his predecessors, required members of the military to submit public speeches for clearance and had the State Department review those regarding foreign policy.

The senators subjected McNamara to hours of hostile questioning. Several charged him with allowing salacious literature to be sold on the bases. Thurmond held up a copy of the *Overseas Weekly* and asked McNamara to describe its front—a photo of a scantily clad, buxom woman, somewhat daring cheesecake by the day's standards (a picture that any tabloid in 2004 would reject as too tame). Motherly types in the hearing room hissed as McNamara tried to make light of the picture.

To prepare for the hearings, I had set up a team of a half dozen individuals to look at more than one thousand speeches by military personnel that the Directorate of Security Review had examined in 1961. Senator Thurmond demanded copies of all the speeches that had been studied. McNamara reluctantly agreed to provide copies of the speeches and names of the reviewers (who were listed in the Pentagon phone directory), but he refused to identify which person had reviewed which speech. By moving fast and cooperating, McNamara hoped to end the hearings. That hope was dashed when a special subcommittee was established to continue the investigation; Senator John Stennis of Mississippi was named chair with Strom Thurmond (then a Democrat) the ranking majority member.

When Thurmond insisted that McNamara link the reviewers' names to the speeches each reviewed, I alerted Senator Stennis that the secretary intended to plead executive privilege in refusing to respond. Stennis believed that only the President could invoke executive privilege to withhold information from the Congress.

So I went to the Justice Department to sit down with Nicholas Katzenbach, assistant attorney general for the Office of Legal Counsel, the division that prided itself on being "the President's lawyers." Katzenbach, a law professor at Yale and the University of Chicago before joining the administration, agreed with our analysis. Together, over much coffee and many cigarettes, we drafted a letter for President Kennedy's signature directing McNamara to invoke executive privilege to deny identifying which individual had reviewed which speech.

In late January, hearings before the Special Preparedness Subcommittee on Military Cold War Education and Speech Review Policies began. Senator Thurmond asked Willis Lawrence,[19] a civilian speech reviewer, to identify the reviewer who had censored testimony prepared for Lieutenant General Arthur Trudeau, Army chief of research and development. McNamara, who accompanied Lawrence, instructed him not to respond and invoked executive privilege. Over Thurmond's objections Stennis allowed McNamara to read aloud President Kennedy's letter, which concluded "that it would be contrary to the public interest to make available any information which would enable the Subcommittee to identify and hold accountable any individual with respect to any particular speech he has reviewed." To me it was remarkable that the words of the President were those that Katzenbach and I had drafted.

Stennis ruled that the privilege was properly invoked. That confrontation ended McNamara's involvement in the hearings.

But not mine. I prepared seventy witnesses to appear before the hostile committee and accompanied them throughout the winter and spring when they testified. Each time, Thurmond would ask the witness, "Is that your lawyer?"

"Yes, Mr. Chairman," each responded.

Thurmond would shoot back, "No it's not. It's the secretary of defense's lawyer."

At that point, Thurmond would insist that I raise my hand and be sworn in. Thurmond staged this preposterous minuet repeatedly before the hearings ended.

By selectively reciting changes ordered in speeches, Thurmond found them a political bonanza to demonstrate that administration appointees were softening the line on communism. In fact, of the fourteen Defense Department reviewers, eleven were military officers (most of whom had seen combat in Korea) and the other three were career civil servants. Some changes were made to bring military rhetoric into line with a specific foreign policy objective—for example, eliminating the term "Sino-Soviet bloc" because the Kennedy administration was trying to separate Russia and China and create tension between the two communist powers. Others did soften anti-communist rhetoric. Years later, McNamara told me that the softening was at his personal direction; he wanted to get some of the emotion out of the confrontation with the Soviets: "The situation was tough enough without exaggerating or inflaming it, so I thought that all speeches by officers should be reviewed for excessive and inflammatory language."

The entire climate of the hearings changed when General Walker testified. By the time Walker appeared before the subcommittee in April 1962, he had resigned from the Army and was seeking the Democratic nomination for governor of Texas. On his first day of testimony, Walker read a nine-thousand-word prepared statement. He described himself as a "scapegoat" to a "no-win" policy against communism and cited many prominent Americans, including President Kennedy, Dean Rusk, and CBS reporters Daniel Schorr and Walter Cronkite, and publications, including Max Ascoli's (consistently anti-communist) *The Reporter,* as being in "collusion with the international Communist conspiracy." The next day, with no prepared statement, Walker's comments were so incoherent that Mary McGrory wrote in the *Washington Evening Star,* "In the world of Mr. Walker sentences have no beginnings, no endings, no verbs."

During the hearing, George Lincoln Rockwell, leader of the American Nazi Party, was ordered out of the room because he was wearing a swastika on his lapel. As Walker completed his testimony and left the hearing, *Washington Daily News* reporter Tom Kelly asked Walker a question about

George Lincoln Rockwell. Walker turned and with his right fist hit Kelly in the left eye. That outburst branded Walker's appearance as a farce. It was only a matter of time (and several boring witnesses called by Thurmond) before the hearings ended. The special subcommittee issued its report on October 25, 1962, finding that the policies governing the review of speeches were appropriate. The committee did criticize us for inconsistent application of those policies, a view with which I agreed and considered an example of the limits of censorship even in such a narrow area. I was pleased that the hearings ended with a political whimper, not a bang.

But it would not be my last encounter with General Walker.

CHAPTER 12

In the Army on the Home Front

A S THE MUZZLING-THE-MILITARY hearings wound down, and with my first child due in July, I resumed my conversations with Arnold, Fortas & Porter. In May as I was interviewing at the law firm, Cy Vance called me into his office. "Bob has asked me to succeed Elvis Stahr as secretary of the Army," he said. He told me that McNamara was disappointed with Stahr's failure to get control of the Army and move aggressively to create air cavalry (helicopter) divisions and Special Forces.

I congratulated Vance, thinking I had better tell him that I myself was planning to move to private practice. Before I could continue, Vance interrupted, "I have something difficult to tell you. Bob is thinking about making you general counsel of the Department of Defense."

My thirty-one-year-old heart beat with excitement at the thought of succeeding Vance. There's nothing difficult about that, I thought.

Then he added. "I told Bob it was his decision, but that I was going to urge you not to accept."

What's going on? I wondered.

"You're as bright a young lawyer as I've come across," Vance continued. "But you need more experience before taking on a job like this. There are political minefields everywhere in this position and the Pentagon. There are complex and sophisticated military-industry issues. Bob can be headstrong, and I'm not sure you're yet seasoned enough to argue with him—or for him to listen to you—and that's essential for the good of the department."

What he's really saying, I thought, is that I'm too young and green for McNamara to respect my judgment. Vance added, "No doubt in another year or so you will be. I have seen bright young men in Washington move too fast and as a result stumble and lose what could have been brilliant careers. I don't want that to happen to you."

"Is McNamara offering me the job?" I asked.

"He will, unless I tell him that you agree with me that you should have more seasoning."

"If I agree with you, what happens?"

"I'd like you to come with me as special assistant to the secretary of the Army. You'll work on lots of non-legal matters and get experience at the top of a military department."

Vance told me to come back to him when I had thought about it.

While I was thinking about it, I had an interview with Victor Kramer, an original character and iconoclastic partner at Arnold, Fortas & Porter. Short, balding, tightly built, and tautly spoken, Kramer punctuated his ordinary conversation with forefinger-extended punches. "Don't come here now. You have your wagon hitched to two stars, Vance and McNamara. Stay with them. There's nothing here that won't be here years from now. I don't know why you're even talking to us. Stay with them and listen to Vance."

It was like a bracing bucket of cold water in the face. As soon as he said it, I woke up knowing it was the right thing to do. The next morning I told Vance I would go with him to the Army and in a letter to Kramer expressed my gratitude: "Of all the people I spoke to during the last two or three days, you gave the most help in crystallizing the alternatives for me. . . ."

The decision would involve me in the government's actions in just about every civil rights event in the 1960s, and open my eyes to the difficulty and significance of the battle to eliminate racial discrimination in our nation. I had read about Eisenhower enforcing the Supreme Court's decision to desegregate the high school in Little Rock in 1957 and of the Catholic archdiocese in New Orleans desegregating its parochial schools in April 1962. But I didn't see them as opening skirmishes in a sometimes violent racial revolution. I certainly didn't see myself as a participant in that upheaval, which would expose the best and worst of America. The key role the Army would play and my position with Vance would put me at center stage.

.   .   .

Just two months after Vance and I arrived in the secretary of the Army's office, a twenty-eight-year-old former Air Force enlisted man sought to be the first black admitted to the University of Mississippi at Oxford. Convinced he had a "divine responsibility" to "break the system of 'White

Supremacy'" in his home state, and with the help of the National Association for the Advancement of Colored People (NAACP), James Meredith had obtained a federal court order directing the university to admit him. Mississippi governor Ross Barnett invoked something he called "the doctrine of nullification," declaring all pubic schools answerable only to state officials. He urged every citizen to be prepared to go to jail to prevent desegregation.

Faced with Barnett's defiance, President Kennedy sent Deputy Assistant Attorney General for Civil Rights John Doar and U.S. marshals to accompany Meredith on September 25, 1962, when he first attempted to enroll. Barnett blocked Meredith's attempt to register and was held in contempt for doing so on Friday September 28. That set the stage for a second try.

As the Mississippi governor promised to defy the court order and crowds of angry segregationist demonstrators streamed into Oxford and the university campus, President Kennedy federalized the Mississippi National Guard (thus bringing them under his control) and dispatched regular Army troops to the Naval Air Station in Millington, Tennessee, north of Memphis. Though the base was one hundred miles from Oxford, Attorney General Robert Kennedy wanted the troops moved no closer for fear of increasing tension if they were visible around the university. He sent to Oxford several hundred U.S. marshals, prison guards, and Border Patrol officers, none with much, if any, experience in riot control. Deputy Attorney General Nicholas Katzenbach assumed the role of field commander, but since we had given no thought to communications, he had to use a pay telephone, constantly inserting coins when he called the White House or the Justice Department. On Sunday, as the situation deteriorated, Robert Kennedy rejected Vance's repeated requests to move troops closer. Vance, suffering a ruptured disc in his back at the time, lay on his office floor, telephone in hand, arguing with the attorney general to no avail.

Late that afternoon, Meredith arrived at Baxter Hall dormitory on the university campus to spend the evening before registering the following morning. By this time, a thousand protestors were chanting, "Go to Cuba, nigger lovers!"[1] As the crowd began slashing tires and throwing bricks, pipes, and Molotov cocktails (gasoline-filled bottles with a flaming rag wick), marshals put on gas masks and fired tear gas.

Under the mistaken impression that Meredith's entrance to the campus had gone smoothly, President Kennedy reported it that way in his address to the nation early that evening. Within an hour of his speech, the first shots were fired and the mob exceeded two thousand. As casualties mounted and marshals ran out of tear gas, Robert Kennedy told Vance to move 3,000 soldiers from Memphis to Oxford to stop the rioting. Inexperienced in military operations, we misjudged how long it would take troops to get to the university, because we assumed they could travel in convoy as fast as a single car, about forty to fifty miles an hour. Worse, because we held everything so closely until the last minute, the troops didn't even have adequate road maps. Often they had to depend for directions on Mississippi state troopers under the control of Governor Ross Barnett.

Because of our miscalculation, the forces could not get to Oxford in time to restore order before Paul Guihard, a thirty-year-old correspondent for Agence France Presse, and Ray Gunter, a twenty-three-year-old local jukebox repairman, were shot and killed, and 375 others, including 166 U.S. marshals, were injured.

In an inflammatory twist, former Army general Edwin Walker (who, after the muzzling-the-military hearing, had lost his bid for the Democratic nomination for Texas governor) appeared on campus in a ten-gallon hat to incite the rioters into action and lead two charges of students against U.S. marshals. During his tirades, Walker called for 10,000 volunteers from all parts of the U.S. to take up arms. Robert Kennedy had him arrested and charged with assault, resisting arrest, conspiracy, and inciting an insurrection. Both Kennedy brothers blamed the Army for the colossal mess at Oxford, and on hearing of Walker's stirrings, President Kennedy said, "Imagine that son of a bitch having been commander of a division . . . up till last year. And the Army promoting him."[2]

The next morning, in a car pocked with bullet holes, Doar and U.S. marshals drove Meredith to the Lyceum building, where he registered. Soldiers held back the students and Meredith listened to shouts of "nigger" as he registered. Later that day he attended his first class—in Colonial American history.[3]

That same morning, Walker was arraigned and flown to the United States Medical Center for Federal Prisoners in Springfield, Missouri. The *New York Times* noted that "committing him to a hospital while awaiting trial on the charges, rather than to a jail or reformatory, was regarded as unusual." What the *Times* didn't know was that the attorney general had decided that Walker was not getting back out on the street, whatever it took.

As an expert on General Walker, I was rushed by Vance to the attorney general's office to help draft papers to keep Walker behind bars. When I arrived, his secretary, Angie Novello, waved me in. "They're in the conference room. They told me to send you right in."

Without even saying hello, Robert Kennedy said he did not want General Walker released on bail. My job was to give the Justice Department psychiatrist enough ammunition to sign an affidavit to support a court order requiring Walker to undergo psychiatric examination before release. There was no discussion of Walker's rights—no echoes of the right to bail that was stressed in my criminal law course at Harvard. "Whatever it takes to keep him locked up in that hospital, that's what we need" was the message from the attorney general as he stared at me. I knew Kennedy had mercilessly chewed out Vance for not getting Army troops to Oxford in time to avoid the violence. His chilling glare said, "Maybe you guys in the Army can at least get something right."

I had plenty of material to nail Walker. We drafted the affidavit in less than two hours and sent it to the court in St. Louis. There federal District Judge Claude Clayton ordered Walker held for psychiatric examination, which the U.S. attorney in Kansas City said would take sixty to ninety days. At that time, I relished the task. Reflecting on my part in holding Walker, I wonder if the excitement of the moment and my desire to impress Robert Kennedy led me to ignore the lessons of fairness and rights of defendants I'd learned at Harvard Law School. After seven days, with the situation in Oxford under control, Walker was released on his promise to return to Texas.[4] Though both Kennedy brothers were furious with the Army, in their public statements they laid all the blame on Mississippi governor Ross Barnett. At the Pentagon, we were told to keep our mouths shut and not admit any deficiencies. The press remained so anti-Barnett and pro–federal government that we never were called to public account for our blunders.

President Kennedy ordered the Army to remain at the University of Mississippi as long as necessary to assure Meredith's safety. We created Camp USAFOX (U.S. Army Forces Oxford), and in shifts over the school year some 23,000 soldiers served there.[5] Meredith's dormitory, Baxter Hall, was patrolled around the clock. When Meredith moved around the campus or Oxford, a twelve-man security group with a sedan and three jeeps accompanied him.

In the spring of 1963, I visited the university with Justice Department representative John Doar to assess the situation. We arrived in the late morning and toured the campus with the commander of the troops. We were told that the evening before, students had hanged Meredith in effigy, exploded cherry bombs in Baxter Hall, where he lived, and thrown a couple of Molotov cocktails. Campus police had confiscated rifles from students.

When we visited Baxter Hall, I saw that Meredith was living like a prisoner. His windows were boarded up with plywood; a marshal sat outside his door. This guy is committed to suffer through this, I thought, but how the hell can he study?

Doar and I went to dinner with Meredith that evening. As we walked the campus lane to the mess hall, students hung out the windows shouting, "Nigger lovers! Nigger lovers!" and threw objects at us. In the cafeteria, we got our trays of food and sat down at a table. Students immediately left all the tables surrounding us, leaving a circle of empty tables, as though we had some terrible contagious disease. It reminded me of a scene from the movie *Hellzapoppin* (the 1941 film adaptation of a hit Broadway play written by the comedy team of Olsen and Johnson), which I had seen as a kid: the silhouette of a little black boy comes on the screen as he sits in a movie theater and people sitting around him hold their noses and move away. With the empty circle of chairs surrounding us, I felt embarrassed that I had once laughed at that scene.

We had heard that Meredith was not easy to get along with, but he gave us no sense of it that evening. The experience was taking its toll on him and he wanted it over with. He said he might go right through the summer to earn his degree and get out. We walked Meredith back to his dorm and then went to Camp USAFOX to sleep in tents. Every soldier I saw there was white.

The next morning we returned to Meredith's dorm. Parked out front was his car, a large four-door sedan with a crenellated roof, covered with broken raw eggs. The cruelty of these actions struck me, but even more the comments of a couple of the marshals. "Meredith shouldn't drive a car like that on campus. Then this wouldn't happen."

Doar and I recommended that the troops be withdrawn. We believed the few recent incidents were related to our arrival. We were convinced that now the marshals alone could do the job. The Army disbanded Fort USAFOX on June 10, 1963.[6]

We learned from the riots at Ole Miss that we needed to plan well ahead and have troops close by or leave plenty of time—convoy time—for travel; we needed reams of physical intelligence about where we were going, and ample communications. We needed to let the military prepare as if their objective were to take over hostile territory. We needed never to use U.S. Army troops if we could avoid it; it was too difficult to get them out. It was far better to have the President federalize a state's National Guard, whose members (and their families) would press to return to civilian status.

For me, the most important lesson came on my visit to Oxford. I was shaken by how vehemently the white students resented even one black student on campus. I began to appreciate how nasty and violent the struggle for civil rights was going to be. We could force the door open for schools in the South to admit blacks, but we could never force the white students to accept them. I realized how critical it was to change the culture—the hearts and minds of men and women—to make progress. All thoughts of returning to the private practice of law vanished. This was a battle worth fighting and I was up for it.

·   ·   ·

With his 1963 inaugural speech bellowing, "Segregation now, segregation tomorrow, segregation forever," Alabama governor George Wallace gave us early warning of the problems we would face when the University of Alabama received the next federal court order to admit black students. As a result we had the time to prepare. Determined not to repeat the mistakes at Ole Miss, we at the Pentagon took aerial photographs of the campus and surrounding areas. I had Army Intelligence personnel in civilian clothes reconnoiter campus buildings, local hospitals, firehouses, assembly areas, and escape routes. We set up our own independent communications system as though we were going into enemy territory. We arranged to have Coca-Cola remove all soda machines from campus to eliminate use of the bottles as Molotov cocktails. With the Army brass determined never again to suffer the embarrassment of Oxford, and Vance telling me to "make absolutely certain to take every precaution," I knew we would be ready when twenty-year-old Vivian Malone and nineteen-year-old James Hood, two black students, arrived at the University of Alabama to register.[7]

In early May 1963, as we were making these preparations, Birmingham, Alabama, a city sixty miles from the University at Tuscaloosa, became the target of a civil rights campaign to desegregate lunch counters, public spaces like libraries, and downtown businesses. Led by Reverend Martin Luther King, Jr., the campaign began with sit-ins on April 3 resisted by Commissioner of Public Safety Bull Connor. King was arrested and incarcerated in the cell where he wrote *Letters from a Birmingham Jail.*

Upon release, King launched the "Children's Crusade," in which hundreds of children marched in protest. When Connor unleashed dogs so vicious and fire hoses so powerful (100 pounds per inch) that they knocked children over—to the horror of the nation and the world viewing it on television—I became concerned that whatever we did, violence might be inevitable. Negotiations between civil rights leaders and local businessmen eventually desegregated Birmingham lunch counters, but I remained fearful of a redux of Oxford as sporadic bombings and outbursts of violence and vandalism continued. With the desegregation of the University of Alabama just weeks away, we secretly alerted troops and drafted papers to call the state National Guard into federal service.

Wallace played publicly and loudly to the segregationists, but he was sending secret signals to us that he preferred to star in the theater of segregation without the violence that had shattered the campus at Oxford, Mississippi. Nevertheless, when he announced his intention to stand in the schoolhouse door to block the admission of Malone and Hunt, we federalized 16,463 men of the 31st Alabama guard division. When federalized, the Mississippi guard had obeyed orders, so we expected the Alabama National Guard to do so. Deeply committed and totally engaged, Robert Kennedy wanted to confront Wallace personally at the schoolhouse door. We in the Army—and Kennedy's own aides—opposed the idea. We feared his presence would inflame an already smoldering situation. Because it appeared that Kennedy's presence might tilt Wallace from his tentative willingness to step aside after making his points on live television, the attorney general acceded to our recommendation and deputized Nick Katzenbach to escort the two students.

As Wallace stood at the door of Foster Hall on the steamy afternoon of June 11, 1963, Cy Vance and I were sitting in the Army war room at the Pentagon, with sophisticated communications and television capabilities at our fingertips. In a tan sedan, Katzenbach arrived on campus with Hood, dressed in a dark four-button suit and natty snap-brim hat with red feather, and Malone, a tall slender woman wearing a pink knit dress. Army general Creighton Abrams[8] was stationed at the Black Warrior River bank on the edge of the campus. We had a speedboat parked there, motor idling, ready to whisk the two students off, if necessary for their protection. To be certain that this time we would know everything the White House and Justice Department were doing, we secretly ran all their communication lines through the Army war room. Sitting there, Vance and I were able to listen to any conversations the President or attorney general had with Katzenbach or other officials on the scene. Because we assumed Robert Kennedy would have objected to our eavesdropping, we never let him know.

When Katzenbach arrived with the students, Wallace blocked the doorway. As Vance and I watched live television reporting the event, Katzenbach asked him to "cease and desist" from "unlawful obstruction" to a federal court order. Wallace refused. Wallace, wearing a microphone, stood in the shade as Katzenbach sweltered in the hot sun. After Wallace had his segregationist say, Katzenbach responded, "From the outset, governor, all of us have known that the final chapter of this history will be the admission of these students."

He then summoned the Alabama National Guard commander, General Henry Vance Graham, to force Wallace aside upon pain of arrest. Dressed in combat fatigues, General Graham stepped up to the doorway, gave the governor a salute (which Wallace returned), and said: "It is my sad duty to ask you to step aside on order of the president of the United States." Wallace urged Alabama citizens to remain "calm and restrained" in this fight against "federal interference" and assured them he would continue his battle in Montgomery, the state capital. He then stepped aside. Malone and Hood were whisked through to the university gymnasium, where they registered as hundreds of white students jeered.

That night we sighed with relief, hope, and pride as President Kennedy addressed the nation:

> We are confronted primarily with a moral issue. It is as old as the scriptures and is as clear as the American constitution. The heart of the question is whether all Americans are to be afforded equal rights and equal opportunities, whether we are going to treat our fellow Americans as we want to be treated. . . . A great change is at hand and our task, our obli-

gation, is to make that revolution, that change, peaceful and constructive for all.

Later that evening, as we congratulated ourselves that all had gone well in
Alabama, Medgar Evers, the thirty-seven-year-old civil rights leader and
NAACP field secretary, was shot in the back, assassinated outside his home
in Jackson, Mississippi.[9]

We kept the guard, about twelve hundred strong, federalized and around
the campus throughout the summer session. We barricaded no dormitory
rooms, but the pressure of being escorted everywhere by federal marshals
and ugly phone calls at night, as well as the strain on his family, was too
much for James Hood. He left for Detroit at the end of the summer semester to pursue his degree in Michigan.[10]

The University of Alabama campus at Tuscaloosa remained calm
throughout the fall, despite segregationist outbursts of Governor Wallace
and the bombing of the Sixteenth Street Baptist church in Birmingham that
killed four black girls in September. In November John Doar and I visited
the university. We found Vivian Malone playing bridge with three white students, all four of them dressed in plaid skirts, white socks, and buckskin
shoes, the style of college women in the South in those days. The situation
and ambiance were entirely different than with Meredith, in good measure
because of Malone's engaging personality.[11] I was heartened by the way in
which her white female classmates accepted her, and hoped that this would
be the last university to be desegregated by troops.*

.   .   .

In June 1963 when Cy Vance named me general counsel of the Army, I
wanted to pick up the phone to thank Victor Kramer for urging me to stay

---

*We would need troops in March 1965, when Martin Luther King led marchers fifty miles from Selma to
Montgomery, Alabama, to dramatize the need for a federal voting rights law. In their initial attempts,
marchers were clubbed and tear-gassed; a white minister from Boston was killed. President Lyndon
Johnson federalized the Alabama National Guard to protect the marchers and I was charged with monitoring the situation. I received hourly reports and kept McNamara, Vance, Attorney General Katzenbach, and the White House informed. The 392 marchers at the start grew to 25,000 by the time they
reached the state capitol on March 25. There were few other incidents along the way. But, taking no
chances, we positioned a military force of about 3,000 at the capitol in Montgomery to maintain order.

in the government. Just thirty-two, I became the youngest top legal officer in the history of the Army.

"Your first assignment as general counsel," Vance said, "is to take charge of the Defense Department's responsibilities in connection with the civil rights march on Washington planned for August 28."

The seventy-four-year-old civil rights veteran A. Philip Randolph was organizing a march on the nation's capital, in support of public-school integration and passage of fair-employment practices and civil rights legislation.[12] Randolph enlisted Bayard Rustin, Martin Luther King, Jr., James Farmer, Roy Wilkins, and John Lewis to put it together. They hoped to bring 100,000 people to Washington.

Vance told me that he and Robert Kennedy feared the march was fraught with potential for violence. John Douglas, assistant attorney general for the civil division, and I were to represent the federal government in meetings with the march organizers. At our first meeting, it became clear to Douglas and me that the situation was dangerous. Bayard Rustin, the two-hundred-pound, six-foot Quaker and veteran civil rights leader,[13] whose hair was perpetually awry, and Walter Fauntroy, the thirty-year-old clergyman,[14] who was invariably neatly groomed and dressed, were a combustible mixture of total commitment and utter disorganization. They had not given the slightest consideration to what was involved in logistics or protection for thousands of civil rights marchers assembled on the Mall.

Much as Kennedy and Vance had hoped to discourage it, Douglas and I reported, this march would happen. We all agreed with the objectives of the civil rights leaders but feared that an unruly demonstration could set back efforts to desegregate southern schools. The President's civil rights legislation was already in terminal trouble in Congress, and the attorney general thought the march—especially if violence erupted—would kill what little hope remained for action on the Hill.

The D.C. police wanted to use dogs. The National Guard wanted to carry firearms, at the very least pistols for all its officers. At the attorney general's office on August 16, we quickly agreed that the D.C. police would not be permitted to use dogs. Vance and I wanted the National Guard to have only billy clubs. We feared that someone in the guard, which was not nearly as well trained and disciplined as regular Army troops, might fire a gun unnecessarily. John Douglas thought officers should be allowed to carry side arms.

But Kennedy wasn't "going to take that kind of chance" and sided with Vance and me. None of the guardsmen were permitted to carry weapons.

There were a hundred logistical details: how to get trains in and out D.C., where to park buses, whether to alert troops in the area, whether to pre-position the 82nd Airborne, what federal leave policy should be, whether to close all bars and liquor stores, how to get ready for a blistering hot day in terms of water and medical facilities, how to prepare for the worst.

No administrative leave was granted to federal employees. Already accused of promoting the march, the Kennedy brothers wanted to give political opponents no ammunition that could be used in the 1964 presidential campaign to accuse them of swelling the number of marchers with federal workers.

Robert Kennedy wanted to encourage as much religious participation as possible. The Kennedys pulled out all their Roman Catholic connections to produce priests in their Roman collars and nuns in their habits.

Kennedy wanted the marchers in and out of the district on the same day. He worried that demonstrators staying overnight unacceptably increased the risk of violence and clashes with angry whites opposed to the march, even though we had decided to close all liquor stores and bars. We insisted, therefore, that charter bus companies and trains transport marchers out of town that afternoon and evening and that district police prohibit buses and cars from parking overnight. We quietly encouraged hotels to demand gouge prices for their rooms, which they were happy to do; still crawling with racism, they did not want their rooms to be filled up with blacks.

Robert Kennedy did not want civil rights leaders to know that he was behind the push to get them out the same day. I was ordered to attribute the decision entirely to the Army's concern about security (which was real enough). The greatest resistance to this tactic came from Patrick O'Boyle, the first Roman Catholic archbishop of Washington, D.C., and a champion of civil rights. He was placing cots in church basements and Catholic school gymnasiums for the marchers and calling other churches to do the same. Douglas and I visited O'Boyle in offices next to Annunciation Church on Massachusetts Avenue in order to stop this activity. I took the lead in pressing him not to provide overnight accommodations for the marchers.

The archbishop was shocked. "What about old people? People who get sick? Who might collapse from exhaustion or have heart attacks if they have to go back that evening?"

Douglas said he could see the difficulties; he understood the archbishop's concern. By prearrangement, I played the bad cop, at one point saying, "To be blunt, we're so concerned about the danger of violence if marchers stay overnight that we'd rather have them drop of exhaustion, get sick on the buses on the way home, or—God forbid—even have a heart attack. We want them moved out the same day they arrive."

O'Boyle was appalled. He looked at both of us and asked, "What is your religion, gentlemen, if you don't mind telling me?"

Douglas responded, "Not at all, Your Eminence. I'm a Presbyterian."

O'Boyle looked coldly at me.

"I'm Roman Catholic," I responded, anticipating this might gain me some points.

Glowering at me for a moment, then gently looking at Douglas, O'Boyle said, "Well, you know, sometimes those who are not of our Catholic faith have more of the milk of human kindness in their hearts."

O'Boyle ignored our pleas. He continued to place cots in the gyms and basements of schools and churches and to publicize their availability.

In the dark hours of early morning on August 28 while the press (and most everyone else) slept, we quietly positioned 4,000 regular Army troops in the immediate Washington area at Bolling Air Force base, the Anacostia Naval Air Station, and Fort Myer. We stationed Justice Department officials and Army personnel atop the Lincoln Memorial and secretly planted among the marchers government agents in civilian clothing—local police, national guardsmen, FBI agents, Army intelligence personnel.

Although the organizers worried whether the crowd would be sufficient to attract national attention, some 200,000 people from every state arrived by foot, car, bus, and train. They were black and white, rich and poor, educated and blue collar, famous and ordinary. Volunteers made signs and 80,000 cheese sandwiches.[15] The marchers walked from the Washington Monument along the reflecting pool to the Lincoln memorial and sang "We Shall Overcome" as they waited for the speeches from the steps of the Lincoln Memorial.

Beneath the statue of Abraham Lincoln, civil rights leaders lined up to speak. Vance and I watched apprehensively on a television screen in the Army War Room, monitoring communications among federal and local law enforcement. We were especially concerned about the speech of John Lewis, chairman of the Student Nonviolent Coordinating Committee

(SNCC). Lewis had drafted a rabble-rouser blistering attack on the Kennedy administration for its lack of support. White House aides had pressed Randolph to get Lewis to tone it down. Just moments before he addressed the crowd, we got word that Lewis would temper his speech. His most inflammatory line was, "We want our freedom and we want it NOW!"

Martin Luther King, Jr., with supreme eloquence and dignified passion, delivered his "I have a dream" speech. The marchers conducted themselves peacefully and dispersed late that afternoon, boarding their buses and trains and leaving the city before dark. That evening, at the Pentagon and the Justice Department, we felt palpable relief. A. Philip Randolph walked around the grounds of the Lincoln Memorial and wrote later, "There was nothing but the wind blowing the left over programs and scattered litter across the way. . . . We were so proud of the fact that no violence had taken place that day. . . . It was the greatest day of my life."[16]

That evening, excitement and adrenaline kept me awake most of the night. I finally fell asleep, knowing I was at the moral and political epicenter of a revolution. The next day, when I picked up the Washington *Evening Star* I saw a picture of the Catholic University gym filled with empty cots. They had never been used.

It is difficult to overstate the satisfaction I felt being a small part of the nation's initial desegregation effort. I admired the way the regular Army and the National Guard of states like Mississippi and Alabama enforced unpopular federal court orders and protected civil rights workers in tense situations where such actions were angrily opposed. The professionalism of the military stood in sharp relief against the recalcitrant attitudes of other government agencies and much of Congress. On January 14, 1965, when Burke Marshall resigned his post as assistant attorney general for civil rights, he sent me a note that captured this atmosphere and which I cherish to this day:

> During the past four years, I have had some business or other with virtually every agency of the government and the business on virtually every occasion was unpleasant. So I saw a lot of people on difficult matters. There is no one who gave me more confidence than you, or whom I more enjoyed seeing.

CHAPTER 13

Getting Fidel

To THIS DAY I harbor pride about my role in the Pentagon's activities in desegregating the South and a moral certainty about the justness of that cause. I cannot say the same about my personal involvement in the nation's Cuba policy, aiding and abetting the obsession of the Kennedy brothers to get Castro.

Castro's emergence as Communist Russia's first ally in the Western hemisphere, his threat to foment revolution in other Latin American countries, and the possibility of a Soviet foothold ninety miles from our shore led President Eisenhower in March 1960 to approve a secret Central Intelligence Agency plan to organize a "paramilitary force of Cuban exiles to overthrow the Cuban government." And the situation set off an "I'm tougher than you are" battle between John Kennedy and Richard Nixon during the 1960 presidential campaign.

On April 17, a week after I arrived at the Pentagon, with the blessing of President Kennedy some fifteen hundred Cuban exiles, known as Cuban Brigade 2506,[1] landed on Giron Beach, the Bay of Pigs. As the invasion faltered and the extent of U. S. involvement became known, I was astonished. I had been disillusioned by Castro since my days in New York, but had not yet relegated him to the garbage heap of unreconstructable communists like Nikita Khrushchev and Mao Tse-tung. I quickly fell in line, however, with the widely held view in the Pentagon: the CIA and the President had botched it; if the military had been in charge and if the President had authorized air cover, the invasion might have succeeded. When Kennedy took responsibility for the failure, most military officers I knew considered it the least he could do.

The President's Bay of Pigs failure and his trepidation after the 1961 Vienna summit emboldened Russian premier Nikita Khrushchev, who launched a plot to build nuclear-missile sites in Cuba. The Soviet leader's move precipitated the Cuban missile crisis in October 1962, less than a month after James Meredith had entered the University of Mississippi.

My primary duty during those fateful thirteen October days was to hold charts displaying pictures of the missile sites while Secretary McNamara briefed legislative leaders. On October 28, when Khrushchev blinked, agreeing to dismantle the offensive missiles in Cuba, I admired our young president for not giving an inch to the Kremlin dictator.*

In the following months, Robert Kennedy ransomed the 1,100 Cuban Brigade members captured at the Bay of Pigs with $53 million in food, medicine, and supplies for Castro. On December 29 as President Kennedy received the Brigade 2506 flag, he promised thousands of cheering Cubans at Orange Bowl stadium in Miami, "I want to express my great appreciation to the Brigade for making the United States the custodian of this flag. I can assure you that this flag will be returned to this Brigade in a free Havana."

A week later, on January 8, the President created the Interdepartmental Cuban Coordinating Committee. Nominally chaired by State Department representative Sterling Cottrell, the committee was in reality run by Robert Kennedy. Its mission: to plan the future of the liberated Cuban Brigade and design a covert program to overthrow the Castro regime.[2]

The President and Secretary McNamara charged the Army with responsibility for assimilating Cuban Brigade members into American life and making available, on short notice, a military unit of Cubans to participate with U.S. troops in any future action against Castro. Vance gave me this task and designated me his alternate as the Defense Department member of the Interdepartmental Cuban Coordinating Committee.

To help me provide Pentagon support for covert activities, I recruited Lieutenant Colonel James Patchell, who had experience in dirty tricks and counterinsurgency. I interviewed a number of junior officers in search of someone to help organize a training program for the Brigade members, finally settling on a young lieutenant colonel who had graduated from West Point in 1947 and served in Japan, Korea, Europe, and Vietnam. He had recently received a master's degree in international relations from Georgetown University. His name was Alexander Haig, and our paths would cross at critical moments for a quarter of a century.

In these Cuban Committee meetings, I first learned that in late 1961 Pres-

---

*At the time, Kennedy denied his secret quid pro quo for the withdrawal: his commitment to remove our missiles from Turkey and Italy. He feared a political firestorm costing him reelection if the public discovered the deal.

ident Kennedy had established a program of covert operations designed to overthrow Castro. Code-named Operation Mongoose, this clandestine program constituted the core of our Cuba policy until the missile crisis in October 1962. Spearheaded by Air Force brigadier general Edward Lansdale (then an assistant to the secretary of defense for special operations but reporting directly to the President),[3] a series of covert actions were mounted to disrupt and destroy Cuba's sugar crop, oil refineries, electrical systems, rail transportation, and bridges. Operation Mongoose's psychological warfare even included this effort to enlist the Almighty:

> [Have] prayers said—for the people of Cuba suffering under Communist tyranny—in all U.S. military units which have significant numbers of Cuban refugees serving in the U.S. armed forces. Service chaplains and public information officers should team up on this, to assure the event is publicized widely. Cubans should be in the front ranks, where they will loom up in photographs. Defense, in collaboration with CIA, will assure that some photographs of troop units with Cubans in them are passed effectively to Cuban intelligence collectors, with a story of invasion plans sufficiently convincing to cause the Communist regime to begin an alert of the militia (including cane field workers).[4]

When I read these files of past covert activities and CIA involvement in guerilla warfare, I saw that in a March 21, 1962, meeting on Operation Mongoose, Attorney General Robert Kennedy called the Cuban problem the "highest priority project in the Government. . . . We must be ready to exploit any change that occurs for us. . . . The President is prepared to do whatever has to be done, we must use our imagination."[5] I realized that Castro had every reason to accuse the United States of trying to destroy him and destabilize his island. Little did I realize that I would soon help conduct a new round of similar activities and Keystone Kop capers, this time around driven by Robert Kennedy.

.   .   .

My first task was to enlist the Cuban Brigade in specially tailored military training programs, which also taught American history, culture, and customs, as well as the English language. The Army joined in enthusiastically; the Air Force reluctantly bowed to the inevitable. The Navy, however, wanted no part of the program; the admirals claimed it would "dilute the integrity" of their service to waive traditional requirements and accept Cuban exiles.[6] When I reported this attitude to the attorney general, he pounced on the secretary of the Navy. An hour later, the Navy was in line.

I learned that before the Bay of Pigs, Brigade members were soldiers, priests, farmers, and fishermen, rich and poor, professionals and laborers. Most were well educated; a number had graduated from American universities such as Harvard, Pennsylvania, and Georgetown. Many were devout Catholics, fighting for a democratic Cuba that would allow them to practice their religion. Most were in their twenties and thirties, and they knew how to use the media. Robert Kennedy did not want them agitating in Miami's Cuban community, noisily demanding actions the administration had no intention of taking. Such outbursts from Brigade members, he feared, could provide ammunition to Republicans in the 1964 election.

To Kennedy's delight, we signed up virtually all the Brigade into military assimilation programs:[7] 209 in officer training at Fort Benning, Georgia; most enlisted men at Fort Jackson, South Carolina. We detailed Cuban Air Force officers to Lackland Air Force base in Texas, but did not permit them to pilot planes, for fear they might fly over Cuba and precipitate yet another incident. Naval personnel were assigned to the San Diego Naval Base.

Robert Kennedy extended himself personally to Brigade members to placate their concerns—and perhaps to allay a guilty conscience. The failure to provide air cover during the Bay of Pigs invasion had cost more than a hundred Cuban lives. Brigade members often took their complaints to the attorney general about restrictions I placed on their activities; more than once he overruled me, even when it meant backing off his own prior orders.[8] Most troubling (and greatly complicating my job), he could not admit to them, and perhaps even to himself, that the United States was unlikely to support another invasion.

But President Kennedy had to do something about Cuba and Castro. Though Soviet missiles were removed, some seventeen thousand Russian troops remained on the island.[9] With Republicans (and conservative Democrats) reminding the American people of the Monroe Doctrine, eliminating the Soviet military presence in Cuba became a key objective of the

Kennedy administration. This provided a powerful added argument for ending the Castro regime. Presidential demands for a covert program to achieve that objective intensified.

Helping develop this covert program and direct the Defense Department's role in it occupied much of my time in 1963. When General Lansdale retired that year, Marine Corps general Victor Krulak—whose nickname, "Brute," was well deserved—became the ranking military officer for covert Cuban operations.

Under pressure from the attorney general and often at the suggestion of the CIA, our committee entertained a sometimes bizarre range of ideas. To disrupt the Cuban economy, we discussed financing a Radio Free Cuba to urge all Cubans to turn all their water faucets on at the same time if they didn't like Castro. We encouraged putting sugar in gasoline supplies to ruin gears of trucks and tractors. We pondered destroying ships (but close to shore, so that innocent civilians would have an opportunity to swim to land). We reviewed proposals to shell power stations and parachute Cuban saboteurs, trained at our military installations, onto the island.[10]

The unrelenting pressure from Robert Kennedy to get rid of Castro led to some exotic suggestions. On February 14, 1963, I received a memorandum from the Office of the Chief of Naval Operations with this one: "Attach incendiary devices to bats and drop over training centers. Bats retire to attics during daylight. Incendiaries ignite by timers and start fires." The memo cautioned that the suggestion was "politically risky" because bats would have to be conspicuously air dropped.[11]

I felt I was working directly for the attorney general and, through him, for the President, and with one exception I enthusiastically joined the administration's effort to topple Castro. That exception erupted at a meeting where someone suggested mounting an effort to assassinate or encourage the assassination of Fidel Castro. Joe Dolan, an assistant deputy attorney general, and I argued against such a policy. We insisted such a course of action was inconsistent with American principles and inappropriate for us to consider. Throughout a lengthy and sometimes heated discussion, the CIA representatives sat silent.[12]

The only meeting I ever attended with President Kennedy involved Cuba. Tensions between the State Department on one hand and the Defense Department and CIA on the other were running high only a month after the committee had been established. Vance requested a meeting with the President after Ambassador Raymond Thurston had circulated to the Cuban Committee a State Department paper that relied largely on travel controls and propaganda to deal with Castro/communist subversion in Latin America. At the Pentagon, we wanted "affirmative actions in the area of counter propaganda, exposure of Latin Americans to U.S. training and measures to attrit Soviet/Cuban resources [a euphemism for covert paramilitary activities inside Cuba]."[13] Vance and I believed the State Department proposals were so weak that they would have no impact on Castro and hence betrayed the Cuban people and the Brigade. As he lay on the hard wooden bed for his bad back in a room adjoining his office, Vance talked to me. He was considering resigning rather than participate in such a betrayal.[14]

On February 18, 1963, Thurston, Vance, and I, along with Sterling Cottrell, White House aide Ralph Dungan, General Brute Krulak, and J. C. King, a CIA Western Hemisphere expert,[15] met in the Oval Office.[16] Vance, Krulak, and I sat on the sofa to the President's left, the State Department representatives to his right. Dungan sat in a chair behind us. Kennedy was in his famous rocker, facing the fireplace.

Vance handed the President a memo he and I had prepared. It proposed purchasing defection of Cuban personnel, aircraft, ships, and other valuable items. It recommended non-attributable actions against petroleum resources extending "all the way from direct destruction to sabotage through chemical and potential bacterial contamination of carriers and storage." We urged a misinformation campaign to keep Cuban forces on constant state of alert. We wanted to create a pro-American press in Latin America and greatly expand training of Latin American military, nurses, reporters, and technicians to enhance their capability and expose them to U.S. influences. The memo suggested printing counterfeit currency to disrupt the Cuban economy.[17]

As the President read the memo, Vance argued with the State Department representatives. When Kennedy finished reading, he ignored the argument, rose, and said he had to go to another meeting but would return. Presidential aide Kenny O'Donnell came in shortly to say that the President was not returning. "Presidents do not like to preside over such disagreements and scenes," O'Donnell said. "That's what presidential aides are for."

It was my first lesson in presidential governing. No president wants to take sides in a dispute over covert actions that he would prefer to deny he knew anything about. Kennedy was not about to signal his approval or disapproval in front of people like me whom he did not know and career civil servants whose political loyalty he could not count on.

Though the President did not act on our specific proposals, his brother kept up the pressure for an effective covert program. On April 1, the Cuban Coordinating Committee recommended new covert actions to step up pressure against Castro: balloon operations to drop leaflets in Cuba, training of exiles to be saboteurs, sabotage of Cuban ships, propaganda to incite Cubans against Soviet troops.[18]

Two days later Robert Kennedy reviewed these and other proposals at a White House meeting I attended with Vance, Ralph Dungan, Desmond FitzGerald and Richard Helms from the CIA, and Ed Martin, Thomas Parrott, and Bob Hurwitch from State.[19] As Robert Kennedy pressed for tougher actions, I thought: he is obsessed with Castro; he is pursuing a total war with Castro. The intensity I had admired in his dealing with Mississippi governor Ross Barnett and Alabama governor George Wallace now struck me as vengeful with respect to the Cuban leader. I left the meeting deeply troubled—and sensing that there was some other track upon which Cuban policy was running, involving the Kennedy brothers and the CIA, but not the Defense Department. Vance was furious. He deplored what he called "the barbershop atmosphere" of the Cuban project—too many people at the table, low-level aides sitting against the wall—when "actions like this, however discreetly, are being discussed." I took his comment to mean that he understood what I suspected: Bobby Kennedy and his brother wanted Castro assassinated. I guessed that Desmond FitzGerald, head of the CIA's Special Affairs Staff, was involved in the assassination plots, since he was the point man for covert raids and other dirty tricks to disrupt Cuba.

FitzGerald, father of Frances FitzGerald, who later wrote *Fire in the Lake,* an attack on U.S. policies in Vietnam, was the quintessential undercover agent. I once met him in Miami en route to Panama to meet Jake Esterline, the CIA station chief in Panama, who was directing covert Cuban activities mounted from there. As I entered his hotel room, FitzGerald placed his forefinger over his lips, turned on all the water faucets, set the radio blaring as loud as it would go, and then whispered in my ear, "O.K. Go ahead." I felt I was in a scene from a Hollywood thriller.

The same day of my meeting with the attorney general, the President held a late-afternoon press conference to announce that 1,000 Soviet troops had left Cuba. The announcement served largely to attract Republican attacks that he was unable to rid our hemisphere of the entire Soviet presence in Castro's Cuba—12,000 troops remained. The *Washington Post* reported the next day that the "Kennedy Administration is caught in a sliding squeeze," since each "announcement of how many Russian personnel have been withdrawn inevitably focuses new attention on the remaining number." Such attacks fueled the determination of the Kennedy brothers to get rid of Castro.

A week later, I learned that the President had approved many of the covert actions Vance and I had recommended at the April 1 meeting. The President rejected dropping balloons with anti-Castro leaflets over Havana and Russian-language radio broadcasts by exile groups. But he okayed the sabotage of Cuban ships and propaganda "inciting Cubans to harass, attack and sabotage Soviet military personnel in Cuba," and he approved use of Defense facilities and personnel to support and train Cuban CIA agents.[20] We in the Army agreed to identify twenty Cubans at Fort Jackson who had the necessary characteristics for CIA operations inside Cuba.[21] My memo to Vance reporting these presidential decisions reflected the unrelenting hard line the Kennedys were taking toward Castro; even an invasion of sorts had not been ruled out. "These personnel [along with those given parachute jump training on a military reservation]," I wrote, "would also be used in advance of the introduction of Special Forces, should there be a decision to invade Cuba."[22]

At Robert Kennedy's insistence, covert actions were stepped up all that summer and fall. I felt overwhelmed with endless meetings in the Pentagon to assure that the necessary military training and equipment support was available; with an increased number of sessions of the Cuban Coordinating Committee; with my efforts to help integrate the University of Alabama; with Defense Department preparations for the March on Washington. I had little time for my additional duties as general counsel of the Army and my responsibility to supervise the civil works functions of the Army Corps of Engineers.*

---

*I soon learned that Vance and McNamara could not have cared less about the Army's public works, such as construction of dams and waterways, but the White House political staff and members of Congress seemed more interested in these projects than almost anything else. I got a crash course in pork barrel politics that proved invaluable in later years in government and Washington law practice. I also had a sense of helping the President with his legislative program as I found that on-the-fence senators and representatives could be swayed by giving higher priority to their Corps of Engineers projects.

So much was going on that my secretary Anne Ihnat joked that my concept of the perfect secretary was an octopus. I was completely submerged in work, returning home most nights at 11 P.M. or later. That summer, Father Raymond Swords, S.J., then president of Holy Cross, wrote after a brief visit, "It was quite obvious to me that you were very tired. . . . Your work is so interesting and so challenging that you do not realize how much it exhausts you. Your obligations to your self and family are the most important ones— and these take preeminence over your obligations to your work. Please be sure to take time off regularly." I barely had time to read his letter. I didn't heed his wise advice.

Some anti-Castro raids set for July were postponed until mid-August, since Secretary of State Dean Rusk was scheduled to sign the Nuclear Test Ban Treaty in Moscow on August 5.[23] There was no relief, however, from the attorney general's pressure to devise tougher policies and more disruptive covert actions to topple the Castro regime.

But Castro wasn't weakening. In July 1963 my office conducted a dispassionate and candid analysis of where we stood and what it would take to achieve the administration's objective. On our present track, we concluded, "Barring unforeseen breaks which the US has no good reason to expect (the natural or accidental demise of Castro himself might be one such break), there seems to be little assurance of either the elimination of Soviet presence and influence in Cuba, or the reestablishment of a non-communist regime on the island."[24] Taking account of international and domestic political realities, the most I thought we could hope for was increasing economic pressure on Cuba, tightening the island's isolation, devising carrots and sticks to pressure Soviet troops to leave, not letting the Cuban people believe that we had given up, military contingency planning to take advantage of opportunities for major change, and playing for breaks. Along with the covert actions planned and likely to be approved, I concluded "such a policy . . . does not offer high or even moderate assurance of success—if the criteria of success are a non-communist solution for Cuba and the exclusion of a permanent Soviet political-military forward base from this hemisphere." I wrote that failure of current policies would leave the United States with two alternatives: accommodation to a communist regime or aggressive military action to get the Russians out and topple Castro. The longer the present situation continued, I concluded, the likelier the U.S. would have to resign itself to the continuation of a communist regime in Cuba.[25]

In the fall of 1963, pressed by Robert Kennedy and operating out of a secret base in Costa Rica, the CIA carried out sabotage raids in Cuba with arms and transportation provided by the Defense Department. We bombed railroads, bridges, piers, warehouses, power plants, and transformers. We continued to infiltrate radio equipment, arms, and supplies to resistance forces on the island.[26]

At the direction of the Cuban Committee, I compiled all the data we had in the Pentagon on key Cuban military personalities to help the CIA find a "mole" in Castro's inner circle. Desmond FitzGerald said the CIA needed this to enhance its intelligence on Castro and his government.[27] I took FitzGerald at his word, though I doubted he was revealing all his motives.

As I had suspected and later learned, FitzGerald was also operating on another, entirely separate track.[28] The Joints Chiefs of Staff were concerned that the CIA program was not effective. I asked FitzGerald to brief the military chiefs on CIA raids; he began to do so in August. He requested military support for CIA Cuban agents who were attempting raids on Castro's facilities. The Joint Chiefs responded that the individual raids of which they were aware were too minor to merit such support, given the risk of discovery by Castro. They said they could make a more refined judgment—and implied that they might change their view—if they were informed of the entire CIA covert program. That led to a secret briefing of the Chiefs by FitzGerald on September 25, 1963.[29] I repeatedly asked to attend that meeting, but the Joint Chiefs of Staff refused to invite me.[30] The JCS memorandum for the record—which I pressed the Pentagon to declassify and first read in doing research for this memoir—revealed that the CIA was studying how German generals plotted to kill Hitler, in order to develop a way to organize high-ranking Cuban officers to kill Castro:

> . . . [FitzGerald] felt that there had been great success in getting closer to military personnel who might break with Castro, and stated that there were at least ten high-level military personnel who are talking with the CIA but as yet are not talking to each other, since that degree of confidence has not yet developed. He considers it as a parallel in history; i.e., the plot to kill Hitler; and this plot is being studied in detail to develop an approach.[31]

Had I attended that meeting, it would have confirmed my suspicions as to why FitzGerald wanted all our intelligence on Cuban military officers. A month later, on October 29, 1963, FitzGerald met in a CIA safe house in Paris with Rolando Cubela Secades, a disillusioned member of Castro's inner circle who was code-named AMLASH. Identifying himself as Robert Kennedy's representative, FitzGerald said the U.S. was prepared to support an anti-Castro coup. AMLASH asked for a high-powered rifle with a sniper's scope and silencer. On November 19, the CIA promised to get him what he wanted. At a meeting on November 22—the day Kennedy waved to crowds for the last time from his Dallas motorcade—the CIA offered Secades a poison pen that could be used to kill someone at close range. It is inconceivable to me that FitzGerald might have taken these actions without the approval of both Kennedys—or an explicit communication from Robert Kennedy.

The covert Cuba strategy seems to me consistent with President Kennedy's handling of the conflict in South Vietnam. For years the United States had supported South Vietnam's non-communist government, led by a Catholic President, Ngo Dinh Diem. When Diem proved corrupt and out of touch, President Kennedy endorsed a coup, in which Diem and his brother Nhu were killed on November 1, 1963.[32]

I did not gain full knowledge of these activities until the mid-1970s, when the Senate Select Committee to Study Governmental Operations with Respect to Intelligence Activities—known as the Church Committee, after the Idaho senator who chaired it—uncovered "concrete evidence of at least eight [assassination] plots" concocted by the CIA between 1960 and 1965, including use of "American underworld figures and Cubans hostile to Castro," and running "the gamut from high-powered rifles to poison pills, poison pens, deadly bacterial powders, and other devices [poison cigars] which strain the imagination."[33] Not surprisingly, the committee could find no direct order from President Kennedy (or President Eisenhower) ordering the assassination. It did uncover evidence of presidential involvement through a recurring euphemism: approval by "higher authority."

No one on the Warren Commission, which investigated the assassination of President Kennedy, talked to me or (so far as I know) anyone else involved in the covert attacks on Castro and Cuba about those attacks. The commission was not informed of any of the efforts of Desmond FitzGerald, the CIA, and Robert Kennedy to eliminate Castro and stage a coup.

Years later, when I was on his White House staff, Lyndon Johnson told me, "Kennedy tried to kill Castro, but Castro got Kennedy first." Though Johnson had set up the Warren Commission, he never accepted its conclusion that Oswald was a loner.* I have come to share LBJ's view. With the step-up in covert activities and outright attempts on Castro's life—and with the assassination of Diem on November 1, 1963—the Cuban leader had reason to conclude that the Kennedy brothers were seeking an opportunity to kill him. Indeed, on September 7, 1963, Castro gave an impromptu interview to an Associated Press correspondent in which he warned against assassination plots directed at Cuban officials. "We are prepared to fight them and answer in kind," Castro said. "United States leaders should think that if they are aiding terrorist plans to eliminate Cuban leaders they themselves will not be safe."[34] Over the years I have come to believe that the paroxysms of grief that tormented Robert Kennedy for years after his brother's death arose, at least in part, from a sense that his efforts to eliminate Castro led to his brother's assassination.

Soon after he assumed office, Lyndon Johnson ordered an end to covert activities in Cuba. He prohibited any attempts to kill Castro or encourage his assassination.[35] I was told to deliver his message to Cuban Brigade officers still in the U.S. military. In late February 1964, I traveled around the country to tell them personally. I offered Brigade members two options: to continue in the Armed Services or, with our help, to enter civilian life. We offered student loans and grants if they wanted to go to college or graduate school and preference in obtaining government jobs.[36]

I remember a wrenching meeting at Sheppard Air Force base in Wichita Falls, Texas, on February 24, 1964. Lieutenant Erneido Oliva, the leader of the Brigade, had on several occasions visited me to press for creation of "a re-born Brigade 2506" to invade Cuba and overthrow Castro. Tears came to his eyes as he heard our decision against such a plan. He made one last plea to use the Brigade to invade Cuba. Then, as he came to realize there was no room for discussion, he slumped into a wooden chair. I urged him to make a career in the U.S. Army; we hugged when I left. Four days later, he called to say that he and the three other top leaders of the Brigade were resigning from the Army. We remained friends, however, and I had Erneido and his family for Thanksgiving dinner at our home that year.[37]

*Oswald had lived in the Soviet Union from 1959 until 1962 and in September 1963 he had visited the Cuban Embassy in Mexico City, identifying himself as a friend of the Cuban movement.

.   .   .

My work on the Cuban Coordinating Committee during the Kennedy years aroused the interest of President-elect Jimmy Carter when he was considering me for a cabinet post in his administration. He told me he "had heard rumors" about it. In December 1976, Fritz Mondale called me and asked for a letter describing my involvement. I was eager to be secretary of Health, Education, and Welfare—Mondale was urging Carter to nominate me—and I was determined not to let my work on Cuba disqualify me. In my letter to Mondale, I recounted in general terms the work of the Cuban Coordinating Committee. I said—truly—that I was never engaged in efforts to assassinate Fidel Castro. He didn't press me to elaborate; I didn't offer to. I never shared with Fritz or with President Carter my misgivings about the covert activities of those years. Those misgivings were—and are—real and deep. My own hands were hardly clean, however—and so I remain reticent to judge others who participated.

CHAPTER 14

When Kennedy Was Shot

A T T H E M O M E N T John F. Kennedy was shot, on November 22, 1963, I was inspecting an Army Corps of Engineers dam in West Virginia.

I dashed back to the Pentagon.

As I drove from the airport to the Pentagon, I ached with grief and with a sense that this bullet had snatched the best years of life from my country and from my generation.

I went straight to Vance. I told him I intended to leave government. I didn't think a Johnson presidency was much to stay around for.

Vance's wistful smile did not hide his own sadness. "I thought that's why you wanted to see me," he said. "You're wrong." He had worked for Johnson when the Texas senator had conducted a Senate investigation of the "missile gap" between the U.S. and the U.S.S.R. "This town has never seen a president like Lyndon Johnson," Vance told me. "Stay around for a while. You're going to see things move."

I didn't believe it.

"I've got some work for you," Vance said. "Jacqueline Kennedy wants the President buried in Arlington Cemetery. You should meet the attorney general over there tomorrow."

On Saturday I met a shattered Robert Kennedy. I have never seen a sadder man or woman. In pouring rain, we walked the perimeter of a 3.2-acre site on the rolling hill above Memorial Bridge and below the Lee Mansion as I outlined it on a cemetery map. Walking like a zombie, eyes hollowed from lack of sleep, Kennedy nevertheless was determined to do this task. He said almost in a whisper, "This is where we'll bury the President," then got in his car. I returned to the Pentagon, where a call from McNamara awaited me.

"Joe, I want to tie up that land for President Kennedy so that no one can ever take any of it away for any other purpose," McNamara said. "And I want to be damned sure we own it."

"It's in the middle of Arlington Cemetery," I said.

"I don't give a damn. Get a title search made. Write a legal opinion nailing down the title to the land. I want to sign the deed that sets this land aside forever."

McNamara soon called again. "Mrs. Kennedy wants an eternal torch above the grave that will never go out. Set up a temporary one, so it can be lit at the burial."

I returned to the gravesite with a Corps of Engineers general and blocked out a location for the torch. We would have copper pipe in the ground running to a temporary propane tank. I worried. "Make damn sure that pipe is buried deep so some woman's spiked heel doesn't rupture it. Once that flame is lit, it can never go out."

On Sunday I signed a legal opinion describing the results of the title search conducted by one of my attorneys and Ramsey Clark, head of the Justice Department Lands Division. I prepared an order setting the 3.2 acres aside in perpetuity, which Vance signed.

Though it wasn't necessary, McNamara insisted on signing the order as well. He was so distraught that he had to do something to relieve his sense of helplessness. I took the order over to Arlington Cemetery, where he was making certain the gravesite was squarely in the center of the view from the bridge. Sitting in his car, McNamara signed the order. He handed it back to me, and added, "Set the pipe for the gas plenty low so no high heels can break it if they sink into the ground."

"Already done," I assured him. I was not surprised that even in his grief McNamara would cover all details.

"Thanks," he said, and added, "We're counting on people like you more than ever."

I wasn't convinced by McNamara any more than by Vance, but I respected them both and decided to stay for a while.

CHAPTER 15

Isthmus Insurrection

L YNDON JOHNSON's first foreign policy crisis became my first case as a trial lawyer, as I shifted from covertly fighting communists in Cuba to battling them in open hearings in Panama.

On January 9, 1964, the most virulent anti-American riots in the history of Central America erupted on Fourth of July Avenue—that unique street, one side of which was within the U.S. Canal Zone and the other within Panama. The riots were steeped in bitter resentments that had been festering before the ink was dry on the 1903 treaty that established the Canal Zone.[1] Panamanians claimed that the treaty gave the United States sovereignty over only the operation and protection of the canal; the U.S. claimed it had been granted exclusive and complete sovereignty over the entire 650-square-mile Canal Zone. Panamanian agitation over the issue of sovereignty, the size of the U.S. presence, and the wealth of Americans living in the zone rose steadily during the 1950s and early 1960s.

To undermine communists exploiting this situation, shortly before his death President Kennedy agreed to fly the Panamanian flag wherever the U.S. flag was flown in the zone. U.S. residents there demonstrated against that decision and sparked a firestorm in Congress. In a misguided move to ease tension, Canal Zone governor Robert Fleming, Jr., ordered the American flag taken down in front of all schools so that there would be no need to fly the Panamanian flag alongside it. His decision outraged both Americans in the zone and Panamanians.

On January 7 students raised the American flag on the pole in front of Balboa High School in the Canal Zone. Canal Zone authorities immediately took it down. The students again raised the flag and, along with friends and parents, surrounded the pole throughout the night to prevent anyone from lowering the flag.

Word of this incident spread through Panama like a gasoline fire. On January 9 two hundred Panamanian students, carrying their country's flag, marched to the high school. They displayed banners asserting Panama's sovereignty over the zone. They demanded that their Panamanian flag be raised alongside the American flag. Canal Zone police failed to keep American and Panamanian students apart; the first clashes broke out. Panamanian students were forcibly driven away from the school and out of the zone. In the turmoil, the Panamanian flag was torn.

As students paraded their torn flag up along Fourth of July Avenue, rioting broke out in Panama City. Panamanians tossed Molotov cocktails into the zone, igniting fires and destroying buildings and vehicles. Panamanian authorities made only token efforts to control the crowd.

General Andrew O'Meara, commander of the U.S. Southern Command, promptly took charge and deployed Army troops to restore order. The headquarters of the U.S. Southern Command, with its 20,000 military personnel and dependents, was situated in the Canal Zone. The troops constituted the U.S. military presence in Latin America—a force of signal political and emotional importance during the cold war, especially in light of Castro's cozy relationship with the Soviet Union and the guerilla games he was playing in South American countries like Venezuela.

Even though O'Meara's troops were subjected to sniper fire, they were forbidden to fire weapons without specific permission. The general ordered them to use tear gas to clear the zone of Panamanians. At about 12:30 A.M. on January 10, after five U.S. soldiers and one civilian had been wounded, General O'Meara gave permission for U.S. sharpshooters to return fire. Still he ordered restraint: "When you fire, two marksmen must identify the sniper you fire at. You first fire to chip the cement or wood near him and scare him; and then you fire to wound him, and only as the last resort do you fire to kill him."[2]

Throughout that night Harry McPherson, then undersecretary of the Army for international affairs, and I worked in the Army War Room, piecing facts together as best we could from cables and phone calls in order to prepare Army Secretary Vance for a 9:30 A.M. meeting with President Johnson. LBJ decided to send immediately to Panama a top-level delegation led by Thomas Mann, his friend and assistant secretary of state for inter-American affairs.[3] McPherson went with Mann and Vance to Panama. I was dispatched to Capitol Hill to brief Mendel Rivers and Richard Russell, conservative chairs of the House and Senate Armed Services Committees.

Late that afternoon, I went home for some sleep. Trudy was at the front door, a suitcase at her feet. She was in labor with our second child. We rushed to George Washington University Hospital. During the several hours of her labor, I fielded repeated calls about the situation in Panama. Our second child, Joseph Anthony III, was born late that evening.

By the time Panamanian national guardsmen ended the rioting and sniper fire and the U.S. Army returned control of the zone back to Governor Fleming on January 16, 3 American soldiers, 1 American civilian, and 18 Panamanians had been killed and more than 150 Americans and 95 Panamanians wounded.[4]

At the behest of Panama's president, Roberto Chiari—and fired up by nationalistic, anti-American, and communist elements—the Panamanian Bar Association charged that the U.S. had violated three articles of the U.N. Declaration of Human Rights.* The lawyers' group sought an investigation by the International Commission of Jurists, an organization based in Geneva, Switzerland, and affiliated with the World Court and the United Nations. Dismissing recommendations of Latin American desk officers in the State Department to quietly negotiate with Panamanians and squelch any such investigation, President Johnson, Secretary of State Dean Rusk, and Mann decided to fight the charges.

To my surprise—and the dismay of my wife at home with a six-week-old baby and his eighteen-month-old brother—when Vance told me of this decision, he said, "Assemble a team of lawyers. You're going down there to try this case." I didn't tell him that I'd never tried a case in my life. I wanted this opportunity.

I brought with me John McEvoy, a tenacious young Army captain assigned to my office, and John Wolfe, an experienced career litigator from the Justice Department. We left for Panama in the third week of February. In preparing for the hearing, we discovered that although the initial disturbances may have been sparked by nationalistic fervor, Communists in Panama had quickly shaped the rioting for their own incendiary purposes. Members of the outlawed Communist Party of Panama and the Vanguard of National Action, the Castro party there, had encouraged and manipulated rioters.[5]

The hearings were held in a meeting room of the Panama Hilton Hotel

---

*The individual rights to life, liberty, and security of person; to freedom from cruel, inhuman, or degrading treatment or punishment; and to peaceful assembly and association.

in Panama City. Each day as I arrived and departed, photographers for Panama papers snapped pictures of me; each following morning the ugliest, angriest resulting photo was published. After a week of procedural wrangling, testimony began and continued over several days. Late in the evenings, I called my wife to see how she was doing with the new baby. The situation placed an enormous strain on her—and on us.

A central issue was whether U.S. Army tanks and troops had "invaded" Panama by crossing the Canal Zone border. General O'Meara and the officers and enlisted men we interviewed vehemently denied it. At one point in the proceedings, Jorge Illueca, the lead Panamanian lawyer, put a witness on the stand who introduced a photograph showing an Army tank and U.S. troops on Panamanian soil. In lengthy cross-examination, I was unable to shake the witness. I was devastated, and furious with O'Meara and his troops.

That evening, O'Meara said I had to remember that this was a disturbance and "nobody's perfect." I told him it shook the credibility of everything else in our case. Then a Canal Zone lawyer rushed into my office and pointed to a section of the photo that had been introduced. "Look at that, look at that!" he exclaimed. He was pointing to a street light.

"So what?" I said.

"Those street lights were removed years ago. This is a picture from the 1959 riots!"*

I was so shaken by the earlier testimony that I insisted on going out that evening with the lawyer and driving slowly all along Fourth of July Avenue to make damn certain there were no such lights.

The next morning, feeling like Perry Mason, I recalled the witness and excoriated him and his attorney, Illueca.

On the searing emotional issue whether an American high school student had deliberately torn the Panamanian flag, I was not so secure. Panamanians claimed that the rage and violence that followed the incident at Balboa High School was set off when one of the American students tore the Panamanian flag. This had been widely reported in the Panamanian press; it created the most exposed nerve in our case. After interviewing scores of

*In November 1959, rioting broke out as Panamanians tried to raise a Panamanian flag in the Canal Zone. To avoid more disturbances, the Eisenhower administration issued a statement recognizing Panamanian "titular sovereignty" in the zone.

students at the high school, I found the one involved in the flag tearing. The boy said he had been pushed into the Panamanian flag, that he did not tear it deliberately. After questioning him alone for well over an hour, however, I doubted he was telling the truth. I decided not to put him on the stand—and not to tell anyone, even the other lawyers who were working with me, that I disbelieved this version of what happened. Even if he were telling the truth, he was so wobbly about details that I thought the Panamanian lawyers would crucify him on cross-examination. Instead, I took the position that the Panamanians had the burden of proving that the flag was deliberately torn by an American student. Absent such proof, I argued that in the chaos of heated physical and verbal exchanges, it was just as likely that some Panamanian student tore it accidentally.

Castro-sympathetic lawyers representing Panama disputed every issue, procedural and factual. I was attacked personally. Lies were repeatedly told. Testimony was perjured. There were phony accusations, one even charging that the State Department representative sitting at the counsel table with me was one of the attackers and a shooter of Panamanians. Preposterous as such allegations were in the courtroom, they played well in the left-wing Panamanian press.

For my part, I repeatedly took the accusations head on. I charged that communists were behind the riots and unfounded allegations of human rights violations. One reporter covering the hearings, Peggy Poor, wrote in the *New York Journal-American*: "Mr. Califano threw the book back at the Panamanians, in effect charging them with aggression and violation of human rights. Observers of long memory here believe this makes the young Brooklyn lawyer the first American official to take the initiative or the offensive since World War II."[6] When I saw the clipping, I was amused and knew that my mother would be proud. She read it and she was. From her point of view, it was almost as good as getting a favorable mention in Westbrook Pegler's column.

On June 9, 1964, the International Commission of Jurists found for the United States on every count. On the torn flag, the Commission concluded:

The Panamanian students, who were bearing the Panamanian flag, were exposed to considerable stress, especially when two of them stumbled over the hedge and when, some 25 feet further, some fell a second time. It was not proved that American adults or students tore the flag on purpose, nor was it proved that the flag was not slightly torn before the six students proceeded to the flagpole. . . . It is quite likely that the flag, made of silk, was not able to resist the stress and strain of the occasion.[7]

The capstone for us was the finding by the three jurists—a professor of law from the Netherlands, a judge from Sweden, and a practicing attorney from India—that "if the Panamanian Guardia Nacional had taken charge of the situation early on the evening of the 9th or soon thereafter, the violence and the damage to property and the tragic casualties would not, in all probability, have taken place."[8]

I was elated. Mann and Vance were generous in their congratulations. But I have often had second thoughts about keeping to myself my hunch that an American student may have deliberately torn the Panamanian flag and set off the initial disturbances.

To this day I can feel the resentment, anger, and indeed hatred of non-communist Panamanians who looked at me walking to and from the hearing room and who sat there during the hearings. Not only did Panamanians feel hoodwinked by the treaty. The economic contrast between Panama City and the Canal zone was startling. The zone was affluent, generously sprinkled with all the modern conveniences. Panama was poor; what income it derived came largely from the Canal Zone and its financial ripples. Panama was like a colony. Americans lived much like British colonists in a 1930s movie.

One incident captured the precious world of the Americans in the Canal Zone. To unwind while I was there, I played squash with General O'Meara in a freestanding air-conditioned court. I once asked him, "How did you ever find a squash court like this down here?" He laughed. "When I arrived here, I couldn't find one," he said. "Then I kept asking, and presto! It appeared."

In August I returned to the Canal Zone for a week. To the Americans living there, I was a hero. I had helped vindicate not only their conduct during the riots, but also their way of life. There were parties in my honor; deep-sea fishing on a government yacht air conditioned to sleep ten comfortably. But I was not permitted to go into Panama, as a "precaution" (the Army's word) for my protection, since Panamanians had a different view of me. We had repelled the communist efforts to manipulate the riots and distort what happened, I thought, but I returned to Washington knowing that the question wasn't whether the American way of life in the Canal Zone would end, but when.*

---

*In 1966, President Johnson named Sol Linowitz U.S. Ambassador to the Organization of American States, to negotiate with the Panamanians on the Canal Zone. In 1977, during the Carter administration, an agreement was reached to return the Canal Zone to the Panamanians on December 31, 1999.

CHAPTER 16

Troubleshooting for McNamara

IN APRIL 1964, Robert McNamara tapped me to become the special assistant to the secretary and deputy secretary of defense, a post he had established for his chief troubleshooter.[1]

Mother and Dad were excited at my promotion. In handwritten notes, they reminded me of the source of my success. As Dad wrote, "We know that you will continue to make use of and prove yourself with the gifts that God has given you—and never forget to be thankful for them."

My first assignment in my new job came a week before I left my position as Army general counsel. McNamara tossed across his wide desk a draft presidential executive order. "There's disagreement whether the government should provide financial support for a commercial supersonic transport," he said as I picked up the document. "The President's setting up a special committee to recommend a course of action. He's asked me to chair it and you're going to be the executive director."[2]

As I read the draft executive order, McNamara kept talking. "Borrow some people from Systems Analysis. Set up a blue team and a red team—one to make the case for government funding; the other, the case against. We'll use Harold Brown [director of Defense Research and Engineering] to deal with the science. Put together an agenda for the first meeting, which I want to hold in a couple of weeks." McNamara then looked down at some other papers on his desk, his signal, I soon learned, that he was finished with me.

I left the office in a daze. I knew nothing about this subject. The only thing clear to me was that there would be no time off between my departure as general counsel of the Army and my new job. Once again I had to tell Trudy that a brief vacation we had planned would have to be cancelled.*

I frantically put the teams together to study the commercial supersonic

---

*When I took up my new post, I learned that McNamara expected me to keep the same hours he did. But arriving at 6:30 A.M. and not leaving until 8 P.M. meant that I never saw my young children, since I

transport issues. Should our government finance an SST to compete with the British and French, who had already combined efforts to develop the Concorde? That question rumbled around in my head even at the farewell party that Steve Ailes, Vance's successor as secretary of the Army, held for me as I left my position as Army general counsel. "Thank God this paesano has gone straight," Ailes said in his remarks. "If he hadn't, an army of Elliott Nesses would never be able to catch him!" Hardly politically correct, but at the time I considered it a compliment.

The first meeting of the SST committee was a lesson in bureaucratic control. McNamara permitted only committee members and me to sit at the table. He had initially limited the meeting to principals, but FAA Administrator Najeeb Halaby—an SST proponent—complained. McNamara agreed to allow each member to be accompanied by one staffer who was not permitted to speak during the meetings. To make it difficult for staffers even to pass notes, McNamara had me seat them against the wall of his conference room, a distance of at least ten feet from their principals at the table.

McNamara read everything on this subject that I sent him. One evening, I gave him a detailed analysis of the economics of the SST versus a jumbo jet, the commercial plane certain to evolve from the big Defense C5A transport. The next morning he called me to his office. With his forefinger and pinky guiding his eyes down two columns, he asked, "What factor did you use for fuel inflation over the life of the planes?"

"Three percent annually," I whipped back. I was relieved that I knew the answer to this probing question—and grateful that I had learned never to give him a paper I hadn't mastered.

"Too low," he snapped. "Run the calculations at five and six percent."

Our analyses of the commercial jumbo jet told us that, against the competition of such high-capacity planes, the SST, which had to be much smaller in order to maintain supersonic speeds, would never be economically viable without significant government subsidy (and even then might require a much higher fare). Moreover, McNamara found that there was no defense need for a military supersonic transport, thus foreclosing Defense Department research and testing. With that nail in the coffin, the commit-

---

was out before they were awake and home after they were asleep. Eventually I explained the situation to McNamara, noting that I was prepared to stay later if I could be home in the morning when they woke up. "Fine," he said. "You don't have to be here until eight A.M."

tee recommended against the government's subsidizing the development of an American SST. Halaby and the two powerful senators, Warren Magnuson and Henry Jackson, from the state of Washington, where Boeing was headquartered, were disappointed and angry. In later years, as I got to know Lyndon Johnson, I realized he picked McNamara to chair this committee because he wanted to kill federal funding for this project.[3]

.   .   .

McNamara was a superb bureaucrat. He understood how to keep control of his department. He accepted (reluctantly) the legal right, established by Congress in the National Security Act, of the Joint Chiefs of Staff to go directly to the president. But that legal technicality aside, all White House contact with the Pentagon or with any of the military services was routed through my office. That's how I came to know McGeorge Bundy, Bill Moyers, and Jack Valenti, as well as other LBJ staffers—and how I began to get a sense of what a demanding, driving president the nation now had.

During the 1964 presidential campaign, the defense secretary became a preferred target of Republican candidate Barry Goldwater. Two of Goldwater's charges stung Bob like a pair of vicious wasps: that while at the Ford Motor Company McNamara was responsible for the Edsel, the car that was dead on arrival in the market, and that "no new weapons systems" had been developed during McNamara's tenure at the Pentagon.

In all my years with McNamara, I saw nothing dig further under his nails than these Goldwater charges. McNamara asked me to get Henry Ford to sign a letter exonerating him from any responsibility for the Edsel. Ford was so vocal a Johnson supporter that I feared Goldwater would dismiss such a letter as political. McNamara agreed. When we learned that Ernest Breech, Ford's executive vice president, was an outspoken Goldwater financial supporter, we asked Henry Ford to have Breech write to the Arizona senator. Breech readily agreed. He sent a letter to Goldwater saying that "Mr. McNamara . . . had nothing to do with the plans for the Edsel car or any part of the program."*

McNamara also winced at the claim that no new weapons systems had

---

*Years later as head of the World Bank, McNamara would distribute a copy of the letter whenever he was charged with being "the father of the Edsel."

been produced on his watch. Goldwater convinced the American public, and the media, that the Minuteman II missile was merely a "face-lift" of Minuteman I. In truth, the new missile was a distinctly different and more effective weapon. It gave the nation a spectacular second-strike capability. We suspected that the Air Force, a cauldron of Goldwater supporters, had deliberately used the name Minuteman II to play down the significance of the new weapon.

On September 16, 1964, Bill Moyers called me. "The President's speaking in California tomorrow. Goldwater's still beating up the administration on 'no new weapons systems,' and this state lives off defense contracts. The President wants a new weapons system to announce."

I scratched around the Pentagon for something dramatic and learned that we had perfected a new over-the-horizon radar. But the Joint Chiefs insisted that revealing this new capability might jeopardize our national security.

I talked to McNamara. "Nonsense, Joe. You've found the perfect announcement for the President. I'll declassify it right now."

With that assurance, I wrote three paragraphs that evening and wired them to Air Force One. The next day, from the steps of the capitol building in Sacramento, with Governor Pat Brown at his side, the President made his announcement:

Today I am able to tell you, and . . . the entire world, we have a major increase in our capacity to detect hostile launches against the free world.

Previously, our radar capability had been limited to the detection of objects within the line of sight, but now we have produced, and we are installing, our first facilities for "over-the-horizon" radar. This radar will literally look around the curve of the earth, alerting us to aircraft, and especially to missiles, within seconds after they are launched.

This capability will give us earlier warning than ever before of any hostile launches against this country. This means more time to prepare our retaliatory strike and more time for us . . . to decide with prudence and reason the scope and the extent of our retaliatory strike.

There was a thrill to knowing that I had written part of a presidential speech.

The Minuteman II incident had its aftermath. In 1965, when the Navy proposed to call a new submarine-based missile Polaris II, McNamara erupted. "Joe, get your ass down there and find a new name for this missile. It's a huge step forward in weaponry. I'll be damned if we're going to let them name it Polaris II."

When I called Admiral David McDonald, chief of Naval Operations, after considerable sputtering about the secretary of defense's lack of authority to name military service weapons systems, he refused even to meet with me. As I persisted, he referred me to four-star admiral Horacio Rivero, Jr., the deputy chief of Naval Operations.[4]

I asked McNamara if renaming the missile was worth all the grief we'd get. The Navy inevitably would leak that we had overruled them for political reasons. "I don't give a damn," he said. "You see this Rivero right now and get a new name for this missile *this afternoon*."

Rivero was adamant. "The entire Navy command and public affairs operation is geared up to announce it under the Polaris II name," he stressed.

"They'll just have to change," I said.

Eventually Rivero softened. The two of us started leafing through a book of naval expressions and nautical things. We came across a drawing of Poseidon—the God of the sea riding the waves in a chariot. I said, "That's it. That's perfect."

I went back to McNamara. "How about Poseidon?" I asked, describing the mythical character. He approved it on the spot. On January 18, 1965, in a special message to the Congress on the state of the nation's defenses, President Johnson revealed "a new missile system, the Poseidon, to increase the striking power of our missile-carrying nuclear submarines."

.   .   .

My first close-up view of Lyndon Johnson in action came on October 14, 1964, after reports that Walter Jenkins, a long-time Johnson aide, had been arrested a week earlier for making advances to a sixty-one-year-old man at the downtown Washington YMCA. The story broke less than three weeks before the presidential election. It promised to fuel Goldwater's charges of improprieties in Johnson's past.

Around seven that evening, McNamara called me into his office. "Walter Jenkins was a member of an Air Force Reserve unit on Capitol Hill," he said, speaking sharply. "The President wants a copy of his Reserve personnel file immediately. Get it. Make damn sure that everything is copied and nothing is removed. Have one of your guys do the copying himself or watch it being done."

I called the Air Force deputy chief of staff for personnel, Lieutenant General William Stone. "The secretary of defense wants a complete copy of Walter Jenkins's Air Force Reserve personnel record," I explained. "This is so sensitive I'm asking you to copy it yourself. One of my staff will come down immediately to help you. After it's copied, I suggest you keep the original in a safe in your own office."*

As soon as we had a copy, McNamara and I rushed to Moyers's White House office. As Bundy, McNamara, and I gathered around a speaker phone, Moyers called Valenti at the Waldorf-Astoria in New York City, where the President was speaking to the Alfred E. Smith Memorial Dinner. Lady Bird Johnson was preparing a sympathetic statement supporting Walter Jenkins and his family. When the President got on the phone, he expressed his suspicion that Jenkins had been framed, set up by the Republicans. He asked McNamara to read him texts of Jenkins's Air Force Reserve fitness reports signed by the commanding officer of the Capitol Hill Air Force Reserve unit. Each was more glowing than the last.

"Well," said the President, "I'd better call Walter's commanding officer. He'll be shaken by what's happened to Walter. And, in any case, I know he wouldn't want to embarrass himself by making any damned-fool statements."

Moyers and Bundy smiled. McNamara and I exchanged glances. The commanding officer who had signed Jenkins's glowing reports was Air Force Reserve major general Barry Goldwater.

.   .   .

In the wake of the Jenkins incident, McNamara ordered me to "have the FBI reinvestigate all Defense Department presidential appointees and yourself. Make damn certain that all military personnel at the White House have been checked and cleared for top secret."

When I sent the request to the FBI, Deke DeLoach, assistant director of

---

*I sent Lt. Col. Al Haig rather than my Air Force staff aide, Lt. Col. Alexander Butterfield, to avoid putting Butterfield in an impossible position with his own service.

the Bureau, told me that this was not the FBI's responsibility, that J. Edgar Hoover would charge thousands of dollars for each security check—if he agreed to do them. When I reported to McNamara, he laughed. "Call Nick [Katzenbach, then acting attorney general] and tell him it's not our responsibility to fly him, Hoover, and other Justice Department people around in Defense Lear jets and if we decide to do it, we're going to charge them full cost, not just a first-class fare." I did. Hoover conducted the checks quickly and at no charge.

I was astonished to discover that the Defense Department had never run any security checks on the Navy Filipino mess stewards who served in the White House, or on the military band members who played there almost daily. As one of their duties, the Navy mess crew took turns sitting in a tiny room next to the Oval Office so that they could instantly provide the President and his guests coffee or sodas. When I informed McNamara of this oversight, we decided not to let the President or anyone on the White House staff know, and we rushed to perform security checks on the mess crew. Happily, all passed.

We were not so fortunate with members of military bands. When I ran those checks, I learned that a good many had been convicted of marijuana possession. We decided to replace them, but we had to do it over a lengthy period in order to avoid decimating the bands. Again, I concluded that the President and his top staff had enough on their minds, so I didn't tell them about it.

.   .   .

On the morning of November 4, 1964, the day after LBJ's unprecedented landslide victory over Barry Goldwater, National Security Adviser McGeorge Bundy asked me to come to the White House to meet with him and Bill Moyers, the President's special assistant. When I did, they said the President (whose only personal contact with me was a handshake in August 1964) wanted me to join the staff as headhunter and White House expert on Latin American affairs. I said I'd have to talk to McNamara. They urged me to wait until the President had talked to him, but I said I couldn't.

I told McNamara over lunch and he bristled. "Out of the question. First, they should never have talked to you without talking to me. Second, the work you're doing here is far more important. . . . Forget about it. I'll talk to the President." The only two White House staff jobs that McNamara considered more important than my Pentagon position were Bundy's and Moyers's—and Moyers's "only if Johnson would turn his job into a new post, a domestic affairs adviser comparable to the NSC job."

Returning from the LBJ ranch a week later, McNamara told me, "As I suspected, the President knew nothing about this. He said he didn't know his aides did a damn fool thing like this. For the time being at least you'll stay here with me, though we may have whetted his appetite." Years later, listening to the LBJ tapes, I learned that the President knew everything about it. In conversation with the President an hour before Bundy called me, he and Moyers had recommended me to LBJ for his White House staff. LBJ said McNamara would resist any such move, so he didn't want to talk to him directly. Instead he told Bundy and Moyers to "see about" me.[5] That afternoon, Johnson told Abe Fortas, "We've got to bring in a lot more people. . . . Like this . . . fellow over in McNamara's—" Fortas interrupted, "Califano."[6]

.   .   .

As it became obvious that Johnson would defeat Goldwater in a landslide, McNamara had called several of his most trusted aides, including me, into his office. "The President is going to lick Goldwater by an enormous margin. With such a decisive victory, we have the opportunity to take all kinds of important actions, no matter how unpopular—if we're ready. I want you to get a hundred new initiatives from throughout the building of things we ought to do." Turning to me, he said, "Joe, you pull it all together. Scour the Pentagon for every good idea. Don't worry about the political consequences. We'll pick the best and move out with them right after the election. Keep them secret until then."

On November 10, less than a week after the election, McNamara met with LBJ at the ranch, to outline several of his new initiatives. At the top of the list was the Pentagon's first base closure program, a slate of almost one hundred major military installations he wanted to eliminate in order to save a billion dollars a year.

McNamara called me from his plane on the way back. "Assemble all the troops tomorrow so we can put the final touches on an announcement." He had gotten the President's approval for closing the bases but it was, he said, "the only time I've ever seen the President's face pale appreciably." The list included installations in Texas. It included the Navy Yard and Army Terminal in Brooklyn, and Glasgow Air Force base in Montana, a major employer and source of income for Senate Majority Leader Mike Mansfield's home state. "I'm afraid if we don't act immediately he might change his mind."

McNamara announced the closures a week later. True to his word, the President stuck by him when all political hell broke loose. The new senator from New York, Robert Kennedy, was particularly outspoken in opposing the closures of the Brooklyn Navy Yard and Army Terminal. He demanded a meeting with McNamara. Kennedy had won election in New York by just over 700,000 votes, while LBJ had carried the state by 2,700,000 votes. Kennedy had called LBJ in to help him in the final days of his campaign and Johnson had come through. On the night of his election, after Kennedy had thanked just about everyone else, he mentioned Johnson, briefly and grudgingly. Johnson was livid about the snub. McNamara and I knew these were base closures that the President would never rescind.

As I gathered the material for the secretary's meeting with Kennedy, we found that the case for closing the Brooklyn Navy Yard was weak at best. Kennedy arrived at McNamara's office with Anthony Scotto, who controlled the Brooklyn docks for the International Longshoreman's Union.[7] Kennedy made an excellent argument for keeping the installation open. As he finished, he smiled a tight, self-satisfied, almost arrogant smile, signaling his satisfaction that that he had bested McNamara.

McNamara responded coolly. "Bobby, we're going to close the Brooklyn Terminal and Navy Yard. I believe it's the right decision. But even if the Navy has sandbagged me by putting together an analysis that won't stand up, I'm going to follow the gold watch procedure."

Kennedy asked what that was.

"When I was at Ford," McNamara continued, "I ordered a five percent reduction in costs by every component of the company. Everyone bitched. One of the division heads stopped giving gold watches to employees who had been with company twenty-five years and blamed the change on me. I got letters from scores of angry employees. It was a terrible decision, one designed to embarrass me and pressure me to back off the cuts. Clearly, taking away the gold watches was a mistake."

Kennedy smiled, "So, what did you do?"

"I kept the decision in place. I had committed to stand by every decision made to reduce costs. And I fired the guy who cut off the gold watches."

Kennedy laughed nervously.

"Someone here may lose his job," McNamara said. "But these bases will be closed."

.   .   .

The first time in my government service that I was asked to lie came in April 1965. On April 14 the *Washington Evening Star* reported that the Democratic Party had not reimbursed the Pentagon for LBJ's political trips on Air Force One during the campaign. White House aide Bill Moyers called me to inquire as soon as the story broke. I investigated and found that the report was correct: In late 1964, the Pentagon had billed the Democratic National Committee $149,019.69 for the cost of political campaign trips. The committee had complained about the amount and hadn't paid; the Pentagon had made no effort to press for payment.

Late that afternoon, Moyers set up a conference call with Treasury Secretary Henry (Joe) Fowler, who had just assumed his post, and me. Moyers said the DNC would backdate a check, and he wanted us to say that the bill had been paid and the story was incorrect.

I said it wasn't worth lying about because it would hurt our credibility on other matters, and noted the fearful price President Kennedy and the Pentagon had paid for some corner cutting in connection with the Cuban missile crisis.

Fowler agreed.

Moyers—obviously under enormous pressure from the President—pressed hard for us to say the bill had been paid. I stood fast and finally said that I would not lie. So did Fowler. "The check is written, dated April 1, two weeks before this story. It's probably already at the Treasury," Moyers said. "So the bill's been paid. You have to make some kind of a statement."

"All right," I said. "I'll issue a statement that the Democratic National Committee paid the bill in full by a check dated April 1."

Fowler stuck with me. Moyers backed down, hoping the reporter would not pick up the artful wording (which in turn would subject him to the

President's wrath). Walter Pincus, the reporter for the *Star,* was too smart for that; he wrote a page 1 story the next day:

> Califano, special assistant to Defense Secretary Robert McNamara, released a statement to the press that said "the Democratic National Committee paid the bill (for the use of presidential aircraft) in the full amount . . . by check dated April 1, 1965."
>
> Califano in making his statement failed to add that the check—though dated April 1—was delivered to the Treasury Department less than an hour before he made his announcement.

When I read the story, I thought, I'm glad I love working for McNamara, because there's no chance now of my ever being on the White House staff.[8]

.   .   .

As President Johnson rode his landslide victory to launch his Great Society programs at home, Castro stirred the revolutionary pot in our back yard. On Saturday April 24, 1965, rioting broke out in the Dominican Republic. Known communists, some trained in Cuba for guerilla warfare, sought to overthrow the government of Donald Reid y Cabral by handing out rifles and urging the citizens to revolt.[9] I was McNamara's civilian point man during the crisis.

On the Cuban committee I had seen numerous reports of Castro's actions to subvert other governments in Latin America. As the violence escalated, we were convinced that Castro had targeted the country for a communist revolution and trained many of the Dominican rebels. On April 28, with the American embassy under fire and the ambassador calling for more troops to protect lives of evacuating Americans, President Johnson ordered U.S. Marines into Santo Domingo.

We poured American troops into the Dominican Republic for two weeks until they numbered around 23,000.[10] Eighteen U.S. military personnel were killed and 100 wounded before we ended the insurrection on May 25. The country did not fall to the communists, and Dominicans would elect a U.S.-backed candidate, Joaquin Balaguer, their new president in 1966. We had thwarted Castro's attempted communist insurgency—and cooled his subversive activities elsewhere—by applying the lessons we learned from the Bay of Pigs, intervention in civil rights disturbances, and the Panama riots: when moving militarily, we knew to do it with a massive force directed with extreme restraint.

.   .   .

During the Dominican crisis, a group of clergy, the Inter-Religious Committee on Vietnam, held a May vigil at the Pentagon to protest U.S. involvement in Vietnam. The President had just approved McNamara's recommendation to more than double the number of American troops in Southeast Asia.[11] Members of the committee included Protestant ministers, Catholic priests, and Jewish rabbis. As McNamara was debating whether to meet with the group, I asked the FBI to provide us with background checks. The Bureau reported that eight of the twenty-three were associated with socialist or communist organizations or were pacifists or conscientious objectors.[12] "Nevertheless," William Sullivan, Hoover's right hand at the Bureau, said, "we urge you to permit the vigil to take place."[13]

McNamara met with the group on May 12. It was an extraordinary session, in which the defense secretary defended our involvement in Vietnam, noting that the South permitted freedom of all religions and emphasizing that there were millions of Catholics in South Vietnam, while the communist North was militantly atheistic. "We are protecting souls in South Vietnam," McNamara said. I never had any discussion with McNamara about religion. I knew nothing of his religious beliefs. But I was struck by the arguments made by this quintessentially rational man.

.   .   .

As the Vietnam War consumed more of McNamara's time, he spent entire days, sometimes several in a row, in meetings at the State Department or White House, and in travels to Vietnam. Stacks of decision papers on other subjects, with lines for him to check indicating approval or disapproval, began to pile up. He told me to review them; where there was little or no disagreement among his advisors and the recommended actions were in line with his objectives, he instructed me, I was to check the decision box and move the paper along. On one occasion, I checked a decision in favor of the Joint Chiefs that the Army secretary opposed. The Army appealed for reconsideration. McNamara had Secretary Ailes and General Wheeler, chairman of the Joint Chiefs of Staff, troop to his office to argue it out. I sat and listened, knowing that by this time Pentagon sophisticates were aware that I was checking off decisions when McNamara was otherwise occupied. At the end of their discussion, the defense secretary said, "I stand with the decision that Joe made."

As the group left his office, McNamara asked me to stay back. "You were wrong, Joe," he said, "but it's a relatively minor decision. It's more important to my ability to run this department that they know you speak for me than it is to be right on a relatively small matter."

.   .   .

Though McNamara eventually developed deep emotional pain over the war, in the fifteen months I directly worked for him, I never witnessed any such expression. He seemed—and, I believe, was—convinced we were on the right track. He thought that we could send signals to the North Vietnamese by gradually tightening the screw—with more troops, increased bombing, or other activity—and they would eventually respond.

McNamara struggled mightily to measure precisely successes and setbacks in a messy guerilla war. In conventional warfare, measurement was straightforward: one side or the other moved ahead and took control of more land, as the Allies did in World War II as they moved from Normandy across Europe to Berlin. But progress in a guerilla war was much dicier to assess. McNamara's insistence on measures of success led to orders that troops keep track of weapons captured, weapons lost, whether schools were operating, and whether the town leader had been assassinated. He also demanded body counts of enemy dead. When news reports suggested that body counts might be exaggerated, McNamara sought to develop ways to prevent that: double checks, psychological tests that might provide a measure of the extent to which a sergeant, first lieutenant, or captain might exaggerate body counts. What we couldn't measure, of course, was the will of the North Vietnamese and Viet Cong. Their incalculable resolution proved the decisive factor in determining how well we were doing in the war.

McNamara was the preeminent hawk of the Johnson administration until he developed profound doubts in 1967. In 1965 and 1966 he repeatedly proposed more aggressive military activity than the President was willing to undertake. Had I not moved to the White House just days before President Johnson announced on July 28, 1965, that U.S. military forces in Vietnam would increase from 75,000 to 125,000, I would almost certainly have been at McNamara's side, helping draft position papers and options.

Over my years at the White House, I watched the war exact a devastating toll on McNamara. His own children opposed it. His wife, Margie, and his son, Craig, McNamara said, "got my ulcers." She had surgery for them in the summer of 1967 and, after growing increasingly frail, died prematurely of cancer in 1981.

McNamara never used me to work on Vietnam policy matters; he relied on the Joint Chiefs of Staff and his assistant secretaries for international security affairs. At this stage of my life, almost forty years later, I can't say that I would have eventually urged McNamara that we get out of Vietnam had I stayed in the Pentagon as his special assistant. I must admit that I felt fortunate to move to the domestic side of the Johnson presidency, helping to craft Great Society programs. In those, I believed—without a doubt.

CHAPTER 17

The LBJ Years

THE CALL THAT brought me to the White House came on July 8, 1965, after this foreplay with Defense Secretary Robert McNamara captured on the Johnson tapes:

> LBJ: "We would like for Califano to take over . . . pulling together the budget and the various departments on all of our 137 proposals that we make, everything from beautification to disarmament. . . . My only knowledge of Califano is what he does for you. I really think you've got enough executive ability that you could equip anybody to do what he's done. . . . You want to give me your reaction?"
>
> McN: "Joe's training and education and experience and interest has all been the law. . . . Joe is bright, he is able, he is sensitive to the individual's requirements. I think he'd work well with you. . . . I think he understands Congress. . . . I don't think he would initiate new proposals as well as others simply because he's inexperienced in this whole field. . . ."

McNamara then suggested alternative candidates. Johnson interrupted. Turning what McNamara cited as a weakness into an asset, the President said he had plenty of new education and urban proposals and what he needed was "practical judgment. . . . I thought if it met with your approval, I'd ask Bill [Moyers] to talk to Joe. . . ."

McNamara, sensing LBJ's mind was made up, said, "But my answer to you on Califano, obviously, is I wouldn't think of taking him away."

LBJ already had McNamara talking as though he, McNamara, were taking me, McNamara's special assistant, away from the President!

The President boxed McNamara in, as I later often saw him do when locking up a congressman's vote:

LBJ: "Will you tell Califano that Bill will be calling him . . . and that he's
free to do whatever his judgment thinks?"
McN: "Absolutely."

Jack Valenti and Moyers called me over to the White House later that
morning. When I returned I reported to McNamara: "They want me to prepare legislative programs, handle domestic crises, and be a utility infielder
on the domestic scene."

McNamara never mentioned his conversation with the President. "It's
important for you to coordinate economic policy as well," he said. "The economic problems are bound to be severe as Great Society programs need
more and more funds, since the cost of the war in Vietnam is likely to rise."

An hour later, McNamara told me the President agreed with him. "What
a job!" I exclaimed.

"It's an opportunity, not a job or even a job description," McNamara
remarked. "I assure you of this," he continued. "You will never work for a
more complicated man as long as you live. But you're not likely to work for
a more intelligent one." Then he told me to take a vacation.

"Enjoy it," he said smiling. "It will be the last week you'll have off until you
stop working for him."

I took Trudy and our sons, Mark and Joe, to my parents' home in Spring
Lake on the New Jersey shore, where we spent the only full week we had
away together until I left the White House in 1969.

I was barely two months beyond my thirty-fourth birthday. I was totally
inexperienced in domestic policy. Nevertheless I was brashly confident I
could do the job.

That confidence—however unjustified—came most immediately from
McNamara's encouragement and the experience as a troubleshooter that I
had gained under him and Vance. I had learned other lessons from McNamara's systems analysis and budget-planning techniques, and from his
management style. Brash or not, I believed I could organize and manage
legislative programs and domestic policy. My temerity also stemmed from
influences outside the Pentagon. Didn't Harvard Law School expect its
graduates, especially its *Law Review* editors, to run the country, as so many
had during the New Deal? The support and love of my parents and aunts
and uncles was another source of my self-assurance. "Joe Cal is going to do

something big with his life," they said. Not in their wildest dreams—or mine—did that "something big" entail being the President's chief domestic advisor. But, as ready as I was to go, I was unprepared for the magnitude of LBJ's ambition and the tenacity and intensity of his drive to recast the role of the federal government and to reshape America. Those hit me five days into the job with him, on Saturday morning, July 31, 1965.

The President called me from Washington to his Texas ranch to discuss the legislative program. Johnson was in the pool when I arrived; he signaled me to join him. We swam for a couple of minutes, then stopped about two-thirds of the way toward the deep end of the pool. At a husky and imposing six feet three, he could stand on the pool floor; at five feet ten I had to tread water because my feet couldn't quite touch the bottom.

Poking my shoulder with a strong finger as though punctuating a series of exclamation points, Johnson started talking. He saw America as a nation with many needs: "We'll put together lots of programs and we'll pass them. But there are three big ones I want to be damn sure you do. One, I want to straighten out the transportation mess in this country. We've got to start by getting our own house in order. There are too damn many agencies fiddling with transportation. I want to put them all together in one cabinet department."

I nodded, treading. He was so close to me, almost nose to nose, that I couldn't move around him so I could stand on the bottom of the pool.

"Next, I want to rebuild American cities."

I was breathing hard.

"Third, I want a fair housing bill. We've got to end this Goddamn discrimination against Negroes. Until people"—he started jabbing my shoulder as he recited each color—"whether they're purple, brown, black, yellow, red, green, or whatever—live together, they'll never know they have the same hopes for their children, the same fears, troubles, woes, ambitions. I want a bill that makes it possible for anybody to buy a house anywhere they can afford to. Now, can you do that? Can you do all these things?"

"Yes, sir, Mr. President," I responded, not having the faintest idea how.

We were setting course on a daring and high-risk adventure, and I was electrified by his energy and awed by his ambition even while breathless from treading water as his finger against my shoulder kept pushing me down. Not until months later, as I got to know him, did I realize that for this early exchange Lyndon Johnson had instinctively and intentionally picked a depth of the pool where he could stand and I had to tread water.

During that weekend at the LBJ ranch and the weeks that followed, I saw Lyndon Johnson as a complex man who stuffed rooms with his dominating presence and determination. I saw how committed he was to use his power to mount a revolution in America. He was a singularly prodigious worker—the most remarkable thing to me about the LBJ White House tapes is the absence of chit-chat or small talk; every conversation is related to achieving some policy or political goal or persuading someone to do something he wants them to do. He was a man-eater willing to use his staff up in his drive to be the education president, the environmental president, the health president, the housing president, the consumer president, the anti-crime president, and most of all the anti-poverty and civil rights president. I couldn't know then how he intended to use me, or use me up, in that drive.

Johnson had sketched his concept of a Great Society at his University of Michigan commencement address in May of 1964 in broad and grand strokes. Reading that speech and seeing him drive through Congress the 1964 Civil Rights Act, the 1964 tax cuts, which set off an unprecedented (to that time) period of economic prosperity, and the Office of Economic Opportunity to wage a war on poverty provided a hint of the gargantuan scale of his legislative appetite. But no one—and certainly not I—realized that for LBJ, "Great Society" was a code word for a revolution in our society. I had no idea how vastly he would change our nation or how deep a role I would play—to say nothing of how significantly he would affect my life.

.   .   .

To my surprise, I, the kid from Brooklyn and Harvard Law School, and he, the oversized Texas politician from the hill country, hit it off well from the get-go. As I learned from him, my commitment to his revolutionary goals deepened and my confidence that we could achieve them surged.

It helped that several White House staffers—Jack Valenti, LBJ's close advisor and first appointments secretary; Larry O'Brien, his congressional liaison; Harry McPherson, his senate counsel; and Bill Moyers, his press secretary—went out of their way to advise me on dealing with this political dervish. On my first day, Johnson told me, "I want you to read all my mail, attend every meeting I have, be with me at the National Security Council, travel with me." When I expressed my doubts about such grandiose involvement, Valenti told me, "The President says that to every new staff member. Ignore him and stick to your job."

I didn't need Valenti, or the others, to teach me about press leaks. I had already seen McNamara banish to an Alaskan outpost an Air Force general he suspected of leaking. Lyndon Johnson, I knew, considered leaking the highest measure of an aide's untrustworthiness. Chronic leaking to reporters had caused LBJ to lose trust in Richard Goodwin (as John F. Kennedy had). When Valenti and I wanted to bring Goodwin back to the White House to help write the 1966 "guns and butter" State of the Union address, Johnson resisted. "When Goodwin works on a speech, the press knows it before I deliver it." LBJ also came to suspect that Bill Moyers disclosed information for his own benefit; this contributed to a final rift between the President and the young man whom he had treated like the son he never had.

Johnson believed that White House aides should be anonymous. When the New York Times Magazine was doing an article on me in 1968, the President, to my irritation, refused to release any White House picture of the two of us together—and prohibited me from giving them any of mine. The only part of the magazine piece he liked was this: "If you are neither a Washingtonian nor a politician, you can be forgiven if you have never heard of Califano. His round, forgettable face has graced no newsmagazine covers. . . ." I was delighted with the conclusion of that section, which angered him: "Yet in the past year, with no fanfare, Califano has come to be, in function if not in title, the Deputy President for Domestic Affairs."

I had one important advantage from the first day at the White House: I came to LBJ something of my own man, with an independent reputation developed working for McNamara. Johnson could crush an aide with brutal criticism, just as he could mount his staffers on pedestals with extravagant praise. Cliff Carter, then executive director of the Democratic National Committee, warned me on our first trip together, "To work for this man, you've got to remember two things: You're never as good as he says you are when he praises you and you're never as bad as he says you are when he chews you out." I watched as LBJ mercilessly chewed out Valenti, Moyers, and others, like Horace Busby—aides he viewed as his creations and who he believed owed their careers to him. He chewed me out, too, but rarely, and never as personally. He spared me not because I made any fewer mistakes, but because I came from McNamara, whom LBJ held in high esteem. Thanks to McNamara, Johnson accorded me enough respect and gave me a long enough leash to show what I could do. And early on I had several lucky breaks.

The first crisis we faced together was a riot in Los Angeles, three weeks after I arrived at the White House. Erupting in Watts just five days after LBJ had signed the Voting Rights Act, this urban violence so depressed Johnson that for three days and nights he would not return my phone calls, the only time that happened during the years I worked for him.*

California called up national guardsmen to assist local police, but the rioting and looting intensified. The state National Guard asked the U.S. Army for help. General Creighton Abrams, then vice chief of staff of the Army, asked me for permission to "support" National Guard troops with supplies and Air Force planes to transport them to Los Angeles. After repeatedly calling the President at the ranch and receiving no response, I made a decision. In my Pentagon experiences handling earlier disturbances, we had achieved the most success when the federal government assisted, but left state and local officials primarily responsible for maintaining law and restoring order. I said very carefully to Abrams, "You've got White House approval." But I stressed the importance of keeping a low profile. "Keep it to support and stay in the background."

When the President finally called me later that same night, he sounded more sorrowful than angry. He was pleased that I had left state officials responsible for law and order. He did not "want to admit," he said, "that city government, state government, and county government is impotent in this country. . . ." He made no apology for his failure to answer my calls. He admonished me in a backhanded way for acting on my own: "I'll give you a decision on anything you recommend within five minutes. . . . I'd like for them to do what they can on their own but what they can't, why then we'll be glad to do it, but I want to see what I'm approving and rejecting. . . ."[1]

*On the evening of August 11, 1965, a highway patrolman arrested a twenty-one-year-old black youth suspected of drunk driving in the Watts area of Los Angeles. Hundreds of people gathered at the scene, and by the following night, five thousand blacks were rioting and looting in Watts. Thirty-four people were killed and more than one thousand injured by the riot's end. Almost unnoticed, on August 13 the black youth arrested pleaded guilty to drunk driving in Los Angeles Municipal Court.

Next, I had the good fortune to have a tough and delicate assignment work out well for the President. In September, LBJ decided to relieve Vice President Hubert Humphrey of his responsibilities for coordinating the administration's civil rights activities. Johnson considered civil rights his central mark on history. He could not bear to entrust it to anyone else, especially Humphrey, whom he pegged as neither shrewd enough nor tough enough for this job. In relieving Humphrey of his civil rights responsibilities, LBJ was ending the vice president's only substantive role, one the Minnesotan cherished. Johnson asked me to put together a plan to take this task from the vice president, and persuade Humphrey to sign a memorandum recommending the action and hold a press conference announcing it as his own idea. Less than two months on the White House staff, I faced some tense and testy conversations with Humphrey. The vice president knew he was being politically emasculated, and he was hurt. Eventually he gave way gracefully, and I gained points for handling a painful diplomatic chore.

My third break came in late August when I was charged with leading the government's effort to avert a steel strike and settle the dispute between the steel companies and their union. LBJ wanted any pay hike held within the wage-price guidelines that he had established in an effort to limit wage increases to increases in productivity. With intense hard work and plenty of presidential persuading, we achieved his goal. Johnson later told McNamara, "The man most responsible for the steel strike settlement is your boy Califano."[2]

My fourth opportunity occurred just after 5 P.M. on November 9, 1965. Driving around the ranch with Mrs. Johnson and A.W. Moursund, LBJ's lawyer and business advisor, the President heard on the radio news that the electricity and lights had gone out in New York City. "Find out what caused it. See if it's sabotage or what," the President said in his call to me, and clicked off. He then told his pilot, Colonel James Cross, to prepare planes for an emergency departure. Cross and his aides carried the President's "Football," the black satchel with instructions LBJ needed to launch a nuclear attack.

A few minutes later, at 5:17 P.M., I reached the President in his car with ominous news: "The lights have also gone out in Boston and Canada, and the 'Hotline' water and land lines to Moscow and [Soviet Premier Alexei] Kosygin have gone dead."[3] Fearing a Soviet military move, I suggested that the President get to a regular phone as quickly as possible. LBJ rushed to the

Moursund ranch house and stayed there for the next hour and a half, barking orders to Secretary McNamara, me, and others. McNamara put U.S. forces, including our nuclear capability, on highest alert. LBJ then helicoptered back to his own ranch, where communications were secure.[4]

Hurriedly I tried to learn what was going on. We discovered that a power failure had blacked out 80,000 square miles and 30 million people in the Northeast and parts of Ontario, Canada. Much about the situation was still unclear, but after several conversations with CIA Director William Raborn and the FBI, I grew less worried about sabotage or a Soviet attack. Nevertheless, 600,000 people were stranded in New York City's subway system and high above Manhattan in elevators stalled between floors. Fewer than half of the city's hospitals had adequate standby power. Traffic was gridlocked and the threat of tragedy and looting loomed. Only a bright moonlight and auxiliary power for air traffic control towers provided some mitigation of this disaster.

The President ordered me to get in touch with New York City mayor Robert Wagner, New York governor Nelson Rockefeller, and the other northeastern governors. I should find out what was going on and offer help. Shortly before ten, the President called to say that he and Governor Rockefeller wanted me to rush over to the CBS Washington studios. My job: to appear on a special television broadcast and inform New Yorkers of our actions and concern.[5] I dashed down to a waiting White House car and over to CBS. As I ran into the studio, it suddenly dawned on me. Who the hell in New York City would see me? The city had no power. The President of the United States and the governor of New York had rushed me over to this television studio to put the people of New York City at ease, and none of them would be able to see or hear me!

I went on, in any case. I talked to the rest of the nation for about ten minutes about what Lyndon Johnson was doing for the people of the Northeast. In truth, I thought I was laying it on a bit thickly. But when I returned and spoke with the President, he mentioned several points I could have added. I learned that it was simply not possible to lay it on too thickly for him (or most other politicians).

The morning after, calls and wires poured in from citizens and others thanking the President for staying on top of the problem and for the continuing reports issued throughout the night. I realized that from the President's perspective, it had mattered little that New Yorkers could not see or hear me. The power of television had amplified his concerns and served him well.[6]

At the ranch on December 29, 1965, I presented "The Great Society—A Second Year Legislative Program," as vast an agenda as he had sent to the first session of the 89th Congress. He loved it. I think he realized that I had internalized the words he spoke at least once a day, "Do it now. Not next week. Not tomorrow. Not later this afternoon. Now."

A month later, I basked when I heard the President say in a cabinet meeting, "When Joe speaks that's my voice you should hear." It was heady stuff. His affirmation gave me the clout and the confidence, young as I was, to push cabinet officers and agency heads to action, and to negotiate with senators and representatives on Capitol Hill.

The President and I got along, I think, because we were both true believers and driven. Johnson was prepared to fall on his sword for what he believed in, whether it was his crusade for civil rights or the War on Poverty. To both of us, civil rights, increased opportunity, and a redistribution of wealth were moral mandates, not political positions. These were goals worth fighting for, worth maneuvering around, or even moving aside, through, or over those who did not share our vision or could not be persuaded to do so. If McNamara taught me how important a week or a month could be in deciding and executing Pentagon initiatives, Johnson showed me how important it was to use every hour of every day to shape national policy while we had the power to do so.

I awoke each morning and rushed to a job that I believed in. Of course I enjoyed exercising the power that the President had given me; that was exhilarating for a thirty-something kid from Brooklyn. But I was conscious too that all my power came from the President. Given the rewards of belief and influence, I didn't mind working harder than I ever had.

When I was beyond exhaustion, LBJ would push me to do more. He was brave and brutal, compassionate and cruel, incredibly intelligent and infuriatingly insensitive. He could be altruistic and petty, caring and crude, generous and petulant, bluntly honest and calculatingly devious—all within the same few minutes. He ran over or around whomever and whatever got in his way. His prodigious energy spilled over to produce second, third, and fourth winds in me. He used all that energy, cajoling, and unceasing drive to get me and others to do more than we thought possible.

He wanted me available at all times. He was mightily annoyed if he called any of his staff and we were not at the other end to answer. Soon after I arrived at the White House, around eight o'clock one morning, Johnson called on my POTUS (President of the United States) line, a direct line from him that emitted a constant uninterrupted ring until it was answered. Down the hall from the Oval Office, my office had its own adjoining bathroom, which is where I was when he called. My secretary, Peggy Hoxie, picked up. "He's not here, Mr. President," she answered a little nervously.

"Where the hell is he?" the President asked.

"He's in the bathroom, Mr. President," Peggy responded.

"Isn't there a phone in there?" Johnson asked incredulously.

"No, Mr. President," she responded, just as incredulously.

"Then have a phone put in there right away."

"Yes, sir."

When I emerged from the bathroom, Peggy told me to call the President immediately. Then she repeated what he had said about the phone. "Like hell," I responded. "Just forget about it."

The following morning, at almost exactly the same time, the President called me on the hotline. I was, unfortunately, again in the bathroom. "I told you to put a phone in that toilet," Johnson shouted at my secretary. "I want that phone installed this morning. Do you hear me?"

"Yes, Mr. President."

Within minutes, as I came out of the bathroom, Peggy was standing in my office, a little shaky, with two Army Signal Corps technicians from the White House Communications Agency. "The President wants a phone installed in your john immediately, sir," one of them said. I shrugged my shoulders, smiled, and surrendered. The phone, complete with POTUS line, was installed and functioning in less than an hour.

LBJ had a laser-like focus on his priorities. Whatever the distractions—including the colossal one of the Vietnam War—Johnson kept me focused on his domestic priorities. As the war drained his power and energy, he insulated me from its corrosive effects. He pressed me to keep the domestic engine going, for that's where permanent achievement lay, even as the foreign policy machine sputtered in Southeast Asia.

As the Vietnam War chipped away at LBJ's time, I tried never to lose momentum or be distracted from producing and sustaining Great Society programs, sensing that if we could just get them on the legislative books, they would survive. The Vietnam War would eventually end; the programs we wrote into law would be in place for a long, long time. (Indeed, the resilience of these programs has been remarkable, even in hostile political environments. Virtually every one of those programs is in place as this memoir is written forty years later and, while ideological conservatives continue to attack them and starve them of funding, for the most part the political debate is how to improve them and adjust them to changed conditions, not whether to repeal them.) We were filled with pride—and a deep sense that on the domestic side, at least, we were the good guys; our proposed changes were for the better.

But at times we used questionable means to achieve our noble ends.

No halo floated above our heads. In the street fights over Great Society legislation I learned that politics was not Ping-Pong; it was played with metal bats and hard balls. The game could turn vicious when pushing legislation freighted with controversy, such as the poverty and civil rights laws, or consumer laws that gored vested economic interests—for example, auto safety laws or highway beautification laws that would eliminate billboards. The applicable moral maxim then became not simply whether the end justified the means, but rather what means did a particular end justify. In catechism class, the nuns at St. Gregory's elementary school taught right and wrong in stark colors, as sharply contrasting as the white chalk writing on their slate blackboards. At the White House, I quickly learned that the political paper on which we were writing the Great Society featured more subtle shadings. I came to realize that the dominant color of politics is gray; difficult choices and compromise are required at almost every step of the journey toward a major new program; men and women are moved by love and fear (the trick is finding the persuasive mix); and today's enemy may be tomorrow's ally (and vice versa). In politics, LBJ reminded us, "Never tell a man to go to hell unless you can send him there."

In order to get votes for legislation on the Hill, we tolerated pork-barrel projects of marginal value in key congressional districts. To win a member's support we sometimes hired people who were less qualified than others applying for the same job. If placing an unqualified crony on a commission got Senate Minority Leader Everett Dirksen's vote to end a filibuster or pass a civil rights act, we were willing to pay that price.

I remember once alerting the President that a secret grand jury was about to conduct a criminal investigation of two senators. I had no idea how he would react. Would LBJ ask the Justice Department to lay off? I wondered. The President told me to have the Justice Department let the senators know, "as a courtesy," that they were under investigation and to keep the investigation going until we could get their votes on a couple of key bills. "After that," Johnson said, "tell them to do whatever's right. But keep this grand jury going until we've gotten their votes on our legislation."

In the push to establish a new cabinet-level Department of Transportation, I realized how far I had come from the classroom at St. Gregory's. John McClellan, a stony faced, crafty Arkansas Democrat, chaired the Senate committee with jurisdiction over the bill. He was refusing to let the bill out of his committee unless the administration relaxed its demanding standards for approving waterway navigation projects. McClellan couldn't find time even to meet with me.

I reported my frustration to the President one night over dinner in the mansion. Johnson suggested that I leak, off-the-record to a friendly reporter, that "there are some who say McClellan is holding up the Transportation Department because he wants the Corps of Engineers to build a dam on land he owns. That way he'll get a lot of money when the government buys the property."

"Is that true?" I asked.

Johnson leaned back in his leather chair: "The first time Mr. Kleberg* ran for Congress, he was back home making a tub-thumper campaign speech against his opponent. I was sitting nearby listening. Mr. Kleberg said: 'It isn't easy, but I guess I can understand why the good citizens of the hill country might let themselves be represented in Washington by a man who drinks too much. It isn't easy, but I guess I can even understand why the good citizens of the hill country might even let themselves be represented by a man in Washington who carouses with city women while his wife and children are back here working the land. But, as God is my witness, I will never understand why the good people of the hill country would let themselves be represented by a man who takes female sheep up into the hills alone at night!'

"Well," pausing for emphasis, the President continued, "when he finished, I said, 'Mr. Kleberg, that's not true!'"

*Richard Kleberg, part owner of Texas's huge King Ranch, was the congressman who first brought LBJ to Washington as an aide.

"And you know what Mr. Kleberg did?" Johnson asked, leaning toward me as he peered into my eyes. "He just looked at me and said, 'Then let the son of a bitch deny it!'"

Johnson and I both laughed, and then he paused and said quietly, "You just let John McClellan deny it."

As it turned out, we reached a compromise without having to leak the charge. But I was ready to put the story out if the Arkansas senator had persisted in blocking the bill. McClellan was playing hardball with the President's proposal, and I saw leaking such a story simply as sliding into his base, spikes high à la Ty Cobb.

Despite an occasional nagging misgiving, I quickly found myself prepared to use the serrated edge of the political knife in the Johnson White House. I rationalized that we wielded this weapon to pass legislative programs that were desperately needed by the poor and to give average citizens a fair chance to share in the benefits of our society; programs to deal with the growing number of large national corporations and the increasing size of union and government bureaucracies average Americans faced, as the corner grocer, neighborhood butcher, and town hall meetings disappeared from American life.

.   .   .

The White House staff was a far cry from the caricature of Texas politicians I had expected from reading the press and hearing comments of Kennedy appointees scattered throughout the government.

Among my colleagues was Douglass Cater, who had authored *The Fourth Branch of Government,* a prescient classic that foreshadowed the media's extraordinary power, and who was later named publisher of the London *Observer.* Larry O'Brien, LBJ's congressional liaison, became president of the National Basketball Association; Jack Valenti, president of the Motion Picture Association of America. Bill Moyers built a career as a distinguished television producer and commentator. Harry McPherson established a top law firm in D.C. Tom Johnson, a deputy press secretary, became publisher of the *Los Angeles Times* and chairman and CEO of CNN.[7]

The speechwriters were remarkable: Ervin Duggan went on to be a commissioner of the Federal Communications Commission and president of the Public Broadcasting Service. Robert Hardesty became chairman of the board of governors of the U.S. Postal Service and president of Southwest Texas University at San Marcos. Harry Middleton, as head of the LBJ library, redefined the role of presidential libraries. Peter Benchley went on to write the best selling novel *Jaws*.

The Johnson White House, like Kennedy's and the city itself in the 1960s, was a male bastion. Aside from Lady Bird, the only feminine voice of any moment was Liz Carpenter, the First Lady's staff director—a savvy politician and clever jokester who penned many of LBJ's funniest lines. Juanita Roberts and Marie Fehmer, the president's senior secretaries, were recognized for their discretion and devotion as well as their intelligence; his other secretaries were regarded at least as much for their physical beauty as for their efficiency. Johnson saw "the women of America [as] one of the largest untapped resources for the great tasks of this Nation."[8] But in positions of power and influence, on domestic and foreign policy, ours was a male locker room. We named prominent women to our task forces—and Johnson had the highest regard for bright ones, like Barbara Jordan. But I can recall interviewing only two women for any job on the White House staff: NBC reporter and *Today Show* regular Betty Furness and Esther Peterson, a New Deal veteran stationed in the Labor Department. The two competed for the consumer affairs position under me. LBJ picked Furness, the more glamorous candidate and seasoned communicator.

I used the President's staffing techniques as a model for building my own, the first domestic policy affairs staff at the White House. I never asked the political affiliation of anyone I hired. I looked for brains, judgment, talent, commitment to our domestic agenda, and a willingness to work around the clock. My staff never exceeded four or five (by 2001, under George W. Bush, it had grown to more than one hundred).[9]

To be sure, with Republicans and conservative Democrats there were always spirited, often angry, sometimes partisan differences over Great Society programs, consumer protection, civil rights, education, and health care—and certainly about the Vietnam War. But these were usually intellectual and political battles over public policy, not extreme partisan trench warfare. There were battles over judgeships, not just over the losing attempt to name Abe Fortas chief justice of the Supreme Court, but also over LBJ's determined effort to put pro–civil rights judges on the lower federal bench.

Through it all, however, we worked with our Republican and conservative adversaries. My instructions were to give Senate Minority Leader Everett Dirksen (always) and House Minority Leader Gerald Ford (most of the time) the same deference I gave Democratic Senate Majority Leader Mike Mansfield and House Speaker John McCormack. It was enlightened self-interest: we needed Dirksen, particularly, to pass civil rights and other progressive legislation in the Senate. Besides, Johnson genuinely liked him. In 1967 and 1968 we needed moderate Republicans in the House if we hoped to pass Great Society bills. Though LBJ thought Gerry Ford was too partisan—and he lacked the fondness for Ford that he felt for Dirksen—the President was careful never to alienate the House minority leader.

As intent as Johnson was on recasting the role of the federal government in American life, he subjected me to surprisingly little micromanagement as we drafted programs. His admonition was: "Give me the best ideas. Forget about the politics. I'll worry about that after we know what the best program is." He would say that he wanted "a program for the cities," or an "Asian development bank," or "something to help the Negro male and his family," or a "balance of payments program." At other times he spoke of a "clean air bill," or a "consumer program to help housewives buying groceries and veterans buying cars and homes." But he expected me to put the flesh on the skeletal ideas he put forward.

Over the summer and fall of 1965, in my first efforts at preparing a legislative program, I set up task forces of outside experts to develop programs in transportation, job training, air and water pollution, population and family planning, income maintenance, tax reform, education, public assistance, urban affairs, housing, health care, crime, foreign aid, civil rights, and agriculture. My staff and I sought ideas from a broad sweep of individuals, from United Auto Workers president Walter Reuther to Yale University president Kingman Brewster, from economists like John Kenneth Galbraith and Barbara Ward to writer John Steinbeck and former secretary of state Dean Acheson. The task forces we set up had the best minds we could enlist regardless of party affiliation. Conservative Republican George Schultz, for example, headed our manpower and jobs task force.

By late fall each year my office was the storm center. Hot tempers and heated arguments raged over the details of these programs and which department or agency would run them. Occasionally, I sought guidance from the President, but he pressed me to resolve as many issues as possible. Remarkably, the political judgments Johnson rendered on my legislative proposals focused not on their impact on his reelection or popularity— though he certainly wanted Americans to love him—but on the feasibility of passage in Congress.

.   .   .

Johnson understood the power of the presidency to set an example, and he lived in fear of a race riot in the overwhelmingly black nation's capital. He was acutely conscious of the de facto segregation of Washington, D.C., with affluent whites concentrated in the northwest Georgetown and Cleveland Park sections and poor blacks in the rest of the city.

On July 19, 1966, the *Washington Post* reported that only one of three district swimming pools scheduled to open during the summer would be completed by Labor Day. "That's why these kids get into so much trouble," the President told me that morning in his bedroom as he punched with his forefinger at the story in the *Post*. "They don't have anything to do." Only a week earlier a Chicago ghetto had erupted in four days of rioting after police arrested two youths who had turned on a hydrant to beat the heat. Johnson wanted even more pools and hydrants than originally planned—in operation "yesterday, not tomorrow"—and he told me to get Secretary of the Interior Stewart Udall, Office of Economic Opportunity Director Sargent Shriver, president of the D.C. Commissioners Walter Tobriner, the Army Corps of Engineers, and "anyone else who might be responsible for this fiasco and haul their asses into your office."

The meeting I held that morning was bureaucratic theater of the absurd. As I pressed for action, I heard all the reasons why nothing could be done. The Corps of Engineers said that a larger hydrant program would use too much water. "How much?" I asked. They didn't know exactly. "Pick up the phone and find out." After calling, they reported that it wouldn't use too much water after all.

District commissioner Walter Tobriner then said that there weren't enough shower heads to open more hydrants. "Why not?" I asked.

"Because prisoners make the shower heads and cannot make enough in such a short time."

"Ever try to buy any?" I shot back.

"No."

"Well, do it."

Another D.C. official claimed there wasn't enough manpower to run the hydrant program. Why not use jobless people from local neighborhoods? They weren't reliable. Why not temporary pools? Not enough college students wanted to be lifeguards in ghettos. Why not use local people? It takes a long time to train a lifeguard. "How long?" I asked.

No one knew.

"Call the Red Cross."

The Red Cross reported that lifeguards could be trained in a week if they knew how to swim; in four, if they didn't.

If LBJ had been at the meeting, he would have fired nearly everyone there. Within a few weeks, we had a dozen temporary pools and scores of hydrant showers in operation to give the kids something to do in the scorching Washington summer. We also put local residents to work.[10]

The incident made Johnson realize that neither he nor his staff knew enough about what was going on in the nation's ghettos. Johnson had the dirt of rural and Mexican-American poverty embedded in his skin, but not the grime of urban slums. He suspected that most local white politicians had no whiff of what was happening under their own noses.

The President ordered me to send White House aides out to live in the slums for a night or two in order to get a better sense of what people were doing and complaining about, what they wanted and were angry about. Buttoned-down White House staffers and other officials visited ghettos in New York, Detroit, Chicago, Cleveland, Los Angeles, San Antonio, Washington, and Baltimore. Their reports led us to expand summer recreation, education, health, and job programs in 1967. Repeated complaints about urban rats prompted the 1967 Rat Extermination Bill. For a time, the President and I were the only proponents of this legislative proposal. But Johnson began asking those opposed, "Have you ever been scared of a wasp in your home? Scared he'd bite you? Well, how'd you like to have fifty rats in your house?" I picked up that question and we picked up supporters.

·   ·   ·

After the loss of forty-seven House seats in the 1966 congressional elections, Johnson invited governors from the South and border states to his ranch on December 21, 1966. It was a nasty meeting, with the governors making it clear that they thought the President's policies on civil rights—his 1964 Civil Rights Act and 1965 Voting Rights Act, as well as his vocal support of expanded rights for Negroes—had cost our party House seats and threatened several statehouses in 1968.

After the meeting, the President was steaming. Red-faced, he almost shouted at me. "Niggah! Niggah! Niggah! That's all they said to me all day. Hell, there's one thing they'd better know. If I don't achieve anything else while I'm President, I intend to make it impossible for people to come here and shout 'Niggah! Niggah! Niggah!' to me and the American people."

I listened but then shifted to my reason for being there: to review the full menu for his State of the Union message and his coming legislative program. In 1964, the first surgeon general's report had targeted smoking, pointing out that smokers had a nine to ten times greater likelihood of getting lung cancer. The report also raised early concerns about a link between smoking and heart disease. In the wake of that report, Paul Rand Dixon, chairman of the Federal Trade Commission, recommended to me that the administration seek to ban cigarette advertising on television. I urged that LBJ include it in his legislative program, expecting ready approval. After all, Johnson himself had quit smoking on doctor's orders after a near fatal heart attack in 1955.

As we rode around his ranch together, he stopped the car when I lit a cigarette* and turned toward me. "The day you quit smoking, I'll send your bill to Congress," he said, chuckling as he resumed driving. He knew I couldn't quit under the stress of working for him. When his physician had told him that he had to quit after his heart attack, then Senator Johnson sighed and said, "I'd rather you have my pecker cut off."[11] Though he quit, LBJ often said that one of the first things he would do upon leaving the White House was resume smoking; he lit up on the plane taking him to Texas on January 20, 1969. More significantly, Johnson had decided that there was only so much we could take on in the South. At war with the old Confederacy over desegregation and determined to move aggressively on civil rights, he would not further alienate senators and representatives from states like Virginia, North

---

*Working for LBJ had increased my smoking from one to as many as four packs a day; by early 1967 I carried regular cigarettes in one pocket and menthol in another so I could continue to smoke when my throat grew raw.

Carolina, and Kentucky. Nor would he risk driving all the tobacco money to the side of the segregationists and against civil rights. The public health battle against smoking was for another president and another day. I had no idea that a decade later it would become my battle.

Despite Lyndon Johnson's pay-any-personal-or-political-price commitment to provide equal opportunity to blacks—reflected not only in his civil rights acts and anti-poverty programs, but also in his appointments of the first blacks to the Supreme Court (Thurgood Marshall), the cabinet (Robert Weaver), the Federal Reserve Board (Andrew Brimmer), and the mayoralty of a major city (Walter Washington in the nation's capital)—in the two years following the 1965 riots in Watts, race riots broke out in twenty American cities.

The most violent disturbances erupted in the steamy July of 1967, first in Newark and then in Detroit. The motor city experienced the worst race riot since federal troops had been sent there a quarter century earlier when racial violence broke out in 1943. I was LBJ's point man on these disturbances. I remember a late dinner in the White House living quarters on July 24 and an even later meeting in the Oval Office. McNamara, FBI Director J. Edgar Hoover, Supreme Court Justice Abe Fortas, Attorney General Ramsey Clark, Army Secretary Stan Resor, and Army Chief of Staff Harold Johnson were there. Hoover was convinced that Communists were stirring up trouble. "Harlem will break loose in thirty minutes," he said. "They plan to tear it apart." He urged the President to move armed troops in immediately. Michigan governor George Romney, then a potential presidential candidate against LBJ, was loath to request federal troops and thus admit publicly that he could not control the situation in his state's largest city.

Johnson was distraught. When after 11 P.M. he signed the order to federalize the Michigan National Guard and send Army troops into the riot-torn city, he insisted that they carry no ammunition. "I don't want American citizens killing American citizens," he said. The Army strenuously objected and LBJ finally agreed to let the soldiers carry ammunition, but he forbade them to load any guns except on the orders of a regular Army officer at the scene. "Well," he said sadly, sinking into his chair as he handed me the signed order, "I guess it's just a matter of minutes before federal troops start killing women and children." Before order was restored, forty were dead, two thousand injured; none were killed by regular forces.[12]

Frustrated, scratching for some action he could take to stem the violence—and fearing that worse might lie ahead—Johnson decided to set up the National Advisory Commission on Civil Disorders and to proclaim July 30 a national day of prayer and reconciliation. I expressed my concern that the reaction would be: "The cities are aflame, the country's coming apart, so what does LBJ do? Set up a commission and say a prayer."

The President dismissed my objections and I did not press them. He was so forlorn, frustrated, and depressed that evening that I did not push my position as firmly as I should have. I knew what was bothering him and I shared his concern: the Great Society programs and civil rights initiatives might be in most danger not from the enemies of social legislation but from those we were trying to help. As LBJ's policies were giving American blacks hope they'd never had, they found intolerable what they had once accepted as inevitable. Were we in a losing race against high expectations? Maybe, I thought, prayer was the only thing that would get the nation through.

.   .   .

Athough I had been turned on by liberal and socially active Catholics in New York, I arrived at the White House a traditional, non-ecumenical, Baltimore Catechism Catholic. I viewed religion through the lens handed me by the nuns in elementary school, the Jesuits at Brooklyn Prep and Holy Cross, and my parents. The church's fine-print rules and regulations set the boundaries for American Catholics at that time. I believed my faith was a gift from God and that the world was full of good people who did not have that gift—Jews, who did not accept Jesus as the Messiah; Protestants, who had split from the church; agnostics and atheists unmotivated by love (or fear) of God. For me, the Catholic Church was "The One True Church" and I was not about to provide any support to other religions.

For the most part, President Johnson liked it that way. He brought me along to every Catholic celebration and funeral he attended and made sure those there knew I was "Roman Catholic."[13] When he held his unprecedented meeting with Pope Paul VI in October 1965, he marched me into the meeting at the Warldorf-Astoria and beamed when I knelt to kiss the pontiff's ring.

When the President took me to Sunday services at the First Christian

Church in Johnson City on the morning of August 1, 1965, during my second weekend at the ranch, it was the first time I had ever been in a Protestant church, aside from visiting Westminster Abbey in London as a tourist.
I was rattled when the usher came around for the collection; it never
occurred to me to make a contribution. Sitting next to my fellow Catholic
Larry O'Brien, I was shocked to see him drop a $20 bill into the wire basket.
(He told me on the way out that he had nothing smaller in his wallet.)

Later in the service, the ushers passed a tray with tiny cups of wine and
small pieces of bread. When it came to me, I froze and uncomfortably
passed it on without taking either. Johnson teased me on the drive back to
the ranch, saying that the wine wasn't sour and adding, "Joe didn't even
drop a dollar into the basket." He then cited all the money he'd given to
Catholic churches like St. Francis Xavier in Stonewall, Texas, as well as all the
help he had given to Father Wunibald Schneider, pastor of the Stonewall
church.

Years later I learned how obvious my discomfort had been when I read a
transcript of Lady Bird's tape for that day, "We got off in a great flurry for
church, nine of us in the station wagon . . . I could hardly keep from gig-
gling—at least three Jews and two Catholics. . . . Father Akin's* helpers,
pausing in front of everybody, with the bread and the wine, would simply
shove it a little close, for a moment, until they understood the gentle shake
of the head. . . . Lyndon has certainly shaken things up around Johnson
City, indeed around much of this nation."[14]

As uneasy as these early brushes with non-Catholic religious services
were for me, I soon got used to them as Johnson took me along to a number of Protestant and Jewish services. As his Brooklyn aide, I accompanied
him to a synagogue there in House Judiciary Committee chairman
Emanuel Celler's district. LBJ publicly trumpeted my Brooklyn roots and
privately teased me for not putting a yarmulke on my head: "You won't get
dandruff."

Working on domestic legislative policy, I had a deep sense that we were,
as my parents and relatives used to say, doing the Lord's work, pressing for
racial equality and to provide the poor with things that most of us got from
our parents—food, health care, housing, education, clothing. I even gained

*Ray Akin was lay minister of the First Christian Church of Johnson City.

a new insight to the importance of protecting the earth that God had created; being raised in Brooklyn hadn't offered much sensitivity to land, water, and natural resources.

I saw my work on the Johnson staff as remarkably in tune with Pope John XXIII's 1961 encyclical *Mater et Magistra: Christianity and Social Progress.* While recognizing that "the economy is the creation of the personal initiative of private citizens," the Pope wrote that "public authorities also must play an active role in promoting increased productivity with a view to social progress and the welfare of all citizens." Failure to do so, the Pope warned, would pave the way to "political tyranny" or "civil disorder." Pope John XXIII's 1963 encyclical, *Pacem in Terris,* produced shortly before his sudden death that year, proclaimed that men, women, and persons of all races deserved equal rights. Our legislative drive lacked the evangelical timbre of the Vatican's pronouncements, and some of our methods might have offended the Pope. But I was sure we were waging the same battle.

I was working seven days a week, well into the night most of those days, but surprisingly I was rarely tired. I was exhilarated by the prospect of putting the thumb of the federal government on the scale for the most vulnerable in our society and, for the first time, putting muscle behind the rhetoric of equal opportunity for all.

Not everything I did fit readily into the contours of Catholic doctrine. As the President's chief domestic aide, I became one of his instruments for promoting birth control programs as part of the war on poverty.

Johnson was the first president to put the government deeply into the business of family planning at home and abroad. In 1960, the Food and Drug Administration had approved The Pill. Shortly before I joined the White House staff, the Supreme Court had declared unconstitutional a Connecticut statute prohibiting distribution of information about contraceptive devices and their use.[15] Although I had struggled with the use of the pill while Trudy and I were trying to conceive, I had not seriously revisited this subject until the President asked me to mediate a battle over the Food for India program before a state visit by Prime Minister Indira Gandhi in March 1966.

LBJ insisted, over the objection of many of his advisors, including Secretary of State Dean Rusk and Averell Harriman, that he would not provide food to ease India's famine until that nation adopted a family planning program that included widespread education about all methods of birth control and made available devices such as condoms to India's poor. "I'm not going to piss away foreign aid in nations where they refuse to deal with their own population problems," Johnson told me. Pressing his reluctant advisors, I put together a plan to provide some relief to India conditioned on its commitment to family planning. Johnson was able to announce during Gandhi's visit that "there can be no effective solution of the Indian food problem that does not include population control."

I was comfortable with my involvement—and got reluctant administration officials to go along—after concluding that, among the Indian population, Hindus, Muslims, Catholics, and other Christians could choose their own way of family planning. I reasoned that no segment would be forced to adopt methods of birth control contrary to their religious beliefs, but no single set of religious beliefs would limit the means available.

Johnson became an aggressive promoter of family planning. He accepted the first Margaret Sanger Award, named after the founder of Planned Parenthood, the nation's leading proponent of contraception (and an organization that my parents and I, and most other Catholics, viewed as virulently anti-Catholic). Initially uncomfortable, I came to the conviction that I had an obligation as a public official in a pluralistic society to promote presidential policies, including birth control, so long as the government did not require anyone to adopt practices contrary to their religious beliefs.

Johnson's promotion of birth control as a national policy, however, earned him a stinging rebuke from the Catholic bishops in 1966. LBJ typically wanted it both ways: he was "not going to deny contraceptives to any poor person who wanted them," but he sent me "to make peace with the Catholic bishops, because before long they may be the only allies we have on Negro rights and the poverty program."

It was my first experience of political negotiation with the bishops. I met initially with their lobbyist and liaison with the White House, Father Francis Hurley. We crafted an uneasy truce: if the President used the term "population problem" rather than "birth control" or "population control," Hurley could persuade the bishops to stay silent. Johnson kept his part of this bargain. So did the bishops. Even when the President signed a global agreement on the subject with the United Nations, because the words "birth control" and "contraceptives" were nowhere to be found, the bishops remained quiet.

During our negotiations I came to understand that the American bishops had their own political agenda. Throughout history, popes and their representatives had negotiated with nations, friendly and antagonistic. Indeed, the establishment of the Vatican as an independent state was the result of a political pact with the dictator Benito Mussolini. I had been raised to see bishops as above such secular stuff. To me, they were the spiritual leaders of the American hierarchy who came to parishes once a year to remind candidates for confirmation, usually by a symbolic slap on the face, that they were soldiers of Christ and must be ready to suffer for Him. Now I knew that it was possible to cut a deal with the bishops on political issues even where they held different views on the morality of the conduct. Throughout our negotiations, I had reminded Father Hurley, and I'm sure he reminded the bishops, that LBJ was doing God's work on poverty, helping the elderly, and promoting equal rights for minorities. I urged that they not attack and wound a president who, on balance, was advancing so many of their causes.

I felt comfortable pursuing a policy to promote family planning for those who were prepared to use it in order to relieve poverty in our nation and the world. I had no hesitation in pressing the Office of Economic Opportunity to push the President's family planning programs and encouraging Health, Education, and Welfare Secretary John Gardner to make contraceptive devices available to poor married women who asked for them. (In 1966, we knew that if the government made such devices available to unmarried women, Congress would end all funding for the program.)

In the course of these years, I came to question the church's absolute ban on contraception. Here, Vatican II's unprecedented encouragement of ecumenism—and its recognition of the significance of individual conscience in relation to conduct expected of a practicing Catholic—both influenced and relieved me. I read moral theologians questioning papal pronouncements on the subject. Parish priests were relegating the practice in many circumstances to a venial sin (if that) and rarely heard confessions of artificial birth control use, because to most American Catholics it had become a non-issue. (When Pope Paul VI issued his 1968 encyclical *Humanae Vitae,* prohibiting Catholics from practicing artificial birth control, and overruling a Vatican commission's contrary view, I agreed with the 87 Catholics, including some prominent priests and theologians, who objected in a statement published in the *New York Times.*)

.   .   .

In those years at the White House, I watched Lyndon Johnson become more dependent on the Almighty. LBJ attended services at the National City Christian Church in Washington or the First Christian Church in Johnson City. In 1967, LBJ went to Roman Catholic Mass fourteen times; in the last year in office, almost every other week. (His daughter Luci converted to Catholicism on her eighteenth birthday, in July 1965.) Over time, the President talked more often about seeking spiritual guidance from the Almighty and praying. I had a sense that he found comfort in his relationship with God, particularly during his final year in office.

In this regard, LBJ made me think of my own parents, especially my mother, when he spoke of Rose Kennedy as we were waiting for the train from New York to arrive at Union Station in Washington bringing the casket with Robert Kennedy's body, in June 1968. Sitting in the presidential limousine, Johnson said softly, "That woman has suffered more than anyone I know. Her religious faith is what brings her through these tragedies."

My mother said the rosary every day; my father by this time was going to Mass every morning. They found a solace in their faith that I wondered if I ever would experience. I certainly held firm to my belief in God and commitment to the Catholic Church, but I lacked their simple, total reliance on God and His will. Though I prayed, especially in moments of severe pain or high anxiety, and usually to the Blessed Mother, I did not share their complete faith in the efficacy of prayer. Mass on Sunday was one of the most important moments of my life, but more because I felt an obligation to pass the Catholic faith on to my own children (then just Mark and Joe) and because it was the only time I consistently set aside for them.

.   .   .

When Robert Kennedy was shot that June of 1968, the President invited me to accompany him to the senator's funeral. Then threats to LBJ's life streamed in. The Secret Service urged him not to attend and Johnson said that I didn't have to go because I had young children. I said I wanted to go with him. Though Kennedy's attitude of entitlement to the Oval Office and his treatment of LBJ as a usurper left me cold—and sometimes angry—I shared none of Johnson's paranoia toward the Kennedys. I considered myself a friend of Robert Kennedy and his wife Ethel, and I was greatly shaken by his assassination. Kennedy was a lawyer, anti-communist, pro–civil rights Catholic committed to social justice, and I admired him.

On the morning of June 8, we landed in the helicopter in Central Park. We were greeted with a report that a man had been stopped entering St. Patrick's Cathedral with a gun in an attaché case. The President again offered to let me wait for him in the park. I declined and walked into the church and down the aisle of St. Patrick's Cathedral with him. So many committed people—including my wife Trudy—felt that the shooting of Bobby Kennedy signaled the end of what was good about America. I experienced no such despair. I considered it important to show my flag with the President and to keep going, demonstrating that though a good man had died, the good work of others would continue.

.   .   .

The White House years took an enormous toll on my marriage. When I look over calendars for that three and a half years, I see that I was at the White House, at the LBJ ranch, or travelling with the President all but a few days. Even at home, I was invariably on the phone. No Thanksgiving or Christmas passed without some crisis that pulled me back to the White House or engaged me in repeated phone conversations with the President.

Johnson liked to review the budget and make his final decisions over the Christmas holidays at his ranch. One year, I arrived back in Washington about 10 P.M. on Christmas Eve. I asked my White House driver to stop by a Christmas tree lot on Massachusetts Avenue where only a few trees and no sales person remained. I picked up a tree, put it in the trunk of the car, and took it home to decorate before the kids woke up the next morning.

LBJ imposed a family planning program on Trudy and me: our two sons, Mark and Joe, were born in 1962 and 1964 before I joined the White House staff. From 1965 to January 1969 I worked for LBJ at the White House. My daughter Claudia was born in 1970, seventeen months after I moved out of the West Wing.

Trudy, like other White House spouses, came to look upon the President as a competitor who was taking away her husband and destroying her family life—and she was right. Moreover, as the Vietnam War became more controversial, Trudy, like many other administration wives, became an opponent of U.S. policy in Southeast Asia. On one occasion, she asked if I would help get Father Richard McSorely into the White House on a tour. McSorely was a Berrigan brother–type Jesuit[16] whose courses on nonviolence at Georgetown University were packed to capacity; he later became director of Georgetown's Center for Peace Studies. In the days when antiwar demonstrators were outside the White House chanting, "Hey, Hey, LBJ, how many kids did you kill today," I feared McSorely might spill animal blood on White House rugs or walls in protest. I refused. Undaunted, Trudy supported public protests against the war.

Her alienation deepened to the point where she declined to go to most White House dinners and other official functions; she turned down all invitations to go to the ranch. Initially angry, I resigned myself and accepted her disaffection as inevitable. I was so involved in my work, so consumed with its importance, that I largely dismissed her concerns. I would put off dealing with them, I thought, until I left the White House.

Trudy was especially close to her father, Dr. Edmund Zawacki. He was an extraordinary man—a psychiatrist and the administrator of the state hospital for the mentally ill in Taunton, Massachusetts. In the evenings and on weekends, he provided psychiatric treatment to Taunton residents for modest fees or at no charge for those who could not afford to pay. On September 14, 1967, Trudy's brother Bruce called me at the White House to tell me that Dr. Zawacki had died unexpectedly. I went home and told Trudy. We boarded the next available plane, arriving in Taunton that evening.

When President Johnson heard about it, he rushed a letter to Trudy in Taunton, recalling having met her father when I had brought my in-laws to the White House:

> Dear Trudy:
>
>   Lady Bird and I, and all your other many friends here in the White House, were deeply saddened to hear of the sudden loss of your father. I remember him as a warm and loving gentleman, so I can appreciate what his loss must mean to you. These are tragedies which eventually enter all our lives, but knowing this really does nothing to lessen our grief. I just wanted you to know that our hearts go out to you and Joe, and our prayers go with you.

The letter from the President became the talk of Taunton as her mother showed it to each family member and to numerous friends and patients who came to the house to pay their respects. I could sense Trudy cringing, however, resenting what in her grief she considered an intrusion and yet another infringement on her personal privacy.

I made matters worse. Immediately after the funeral, I returned to the White House and resumed my fifteen-hour days. Trudy was left at home alone with the children to deal with the loss of the one person in her life who had given her unconditional love and support. I didn't comprehend her loss at the time, and wouldn't until my own father died twenty-five years later.

With the death of Trudy's father and my chronic absences, our increasingly troubled relationship deteriorated even more. Trudy sought help and refuge in therapy to deal with her depression and disappointment. I took little time to appreciate her pain. I doubted the value of the psychiatric treatment she was receiving, especially as our relationship continued to unravel. I felt she was failing to appreciate the pressures on me, and I made little effort to relieve her suffering.

I felt torn between two powerful goods—family and the work of promoting the social revolution of Great Society programs for the vulnerable—and I was choosing work. With the demanding ambition of Lyndon Johnson and my own consuming conviction about what we were doing, it was impossible to do justice to both, and my family paid a price. At no time was the tension greater than immediately after the assassination of Martin Luther King in April 1968.

When riots and vandalism exploded in Washington and across the nation in the wake of King's murder, the President asked me to live in the White House so I could work uninterrupted throughout the crisis. Trudy remained at our house on Albermarle Street. Isolated there with young Mark and Joe, and our elderly maid, Emma, Trudy felt that I had abandoned her for President Johnson. On television, she watched hundreds of young blacks as they shouted, "Burn, baby, burn!" and set fires to buildings in their own neighborhoods. Coverage of violence and destruction in the district was terrifying. National guardsmen patrolled the streets around our home. Trudy could not understand how President Johnson could insist that I stay in the White House living quarters, with all the security in the world, while she stayed alone with our two children. Nor could she understand how I could accede to obeying the President's edict. I had no trouble understanding that I needed to be on hand around-the-clock to direct our response to rioting and civil disorder in more than one hundred cities, as the President had to decide to send Army troops into several of them. We were trying to hold a shattered nation together, and the challenge energized me; it depressed and alienated Trudy.

By Palm Sunday, the violence was subsiding. The President took his daughter Luci and me to 12:15 Mass at St. Dominic's Roman Catholic Church. I planned to go home that afternoon, when Mrs. Johnson called my office to invite me to have supper with the family that evening. "I'd love to, Mrs. Johnson," I said, "but I haven't been home since Wednesday night. I think I'd better go see my wife and kids."

"I can certainly understand that, Joe," Mrs. Johnson said. "But Lyndon and I are having some people he truly likes—Lynda, Luci, and Pat, the Brookses [the Texas Congressman Jack Brooks and his wife], Vicky [Mc-Cammon]—and I'd like you to be there."

I tried to beg off.

"Joe," Mrs. Johnson said, "this is going to be a nice evening for Lyndon. This has not been a good week. You've been bringing a lot of bad news to him. I want Lyndon to see you in some pleasant circumstances. You know Lyndon sometimes can confuse the messenger with the message, and I wouldn't ever want that to happen to you."

Touched, I accepted the invitation. It was a warm evening, with Lady Bird doing everything she could to relax her husband and saying some very complimentary things about me.

As I watched how supportive Mrs. Johnson was of her husband, I resented—fairly or not—Trudy's anger and lack of understanding about my staying at the White House, especially when during dinner I had to hand Johnson an executive order to sign, sending troops to restore order in yet another American city, Baltimore.

Despite the tensions on our marriage, I thought only once of leaving the White House before the end of Johnson's term. On a particularly grueling day, the President told me to give some background information to a United Press International economic reporter. LBJ wanted to point up the need to slow investment in capital spending, which was fueling inflation. "Do it carefully," he stressed. "Make damn sure there's no suggestion that we might try to repeal the investment tax credit or you'll set off another round of investment in plant and equipment." It was a delicate balancing act, and the wire service story suggested that the investment tax credit might be repealed. Johnson was at his ranch, but I knew he would eventually see the story. I went home that evening after midnight, expecting to be awakened the next morning by a Presidential explosion. To unwind, I filled a water glass with scotch and a couple of ice cubes and gulped it down.

Early the next morning, speechwriter Bob Hardesty came into my office to go over some drafts. "You know," I said to him, "I've got to think about leaving this job. My marriage is in a perpetual state of tension. And last night, for the first time in my life, I couldn't sleep without filling a water glass with scotch and gulping it down."

"Christ," the overworked Hardesty, responsible for producing several statements and speeches a week, replied. "I've been whacking down double martinis every night for a year to get to bed!"

By the end of President Johnson's first term, I had decided to leave after the 1968 election, no matter who won. On March 28, 1968, the President told me in the Oval Office that he thought I was the person to run the poverty program when Sargent Shriver became the American ambassador to France. I was stunned. I tried to control the expression on my face. I knew how impossible it could be to say "No" to this man.

"Mr. President," I responded, "I think I should tell you something. I hadn't planned to tell you until after the election. But I've decided to leave next year, even if you win, and I assume you will. I'll stay in this job to put together your legislative program. Then I plan to leave. I don't think I should start a new government job."

Johnson interrupted, looking at me as though I were crazy. "I don't want you to leave your job at the White House," he said in his booming Texas accent. "I'm just adding the poverty program to your responsibilities."

"Mr. President, for myself and my family, I've got to leave after next year's legislative program goes to the Hill."

Then the President said—"If I run again"—he would name me attorney general so I could leave government as "a distinctly independent man." There was no way I could accept the President's offer. I was concerned that my marriage would not last if I signed on for another term.

Mother and Dad, the honeymooners: Joseph A. Califano, Sr., and his bride, Katherine Gill Califano, on Atlantic City's boardwalk. November 29, 1929.

A sassy six-month-old in Brooklyn. November 8, 1931.

Seven years old, dressed for my First Holy Communion. May 26, 1938.

1955 Navy Officer Candidate School graduation picture. I would never be in better shape, and I would never spend a day at sea.

The "guns and butter team" in my White House office, searching for a way to finance the Vietnam War and the Great Society. Left to right are: Treasury Secretary Henry Fowler, me, Larry O'Brien, President Johnson, Budget Director Charles Schultze, Defense Secretary Robert McNamara, White House aide Barefoot Sanders, Council of Economic Advisers Chairman Gardner Ackley. January 3, 1967.

Making a point for the President's tax bill in the Cabinet Room. Left to right: President Johnson, House Ways and Means Committee Chairman Wilbur Mills, Council of Economic Advisers Chairman Gardner Ackley, me, Treasury Secretary Henry Fowler. July 26, 1967.

Whispering in the President's ear as he listens on the speaker phone in the Oval Office to Governor Richard Hughes of New Jersey discussing the race riots in Newark. The disturbances in that state were finally winding down. White House press secretary George Christian is seated. July 17, 1967.

For LBJ's ear only. I didn't even want my former boss, Defense Secretary Robert McNamara, to hear this.

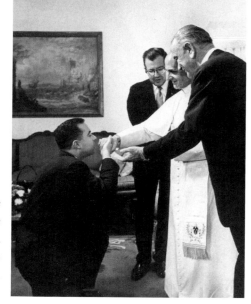

LBJ loved parading me as his in-house Catholic. Here he beams as I kiss Pope Paul VI's ring at the Warldorf-Astoria in the first meeting in the United States between an American president and a Pope. October 4, 1965.

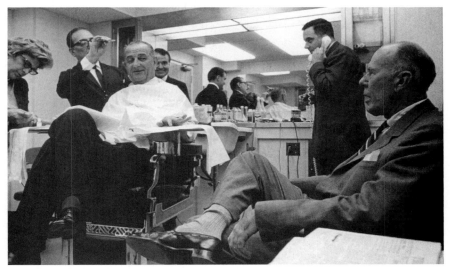

LBJ never stopped working and never let me stop. In the White House barbershop. Left to right: manicurist Mrs. Steve Martini, White House barber Steve Martini, LBJ, Jack Valenti, me, Ford Bell, Sr. April 26, 1966.

Four-year-old Joe Califano III and six-year-old Mark Califano with President Johnson and their proud father in the Oval Office. July 2, 1968.

Late on the evening of July 24, 1967, in the Oval Office shortly before LBJ ordered federal troops to Detroit to end rioting that killed forty and injured two thousand. Left to right: Army Chief of Staff Harold Johnson, Army Secretary Stanley Resor, FBI Director J. Edgar Hoover, Supreme Court Justice Abe Fortas, me, Defense Secretary Robert McNamara, LBJ, White House aide Marvin Watson.

After 3 A.M. in my office on April 5, the early morning after Martin Luther King, Jr.'s assassination. The map identifies fires then raging throughout the nation's capital, some just a few blocks from the White House. LBJ is in the background.

Three days after the Watergate break-in, announcing that I was filing, on behalf of the Democratic National Committee, a $1 million suit against the Nixon campaign Committee to Re-elect the President (CREEP). With me, DNC chairman Larry O'Brien. June 20, 1972.

As a lawyer I saw more of Capitol Hill than of courtrooms. At this press conference on July 27, 1982, the Speaker and the minority leader of the House of Representatives named me special counsel to the House Ethics Committee to investigate allegations of sexual abuse of pages and illegal drug use by some members. Left to right: House Minority Leader Robert Michel, House Ethics committee's ranking minority member Floyd Spence, Committee Chairman Lou Stokes, me, House Speaker Thomas P. O'Neil, House Majority Leader Jim Wright.

Counseling CBS correspondent Daniel Schorr during his September 1976 contempt hearing before the House Ethics Committee. Schorr refused to reveal his source of a top secret House Intelligence Committee report on CIA covert activities that he had given to the *Village Voice*.

With Alexander Haig, Ronald Reagan's controversial nominee for secretary of state, at Haig's confirmation hearing. January 13, 1981.

As it turned out, we both left on January 20, 1969.

When Johnson jolted the nation by withdrawing from the presidential race on March 31, 1968, he hoped to free the country from its division over Vietnam—and to free himself. But Johnson did not walk out of the White House a free and independent man. He was chained to the Vietnam War until he died. The Great Society programs we constructed and civil rights laws we passed, however, sailed on. Only at the dawn of the twenty-first century did historians—and Americans generally—begin to recognize how his domestic achievements had reshaped the nation for the better.

.   .   .

The end of a career for LBJ was the start of a new life for me. For three and a half years, I had been the President's man, completely captive to his wants and whims. Soon I would be my own person.

The war had taken a savage toll on Lyndon Johnson and his foreign policy aides.[17] I had a happier fate. Being young and being crowned by the *New York Times* as the "Deputy President for Domestic Affairs" positioned me as a hot commodity. Offers beyond my expectations flooded in. Ben Heineman, Sr., chairman and CEO of Northwest Industries, talked to me about moving to Chicago to be his executive vice president.

Lew Wasserman, head of MCA and Universal Pictures, invited Trudy and me to Los Angeles, where we stayed for several days in August at the Century Plaza Hotel. We were wined and dined at MCA's Universal Studios, and Lew asked me to start an education and training movie company. Trudy was reluctant. At dinner at the Wasserman's house with Kirk and Anne Douglas, Trudy became annoyed at the pro-Johnson conversation and got into a tense debate with other guests. Her anger reflected her fear that I would go to California and climb aboard another all-consuming merry-go-round. I was annoyed, in turn, at Trudy's dislike of the high-powered world I wanted to be part of. I decided not to go to work for Wasserman; Los Angeles was too far from my parents and my extended family. But Lew and his wife Edie became dear friends over the years.

Governor Tom Dewey asked me to come up to New York. On a Monday afternoon in November, I stopped by Dewey's office at 140 Broadway. The governor urged me to return to his firm, and the talk soon turned to money.

If I returned, I wanted to be at the top, just below him, astride the senior partners. He said I would probably have to take my place in terms of law school class. When I asked him to put dollars next to the percentages on the "sharing rate" list, I noted that Wall Street lawyers made no more than Washington lawyers—and it cost a lot less to live in D.C. I told Dewey I had no money to buy an apartment. He said the firm would give me a loan. I balked. He offered an interest-free loan. I balked again. He then said the firm would pay for most of a Manhattan apartment as a signing bonus if I would agree to go into line with my class. We left our negotiations open and I promised to get back to him. But as I taxied to the airport, I concluded I would not return to Dewey Ballantine or New York at that point. I had become addicted to Potomac River water.

The most interesting offer came from McGeorge Bundy, my former colleague, now president of the Ford Foundation. My four years immersed in domestic policy, he said, qualified me for a Ford Foundation grant to travel around the world "to help you prepare for more public service and get involved in world citizenry." The foundation would also underwrite my living expenses for up to a year so that I could write a book about my experiences with Lyndon Johnson.

This was an offer I couldn't refuse. On top of everything else, it gave me time with Trudy and time to decide my future. Bundy and I settled on a three-month trip around the world with my wife, followed by a nine-month subsidy to write a book. Bundy put me in touch with Evan Thomas, W.W. Norton's top editor.

Unknown to me, Lyndon Johnson had another idea. Within days after withdrawing from the 1968 presidential race, LBJ turned to building his presidential library and establishing the LBJ School of Public Affairs at the University of Texas.[18] He tapped me to brief potential donors. The President wanted me to come to Texas to get the library and the LBJ School of Public Affairs off the ground. Exhausted, not wanting to live in Austin, and desperately needing some relief from this voracious boss, I declined. I never dared even mention it to Trudy. LBJ tried a couple of more times to lure me to Texas, but I declined and he stopped pressing me. I heaved a sigh of relief.

Then I got a call from Ed Weisl, Sr., head of the New York law firm of Simpson, Thacher & Bartlett. He and his partner Cy Vance, who had brought me to Washington, were urging me to join them. Weisl informed me, "Joe, just between us, you should know that the President called this morning and asked me not to offer you a job for the next two years because you were going to Texas with him. He said he needs you to start his library and school." Within the next twenty-four hours, I got a similar call from Lew Wasserman.

Then Bundy called. "He's at it again," Mac rasped with a chuckle. "The old man wants me to make a condition of any grant that you do your writing at the University of Texas in Austin."

"What the hell am I going to do?"

Bundy chortled and promised that he would not add any such clause to the grant.

I called Weisl for advice. "Make up your mind as fast as you can," he said. "Then go in and tell the President that you've accepted the job you want. That should end it."

By then, I knew I wanted to become a Washington lawyer in the tradition of Thurman Arnold and Clark Clifford. I thought about starting my own firm with the young lawyers on my staff, but they needed independence from me as much as I needed it from LBJ.[19]

The Washington firm of Arnold & Porter held the most appeal. Abe Fortas had first recommended his firm in November 1966 (while he was a sitting Supreme Court justice), when together we drafted the President's message vetoing a District of Columbia crime bill as unconstitutional.[20]

"You've got to go to Arnold & Porter when you leave here," Fortas said.

"Why?" I asked.

"Because you'll make a lot of money," Fortas shot back.

As soon as I hung up with Weisl, I called Paul Porter, Fortas's former partner. "I'll meet you for lunch at the Madison Hotel," he said. I wasn't certain that I wanted to spend my life at Arnold & Porter; I saw it as an immediate safe haven.

Over a heavy lunch, I agreed to join Arnold & Porter as a full partner.

I was $13,000 in debt. Arnold & Porter offered an income of more than $100,000, and Paul Porter agreed to guarantee personally for five years mortgage payments on a house I hoped to buy on Springland Lane in Washington's Cleveland Park. Porter welcomed my desire to stay involved in public policy and Democratic politics as part of the firm's tradition, and he respected my desire to avoid lobbying.

"When can we announce it?" Porter asked.

"As soon as possible," I said.

"I'll have to clear it with my partners," he responded, but he anticipated no problems.

I told him I was going to inform the President immediately; if Johnson called Porter, he should say it was a done deal. We agreed that we would both tell LBJ that my decision would position me to help the former president in Washington.

As soon as I returned to the White House and Johnson rose from his nap, I told him that I had accepted a job at Arnold & Porter and was ready to be his man in Washington. To my surprise, Johnson knew the financial structure at the firm and wanted to be sure I was a 100-point partner. Without revealing that he had tried to derail my plans (I never indicated I knew), LBJ wished me well.

I was elated. In the short term, my years with Johnson had turned me into a highly marketable legal commodity in the nation's capital. Those years also promised an invigorating social life. I had met a small army of movers and shakers in politics, academia, business, entertainment, sports, labor, medicine, law, and journalism. Upon leaving the White House, I had a rude awakening. The A-list invitations declined to a trickle. Suddenly, I had to buy tickets to events I was once begged to attend free. Nevertheless, I had accumulated many pals in Washington, New York, and Los Angeles who continued to work and play with me.

The White House years had deeper impacts as well. My marriage had suffered, but the experience with LBJ had nourished a commitment to social justice, opened enormous financial opportunities, and taught me important, profound lessons.

I intended to write a book about Lyndon Johnson shortly after leaving the White House staff. But I was so emotionally, intellectually, and physically drained by those years and so tangled up in swirling images of successes and failures that I soon realized I had no perspective from which to assess him, those times, or even myself. I doubted my ability to see those forty-three months clearly—or even accurately record events in which I was involved. It would take a twenty-five-year hiatus before I could write that book.

With another decade of reflection, I can appreciate the immensity of the imprint this man has had on my life.

No quality of LBJ's had a greater impact on me than his courage. His means were Machiavellian even as he gave new hope to the disadvantaged. He fought for causes in which he believed. And he fought no matter how his perseverance hurt him politically. He fought for racial equality even when it hurt him personally and clobbered his party in the South. He fought to end poverty, even when the Congress resisted and some subjected him to ridicule. He fought the war in Vietnam—and that really hurt. Johnson passes with flying colors the historian David McCullough's threshold test of a good president, because he was "willing to risk his political life for something he believed in." Lyndon Johnson didn't have much of a profile—but he did have courage. I admired that quality—one in very short supply in Washington and in life—and hoped I would be able to display it when called upon in the future.

LBJ's determination to enact his programs whatever the political cost struck me most. He would complain, sometimes rant and rave, that this or that proposal would kill him in the polls, destroy the Democratic Party, or precipitate the loss of a long-time political ally or personal friend. But when push came to shove, he stuck with his commitment to provide equal opportunity for blacks, eliminate poverty, and level the commercial playing field for individuals facing the lopsided power of auto companies, big banks, and sophisticated marketers.

Those years also gave me an appreciation of the importance of tenacity, not simply in governing and in the grueling battles to pass controversial legislation or shake up the executive bureaucracy, but in virtually every aspect of life. I learned that what was worth fighting for was worth pursuing for a long time, taking a step backwards if necessary, in order to take two forward later on.

Perhaps most important, in those years I experienced a satisfaction that comes to too few people: the satisfaction of committing my talents and energy to tasks that I believed in. I had a sense of fulfillment that came from, as my parents admonished, "using the talents that God has given you in a way that will please Him." And I had one helluva good time doing it. I left the White House proud of the President's comments in his farewell letter to me: "You were the captain I wanted and you steered the course well." LBJ wound me up to be a social activist, to stay involved in the quest for social justice, and by action, example, and total immersion, he taught many skills to continue that quest.

He opened my mind and energy to a vast new world of powerful people, institutions, and concepts. I learned that to achieve a goal that challenged powerful interests required laser-like concentration; it was essential to detect the jugular of every ally and enemy relevant to success—and go for it when necessary. "Find out the real reasons why someone wants (or doesn't want) something," he often instructed, as he reminded me that those reasons were rarely expressed—and in many cases not even known to the subject himself. I saw that the key to making good decisions was in understanding every point of view, in testing arguments of proponents with opponents, and vice versa. I learned how critical it was for leaders to be surrounded by aides who would, as Johnson often insisted, "Give it to me with the bark off." I learned I could call anyone in the nation to ask for help or cooperation; at worst, they wouldn't take the call, or when they did, they would just say no.

To this day, LBJ adages stick in my head: "Sex and envy make people do more mean and damn fool things than anything else." "When you deal with ambitious politicians, keep one hand on your wallet and the other on your balls," advice applicable to dealing with many lawyers and corporate executives as well. "Don't ever ask a member of Congress to do something he thinks might cost him re-election," and "Don't ever send someone who has lost an election up to the Hill to persuade a sitting senator or representative to do something."

Those years gave me an appreciation that, properly led with drive and inspiration, most men and women can achieve far more than they realize. I came away from the White House with a greater understanding of human frailty and an appreciation that gray, not black or white, colors most controversial political conduct. LBJ knew how to persuade men and women by appealing to their noblest—or basest—instincts, or both. I left the White House a far more effective advocate. I also had a far better understanding of human nature.

To me the public legacy of those years was nothing short of a revolution that saved this nation. It was during those years that Johnson proposed and Congress enacted hundreds of bills that forever changed America, by establishing: civil rights and voting rights for blacks and minorities; the Head Start program for pre-school children; aid to elementary and secondary education; financial aid programs that made college available based on talent, not on the thickness of daddy's wallet; the first air-, water-, and noise-pollution laws; the public television and radio systems and the National Endowments for the Arts and Humanities; a raft of consumer laws; health care for the old and the poor; immigration reform, which reshaped the demography of America. The role of the federal government was forever changed; its expanded responsibility has been accepted by every successive president regardless of political party or ideological bent. Even Ronald Reagan would later ask for $10 billion to continue funding eleven of the twelve programs started by the controversial Office of Economic Opportunity. Forty years later, two of his outspoken anti-war opponents, Senator George McGovern and the economist John Kenneth Galbraith, concluded that LBJ's domestic programs achieved more for social justice in America than those of LBJ's idol, Franklin Delano Roosevelt.[21]

I always thought Johnson said it best in December 1972, a month before he died, when he released his civil rights papers at the LBJ library: "I believe that the essence of government lies with unceasing concern for the welfare and dignity and decency and innate integrity of life for every individual. I don't like to say this and wish I didn't have to add these words to make it clear but I will—regardless of color, creed, ancestry, sex, or age."

Did we legislate too much? Perhaps. Did we stub our toes? Of course. We made mistakes, plenty of them. Often, we failed to recognize that government could not do it all and to anticipate unintended consequences. And, of course, there were overpromises. But our excesses were based on high hopes and great expectations and were fueled by the frustration of seeing so much poverty and ignorance and illness amidst such wealth. We simply could not accept poverty, ignorance, and hunger as intractable, permanent features of American society. There was no child we could not feed; no adult we could not put to work; no disease we could not cure; no toy, food, or appliance we could not make safer; no air or water we could not clean. It was all part of asking "not how much, but how good; not only how to create wealth, but how to use it; not only how fast we are going, but where we are headed."

On the domestic front, I saw that by shooting high and working relentlessly we got things done. After sitting in an office a few steps from the President's for three and a half years and seeing hundreds of bills I worked on enacted into law, I believed I could do anything I put my mind to next.

CHAPTER 18

Recharging Batteries

L BJ KEPT ME AT THE White House until the day he left. Though he made it clear that he did not want me to get involved in the presidential campaign, I quietly moonlighted for Democratic presidential candidate Hubert Humphrey late at night and on some weekends, helping prepare speeches on domestic policy, including a nationally-televised address on crime, and working with Larry O'Brien who was managing the Democrats' campaign for the White House. Republicans Richard Nixon and Maryland Governor Spiro Agnew narrowly defeated the Democratic ticket of Humphrey and Maine senator Edmund Muskie.

On the morning of January 20, 1969, I went by my office for one last time and stopped to watch President and Mrs. Johnson welcome Nixon and his wife, Pat, to the White House. Then Paul Porter and I drove in his limousine to Andrews Air Force base to say goodbye to the Johnsons as they boarded their plane for Texas. Only a few people came to bid farewell, and I wondered aloud how this giant of a man would bear being out of the center of national politics for the first time in his adult life.

Two days later Trudy and I began our travel around the world on my Ford Foundation grant.

In Europe we visited London, Paris, Bonn, Berlin, and Rome; in the Mideast, Israel; in Africa, Kenya and Tanzania; in Asia, India, Hong Kong, and Japan. Early in our trip, while still in Europe, we got word that someone had fired gunshots at our home. The Secret Service and the FBI feared it was either antiwar activists or those who opposed the Great Society's racial desegregation policies. The Secret Service placed guards at our home and followed my children to school. Officials eventually discovered that the shots were fired by a man who had mistaken our house for that of one of our neighbors; the shooter believed the neighbor was having an affair with his wife.

Before embarking on my trip, I had talked to Bob McNamara, who had become president of the World Bank in the spring of 1968. Bob suggested that I pick a specific topic to investigate on the trip: "You'll go crazy just sightseeing for two months." I decided to look at student unrest. I had left the White House after navigating two revolutions—that of the Great Society in our nation and that of Vatican II in the Catholic Church. What I had yet to understand was the cultural revolution—the crisis of faith in traditional values and dwindling confidence in the integrity of our institutions—underway among America's youth.

Working in the White House I had been acutely aware of student unrest and anger. I had dealt with college students who went south to sit at lunch counters, ride buses, and march to Selma with Martin Luther King, who stepped up protests against the Vietnam War and rioted on college campuses when threatened with being drafted to fight for a cause they didn't believe in,[1] and who gave Minnesota Senator Eugene McCarthy his fifteen minutes of fame, morphing him from enigmatic dreamer into presidential candidate in 1968. Like other Americans, I knew of their actions, but in the frenetic life of a White House aide, I had never been able to pause long enough to probe the underlying motivations of these young men and women.

The other purpose of my trip was personal—not only to recharge my own batteries but also to try to revive my marriage. The endless cancellations of dinners, birthdays with children, and family weekends had taken a heavy toll. I hoped that our two months abroad would ease our marital tension. Indeed it did, leading to the birth of our daughter Claudia Frances, who was born on June 15, 1970.

My grant sparked some controversy. In February, while I was in India lunching with Ambassador Chester Bowles in the garden behind his New Delhi residence, an aide brought him a copy of the *International Herald Tribune*. The paper contained a report of House Ways and Means Committee hearings on tax reform and tax-exempt foundations, which were regarded by many as a major tax dodge for the wealthy. The story recounted the testimony of Ford Foundation president McGeorge Bundy in response to committee chairman Wilbur Mills's questions about individual travel grants that the Foundation had given to a number of liberals, including eight members of Robert Kennedy's senate staff after his assassination. Mills viewed those grants as motivated by politics—an abuse, he charged, of the Foundation's tax-exempt status. Bundy responded that the grants were "fully justifiable in educational terms."[2] Under persistent questioning by Mills, Bundy confirmed that Ford had given me a $12,000 seven-week grant to travel around the world with my wife.[3]

I told Bowles that I was sure Wilbur Mills relished the questions targeting me. During negotiations over tax and welfare legislation, when President Johnson became annoyed, he would needle Mills, who was at the bottom of his Harvard Law School class, and make my job harder by saying, "Now, Wilbur, you listen to Joe on this issue. You know he's into all the details of this and he was at the top of his class at Harvard Law." Mills's normally red features and bulbous nose would light up with irritation.

When I returned to Washington, Bundy asked if I could produce a report for the Ford Foundation. Fortunately, I had kept notes of the scores of interviews I had conducted. Bundy sent my report to Howard Simons, then editor of the Outlook section of the Sunday *Washington Post*. Simons asked me to recast it into an article, which the *Post* published on Sunday, May 4, 1969. In turn, Evan Thomas asked me to turn the article into a short book for W.W. Norton; it was published in 1970 as *The Student Revolution, A Global Confrontation*.

The interviews of students, professors, and others in ten nations overseas and the disciplined thinking required to write about them led me to conclude that students around the world and in our nation were experiencing a widespread and profound crisis of belief—one that went to the very purpose of life for large numbers of young people.

I found four major distinctions in the student unrest abroad: there were no black-white racial tensions at their universities; there was no drug abuse like that mushrooming in the U.S. and no significant hippie element; while opposition to the Vietnam War was common, abroad the issue was not aggravated by a draft, which in the United States alienated students and rendered universities reluctant to expel the disruptive ones; and adults abroad—whether politicians or parents—did not suspect that student unrest was part of some international communist conspiracy.

One similarity, however, overshadowed these differences: the common widespread crisis of belief in values, institutions, God, and themselves.[4]

As I recorded these observations, I vowed to do all I could to instill in my own children a set of beliefs and values that would carry them through their lives.

CHAPTER 19

Washington Lawyer: Arnold & Porter

W ASHINGTON LAWYERS and politicians have been bedfellows from the moment our nation was conceived. Of the fifty-six signers of the Declaration of Independence, twenty-five were lawyers. I had seen how Lyndon Johnson had used not only Fortas but Clark Clifford, David Ginsberg, Jim Rowe, and other attorneys as advisors and for delicate assignments. I had dreams of being used that way by future presidents and members of Congress. But my first taste of Washington lawyering was none of the above; it was a bare-knuckled dispute that almost destroyed the firm I had just joined.

When Richard Nixon took office on January 20, 1969, Supreme Court Justice Abe Fortas was in his sights and those of conservatives set on recasting the Court in their image. They had defeated LBJ's attempt to have Fortas replace Earl Warren as chief justice. Now they viewed Fortas as far too liberal to leave on the Court.*

On Monday, May 5, 1969, *Life* magazine reported that in 1966 Fortas had received a $20,000 payment from the foundation of Louis Wolfson. At the time Wolfson was under an investigation by the Securities and Exchange Commission that had led to his imprisonment in April 1969. Although Fortas had returned the check, the revelation of an arrangement through which he would have received $20,000 a year for life from the Louis Wolfson Foundation set off demands that he get off the Court. With Nixon's Justice Department poised to investigate him, Fortas resigned on May 14.

*When it appeared that Richard Nixon might succeed Johnson, Chief Justice Earl Warren offered his resignation in time for LBJ to nominate his successor. When LBJ nominated Fortas, Republican senators, eventually joined by the influential Democrat Richard Russell of Georgia, fought the nomination. Fortas was vulnerable, having received $15,000 donated by former clients for lectures he gave at American University Law School. Even more devastating to Fortas's chances for confirmation was his relationship with LBJ. After Fortas became a Supreme Court justice, Johnson continued to treat him as his personal lawyer and advisor. Fortas's equivocal testimony during his confirmation hearings heightened senatorial concerns. Unable to stop a filibuster, Johnson withdrew the nomination in October 1968.

Fortas expected to return to his old law firm and revive the name Arnold, Fortas & Porter, but a number of young partners objected. They drew their battle lines on moral grounds: Fortas had violated ethical standards and professional integrity appropriate for a Supreme Court justice; so flawed, he should not be permitted to return. The arguments became so heated and venomous that they stunned Thurman Arnold and reduced Paul Porter to tears on more than one occasion. These founders viewed the younger partners' reaction as selfish arrogance and ingratitude.

I was shaken by how deeply the young partners resented—in some cases despised—Fortas. It was a mess I hadn't bargained for and wanted no part of. The final battle stations were mounted when key partners met at the home of Norman Diamond on a Saturday morning, ten days after Fortas resigned from the Court.

We sat around a long rectangular table with coffee, doughnuts, and danish. Neither the emotionally shattered Porter nor the ailing Arnold was there. As partners began to speak about morality, ethical standards, and professional integrity, Victor Kramer, a short but powerfully built graduate of Harvard University and Yale Law School and a veteran litigator, stood up. Years before, Kramer had bluntly told me to stay with McNamara and Vance and it had been among the best pieces of advice I'd ever received. Kramer could not tolerate posturing. Now, he began cross-examining his partners.

He started with Abe Krash, who had succeeded to the first chair in the Phillip Morris account when Fortas left for the Court. Kramer drew out the real objection: Krash did not want to return to second seat. Kramer's rat-a-tat questions exposed the concern of several partners to be fear of diminishing their personal status, not their professional standards. Finally, he asked each partner around the table who opposed the return of Fortas if they would feel the same way if the person involved were Paul Porter. Despite the hedging, it was clear: they would never shun the affable Porter, who delegated client responsibility shortly after it stepped in the door. Fortas, who had cracked the whip at the firm and who preferred to keep tight control of his clients, commanded no such affection or loyalty.

I had entered the meeting knowing more about the chalk on Fortas's shoes from stepping over the line—and how much he had bent the truth about his relationships with Johnson during his Senate testimony—than anyone in the room. For that reason I had sympathized with partners who opposed his return. But when Vic Kramer exposed the hidden sources of the opposition, I decided to support Paul Porter's efforts to bring Fortas back. However, the issue never came to a vote. Kramer saw that Fortas had no chance. Finally, he said, "We're not going to change any minds here. But I want you all to reflect on the real reasons for your positions."

Thurman Arnold died six months later, on November 7, 1969, broken-hearted. Paul Porter's heavy drinking increased; he never recovered from this shattering split in his firm and the loss of his friend as a partner. Victor Kramer took a leave of absence to help found the Center for Law and Social Policy. He never returned to the firm. I realized within a few months that this trauma would sear the firm for many years to come and decided that for me Arnold & Porter must be a way station, not a destination.

.   .   .

By forcing Abe Fortas off the Supreme Court, Richard Nixon obtained a vacancy with which to promote his Southern strategy and play to racial resentment among whites about LBJ's civil rights policies. He nominated Clement Haynsworth, Jr., to fill the Fortas seat. A conservative judge on the Fourth Circuit Federal Court of Appeals covering Virginia, West Virginia, Maryland, North Carolina, and South Carolina, Haynsworth was regarded as pro-segregationist and anti-labor.

Senator Birch Bayh of Indiana led the effort to defeat Haynsworth. At his request I helped organize a number of attorneys in private practice to oppose the nomination. We wanted to sustain the philosophy and momen-tum of the progressive Earl Warren Court. The Senate battle was brutal. Despite lopsided Democratic control (58 to 42), the outcome was in doubt until we learned that Haynsworth had failed to recuse himself from cases involving several companies in which he owned stock. Armed with that information, Bayh led Senate Democrats, and some Republicans, to a 55-to-45 vote to kill the nomination.[1]

Furious about Haynsworth's rejection and determined to pursue his Southern strategy, Nixon calculated that Senate Democrats would be loath to take on another bruising battle. In January 1970, he nominated a conser-vative Florida federal district court judge, George Harrold Carswell, to fill the Fortas vacancy. The initial reaction of Senate Democratic liberals was resignation. Civil rights activist Joe Rauh and I tried to interest a number of senators to lead the charge against Carswell. We found little stomach for another nomination fight—even after two Republican senators, New York's Charles Goodell and Massachusetts's Edward Brooke, the only black member, announced their intention to vote against the nominee.

As Carswell's record became known, however, Senate liberals began to take notice. Years earlier, Carswell had said in a speech: "I believe that segregation of the races is proper and the only practical and correct way of life in our states." In Tallahassee in 1953, he had represented a fraternity in its fight to stay white only. In 1956, while U. S. attorney in the Northern District of Florida, he had helped take a public Tallahassee golf course private in order to circumvent a Supreme Court ruling that desegregated public recreational facilities.

Herb Block began sketching anti-Carswell cartoons in the *Washington Post*. One depicted White House lobbyists as used-car salesmen with a banner above a broken-down old car reading: "Used Carswell: Racist Model— All White Sidewalls."[2] A group of Columbia Law School students compiled a collection of Carswell's published decisions that revealed that he was reversed at more than twice the rate of other district court judges in his circuit. When Attorney General Mitchell belittled the students' work, they examined (in a non-computer age) fifteen thousand decisions of federal judges across the nation, revealing that Carswell was reversed a third more often than the average of *all* his fellow district court judges. The number of senators publicly declared against Carswell rose from a handful to twenty-two, far short of the majority needed to defeat the nomination.

Still Rauh and I could find no Democratic senator to lead the attack. Then the Senate confirmation hearings in March 1970 provided one of those major media breaks that can turn the tide in Washington. Roman Hruska, Republican senator from Nebraska, indignantly defended Carswell in these words: "Even if he were mediocre, there are a lot of mediocre judges and people and lawyers. They are entitled to a little representation, aren't they, and a little chance?"

I called Derek Bok, then dean of Harvard Law School and a friend who had graduated there a year ahead of me, urging him to help organize law school deans to oppose the nomination. An energized Senator Bayh held a meeting with Harry McPherson, Lee White, Lloyd Cutler, Clifford Alexan-

der, and me. We went over head-count sheets and discussed ways of influencing individual senators through their more important constituents and
campaign contributors. Bayh was in his shirtsleeves; our meeting reminded
me of going over head counts on Great Society bills with Lyndon Johnson.

Time was of the essence. Immediately after the meeting, Cutler and I
went to my office at Arnold & Porter and drafted a telegram to Lawrence
Walsh, chair of the American Bar Association Judiciary Committee, which
had been established during Eisenhower's presidency to review judicial
nominees. Walsh, an intimate of President Nixon, for a time his representative at the Paris peace talks, had been deputy attorney general, responsible
for recommending federal judges when Eisenhower had named Carswell to
the federal bench in 1958. Working the phones, Cutler and I persuaded six
leading members of the bar, including Derek Bok and three other law school
deans, to join us in signing our telegram to Walsh. The telegram was blunt:
"We are members of the American Bar Association who do not believe that
Judge Carswell meets the minimum requirements of professional ability
and judicial temperament to sit on the Supreme Court of the United States."

During this time, I had been talking to Charles Horsky, who had worked
with me on the LBJ staff on District of Columbia matters. Horsky was a
member of Walsh's ABA Judicial Review Committee. I pressed him on Carswell's lack of qualifications and the fact that many of us thought Walsh was
in the tank for Nixon. On March 25, Horsky wrote a memo describing his
meeting with Carswell on January 26. In that meeting, Carswell told Horsky
that he had been an incorporator of the segregated private Tallahassee golf
club. This admission conflicted with Carswell's sworn testimony before the
Senate Judiciary Committee, in which he admitted no such role. When
Horsky's memo leaked to the press on April 4, he became the first member
of the ABA Committee to break ranks with Walsh.

We tried to enlist all our important professional contacts, however
remote, to publicly oppose the nomination. Absent some personal advantage, most lawyers are reluctant to get involved in judicial appointment
political controversies in Washington. But this time, in short order, hundreds of attorneys, including some of the nation's most distinguished law
professors, bar association heads, former government officials, and retired
judges, joined in announcing their opposition to Carswell. One lawyer I
called was a man of considerable influence in his state; I hardly knew him

and had nothing to offer in return. He responded immediately, saying that he was utterly opposed to Carswell and was willing to do anything to stop him from going on the Court. I found widespread conviction that the integrity of the judiciary was at stake. Whether lawyers favored or disapproved the Warren Court's liberal opinions, they had respect for the nation's highest judicial body. Largely due to the revolt of the attorneys, the Senate rejected the Carswell nomination on April 8, 1970, by a vote of 51 to 45.[3] To me, the moment ranks among the finest hours of the legal profession in our time.*

.   .   .

One of the main reasons I had chosen Arnold & Porter was that I knew the partners would allow me to stay involved in Democratic politics. Neither they nor I realized how involved I would become.

On March 5, 1970, Larry O'Brien was elected chairman of the Democratic National Committee, replacing Oklahoma senator Fred Harris. The Democrats were in a snappish state of political and ideological exhaustion and irritation. Lyndon Johnson had enacted the progressive agenda, and much more, with his hundreds of Great Society programs. His all-out attack on racial prejudice put big teeth in Lincoln's Emancipation Proclamation, but at a fearful political price in loss of conservatives in the South and blue-collar whites in the North. His pursuit of the war in Vietnam sparked bitter opposition among the liberal and academic base within the party.

The 1968 Democratic convention in Chicago was such a disaster that two years later political pundits were still writing the party off, even though Hubert Humphrey had come within a hair of beating Richard Nixon (he got 42.7 percent of the vote to Nixon's 43.2 percent; third-party candidate George Wallace won 13.6 percent).

I was delighted with O'Brien's willingness to take on the thankless task of chairing the fractured party. If anyone could put the Democratic Humpty Dumpty together again, it was this shrewd, committed professional. From the moment I joined the White House staff in 1965, O'Brien had given me a

---

*Nixon nominated Minnesota judge Harry Blackmun to the Supreme Court later that April. Blackmun was unanimously confirmed one month later, and became one of the more liberal justices; in 1973 he wrote the Court's controversial *Roe v. Wade* decision.

crash course on how to negotiate the minefields on Capitol Hill. We had been an effective team lobbying for social programs and had become close personal friends.

On Sunday afternoons in the spring and summer when Congress was in session, I often went to O'Brien's house on Normanstone Terrace in northwest Washington. Sitting for a couple of hours on the terrace between his pool and house, we would plot out the coming week in Congress while his son, Larry, then a law student, helped teach my much younger sons, Mark and Joe, how to swim. O'Brien and I reviewed bills to pass, committee members to massage, and compromises needed to push the President's legislative agenda, and prepared for Johnson's weekly meeting with the congressional leadership. He was a team player who believed fervently in the ideals of the Democratic Party.

When Larry asked me to succeed David Ginsburg as general counsel of the Democratic National Committee, I was excited. "This is going to be a bitch of a job," he warned. "I need someone I can trust, who will give it to me straight."

"I have to clear it with my partners and Paul Porter, since I assume the DNC has no money to pay me."

"Or me," O'Brien said. "But let me warn you, there could be some heavy lifting related to the party reforms."

Good Democrat Paul Porter sold the idea to our partners as a "superb recruiting and business-getting device for the firm." O'Brien announced my appointment on March 21, 1970.

O'Brien and I knew major changes were called for. But neither of us realized how drastically we would shake up the presidential nomination process and stir the most radical reform of Democratic Party structure in its history, with changes as vast in the political arena as Lyndon Johnson had crafted in the role of the federal government and Vatican II had spawned in the Catholic Church.

In the wake of the Carswell nomination, one of my first acts as counsel for the Democratic National Committee was to take a hard look at the membership and procedures of the American Bar Association Committee on the Federal Judiciary. The committee was an all-white bastion of establishment attorneys. Lawyers like Walsh, a partner in the Wall Street firm of Davis Polk & Wardell and a man with impeccable Republican credentials, controlled the committee. Three days after Carswell's defeat, I wrote Walsh, ABA president Bernard Segal, and immediate past president William Gossett, asking for more specific standards of review, a more open process, and a major overhaul of committee membership:

> As currently constituted, the Committee appears to be singularly unrepresentative of the Bar at large in our nation. . . .
>
> We strongly recommend that changes be made which would provide formal representation to reflect the view of the thousands of young lawyers in America. The average age of the Committee is over 61 years, with only one member under 50 and five members 65 or over.
>
> We also strongly recommend that the various types of legal practice in which lawyers now engage (for example, poverty law), in addition to the older legal specialties, be given some representation on the Committee. Moreover, it is inexcusable that the Committee contain no representative of the academic legal community, such as a law school dean.
>
> Finally, we believe that the Committee on the Federal Judiciary can no longer be all-white. Minority groups, particularly the black lawyers of our nation, should be represented. . . .

As a result of that letter and other pressures on the committee, membership was changed to include minorities, academics, and a more representative set of lawyers.[4] Twenty years later, many Republicans would complain that the ABA and its Federal Judiciary Committee had become too liberal. In March 2001, President George W. Bush, bowing to conservative pressure within his own party, announced that he would no longer submit names of judicial nominees to the committee for their review.

·   ·   ·

Though shattered personally over the Fortas battle in the firm, Paul Porter never lost his zest for preserving the constitutional rights of unpopular clients and causes. At his insistence, he and I represented the Black Panther Party in connection with its application to rent the D.C. Armory for a convention in November 1970. At the time, a less popular client would be hard to imagine. We lost; the U.S. Court of Appeals upheld the Armory

Board's denial of the application. But the court admonished the board to evaluate such matters in the light of published "rules, or criteria, or guidelines." We had undertaken the case, as we wrote D.C. mayor Walter Washington, "as a professional responsibility in the belief that the right of peaceful assembly of any group of citizens was a constitutionally protected privilege and that the Armory was the only available facility which would accord these groups such an opportunity and at the same time minimize any prospect of civil disorder."

.   .   .

Several of Johnson's longtime aides had told me, "Once you work for him, you always work for him." So it was inevitable that within my first few months at Arnold & Porter the President would call on me.

During the final hours of LBJ's presidency, we had raced to approve a federally financed home for the elderly in Austin, Texas.[5] Its concept of "life care" was novel at the time: a senior citizen living in the complex could receive every level of assisted living, from independent apartment housing to full nursing home care. It was to be the first such undertaking financed by the federal government.

We had the Department of Health, Education, and Welfare deed a 26.5-acre former fish hatchery to the Austin Geriatric Center in December 1968 and guarantee loans of the nonprofit corporation that would operate the center. I had dispatched Wilbur Cohen, then HEW secretary, to Austin on January 19 to get the papers signed. The loans for construction were approved on the morning of January 20, minutes before LBJ left office.

On October 30, 1969, Senator John Williams, a cantankerous Republican pit bull from Delaware, moved to embarrass President Johnson and block the arrangement. Williams charged that government-guaranteed loans of $8.7 million to a non-profit corporation controlled by Johnson cronies* constituted an improper use of taxpayer dollars. Williams called for a Justice Department investigation; HEW demanded return of the land.

Johnson called me, saying that he had talked to Nixon, who had agreed

*Three directors of the nonprofit corporation were LBJ intimates: Frank Erwin, Jr., former state Democratic chairman in Texas; J.C. Kellam, manager of the Johnson family's broadcast stations; and Roy Butler, an Austin automobile dealer.

to let the project go forward. I was to work out the details with Robert Mardian, general counsel of HEW.[6] In a meeting the next day, I made some suggestions to Mardian as to how we could go forward with the arrangement. To my amazement, Mardian expressed concern that I was in violation of criminal statutes by representing a client in a matter on which I had worked in the government.

"I'm here to work out a situation between two presidents," I said.

"But you worked on this at the White House," Mardian responded, looking at a folder on his desk. "Your name is all over the papers about this project. If you do this as a private attorney, we'll have to investigate you for possible criminal law violations."

"Those conflict laws apply only if I were getting paid for the representation. If you think I'm getting paid, you don't know Lyndon Johnson," I said, trying to lighten the mood.

Mardian wasn't smiling. The meeting ended with his admonishing me, "I don't want to be involved in a situation where I know the lawyer I'm dealing with is violating the law."

As soon as I returned to my office, I called Bryce Harlow at the White House. One of Nixon's top aides and a political pro, Harlow had suggested I talk to Mardian.

"There must be some misunderstanding," Harlow said, and agreed to meet with me himself.[7] After we discussed it and I met with Treasury Department officials, HEW backed off, the Internal Revenue Service granted the Austin Geriatric Center non-profit status, and the project went forward.

In November 1970, Nixon promoted Mardian to assistant attorney general in charge of the Justice Department's Internal Security Division.*

.   .   .

Despite my intent to devote myself to litigating, I soon learned that corporate clients were more interested in my ability to negotiate the treacherous rapids of Capitol Hill than in my largely untested courtroom talents.

---

*Mardian was indicted on March 1, 1974, and convicted along with others on January 1, 1975, of conspiring to impede the Watergate investigation; his conviction was overturned on the grounds that he should have been granted a separate trial.

In the early 1960s the pharmaceutical giant Hoffman-La Roche introduced Librium and Valium to the market, opening the floodgates to a new family of anti-anxiety drugs called benzodiazepines. Millions of Americans, especially women and the elderly, began taking these presumably safe tranquilizers to combat stresses of daily life; Hoffmann-La Roche reaped enormous profits. By 1966, the Rolling Stones released their song "Mother's Little Helper," which topped the charts with its Valium lyrics, "Mother needs something today to calm her down. And though she's not really ill, there's a little yellow pill." In August 1969, more than half a million people gathered at Woodstock in upstate New York to hear performers like Janis Joplin and Jimi Hendrix in a flagrant display of the American culture of sex, drugs, and rock 'n' roll.[8] With growing awareness of the easy availability of dangerous and addictive drugs and the explosion in their use, Congress moved to legislate controls for dangerous substances. Inevitably, the tranquilizers Librium and Valium were targeted.

On January 28, 1970, the Senate passed the Controlled Dangerous Substances Act, which established four schedules for drugs based on their medical usefulness and potential for abuse. Schedule I covered drugs such as heroin and LSD (lysergic acid diethylamide) with a high potential for abuse and no accepted medical use; Schedule II, drugs such as morphine with high potential for abuse but restricted medical use. Schedule III included amphetamines and short-acting barbiturates with medium potential for abuse and some accepted medical use. Schedule IV embraced drugs with widely accepted medical use and low abuse potential, such as cough medicine with codeine.

Librium and Valium were included in Schedule III. Misuse or unlawful sale, manufacture, distribution, or promotion of drugs in Schedule III was a felony carrying a five-year sentence. Shaken by the inclusion of Librium and Valium—by far the company's most profitable drugs—Hoffmann-La Roche came knocking on my door. Hesitant at first to jump into the lobbying pool, I bowed to the reality of my "responsibility" to the law firm and my partners.

The company's general counsel, Ellis Anderson, a tall, thin, nervous Uriah Heep of a man with a neatly trimmed gray mustache, made clear that he must get Librium and Valium out of that schedule. "Lumping our pharmaceuticals in the same schedule with 'bennies' and 'goofballs' is appalling and unfair," he said. "It would hurt millions of patients who are helped by the tranquilizers." Hoffman-LaRoche feared that doctors would become reluctant to prescribe these drugs and patients would shy away for fear of getting hooked.

Competing pharmaceutical companies would benefit from keeping Librium and Valium in the same schedule as bennies and goofballs, so we couldn't expect any help from the industry. After convincing Anderson that some level of control was inevitable in the congressional stampede to stem rising drug use, I suggested that our best hope was to persuade the House to create a fifth schedule—one designed for minor tranquilizers like Librium and Valium.

We gathered research papers showing that use of Librium and Valium did not lead to dependency and that these pills were prescribed for patients suffering serious stress, anxiety, insomnia, panic, depression, muscle spasms, and back pain. The company argued that the drugs were not implicated in suicide attempts—to kill oneself with either tranquilizer would require a person to take more pills than most people would be able to swallow. So limited then was the knowledge of poly-drug abuse that questions of the tranquilizers' use with other drugs, including alcohol, never came up.

I went for help to Carl Albert, the short, affable Democrat from Oklahoma who had just become Speaker of the House. Albert had been the majority leader during my years with Lyndon Johnson, so I knew him well. Sitting in the Speaker's office in the spring of 1970, I was making the public health case for a separate schedule for Librium and Valium. "It's just not fair to consign them to the same schedule with bennies and goofballs."

As I made that remark, Speaker Albert stuck his hand in his pocket and pulled out a plastic container filled with Valium. "You talking about these?"

Hiding my concern about what was to come next, I said, "Yes," and began to explain.

But he interrupted me. "These pills aren't dangerous," Albert said. "They're great. I take 'em all the time. I couldn't get through the day around here without them."

With that I knew we had Albert's support for a fifth schedule. The legislation passed by the House in October 1970 had five schedules, inserting a new fourth one designed for minor tranquilizers like Librium and Valium, with reduced penalties for improper manufacture, distribution, or possession.

On the day the House and Senate conferees reported the bill with our fifth schedule,[9] thus assuring its passage, Hoffmann-La Roche's Washington representative Travis Stewart, Ellis Anderson, the company's general counsel, my partner Stuart Land, and I went out for celebratory drinks, fine wine, and dinner. The following morning, I told Paul Porter about the celebration. He said, "You've got to ask them for a bonus." I remarked that we had already billed them several hundred thousand dollars (a hefty fee in 1970 in Washington).

Porter's eyes twinkled and in his marvelous voice, hoarse from too many martinis and cigarettes, he said, "You've just put millions of dollars into that company's coffers. You've made Dr. [V. D.] Mattia [the company's president and chief executive officer] a hero with the Swiss gnomes. You've jacked up the company's stock. It's bonus time."

"What kind of a bonus?" I asked.

Without hesitation Porter said, "One million dollars."

"Who the hell can I ask for that amount?"

"Put it to Ellis Anderson. You just guaranteed his job right through to a fat retirement," Porter said, chortling.

A few days later I went up to Nutley, New Jersey, to the company's U.S. headquarters. When I finally sat in Anderson's office, I clammed up. I couldn't get the phrase "million dollars" out. So I simply told him I thought we should receive a bonus.

"How much?" Ellis asked warily, tapping the tips of his fingers on his desk.

"Five hundred thousand dollars," I blurted out.

"I think we can do that," he said, indicating that he had to check first with Switzerland.

I detected a sense of relief in his demeanor. So I pressed him, "We put in all our chips for you. I'd like to go back with a commitment."

Ellis smiled and said, "You've got it. I assure you. What you've asked for is eminently fair." He hesitated a moment and added, "To be perfectly frank, I thought you might ask for a million dollars."

Damn, I thought, Porter was right! He's going to tell me I've blown it.

Back in Washington, I went right to Porter's office. When I reported what happened, he said. "You know, you've just told it to me the way it really happened. At least you didn't do what most appellate lawyers do."

"What's that?"

"Most appellate lawyers have four versions of their arguments in court: the one they prepare, the one the give, the one they wish they'd given, and the one they tell the client they gave."

We both laughed. Then Porter said, "Learn a lesson from what happened. Next time give the one we prepared. Don't ever undersell your services. That's how we get the money to do good deeds."

Using delaying tactics during the administrative process, we managed to keep Librium and Valium out of any of the five schedules until 1973. In May of that year, however, evidence was mounting that suggested that Valium combined with alcohol might be implicated in a number of suicides and emergency room visits. There were also reports that patients were becoming dependent on both drugs. The Bureau of Narcotics and Dangerous Drugs was fed up with our tactics and eager to control these tranquilizers. It threatened to institute proceedings to put them in Schedule III along with amphetamines and short-acting barbiturates, exactly what Hoffman-La Roche most feared. We vowed to fight any such effort and tie it up in the courts for years. To get some timely controls on these drugs, the Bureau offered to put them in the schedule IV that we had drafted for them. With rising concerns about the diversion of these pills, their increasing street value, their involvement in more suicides, and indications of dependency, the company acceded to this listing.[10]

Throughout my representation of Hoffmann-La Roche on Capitol Hill, I had few second thoughts about what we were doing. After getting over my reluctance to lobby, my focus was on making the case for the client. I was comfortable devising the special schedule for Librium and Valium. I was less comfortable with the tactics in holding off controls for three years after the law was passed, especially when evidence of potentially dangerous side effects developed, but I never raised any serious objections.

In 1966, when President Johnson proposed the Traffic Safety Act to curb highway deaths and injuries, I had criticized lawyers who represented the auto industry and tried to block the provisions of the law we had proposed to require seat belts, padded dashboards, and a host of other safety features. I shared LBJ's frustration when, as he was signing a Transportation Day proclamation, he charged the industry's executives and lobbyists with responsibility for highway deaths and deplored the "blood on their hands." Was I slipping into the mold of every other Washington power broker, strutting my political stuff to fill my pockets with big fees and build a high-priced legal practice?

By 1978 the government would estimate that 68 million prescriptions for Valium and Librium had been written annually (80 percent of them for Valium). Believing it was safe and nonaddictive, doctors were dishing out Valium so promiscuously it had become America's most commonly prescribed drug; an estimated 20 million Americans were using Valium in the late seventies, most often to relieve anxiety.[11] That same year, Betty Ford entered treatment for alcohol abuse and dependence on Valium, which her doctors had continually prescribed for her painful arthritis. And I learned that most alcoholics also abused some other drug, commonly Librium or Valium, often because physicians frequently prescribed these tranquilizers to alcohol-abusing patients.

In 1979, Barbara Gordon's book *I'm Dancing as Fast as I Can* was a bestselling description of Gordon's agonizing withdrawal from Valium dependence, and Senator Edward Kennedy's Subcommittee on Health and Scientific Research held hearings on the misuse of benzodiazepines, with a focus on Hoffmann-La Roche's promotion of Valium. To this day, I wonder how many patients developed problems as a result of my lobbying to keep these tranquilizers free of stricter controls. I remember it as a dark moment in my private practice of law.

.   .   .

On April 30, 1970, President Nixon ordered U.S. ground forces into Cambodia in search of Viet Cong guerillas. Sending U.S. troops into a neutral nation—with no advance notice to a Congress where leading members of both parties opposed continuing the war—sparked a wildfire on Capitol Hill that rapidly spread across the nation and set off disruptive demonstrations on college campuses.

In a speech to Pentagon employees, Nixon assailed "these bums" on college campuses who "burn books" and "blow up buildings."[12] Three days later, national guardsmen shot and killed four students, two men and two

women, at Kent State University in rural Ohio. The nation was horrified by
the television pictures of students dead on the ground and by the *Life* cover
photo of a young woman holding one of the dead students in her arms.[13]
Many liberal Republicans and Democrats attacked the President for escalating an "immoral and unwinnable" war. Far-left activists advocated moving beyond civil disobedience to violence, urging that railroad tracks and
troop trains be blown up. Across the nation, colleges and universities were
paralyzed.

During my years at the White House, LBJ had kept me focused on
domestic matters with few exceptions. One had been in early 1968 working
with Harry McPherson on the President's March 31 speech announcing a
bombing pause in Vietnam and pressing for a tax surcharge (the same
speech in which he announced his intention not to seek reelection).
McPherson and I went to the secretary of state's dining room to discuss the
speech over lunch. It was the most depressing three hours in my years of
public service.

This was the first time since early 1966 that I had heard the President's
advisors in an intimate discussion of Vietnam. McNamara, Katzenbach,
then undersecretary of state, and Assistant Secretary of State William Bundy
sounded a chorus of despair. Rusk was pessimistic, exhausted, and worn
down. Clark Clifford, who was about to succeed McNamara as defense secretary, called for a "reevaluation of our entire posture in South Vietnam."
With the exception of Walt Rostow, Johnson's national security aide, no one
expressed a sense that any increased number of troops (the Joint Chiefs
were asking for 205,000 on top of the half million already there) would
bring a victory in Vietnam.

McPherson and I drove back to the White House in a state of depression.
I was physically shaken. Both of us were completely drained.

"This is crazy," I said.

"You bet," McPherson said.

"It's really all over, isn't it?" I asked.

"You bet it is," McPherson responded.

It was at this moment, riding in the car, that I knew Lyndon Johnson had
to get out of Vietnam.

Another involvement in Vietnam was in April 1968. The President had
me (as the designated White House Catholic) contact the apostolic delegate

to the United States, Archbishop Luigi Raimondi, to get Pope Paul VI to offer the Vatican as a neutral place where the United States and North Vietnam could sit down and decide where and when to negotiate. The Pope made the offer. Within forty-eight hours after President Johnson accepted it, the North Vietnamese suggested that negotiations begin in Paris a week later.

When I left the White House, and after my trip around the world, I decided that I would keep my public activities focused on domestic policy and on the widespread crisis of belief among American college students. As I struggled in my own mind to find some way to work with students, Nixon charged that Kent State demonstrators should have known "that when dissent turns to violence it invites tragedy" and Vice President Spiro Agnew called the shootings "predictable."[14] Students at hundreds of colleges, from MIT and Rutgers to Stanford and the University of Texas—cheered on by their professors—went on strike in the middle of exams. On May 5, the New Mobilization Committee to End the War in Vietnam called for a mass student demonstration across from the White House to protest the Kent State shootings and the war and paralyze the nation's capital.

I longed to find some way to give these young men and women a sense that our system was the best in the world. On May 6, Kingman Brewster, then president of Yale, asked me to meet with a couple of law school students who wanted to organize a lobbying effort against the war. Brewster thought their idea needed refining to make it realistic, but said, "If you work with them, do a little lobbying yourself and guide them, it would certainly offer a constructive outlet for anti-war energies on the campuses." Brewster shocked me when he added, "I fear that the students will destroy some of our major universities if offered no constructive alternative."

The following evening, I met with Greg Craig and Steve Cohen. They wanted to organize students to lobby Congress to cut off funds for the war, thus ending it. I told them that the Congress would never cut off funds completely, because it would endanger our troops. Moreover, such an action would allow Nixon and Agnew to excoriate the Democrats for refusing to support our men and women in uniform. These two young men, however, were persistent and remarkably resilient. They wanted to mobilize American businessmen and university presidents. They were clean-cut, decidedly mainstream and presentable. They bore none of the deliberately sloppy, offensive, shabby-clothing or in-your-face attitude of protestors that turned off many Americans.

I called John Gardner, former secretary of Health, Education, and Welfare in the Johnson administration, who had resigned in January 1968 because he felt LBJ could no longer lead the nation effectively.[15] Gardner was leaving his position as head of the Urban Coalition to found Common Cause, a nonpartisan citizens' lobbying organization that he would launch publicly on August 18, 1970. I took Craig and Cohen over to his office that evening.

We focused on passing legislation to restrict the use of appropriations, a constitutional prerogative of Congress. When I suggested that we concentrate the lobbying operation on prohibiting the use of any funds to fight in Cambodia in the air or on the ground, John Gardner immediately liked it. Craig and Cohen argued that to get students off the streets and into the halls of Congress the rider would have to be a total prohibition against using any appropriations to fight in Southeast Asia. Understanding that, Gardner and I agreed we could start there, but stressed that we should measure success by our ability to stop the use of funds for troops or bombers in Cambodia.

We cast about for a name and decided on "Project Purse-Strings." The effort became the key lobbying force for an amendment, introduced by Republican senator John Sherman Cooper of Kentucky and Democratic Senator Frank Church of Idaho, to prohibit use of Defense Department appropriations for any operations in Cambodia. That was as far as any members of Congress were willing to go.

Gardner and I then sought to raise funds for Craig, Cohen, and their band of articulate student activists. I called a couple of dozen business leaders and asked them to fund a movement of students with this mission:

We pledge ourselves to form a National Movement to:
1. Encourage Congressional and other government efforts to end the war.
2. Support candidates in the 1970 election who will oppose the war and who will work and vote to end it as soon as possible.
3. Work to make it easier for Americans to have an effective political voice and to make all branches of government responsive to youth and change.

We pledge ourselves to provide a constructive role for everyone who wants to work in this cause. . . .[16]

I was astonished at how favorable the response was. Within a day, Coca-Cola chairman Paul Austin, Hoffman-La Roche president Barney Mattia, Stanley Marcus of Neiman Marcus, Bernie Rappaport of American Incorporated Life Insurance, Al Stokely of Stokely-Van Camp, Ed Land of Polaroid, and several others put up the $15,000 I had requested of each. Edward Bennett Williams agreed to give the students office space at 1776 K Street, a building he owned.

Each of these corporate leaders was convinced, as I was, that there was real danger of losing the best of a generation. We feared they might turn into a rabid, persistently negative force in our society. Most of us thought Nixon had gone over the line in Cambodia, but even those who supported him (or gave him the benefit of the doubt on the Cambodian invasion) felt it was important to nourish a student movement pledged to work within the system.

On Saturday, May 9, some 100,000 students descended on the nation's capital to protest the war in sweltering 90-degree heat. They gathered on the Ellipse, spreading from just behind the south lawn of the White House to the Reflecting Pool, where the police looked the other way as they jumped into the water to cool off. A couple of senators attended the rally, but most speakers, like most protestors, were college students. The troops Nixon had alerted to keep order were never needed.

For several weeks—from May 13 to June 30—the Senate debated the Cooper-Church Amendment as hundreds of students and businessmen supporting Project Purse-Strings paced the halls of senate office buildings. In an effort to derail its passage, Nixon committed to pull all U.S. troops out of Cambodia by July 1. Nevertheless, on June 30, a skeptical Senate adopted, by a 58 to 37 vote, the Cooper-Church amendment to the Defense Appropriations bill of 1970, which prohibited spending any funds for military action in Cambodia on the ground or in the air.

Despite the students' lobbying, on July 9 the House rejected the amendment by a 237 to 153 vote. After six months of legislative jockeying, House and Senate conferees agreed to a revised Cooper-Church Amendment that prohibited the use of funds to support ground troops in Cambodia but did not restrict the use of funds for bombing that country. On January 5, 1971, Nixon signed the bill, which contained the first legislative restrictions placed on a President's power during wartime.

I had spent more time than my law partners liked that summer working with these students. I had gotten involved in order to help restore their faith in our system of government. In fact, the experience restored my faith in young Americans—their dedication, intelligence, and common sense— and in the responsiveness of our government. No savvy Washingtonian (myself included) would have placed a bet on passing any version of the Cooper-Church Amendment. As it turned out, these "kids" were less cynical about the system than I was.

I never spoke out publicly against the war, however, because I knew the pain such an act would cause Lyndon Johnson, and I considered that pain far greater than any good my voice in opposition might do. Media caricatures of LBJ as a blood-thirsty, gun-slinging Texan angered me. On more than one occasion, I had heard him express privately his discomfort over the war. I'd seen his tears as he signed condolence letters to parents and loved ones of men killed in Vietnam. I knew the agony he had suffered and how reluctant he had been to wage the Vietnam War—a state of mind that the release of the LBJ tapes thirty-five years later made clear. But from Project Purse-Strings on, I refused to do anything to support our involvement in Vietnam, and I did what I could to help those opposing it.[17]

.   .   .

Paul Austin, chairman and CEO of Coca-Cola, retained me to represent his company in Washington. Austin was a committed political and financial supporter of Lyndon Johnson. He had served as the vice chairman of the National Alliance of Businessmen, LBJ's effort to get private corporations to hire the hard-core unemployed. Though Austin was a socially conscious corporate leader, Coca-Cola, as a result of its 1960 acquisition of Minute Maid, became an object of Congressional fury over the plight of migrant workers in Florida.

In the very same year Coca-Cola acquired the citrus fruit juice company, *Harvest of Shame*, a legendary CBS documentary, exposed the exploitation of migrant workers. Later in the decade, Cesar Chavez organized migrants and farm workers in California to improve working conditions and create an effective union. He mounted a boycott of the California grape industry that attracted national attention—network television coverage, support of the AFL-CIO and the National Conference of Catholic Bishops, and the interest of Senate Democrats, including the Democratic senator from Minnesota, Walter (Fritz) Mondale.

Seeing pictures of California migrants on television, Paul Austin sent the head of the Coca-Cola foods division, Luke Smith, to examine the Minute Maid groves in Florida. Smith was so shocked that he came immediately to Coke's headquarters in Atlanta. The migrants, he reported to Austin, were living in conditions that "could not in conscience be tolerated by the Coca-Cola Company." Donald Keough (then director of public affairs for the company's food division, later to become president of Coca-Cola) and I were dispatched to investigate conditions in the groves and put together a program to remedy the situation.

We were appalled. The problems went far beyond inadequate housing and transportation. The migrants were illiterate. Families were separated, with parents and children working in different groves and staying in different, often unsanitary, dormitories. Mental illness, alcohol abuse, and violence were common. These migrants had never lived in stable situations, so having to pay rent, a phone bill, or any other monthly expense was foreign to them. What little they made they promptly spent, commonly within hours after they were paid.

Keough and I put together a plan of housing, transportation (buses to take them to the groves and home at night, equipped with sanitary toilets so the workers did not have to use the open fields), literacy training, social services, and health care. Coca-Cola met resistance in Frostproof, Florida, where it planned to construct the living quarters and establish its social programs. Other farm owners opposed the company's program, claiming they could never afford to match it. The town refused to provide water and sewerage for the project, so Coca-Cola had to install such systems itself.

Before these good intentions became reality, Mondale, chairman of the Subcommittee on Migratory Labor of the Senate Committee on Labor and Public Welfare, began a searching investigation of migrant labor problems. By early 1970, he had compiled a shocking record of abuse. All that was needed for a spectacular Senate Caucus Room hearing was a corporate scapegoat. When the committee discovered that Coca-Cola owned Minute Maid, Mondale knew that the world's most visible corporation was perfect for the part. He demanded that Paul Austin testify.

To set the stage for Austin's testimony, Mondale called a series of witnesses who described the sordid conditions and often sadistic treatment of migrant workers in America. A week before Austin was scheduled to appear, NBC aired its own documentary, *Migrant*, on its *NBC White Paper* series, which included disturbing scenes filmed in Coca-Cola's Florida groves. Testifying two days before Austin, Philip Moore, coordinator for Ralph Nader's Campaign for Corporate Responsibility, described workers in Minute Maid groves in housing with no running water or inside plumbing, an average annual wage of $890 with no health or unemployment insurance, crew bosses with the power to reduce salaries or fire workers on a whim. Coca-Cola had not moved fast enough to get out of the line of fire.

As Austin, Luke Smith, Don Keough, and I met in the boardroom at Coca-Cola headquarters in Atlanta preparing for the hearing, Mondale called. He asked me how Austin would answer a question whether farm workers should be given the protection of the National Labor Relations Act and permitted to organize. I promised to get back to him. This was the gut issue for Chavez and the unions. I wanted Austin to answer "Yes," because I believed it was the right public policy response—and because with the right answer, Mondale would go a lot easier on him.

We discussed the issue for about an hour, after which Austin concluded that he should support amending the National Labor Relations act to cover migrant workers and permit them to organize. It was not simply altruism that led to this decision. It was also the advantage of having the workers bound by a set of rules, especially when they were being led by such a charismatic leader as Cesar Chavez.

I called Mondale. He agreed to praise Austin if the executive supported coverage of migrant workers under the labor law.

On July 24, 1970, at 10 A.M., the hearings were held in the Senate Caucus Room in the Russell Building, the scene of many great Senate confrontations, including the McNamara muzzling-the-military hearings, which I had lawyered almost ten years earlier. As Austin, Luke Smith, and I entered the Caucus Room on that steamy Washington morning, it was so jammed with spectators that many were standing and sitting on the floor. A large number were student interns working on the Hill that summer, angry about Nixon's bombing Cambodia, dispirited about the four students killed at Kent State University that May. Many in that room had been among the 100,000 young Americans who had earlier that summer clogged the city to protest the war. Anti-establishment fervor, at a fever pitch that July, was palpable in the hearing room.

About half way down the aisle, a young woman with dark hair and thick-rimmed glasses abruptly came in front of me and said, "You sold out, you motherfucker, you sold out!" I kept walking, pretending to ignore her. Two and a half years later, at 11 A.M. on Monday March 19, 1973, that same young woman walked into my office at Williams, Connolly & Califano for a job interview.[18] It was Hillary Rodham, who was graduating from Yale Law School later that year. Neither of us mentioned the incident in the Senate Caucus Room. I offered her a job, but she decided to go to Arkansas rather than practice law in Washington.

Austin handled himself well and Mondale kept his word. Referring to a *New York Times* editorial that morning which recommended that Congress and state legislatures give farm workers the right to organize into unions and to negotiate and bargain for contracts, Mondale asked, "Would you object to legislation that extended these rights to farm labor?"

"I would not. May I broaden my answer?" Austin responded.

"I like the one I heard," said Mondale.

Austin went on to point out that the situation was so grave for these farm workers that they needed far more than unions alone could provide.[19]

Austin was followed by George Wedgworth, president of the Sugar Cane Growers Cooperative of Florida and president of the Florida Fruit & Vegetable Association. Wedgworth defended the status quo. He attacked NBC, the committee investigators, and the press generally for biased reporting on the migrant situation. The contrast was a big plus for Coca-Cola. To his credit, Paul Austin made sure that the Coca-Cola Company cleaned up its groves and improved working conditions for the migrant farm workers.

Austin and his colleagues at Coca-Cola were open to new ideas and conscious of their larger responsibilities. They also had the sense to get a jump on the regulators in those early days of rising consumer consciousness. In 1970 Robert Pitofsky, a friend and former colleague at Dewey Ballantine who was then director of the Bureau of Consumer Protection at the Federal

Trade Commission, charged Coca-Cola with false and misleading advertising in the very name of a profitable Coca-Cola fruit drink, Hi-C. Since the drink contained only the minimum daily requirement for vitamin C, Pitofsky charged that it was not "high" in that vitamin. The company feared that it might lose this valuable name and product. After struggling with alternative strategies for dealing with Pitofsky, I asked executives at the company how much it would cost to double the amount of vitamin C in the drink. "A penny or two per case," was the response. "Let's do it!" I said, and Austin agreed. When we met with Pitofsky and his lawyers, I was delighted to report that we were indeed making the drink "high" in Vitamin C by doubling its amount. "You've mooted the case," Pitofsky replied, smiling wryly.

Austin and I visited the head of the Food and Drug Administration, Dr. Charles Edwards, on October 15, 1970, to tell him that the company wanted to identify caffeine as an ingredient on the label of its Coca-Cola drink. Edwards responded that regulations prescribed a general definition for all "cola" drinks and that going beyond that word on the label would violate those regulations. Edwards refused to budge from his position, despite our arguments that consumers needed this information. When we left, I urged Austin to go ahead, to label the caffeine to get the jump on consumer advocates. "Let the FDA object," I said. Austin loved the idea. Coke started using its new labels. We never heard from the Food and Drug Administration.

.   .   .

At Arnold & Porter, as in other capital firms, we practiced the hired-gun theory of lawyering: everyone was entitled to an attorney and our role was to represent our clients' interests, not to judge them. As ethically acceptable as that theory was in the courtroom, I felt uneasiness about translating it to the playpen of Washington lawyers: the political dark alleys and back rooms of the nation's capital. We Washington lawyers represent not merely an individual client but often an entire industry or combination of clients—sugar growers, the housing or oil industry, or environmentalists. The Washington lawyer rarely litigates cases; he tries to influence the appointment of judges. Instead of writing to his congressman, he seeks to deliver a majority of the committee. He is not reviewing tax returns; he is helping write tax laws. In his private practice he steps on the brass rail of public policy every time he has an expense account drink or dinner. The Washington lawyer operates at the interface between public and private interests and is an active participant in the exercise of governmental power.

There is a sharp difference between representing a client in the courtroom on the one hand and legislative lobbying and informal executive and administrative agency relationships on the other. In the courtroom, it all hangs out on the public record. Ex parte communications between the judge and lawyer-advocate are generally prohibited. The public and its representatives in the press have a full view of the proceedings. A host of procedural rules protects the interests of both sides and governs the entrance of additional parties into the proceedings.

Lobbying on Capitol Hill is another, murkier world. Ex parte communications are the accepted rule, not the disparaged exception. Lobbying lawyers do not consider themselves "officers of the Congress," as courtroom lawyers accept responsibility as "officers of the court." Too often money opens the doors to the offices of senators and representatives desperate to finance their campaigns.

I was enjoying the excitement and rewards of being a Washington lawyer; prowling the corridors of power has a special edge. But the pressures to use skills honed in public service to lobby for private interests—and the need to bend my personal views to a large partnership—were beginning to wear on me at Arnold & Porter.

CHAPTER 20

Washington Lawyer:
Williams, Connolly & Califano

I N THE SUMMER OF 1967, President Johnson had persuaded Congress to approve a reorganization of the District of Columbia government that gave him power to name the first mayor and deputy mayor of the nation's capital. Katharine Graham, chairman and publisher of the *Washington Post* and deeply involved in local politics, had supported the plan personally (as had her paper's editorial page). Graham's involvement troubled *Post* executive and managing editors Benjamin Bradlee and Howard Simons, who believed in separation of press and personal politics.

Kay called me to promote her candidate for mayor—Edward Bennett Williams, the best-known criminal attorney of his day. In 1963, Williams had saved her from losing control of the *Post* after her husband committed suicide. LBJ had other ideas and told me to tell her—"Nicely but firmly; we need her to keep her paper with us"—that Williams was out of the question.

"Much as the President loves you and appreciates your interest in the district and your support, he feels that Williams is not the man for the job," I told Kay over the phone.

"I don't see why," she responded.

"First, he's white and the President wants to appoint the first Negro mayor of any major city. Second, Williams has no experience running cities. Third, he's been representing Bobby Baker,* who needs him more than the President does. And the President wouldn't want to be accused of rewarding Williams for that."

"Do *you know* Ed Williams?" she asked a bit huffily.

"No, but there's no need for me to meet him."

"I don't quite see how you can dismiss him out of hand without ever having met him," she said in her heightened aristocratic accent.

---

*Baker had been a top aide to Senate Majority Leader Lyndon Johnson. His conviction for income tax evasion, theft, and conspiracy to defraud the federal government was on appeal.

Kay Graham made no effort to hide her disappointment at the President's decision and her annoyance at my unwillingness even to meet Williams. Then she decided to take matters into her own hands. At several of her star-studded dinner parties, she seated us at the same table.

When I left the White House, she asked Ed Williams and me to join a Special Committee on Crime Prevention and Control in Washington. The district was the nation's poster city for crime in 1969. Businesses were leaving town; affluent families were fleeing to Virginia and Maryland. Many citizens were fearful of walking the streets, by day as well as night. Heroin use was soaring, and with it, robberies and violent crime. Kay Graham, along with John Kauffman, president of the *Washington Evening Star* and a member of its founding family, had formed the committee. Her request to join was a command for anyone with ambition in the nation's capital. Like Ed Williams, I immediately accepted.

In short order, Ed and I became close friends. We were both practicing Catholics and both Jesuit-educated at the College of the Holy Cross, and we both had young sons at Mater Dei, a school for boys taught by lay Catholics. Washington workaholics, we were accustomed to spending Saturdays in the office. Soon we began having lunch every Saturday, just the two of us, or with Bradlee, Art Buchwald, and other pals from the *Post*. Ed invited me to sit in his box at Washington Redskins football games, and for the first time since the Dodgers had left Brooklyn in 1957, I became an ardent and devoted sports fan.

I didn't share with Ed my discomfort about Arnold & Porter, my worries about the lingering bitterness over Abe Fortas, and the increasing pressure I felt to lobby for the firm's clients. Second only to Lyndon Johnson, however, Ed was the shrewdest judge of the emotions, strengths, vulnerabilities, and ambitions of others that I had ever met. He sensed I was chafing.

Williams began talking to me about joining him in early 1971. His firm was much smaller, less well known than Arnold & Porter. It was dependent on him and narrowly focused on criminal and, thanks to his partner Paul Connolly, civil litigation. Ed had a reputation for litigating high-profile, white-collar criminal cases, not tax, public interest, or corporate matters. I enjoyed litigating, but did not consider myself in a class with Williams or Connolly.

I resisted Ed's first overtures. But he persevered, and we had the same conversation on so many occasions that it became a refrain. "I'm committed to continuing as counsel to the Democratic Party as long as Larry O'Brien is DNC chairman," I told him. "That takes up a quarter of my time."

"That's a big plus," he would say.

When I said I'd want to be in another Democratic administration, he'd respond, "That's way down the road."

When I pointed out that I was nowhere near the litigator he and Paul Connolly were, he smiled. "That's the point. We'll be the War Department and you'll be the State Department. Together we'll be more powerful than we are apart."

Finally, over drinks and small steaks with butter anchovy sauce at a late March Saturday lunch at Sans Souci, Ed made his most persuasive case. "Together we'd have a real shot to get the *Washington Post* as a client. I'll give you a free hand to build the firm, bring in all the young talent we need. And your name will go in the firm."

We closed the deal on April 22, 1971, over lunch with Ed and Paul Connolly at Rive Gauche, another expensive French restaurant. With a toast and a handshake, we agreed to form our partnership and split the profits: of each dollar, fifty cents to Ed, twenty-five cents each to Paul and me. That was the arrangement for all the years we were together. We never signed any piece of paper.

I told Paul Porter of my decision that afternoon in a meeting that was one of the most wrenching of my life. I loved and admired this courageous lawyer who never hesitated to take on unpopular clients. He was a hero to me, a Robin Hood who took big fees from the rich and powerful not simply to live well but to amass the resources to represent unpopular clients and causes.

"Paul, I have thought long and hard about Ed Williams's invitation and I am convinced it is the right decision for me. As you know, Ed and I have become close personal friends. I want to practice in a smaller firm with a friend like Ed." When I told him of my decision and made it clear that it was irrevocable, his broad frame seemed to shrivel into his leather chair.

I also gently told him what he had so painfully come to accept: Arnold & Porter was not the firm it once had been, and I had joined—ever since the nasty dispute over the return of Fortas.

After a few moments of silence, Porter said sadly, "Joe, I understand how important it is to practice law with close personal friends, ones you trust, and to have an opportunity to build a law firm. But you tell Ed I'll not forgive him for this for a long time."*

When the story broke in the *Washington Post* on April 29, just two weeks before my fortieth birthday, the temperature dropped below zero at Arnold & Porter. A large picture of me accompanied the lead story on the Metro section's front page. It didn't help that the story read: "The move by Califano was described in legal circles yesterday as the most serious setback to Arnold and Porter since one of its founders and former partners, Abe Fortas, resigned from the Supreme Court in 1969 amid charges of financial impropriety. . . . He is widely credited with having brought back to the firm—long considered one of the top six in Washington—both corporate and public service business lost when Fortas initially left to join the Supreme Court in 1965."[1]

The move was traumatic in a day when partners rarely, if ever, left one firm for another. But it opened for me, and I believe for Ed Williams and Paul Connolly, the most exciting and satisfying years we would have as practicing attorneys.

.   .   .

From the moment we became partners, Ed and Paul were the brothers I never had. Of the three of us, Ed was the oldest; he was born in 1920, Paul in 1922, and I in 1931.

Tall, with the husky thickness of a former running back, Ed was the greatest trial lawyer of his day, the premier criminal defense lawyer of his generation. Ed had presence not just in the courtroom but across a booth at a restaurant, at any party, on the street. He was a penetrating and sensitive counselor. He gave his advice with humor, with grim foreboding, angrily, thoughtfully, sitting at the end of his conference table, in whispered confidence over breakfast, lunch, dinner, drinks, or late at night over the phone—but always, as he put it, "coooooold and truuuuue"—to clients, young lawyers, partners, children, friends and spouses of friends, and thank God, often to me.

*I remained close to Paul Porter until his sudden death in December 1975 as a result of choking on a piece of lobster while dining at Washington's Palm restaurant.

Paul Connolly was equally admirable: as decent as any person I ever met. He was a devout Catholic, Jesuit-educated at Baltimore's Loyola College. A Navy veteran of World War II, he was the first American officer to enter Hiroshima after the atomic bomb was dropped, an experience that indelibly marked him. Paul's integrity was a bedrock of our firm. Without preaching or patronizing, he knew how to pull Ed and me back when we lifted a foot to step over the line. He had no ego—none of the flair for publicity that afflicted Ed and me. He had the short temper of many Irishmen, but never held a grudge. Tall, white-haired, florid, always dressed impeccably, Paul was the style of the firm. He was perpetually telling Ed and me that we didn't know how to dress (we both wore baggy Brooks Brothers suits and rumpled shirts).

To younger lawyers, Ed was a figure of heroic proportions, bigger than life. I was the taskmaster driving the firm's hours and billings, recruiting bright young lawyers. Paul Connolly was the lubricant eliminating the squeaks.

We were three ambitious Catholics. Ed and Paul were all Irish; I was half Italian, half Irish. Ed was from humble beginnings in Hartford, Connecticut; Paul grew up in Baltimore during the Great Depression. Our parents remembered the "Irish need not apply" signs, limits on the number of Italians and Irish admitted to Ivy League schools, and the discrimination that kept Catholics out of the best prep schools and the executive suites of large corporations. Our parents had sacrificed to educate us. We cared about our church, about the Jesuits, about our often neglected families, and we had great times together with our kids.

We led a life of extremes—hard work, hard play. We were highly competitive in the courtroom, in negotiations for clients, and on the playing field.

We had a great partnership, and our firm began growing like Jack's beanstalk. Ed would say, "We're alive! We're alive! Look! Williams, Connolly, Califano! Where's Covington? Where's Burling? Where's Arnold? Where's Hartson? Where's Hogan? They're dead. We're alive!" We were hot. We were celebrities.

We believed that no act is so heinous as to deny the individual who committed it an aggressive advocate. We understood what it meant when the forces of government are turned on someone. We knew that once the prosecutors designated a client the target of a criminal investigation, or the indictment was handed down, we were working for the underdog. For the client targeted in those proceedings, it is the beginning of an ordeal often so draining that hardly any punishment can exceed the terror and experience of investigation and trial—and all the savage sidebars of tax audits, securities investigations, nights without sleep, days crowded with "if only" thoughts, brutal media coverage, loss of job, public ostracism, private slights from friends and acquaintances, and psychological devastation of spouse and children.

Williams considered a lawyer analogous to a doctor or priest who would never turn down a patient or penitent. He often pointed out privately and in speeches that a physician trying to heal an injured or sick patient did not make any moral judgments about his patient, and then asked, Why should a lawyer be expected to? Individuals who are under investigation or indicted are in trouble; that's why they come to lawyers.

To the contrary, I always believed that unlike doctors and priests, lawyers were free to choose whom to represent. Particularly in the halls and tunnels of Capitol Hill and in the executive departments, lawyers had some obligation to make a judgment about their clients. Our different views stemmed from our experience—his as a criminal lawyer, mine in government, seeing the enormous advantage of the rich and powerful behind the scenes in Washington.

.   .   .

On the afternoon of May 25, 1971, just a few days before I was to join the new firm, I had a call from Tom Fletcher, whom I had recruited and LBJ had named Washington's first deputy mayor, and who was now city manager of San Jose, California. His voice was frantic, his phrases punctuated by sobs.

"Heidi, my daughter, has been arrested in connection with a bank robbery and murder in northwest Washington," Tom blurted. "Can you help me?"

I immediately called Ed, who rushed an associate down to the woman's detention center, where Heidi was being held.

Heidi Fletcher was in a Mansonesque relationship with her boyfriend, Eros Timm, and a former symphony clarinetist, Lawrence Caldwell. On the morning of May 25 Timm and Caldwell held up the National Permanent

Savings and Loan Association on MacArthur Boulevard. As Heidi drove the getaway blue panel truck, D.C. police officer William Sigmon was killed, shot in the back by Caldwell. Seven minutes later, police closed in on the truck. Heidi was still driving. All three were arrested.

Tom Fletcher flew in from San Jose the next evening. He wanted to see his daughter and be present at her arraignment. The arraignment was brief. Heidi faced a felony murder charge. The prosecutor said he would seek the death penalty.

The sidewalk outside the federal courthouse on Third Street off Constitution Avenue, one block from the Capitol, is unusually wide. As we left after the arraignment, I pressed Tom to come with me directly to the car at the curb. He refused, saying that he wanted to show his support for his daughter. I'd seen many journalistic melees during my years at the Pentagon and White House, but I was not prepared for what happened.

Fletcher stepped up to the microphones just outside the door, eyes swollen from a sleepless night of crying, and said, "The only thing I can say is I'm here to support my daughter. We love her. I'd like to have her with us. I love her very much."[2]

He burst into uncontrollable sobbing. I took Tom's arm, pulling him rapidly toward our waiting sedan. As I nudged his elbow to speed up, one of the reporters shouted to his television technician, who held a long pole with a microphone at the end, "Get it above his head! Get the sobs! Get the sobs!"

The case attracted enormous attention. Senator Thomas Eagleton, then chair of the Senate District of Columbia Committee, introduced legislation to provide payment for widows of district policemen killed in action. Because Ed Williams feared that public hearings on the bill could hurt Heidi's chances in court, I asked Senator Eagleton to postpone the hearings to preserve Heidi's right to a fair trial.[3] He agreed, and Ed said, "See what I mean? We're better as a team than separately!"

Heidi's best hope was to plead guilty of murder and armed robbery before her twenty-second birthday, which would make her eligible for a lesser sentence under the Youth Corrections Act. If tried as an adult, she would be subject to the death penalty.

Williams and I met with a shattered Tom Fletcher. For most of his daughter's life, he said, he had been either a city manager or deputy mayor. "These are the most demanding jobs in the country," he said. His description of his life for many years confirmed it: an endless round of funerals, fires, break-

fasts, dinners, weddings, baptisms, bar mitzvahs, store openings, gradua-
tions, anniversaries. "I was just never home. Never there for Heidi," Fletcher
said again and again. He was the greatest city manager in the nation, I
thought. That's why we picked him to be the deputy mayor of Washington.
But the price of being the greatest city manager in the nation and the first
deputy mayor of the nation's capital was to be an AWOL father. I couldn't
help thinking about my own years on the White House staff and how hard
I was now working to build our law firm. I said a silent prayer that nothing
like this would happen to my own children (but I didn't trim back my work
at the firm).

Williams said to Fletcher, "Well, you have your chance now—if you're
willing to take the stand and say publicly what you've been telling Joe and
me." I could see the agony on Tom's face.

"What I'm asking is that you confess publicly that you have been a miserable excuse of a father to Heidi. That's the only way I can help your daughter." Ed kept his eyes locked on Fletcher.

Sagging in his chair, Tom's eyes filled with tears. "I'll do it."

On December 15, 1971, a week before her twenty-second birthday, Heidi
Fletcher pled guilty to ten counts of first degree murder, armed robbery, and
illegal possession of dangerous weapons. Ed put Tom Fletcher on the stand.
Then he made his case to Judge June Green.

Our biggest concern was that Heidi was a white girl represented by the
nation's top criminal attorney, also white, in a predominantly black city. Ed
turned the issue on its head: "Your honor, all I ask is that you not discrimi-
nate against Heidi because she is white and her father is prominent. All I ask
is that you treat her as you would treat any poor black girl who came before
this court, twisted and used by two older, Mansonesque characters. Treat
her the way you would treat a poor black girl in the district."

It worked. Judge June Green gave Heidi the maximum sentence under
the Youth Corrections Act—nine years with the possibility of release any
time before then. Heidi was sent to Terminal Island near Los Angeles, so that
she could be near her parents, who could help in her rehabilitation. Ironically, Tom Fletcher would have a chance now to establish the kind of
parental relationship he had so far denied his daughter.[4]

Heidi's first request for parole was denied in 1972. She was caught smoking marijuana. I went out to Terminal Island to see her and lay the ground-
work for a successful parole hearing the next time around. I flew to Los

Angeles and got into a limousine for the drive to the Terminal Island facility. Because I had never been to Watts, I asked the driver to take me around the area before going to the prison. After visiting Watts, he kept asking me whether I wanted to stop for coffee, buns, or a meal. I repeatedly declined.

When we got to Terminal Island, I got out of the limo. He started to drive away. I hailed him back.

"Wait for me," I said.

"Sorry," he said. "I thought you was going to stay here awhile."

"How the hell could you think that? I'm just going to visit a client."

"Mr. Califano," he said, lingering on the name, "when you had me drive you through Watts, I thought you was looking over your drug and numbers sites."

It's the only time in my life I felt ethnically profiled.

.   .   .

From the moment we became partners, Williams and I shared one great ambition: to be the lawyers for the *Washington Post*. The first opportunity came less than two weeks after I had joined the firm.

In 1971, the *Washington Post* was rising in readership. It was poised to surpass the circulation of the *Washington Star*.* Kay Graham, still less than a decade into her role as the paper's owner and the only woman of such power in Washington, had decided to take the company public.[5] The paper was at a crucial, potentially vulnerable point, financially and journalistically.

On June 13, 1971, I read in the *New York Times* the first story based on the leaked Pentagon Papers, forty-seven volumes of documents and narratives tracing the nation's path into the Vietnam War. Secretary of Defense Robert McNamara secretly had them assembled to help future policymakers understand how we got into the war that would torture him for the rest of his life.

I knew the Nixon administration would be outraged and so would *Post* editor Ben Bradlee—for different reasons. Publication set off a surge of White House efforts, including wiretaps and formation of what would be known as "the plumbers," to stop leaks of classified information. The ad-

*In Washington, there were three papers at the time: the morning *Post*, *Evening Star*, and tabloid *Daily News*, with the *Star* leading in circulation.

ministration sued the *New York Times* to enjoin further publication. Bradlee was furious that he did not have the Pentagon Papers. He charged street-smart reporter Ben Bagdikian to get a set, "whatever it takes." Bagdikian delivered.

Bradlee wanted to publish immediately, especially since the *Times* had been temporarily restrained from further publication. The *Post* lawyers at Royall, Koegel & Wells advised awaiting the final outcome of the government suit against the *Times*. Since Daniel Ellsberg, who had given the papers to the *Times*, was also Bagdikian's source, the lawyers feared the *Post* would be held in contempt for colluding with the *Times*.

Bradlee called Williams, who was in Chicago, representing former McDonald's president Harry Sonneborn in a bitterly contested civil fraud case arising out of his divorce settlement. To Ed the decision was easy: "Publish."

Bolstered in what he was determined to do anyway, Bradlee persuaded Kay Graham to let him go with the first story, but they both expected trouble.

Seeing the *Post* story on June 18, the Nixon administration asked Bradlee to refrain from continuing the series until the Supreme Court had ruled in the *Times* case. Bradlee was not about to be the wagging tail of the *Times* litigation. He "respectfully refused," and the government sued that day to stop further stories.

Federal District Judge Gerhard Gesell declined to block publication at 8:05 P.M. The government rushed to the Court of Appeals, which issued a restraining order at 1:20 A.M. on the morning of June 19, but permitted the *Post* to deliver papers already on the street.

Unhappy with "the fancy-pants lawyer from New York"—the Rogers firm had sent William Glendon, a litigator with no previous experience on *Post* or First Amendment matters—Bradlee agitated for Kay Graham to hire Williams to argue the *Post* case in the Court of Appeals and the Supreme Court. Bradlee called Ed to ask him if he would take the case.

It was our big chance to get the *Post* as a client. But Ed was in the middle of a major trial in Chicago, so he called me. "I can't break my commitment to this guy," he moaned. "Every trial has a rhythm. This is a tough case before a jury. I've got to stay with it if my guy is going to have any chance. If only this guy had taken my advice to settle."[6]

We both agonized. Then Ed came up with an idea: "Maybe I can sell them on you writing the brief and I'll get a stay of a day or two here and come in and argue the case."

Before I could respond, he hung up. He called me back a few minutes later. "I think Bradlee might go along with your doing the brief and me arguing the case."

But I was preparing to try a case before the Interstate Commerce Commission in Oklahoma City. We finally concluded that Ed had to call off Bradlee and tell him we couldn't do a first-class job. On June 30, the Supreme Court decided in favor of the press and publication of the Pentagon Papers resumed.[7]

Ed and I thought we had lost our best chance to represent the *Post*. Then, in December, Kay Graham asked Ed to come over to her office. She thought it made sense to have the *Post* represented by our firm, which was based in Washington, rather than a New York firm with a branch office in Washington. There was one condition: since we did not have an experienced libel lawyer, she wanted us to hire Roger Clark from the Washington office of the Royall firm.

Ed returned to the office and called me immediately. "Let's go to Duke's for drinks and dinner. Now. I've got something to tell you."

As soon as he had taken a sip—more like a gulp—of his gin martini, Ed said, "She offered us the *Post* this afternoon, and I've got to tell you, I think I've blown it again."

"What happened?"

Ed recounted Katharine Graham's conversation, saying, "I told her that we wanted to represent the paper, but that we decide who we hire as lawyers. No one tells her what to print and no client can tell us who to hire."

"So, what'd she say?"

"She said she'd have to think about that. She'll talk to Fritz Beebe"—a former Cravath, Swaine and Moore lawyer who in 1961 had become chairman of the Washington Post Company and Kay Graham's key financial advisor—"and let me know."

We both worried that Beebe would favor having the *Post* represented by a Wall Street firm.

A week later, Ed barged into my office just before lunch. "Let's get Paul and celebrate," he said. "We've got the *Post* on our terms!"

"Fantastic!" I shouted. But I had no idea how fantastic it was going to be.

. . .

In the spring of 1971, incidents of brutality by American officers and non-coms in Vietnam were the stuff of front-page headlines. On March 31, Lieutenant William Calley was sentenced to life at hard labor after his conviction for leading the slaughter of several hundred unarmed men, women, and children in a Vietnamese village. The My Lai massacre, as the incident became known, was but one, though perhaps the worst, of several incidents of improper conduct by American soldiers in Southeast Asia.[8]

Disgusted by the lack of self-control this incident and others revealed, Army colonel David Hackworth spoke out in an interview for ABC's *Issues and Answers* that aired on June 27, 1971. He pulled no punches about the conduct of some officers and soldiers in Vietnam, charging that "great mistakes were made because of improper training" by the U.S. Army.[9] The interview infuriated Army brass, including Chief of Staff General William Westmoreland, who had commanded U.S. forces in Vietnam from 1964 through 1968.

Hackworth was a soldier's soldier. He lied about his age during World War II, first to join the merchant marine at fourteen and then to enlist in the Army at fifteen. While serving in Korea, he was wounded four times, once taking a bullet in his head. During the 1960s, Hackworth served repeated combat tours in Vietnam, where he was wounded on several occasions and accumulated a full breast of medals.

By the time his interview aired, Hackworth had put in for retirement, but angry Army generals were determined to punish him and set an example to discourage others from speaking out. A team of Army criminal investigators descended on Hackworth's headquarters at Cao Lanh near the Cambodian border to search his records. Shortly thereafter, Hackworth went on leave to travel along his way back to the United States to retire.

Throughout his trip home, including a stopover in Australia, Army criminal investigators followed Hackworth. They tailed him as he drove across the country from California to Washington, where he arrived on August 23, three days after Nixon had reduced Calley's sentence. Concerned about constant Army surveillance, Hackworth contacted Ward Just, whom he had met when Just was covering the Vietnam War for the *Washington Post*. Just called me, vouched for Hackworth, and asked me to help the Army colonel.

A few minutes later Hackworth called me from a pay phone. He said he was being watched as he was calling; he believed that his motel phone was tapped by Army criminal investigators trying to get something on him before he retired. I told Hackworth to get some sleep and lie low until we met.

The next morning, two Army criminal investigators banged on the door of Hackworth's motel room. When Hackworth opened it, they told him that his leave had been cancelled and his request for retirement denied. He was being ordered to return to Vietnam. He was to report immediately to Walter Reed Hospital.

Hackworth called me. I told him under no circumstances was he to go to Walter Reed Hospital. "You can't go there," I said. "We have no idea what they want to do to you. For all we know they'll give you a prefrontal lobotomy."

"What about the orders to Vietnam?" Hackworth asked.

Both of us feared that they wanted him in Vietnam to put him in a situation where he would be killed.

"Tell them I'm your lawyer and I told you that if you go to Vietnam you'll be taking me with you."

He did and later that day the Army assigned him to Fort Meade, outside Washington in nearby Maryland.

Army investigators continued to trail Hackworth wherever he went, including his visit to my office, where they ostentatiously waited outside the building. Seeing his exasperation, I told Hackworth that I would have the surveillance stopped that evening, even if we had to go to court for an emergency restraining order against the Army.

But we never had to.

In the face of our threat to go public and take the case to court, the Army blinked. Fearful of media scrutiny—Hackworth had earned eight Purple Hearts and nine Silver Stars, among other decorations—newly installed Army Secretary Robert Froehlke ordered that Hackworth be permitted to retire with the honor his heroism and career deserved. As soon as the Army informed me, I told Hackworth to fill out his retirement papers at Fort Meade.[10]

Only three months into our law practice together, I could see Ed's vision was taking shape. As the "State Department," I had killed the government's move to get Hackworth without resorting to the courtroom. The experience left me with an ominous sense of foreboding, however, about the tone that Nixon and Agnew were setting. They seemed callous about the killings at Kent State; the President had defiantly reduced Calley's sentence. If the Army brass thought they could harass the nation's most decorated active-duty officer with impunity, how would other military and federal law enforcement officers treat other voices of dissent?

.   .   .

On December 15, 1971, a grand jury indicted federal Court of Appeals judge Otto Kerner on charges of fraud, bribery, conspiracy, and income tax evasion arising from his purchase and sale of racetrack stock while gover-nor of Illinois. The government charged that in exchange for the money that Kerner made on the transaction, he had assigned the track prime dates, such as holiday weekends, for its races.

Two days later Ben Heineman, chairman of Northwest Industries, called me to say he had urged Kerner to retain Ed Williams to represent him. Heineman thought it important for Ed to take the case "both in Otto Kerner's interest and in the interest of the Democratic Party in Illinois."[11]

Kerner flew into Washington to meet with Williams and me on Wednes-day, December 29. As Kerner recounted his recollection of what had hap-pened, I thought back to my final night in the White House, January 19, 1969, at LBJ's party for his immediate staff. Talking to me alone, in a corner of the living quarters near the elevator, poking his right forefinger into my chest, LBJ had given me some advice I've never forgotten. Almost eyeball to eyeball as he bent over me, speaking just above a whisper, he said, "You're going to make some money now for the first time in your life. . . . When you pay your income taxes, after you figure them out, pay an additional five hundred dollars. It's not enough for Nixon to win. He's going to have to put some people in jail."

Kerner, I thought as I took notes of his answers to Ed's questions, was someone Nixon would love to put in jail. He had been elected governor of Illinois in 1960 when Kennedy's victory over Nixon was secured by his razor-thin majority of Illinois votes. Nixon always believed that Chicago Mayor Richard Daley and Kerner had stolen the state from him by a fraud-ulent vote count. I suspected this indictment was Nixon's way of getting even. Since Kerner was a federal judge, Attorney General John Mitchell had to sign off on the indictment; that just confirmed my suspicion.

I knew Kerner from my White House years. In July 1967, during a summer of racial violence in American cities, President Johnson named Kerner chair of the National Advisory Commission on Civil Disorders. He performed with distinction and LBJ later nominated him for a seat on the Seventh Circuit Court of Appeals. Kerner was promptly confirmed; he resigned as governor to take a seat on the same appellate court on which his father had served.

On January 6, 1972, I flew to Chicago to tell Kerner that Ed could try the case only if it went to trial after the presidential election that November; if it went to trial before the election, Paul Connolly would have to try it. Kerner agreed to that condition and the financial arrangements.

Our "State" and "War" departments held several joint sessions. Ed, Paul, and I concluded that it was essential for Kerner to resign as a federal judge before the trial. If he were still on the bench, the jurors would determine his guilt based on whether they thought he was fit to be a federal judge, rather than whether he was guilty beyond a reasonable doubt of the crimes charged.

The three of us spent most of a Saturday laying out this proposition to Kerner, who balked. "I'm not going to resign from the bench. That looks like an admission of guilt."

After several hours, Ed played his trump card: "I will not try the case unless you resign from the court of appeals. There's no way—nooooo way—we can win if the jury is simply deciding whether you are fit to be a federal judge."

Kerner was silent for several moments. Then he turned to Paul Connolly. "Will you try the case if I'm still on the bench?"

Paul hesitated and said, "I agree with Ed. It may be impossible to win if you are a sitting federal judge as the case is tried." Then he took a deep breath and added, "But if you want me, I'll do my best for you."

"That settles it," Kerner said. "I'll go with you."

I don't think Paul ever worked harder on any case. He moved into Chicago's Ambassador Hotel well before the trial began. He faced two ambitious and bright Republicans: U.S. Attorney James Thompson (who became a four-term governor of Illinois) and Sam "the Hammer" Skinner (who later served as secretary of transportation and White House chief of staff under President George Bush I).

I visited Paul during the trial on my way back from a hearing in Oklahoma City. When I arrived at the Ambassador, he expressed his sympathy to me. I was puzzled. It was he who deserved sympathy for the rough trial he was going through.

"Haven't you heard?" he said. "Lyndon Johnson died of a heart attack this afternoon."

I learned that LBJ had died alone at his Texas ranch. Tears came to my eyes. I knew how he hated to be alone, ever since his heart attack in 1955. He would not live to see the American people and historians appreciate his triumphs on civil rights, Medicare for the elderly, and dozens of other domestic programs. His fate had been to suffer their opprobrium over the Vietnam War, and then to die five days before the signing of the cease-fire agreement in Paris.

We went down to the Pump Room for dinner, where I talked, wistfully and endlessly, about LBJ and my experiences with him. Near the end of dinner, realizing how self-absorbed I'd been, I asked Paul about the Kerner trial.

"I think we may be able to pull it out," he said. "But Sam Skinner is one tough sonuvabitch. He and Thompson are both damn good lawyers."

On February 19, President's Day, 1973, the jury convicted Kerner, a crushing blow both to Kerner and to Paul Connolly. It seemed to me that Paul never got over losing this case. He died believing that a terrible injustice had been done and—wrongly—held himself largely responsible.[12]

The Kerner indictment in 1971, coming as it did after the Nixon administration's effort to suppress the Pentagon Papers and the Army's harassment of Colonel Hackworth, sharpened my concern about the dangers of abusive government power. I began to see how essential it was to restrain that power. I had no idea, however, that the opportunity to do just that was heading my way.

.   .   .

I had always enjoyed the company of reporters. During my White House years I was on guard around journalists lest I make some mistake. I learned early in those years that nothing stayed off the record for very long in Washington. Even casual dinner table conversation that had some juice eventually spilled over into columns or news stories. In private life now, free from the danger that my words might be taken for national policy or reflections of the President's position, I came to rejoice in the company of journalists. I liked their toughness and irreverence; their macho posturing and rough sense of humor fit my attitudes about life. In Washington, there is no one better to eat, drink, party, gossip, laugh, or argue with.

Until Ed Williams and I landed the *Washington Post* as a client, however, it had never occurred to me that I would be in the position of representing the *Post* and its reporters. From the Pentagon Papers forward, no editor was bolder in pushing the envelope of First Amendment rights than Ben Bradlee—and no news gathering institution was more aggressive in this regard than the *Washington Post*. It was an exciting time to be the paper's lawyer.

The stage for aggressive reporting was set by several events. In April 1961, the *New York Times* had the story that the Bay of Pigs invasion was imminent but held it at President Kennedy's request. Bradlee, managing editor Howard Simons, and editorial page editor Phil Geyelin—indeed everyone at the *Post*—considered that a major mistake. "If we had had that story, we would have run it and saved the nation a major embarrassment," Bradlee and Simons said a thousand times, drumming it into every reporter in the newsroom.

In March 1964, the press began to flex its First Amendment muscle after the U.S. Supreme Court decided, in *New York Times v. Sullivan,* that public figures had to prove intentional malice to win libel lawsuits. The opinion created a storm of controversy; it disturbed every public official and many judges.*

Then in 1966, at President Johnson's urging Congress passed the Freedom of Information Act, which gave the public access to most government documents and previously inaccessible files. The Bay of Pigs lesson, the *Sullivan* decision, and the Freedom of Information Act led to more aggressive reporting by the mainstream press covering politicians and celebrities. It was a media environment in which Ben Bradlee thrived.

---

*Years later when I cited *New York Times v. Sullivan* in a libel suit filed in Frederick, Maryland, by a local school board official against the *Washington Post,* the county court judge interrupted me from his perch on the bench. "The *New York Times* is not printed in this county, counselor," the judge admonished.

My zeal for the First Amendment as we began representing the *Post* was limited and Ed Williams's was non-existent. His commitment was to the constitutional rights of defendants in criminal trials. He thought that the media's scramble to be first with the most sensational elements of any criminal story too often trampled the Sixth Amendment rights of the accused to a fair trial. That meant that when the *Post* became our client, the assertion of First Amendment rights in the courtroom (and clearing news stories for libel) fell to me. I found it exciting to be a legal gladiator for a newspaper led by Bradlee and Simons, but I joined their team with misgivings I had acquired from my government experience.

Working in the Pentagon for Secretary McNamara and in the Johnson White House, I had at times resented what I saw as only-half-right stories by the press. I sang the common refrain of insiders when I read a newspaper story: "It's not quite correct. I was there and I know exactly what happened. *They never get it right.*" I shared the view of military and intelligence officers that the press endangered our national security when it published classified information, although I had learned that it was fruitless to chase after the individual responsible for a particular leak.

At the same time, I had a grudging respect for the power of the media. In the LBJ White House, I saw how the press drove so much of what we did. The President kept three television sets blaring every evening near his desk in the Oval Office so that he could watch all networks at the same time.* Next to the television sets, the Associated Press and United Press International teletype tickers clicked away all day. LBJ would often stand over them, pulling at the unfolding rolls of paper as though that might make them print faster. He read several papers each day; he received the earliest edition of the *Washington Post* each evening before it was delivered the next morning.

In preparing messages to Congress describing our legislative programs, I had learned that members of Congress read *Washington Post* and *New York Times* stories about the message; they rarely read the message itself. It took heavy lifting to overcome first impressions that news stories in those papers gave members about our proposals. I was also aware of how many times in the government we had avoided cutting some corner or taking a question-

---

*ABC, CBS, and NBC; CNN, MSNBC, and FoxNews, with their 24/7 news coverage, did not exist then.

able action when someone said, "If it leaks to the *Washington Post* or *New York Times*, there'll be hell to pay." The press kept us honest on more occasions than I liked to admit.

Out of government, involved with the Democratic Party and occasionally playing hair shirt to the Nixon administration, I enjoyed the media penchant for needling those in power. It was fun to be on the attack, free of the responsibility to govern, able to criticize even when I had no alternative to propose. Having a receptive press corps that couldn't stand Nixon made it even more fun. My wariness about the press was changing as my vantage point changed. But still, I had only a law student's academic appreciation of the First Amendment until I got into the legal trenches for the *Washington Post*.

.   .   .

My initial First Amendment case for the *Washington Post* started with a prison riot. On September 9, 1971, more than one thousand inmates rioted at Attica State Correctional Facility in upstate New York, protesting harsh conditions and cruel treatment. The rioters took thirty-two guards hostage and seized Cellblock D of the prison. After a tense five-day standoff, state police blasted their way back into control, firing a barrage of two thousand bullets in six minutes. Thirty-two inmates and eleven corrections officers were killed. The incident gripped the nation's attention, and New York governor Nelson Rockefeller created a special commission to investigate and recommend changes in prison policy.[13]

In the wake of Attica, prison conditions and treatment of inmates became a hot issue, and the *Post* wanted its piece of the story. Bradlee assigned Ben Bagdikian to do a series of articles. Bagdikian's series, which ran for a week beginning on January 30, 1972, created a sensation. It revealed that 97 percent of all prisoners were eventually released back into society and almost all soon committed new crimes. He exposed deplorable conditions from Pennsylvania's Huntington State Correctional Institution to the Manhattan House of Detention (The Tombs), with its twelve floors of cages and eleven suicides a year. Bagdikian reported several bombshells: 80 to 90 percent of female inmates practiced homosexuality; three of every six serious crimes were committed by a child between the ages of ten and seventeen.[14]

Letters and telephone calls about federal prisons poured in to the *Post*. Not long afterward, all 356 inmates at the federal prison at Lewisburg, Pennsylvania, organized a work stoppage for two weeks, protesting conditions there. Bradlee wanted Bagdikian to interview these inmates. But Norman Carlson, director of prisons, refused, citing a Bureau of Prisons policy statement that prohibited all press interviews of inmates.

Bradlee called me. "What are our chances of winning a lawsuit to gain access?" After a quick check of the law, I told him they were good. "File it," he said, "as fast as you can. There's something going on there. That place is ready to explode and I want the story."

I did. Our suit was assigned to a liberal judge, Gerhard Gesell, who ruled that Bureau of Prisons policy violated the *Post's* First Amendment rights.

Before appealing Judge Gessel's decision, the Bureau of Prisons amended its policy to permit interviews in minimum-security prisons, limiting its press ban to medium- and maximum-security prisons—a policy that would keep the *Post* out of Lewisburg. Notwithstanding, the Court of Appeals unanimously affirmed Judge Gessel's opinion. The Bureau of Prisons went to the U.S. Supreme Court, where I argued the case and found the justices closely divided. A bare majority of five justices held that the Bureau of Prisons ban did not violate the *Post's* First Amendment rights. Four justices—Douglas, Powell, Brennan, and Marshall—dissented, concluding that the "interview ban impermissibly burdens First Amendment freedoms," especially in view of the "factual showing that the interview ban precludes effective reporting on prison conditions and inmate grievances."[15]

Despite this setback, we ultimately triumphed. Dogged by the *Post* and other news organizations, the Bureau of Prisons eventually changed its policy to permit interviews in all federal prisons of inmates willing to talk to the press.

CHAPTER 21

The Democratic Party's Cultural Revolution

Y OU KNOW THE difference between liberals and cannibals?" Lyndon Johnson asked me after a difficult Oval Office meeting with some members of the Democratic Party's left wing.

"No," I responded.

"Cannibals eat only their enemies!" Johnson roared, and then launched a tirade about his guests' demands.

In my years on the Johnson staff, I usually smiled at such LBJ complaints and shrugged them off. But in my years as general counsel to the Democratic National Committee, I lived the lesson of his quip.

As titular head of the party after Richard Nixon's election in November 1968, Hubert Humphrey faced the impossible task of rebuilding out of the rubble of a divided and violent Democratic Convention in Chicago. The party was a political storm without an eye of calm. Anti-war activists had watched Humphrey get nominated inside the hall despite their noisy demonstrations outside on Michigan Avenue and in Grant and Lincoln Parks. They were determined to be inside at the 1972 convention. A new generation of politically active blacks—among them Ralph Abernathy, Jesse Jackson, Stokeley Carmichael, Black Panther leaders Huey Newton and Bobby Seale, Eldridge Cleaver, Roy Innis, and representatives Shirley Chisholm (New York) and Julian Bond (Georgia)—were battling to succeed Martin Luther King, Jr., Whitney Young, and Roy Wilkins. A zealous and street-smart feminist movement, led by Gloria Steinem, Betty Friedan, and Bella Abzug, was pressing for equal status with men at the party's table. The quest for political power became so righteous in the eyes of New Left reformers that any means to get it were justified.

Delegates sent to a convention are like electors sent to the Electoral College: chosen to cast their state's vote to select the party's presidential candidate. In twenty states, there were no rules for the selection of 1968 convention delegates, leaving state party bosses in full control. Those bosses had named more than a third of convention delegates prior to 1968,[1] well before Johnson announced his decision not to run. As a result, the delegates in 1968 were overwhelmingly white, male, middle-class, middle-aged, most of them tied to state and local political machines. Out of the grueling labor pains of that raucous convention had come two political offspring of the effort to open up the party: the Commission on Party Structure and Delegate Selection to construct a new set of procedures for selecting delegates to the 1972 national convention and the Commission on Rules to democratize the business of the convention.

In February 1969, a year before Larry O'Brien was elected Democratic Party chairman, South Dakota senator George McGovern was named chair of the Commission on Party Structure and Delegate Selection, as part of an effort to placate the party's disaffected left. An early opponent of the Vietnam War and now the darling of most party liberals, McGovern had taken up Robert Kennedy's banner after the assassination, and sympathized with protestors in Chicago during the 1968 convention. To the party's energized and ambitious New Left, Humphrey was seen as a tired, aging cowpoke struggling in a political rodeo as aggressive, agile young cowhands mounted the angry bronco to compete for first prize. From my years in Johnson's White House, I thought I knew how down and dirty politics could get, but I was in for a surprise. Working with O'Brien to hold the party together, I experienced politics as extreme sport.

In November 1969, Humphrey asked me and Morris Abrams, president of Brandeis University, to co-chair the Committee on National Priorities of the Democratic Policy Council.[2] Our task was to listen to various constituents of the party—simmering forces like environmentalists, blacks, Mexican-Americans, and especially women—and issue a report recommending new positions and identifying key issues facing the party. I didn't need the March 23, 1970, *Newsweek* cover story, "Women in Revolt," to tell me women were fed up with male patronizing.* I was about to be embroiled in an angry dispute arising out of a Committee on National Priorities meeting.

---

*Three years later, in June 1973, on behalf of the Washington Post Company, I would negotiate a settlement between *Newsweek* management and its female employees establishing goals and timetables for women to be named as reporters and bureau chiefs, and under which Lynn Povich Young became the first female senior editor at the magazine on September 1, 1975. Until then, women had been locked into jobs as researchers and concentrated in "back of the book" sections like Life and Leisure, Religion, Art, Movies, and Books.

I had invited Patsy Mink, the diminutive Asian-American congress-woman from Hawaii, to testify on women's rights before the committee at a meeting in April. Her presentation, "Equal Rights for Women—A National Priority," was an eloquent plea for increased party support of equality for women and more active engagement in women's causes. Noting that in 1970 42 percent of all adult women were working either by choice or necessity, Mink called for increased funding for daycare for children and measures to combat discrimination in wages and executive positions. In her testimony, Mink contended, "Women . . . are just as capable of being heads of state as men. Some of the most forceful leaders of history, from the time of Queen Elizabeth to Israel's Golda Meir and India's Indira Gandhi in our own time, have been women. Mrs. Gandhi, incidentally, is prime minister of 530 million people, more than twice the population of the United States."[3]

Mink responded to questions, and our meeting seemed to be going smoothly. Our party, after all, was already positioning itself behind the women's movement. Then commission member Edgar Berman, Humphrey's personal physician (who I assumed was there to protect the former vice president's interests) spoke up.

"As equal as women are, there are certain basic differences that make an inequality," Berman began. "There are certain biological conditions that may be lunar, may be at puberty, during pregnancy, and menopause, whereby women are much, much different."

Patsy Mink looked as astonished as I felt.

"If you had an investment in a bank," Dr. Berman continued, "you wouldn't want the president of your bank making a loan under these raging hormonal influences at that particular period."

Patsy Mink's face so reddened with anger I thought her skull would explode. Berman, oblivious, continued. "Suppose we had a president in the White House, a menopausal woman president who had to make the decision of the Bay of Pigs, which of course was a bad one, or the Russian contretemps with Cuba at the time. Now, anything can happen, knowing women, psychologically during this period, or during their lunar problem. Anything can happen from going up and eating the paint off the chairs—"

Mink interrupted Berman, "Certainly all of the mistakes that have been made that we are now passing resolutions on have been made by men," she said. "I don't know what kind of lunar period they were in when they made these decisions."

"Men can of course make the same mistakes as women, but women have this added encumbrance," Berman shot back. Our entire panel was speechless as he spouted his concern about "a female airline pilot, during her lunar problems, making a very tense decision when she is probably about ready to be cut in half by her own hormonal influences."[4]

Flabbergasted—and thinking of the achievements of the women in my own family—I cut Berman off. I thanked Patsy Mink profusely and adjourned the hearing. Since no reporters were present, I hoped this bizarre incident might all blow over. I feared, however, that it was only a matter of time before the exchange would erupt into open controversy.

Enraged, Patsy Mink wrote a blistering letter to Humphrey. Citing "the great awakening of women who no longer will tolerate these insults," she demanded that Humphrey "have [Berman] removed" from the commission.[5]

Humphrey passed the letter on to Berman, who wrote Mink: "I would cite your little screed (which I am sure you are now sorry for) as a typical example of an ordinarily controlled woman under the raging hormonal imbalance of the periodic lunar cycle—thus proving the point against which you rail." Berman added a P.S. reminding Mink of "the small favor I tried to help you with some time ago."[6] (Berman later told me that Mink had asked him to find her husband, then a hydrologist working in Maryland, a federal job in Washington, which he was not able to do.)

Berman sent me the letter with a handwritten note saying, "Would you want your brother to marry one?"[7] As soon as I saw the note and letter, I called Larry O'Brien. "Berman has to go," I told him. O'Brien agreed, but knew that Humphrey would find it impossible to ask an old friend to resign. O'Brien suggested that I do it. Before I could speak with Berman, the story broke in the *New York Times* and *Washington Post*. Both papers quoted Berman holding fast to his position about women and vowing that he wouldn't quit the committee.

I called Humphrey. I was going to issue a statement, I said, calling on Berman to resign. Humphrey asked me to soften it to suggest gently that Berman step down. "I am in total disagreement with Dr. Berman's views," I said in my statement. "Dr. Berman should be permitted to decide for himself whether in light of recent events, it is in the best interests of the Democratic Party for him to remain on the Committee on National Priorities."

The next day Shirley Chisolm, the wiry Democrat who represented the congressional district where I had been born, called for Berman's resignation. The *Washington Post* interpreted my statement as I had hoped, reporting that I had "suggested that . . . Berman resign from the committee following his dispute with Rep. Patsy Mink. . . ."[8] The *New York Times* ran a story reporting on interviews with other physicians: "Doctors Deny Woman's Hormones Affect Her As Executive," inadvertently, I thought at the time, revealing its own sexist bias by placing the story in the Food/Fashions/Family/Furnishings section.[9]

The next day, Berman quit.

.   .   .   .

With Richard Nixon using television more boldly than any prior president, O'Brien and I searched for ways to get our party leaders on the airwaves. Within weeks of assuming office, Nixon began commandeering free airtime for political purposes. He moved press conferences to prime time; he barraged the public with regular television appearances on the Vietnam War and his economic programs.

We battled on two fronts: one, to obtain time to respond to Nixon's speeches under the Federal Communications Commission fairness doctrine, which mandated coverage of both sides of controversial issues; the other, to buy time for issue advertising. The three networks responded by permitting congressional leaders to respond to many Nixon appearances. But we hit a stone wall in our efforts to buy time to present the Democratic side of issues.

In May 1970, I filed an action asking the Federal Communications Commission to order CBS to sell us time. I posed this question: "Are the public airways—the most powerful communications media in our democracy—to promote the sales of soap, brassieres and deodorants and not to promote the exchange of ideas?"[10]

The FCC turned us down. We appealed to the U.S. Court of Appeals for the District of Columbia. Over my objection, the case was consolidated with a petition for review of an FCC decision upholding a station's refusal to sell broadcast time to a business group opposed to U.S. involvement in Vietnam. With demonstrations against the war prominent in the news, I feared that courts would be concerned about crafting a decision that might open the airwaves to "radical" groups.

My fears were allayed. Judge Skelly Wright, writing for a two-to-one majority of the D.C. Court of Appeals on August 3, 1971, held that "a flat ban on paid public issue announcements is in violation of the First Amendment, at least when other sorts of paid announcements are accepted." I was elated with the sweep of Judge Wright's opinion. That evening I went out to celebrate with Ed Williams and Paul Connolly.

The next morning, after he had read the opinion, Ed said, "You've got a big problem before the Supreme Court."

"How so? I'm golden with Skelly Wright's opinion."

"No," said Ed. "You won too big. Wright's opinion is so broad that it will scare the hell out of most of the justices."

Williams turned out to be right.

On October 16, 1972, as I argued the case before the Supreme Court, I could sense the concern of several justices. They were edgy about requiring networks to sell time to anyone who might want to place an issue ad. In May 1973, the Supreme Court reversed Skelly Wright.

.   .   .

The McGovern Commission, as the Commission on Party Structure and Delegate Selection became known, had sent its reform proposals to the Democratic National Committee in April 1970. All that spring, summer, and fall, O'Brien and I did our best to shape the proposals into a set of rules more acceptable to party regulars and elected officials. We wanted harmony, not conflict.

The commission proposed to prune back sharply the power of party bosses to select delegates and to uproot the traditional delegate-selection process. For the first time delegations would be required to give equal weight to population and Democratic Party strength and reflect their states' population mix in terms of gender, race, and age, down to eighteen-year-olds.[11] The commission recommended allocating state delegates in proportion to each candidate's share of primary votes and abolishing the unit rule—then a time-honored practice requiring all delegates to vote only for the winner of their state's primary. All delegates, moreover, would have to be selected during the election year, in order to avoid early stacking by state party machines.

The reaction from many state Democratic organizations was rage stoked by fear of losing power and forfeiting the national election. George Meany, the AFL-CIO president, opposed the McGovern reforms, as did most elected officials in state houses and city halls. Many members of Congress and senators called O'Brien and me; if these reforms were imposed, they told us, any chance of beating Nixon's reelection bid would evaporate.

O'Brien and I shared their concern; but the determined reformers would not budge. The Democratic National Committee adopted most of the delegate-selection proposals on February 19, 1971. At my recommendation, national party officials instructed states that half their delegations had to be women. The number of states announcing primaries rose from seventeen in 1968 to twenty-three in 1972. For the first time, a candidate could gather through primaries enough delegates to lock up the nomination.

O'Brien and I quickly learned how political pros were reacting to the new world of reform when party officials and members of Congress, one after another, turned down our requests that they chair—or even serve on—the three convention committees: credentials, platform, and rules. The Speaker of the House, Carl Albert, declined to chair the convention, ending a long-standing practice.

Finally, Michigan congressman James O'Hara, a moderate Democrat pressed by the labor movement to take the post in order to protect its interests, agreed to chair the rules committee. He was the only elected politician that we were able to interest in heading any key committee. Faced with a revolt by the party's elected leaders, we persuaded Richard Neustadt, a Harvard government professor, to chair the platform committee. Washington lawyer David Ginsburg agreed to be committee counsel. We sought someone tough and unimpeachable to chair the credentials committee and found her in the eminent lawyer Patricia Roberts Harris.[12]

The McGovern changes in party structure and those of the rules commission were liturgical, not substantive. Our party needed a vision: programs to attack poverty, enact national health care, revitalize cities, and end racial discrimination. I feared that McGovern and his band of anti-war advisors were steering the Democratic Party into a one-dimensional campaign against the Vietnam War. They were convinced that had Humphrey broken earlier with Johnson on Vietnam, he would have defeated Nixon in 1968. To me, the war had become a moral issue, but it was not the only one. Neither O'Brien nor I considered Vietnam a stand-alone political winner.

We believed the Democratic candidate should run, and could win, using the Great Society as a foundation for a host of new initiatives on the domestic front. In February 1971 I published an article in the *New Democrat*, "Vatican II For a Party." I argued that the party had lost its ideological bearings and was urgently in need of an "aggiornamento." (For a sense of how leftward the party and I were tilting in those days, I suggested that to combat pollution, Congress should require every family to meet strict standards in order to own more than one car!)

By January 1972, six men had announced their intentions to seek the Democratic Party's nomination for the presidency: in addition to Humphrey, McGovern and Maine senator Edmund Muskie (who had been Humphrey's running mate in 1968) were the top contenders. Also announcing were New York mayor John Lindsay, Senator Henry (Scoop) Jackson of Washington, and racist George Wallace of Alabama whom Lyndon Johnson once called a "runty little bastard . . . just about the most dangerous person around [with a] powerful constituency."* With the Chappaquiddick tragedy of July 1969, when Ted Kennedy drove off a bridge and his companion Mary Jo Kopechne drowned, the Massachusetts senator decided not to walk in his brothers' footsteps, although Larry O'Brien told me that he thought 1972 was Kennedy's only chance to be the party's nominee. "The longer he waits," O'Brien said, "the slimmer his chances. This story will fester and grow." I considered the fatal incident a serious blow to our party and country. I shared the view LBJ had expressed to me in 1968: "Of the three brothers, Teddy has the most potential to be the greatest senator and president."

Muskie was the early favorite. Though he won the New Hampshire primary on March 7, the media trumpeted the surprising performance of Senator George McGovern, who took 37 percent of the Democratic vote, a haunting redux of 1968, when Lyndon Johnson's primary victory there was overshadowed by Eugene McCarthy's 42 percent showing. Overnight, McGovern moved from quixotic anti-war critic to serious candidate.

The Democratic candidates devoted most of their rhetoric to the war in Vietnam. But the racial issue continued to haunt the party's political house.

*North Carolina governor Terry Sanford and House Ways and Means Committee chair Wilbur Mills also considered themselves candidates, but few took them seriously.

In his 1968 campaign, Richard Nixon had introduced his "southern strategy" to capture white voters angry at Lyndon Johnson's civil rights policies. The rawest racial nerve in 1970s America was school busing, as federal courts moved white and black children to schools outside their neighborhoods to end de facto segregation. To avoid having their children bused to schools in black neighborhoods, affluent whites placed their kids in private schools or fled to suburban communities. White families without the resources to escape court-ordered busing were enraged, seeing themselves as victims of forced racial integration that undermined the quality of their children's education.

Now, Richard Nixon took his southern strategy north on March 16 in a nationally televised address designed to capitalize on the resentment against school busing: "I am opposed to busing for the purpose of achieving racial balance in our schools," he said, and expressed support for a constitutional amendment to end court-ordered busing. Then Nixon trumped himself. "But as an answer to the immediate problem we face stopping more busing now, the constitutional amendment approach has a fatal flaw: It takes too long." He demanded that Congress pass legislation to "call an immediate halt to all new busing orders by federal courts. . . ."

I watched the speech in the family room of my house in Washington, D.C. I was appalled at the crude cynicism of his speech, laced with racist code words pandering to the worst instincts of white Americans. The jury was out on whether busing was sound policy, I thought, but Nixon's craven appeal to fear and hate will dash all hope for a racially peaceful society.

President Johnson had urged his staff to stand back from criticizing Nixon. "We only have one president," he often said, "only one pilot. We're all on the same plane, so look for ways to support him." But this speech so threatened to unravel the civil rights advances we had made that I couldn't sit silent. I picked up the phone and called LBJ at his ranch. He had watched the address on television.

"Mr. President, you need to speak out against this. He'll turn the clock back if you don't." It was the only time I asked him to publicly oppose Nixon.

Johnson listened, noncommittal, as I urged him to respond.

Typical of when he was brooding, he listened, grunted, "Uhuh, thanks," and hung up.

I heard nothing for the next two weeks, and I assumed he would say nothing. Then, on Easter Monday, Harry Middleton, director of the LBJ Presidential Library, called me. "The President is scheduled to give a speech in two weeks. He told me to tell you he wants to see a draft along the lines you discussed with him."

Ecstatic, I cut short a vacation in Hot Springs, Virginia, to return to Washington to write the speech. As Trudy and I were driving back on April 7, listening to the car radio, we heard that President Johnson had suffered a heart attack while visiting his daughter Lynda and her husband, Chuck Robb, at their home in Charlottesville, Virginia.

I knew then that LBJ would not be able to make the speech we had discussed. And I wondered if he ever would speak out on civil rights again. Months later, at the unsealing of his civil rights papers on December 12, 1972, the ailing ex-president ignored his doctor's orders and spoke to a conference at the LBJ Library. Popping a nitroglycerine pill to ease his chest pain, he said:

> Not a white American in all this land would fail to be outraged if an opposing team tried to insert a twelfth man in the football lineup to stop a black fullback on the football field. Yet off the field, away from the stadium, outside the reach of the television cameras and the watching eyes of millions of their fellow men, every black American in this land, man or woman, plays out life running against the twelfth man of a history that they did not make and a fate they did not choose. In this challenge, our churches, our schools, our unions, our professions, our trades, our military, our private employers and our government have a great duty from which they cannot turn. It is the duty of sustaining the momentum of this society's effort to equalize the history of some of our people so that we may open opportunity equally for all of our people.

It was Johnson's last public statement before dying a month later. I was never prouder to have been on his team.

.   .   .

Five days after Nixon's televised speech on busing, Muskie won the Illinois primary and captured that state's fifty-nine delegates. But at the end of

April, after McGovern took the Wisconsin and Massachusetts primaries, Muskie abandoned active pursuit of the nomination. He did not formally withdraw, because he wanted some influence in shaping the party platform and in naming a nominee other than McGovern.*

George Wallace, preaching his segregationist gospel, jolted the nation by winning the Florida primary with 42 percent of the vote. Drawing votes—and big, enthusiastic crowds—in the North as well as the South, Wallace demonstrated that he had become a national force. Then, campaigning in Maryland on May 15, he was shot by Arthur Bremer, a white man, in an assassination attempt that would leave him paralyzed for life. His candidacy had provided a grim reminder that Lyndon Johnson was right when he remarked to a young aide the same night he signed the 1964 Civil Rights Act: "We just delivered the South to the Republican Party for your lifetime and mine."

The race was now between Humphrey and McGovern. On June 6, the South Dakota senator won the California primary by a five-point margin, 44.3 percent to 39.2 percent for Humphrey. The remaining California votes sprinkled among the fractious assemblage heading for Miami, including segregationist George Wallace; black Brooklyn liberal Shirley Chisholm; floundering moderate Muskie; Los Angeles mayor Sam Yorty, who had accused communists and LBJ's new Great Society programs of instigating the 1965 Watts riots; enigmatic and mischievous dove McCarthy; pro-defense hawk Jackson. But California's winner-take-all primary law had not been amended to conform to reform guidelines of proportional representation. If McGovern took all 271 of California's delegate votes under that law, he would almost certainly get the nod at the Miami convention. For any shot at the nomination, Humphrey needed his proportionate share of California delegates (106) as well as the Illinois delegates that Muskie had won with Richard Daley's help.

The political combatants for Humphrey and McGovern prepared to slug it out in the credentials committee, on the convention floor and in the courts. By late spring it was clear that half the delegates selected by the states would be challenged before the party's credentials committee—an unprecedented situation that promised chaos on the convention floor. Worse yet, even before the credentials committee met, I found myself dealing with dele-

---

*New York City mayor John Lindsay, a liberal Republican turned Democrat, had dropped out after the Wisconsin primary on April 4.

gate challenges in federal district courts in Illinois, Mississippi, California, and the District of Columbia, and several other challengers promised to seek judicial review of adverse credentials committee actions. With the committee meeting at the Sheraton Park Hotel in Washington during the last week of June, any subsequent court battles threatened to delay and disrupt the scheduled start of the Democratic National Convention in Miami.

On June 10, as counsel for the Democratic Party, I wrote to David Bazelon, chief judge of the United States Court of Appeals for the District of Columbia: "Presently the rights of roughly fifty percent of the delegates that have been selected in various states to sit at the Convention are being challenged. [It is essential that these cases] be considered on an emergency basis if the Democratic National Convention is to go forward in an orderly manner beginning on July 10."

.   .   .

As the fight for the nomination became a struggle for the soul of the Democratic Party, the credentials contests turned into political blood sport.

In my years working in the Kennedy and Johnson administrations, I had learned that those who seek the presidency are prepared to stop at almost nothing to get their party's nomination. In my experience a notable exception to this code of conduct for presidential aspirants was Hubert Humphrey. In 1968, Humphrey decided not to use information that LBJ had derived from intelligence sources—that Nixon was subverting the Vietnam peace talks by signaling the South Vietnamese leaders to drag their feet because they would get a better deal under the Republican candidate than under Johnson or Humphrey.* Johnson did not believe Humphrey was tough enough then. I wondered now if Humphrey had the political brass knuckles he needed for this street fight with McGovern over the California and Illinois delegates.

McGovern supporters moved before the credentials committee to unseat

---

*Johnson knew from National Security Agency intercepts and other intelligence sources that Anna Chennault, the Chinese-born widow of World War II hero General Claire Chennault, had been pressing Nixon to send word to the South Vietnamese that as president he would give them a much better deal, so Saigon should not go along with Johnson. On October 31, the Thursday before the 1968 election, Johnson announced a complete bombing halt. The next day South Vietnamese president Nguyen Van Thieu backed out of the peace talks. Johnson was certain that Nixon had torpedoed the arrangement.

Chicago mayor Richard Daley and the other Chicago delegates that Muskie had won and committed to Humphrey. McGovernites contended that Daley hand-picked the Illinois delegates privately with the help of party leaders, violating reform rules that required openness at every stage of delegate selection. Daley *was* the Democratic Party in Illinois. He had chaired the state's delegation to every convention since 1956. During my years on the White House staff, one call to Mayor Daley brought the entire Illinois congressional delegation into lockstep behind an LBJ legislative program. It was inconceivable that Daley would not be seated at any Democratic convention.* Inconceivable to me, but desirable in the reformers' eyes. Daley was the bull's-eye they were targeting in the ring of political bosses. They loathed him for what they (and an independent investigation) called a "police riot" in the city's handling of demonstrators at the 1968 convention. On May 19, Chicago alderman and Daley intimate Thomas Keane asked the federal district court in Washington to enjoin the credentials committee from considering the McGovern challenge because state law superseded party rules.

To my astonishment, on June 19, the day the credentials committee began meeting, George Hart, chief judge of the federal district court, rejected my argument that delegate selection was a political question outside the jurisdiction of the courts. He ruled that the Democratic National Convention could not unseat the elected Daley delegates. I filed an appeal that evening. The appeals court reversed the district court the next day and permitted the credentials committee to consider the challenge.

On June 24, I went to a buffet dinner at the home of Alan and Adrian Barth. Alan was an editorial page writer for the *Washington Post* and father of the "Liberals Softball Game."† Joe Rauh, McGovern's attorney and avid supporter, was at the Barths' buffet, as was U.S. Court of Appeals chief judge

---

*Emblematic of Daley's confident attitude was his request, while this challenge was pending, to split the ten at-large delegates into half votes, thereby getting twenty seats at the convention for the ten votes, even though the reform rules explicitly limited the number of delegates to the number of votes. Daley was seeking seats for Jacob Arvey (long a behind-the-scenes political boss and money man in the state) and a number of allied labor leaders—precisely the kind of people who waved a red flag before the raging bulls in the McGovern camp. Since the convention call explicitly put an end to the practice of half votes, which had been used to provide political patronage seats, as party counsel I ruled against Daley's request. That infuriated the Chicago mayor.

†Each May and June, a group of us played on a field in Cleveland Park behind my house on Springland Lane and across the street from the Barths. Men, women, and children from seven to seventy were eligible to play. Joe Rauh and I pitched against each other in these Sunday afternoon games, after which we would go to the Barths' for beer, soda, potato chips, and political gossip. The game had become a family tradition and acquired its name because so many players were regarded as liberal Democrats.

David Bazelon. I knew Bazelon and admired him for having written in 1954 the controversial opinion in *Durham v. United States*, which introduced for the first time principles of modern psychiatry into the determination of criminal responsibility. I was polite but kept my distance from him, because I expected to appear in his courtroom on the credentials cases, arguing against Rauh.

Alan Barth surprised me when he said that Bazelon wanted to talk to me on the screened-in porch. When I went there, Bazelon signaled me to sit down next to Sid Yates, a liberal Democratic House member from Chicago. Bazelon got right to the point: "Sid Yates and I think these credentials disputes must be settled so the party can have a peaceful convention." Yates supported McGovern for the nomination, and during this discussion Bazelon made no effort to disguise his own preference for the South Dakota senator. I listened awkwardly, trying to cover my shock with a poker face. Humphrey had been Bazelon's friend for years, and they had earned many political Purple Hearts in progressive skirmishes together. The liberals are abandoning Hubert, I thought, and Bazelon must believe McGovern is his best shot for a seat on the Supreme Court. When we rejoined the party inside, shaken by Bazelon's undisguised partisanship, I assumed he would surely recuse himself from any case involving the party's credentials battles.

In the battle for California's delegates, the McGovernites scuttled their objection to the unit rule. They claimed that under California's winner-take-all primary law, George McGovern's plurality of 44 percent gave him all 271 of the state's delegates. The other candidates insisted that the reform rules—requiring apportionment of delegates on the basis of the percentages of votes garnered—superseded state law.

The credentials committee by a narrow vote apportioned the 271 California delegates among all the candidates, giving Humphrey 106, leaving McGovern with only 120, and distributing the remaining votes to the other candidates. The decision enhanced Humphrey's chances and left McGovern shy of the votes needed for nomination. Most other candidates were prepared to pass their delegates to Humphrey in a desperate effort to stop the McGovern movement, which they believed would doom the party in November. McGovernites vowed to fight.

The next day, by a vote of 71 to 61 that brought loud cheers from an audience composed largely of McGovern supporters and anti-Daley activists, the credentials committee unseated the 59 Daley delegates in Illinois, only 9 of whom were women and only 12 black. They were replaced by a racially and gender-balanced delegation headed by Jesse Jackson and William Singer. It was a slap in the face to Daley, who despised Jackson for encouraging Martin Luther King, Jr., to stage his initial marches in support of open housing in Chicago in the summer of 1966.

As expected, disappointed California McGovernites and Daley's Illinois forces raced to court. Their cases were consolidated; a hearing was set for July 3, a week before the national convention was to open.

A frantic O'Brien asked me if he could ignore the court cases. "These judges have no business getting into party politics," he said. I agreed, assuring him that I expected to win.

"And what if we lose?" Larry asked.

"We can decide what to do at that point." I had no idea what that might be.

I told O'Brien that we would be within our legal rights to ignore any court interference in our party convention. We both were concerned, however, about how it would look for the Democrats to defy court orders. "The Republicans will have a picnic," I said. "They'll paint us as a lawless party that can't stop violence and won't obey court orders."

"Joe, take one more shot at trying to settle some of this," O'Brien urged. "We've got to try to keep Daley on the reservation."

On the eve of the hearing before Judge George Hart, I had dinner with Daley's man Tom Keane at Duke Ziebert's. There was no chance of carrying Illinois in November without Daley, I told Keane; O'Brien and I wanted to work out a compromise between the McGovern camp and the mayor. Keane was antsy and non-committal throughout dinner as I probed for a deal. Finally, with a few drinks under his belt, Keane told me that the Chicago mayor would never make a deal with me; Daley was outraged that I had referred to the delegates as "The Daley 59" during a court hearing on June 29. I had considered it a clever and witty allusion to the Chicago 7, who had been indicted on federal charges of inciting violence during the 1968 convention.[13] The remark had achieved my objective of infuriating and distracting Daley's lawyer, Jerry Torshen.

"The mayor thinks you're an ungrateful son of a bitch," Keane reported. "I think he's as pissed off about your crack about the Daley 59 as he is about McGovern teaming up with Jesse Jackson. If that's possible."

What helped in court had obviously hurt in politics.

"Tell the mayor it just came out in the heat of argument," I suggested to Keane. "Tell him I apologize and won't use the term again. There's no way to carry Illinois, much less win in November, without Daley. The McGovernites may be on a political kamikaze mission, but O'Brien and I see it as our obligation to take the party into the campaign in as strong a position as possible. Daley can't possibly want Nixon reelected."

"Compared to who?" Keane said. "Don't be too sure, if McGovern gets the nomination."

The McGovernites espoused promoting abortion rights, accepting homosexual lifestyles, and legalizing marijuana. Their cultural agenda was offensive to a traditional and devout Roman Catholic like Richard Daley, and (before the Watergate scandal unfolded) Nixon appeared a moderate God-fearing Republican. The Republican president had funded most Great Society programs (despite his attack on them during the 1968 campaign) and pushed to enactment several legislative initiatives (occupational safety and health, pension reform, and an independent postal service) that Johnson had proposed but did not have time to get through Congress. O'Brien and I shared Daley's distaste for the New Left cultural agenda, but we distrusted Nixon.

Keane promised to talk to Daley. He called me at home late that evening to say that the mayor would take his chances in court and on the floor of the convention. Despite my warnings to Keane, Daley assumed, I suspected, that O'Brien and I would bend the rules to seat his delegation.

.   .   .

At the court hearing on July 3, Joe Rauh represented the McGovernites in the California case; Torshen continued as attorney for Daley in the Illinois case.

I argued that the Democratic Party had the right to determine which delegations to seat at its convention; these were political questions that had no place in court. "If the courts get into this case, we might as well move the court up to the Sheraton-Park and then move it to Miami next Monday," I said. Judge Hart raised his arthritic hands, palms tilted out and upward, and sighed, "Heaven forbid."

To underline the point that this was all politics, I noted that in Illinois the

McGovern campaign was arguing for meticulous compliance with the non-discrimination and open-selection rules—even if it involved overriding state law. In California, however, the McGovernites claimed that the winner-take-all state law overrode the party's proportional-representation requirement.

During my presentation, Judge Hart was handed a note. He interrupted me and left the bench. When he returned, he reported that Chief Judge David Bazelon had called to inform him that the Court of Appeals would hear any appeal of his ruling the following morning, July 4, at 11 A.M.

At the end of our oral arguments, Judge Hart let stand the credentials committee actions that stripped McGovern of 151 California delegates and unseated the 59 Daley delegates. He agreed that these were purely political questions, inappropriate for judicial review. Obviously referring to Judge Bazelon's call, Judge Hart concluded his oral opinion with a mischievous twinkle. "That's the law," he said, "at least for this evening."

The following morning was Independence Day and the political fireworks began in the main hearing room for the U. S. Court of Appeals. As I walked in, partisans wearing McGovern, Humphrey, Chisholm, and Muskie buttons and T-shirts filled the courtroom. The clerk asked all to rise, and I was stunned to see David Bazelon take the seat as chair of the three-judge panel. Sitting with him were Judge Charles Fahy, a moderate appointed by President Truman, and Judge George MacKinnon, a conservative appointed by President Nixon. Fahy and MacKinnon were strictly by-the-book jurists; if they had known about Bazelon's conversation with me at Alan Barth's, I thought, they would have been appalled at his failure to recuse himself.

Rauh and Torshen presented their arguments. When I rose to speak, I swung toward the audience, waved my arm broadly, and said, "If this court has any doubt that these are political questions, all your honors need do is look at the audience. They are festooned with political paraphernalia more appropriate for the floor of the Democratic convention than for a courtroom."

Bazelon slammed down his gavel and reprimanded me. "Counsel, you are in the United States Court of Appeals for the District of Columbia. Let me remind you of that. Please face the court and discuss the legal issues."

As I resumed, Judge Fahy interrupted me to wonder aloud "if the actions of the credentials committee were consistent and made any sense."

"A judge, in his wisdom, might think the shrewd political decision for the Democrats would be to seat the McGovern 151 and Daley 59," I said. "But if the Democratic Party wants to push the self-destruct button on this, that's the First Amendment right of the Democratic Party." The audience broke into laughter.

Bazelon again slammed his gavel, calling for order.

Then Bazelon questioned me sharply. *This guy,* I thought, *is looking for a way to give all these delegates to McGovern.*

After two hours of oral arguments, I called O'Brien. "We'll be in the Supreme Court over this before the convention begins."

The following day, the Court of Appeals decision was handed down. As soon as I read it, I called O'Brien. "Bazelon's done it," I shouted into the phone. "He's figured out a way to give all the California delegates to McGovern and keep Daley out!"

Unanimously, the three judges affirmed the decision of the credentials committee unseating the Daley delegates. Bazelon and MacKinnon reversed the credentials committee in California and, with Fahy dissenting, awarded all that state's delegates to McGovern.

"Christ Almighty!" was all O'Brien could say.

"We'll go right to the Supreme Court," I said. "I don't know whether they'll take it or not. But if they do, I think we'll win."

"Win what?" O'Brien asked. "Whatever happens, this is one helluva mess."

The Supreme Court, already in its summer recess until October, had reconvened during that recess only three times since 1932.*

I had no idea whether the Supreme Court would hear our appeal to stay the Court of Appeals order and let the convention handle its own delegate disputes. I didn't know what O'Brien and the convention would do if I failed to get the lower court order stayed.

We worked through the night preparing papers.[14] On Thursday morning, July 6, I filed a request that the Supreme Court review the case, or at least stay the orders of the court of appeals and permit the convention, due to start in four days, to determine which delegates to seat. I then flew to Miami to deal with the credentials battles steaming up for the first day of the con-

*In 1942 to decide whether President Roosevelt had authority to try alien saboteurs in military courts during World War II; in 1953 to consider the death sentence in the Rosenberg spy case; in 1958 to review the Little Rock school desegregation order.

vention. In addition to Chicago and Illinois, challenges had been filed against hundreds of the delegates. If any significant number went to the convention floor, the first session would go around the clock, well into the second day.

As soon as I arrived at the Fontainebleau Hotel, I began a round of meetings with lawyers representing candidates. Early the next morning, I was told that the Supreme Court would hand down its decision that afternoon. I rushed to the Miami airport to get a plane back to Washington.

At 9 P.M. the clerk handed out copies of the Court's decision to a screaming, scrambling mob of lawyers and reporters. We had won our stay, 6–3. Justices Burger, Powell, Rehnquist, Blackman, Stewart, and Brennan were in the majority; Justices White, Douglas, and Marshall dissented. I called O'Brien to tell him the convention could now go forward. All the harassed chairman could muster was, "Great. Now get down here to settle these other damn challenges, or we'll still have a disaster on opening day."

I raced to the airport and caught the last flight to Miami just as the gate closed. I arrived after midnight and went straight to O'Brien's suite.

We had won what we had sought: the right to determine which delegates to seat. We faced a welter of politically explosive procedural issues on the way to choosing the party's candidate, however. I recalled Oscar Wilde's adage: "In this world there are only two tragedies. One is not getting what one wants, and the other is getting it."

O'Brien now had to rule on two issues that would determine whether Humphrey or McGovern got the nomination. The first: Did the 151 California delegates of Humphrey, Muskie, and others have the right to vote on the challenge to unseat them? I told O'Brien that the rules clearly prohibited challenged delegates from voting on a challenge to unseat them.

An even tougher question loomed: What kind of majority was needed to decide the challenges? Should it be a constitutional majority of all delegates to the convention? Or should it be a majority of only the delegates eligible to vote on a particular challenge?

O'Brien's ruling on this question might determine whether McGovern had the votes to take all the California delegates—and the nomination.

I called Harvard Law professor Paul Freund, the nation's premier constitutional scholar. I called Alexander Bickel, the leading constitutional authority at Yale Law School. They agreed that unless we found something contrary in the rules, a majority of only those eligible to vote was the correct answer. This was consistent with my own thinking and my review of parliamentary precedents. That was it. This interpretation could give McGovern the nomination. I reported to O'Brien and rules committee chair O'Hara. They accepted my conclusion.

O'Hara and I met with representatives of the presidential candidates on Sunday night and told them how O'Brien would rule: the challenged delegates could not vote on their own challenge and a simple majority of eligible voters would decide the challenges.

Max Kampelman, a Humphrey loyalist, jumped up from his seat. He shook his finger in my face. "You bastards are favoring McGovern because you're afraid his supporters will bolt the party and you know Humphrey forces will remain loyal!"

Kampleman attacked my integrity. He claimed I was "out to get" Humphrey. "I never have trusted you," he screamed. Kampleman, I realized, had never forgiven me for telling him that he must withdraw as nominee to be the first chairman of the District of Columbia City Council.*

Representatives of other candidates—John Hoving (for North Carolina governor Terry Sanford), Charles Snyder (for George Wallace), Bill Brawley (for Scoop Jackson), and Pat McGahn (for Wilbur Mills)—were just as disappointed. McGovern's representative, Bobby Kennedy loyalist Frank Mankiewicz, made no effort to temper his elation, grinning from ear to ear as he blew cigarette smoke up to the ceiling.

It was as acrimonious as any meeting in my political experience. I was offended by the lack of trust. I realized that our party would be torn apart at this convention. The frustration and fury of the Humphrey supporters and the zealotry of McGovern's team guaranteed an emotional, irreparable split.

Many state and local elected and party officials had ignored the new party rules. Only contenders seeking the presidential nomination them-

*Kampleman had been Johnson's first choice (and Humphrey's recommendation) to chair the initial District of Columbia City Council. Johnson announced his selection on September 28, 1967, but within a week Kampelman became a controversial nominee. He had been a conscientious objector during World War II, something conservative members of the Senate inappropriately related to Vietnam War protestors seeking to dodge the draft, and he was accused of improper conduct in representing a client in connection with a government loan. He planned to respond at his confirmation hearing. But getting Kampelman confirmed would jeopardize the President's goal of a perfect start for the first D.C. City Council. I told Kampelman that he had to withdraw.

selves or those fighting on behalf of a candidate had paid much attention. For many delegates this 1972 convention, like any other, was a reunion with old friends, parties filled with political gossip, a few days in the Florida sun, and the excitement of lights, cameras, and action on the convention floor.

Even party leaders involved in the presidential quest had failed to appreciate the impact of the new party rules. They assumed the presidential nomination would go to the candidate who won the most primaries, or at least the key ones, and who had the support of the most party leaders. Their failure to grasp the sweep of the procedural revolution left them open-mouthed, shocked at their sudden political impotency. Meanwhile, the McGovern forces, well armed with detailed knowledge of the rules, dominated the Miami convention.

As I negotiated to get most of the challenges other than California and Illinois dropped, I realized the price others had paid for falling asleep at the political wheel. The rules required those who wished to withdraw a challenge to sign a formal statement of withdrawal. Humphrey and other anti-McGovern forces said they would need hours to find their delegates to sign the necessary withdrawals. I turned to McGovern's representative Eli Segal. He opened his briefcase and handed me hundreds of signatures on withdrawals. "We made our people sign the withdrawals at the same time they signed the challenges so we'd be able to deal." So much for the spirit of the reforms. The reformers were playing the kind of political hardball they had deplored when practiced by old-line political bosses.

Shortly after 1 A.M. the McGovern forces challenged the California delegates opposing their candidate. As we feared, O'Brien's ruling that a majority of those eligible to vote was decisive. Had a constitutional majority of *all* the convention delegates been required, McGovern's challenge to the Humphrey delegates would have lost by eleven votes.

The debate over the Daley delegation was the meanest fight of the convention, with the cruelest jabs coming from Jesse Jackson. In a stinging attack on Humphrey, Jackson urged the delegates to oppose "that man from Minnesota who sent blacks off to Vietnam to die."[15]

As I stood on the podium, I realized that we were presiding over not only an anti-war convention, but also an anti-convention convention. Miami 1972 was a revolt against Chicago 1968. McGovern's delegates were determined to cast aside Humphrey, ignore Muskie, oust Daley, alienate George Meany, and disavow Lyndon Johnson.

Eighty percent of the delegates seated on the floor were attending their first convention. Forty percent were women, compared with 13 percent in 1968. The percentage of black delegates had more than doubled. Nearly a third of the delegates had incomes of less than $15,000 compared with 13 percent in 1968. The number of delegates under age thirty had quadrupled.

On the convention floor, Shirley MacLaine, Marlo Thomas, Patty Duke, Julie Christie, and Warren Beatty replaced the older generation of celebrities led by Gregory Peck in 1968. Black delegates thrust their fists high in the angry symbol of black power. Gloria Steinem, in wide-rimmed glasses, and Bella Abzug in a huge, wide-brimmed, red hat and long skirt, pressed the cause of women's rights. John Kennedy's old staffers—anti-war activists now—were there in force, led by John Kenneth Galbraith and Arthur Schlesinger, Jr. Just about everyone was smoking—mostly nicotine cigarettes, but at times the odor of marijuana was pungent in parts of the hall. The convention floor was a colorful mélange of dress, lifestyles, and languages, as votes were cast in Sioux and Spanish as well as English.

Outside, thousands of non-delegates camped harmlessly in Flamingo Park, seven blocks from the convention. The Pot People's Party held smoke-ins among palmettos and eucalyptus trees. Militant gays walked around with "Gay Power" buttons on their bandannas and held same-sex kiss-ins.

Larry O'Brien did his best to keep the convention moving along with an oversized gavel crafted from an oak that had grown on the grounds of Thomas Jefferson's Monticello. He repeatedly pleaded with delegates to clear the aisles as the convention continued into the wee hours of the next morning. At 4 A.M., he reminded the delegates, "You know, we don't serve breakfast here."

.   .   .

The credentials clashes ended at 4:53 A.M. on Tuesday morning, a fitting nine-hour overture for the raucous political cacophony of the next event: the eleven-hour debate over the platform.[16]

Richard Neustadt of Harvard, the tweedy, pipe-smoking committee chair, and Washington lawyer and New Dealer David Ginsburg, its counsel, struggled to rein in a politically unruly platform committee. Most members were as far to the left of the Democratic party and the nation as Barry Goldwater's Republican platform committee had been to the right of the G.O.P.

rank and file in 1964. With the zeal of true believers, they were waging a holy war for the soul of the Democratic Party.

As delegates tangled over controversial planks, I puzzled: Were McGovern and his supporters taking our party to the same sort of political suicide dance that the Goldwater Republicans had choreographed eight years earlier? Maybe you have to burn the political house down to find the phoenix in the ashes, I thought. Many Democrats would see the McGovern campaign as a political kamikaze flight—one they had no intention of boarding. Never had so many elected officials shunned the party's national convention. Eleven of the nation's thirty Democratic governors, most members of the House and Senate, and hosts of elected state and local officials decided it was in their political interest to stay home.[17]

The draft platform recited traditional Democratic bread-and-butter planks: jobs for all, a higher minimum wage, adequate income for the unemployed, and national health insurance. It echoed McGovern's promise of "immediate and complete withdrawal of all U.S. forces" from Vietnam. It held fast to some controversial party positions: opposition to the death penalty, support for gun control, and support for school busing to achieve integration.

But, as I watched and listened, the convention was moving the Democratic Party from the harbor of economic issues like full employment and health care for all into the turbulent seas of cultural revolution likely to infuriate and alienate many middle-class Americans who had been the backbone of the party from Roosevelt through Johnson. How will they react, I wondered as I stood on the podium, to the effort of many delegates to establish cultural issues like abortion rights and gay liberation as litmus tests for what constitutes a national Democrat?

I grew disenchanted with the high pitch of intolerance that rang out from the New Left. Many McGovern delegates, it seemed to me, wanted to silence, not simply defeat, opposing voices. George Wallace, who had amassed votes in northern as well as southern states, proposed a conservative plank against busing and for prayer in public schools. McGovern's legions weren't satisfied simply to defeat his proposals. When the Alabama governor rolled his wheelchair onto the convention stage, McGovern delegates cursed and booed. Wallace found it almost impossible to speak before his planks were screamed down to defeat.

With a lock on the presidential nomination, McGovern and his top aides became a bit more pragmatic. They moved to eliminate some planks they feared would be politically costly in the general election. To avoid angering the most militant, they sought to do this through voice votes rather than roll calls. With no official record of who voted for what, they could deny their culpability.

Oklahoma senator Fred Harris's proposal for a sharply progressive income tax, confiscatory in its impact on the rich, and for a $6,500 minimum annual income for every American, was the first such plank to be sawed off—by voice vote at 2 A.M.[18] A plank to legalize marijuana was then voted down. O'Brien steered the most explosive debates, such as those over abortion and gay rights, to the latest hours.

McGovernites, even though they supported abortion rights, defeated the plank supporting "a person's right to control reproduction"[19] and legalization of abortion.* The abortion rights debate was typical of the convention's rhetorical and political mud wrestling. Shirley MacLaine shouted down Bella Abzug's expletives in order to protect McGovern. Gloria Steinem bitterly attacked McGovern campaign manager Gary Hart for undermining the plank. Tony Chayes, liberal wife of a Harvard law professor, battled against her husband, who opposed the abortion plank because it would hurt McGovern politically. Shirley MacLaine asserted that "nothing is more personal, more individual, more important to women than the plank on abortion," but because such a plank might damage McGovern, she argued that "the matter of abortion should be kept out of the partisan political process and . . . the distortions, which would surely arise in a presidential campaign." There was no way to avoid a roll call, so O'Brien called for a vote when he hoped few Americans would be awake to see the hypocrisy of this debate. McGovernites, abortion-rights supporters, defeated this plank decisively, by 1573 to 1101 votes, shortly before 5 A.M. on Wednesday morning.

Next came the plank on homosexual rights. Since June 27, 1969, when police roughing-up of patrons in Stonewall Inn, a gay night club in New York's Greenwich Village, had ignited a three-day riot, New Left Democrats had been promoting gay rights. To make the proposal more palatable polit-

*The Supreme Court decision in *Roe v. Wade* came a year later, in 1973.

ically, David Ginsburg labeled it the "sexual orientation" plank and brought into the political lexicon a phrase that survives to this day.*

As the plank was to be presented, Ohio Congressman Jim O'Hara, who was the convention's parliamentarian, said, "Joe, you're not running for anything. You take the podium as parliamentarian for this one. I'm running for reelection. I can't be seen anywhere near this."

After I announced that the sexual-orientation plank was next for debate and vote, members of the Gay Activist Alliance cheered and distributed pink and yellow handouts on the convention floor. The hall rocked with the chants, "2–4–6–8, we don't over populate" and "3–5–7–9, lesbians are mighty fine." Despite my political concerns, I was struck by a powerful point made by a delegate speaking on behalf of the plank. Referring to an executive order signed by President Dwight Eisenhower in 1953 that denied government employment to homosexuals, he said, "The truth is a gay person may not push a broom down the hall of the Smithsonian Institution or straighten a picture on the wall of the National Gallery." Nevertheless, in 1972 America even avid McGovernites believed approval of such a plank could sink their candidate. They worked furiously to avoid a roll call vote for two reasons: they would have to use their votes to defeat it resoundingly and they did not want to alienate gay activists and, even more important, they did not want to lose gay money, which was becoming a significant financial factor in national Democratic politics. They defeated the plank by voice vote. O'Brien immediately launched into the next plank, deaf to furious shouts of disappointed gays demanding a roll call.

The bitterness of the homosexual and lesbian community was so pronounced that I quietly worked with David Ginsburg to insert this language in the final version of the platform in a section entitled "The Right to Be Different": "All official discrimination on the basis of sex, age, race, language, political belief, religion, region or national origin must end. . . . Americans should be free to make their own choice of life styles and private habits without being subject to discrimination or prosecution."

As the second insomniac session neared its end, the convention delegates voted to give land back to Native Americans. Then, as dawn broke, an exhausted band of delegates adopted the platform. Ted Van Dyk, a one-time

---

*Minority Report No. 8 proposed a section on sexual orientation affirming "the right of all persons to express their own sensibility, emotionality, and lifestyle as long as they do not infringe on the rights of others."

Humphrey supporter who led the McGovern platform forces, said with a sigh that he had done pretty well. I disagreed. I feared that this convention had appalled any Americans who had stayed awake to watch. I myself felt the first pangs of alienation from the party to which I had devoted so much of my energies since 1960. Whatever this was, I thought, it was not the party of John Kennedy and Lyndon Johnson. McGovern was capturing the Democratic nomination. But on his way to victory, he was paying ruinous tribute to supporters who saw him and the party as tools in their crusade to change the culture of America rather than simply as the means to help distribute economic resources more fairly and assure equal opportunity. Whatever social changes these debates may be signaling, I thought, they did not auger well for victory in November, when voters cluster at the center.

The session, which had begun at 7:30 P.M. on Tuesday evening, ended at 6:30 A.M. on Wednesday morning.[20] When I returned to my room at the Fontainebleau, I found an urgent message that Mother had left during the evening. God, I thought, devout Catholic that she is, she must be horrified at the discussions of abortion and homosexual rights and the conduct on the floor during those discussions. When I phoned, she said sternly, "I've been watching all this on television."

"Yes, Mother." What must she think of her only son, I thought.

"I've been watching you. You're smoking all the time. It looks terrible. You should not smoke when you're on the podium."

Thank the Lord for loving mothers. At least someone cared how I looked during this political debacle.

.   .   .

With McGovern winning the credentials battles and the platform tucked in snugly to the left, Humphrey and Muskie withdrew. They dutifully asked their delegates to support the party and McGovern—in that order. In this, his last run for the presidency, a gracious Humphrey conceded, saying, "This has been a good fight. . . . We bow out now with the spirit of friendship. . . ." Muskie, however, made no secret of his distaste for the direction of the convention and the party. "This is still our party," he said. McGovernites read that remark as a pledge of full support; Muskie told me privately that it was a pledge to fight another day.

The Democrats nominated McGovern on Wednesday evening, July 12.

After much hemming and hawing in the hope that Ted Kennedy would join the ticket, McGovern finally selected Missouri senator Thomas Eagleton as his running mate. Eagleton was forty-two years old, handsome, Roman Catholic (McGovern was Methodist), an urbanite from St. Louis, close to labor, and well within the party's mainstream.

We scheduled McGovern's acceptance speech for prime time on the following evening. But the opportunity for such coverage was trampled in the relentless march of the reformers.

Two routine items were on the agenda: approving a new charter for the Democratic Party and the call to the next quadrennial convention. But the most zealous McGovernites set off a furious—and time-consuming— debate when they insisted that the call to the 1976 convention abolish the unit rule and eliminate winner-take-all primaries. They voted rules to require proportional representation by race, gender, and age. They decreed that all delegate-selection processes must be open to public participation and held during the year of the convention. So many reforms were proposed that the exhausted delegates established yet another reform commission to consider them rather than vote on each in Miami.

Next came the vice presidential nomination, which, being a foregone conclusion, should have been disposed of in a few minutes. But while O'Brien and I watched in disbelief, McGovern and his campaign forces ineffectually stood by as giddiness took hold of the convention. Unruly delegates shouted nominations of eighty other men and women from the floor, and the session slipped into a theater of the absurd. The proceedings ran on, well beyond midnight. There was no indication when McGovern would have an opportunity to deliver his acceptance speech. In a political stream of consciousness, delegate shouts from the floor nominated consumer advocate Ralph Nader, pediatrician and anti-war demonstrator Benjamin Spock, radical priests Phil and Daniel Berrigan, Cesar Chavez, Martha Mitchell, wife of Nixon's attorney general, and Archie Bunker, Norman Lear's wildly popular television caricature of an ethnic bigot opposed to all liberal causes.[21] Not until 1:40 A.M. did the delegates officially vote Eagleton the party's vice presidential nominee.

When Eagleton concluded his acceptance speech, O'Brien motioned the band. As the band played "Hail, Hail, the Gang's All Here," McGovern entered with Humphrey and Ted Kennedy, who had flown in from Cape Cod to introduce the nominee. It was shortly before 3 A.M. eastern daylight time. "McGovern," I whispered to O'Brien, "is now appearing in prime time in Guam."[22]

O'Brien, DNC treasurer Robert Strauss, and I saw the party heading for disastrous defeat. Nixon was the number one bête noir of many Democrats, detested by them. We should have been able to rally these voters—but now, we knew, many of our party would defect to the Republicans. Strauss poured a few drinks in the DNC trailer outside the convention hall and stayed there drowning his despair. He never appeared on the stage when McGovern and Eagleton accepted the party's nomination. McGovern could not win without the party's moderates and big labor. By now, few traditional Democrats remained in the convention hall, and their loathing was palpable. I knew they would never rally behind this Democratic nominee.[23]

McGovern finished speaking at 3:45 A.M. The crowd broke into "This Land Is Your Land." Just below us at the podium an array of young Democrats, many in hippie garb, clapped and swayed. With most of the older and regular party delegates long gone from the hall, dizzying clouds of marijuana smoke rose toward the stage. Watching in disbelief, I remembered a note from Will Sparks, an LBJ speechwriter who had written to me about the party's sharp left turn. Sparks quoted a delegate to a nineteenth-century Democratic convention: "If we go through with this nomination, we will march straight through the slaughterhouse into an open grave." That delegate had referred to Grover Cleveland, who eventually defied the odds and won. But George McGovern was no Grover Cleveland.

Larry O'Brien had done his best to hold the party together. He was eager to disassociate himself from the debacle ahead, but when McGovern asked him to stay on as chairman, O'Brien decided, reluctantly, to accept and soldier on. Pressed by his aides to name a woman, however, McGovern announced he had chosen Jean Westwood, Democratic committeewoman from Utah—without telling O'Brien. Larry resigned immediately.

I also planned to resign promptly after the convention. But I delayed, in the hope of persuading Frank Mankiewicz and Gary Hart, McGovern's campaign managers, to make a major issue of a recent break-in at DNC headquarters in the Watergate office building, which O'Brien and I suspected was a Republican dirty trick that could prove to be Richard Nixon's Achilles' heel. On Friday, July 21, over breakfast in the coffee shop of the Mayflower Hotel, I laid out everything I knew, plus what I suspected we might learn over the summer and fall. I told them O'Brien believed that

Nixon was personally involved; that I was inclined to agree but that as yet I couldn't prove it. Hart and Mankiewicz weren't buying. Convinced that McGovern's commitment to pull out of Vietnam would win the election, they showed no inclination to make the break-in a significant campaign issue.

On the following Tuesday, July 25, the *Washington Post* linked Gordon Liddy, counsel to the Committee to Re-elect the President, to bugging the Democratic National Committee offices in the Watergate building. With that disclosure, I became as firmly convinced as O'Brien that the break-in trail would lead to the White House. I tried to call McGovern. I couldn't get through. For on this same day, Tom Eagleton admitted that he had been hospitalized three times between 1960 and 1966 for psychiatric treatment.*

McGovern was livid. Eagleton had answered "No" when McGovern asked whether there were any skeletons in the closet. Campaigning in Honolulu the day after this revelation, Eagleton acknowledged "a mistake" in failing to reveal his medical history. Rumors circulated that McGovern was reconsidering his choice.

That day, Ed Williams and I—both friends of Eagleton—were having lunch in Sans Souci. The maitre d', Paul Delisle, told me I had a call. When I picked up, I heard Eagleton's excited voice. "Joe, McGovern is announcing that he still wants me on the ticket." He told me McGovern had just said, "I am 1000 percent for Tom Eagleton and I have no intention of dropping him from the ticket." I told Ed. Impressed by McGovern's loyalty, we had a drink to celebrate.

The following morning, I entered my office at 9 A.M. to a ringing phone. It was McGovern calling from South Dakota. "Do you know what the procedures are for replacing a candidate on the national ticket?"

I didn't.

"See if you can get a memo out here," he asked. "Don't talk to anyone about this. Just do a memorandum."

I knew in my gut that Eagleton was toast.

*In a small, pine-paneled auditorium at the Black Hills resort where McGovern was vacationing, Eagleton said he had suffered from "nervous exhaustion and fatigue" after pushing himself too hard. He was hospitalized after running for public office in December 1960 and 1964 and again in September of 1966. During hospitalization, he received electric shock therapy, then a common, though controversial, treatment for depression.

I sent a brief memo to McGovern that day. The press was in full cry: should someone who had received electric shock treatment for mental illness be a heartbeat away from the nuclear trigger?

On Sunday morning, July 30, Eagleton appeared on CBS's *Face the Nation*. Fidgety and perspiring, he vowed to fight for his place on the ticket, but I knew he had reason to sweat.

As Eagleton stood firm, Democratic Party chair Jean Westwood and vice-chair Basil Paterson, the Harlem politician, appeared on NBC's *Meet the Press*. "It would be a noble thing," Westwood said, "for Tom Eagleton to withdraw." Paterson agreed. McGovern did not contradict his party chieftains.

That day, at McGovern's request, I prepared another memorandum, setting out exactly and in detail how to fill a vacancy on the national ticket. On Monday, at 8:30 P.M. in the Senate Caucus Room on Capitol Hill, McGovern and Eagleton announced their "joint decision": the Missouri senator withdrew from the ticket. The reluctance of the red-eyed Eagleton was obvious: "My conscience is clear. My spirits are high. This is definitely not my last press conference, and Tom Eagleton is going to be around for a long time."[24]

Eagleton's resignation kicked off frantic scampering for a replacement. McGovern approached a long list of well-known Democrats—Ted Kennedy, Humphrey, Muskie, O'Brien, Connecticut senator Abraham Ribicoff, Florida governor Reubin Askew—before finally getting acceptance from Sargent Shriver, former director of the Peace Corps and of the Office of Economic Opportunity and former ambassador to France.

We set up a meeting of the Democratic National Committee to make the formal nomination at 2 P.M. on Tuesday, in Washington's Sheraton Park Hotel. Next door, the annual meeting of the American Massage and Therapy Association was in progress. We might need them, I thought, to loosen up the painful knots in the Democratic Party.

I was the meeting's parliamentarian. After we established the formal procedures for Shriver's nomination that evening, another rambunctious session reminiscent of the convention in Miami began to unfold. As Bella Abzug, the rowdy congresswoman from Manhattan's West Side, stormed down the center aisle, I signaled for a motion to adjourn and gaveled the meeting to a close. Abzug called me a "double-crossing son of a bitch" for failing to let her speak, something I had offered to do before the session began to become disruptive.

At the evening meeting to name Shriver the party's vice presidential candidate, Eagleton, O'Brien, Humphrey, Muskie, and Kennedy all made appearances. With his ninety-year-old mother and his wife and children looking on, Shriver praised Eagleton as "an unforgettable example of courage under fire."[25]

My work was complete. I had little enthusiasm for McGovern as a candidate. I resigned as counsel for the Democratic National Committee the following day. I turned my mind and energy to a lawsuit I'd filed against the Committee to Re-elect the President and to representing the *Washington Post*. I believed that Richard Nixon was deeply involved in the Watergate break-in. Now I would try to prove it.

CHAPTER 22

Watergate

OR ME Watergate had begun a few weeks earlier, on Saturday, June 17, 1972. I was awakened by a call from Stan Greigg, deputy chairman of the Democratic National Committee.

"Joe, someone's broken into the DNC headquarters," Stan blurted out. "The place is littered with film and wires and electronic equipment. There are lots of cops here," he added. He wanted to know what to do.

"Cooperate with the police," I said. "But don't let them remove anything until you make a list of what it is."

Immediately, I called Howard Simons, managing editor at the *Washington Post*, who was on duty that weekend. Simons dispatched Al Lewis, the paper's veteran police reporter, to the D.C. jail. There Lewis learned that five middle-aged men[1] wearing suits, ties, and surgical gloves had been arrested at 2:30 A.M. for breaking into Democratic National Committee headquarters on the sixth floor of the Watergate office building with electronic bugging equipment, cameras, and walkie-talkies. They ransacked file drawers and rummaged through papers. Their pockets were filled with new, crisp, sequentially numbered $100 bills.

I called Larry O'Brien, who was in Miami. He agreed that it was a Republican dirty trick. But we had nothing at this point to implicate the G.O.P.

On Sunday morning, the Associated Press reported that one of the burglars, James McCord, had worked at the Committee to Re-elect the President, Nixon's presidential campaign arm. John Mitchell, who had resigned as attorney general to head CREEP, issued a statement. McCord and the others, he claimed, "were not operative either in our behalf or with our consent."

That evening, Morris Dees called me at home to suggest that I file suit against the five men on behalf of the Democratic National Committee. Dees, founder of the Southern Poverty Law Center, whom I had met when we were selected as two of the Jaycees Ten Outstanding Young Men of 1966, agreed to fly to Washington the next day with some notes for a complaint.

On Monday morning, the *Washington Post* carried a story by Metro reporters Bob Woodward and Carl Bernstein saying that McCord was the salaried security coordinator for CREEP and also had a contract to provide security services to the Republican National Committee. Again, Mitchell denied any involvement with the break-in. He said that McCord had left CREEP a month earlier.

Seeing the *Post* story, I asked my secretary Evelyn Ferguson to call the Committee to Re-elect the President. "Say you're going to send social invitations to the top officials there." If McCord was still listed as one of them, I reasoned, it would provide enough of a nexus to justify a suit against CREEP for the break-in. In response, in addition to Mitchell's name, she was given that of James McCord. We then checked the public filings of the committee with the General Accounting Office. McCord, we learned, was the second-highest paid official of CREEP, earning $1,209 a month. His business, McCord Associates, in Rockville, Maryland, had received thousands of dollars from CREEP.

I called O'Brien, who was back in Washington, and told him that we had enough to file suit on behalf of the DNC against the Committee to Re-elect the President, as well as McCord and the others caught breaking in. Dees arrived in my office that afternoon. We drafted a complaint alleging trespassing, invasion of privacy, and conspiracy to violate Democrats' civil rights, constitutional right of free assembly, and right to vote.

The following morning O'Brien and I announced the lawsuit, seeking $1 million in damages, as the complaint was being filed in federal district court. Because of O'Brien's suspicion that Nixon was personally involved, we had added as defendants "John Does and other conspirators whose names are unknown at this time."

During the press conference, O'Brien said that responsibility for the break-in went right to the White House. His unqualified accusation caught me by surprise. When I later asked about it, O'Brien said, "I've studied Nixon since the Kennedy campaign. I've no doubt that the trail will lead to the Oval Office, if we can hang in there long enough."[2] Even if he was right, I had plenty of doubt whether such a charge could be proved. I assumed that Nixon would have taken pains to preserve his deniability. I had seen Presi-

dent Kennedy maintain his ability to deny any involvement in the assassination of Diem in Vietnam and the attempts on Castro's life in Cuba and
President Johnson deny knowledge of actions he had directed White House
aides and cabinet officers to take. O'Brien and I both knew that the mere
absence of a president's name on an order did not mean he hadn't issued it.

Ed Williams and Paul Connolly thought that, in filing the suit, O'Brien
and I might have gone too far. That gave me more pause about O'Brien's
charges. Nevertheless, I set as one of my litigation objectives nailing Nixon
to the Watergate cross.

In its front-page story covering our announcement, the *Washington Post*
wrote that we saw the break-in as a "campaign issue." We certainly hoped it
would become one. Republicans Bob Dole and John Mitchell accused us of
misusing the courts for political purposes. Several Washington lawyers told
me that I was jeopardizing our firm and my own future—at least for the
next four years—since Nixon was sure to be reelected. If Ed or Paul, or any
of the other lawyers at the firm felt that way, however, they never told me.

I couldn't know at the time how much this lawsuit troubled the White
House. I would learn later that the morning of the *Washington Post*'s story
on the suit, Nixon met at 9:30 A.M. in the Oval Office with his chief of staff,
H. R. Haldeman, and his special counsel, Charles Colson, for an hour. Discussing Watergate, Haldeman told Nixon, "Califano's got two men riding
the U.S. attorney's office."

Nixon responded, "We'd do the same thing," and went on to call the civil
suit "very clever."[3]

Our suit was assigned to U.S. district court judge Charles Richey. A former Republican politician, Richey had been appointed by Nixon a year earlier. He was believed to be close to the White House, so I was worried. My
concern heightened when during my first appearance in court, Richey
admonished me for announcing the lawsuit to the press.

I filed notice of a raft of depositions to begin in July after I returned from
the Democratic convention. I also moved to expedite consideration of the
case. This was a lawsuit with dynamite political potential. I wanted it tried
before the election.

During the next three weeks I learned that two of the burglars were
Cuban Brigade members, trained by the U.S. Army at Fort Jackson, South
Carolina. I had been in charge of that program! How ironic, I thought: we

may have taught these guys the techniques of electronic surveillance and document photography that they had tried to use at the Watergate.

I knew we would have to move on several fronts to find out who was responsible for the break-in. I asked Wisconsin senator William Proxmire, chair of the Joint Economic Committee, which oversees the Federal Reserve Board, to demand that the Fed identify the source of the $100 bills found on the burglars. It might be the bank where CREEP had its accounts. The Fed and its chairman, former Nixon counselor Arthur Burns, stonewalled Proxmire.

The depositions of McCord, the other Watergate burglars, Howard Hunt, and White House counsel Chuck Colson were scheduled for our offices on July 20. No one showed. We filed a motion to compel testimony, which Judge Richey granted. At the same time, on his own, Richey issued an order sealing all depositions. I objected. The following day, Richey held a pro forma hearing to cover himself, at the end of which he stuck by his ruling that all pre-trial testimony be sealed. He's trying to protect the Nixon administration from any embarrassment before the election, I thought.

I became more suspicious when I learned that Richey had called *Washington Post* reporter Carl Bernstein, whom he had never met, to justify his ruling. Richey told Bernstein that he feared the release of civil suit depositions would endanger a fair trial in the criminal case expected to be filed. Bernstein remembers Richey saying, "I want it to be very clear that I haven't discussed this case outside the courtroom with anyone, and that political considerations played no part whatsoever."[4] When Bernstein told me that, I knew Richey was protesting too much. Now I was certain someone was talking to him, and suspected it was the White House.

·   ·   ·

In the midst of the political flap over Eagleton's psychiatric treatment, Bernstein was in Florida trying to examine the files of Richard Gerstein, the state's attorney for metropolitan Miami. The suspected Watergate burglars had connections to Miami, so the Florida attorney general had subpoenaed the bank records of Bernard Barker, one of the Watergate burglars, to see if Barker had violated any laws in that state. Seeking to trace the origins of the money found on the Watergate burglars, Bernstein waited all day without getting in to see Gerstein's chief investigator, Martin Dardis, as he had been promised. When told to leave because the building was closing, he called me. He insisted on staying there all night and wanted me to prevent Miami officials from charging him with trespass. When I told him that he had to leave, he said, "This is the people's property! They can't make me leave! I have a right to be here!" Finally, he agreed to leave, but not without muttering in a stage whisper, "What kind of a lawyer have I got?"

Bernstein eventually bulled his way into Gerstein's office. He got copies of the documents he sought, including Kenneth Dahlberg's check for $25,000—a check that passed through Maurice Stans, chair of CREEP's finance committee, into Bernard Barker's account. This provided the first link between the campaign and the break-in: Dahlberg was a fundraiser for Nixon. Bernstein flew back to National Airport in Washington and called me; he was frantic. "They claim they've lost my luggage. I think the FBI has it. And the papers are in my bag! Goddamn, you've got to call Delta!" With everything that's going on, I thought, he may be right about the FBI intercepting his luggage. If the documents were so important, why did he check his bag with them in it?

"Call Bradlee," I advised. "The airline will be a lot more responsive to the editor of the *Washington Post* than the paper's lawyer." Before Bradlee had to call, Bernstein recovered his luggage with the papers in it.

On August 1, the *Post* dropped its bombshell: a $25,000 check for Nixon's re-election campaign given to Maurice Stans, chair of CREEP's finance committee, had been deposited in the bank account of a Watergate burglar. For me, this fact locked up the case against CREEP and Mitchell. The issue now was whether I could prove Nixon's involvement or at least the complicity of his top White House aides.

Ed Williams remained skeptical. He feared that I had filed the lawsuit on flimsy evidence. Now, he was concerned about our firm's reputation. With an edge that betrayed his concern, he teased me incessantly about investing such time and resources in a case for which we'd never get paid. "This is YOUR lawsuit," Ed said, distancing himself. "You'd better win it."

Our first big break came when John Cassidento, a Connecticut attorney (and committed Democrat), called to say he had "a client who can shed considerable light on what happened at the Watergate." I sent one of our firm's lawyers, Alan Galbraith, to meet with Cassidento and his client. We would only know his client by the name "Al." His client would not know where Galbraith was from or who his client was. Al claimed to be the lookout, from the Howard Johnsons hotel across the street from the Watergate, the night of the break-in. Howard Hunt and Gordon Liddy, he said, had visited his room that afternoon. More alarming, he revealed that the DNC headquarters had been bugged prior to the June break-in. Al had been listening to DNC phone calls for weeks; he'd sent memoranda of those conversations via McCord to Mitchell.[5]

We quickly discovered that Al was Al Baldwin, a former FBI agent; he had been granted immunity for testimony before the grand jury investigating Watergate. I wanted O'Brien to go public immediately with Baldwin's explosive revelations. But Ed Williams discouraged me. I held off, sharing a little of Ed's concern about Al's credibility. Al had admitted he was angry with CREEP because it hadn't paid him; he was considering a suit to get his money.

At the end of August, I went to Cape Cod to vacation with my family. Hoping that I might earn his wholehearted support for the suit, I offered Ed Williams something I knew he couldn't resist: the opportunity to take John Mitchell's deposition on September 1. Mitchell refused to answer any questions. The next day Richey ordered Mitchell to reappear at the law firm on September 5 to answer questions or assert some privilege.

Williams sat across the table from Mitchell with thick notebooks in front of him labeled Mitchell I, Mitchell II, Mitchell III. He periodically thumbed through them as he questioned Mitchell about every aspect of the break-in. He sprinkled his questions with allusions to information Al Baldwin had given us. Mitchell and his attorneys were clearly nervous. What they didn't know was that the notebooks contained only blank sheets of paper.

The next day when I returned from vacation, Ed greeted me. "Boy," he exulted, "Have WE got OURSELVES one helluva lawsuit. I may not know much about politics, but I know when someone is lying and when he's scared. John Mitchell had to squeeze his thighs together to avoid wetting his pants."

Now more confident of the reliability of Al Baldwin's information, Larry O'Brien charged on September 7 that for several weeks prior to the June 17 arrests, his phone and that of Spencer Oliver, another Democratic official, had been tapped and monitored from the hotel across the street. O'Brien said that the break-in on June 17 was intended to repair a faulty tap already on his phone and to install an additional bugging device.

With Judge Richey's lid on disclosing the contents of our depositions, I had to find some other way to signal the press and the Democrats on Capitol Hill that we were on to something big. I was determined to interest the major media in this story so they would commit their resources; we couldn't afford to hire investigators. I decided to call additional witnesses for depositions so their names would be filed on the public record at the courthouse. That record would alert the press and politicians that other figures were potentially involved. I filed notice of depositions for the testimony of former secretary of commerce and Nixon fundraiser Maurice Stans; Howard Hunt, a shadowy former spy; and Hugh Sloan, who had been treasurer of the 1972 Nixon finance committee.

To further whet the appetites of the press, I used another tactic: amending our complaint. On September 11, we increased our damage claim to $3.2 million[6] and added to the list of defendants CREEP chairman Francis Dale, who had replaced John Mitchell, as well as Liddy, Hunt, Sloan, and Stans. Dale and Stans fired back with a $2.5 million counterclaim and a $5 million libel suit against O'Brien. (Unknown to us at the time, Stans filed his libel action at the suggestion of Judge Richey.)[7]

.   .   .

On September 15, a grand jury indicted the five Watergate burglars, along with Hunt and Liddy, for conspiracy, burglary, and violation of federal wiretapping laws. A week later Judge Richey, again on his own motion, held an extraordinary private session with the dozen or so lawyers involved in our civil lawsuit. I appeared with Harold Ungar, a seasoned criminal lawyer long associated with Ed Williams, for this closed meeting.[8]

To my astonishment, Richey pressured me to join defendants' attorneys in a joint press release. He proposed that we announce that we would postpone all activity in the case until after the election! I refused. With rising irritation, the judge pressed me repeatedly. I continued to refuse. Then Richey asked that I agree to stop all depositions until after the election. I told him that this too was out of the question. Richey was furious. He demanded that I consult with my client about the press release. Harold Ungar and I went outside to talk. When we found a private corner in the corridor, Ungar slapped a hand to his forehead, "Joe," he said, "in my thirty years of practice, I've never seen anything like this. Never!" He paced in tiny circles muttering, "Never, never, never."

I called DNC chair Jean Westwood—our client—to confirm my position. Then we returned to the meeting. I told Richey that my client would never agree to any such arrangement or joint press release.

Richey then tersely announced that he was ordering an indefinite stay of all proceedings. He suspended, until completion of the Watergate criminal trial, the more than forty depositions that I had set up.

The judge announced his decisions in open court at 2:45 P.M. that afternoon. Richey admitted that ordering counsel to come to a closed preliminary pre-trial conference "was a rather unusual call on the part of the court . . . A pre-trial conference is normally a procedure which takes place after . . . discovery procedures have been exhausted or completed." Richey then unveiled his order staying all proceedings until after the criminal trial.

Richey then invited me to comment. I opened with extravagant and superfluous praise of Richey "for the absolutely extraordinary attempt that this court made this morning to accommodate our present request that at least our original case—the first one filed in this court—be tried prior to the election."[9] I then expressed my disagreement with the court's decision to stay all depositions.

My associate, Galbraith, who was also present, told me that my praise of Richey made him "ill." "Alan," I explained, "it's an old trick I learned from LBJ. Heap so Goddamn much praise on an enemy that no one will believe it."

Coupled with his order sealing the depositions already taken, Judge Richey's stay had effectively shielded Nixon from any potential embarrassment as a result of the civil suit until after the election.

That night I was convinced that Richey was fixed: someone at the White House or on its behalf was telling Richey what to do. I couldn't know it at the time, but Richey was actively *seeking* guidance from Nixon. We learned that later from the Oval Office tapes. As John Dean told Nixon on September 15, 1972, "He's [Richey's] made several entrées, uh, off the bench, to, uh, (1) Kleindienst [attorney general], (2) to, uh, his old friend Roemer Mc-

Phee,* to keep Roemer abreast of what his thinking is."[10] Dean then reported to Nixon—*a week before Richey called his extraordinary session*—that Richey would put our civil suit on hold.

.   .   .

Despite the depositions I had noticed, our amended complaint, and O'Brien's charges that the bugging was part of a wider White House–directed plot, the press remained largely indifferent. The *Washington Post* was the only paper covering the scandal. None of the television networks gave it much attention.

It was the same on Capitol Hill. The only senior Democrat whom I could interest was Wright Patman, chairman of the House Banking and Commerce Committee. At my urging, Patman, a firebrand populist from Texas, invited Maurice Stans to testify about the break-in. Stans refused. Then on October 3 Patman lost his effort to hold a Banking Committee probe of Nixon campaign finances by a 20-to-15 vote; six Democrats joined fourteen Republicans in rejecting any investigation. Members of Congress were involved in their own reelection campaigns. Most Democrats feared that Nixon's twenty-eight-point lead over McGovern put them in jeopardy; they were more concerned to distance themselves from McGovern than to attack Nixon.

On October 4, I was again in Richey's court protesting his decision to seal the transcript of his extraordinary September 21 private hearing and depositions, to no avail. Simultaneously, encouraged by the Department of Justice and lawyers for the seven defendants in the Watergate break-in, chief district court judge John Sirica, who was trying the Watergate criminal case, issued his own gag order. Sirica prohibited all out-of-court comment on the criminal trial by the prosecution, defendants, defendants' lawyers, law enforcement officials, witnesses, potential witnesses—even by complaining witnesses and alleged victims of the bugging incident.

---

*Henry Roemer McPhee was general counsel to the Republican National Finance Committee at the time and a friend of both Maurice Stans and Judge Richey. In a brief telephone interview for this book, McPhee admitted to me that he was "close to Chuck Richey, who was a very good friend." He also admitted that he was in frequent contact with Maurice Stans about the litigation. But he claimed he was not the go-between for Richey and the White House, conduct which could subject him, as a lawyer, to professional disciplinary action, if not more serious charges.

O'Brien and I were outraged. Have these bastards gotten to Sirica as well? I wondered. Is *he* fixed?

The following day I wrote to Judge Sirica. I had advised presidential candidate McGovern and other Democrats, I told Sirica, that the gag order was not intended to apply to them and did not limit their freedom of speech in any way: "Any prior restraint upon free speech which was promulgated in terms so broad, with standards so vague and uncertain, dealing with a matter of public controversy in a political contest for the highest office in the land, would be in clear violation of the First Amendment."

I asked Sirica to confirm my advice immediately, in order to "remove any chilling effect." At my suggestion, Larry O'Brien was prepared to test Sirica's order with some tough public statements. O'Brien was ready to call it "an outrage that Judge Sirica, Nixon's Justice Department, and the Watergate defendants would conspire to gag the opposition party." For openers, the next day O'Brien released my letter and called Sirica's gag rule "nothing less than an act of suppression by the Nixon administration." It was, he said, "evidence of the lengths to which Mr. Nixon and his administration will go to keep a tight lid on this unprecedented act of political espionage."

We were prepared to defy Sirica's order and launch a First Amendment fight. O'Brien asked, "What will happen if we're held in contempt?"

"You go to jail and I go back to my office," I joked. "But it'll be one helluva story."

The next day, Sirica narrowed his order, in effect agreeing with everything in my letter. He took the occasion to indicate that all matters relating to the criminal proceedings would be handled in public view.

·   ·   ·

On October 10, the *Washington Post* revealed that the Watergate break-in was part of a larger scheme of espionage and sabotage against the Democrats financed through a secret CREEP fund. CREEP's activities included investigating personal lives of candidates and their families, forging letters, leaking false information to the press, throwing campaign schedules off, investigating Democratic campaign workers, planting provocateurs at the national political conventions, and stealing confidential files.

On October 13, as the history of all this espionage and sabotage surfaced,

I wrote to Judge Richey again. I objected to his stay of the civil proceedings and all depositions. I again urged Richey to release the transcript of the September 21 pre-trial hearing to the public. "It is my firm conviction that release of the transcript will serve not only the interests of my client, but the interests of justice and the interests of maintaining confidence in the integrity of the judiciary under the circumstances of this case." I thought that release of the transcript would reveal Richey's bias to the press and lead reporters to investigate his relationship with the Nixon White House. I also urged Richey to follow Sirica's lead by declaring all proceedings and papers in the civil suit public.

Richey ignored my letter. Our only hope now—and a slim one—was that the criminal case might be tried before the election. This hope vanished when, on October 27, Judge Sirica postponed the trial until January, blaming the delay on a "pinched nerve." Sirica and Richey thus effectively swept both trials off the election radar screen. I was crushed. I worried that Nixon had subverted the federal court system. I wondered aloud to O'Brien, "What kind of a country do we live in?"

.   .   .

In the *Post* newsroom, Bradlee was getting nervous. Only the *Washington Post* was covering this story. The paper's credibility was under attack. Woodward and Bernstein had written a story charging that Hugh Sloan had told the grand jury that Haldeman controlled the secret fund for espionage and sabotage. As it turned out, Sloan had not given any such testimony (though Haldeman did in fact control the fund). The slip gave the White House ammunition to attack the *Post* for shoddy coverage across the board.

I despaired the lack of media interest. Media competition, I had learned, was a damn good thing. It helped break big stories and spurred reporters to dig deep. Where was it in this case? My efforts had failed to spark any serious interest by any other paper or any broadcaster. The *Post* stood alone.

Then, Walter Cronkite sank his teeth into the story. He ran special Watergate segments on the *CBS Evening News* in late October, a few days before the election. Cronkite, at the time the most trusted man in America, spent fourteen minutes on the evening news, guiding viewers through charts that explained the Watergate scandal. When Cronkite flashed pictures of the

Post's headlines, Bradlee and the cub reporters were vindicated and the *Post*'s news judgment validated. As I had seen with the civil rights movement and the Vietnam War during the Johnson administration, television had compelling power. Suddenly the country tuned in to the scandal. The editors at the *Post* breathed a collective sigh of relief.

On November 7, Nixon and Agnew defeated McGovern and Shriver in the expected landslide. For the first time, the South voted solidly Republican. Nationally, Nixon received 60 percent of the Catholic vote, 61 percent of the blue-collar vote. Only two traditionally Democratic constituencies stayed loyal: 63 percent of Jews and 87 percent of blacks voted for McGovern.[11] The stage was set for presidential revenge. The *Post* and our law firm braced for a counter attack from a bolstered President Nixon.

.   .   .

Once the Justice Department presented the evidence it had of the Watergate break-in to a grand jury, it was inevitable that Woodward and Bernstein would try to learn what the jurors were hearing. This involved pressing witnesses and their lawyers for information, which the eager reporters did with a vengeance.

In December, U.S. Attorney Earl Silbert and his assistant Seymour Glanzer angrily called me. They demanded that, "as lawyer for the *Post* and as an officer of the court," I tell the cub reporters to stop approaching grand jury witnesses about the case. I reminded my callers that witnesses were free to talk about their testimony with the *Post* if they chose. Silbert charged that the reporters were too aggressive; they were interfering with the grand jury. When I relayed the message, Woodward and Bernstein laughed. "We have just come from a one-hour interview with Silbert and Glanzer. They never raised the issue with us."[12]

The next complaint I received from Silbert was that *Post* reporters also were trying to contact grand jury members, who were required under federal rules of criminal procedure to keep secret the testimony they heard. Any reporter who induced a grand juror to violate this rule, Silbert cautioned, would be guilty of contempt of court. I told Bradlee of this call and both Ed Williams and I told the *Post* editor that Woodward and Bernstein could not approach grand jurors. "Suppose the grand juror approaches them?" Bradlee said, chuckling. "Tell them to walk away," Ed and I chorused. Bradlee gave us his mischievous grin and we both left his office wondering what was going on.*

.   .   .

Any doubts that the civil suit had opened a festering political sore evaporated when Frank Fitzsimmons, president of the Teamsters Union, came to see Williams in early 1973. Williams had for years represented the Teamsters—the only union that supported Richard Nixon. When its boss Jimmy Hoffa was indicted in 1957, Attorney General Robert Kennedy had been so certain of a conviction that he said he would jump off the Capitol dome if Hoffa did not go to jail. When the jury voted to acquit, Ed Williams, Hoffa's lawyer, sent Kennedy a parachute. Our firm had won more than a dozen Teamsters cases after that and had never suffered a defeat in either criminal or civil litigation.

Fitzsimmons told Williams he was "concerned about being represented by a firm with a partner who was such an inept lawyer that he filed a frivolous suit against the Committee to Re-elect the President." Unless we dropped the case, Fitzsimmons said, "the Teamsters might have to look elsewhere for better legal representation."

As soon as Fitzsimmons left his office, Ed related the conversation to Paul Connolly and me. I worried about Ed's reaction; his expression was serious. The DNC, a non-paying client, might not even be able to reimburse our expenses. The Teamsters, on the other hand, were a major profit center.

Ed then recounted his experience with Mafia boss Frank Costello. Morris Ernst, the great constitutional lawyer, had brought Costello to Ed in the late fifties, suggesting that the mobster retain Williams to argue his deportation case before the Supreme Court. Near the end of the discussion, Costello asked Ed if he was the same Williams who had represented Senator

*In their 1974 book, *All the President's Men*, Woodward and Bernstein suggest that we had assured Bradlee that their attempts to get at grand jurors would not violate any rules. Williams exploded over the insinuation that he had approved the reporters' contacting grand jurors; it wasn't true. He felt it would hurt him with judges all over the country. I was less concerned than Ed, but he asked me to get Simon and Schuster to have the passage removed. I called Dick Synder, the aggressive new head of the publishing house. I made the usual threats, we had some heated discussions, but he shipped the books to stores unchanged a few days later.

Joe McCarthy. Ed responded yes. Costello said that he didn't want to retain the guy who represented McCarthy. Ed coolly replied, "No client can determine who else I represent." Costello backed off—and Ed blocked his deportation. Williams turned to me. "That rule still goes," he said.

Williams told Frank Fitzsimmons that we would not abandon the Watergate lawsuit. A few days later, the Teamsters dropped us as counsel. They ordered us to transfer all their files to the offices of Chuck Colson, who had left the Nixon White House for private practice. Work for the Teamsters had kept about a fifth of our twenty or so lawyers busy. Ed, Paul, and I scoured the country for more legal work to fill up the gap.

. . .

Unknown to me, on January 13 Nixon and Haldeman had discussed blackmailing Lyndon Johnson to pressure me to back off the lawsuit. Their threatened hammer was to reveal LBJ's bugging of Nixon and Agnew during the 1968 presidential campaign. As Nixon's White House tapes later revealed, Haldeman proposed "to use it on Johnson . . . [to] get Califano and some of those people . . . and if Johnson turns them off, it could turn them the other way. . . ."[13]

The Johnson "bugging" was in fact National Security Agency eavesdropping on the South Vietnamese. NSA learned—and reported to LBJ—that Nixon was trying to scuttle the Vietnam peace negotiations before the 1968 election. LBJ was indeed approached to turn me off; he was threatened with revelation of the eavesdropping a few days before his death. But LBJ showed no fear. He told Nixon's messenger that he would be happy to blow the whistle on Nixon's urging the South Vietnamese to delay the Vietnamese peace talks, hinting that he would give them a better deal after the election. Apparently this stopped Nixon's effort dead in its tracks. President Johnson never asked me to alter my conduct in connection with the DNC lawsuit against CREEP or to soft-pedal my efforts to shine a spotlight on Watergate.

. . .

In January, the criminal trial before Judge Sirica ended. Four Cubans pled guilty. Liddy and McCord were convicted. Convinced that Judge Richey was fixed and would thwart our lawsuit, O'Brien and I appealed to senators Ted Kennedy of Massachusetts, Phil Hart of Michigan, and Birch Bayh of Indiana to press for creation of a special Senate Watergate committee. On February 6, with the criminal trial over, Judge Richey had to dissolve all stays in the pending civil suit, allow depositions to continue, and begin to release transcripts of those already taken. The next day, two weeks after Nixon's Inauguration, the Senate unanimously passed Senate Resolution 60, establishing a seven-member select committee to probe the Watergate scandal.[14]

As the *Washington Post* broke story after story, responsibility for the Watergate break-in moved closer to CREEP, former attorney general Mitchell, and the Nixon White House. The White House was desperate to stop the deluge of *Post* stories. On February 26, Kenneth Parkinson,[15] attorney for CREEP, took advantage of the civil suit I had filed to subpoena *Post* reporters Bob Woodward and Carl Bernstein, managing editor Howard Simons, and Kay Graham. The subpoena demanded all their notes, internal memoranda, and phone logs. CREEP wanted to uncover the identity of the reporters' anonymous source or sources.

Woodward was in the Caribbean at the time. Bradlee did not want Bernstein to be served before talking to me. So on the afternoon the court issued the subpoenas, Bradlee told Bernstein to get out of the building and go see a movie. Bernstein went to see *Deep Throat*—because Howard Simons had named the pair's anonymous source after the title of this notorious pornographic film.

Bradlee made the *Post's* position clear: the paper would never turn over its reporters' notes or reveal the identity of Deep Throat. If the court issued an order to do so, reporters would go to jail for contempt before disclosing their notes or confidential sources.

The law was not nearly so clear. Indeed, if there was a legal tide, it was against us. On June 29, 1972, the Supreme Court had held, in *Branzburg v. Hayes,* that a reporter's notes were not protected under the First Amendment from subpoena by a grand jury in a criminal proceeding. Our resistance would test that ruling in a civil case. To Bradlee, I confessed my doubts whether courts would recognize the right of reporters to refuse to divulge confidential sources or turn over notes used in preparing their stories. In view of Richey's behavior so far, I expected him to rule against us. We would have to win on appeal if at all.[16]

"Well, you sure as hell better bring this one in," Bradlee said, "because there's not a snowball's chance in hell we'll turn over what they want."

Like two heavyweight boxers with glass jaws, the courts and the media had finessed most First Amendment confrontations. Now, however, the *Post* took the gloves off. We were in a barefisted fight not only with the administration but also possibly with the federal judiciary. Sorely in need of a tactical advantage, I insisted that all the notes be given to *Washington Post* publisher Katharine Graham. "It will be a helluva lot harder," I said, "for some judge to put Katharine Graham in jail than to incarcerate Woodward, Bernstein, or Simons." Bradlee, chortling, said that a picture of *Post* owner Kay Graham, in handcuffs, getting out of her limousine to go to prison would be on the front page of every paper in the world. Among us (and unknown to Kay), my tactic became known as the "gray-haired widow" and "widowed grandmother" defense.

Before arguing the motion to quash the subpoena, I signaled the *Post*'s position publicly. I wanted Richey to know that if he ordered compliance with the subpoena, he would have to send someone from the paper to prison—and that it might be Kay Graham. I also enjoyed noting publicly that in 1971 Attorney General John Mitchell's Justice Department had established a policy prohibiting U.S. attorneys from issuing a subpoena to a reporter unless all other possible sources of the desired testimony had been exhausted.[17] In meetings and at dinner parties over the next few weeks, Bradlee voiced the *Post*'s opposition to the subpoena incessantly. He was so frustrated that he would not get the chance to go to jail that we accused him of having subpoena envy.

On Monday, March 5, as counsel for the *Post* I requested a hearing on the motion to quash the subpoenas. The next day, Judge Richey called to court every attorney in the case, by now more than two dozen. Richey asked each to rise and identify his client. I brought Greg Craig, an associate at Williams, Connolly & Califano, with me. He named the Democratic National Committee as his client and I named the *Washington Post*. Richey called me to the bench and publicly accused me of a serious conflict. He ordered me to inform the court by 10 A.M. the following morning which client our firm represented—the Democratic National Committee or the *Washington Post*. He threatened to hold a separate hearing on the conflict and my professional conduct.

Williams had always stretched to the limit the number of clients we could represent in a particular matter without finding a conflict. He considered it particularly important in criminal cases to keep as many witnesses as possible under his control. When I told Ed that afternoon what Richey had ordered, with a twinkle in his eyes, he mocked: "You dumb sonuvabitch. I always said we never have a conflict unless you meet your partner on the other side of a case in the courtroom. Now you've gotten caught on two sides of the same case!"

With my friend Larry O'Brien no longer the DNC chairman, and having served four years as unpaid counsel, the choice was easy. We selected the *Washington Post*.[18] I felt much more comfortable, since I was becoming involved on an almost daily basis in clearing Watergate stories for the paper or advising on legal issues the paper's aggressive coverage raised.

Nixon was concerned about the DNC civil suit. I learned later from the tapes that on March 16, Nixon and Kissinger discussed the suit. Kissinger described me to Nixon as "partisan," a "decent guy, but still very much opposed to you." He recalled running into me in late January and reported to Nixon, "[Califano] was practically salivating then at the prospect of what the trial would do to us."[19] Actually, that day Kissinger had told me outside Sans Souci after lunch that Nixon's reelection meant that the Watergate issue would evaporate and that he couldn't see how "Democrats could recover from their electoral debacle." I replied that judges read newspapers—and that with the *Washington Post* writing a new story each day, Sirica's criminal trial or our civil suit could well be the undoing of Nixon. "Watergate will bring back the Democrats," I contended. Kissinger had passed my comments on to Ehrlichman, who brushed him off saying, "Wishful thinking! If that is what they are counting on, they will be out of office for thirty years."[20]

On Wednesday, March 21, in Court Room 22, I argued that the subpoenas for the notes and sources of the *Washington Post* should be quashed.* My central point was that if reporters were forced to reveal their sources and confidential notes, their ability to gather news would be eviscerated and the First Amendment undermined.

After three hours of oral argument, Richey delivered his opinion from

*At the very moment I was arguing the case for the *Post,* John Dean was meeting in the Oval Office with Nixon and Haldeman, calling Watergate a "cancer on the presidency."

the bench, quashing the subpoenas on First Amendment grounds. He ruled that in measuring the public's right to know against any possible harm to a free press, "the scales were heavily weighted" in favor of the journalists. "This Court," he said, "cannot blind itself to the possible 'chilling effect' the enforcement of these broad subpoenas would have on the flow of information to the press, and so to the public."

It was the first time any federal court had acted so broadly to protect confidential sources of reporters. I was delighted with the ruling and believed it was correct, but I was surprised that it came so swiftly and resoundingly from Richey. Since the judge was no constitutional heavyweight, I chalked some of it up to his sensitivity about how he was perceived in the press. I suspected—and hoped—it might also reflect his reading of the political tea leaves that Nixon was in deep trouble.

The identity of Deep Throat would remain a mystery into the twenty-first century. I never knew who this confidential source was. I never examined the reporters' notes, nor did Kay Graham. I felt that as attorney for the *Post* it was better that I not know the identity of Deep Throat. I didn't need to know to prepare my argument and write the brief—indeed I could use my lack of knowledge as a plus in court. Only Woodward and Bernstein knew at the time. Ben Bradlee learned after President Nixon resigned.

.   .   .

The day after the *Washington Post* subpoenas were quashed, Judge Sirica sentenced the Watergate conspirators and read in open court a letter he had received from James McCord. The letter alleged that others were involved in the Watergate break-in, perjury had been committed at the trial, and pressure had been applied to make the defendants plead guilty.

This moved Watergate to a new level. O'Brien and the Democrats again amended their complaint, increasing the damages sought and adding Nixon aides as defendants. *Washington Post* stories moved in closer to the Oval Office. Several times a week in late afternoon I would rush over to the newsroom to review a story or I would receive a call from Simons or Bradlee about the latest break.

By early spring, it seemed that every day Washington's entire population woke up early and went straight to their front door for the morning *Post*'s revelations. Bradlee reveled in the situation, saying everyone wanted their "daily fix" from the paper. Just being the paper's lawyer put me on almost everyone's "A" list and added a new dimension of celebrity to my life. Friends and colleagues, at lunch, at dinner parties, after tennis games, peppered me with questions for "the inside skinny" on Watergate. For the first time, murmuring doubts of Nixon's survival bubbled up at dinner conversations across America.

In February 1973, as the flood of Watergate stories seeped toward the door of the Oval Office, I began meeting occasionally with Senate Judiciary Committee members Ted Kennedy, Phil Hart, and Birch Bayh. At one of our sessions, we decided to press for an independent prosecutor. Nixon's appointees could not be trusted to investigate the president who appointed them. The civil suit of the Democratic Party was limited to narrow issues of liability, and the Democrats were on the brink of settling, owing to lack of funds. The Senate Watergate committee—formally, the Senate Select Committee on Presidential Campaign Activities—was set up along political lines, and the public would see both Republican and Democratic senators as having an interest in protecting their party's interests. An independent prosecutor would be perceived as searching for truth and justice, with only the public good in mind. At Kennedy's urging I wrote an op-ed piece laying out the case for a special prosecutor. The *New York Times* published it on April 24, 1973.

.   .   .

Four days after my op-ed in the *Times*, the *Post* broke the story of the September 1971 break-in at Daniel Ellsberg's psychiatrist's office. The burglary was directed by White House aides Hunt and Liddy in response to Ellsberg's leak of the Pentagon Papers. Two days later, the two top White House aides, H. R. Haldeman and John Ehrlichman, and Attorney General Richard Kleindienst resigned. White House counsel John Dean, who had begun cooperating with Watergate prosecutors, was fired. In a televised address that evening, Nixon named Elliot Richardson as attorney general and Leonard Garment as White House counsel.

Five days later, on May 3, my friend Al Haig called me. He said that Nixon had asked him to come to the White House as chief of staff. Haig, who had been Kissinger's deputy at the National Security Council, was then vice chief of staff of the Army. I told Haig he was probably on track to become Army chief of staff and eventually chairman of the Joint Chiefs. If he took the post with Nixon, I warned, those opportunities would fade away. "Nixon will either be impeached or resign, Al. It's just a matter of time as more unfolds. If guys like Haldeman and Ehrlichman face jail time, they'll spill on Nixon," I said.

Haig stopped me with a question. "What about the need to protect the presidency?"

We both supported a strong presidency. "The presidency is in dire straits," I said. As we discussed the matter, I agreed that Haig might be able to help. But did he have any obligation to try?

Lyndon Johnson, faced with someone who resisted his fabled persuasive power and refused to take a job offered, would say, "You're not saying 'No' to me. You're saying 'No' to the presidency and to your country. Hasn't your country been pretty good to you?" More often than not, faced with this argument, LBJ's target would end up saying "Yes."

"Al," I finally said, "this isn't what you or I would wish for you. But it's what the country needs."

The next day, Haig became Nixon's White House chief of staff. Unknown to me, on his first day in the job Al urged Nixon to hire Ed Williams and me to represent him. Nixon rejected the idea on the ground that we were both Democrats.[21] (Actually, Ed was a most conservative Democrat; I suspect he voted for Republicans most of his life except for John Kennedy and Lyndon Johnson.)

.   .   .

As the Senate Watergate hearings began on May 17, I called on President Nixon to resign. It was clear to me by then that he had violated the constitutional rights of numerous individuals and had seriously stained the office of the presidency. He was either so paranoid or so determined to save his own skin that he threatened our constitutional government by violating civil rights of citizens with wire-taps and break-ins.[22]

Bowing to the rising demands for an independent investigation, on the next day Attorney General Elliott Richardson appointed Harvard Law

School professor Archibald Cox as special prosecutor. The selection exhilarated me, because I knew of Cox's integrity through his service as solicitor general under Attorney General Robert Kennedy. For the first time I believed the nation would get an aggressive and objective investigation.

John Dean testified before Congress that June. His testimony implicated Nixon in the cover-up dating back to a September 15, 1972, meeting with the President and Haldeman. The strategy of cover-up discussed in that meeting was to slow down the civil suit I had filed. Testifying about the meeting when he appeared before the Watergate committee in July, Haldeman admitted, "There was some discussion about Judge Richey hearing the civil case and a comment that he would keep Roemer McPhee abreast of what was happening."

In his appearance before the committee on July 11, John Mitchell testified that "it was our strategy to limit the progress of the civil suit as much as possible before the election." Mitchell admitted that Roemer McPhee was brought in at the suggestion of Maurice Stans. There was "no question," he said, that everybody knew McPhee was also a good friend of Judge Richey. Now, Richey's bias was coming to light.

. . .

Late on Monday morning, July 16, Alexander Butterfield telephoned my office. As an Air Force lieutenant colonel, Butterfield had been one of my three military aides when I worked as Defense Secretary McNamara's special assistant. He was now one of Nixon's top aides and schedulers. He was calling from the barbershop at the Sheraton Carlton Hotel on 16th Street.

"This past Friday I was interviewed by a Watergate committee investigator, Don Sanders," Butterfield said. "He asked me a lot of questions and in response I told him about a voice-activated taping system in the White House." Butterfield then described the elaborate sound-activated system in the Oval Office. Every telephone call to Nixon went through Butterfield first, even those from Nixon's wife and daughters, because Nixon taped indiscriminately and insisted on knowing what people—even his own family—wished to talk to him about before getting on the phone. "I've been subpoenaed to testify this afternoon," Butterfield said. "I need help."

That's an understatement, I thought.

Butterfield was a straight arrow, a military professional. I knew he would tell the whole truth when he testified. He asked if I could represent him.

"I can't," I said. "Much as I'd like to help you, I've got a conflict. I filed the lawsuit for the Democratic party against CREEP and I'm the lawyer for the *Washington Post*."

"What should I do?" Butterfield asked.

"Get in touch with [White House Counsel] Len Garment."

He did.

Garment, who nearly dropped the phone when he heard from Butterfield, couldn't represent him, because he was the President's lawyer.

Butterfield called me back. We talked about the Watergate imbroglio. After I questioned him in some detail, I was convinced that he had nothing to do with any of it. "Since you are completely clean," I said, "you have nothing to hide. I suggest you testify without counsel. It'll make a much better impression on the committee."

Cautiously agreeing, Butterfield asked if I had any other advice.

"Are you still at the barber?" I asked, remembering his full head of black hair.

"Yes," he responded.

"Then I suggest you get a damned good haircut. They're going to take a lot of pictures of you today."

Butterfield's testimony that afternoon opened a new front in the Watergate war—the battle for the tapes.

The next day Al Haig called. What, he asked, should he advise the President to do about the tapes? The Senate Watergate committee wanted them, but neither the committee nor the grand jury had yet subpoenaed them. We discussed the options for a few minutes.

"What would you do if you were in my shoes?" Haig asked

"Al, we've been through a lot together. I'm not your lawyer. But if I were in your shoes, I'd tell the President to burn the tapes immediately and then proclaim he'd done so as a matter of national security and executive privilege and out of an obligation to protect the office of the presidency."

"All hell will break loose," Haig said.

"You bet," I said. "There will be the biggest firestorm this town has seen. For a week, maybe two or three. But then it will be over so far as the tapes are concerned."

I don't know what Haig's view was at the time, but a few days later he called and again asked if Williams and I could represent President Nixon. He said he had recommended that Nixon retain us. But I told Haig that it was still out of the question.*

Cox and the Senate committee both demanded the tapes. President Nixon was subpoenaed to produce them. His expected refusal set off a constitutional battle that would wind up in the Supreme Court.

.   .   .

On July 26 Bradlee called to say that Jim Doyle of Special Prosecutor Cox's staff was demanding to interview *Post* reporter Marilyn Berger about her article revealing that Ken Clawson, deputy director of White House communications, told her that he had forged Muskie's signature to a letter calling French Canadians "Canucks." The letter, revealed during the New Hampshire primary in 1972, had cost Muskie votes and weakened him as a candidate.

The background of the article was intriguing. On September 25, 1972, Clawson had called Berger to ask her out. She said no, she was too tired, but invited him to her place for a drink. Clawson arrived around nine in the evening and during the visit stated, "I wrote the Canuck letter." When Berger expressed surprise, Clawson responded, "That's politics." Berger later related this to *Post* political reporter David Broder, who said, "That's not politics as I understand it." Broder suggested Berger talk to Woodward and Bernstein, who thought they had traced the letter to the White House but did not know who there had written it. "Woodstein," as we often called the two reporters, asked Berger to see Clawson again, to try to reconfirm his story. Berger had lunch with Clawson on Columbus Day at Sans Souci. Clawson told her that if the *Post* ran her story, he would deny it. He was deeply concerned about the references to Berger's apartment, saying, "My wife would have a fit." The *Post* ran the story. Clawson denied it.[23]

Bradlee had told me that under no circumstances would he allow *Post* reporters to be interviewed by any government prosecutors. When they

---

*Shortly before he died of cancer in 1988, Williams arranged a peace-making lunch with Richard Nixon at Le Cirque in New York. He told the former president that the biggest mistake he had made was not burning the tapes.

approached Berger, I called Jim Vorenberg, special assistant to Cox. I had known Vorenberg since his time as staff director of President Johnson's Commission on Law Enforcement and Administration of Justice. "The *Post* has a consistent policy of not permitting its reporters to testify about such matters," I told him.

Vorenberg said he could understand the paper's point of view. "But others here, including Cox, feel strongly that Berger should be interviewed because no confidential sources were involved."

"The *Post* policy applies to any government interviews of its reporters," I responded. "It is not limited to situations where confidential sources are involved."

"But she wasn't acting as a reporter when Clawson told her about the letter," Vorenberg replied.

"From our point of view," I said, "reporters are on duty twenty-four hours a day and we view your request as analogous to trying to obtain a reporter's unpublished notes. It's chilling our First Amendment rights."

The conversation ended in an impasse. Vorenberg indicated that the special prosecutor's office might well subpoena Berger. I made it clear that such action would kick off a major battle. To my mind, fighting a subpoena from the special prosecutor would add to the credibility of the *Post* and its editors; it would demonstrate that we were prepared to stand on principle even where it might hinder Cox's investigation of the Nixon administration. So I was a little disappointed when the special prosecutor backed off and declined to subpoena Marilyn Berger.

.   .   .

But we had little time to relax. Another subpoena was in the wings. On July 14, a man named Allen Green visited Brendan Sullivan, the hottest young lawyer in our firm.[24] Green needed a lawyer in connection with a federal criminal investigation in Baltimore. Sullivan called me at home that evening. "Something's come up. I need to talk to you."

"Go ahead."

"I can't talk on the phone."

Sullivan had a point. By now we were so concerned that our phones might be bugged that we periodically had the office swept.

We agreed to talk the next day while on the Chesapeake Bay on Sullivan's sailboat, the *Mistrial*. With my sons Mark and Joe at the front of the boat, Brendan and I retired to the stern. Whispering so that even my children could not hear, Brendan said, "You'd better hang on to the railing for this."

Allen Green wanted our firm to represent him in a grand jury investigation of alleged kickbacks and bribes involving Maryland politicians.

"What's so surprising about that?" I asked. We both knew the Maryland state government had a reputation for corruption.

"It involves Vice President Agnew," Brendan whispered. "While Agnew was governor of Maryland, Green claims he paid him $11,000 in return for millions in contracts from the state roads commission."

"Jesus Christ!"

"That's not all," Brendan continued. "Green kept paying Agnew after he became vice president. Green says he delivered Agnew two thousand bucks three or four times a year in Agnew's apartment at the Sheraton Park Hotel. Sometimes he even made payoffs in the vice president's office next to the White House. Green thinks it totals about fifty grand over six years."

"Do you believe him?"

"Yes. This guy's scared shitless. Incredible as his story sounds, this guy's telling the truth. He delivered this money to Agnew in a plain brown paper bag."

Our firm was already representing the *Washington Post*, the Democratic Party, and Robert Vesco, who had skipped the country for the Bahamas, and George Steinbrenner, both charged with making illegal contributions to Nixon's campaign. We were advising members of the Senate Watergate committee. Would we now we have a client who could send the vice president to jail?

I returned to Washington incredulous. Many law firms in town had clients caught up in the scandal. None, however, were sitting on powder kegs like this. Art Buchwald (unwittingly) captured the mounting tension in our firm when he wrote in one of his columns, "Thanks to the Watergate fallout every law firm in this city is now on a 24-hour, seven-day-a-week schedule. Whereas most law offices were sedate, quiet places, they now resemble brokerage offices with everyone screaming into the phones."

As the Agnew investigation came to public light, Nixon was hospitalized with pneumonia. Brendan Sullivan and I speculated about a horrendous possibility: What if a soon-to-be indicted vice president inherited the presidency?

Agnew was a small-time politician. I remembered the first time I had met him. Shortly after the 1968 election, Nixon had announced that his vice president would be the first to have an office in the West Wing of the White House. My office there was by far the largest—and the only one, aside from the President's and the press secretary's, that had its own private bathroom. On a late November afternoon, Agnew came to be briefed on the government's domestic programs—and to see my office. There had been rumors that he and Bryce Harlow were jockeying for my space. When Agnew arrived, he instructed one of his Secret Service agents to stand behind him as he sat at my conference table. When my briefing had gone about twenty or thirty minutes, Agnew became fidgety and distracted. He never asked a question. When I finished, he thanked me, rose, looked around the office, and walked to the door directly opposite the one through which he had entered. He opened it slightly, saw it was a bathroom, smiled, turned to me, shook hands, and left. All he cares about is the bathroom, I realized. (When the transition dust settled, it was Bryce Harlow, Nixon's congressional aide, who moved into my office.)

On August 6, Agnew preemptively announced that he was under criminal investigation and professed his innocence. On August 7, Richard Cohen and Carl Bernstein reported that Agnew was a target of a political kickback probe. As the investigation continued, Cohen, a Maryland Metro reporter at the *Washington Post*,[25] broke a series of stories about the investigation, often based on confidential sources. In San Diego in 1970, in a blistering speech crafted by William Safire, Agnew had assaulted the press as "nattering nabobs of negativism." The vice president was an inviting target for the media.

As press reports piled up and the criminal investigation ratcheted up the likelihood of an indictment, Agnew argued that under the constitution, as a sitting vice president, he could not be indicted unless he was first impeached. On September 24, I discussed this issue on an Eastern shuttle flight from New York to Washington with Representative John Brademas, a thoughtful Indiana Democrat and part of the House leadership. I told him of my concern: if Agnew, using his constitutional argument, sued to enjoin the grand jury investigating him, the Nixon Justice Department might agree. Then we'd have a sweetheart lawsuit designed to kill the investigation. I told Brademas that the House should be ready to intervene in such a suit.

The next day, I sent Brademas a memo written for the House Judiciary Committee: "Both Nixon and Agnew have obvious interests in protecting themselves and the past few weeks would indicate they will do anything necessary to provide themselves all the protection they can. . . . The House is charged with impeachment responsibility; to have its rights and duties defined in a lawsuit (between a Republican President and Vice President) to which it is not a party does not make much sense."[26]

My anxiety calmed when the Justice Department filed a brief in October in Baltimore federal court opposing Agnew's motion to block criminal proceedings and rejecting his constitutional argument. Solicitor General Robert Bork argued that only the president was immune from indictment while in office: "Although the office of the vice presidency is of course a high one, it is not indispensable to the orderly operation of government."

On October 2, Agnew's lawyers, Martin London and Jay Topkis of New York and Judah Best of Washington, asked Richard Cohen of the *Post* to voluntarily identify his sources for the Agnew stories. Cohen refused.

The next day, federal judge Walter Hoffman authorized Topkis to subpoena testimony from anyone suspected of knowledge about press leaks. In authorizing the subpoenas, Hoffman fired a shot across the *Post*'s bow: "Unfortunately, in the present day grab for . . . items, the news media frequently overlooks the rights of others. . . . We are rapidly approaching the day when the perpetual conflict between the news media, operating as they do under freedom of speech and freedom of the press, and the judicial system, charged with protecting the rights of persons under investigation for criminal acts, must be resolved." Agnew's lawyers immediately subpoenaed Cohen, seven other reporters, and two national news magazines, demanding that they identify their sources and turn over all their notes and unpublished materials.

Bradlee sent Cohen to see me. I told Cohen, a street-smart, sassy young reporter, we would fight the subpoena and that I wanted him to turn over his notes to Mrs. Graham. Cohen was worried: Could he trust me and the *Post* to stand firm? he asked. I admitted that it would be more difficult to quash his subpoena than Woodward and Bernstein's. "Here we're dealing

with a criminal grand jury investigation and the defendant's Sixth Amendment rights, not just a civil lawsuit between two private parties."

"How do I know the *Post* won't cave?"

"Because Ben Bradlee is the editor. For Ben and Mrs. Graham this is a
matter of sacred principle."

Cohen sat silent, skeptically so. I added, "It's easy for this judge to send a
brash young reporter to jail. Especially one from the *Post,* which has been
driving this story. I want Judge Hoffman to have to face sending Kay Graham to prison for contempt. That'll force him to think harder." It was the
gray-haired widow defense again.

What I didn't share with Cohen—or Kay Graham—was my fear that this
judge might in fact send someone to jail. As a lawyer, I never revealed such
concerns; I didn't want to rattle clients—even though Cohen would have
exulted in going to jail to protect a source.

Cohen eventually agreed to turn his notes over to Mrs. Graham and we
put them in a safe at the paper. We moved to quash the subpoena, and the
hearing on our motion was set for October 10. Kay Graham was speaking in
Hartford that day, but Judge Hoffman kept signaling that it was time to
tame the press, so we had a plane standing by to fly her to Baltimore; if necessary, she would refuse, in person, to turn over the notes.[27]

As I was editing the final drafts of our papers late on the afternoon of
October 9, Brendan Sullivan walked into my office. "I've been summoned
to Baltimore along with lawyers for the other witnesses against Agnew. This
evening."

"What's going on?"

"I don't know, but the heat is on Agnew. They want sworn statements
from Allen Green and the others and they want them tonight." The urgency
mystified Brendan. I was too busy preparing my motions to quash Cohen's
subpoena to think about it.

Early the next morning, I drove with Richard Cohen to Baltimore. As
Cohen and I mounted the steps of the federal court building, a frantic crush
of reporters and cameras surrounded us. The media knew that Judge Hoffman might send Cohen to jail immediately upon his refusal to turn over his
notes or reveal his sources. Bodies, microphones, and cameras jammed the
court steps so tightly that we couldn't get through. Two marshals had to
escort us to the clerk's office to file our papers and await the afternoon hear-

ing. As we reached the top of the courthouse steps, Cohen whispered to me, "You know, Joe, when I was a kid it was always the Jewish lawyer with the Italian defendant." We both laughed, breaking the tension as we entered the courthouse.

At 2 P.M. we all filed into the court. Judge Hoffman entered and immediately sealed the room. To our surprise, three minutes later, Attorney General Elliott Richardson entered, then Spiro Agnew with his lawyers. Richardson spoke briefly. Then, before our eyes, Agnew resigned as vice president and entered his plea of nolo contendere to a single count of federal income tax evasion in 1967. He accepted a three-year criminal sentence of unsupervised probation and a $10,000 fine. In return, the Justice Department agreed not to prosecute him for extortion and bribery.

The Cohen subpoena was instantly moot. Not a single reporter or other person noticed us as we left the building. It was a vivid lesson of how fleeting Andy Warhol's fifteen minutes of fame is. I fumed on the drive back to Washington. The court, I believed, had allowed Agnew to trade his vice presidency like a Monopoly "get out of jail free" card. Only Vice President Aaron Burr had gotten off more easily, in 1804, when he killed Alexander Hamilton in a duel but was never prosecuted.

.   .   .

Ten days later, on Saturday evening October 20, Trudy and I went to Art Buchwald's forty-eighth birthday party at the McLean Tennis Club. Much of the Washington establishment was there—Kay Graham; the columnist and former Truman press secretary Clayton Fritchey and his wife, Polly; David Brinkley; Ben Bradlee and Sally Quinn; Meg Greenfield, deputy editor of the *Post* editorial page; Rowland Evans; Jack Valenti; Mel Elfin, *Newsweek*'s Washington bureau chief; and a cadre of top television and newspaper reporters and columnists. Most of the fifty or so guests paired off for an indoor doubles tennis tournament.

That afternoon, Archibald Cox had rejected Nixon's offer to hand over mere summaries of the subpoenaed tapes. Cox insisted on listening to the full recordings. Amid rumors that Nixon might dismiss him, Cox claimed that as a special prosecutor appointed by the attorney general, he could be fired only by Elliot Richardson.

At 8:25 P.M., with the Buchwald tennis tournaments in full swing, we got word that White House press secretary Ron Ziegler had announced the firing of Archibald Cox. Over the next hour, we watched as television programs were interrupted with new details of the story. One by one teams stopped playing tennis and gathered around the television set. Even the most cynical, shock-proof reporters and editors were agog as one development topped the next.

Nixon ordered Richardson to fire Cox. Richardson refused and resigned. Then Nixon ordered Deputy Attorney General Williams Ruckleshaus to fire Cox. He refused and resigned. Solicitor General Robert Bork became acting attorney general. When Nixon told him to fire Cox, Bork obeyed the order.

Reporters from the daily papers, TV networks, and news magazines peeled off from the Buchwald party in their sneakers and tennis shorts as they were called to their newsrooms to cover the unfolding story. As I drove home to Cleveland Park, I realized for the first time that the embattled president in the Oval Office might be in terminal trouble. The tapes, I thought, must contain enough material to force his resignation or impeachment. For me, that evening marked the point at which I knew Richard Nixon had to be forced out if he wouldn't resign. We had a desperate man in the White House who was threatening our constitutional system. This was not partisan; now it was a matter of right and wrong, constitution versus conspiracy. I was determined to do all I could to hasten his departure.*

.   .   .

On the Monday after the Saturday Night Massacre, House Speaker Carl Albert called me. With a vacancy in the vice presidency, as Speaker of the House Albert was next in line to succeed to the presidency, a post to which he did not aspire. Aware of his limitations, not only did this mild-mannered Oklahoman, born on a farm and intent to retire to his rural district, harbor no ambition to be president, the possibility terrified him.

On October 12, two days after Agnew's resignation, President Nixon had nominated House Minority Leader Gerald Ford, a Michigan Republican, to

*A year later, on October 19, 1974, Buchwald threw the birthday party again. He called it "The First Anniversary of the Saturday Night Massacre Tennis Party." Archibald Cox, Elliot Richardson, and Bill Ruckelshaus attended.

become vice president. Under the Constitution, Ford's nomination required approval by both houses of Congress. With a real possibility that Nixon might resign or be impeached, Albert wanted to have Ford approved as vice president as rapidly as possible. "We can't live with a situation where it looks as though the Democrats are removing Nixon to take over the presidency," Albert said. He asked me to draft a statement for him indicating that he would have the House act on the Ford nomination before any impeachment resolutions would be considered. That evening I sent him the statement. The next day, Albert emphasized that the nomination of Ford for vice president would not be held hostage to impeachment proceedings. The confirmation of a vice president would be the first order of business, he said, because a "thorough airing of the issues relating to impeachment must be conducted in an atmosphere free of partisan political considerations."

Over the next two days, twenty-two bills for Nixon's impeachment were introduced. Albert referred them to the House Judiciary Committee for hearings in 1974.

On November 1, Nixon appointed Leon Jaworski to succeed Cox as special prosecutor and William Saxbe, a Republican senator from Ohio, as attorney general. The appointments did not quell the growing distrust of the President. Pressure intensified for him to turn over the Oval Office tapes. On November 17, Nixon was reduced to proclaiming in a nationally televised question-and-answer session from Orlando, Florida, "I am not a crook." Ten days later, in a speech before the District of Columbia Federal Bar Association, I called for Nixon's resignation or impeachment.

The Senate approved Ford's nomination at the end of November. The House acted on December 6, and Nixon swore in his new vice president later that day.

.   .   .

As the House Judiciary Committee began devising procedures for its impeachment hearings, Eastern establishment circles of the *Washington Post*, the *New York Times*, and academia questioned whether the committee's chair, Congressman Peter Rodino, was up to the task. Rodino was a first-generation Italian-American, a street politician from Newark. He was proud of every Italian honor and local award he had received. To be sure, he exhibited neither the polish of a sophisticated Ivy Leaguer nor the presence of a southern senator.

I respected and admired Rodino. I was proud of the fact that our nation would have two Italian-Americans—Sirica and Rodino—in charge of the most fateful constitutional crisis since the Civil War. I knew Rodino had the integrity and guts to do the job. I had seen him tested. During the Johnson administration we had enormous difficulty passing the Fair Housing Act.[28] Three years after he initially proposed the act, LBJ finally pried it out of the House Judiciary Committee in the wake of Martin Luther King's assassination—but only after we agreed that Emanuel Celler, a liberal Democrat from Brooklyn who chaired the committee, could keep a low profile on the bill. Celler's Brooklyn district, which included Crown Heights, was predominantly middle-class Jewish, and his constituents resented the movement of blacks into their neighborhood. The ranking Democrat after him was Rodino, who agreed to take the laboring oar in order to steer the bill through the House, even though his action would be unpopular in his Italian-American congressional district in Newark. The House passed the bill in 1968. Rodino almost lost his seat as a result.[*]

Rodino asked me to help prepare a plan for dealing with the impeachment resolutions and to help find a special counsel. He wanted a Republican, and in short order he accepted my recommendation, John Doar, President Kennedy's deputy attorney general for civil rights. My main contribution to their impeachment investigation was urging them to find out all they could from Alex Butterfield about Nixon's day-to-day routines and habits.

On March 1, 1974, the grand jury returned indictments against several former presidential aides in connection with the Watergate cover-up.[29] Nixon was named as an unindicted co-conspirator.

A week later, the House Judiciary Committee began its impeachment hearings. It specified six major areas of investigation: domestic surveillance; intelligence operations related to the presidential election; the Watergate break-in and cover-up; Nixon's personal finances; the political use of executive agencies and campaign fund abuses; and other misconduct, which included bombing Cambodia and scuttling the Office of Economic Opportunity.

Two weeks earlier, the first set of Nixon's transcribed tapes (1,254 pages)

*Years later as Rodino's district became predominantly black, he defeated a number of black challengers seeking the Democratic nomination because of his courage in 1968.

had been released to the public. Al Haig had called and asked me to meet him for a late dinner at Jean-Pierre on K Street. We took a discreet table in the back. A troubled Haig told me he had been subpoenaed to testify before the Senate Watergate committee. "I can't testify about Nixon or any work I'm doing for him," Haig said. "Shouldn't I claim executive privilege?"

"You shouldn't," I said. "But maybe Nixon should. It's the president's privilege. And if Nixon did that, it would be the president that was preventing you from testifying. That's what McNamara did when he refused to divulge which Defense Department employee reviewed which speech in the muzzling-the-military hearings. He read a letter from Kennedy invoking executive privilege."

On May 2, when Haig appeared before the Senate Watergate committee, he produced a letter from Nixon instructing him not to answer any questions. The plea of executive privilege angered several committee members; a year earlier Nixon had promised publicly that "executive privilege will not be invoked as to any testimony concerning possible criminal conduct or discussions of possible criminal conduct, in matters presently under investigation, including the Watergate affair and the alleged cover-up." But the senators accepted that Haig was simply the messenger.

.   .   .

The weeks were racing by, filled with new revelations—and a gathering sense that Nixon's presidency was doomed. On July 17, 1974, Leon Jaworski, the Texan who had replaced Archibald Cox as special prosecutor, asked me to stop by to see him. We met in his office at 1425 K Street in the late afternoon. I had known Jaworski during my days with Lyndon Johnson. He had been a personal friend and financial supporter of LBJ and we had a good relationship during those years. Jaworski and I did some lawyering together and some professional work when he was president of the American Bar Association.

The stocky, white-haired Jaworski was in a blue-striped shirt and glenplaid suit. We exchanged brief LBJ reminiscences. Then Jaworski spoke of the investigation of John Connally (former Texas governor, Treasury secretary under Nixon, and LBJ intimate) that the special prosecutor's office was conducting.

Because of his personal friendship with Connally, Jaworski told me, he had recused himself, but he wanted me to deliver a message to Ed Williams, who was representing Connally. "The lawyers working on the case think they have Connally cold for perjury and bribery," Jaworski said. "Connally made several mistakes before the grand jury when he had lawyers other than Ed. Williams is the best criminal lawyer in the country, but even he can't get John off."

"I would never bet against Ed in any trial," I said.

"John has such pride," Jaworski said, "that I doubt he is capable of leveling with his own attorneys."

The government's key witness against Connally was Jake Jacobsen, who had served on the Johnson White House staff with me. Jaworski said, "I've had numerous personal, professional, and business dealings with Jake and he has always told me the truth. He's never lied to me."

The issue in the case was whether Connally had taken a $10,000 bribe from Jacobsen on behalf of Associated Milk Producers Inc. The payment, Jacobsen said, was in return for supporting price supports for milk. Connally claimed that he had returned the money to Jacobsen when he discovered it was from the milk producers.

Jaworski is convinced they've got an air-tight case, I thought, and he wants me to warn Connally. Though Jaworski's disqualified himself, he wants to spare his friend an ugly and losing trial.

But this was not all Jaworski had in mind. His comments about Connally had been the appetizer. The main course was Richard Nixon and Al Haig.

"I am convinced that Nixon is guilty of a significant number of crimes: the most obvious, obstruction of justice and subornation of perjury," Jaworski said. Now he told me of several meetings he had with Haig, especially about one at the White House in which he told Haig of his conclusions. "Haig was visibly shaken," Jaworski said. "Tears misted in his eyes." Jaworski thought Haig was the only thing standing between Nixon's impeachment and conviction by the Senate or his criminal indictment. "Haig is by far the brightest, shrewdest, and cleverest of the men around Nixon today," he added.

What is Jaworski after? I wondered. Does he want me to deliver a message to Haig?

"Haig and Nixon are calling every single shot," Jaworski asserted. He recounted his proposed compromise on the sixty-four tapes that he had asked for: "I told Haig I would be willing to take eighteen." A few days later, Haig called Jaworski back and said that he and Nixon had listened to every one of the eighteen tapes for two full days and nights. "Haig told me," Jaworski said, "there's no way the President will give up those tapes."

"I assume the tapes are damaging beyond anything we can imagine," Jaworski concluded. He expected to win the Supreme Court case and have an order for the President to turn over the tapes.

When I probed to see why he was so sure of himself, Jaworski told me that the case against Nixon was so overwhelming that he had to stop the grand jury from indicting the President. "There are moments when I fear the grand jury might issue an indictment without my signature," Jaworski said.

"My God!" Jaworski feared he had a runaway grand jury on his hands.

"The foreman has told me privately that he and the jury do not even trust the Congress to deliver justice to Nixon."

I said that I thought Haig believed he was trying to save the presidency, not Nixon.

"That's what he repeatedly says, but I told him to think about whether he was destroying the presidency by using his considerable talents and shrewdness to keep Nixon in office," Jaworski responded.

Jaworski knew his comment had shaken Haig. He assured me that he would never prosecute the general unless a very serious offense surfaced. He believed that Haig, however misguided, was being a good soldier, soldiering the best he knew how. Still, Jaworski shared with me his doubts whether it was possible for anyone to serve Nixon at this point without becoming involved in an obstruction of justice.

Now it was clear to me: Jaworski wanted me to tell Haig that he was getting close to a precipice and it was time for him to start preparing the President to resign before Al got into criminal trouble himself.

"Joe," Jaworski then said, "let me discuss a hypothetical case with you. If we assume that one of the main reasons the President is not resigning is his fear of criminal prosecution and civil lawsuits, then what should I do if he approaches me for a deal in return for his resignation?"

He's trying to learn from me how the *Washington Post* and Democrats would react to such a deal, I thought. And to find out whether Larry O'Brien would sue a defrocked Nixon.

I decided to measure my words with extreme care. "I assume," I said, "that no one can assure the President he will be free of civil lawsuits. Larry O'Brien, for example, has a solid case against Nixon, Haldeman, and Ehrlichman for invasion of privacy."

Jaworski continued to press for my thoughts about a deal not to prosecute criminally in return for a resignation.

"That," I said, "is something only you can measure." I had no idea how I would react, much less how leading Democrats or *Washington Post* editorial page editors Phil Geyelin and Meg Greenfield would greet such a move.

Jaworski then expressed "deep concern about Americans under thirty-five." In the wake of Vietnam and Watergate, he thought "most of them believe the system doesn't work and can't believe that Nixon is still in office."

He also expressed concern about "whether Congress will fulfill its responsibilities."

I expressed confidence in Rodino.

Jaworski remained uncertain. "Do John Doar and Chairman Rodino have a sense of the fact that there is sufficient evidence in the record to convict the President of a crime and know how to accentuate that evidence in their report?"

This is another message he wants me to deliver, I thought.

Jaworski was still getting mail that Agnew had been let off too easily and worried that "young Americans, regardless of their ideology, will be deeply offended by any arrangement whereby the President resigned and was not indicted for his crimes."

I now sensed that Jaworski was struggling with a hard decision he might have to face quite soon. "There are strong arguments for accepting the President's resignation and assuring him he will not be indicted for crimes committed," I said. "But the orchestration of any such arrangement is of critical importance."

Seizing that opening, Jaworski immediately moved to a discussion of how to handle such a situation. We reviewed the need for support from the congressional leadership on both sides and from all presidential candidates. One argument for the deal could be the desperate shape of the economy; prices were rising at the fastest rate in twenty-two years in the midst of a severe economic downturn. Another was the paralysis of the federal government.

"Think about it and get back to me," Jaworski said. "This is moving fast. The evidence is so devastating that Nixon will never survive an impeachment proceeding if they get the facts out."

I expressed concern that Nixon might pardon Haldeman and Ehrlichman. Jaworski agreed, because he felt both aides would spill their guts when faced with serious time behind bars. "But if the President were granted immunity from prosecution if he resigned, there would be no need for him to pardon anyone," I said. Jaworski agreed.

At the end of the meeting, as we stood at his office door, Jaworski cautioned, "It's only a hypothetical we've been discussing," but he asked me to get back to him after I had reflected on our conversation.[30] This, I thought, is a hypothetical that is close to becoming real.

The next day I told Ed Williams only of the conversation that related to John Connally. It was one of the rare occasions when I felt constrained to keep something from him. I reminded Ed that Jake Jacobsen was one of the most liked and trusted aides on Johnson's staff, and added, "Jaworski said that he repeatedly admonished his staff not to even consider indicting anyone with a substantial reputation unless they were absolutely certain that they would win a conviction." Ed had me commit my conversation to writing so that he could show it to John Connally.

Two weeks later, on July 29, John Connally was indicted for accepting a bribe from the milk producers to support increased price supports, for perjury, and for obstruction of justice.

·   ·   ·

A week after my meeting with Jaworski, the Supreme Court ruled unanimously that Nixon must turn over the tapes to the special prosecutor. That same day, I contacted FBI Director Clarence Kelley to report threats against the lives of Woodward and Bernstein.[31]

Over the next week, the House Judiciary Committee—including a number of Republicans—voted three articles of impeachment against President Nixon: for obstruction of justice in attempting to cover-up Watergate, abuse of his powers by violating constitutional rights of U.S. citizens, and defying subpoenas.

On August 5, Nixon released transcripts of three conversations with

Haldeman held six days after the break-in. These "smoking-gun" tapes revealed that Nixon had ordered the FBI to abandon its investigation of the break-in. On August 7, Republican Party elders took matters into their own hands. A delegation, including senators Barry Goldwater of Arizona and Hugh Scott of Pennsylvania, and House Minority Leader John Rhodes, visited Nixon at the White House and told him it was over. On August 9, 1974, Nixon resigned. Gerald Ford was sworn in as president—and the suit I had filed three days after the Watergate break-in was settled for $775,000.

I watched Nixon's resignation on a grainy black-and-white television set at our house in Wellfleet on Cape Cod, where I was vacationing with Trudy and our children. As I sat on the beach in front of our house overlooking Gull Pond that evening, I had no sense of triumph, no high because "we finally got him." I was exhausted. My surging adrenaline from the past few years was whooshing out like air from a punctured balloon. I was satisfied that the system worked, that Sirica and Rodino, both ordinary guys, had delivered, and that Republicans—men like Howard Baker and Barry Goldwater—had put country before party. Most of all, I had a profound appreciation of how precious—and vulnerable—a free press is. Kay Graham's courage and the gutsy determination of Ben Bradlee and Howard Simons, and the tenacity of the young reporters Woodward and Bernstein, were inspiring. I think I knew then that being a part of Watergate would be as important as anything I would ever do as a lawyer and private citizen.

O'Brien donated his $400,000 settlement award to the Democratic National Committee, requesting "that it be applied to a program designed to re-enlist the confidence of the American people in our two-party system," and urged Republican Party Chairman George Herbert Walker Bush to match that amount for a similar effort.

A month later Gerald Ford pardoned Nixon. I considered it an act of presidential statesmanship, but he was criticized by many. I believe his actions cost him the election in his race against Jimmy Carter in 1976, but it was a wise and courageous decision. As part of his effort to heal the bitterness and division that infected the capital, Ford invited several Democrats to the White House early in his administration, including me, despite the fact that I had filed the civil lawsuit against CREEP and represented the *Washington Post.*

．　　．　　．

John Connally insisted on pleading not guilty and going to trial, notwithstanding Jaworski's warning. The trial began on April Fool's Day, 1975. Ed Williams had delayed it for eight months after Nixon resigned to separate it from the scandals. Spectators began lining up at 4 A.M. the day Williams questioned Jacobsen, vying for one of the courtroom's ninety seats. His cross-examination was worth the wait, but equally dramatic was the dazzling cast of character witnesses he assembled for Connally. They included Lady Bird Johnson, Barbara Jordan, Reverend Billy Graham, and Jack Valenti. Valenti was to be the last to testify; he was eager to express support for his friend from Texas, to have the final word. First came Lady Bird, then Barbara Jordan, and then Billy Graham. When Ed finished questioning Graham, he told the court there would be no more character witnesses.

Valenti, waiting outside the courtroom, was puzzled and annoyed. When the proceedings ended, Valenti asked Williams, "Why didn't you call me?"

Williams replied, "When I put Billy Graham on the stand I asked, 'Please state your name.'

"He responded, 'The Reverend Billy Graham.'

"I then asked, 'What is your occupation?'

"He responded, 'I preach the gospel of the Lord Jesus Christ.' I was standing at a far corner of the jury box. I heard two jurors whisper, 'Amen.' One was an elderly black lady who carried a Bible every day with her to the courtroom. Jack, at that point I knew I didn't need any more character witnesses."

Connally was acquitted. That night a grand party celebrated the acquittal at Bob Strauss's Watergate apartment. Everyone was elated, and Ed was rejoicing in another brilliant defense. At one point Strauss pulled out a bottle wrapped in a brown paper bag. He held it high as he spoke to Connally. "Helen and I have saved this bottle of French champagne for more than twenty-five years, waiting to open it on our fiftieth wedding anniversary," Strauss said. "But this is such an important occasion, we're going to open it now!"

Strauss went into the kitchen to open it. When he took it out of the brown paper bag, it was a bottle of Great Western champagne. "Bob, that's no twenty-five-year-old Dom Perignon," I said.

Twinkle in his eye, Strauss said, "Shut up and be quiet. This is a big night for John. I want him to know how much we care. John doesn't drink. He'll just take a sip and won't know the difference."

During the party, Nixon called to congratulate Connally and asked to speak to Williams. Nixon said, "I wish you guys were my lawyers. It's too bad you represent the *Post*," and invited Ed—but not me—to visit him at his San Clemente home in California.

·   ·   ·

Despite all that has been written and filmed about Watergate, remarkably little is known about the lawsuit that we filed on behalf of the Democratic National Committee three days after the crime. John Dean told me while we participated in an American Bar Association panel to mark the twenty-fifth anniversary of the break-in (with Ben Bradlee, Bob Woodward, and Leonard Garment) that Richard Nixon and the administration feared that lawsuit more than anything else.

The *Washington Post*, Dean recalled when I talked to him in California while working on this memoir, was the "only paper in town paying any attention to Watergate. . . . The greatest pressure was without question the civil lawsuit and the threat of depositions that could be very free-wheeling and very wide open, and that was a tremendous concern." Dean added that the unsealing of the depositions in the spring of 1973 gave the *Post* a host of leads that Bradlee, Simons, Woodward, and Bernstein pursued free of the straitjacket of courtroom rules, and that attracted the media in full force to the scandal. With all of that, as Dean said, Watergate began to "fall apart by its own weight."

To me, the overarching lesson of Watergate was how important courage is to our democracy. Nixon used everything he could to consolidate his power—bugging and break-ins to destroy the opposition Democratic Party and its chairman, burglary to get the medical records of Daniel Ellsberg's psychiatrist to destroy the man who leaked the Pentagon Papers. He tried to take away the *Washington Post*'s television licenses. He pushed one of the largest clients of Williams, Connolly & Califano to another firm. I admired the quintessential courage of Katharine Graham and not simply her willingness to go to prison if necessary as part of our "gray haired widow" defense. Kay put her entire fortune and her family's newspaper on the line—her livelihood and that of her children. She put her stack of chips on Ben Bradlee, Howard Simons, Bob Woodward, and Carl Bernstein, and on Ed Williams and me as her lawyers. If serious mistakes were made, those editors and reporters could go to another publication and Williams and I could move on to another client. For Kay, however, a serious mistake and failure to break the Watergate scandal could have devastated her family paper and fortune. I consider her steadfast commitment one of the signal acts of courage in our nation's history, an act that puts her right up there with the great heroes of independence and freedom.

Ed Williams also acted with principle and courage. When the Teamsters—a major client who provided at least 20 percent of our fees—threatened to leave our firm if I didn't drop the DNC lawsuit against CREEP, Ed decided instantly and at enormous personal cost that no one would tell us whom we could represent. He lived up to the profession's highest standards.

A different kind of lesson is that it takes all forums in Washington to unravel a major scandal—courts, Congress, executive branch, and media. That's the four-dimensional chessboard on which the Washington lawyer must play. It was a lesson I had learned in the Johnson White House; this was exactly what Ed Williams, Paul Connolly, and I wanted to show the world our law firm could do, but we hardly expected to put it to work on such a momentous matter.

I was struck by my own involvement in so many sides of the Watergate drama. I had personally represented the Democratic Party and the *Washington Post*. I was a partner in the firm representing Al Green, who bribed Agnew, and also representing George Steinbrenner, Robert Vesco, and John Connally. I found myself advising Haig and Butterfield, suggesting to Haig that he tell Nixon to burn the tapes. I had worked with Democratic senators pressing for a special prosecutor and establishment of the Senate Watergate committee. I helped Peter Rodino and Carl Albert and conferred with Jaworski, the special prosecutor, when he needed a messenger. I tried to be discreet. I never told one client, or friend, what another told me. I did share with Ed Williams and Paul Connally most of what I knew and did, except for my conversations with Jaworski about Nixon's criminal activity and my conversations with Haig.

I had worked hard—struggling at times—to negotiate the political, legal, and media minefields that Watergate presented and to maintain trust across a tangle of personal and professional relationships. At times I was concerned about the propriety of being involved with so many diverging interests. Ed Williams used to talk about our firm representing the situation or problem, a bit of a rationalization he employed to represent as many clients as possible in any criminal case he was defending. I viewed my activities during Watergate differently: as part of a citizen's crusade to protect democracy and eventually to bring down Nixon in order to keep the Constitution from being subverted by stop-at-nothing use of government power.

In those days, I realize now, Washington was quite different from the partisan, often personally nasty and vicious, capital of the 1990s and the early twenty-first century. Ours was a Washington of frequent social intercourse among men and women of opposing parties and political philosophies. Unyielding adversaries during the day could share a friendly drink (or several) in the evening. Ours was also a much smaller town, less corrupted and driven by today's desperate need for piles of political money. Our Washington was a more forgiving place, where knowledge of personal peccadilloes was kept out of the media.

I once said to President Johnson in the Oval Office that Washington seemed like a town of only five thousand people. "More like five hundred," he snapped. In a sense, my conversations with so many of the key players were part and parcel of a web of civility and trust that bound people of different parties and divergent views: Haig, Butterfield, Jaworski, O'Brien, Rodino, Bradlee, Simons, Albert, Ted Kennedy, Howard Baker, Geyelin, Greenfield, Woodward, Bernstein, Cohen, Graham. Whatever those views, we all sensed that we were caught up in a crisis of historic proportions. Of course we were using each other—for protection, to acquire information, to position ourselves, win cases, break stories, avoid embarrassment, stay out of prison, establish a reputation, build a law firm, create a powerful national newspaper. We each knew that. We each knew where the other was coming from and, respecting that, despite all our political, professional, and personal jockeying and ambitions, we trusted each other. Through all the ups and downs, nerve-wracking tension, and mistakes, we remained capable of a measure of civility, communication across political barriers, and understanding for human frailty.

CHAPTER 23

Putting the First Amendment First

A T NIGHT I was meeting with Ted Kennedy to plot strategy as the Senate Watergate committee investigation proceeded and the House Judiciary Committee looked into Nixon's impeachment. During the day I winced as the Massachusetts senator accused my client, the pharmaceutical company Pfizer, of killing patients by encouraging overprescription of its antibiotics. In the morning I worked with Pfizer executives to stay ahead of *Washington Post* stories about its practices; in the late afternoon I found myself at the paper vetting Woodward and Bernstein Watergate stories. In late 1973, as Kennedy stepped up his investigation of pharmaceutical company marketing practices, the *Post* increased its coverage of that investigation, and Pfizer struggled to fight back, I felt like a cue ball in a three-cushion shot.

In the spring of 1974, Kennedy, chair of the Senate Subcommittee on Health, publicly charged that "50,000 to 100,000" patients had died of treatment-resistant bacterial infections because pharmaceutical giants sought to fatten their profits by encouraging doctors to overprescribe antibiotics. One of the world's largest manufacturers of antibiotics, Pfizer exploded at Kennedy's accusation.

Because the financial stakes for the company were so great, it commissioned me to undertake an analysis of all such deaths. I assembled a team that included a Harvard Medical School physician and scientific experts, along with lawyers at our firm. Together we examined all the data and available literature. We consulted a wide variety of experts. We learned that at most only 3,282 patients died from treatment-resistant bacteria—and virtually all who died were afflicted with life-threatening diseases like leukemia and other cancers. Such patients were typically placed on a steady regimen of antibiotics to compensate for the weakening of their immune systems caused by chemotherapy and their disease.

I sent the study to Kennedy and asked him to retract his charges. Instead, we were stunned to see, several days later, a *Washington Post* editorial assaulting the pharmaceutical industry for unethical conduct. Likely inspired by a nudge from Kennedy, the editorial echoed the charge that "50,000 to 100,000" deaths were caused by misuse of antibiotics and industry greed.

Angered by the *Post* editorial, Pfizer chairman Ed Pratt pressed me to "get the *Post* to straighten out their misguided opinion." Like many clients, he thought—mistakenly—that I had an inside track; that somehow I could engender good press coverage in the *Post*.

I normally refused such client requests for good reason: The *Post's* reporters and editorial writers were usually correct or well within the bounds of reasonable criticism of a client's actions, however harsh. In any case, I knew *Post* editors would bend over backwards to resist any approaches by me on behalf of another client. On this occasion, however, I was as annoyed as my client. The *Post* editorial contained several misstatements of fact. I also suspected Kennedy had persuaded the paper to write it before I publicly released our analysis demolishing his antibiotics charges. I felt Kennedy had sandbagged the *Post* and preempted me. This time I bowed to Pfizer's insistence. I sent a stinging note to editorial page editor Phil Geyelin, asking my friend "to correct your editorial and balance the record." I concluded with this shot: "Fortunately for all of us, the stories on the Watergate by those cub metropolitan reporters have been much more accurate."[1]

I enclosed our study, which Kennedy had never mentioned to the *Post* or acknowledged publicly. Geyelin fired back a letter deploring my "snide effort to draw a comparison between the accuracy of this editorial and of the Watergate reporting by our 'cub' reporters." He noted, "We have no reason to believe that . . . Senator Kennedy . . . corrected or repudiated the public record on this matter, and no way of knowing what the senator may have done in response to some memorandum privately sent to him by attorneys for one of the drug firms with a vested interest in this issue." Geyelin fired back concluding: ". . . we trust that your handling of the affairs of the *Post* are conducted more responsibly on a somewhat higher plane than your conduct as counsel on behalf of Pfizer."[2]

I got Geyelin's letter in the late morning of the day I read in the *Post* a Kennedy letter to the editor praising the editorial. All I could do was reflect on how much my life resembled that of a cat on a hot tin roof when I sought to represent an aggrieved client in dealing with the *Post*. I decided never to try it again.

In a toast over a make-up lunch a week later, Geyelin teased, "I hope you represent the *Post* as aggressively as you represent these drug companies."

.   .   .

Representing the *Washington Post* continued to be as exciting and satisfying as any experience in my career as a lawyer. I was helping chart a legal course for the media navigated by editors Ben Bradlee and Howard Simons, whose blood was pumped by pushing the First Amendment envelope.

By the early 1970s, the press in general and the *Post* in particular were skeptical of almost any pronouncement by a government official. Dwight Eisenhower's State Department had lied in denying that the President had any knowledge that U-2 pilot Gary Powers was on a spy mission when his plane was shot down over the Soviet Union in 1960. The Kennedy administration initially dissembled on the Bay of Pigs invasion; his Pentagon stated that it had "no information indicating the presence of offensive weapons in Cuba," as Kennedy feigned a cold to return to the White House to deal with the crisis. And early on the Kennedy administration had put out such misleading reports on the number of troops in Vietnam that Pentagon reporters used to joke that there were more soldiers in Saigon bars than the government admitted having in the entire country. Lyndon Johnson widened the credibility gap, particularly on Vietnam, with unrealistic budgets and optimistic reports on the war's progress—and also on a variety of matters as small as his travel plans and appointments. Nixon turned the credibility gap into a chasm with his Watergate cover-up.

Bradlee and Simons loved living on the edge, and I shared their zest for risk-taking. They helped me appreciate the value of a free, aggressive, relentlessly skeptical press. They were always trying to get it right—and first. Most of my conversations with the two were in the late afternoon; rarely was there more than an hour to deadline. When I complained about the lack of time and asked, "Why can't we run this story tomorrow?" or suggested a change not explicitly required as a mater of law, Simons would snap, "You make too much money to be a reporter."

Working with Bradlee and Simons during those years, I came to understand that it was reporters, not judges, who gave real life to the First Amendment. Good reporters took the Constitution's words to heart, then ran with them to expand that freedom. I came to respect journalists who understood that the public's right-to-know is held in their right-to-print hand. Watergate made me realize how prescient James Madison was when he wrote, "A popular government without popular information or the means of acquiring it is but a prologue to a farce or tragedy or perhaps both." I came to see my job as a mission to persuade judges that they must protect the press and its reporters from government intrusion or pressure.

Even when the reporters stepped over the line, they deserved to be defended, no matter how uncomfortable I felt. One problem, in July 1974, involved the death of Les Carpenter, a syndicated columnist and the husband of Liz Carpenter, who had been Lady Bird Johnson's press secretary. The *Post* reported that he died of a heart attack at the foot of the stairs of the Terminal Hotel, a seedy spot known as a hangout for homosexual prostitutes. The story reported that he had registered at this hotel under an assumed name. A grieving Liz Carpenter called me after reading the story, shattered and enraged. I promised to talk to Bradlee. Ben said that the police blotter facts were not in dispute. Les and Liz, he added, were reporters and celebrities in Washington, and "If you live by the sword, you die by the sword." I called Liz and defended what the *Post* had done. I told her there was no way she could sue successfully. But with a heavy heart for my former White House colleague, I thought to myself that I wouldn't blame her if she never read the paper again.

Despite such uneasy moments, I found myself more comfortable siding with the press. One reason was that I had come to doubt the integrity of many judges. In the Johnson White House I had learned the importance of vetting judges to make sure they agreed with our policies on desegregation and affirmative action. I knew Fortas had lied to the Senate Judiciary Committee about his relationship with Johnson. Moreover, as a sitting justice, Fortas had worked with me to write a portion of the administration's Supreme Court brief supporting the Penn Central merger; he later used the argument we had crafted when he wrote the Court's opinion upholding the merger. I had discussed with Judge Bazelon presidential politics and the 1972 Democratic National Convention only to find him using his appellate court to engineer the nomination of his candidate, George McGovern. I came to realize that Judge Richey was fixed by the Nixon administration to keep the Watergate break-in covered up until after the 1972 election. Nixon's Supreme Court nominees Haynesworth and Carswell were hacks. To be sure, there were plenty of good judges, like John Sirica and most on the Supreme Court. But I'd lost the awe for the judiciary that my Harvard Law School professors had instilled. I'd come to realize that judges were just as biased, corruptible, and ambitious as leaders of the executive and legislative branches and corporate executives. This, I knew, made the vigilance of the free press essential to our democracy.

.   .   .

My sense of the importance of an aggressive, uninhibited press sharpened as I saw some of the excesses of government in the 1970s with respect to the *Washington Post.*

In 1975, the Senate Select Committee to study governmental intelligence activities, chaired by Idaho Democrat Frank Church, exposed improper surveillance, mail intercepts, and wiretaps by the Central Intelligence Agency. The violence of the sixties—civil rights demonstrations, assassinations, anti-war rallies, student disruptions, and the emergence of radical groups like the Black Panther Party—had prompted such activities, illegal for an agency limited by law to foreign intelligence.

Testifying before this Senate committee in January 1975, CIA Director William Colby admitted that his agency had infiltrated domestic groups, used surveillance on U.S. citizens, opened citizen's mail, and amassed files on at least ten thousand "dissidents." He detailed domestic intelligence activities involving physical surveillance, break-ins, and wiretaps. Some of this surveillance involved *Washington Post* reporter Michael Getler, who had broken a number of stories that the government claimed endangered national security by making public classified information.

Bradlee, Simons, and I were outraged. Getler's beat was military affairs; he covered the Pentagon and the Vietnam War. The CIA was forbidden from snooping within the United States. It certainly had no authority to target American citizens. Even the FBI would have been out of line to engage in such activities. I hadn't trusted the CIA since my dealings with them regarding the Cuban Brigade, but after Watergate and Nixon's abuse of power, I wasn't surprised that the agency was out of control.*

I went to see Colby, a Princeton graduate with a Columbia law degree who had been an intelligence officer in World War II. I demanded that the agency turn over all its files on Getler. "On this issue," I told him, "the *Post* is at war with the agency." Colby reluctantly gave us portions of Getler's CIA file, but names of CIA agents conducting the surveillance were deleted. References to third parties and information from other government agencies and classified cables were also redacted. When I protested the deletions, Colby claimed that Getler was subjected to physical surveillance, not eavesdropping, wiretapping, or mail intercepts. I came to realize that the CIA must have rented space in an office or hotel near the *Washington Post* building to watch and follow Getler.

I asked Colby if any photos had been taken. He didn't have to answer; the expression on his face told me they had been. He simply said he would check.

At a later meeting, Colby showed me the photos. Using a powerful lens, CIA agents had photographed Getler with his family in their living room through a picture window, as well as playing in the back yard with his children. Agents had also taken pictures of Getler having lunch with several people.

I wrote Colby that Getler regarded this surveillance "as an outrageous invasion of his privacy, quite contrary to the constitutional principles on which this country is founded." I was so disturbed that I added my personal view, something good lawyers rarely do: "Both as his attorney, and as an American citizen, I share his sentiment and I gather from our conversations that you do as well."[3]

We demanded that all files and photos be destroyed, since they had no relevance to national security. Colby agreed, but he was reluctant to do so while a House committee was holding hearings on legislation that might have prohibited the agency from destroying any files. When George Herbert Walker Bush replaced Colby as CIA director in 1976, I asked him to comply

*When Stansfield Turner, President Carter's CIA director, paid me a courtesy call in my first weeks as HEW secretary, I told him we would get along fine so long as he did not play any covert games with the National Institutes of Health. I did not want to find out that the CIA was testing some dangerous chemical or truth serum in a covert program with NIH. I also insisted that the commissioner of Social Security know when the administration was handing out phony Social Security numbers for the CIA. "No surprises," I said, "and we'll get along just fine."

with Colby's promise. He agreed and soon told me that the records, including all photos and negatives, were destroyed.

In the wake of the Getler revelations, Phil Geyelin, editorial page editor of the *Washington Post,* wanted to see whatever files the CIA had on him. Geyelin's desire became urgent when rumors circulated that he in some way retained ties with the CIA. In 1951, on a leave of absence from the *Wall Street Journal,* he had worked for the agency in Washington. Geyelin was a fiercely independent journalist, and when he became editorial page editor of the *Post* he insisted on reporting only to Kay Graham. She agreed and gave him the freedom to shape editorial policy with one caveat: "I just don't ever want to be surprised."

In April and May 1976, Geyelin and I met with Richard Lansdale, acting general counsel of the CIA, and a representative of the agency's domestic contact division. When we reviewed Geyelin's file, we were astonished. We found that from 1957 to 1968 CIA agents in foreign countries had sent to Washington cables suggesting that Geyelin, then a foreign affairs reporter for the *Wall Street Journal,* might be able to provide foreign intelligence for the agency. The cables were filled with agent reports of insignificant conversations blown out of all proportion. Typical was a memo of an agent's conversation in 1964 after Geyelin's visit to Cuba. The agent reported that Geyelin "seemed friendly and cooperative and provided the interviewer with reportable information on the Cuban budget." Geyelin was shocked; he knew nothing about the Cuban budget.[4]

Our review of the files confirmed that any connection with the CIA terminated with Geyelin's December 1951 resignation from the agency. To dispel rumors that he had any relationship while employed as a newspaperman, we asked CIA Director George Bush in 1976 to publicly, or by letter, make it clear that Geyelin had no connection with the CIA after 1951 "other than the ordinary contacts of any practicing journalist, so that these rumors can be put to rest." Geyelin was troubled that such rumors were not only personally damaging but also, as he wrote Bush, "potentially very damaging to the integrity and effectiveness of the *Washington Post* . . . because in my present capacity as editor of this newspaper's Editorial Page, I am responsible for its opinions on a range of issues involving the CIA, including specifically the question whether the Agency ought to have covert working relationships with the press."

Bush refused to confirm the facts publicly. He argued that any public statement about Geyelin would set a precedent; he said he might have to write to "hundreds" of correspondents who had similar, innocent encounters with the CIA. Grudgingly, as we pressed him, Bush eventually agreed to a letter. In it he confirmed that Geyelin's dealings with the CIA, after leaving its employ in 1951, were solely "in your role as a foreign correspondent and consistent with the usual practice of such correspondents, but you have not been an employee since 1951. . . . Our records reveal no contact at all subsequent to 1964."[5]

.   .   .

Daniel Schorr was an irascible, tireless CBS investigative reporter with unrelenting qualms about government and people in power. In January 1976 he obtained a copy of a report of the House Intelligence Committee about CIA abuses. The document revealed assassination plots against foreign leaders and improper surveillance of American citizens; it chronicled the intelligence community's failure to forecast the 1968 Tet offensive in Vietnam, the Russian invasion of Prague, and the 1973 Mideast War. So sensitive were these findings considered that the House of Representatives had voted to seal the report.

Schorr thought he had something as hot as the Pentagon Papers and was disappointed when CBS broadcast only a few pieces on the radio and rejected his pitch for a television special. Angry, Schorr leaked the report to Aaron Latham at the *Village Voice,* who published it verbatim in the paper's February 16, 1976, edition, with the headline: "The Report on the CIA That President Ford Does Not Want You to Read." Latham was the boyfriend (later husband) of Lesley Stahl, then a fledgling CBS television reporter. On the afternoon that CBS found out about the publication, Schorr let rumors circulate at the Washington bureau that Stahl had slipped the report to her boyfriend. The next morning, the *Washington Post* fingered Schorr as the source of the *Village Voice;* all hell broke loose at the network and on Capitol Hill.

Schorr called me. Filled with rage that the network and political establishments were "ganging up" on him, Schorr said his CBS contract provided that he could select his own attorney. "I don't trust them," he said. "I want you." I met with Schorr the next day and agreed to represent him.

CBS News president Dick Salant was ready to fire Schorr for leaking the report to another news outlet. Salant had the blessing of network boss William Paley. Paley had never forgiven Schorr for an incorrect report the correspondent had filed from Germany twelve years earlier that Barry Goldwater, about to become the Republican presidential nominee, planned a post-convention visit to Germany to link up with neo-Nazis. Paley and Salant were appalled and angry that Schorr had let the false rumor circulate about Lesley Stahl.

On February 18, 1976, CBS took Schorr off the air. The following day, the House of Representatives, by a vote of 269 to 115, authorized the Committee on Standards and Official Conduct to investigate the leak of its classified report. The House floor rang with angry speeches about national security breaches.

Schorr and I flew to New York. We negotiated an arrangement with Salant and CBS president Bill Small that the network would keep Schorr on the payroll with no duties for at least two years, pay his legal fees in resisting efforts to compel him to reveal his source, and provide a severance payment in return for Schorr's resignation when the public furor over the leak cooled off. The agreement to resign would be kept secret to protect the interests of CBS and Schorr.

Forced off the air, Schorr spent much of the spring and summer lecturing on First Amendment rights, shrewdly seeding a groundswell of support on campuses and among local reporters across the country for his coming Congressional battle.

Paley and Salant loathed the prickly, troublesome Schorr. The network tried to renege on its commitment to pay his legal fees; it offered no help in preparing for his appearance before the House committee. Nevertheless, on our own, Ben Heineman and John Kuhns, two attorneys at our firm, and I did a line-by-line analysis of the report, demonstrating that virtually all the material had previously been published. Schorr was initially disappointed, because, to his chagrin, our analysis supported the judgment of his CBS bosses that the House report was no Pentagon Papers story. He soon appreciated, however, that we had eviscerated any contention that its publication might have damaged national security.

As the Schorr hearing approached, Salant, Small, and Paley kept CBS at a long stiff arm from us. But as members of Congress demanded that Schorr reveal the name of the person who gave him the report, the overarching issue became the right of the press to protect confidential sources. The network could not afford to abandon one of its reporters as he asserted a precious First Amendment right. Its failure to defend Schorr would spark a revolt among its other correspondents. Schorr insisted on telling me his source, even though I did not want to know. Noting that I was protected from being asked to reveal it by lawyer-client privilege, he blurted it out at one of our meetings.

Fred Friendly, a former CBS News president who was a broadcast consultant to the Ford Foundation, saw the Schorr hearing as a major First Amendment battle. Friendly had resigned from CBS in 1966, when network chief Bill Paley chose to air a rerun of *I Love Lucy* rather than a fifth day of live coverage of Senate hearings on Vietnam. Friendly persuaded PBS to televise the Schorr hearings live.

On the eve of Schorr's testimony, reporters held a First Amendment rally "in defense of Daniel Schorr" on Capitol Hill. Among others, Dan Rather, then a rising CBS star, Mary McGrory, Carl Bernstein, I.F. Stone, and Seymour Hersh sounded off for Schorr.

By 6:30 A.M., the line outside the hearing room far exceeded the number that could be accommodated. Schorr's speaking around the nation and the First Amendment rally the day before invested him with a heroic aura as we walked past the long line into the jammed House hearing.

Attracted by live television coverage, all twelve committee members were present for our presentation. I counted at most three votes against citing Schorr for contempt for refusing to reveal his source. I expected the committee to hold him in contempt, but hoped that we could build up momentum to win on the House floor. I submitted our analysis demonstrating that just about everything in the report had been published before it was issued. I watched as each member turned the pages with the previously published material marked in red. We're having some effect, I thought.

Then Schorr delivered an eloquent statement of his principles as a journalist and his obligation to protect First Amendment rights: "To betray a confidential source would mean to dry up many future sources for many future reporters. . . . The ultimate losers would be the American people and their free institutions. . . . To betray a confidential source would be to betray myself, my career and my life. To say that I refuse to do it is not quite saying it right. I cannot do it."

I then set out the legal arguments for honoring the confidentiality of his source:

> . . . we believe that . . . the identity of Mr. Schorr's source is protected by the First Amendment. . . . We can spend the entire morning and afternoon in a game of Twenty Questions, asking Mr. Schorr did he speak to A, or did he speak to B, or did he speak to C, and we can spend the morning in a cat and mouse game trying to catch Mr. Schorr in some question in which he will answer this committee, where, at some point later the court would say that might have constituted waiver of his right to protect his source.
>
> I respectfully submit to this committee that the values at stake are too precious to play Twenty Questions with, that the values at stake are too fundamental to our system of Government to play cat and mouse with.

As the hearing continued, I began to sense that some members were changing their minds. The television cameras were keeping them there, so they had to listen to our arguments and Schorr's answers to their questions.

By the time we broke for lunch, I thought we might have a chance. I knew I was not alone in that assessment when Dick Salant sent a telegram to Schorr congratulating him on fighting for the First Amendment and CBS put out the word that Paley was standing behind Schorr in his battle to protect his confidential source. At the end of the afternoon session, I hoped we might have six of the twelve members leaning our way. If so, a motion to cite Schorr for contempt would fail on a tie vote.

Back at my office, I received a call from *Washington Post* reporter Richard Lyons, who was covering the hearings, saying that he counted seven members against citing Schorr for contempt. I called Schorr and told him we had won. The next day, Schorr and I went to New York for his meeting with CBS management, at which he resigned.

When I received a note from Ben Bradlee saying, "Let the record show that you were great—forceful, moving, and above all right," I knew we had delivered big time for Schorr and CBS. I wanted to needle the network bosses; they had failed to come publicly to Schorr's defense until the national press corps had mobilized behind him—indeed, until it appeared from the live television hearing that we would defeat any motion to cite him for contempt. So I sent CBS a substantial bill—$150,000 for a couple of weeks of intensive work. The bill went all the way to Bill Paley, who angrily approved payment after his lawyers said he had no choice: he would be excoriated in the press and it would devastate morale at CBS if he balked at our bill. For years after, friends and acquaintances of the CBS chairman told me that he was still complaining about that fee. Later, in the most unusual circumstances, I would hear about it directly from him.

CHAPTER 24

Washington Pals

FOR ALMOST A quarter of a century, from the mid-sixties into the eighties, a remarkable, disparate group of people worked and played in the Washington world. We had come to Washington at roughly the same time to make our marks there. For a time, there was no restaurant we couldn't get the best table at, no party we weren't invited to, no entertainment or sporting event where we didn't have good seats.

By the early fifties Edward Bennett Williams had established himself as one of the great trial lawyers of his generation. The rest of our capital Rat Pack settled in the city later. What pulled us together was that we were all scrambling to the top at about the same moment, paddling our own boats in each other's currents.

Williams was running the Washington Redskins when football was the town's consuming sport (Monday night football with commentator Howard Cosell started in 1970); basketball was a distant second, and for Washingtonians baseball and hockey did not exist.* We had the finest football carpool in Washington. For a decade in my green Ford station wagon, I drove the renowned Washington columnist and humorist Art Buchwald, his kids, my kids, Phil Geyelin, the television personality Rene Carpenter, and Jack Valenti and his son John to every Redskins home game.

---

*For a brief period, there was a movement among some Native Americans to change the name "Redskins." Williams had no such intention, but at my urging he agreed to meet a delegation of American Indians on the issue. Sitting behind his desk, with me present, representatives of a radical Native American movement argued that the name "Redskins" was demeaning and violated their civil rights. Ed made the case that it was a plus for them, a symbol of excellence, since he intended to make the team the finest in the National Football League. At that point, an Indian almost seven feet tall and built like Arnold Schwarzenegger rose, angrily slammed his fist on Williams's desk, leaned over him, and shouted, "Tontoist. You're a Goddamn Tontoist!" I had to bite my hand to keep from laughing. When they left, Williams turned to me. "You let those guys in my office and if you had laughed, that giant sonuvabitch would have thrown me out the window! Next time you meet with them alone!"

Valenti, president of the Motion Picture Association of America since 1966, and I remained close after leaving the LBJ White House staff. Phil Geyelin, after twenty years at the *Wall Street Journal*, became *Washington Post* editorial page editor. He recruited Meg Greenfield as his deputy (she would succeed him in 1977). I had met Meg while I was at the Pentagon and she was a fledgling magazine reporter. Meg couldn't have cared less about the Redskins; she spent her Sunday afternoons and Monday evenings studying Latin.

We loaded the wagon at noon in Wesley Heights and headed for RFK stadium with a sticker on my car that got us into the closest parking lot, courtesy of Ed Williams. On one occasion, coming out of Buchwald's cul de sac, we almost collided with my law partner Paul Connolly driving his car; Buchwald said he was disappointed, because "it would have been the greatest lawsuit of the year!" On another drive to the stadium, George Stevens, who came to Washington to work for Edward R. Murrow in the Kennedy administration and stayed to create the Kennedy Center Honors, forced me off the road near the Kennedy Center, saying I was trespassing on his property.

At the games we joined Williams and Ben Bradlee in the "Royal Box." A buccaneer Brahmin, Bradlee arrived in Washington in 1957 and became executive editor of the *Washington Post* in 1965, the same year I became Lyndon Johnson's special assistant for domestic affairs. Bradlee and I clashed more than once during my time on the White House staff over stories and leaks. We had a spirited blowup in 1968, when he claimed he had a leaked copy of the controversial Kerner Commission report ("Our nation is moving toward two societies, one black and one white—separate and unequal") with the embargo page torn off. He said he was going to run it since he wasn't obliged by an embargo not to. I considered Bradlee fully capable of asking a reporter to suggest that one of the commission members (I suspected Oklahoma senator Fred Harris) tear off the embargo page before leaking it, so our exchange was fiery, with no expletives deleted.

When I was secretary of Health, Education, and Welfare, I never missed an opportunity to complain to Bradlee about the *Post*'s coverage of my tenure, and he never missed a chance to jab me. When I wrote the preface to a report on the debacle of the Ford administration's effort to inoculate everyone with swine flu vaccine, I received this note: "Did you really need to use the first person singular pronoun 20 times in your three page introduction to 'The Swine Flu Affair'? Editorially yours, Ben."

Dinners at Kay Graham's were a must, both because she always had such interesting people and because we all, in one way or another, worked for her. But these events had their rambunctious moments.

At her seventieth birthday—a bash for six hundred top-tier media, business, and government stars in Washington's Departmental Auditorium—Buchwald began his toast with "There's one word that brings us all together here tonight, and that word is fear."

During one patch beginning in 1971, Katharine hired and fired a series of Washington Post Company presidents. The *Washingtonian* magazine, the paper's media hair shirt, incessantly needled the publisher about her inability to keep someone in the job. For each new president, Kay would have one of her marvelous parties, filling the large dining room at her R Street home in Georgetown wall to wall with capital celebrities—cabinet officers, senators, television anchors, media stars. When in 1981 she brought in Dick Simmons, who had been vice president of Dun & Bradstreet, Kay had the ritual dinner party at her home to introduce him to the Washington scene. As was her custom, she toasted him warmly after dinner before the star-studded gathering. Simmons responded, graciously thanking Kay and adding, "I've met so many interesting people here this evening. I look forward to getting to know each of you better."

Ed Williams, who was sitting at the same table as I, called out, "You'd better hurry up. You don't get much time." All the guests roared with laughter—except Katharine.

Our law firm represented Georgetown University. One evening while Ed Williams and I were having dinner at the Palm, the university's president, Father Tim Healy, was eating with a group of four or five people. When the check came, Father Healy paid it with his American Express card. Ed and I immediately got Tommy Jacomo, the restaurant's maitre d', to deliver a bottle of champagne to his table with our note: "Please celebrate the occasion. We have sixteen years of Jesuit education between us and we've never seen a Jesuit pick up a check before."

Buchwald hosted an Easter lunch every year. He dressed up as the Easter Bunny, had rides, a moon bubble jump, games, and races for the kids. The pièce de résistance was the Easter egg hunt. Every year there was one golden egg and whichever child found the golden egg got a silver dollar. There were always enough prizes so that even children who didn't find a single egg got one. One year, we hid several additional golden eggs and (cheered on by all of us pals) the kids who found them were shouting for their silver dollar while Buchwald threatened never to invite us again.

Saturday lunches were a highlight of the week for Ed and me, Bradlee, Geyelin, Greenfield, Buchwald, and often Kay Graham. We'd go either to Chez Camille on 14th Street or Duke Zeibert's. Our lunches were intimate, uninhibited happenings that gave us a chance to relax and ease the tensions of the hyper-pressured lives we led. The teasing was incessant, tough, and irreverent, but always in good humor. The lunches were celebrations of the bonding that had taken place among us as we played our parts in some of the searing issues and exciting events of our day—anti-war and civil rights demonstrations, Nixon's corruption, the fracturing of the Democratic Party, the perpetual tension among the White House, Congress, the courts, and the media. As Bradlee later said, "We had one helluva ride, didn't we!"

CHAPTER 25

The Last Secretary of
Health, Education, and Welfare

FROM THE MOMENT Jimmy Carter was elected on November 2, 1976, I knew that I wanted to be in his administration. Only two jobs interested me: secretary of Health, Education, and Welfare or director of the Office of Management and Budget. The HEW post was my top choice. The political pendulum was on a conservative swing; I believed it was imperative to demonstrate the effectiveness of Great Society programs, most of which were lodged in that department, or risk seeing them dismantled. My friend Vice President-elect Fritz Mondale knew how much I wanted that job.

I was having so much fun practicing law with Ed Williams and Paul Connolly, and we'd become family. Our law firm represented the Democratic Party when it controlled both houses of Congress in a city that was 90 percent Democratic. We were representing the *Washington Post* at its peak of influence and excellence. I had never let on how much I wanted the HEW job, although both Ed and Paul knew I was still hooked on politics and public service.

A couple of weeks after the election, Williams and I were having dinner at Duke Zeibert's. House Speaker Tip O'Neill had just returned from a visit to Plains, Georgia, and stopped by our table. "Carter's considering you for a major post," he said. "I spent the whole damn ride from his house to the airport this afternoon talking about you. He kept asking me questions about you. He mentioned two or three jobs. When he mentioned HEW, I told him you'd be a great secretary of HEW, but I said, 'Mr. President, Joe isn't going to take a job like that. He served his time with Lyndon Johnson. He makes a fortune as a Washington lawyer.'"

"Tip," I exclaimed, "that's the one I'm interested in!"

"You've got to be crazy," the Speaker said, then recovered quickly. "Hell, I recommended you, and you poor guy, you may just get it."

As O'Neill walked over to his table, Williams started talking about Carter. "You don't want to get mixed up with that guy," he said. "He ran against people like us. He thinks everyone in Washington is corrupt."

"That was campaigning," I said. "He's got to work in this town to get anything done and he needs some people that know it."

"He's not our kind of person," Ed warned.

Ed's life was the superb firm he had founded; he could never understand how anyone could leave. Though periodically he was tempted to other tasks—mayor of Washington, director of the Central Intelligence Agency—nothing could pull, push, or shove him from his law firm.

Now he started to tease me. "And HEW! There's no future in representing welfare clients. They can't afford your fees!"

Over the next couple of weeks, Ed and Paul Connolly tried to discourage me from taking the post, but thoughts of government service washed over me like waves, incessantly. When Carter offered me the post two days before Christmas, I accepted. Ed and Paul, to their credit, were unstinting in their encouragement and support.

But Williams was enraged when Carter insisted, as part of an effort to contrast his integrity with Nixon's sleaze, that all top appointees reveal their income for the year 1976. My law firm income of $505,000 was far more than top Wall Street lawyers were then making. When it became public, it set off a media sensation. The revelation created its share of grief for me as I took over the "poor people's" department, but it had a special sting for Ed—everyone knew that if I was earning that amount, he was making a lot more. Actually, it was twice as much, something Ed didn't want others, especially clients, to know.

When a *Washington Post* reporter asked Ed, "Is it true that Califano made $505,000 last year?" he cracked, "Yeah. It was a terrible year for the firm."

And Williams could not resist making a little mischief for me in the Carter cabinet. A *Time* magazine reporter called and asked, "How do you justify your partner Califano making $505,000 last year when [Cyrus] Vance [secretary of state nominee] made $250,000 and Pat Harris [secretary of Housing and Urban Development nominee] made only $55,000? What do you think about that?"

Williams irreverently answered, "What do I think? I think they were each paid about what they were worth."

As soon as he hung up, he called, chuckling, to tell me what he had just done; he knew the trouble his remark would create. I immediately hung up and called a *Time* editor who owed me one and pleaded (successfully, thank God) to keep Ed's comment out of the story.

My other pals had their fun once the nomination became public. On Christmas Eve, *Washington Post* editors Phil Geyelin and Meg Greenfield ran a warm editorial, praising me, but warning:

> Joseph Califano has been this newspaper's counsel. Knowing him well, we are delighted with his appointment to Health, Education and Welfare. . . . There is a certain poetic justice to his appointment: He will now have to run programs that he had much to do with creating when he was President Lyndon Johnson's top man for domestic affairs at the White House. . . . His work in the apparatus of the Democratic Party should help him in coping with what is not only, in his words, "the people's department," but the politicians' department—the principal arena in which the nation's various social ambitions are worked out. To an old friend, we offer our special congratulations—but no free ride.

Many of my columnist friends needled Carter about appointing such a Washington insider after expressing so much disdain for the corrupt capital during his campaign. Art Buchwald had the most fun. As I was preparing to take office—interviewing candidates for top posts, firing Nixon appointees, and getting briefed for confirmation hearings—Buchwald called. "You'll want to read my column Thursday." He had warned me before about upcoming pieces, but nothing prepared me for his December 30 column, "The Right Man in the Driver's Seat at HEW:"

> I don't know about President-elect Carter's other Cabinet appointments, but I can speak with authority when I say he couldn't have selected a better Secretary of Health, Education and Welfare. . . . You see, Joe Califano has been our football car pool driver to the Redskins games for the past eight years. . . .
> I'll have to admit that the seven of us who ride with Joe to the Redskins games never thought of him as Cabinet material. But then again no football car pool chauffeur is a hero to the people he drives to the stadium.

When the FBI men came to see me to do a check on Joe, I thought they were kidding when they said he was being considered for Secretary of HEW. But I discovered the FBI never jokes.

"What kind of man would you say Mr. Califano is? Does he have any deep-seated prejudices that you know of?"

"He hates red lights. I've seen him cuss and scream at a red light for two minutes. He also has contempt for stop signs. Every time he sees one he goes livid."

"I mean for people. Does he have any prejudice against certain kinds of people?"

"Only pedestrians. Joe thinks pedestrians should stay off the streets during football games regardless of race, creed or color."

"How does he feel about busing?"

"He's for busing people to football games only as a last resort. But if the Supreme Court says you have to bus spectators to the stadium he will follow the law of the land. . . ."

"What would you say are his best traits?"

"He'll always look you in the eye when he's driving even when you're sitting in the back seat. And he's one of the most patriotic men I know. I've seen him sideswipe an ambulance rather than miss the Redskins Band playing the *Star-Spangled Banner*."

As Secretary of HEW I took a 90 percent cut in annual income, to $66,000, but never considered it a sacrifice. I thought I was the luckiest guy in the world landing the best job in the country.

My years in Washington had given me a confidence that sometimes spilled over into arrogance. Toughness is needed to tackle the issues at HEW and I felt I had acquired it. I'd learned plenty about political street fighting from LBJ. I learned the importance of relentless skepticism from the tough-minded editor Ben Bradlee. Ed Williams taught me a lot about legal combat, and my years with McNamara were a crash course in driving bureaucratic behemoths.

My parents worried that I was becoming too tough. Shortly after I was sworn in they sent me a note, quoting from the first letter of Paul to the Corinthians: "There are in the end three things that last: faith, hope, and love, and the greatest of these is love." It was their way of reminding me of the importance of gentleness. But I knew there was no way to run HEW with a gentle touch, and I hoped they would understand that it took a firm hand, sometimes a fist, to imbue a bureaucracy this vast with effective compassion.

During the Johnson years, we had sited the lion's share of Great Society initiatives in HEW; its congressional oversight and appropriations committees were the most liberal and favorably disposed toward such programs. As the cost of these programs soared and as the media recounted one story after another of incompetence, fraud, and mismanagement, the patience of the American people was thinning. I saw it as my job to prove that these programs could be run with competence and integrity, to convince taxpayers that they were getting full value for the dollars they were investing in HEW. The measure of my success would be whether I could get middle Americans to understand that this department and its programs constituted the greatest act of concern by any society for the neediest among them.

Second only to the White House, HEW was the most politically treacherous institution inside the Washington beltway, pinching almost every exposed social, economic, medical, and racial nerve in the nation. With jurisdiction over the issue of abortion and the purity and safety of food, it was the only place in America where both motherhood and apple pie were controversial.

Second only to the President, the HEW secretary had the most power to affect the lives of Americans. I intended to use that power. The issues I faced as secretary were a tangled ball of tradition, morality, education, children, civil rights, dependency, illness, busing, welfare, family life, drinking, drugging, smoking, mental health, teenage sex, disease, old age, and fear of dying. The social conflicts these issues sparked came in bursts of automatic fire and the cartridges were never blank.

HEW's budget then was larger than that of any nation in the world except the United States and the Soviet Union. Its programs served virtually every American—issuing cash payments in Social Security and welfare; providing kidney dialysis, runaway youth shelters, assistance for blind vendors, help for the mentally retarded, rescue for abused children, Head Start for pre-schoolers, funds for elementary and secondary schools, and grants and loans for college students; and paying millions of medical bills each month for the elderly and the poor, assuring the safety of food and the efficacy of pharmaceuticals, and hunting down cures for every known disease.

My Special Ethics textbook at Holy Cross concluded with this admonition for graduating seniors:

> The duty of everyone is to improve the condition of society to such an extent that material wrong-doing will not be forced upon anyone by reason of the social co-operation into which he must enter. . . . If God has given you talents, He will require an account of them. Do not sit with idle hands while there is so much to be done. Do not draw into a narrow selfish circle . . . join some worthwhile organizations; throw yourself into life in its intensest point, and make your impress upon it—the impress of a courageous, right-minded, wise and thoroughly instructed man. Be a doer of the Word, not a hearer only.[1]

As secretary, I experienced "life at its intensest point." On my watch, it was HEW's responsibility to determine whether saccharin was carcinogenic and Laetrile efficacious for curing cancer, how dangerous marijuana was (and if spraying it with paraquat posed a significant additional health hazard). After the Three Mile Island nuclear accident, we tested food and water for safety and assessed the health effects of the radiation; in Philadelphia we did epidemiological detective work to nail the cause of Legionnaire's disease; in Colorado, we assessed the health hazards of moving leaking Weteye (nerve gas) bombs. We taught English, history, and social customs to refugees from Southeast Asia and to Soviet Jews. We worked with the commercial television networks and the Public Broadcasting System to caption programs for the deaf. The Congress and the President vested us with frontline responsibility to fight discrimination on the basis of race, religion, ethnic origin, sex, age, and handicap. When I was secretary, the department had all the functions now dispersed among three separate cabinet agencies: the Department of Health and Human Services, the Department of Education, and the Social Security Administration.

Each morning began with what I called my 6 A.M. "toe test." I opened the door to look down at the folded *Washington Post*. I flipped it open with my toe. If I was above the fold with a story we had released, it was a great day. If I was above the fold with a story about me or HEW that we had not put out, I knew it would be one helluva day.

Would I be "courageous, right-minded, wise"? I had two good examples in my immediate experience. I had learned from LBJ that courage is as important as tenacity if you are to get anything done in government. And I had witnessed Katharine Graham's intrepid commitment during the trying days of Watergate.

I exacted from President Carter a promise that I could hire my own people, a lesson I had learned from Bob McNamara. Jim Gaither, a San Francisco attorney who had been on my staff in the Johnson White House, moved to Washington for three months, abandoning his law practice and family to head up our recruiting effort. With his help, I attracted a group of seasoned experts, executives, and whiz kids—in my judgment the brightest the department had ever seen.

I wanted people around me who would hang tough when they thought I was wrong. That was the only way to negotiate the minefields of social controversy that had disrupted and exhausted prior secretaries and driven one to a nervous breakdown. That's why I worked so hard to persuade Hale Champion to be undersecretary. He had been California governor Pat Brown's budget director and campaign manager, and was vice president of Harvard for finance and administration when I recruited him. Hale recalled those years this way:

Joe eats people alive. . . . It was a very conscious recommendation for the people around him and a conscious choice by him to have somebody who would tell him he was full of shit on a regular basis. . . . He wanted somebody who would tell him when they thought he was wrong and to fight with him about it. He knew how big a job it was and he wanted somebody [to] whom he could simply say, "I'm going to be busy with this, so you do that."[2]

My most publicized appointment was a political misstep and a signal embarrassment. I hired a cook, Wiley Barnes, to take advantage of the elaborate kitchen in HEW to serve the secretary's dining room for breakfasts, lunches, and dinners with staff, members of Congress, and interest groups. I signed a 402-word job description for the chef as "personal assistant," and the words "cook" and "chef" never appeared in it. On March 23, the Associated Press broke a story by Mike Putzel that the personal assistant was in fact a chef. Coming on top of the revelations about my income as a lawyer, the story took off on all television networks and just about every newspaper.

The story also got legs from President Carter's ostentatious trimming of perks: no cars and drivers for White House aides, carrying his own clothing on planes, ordering the cabinet to fly economy class. I offered to fire the chef; the President told me, "Handle it your way. Whatever you do is fine with me."

That afternoon, as I was leaving the White House, ABC correspondent Sam Donaldson stuck a microphone in my face, demanding to know whether I intended to keep the chef. "I'm going to rewrite the job description to set forth candidly his duties," I answered. "But the chef will save time and money over the long haul and I intend to keep him."

House Speaker Tip O'Neill called that evening just after the nightly network news ended. "Joseph," he said, "is it true you hired a chef for twelve thousand dollars?"

"Yes, Mr. Speaker," I responded.

"Well, I've got some advice for you: Any guy in this town that hires a chef for twelve grand had better hire a food taster."

He laughed. So did I (for the first time that day).

"You looked so worn down on the tube tonight. Don't let it get you down," Tip O'Neill added. "It'll pass. You'll do beautiful things. Just get on with it."

A few months later Morrie Leibman, a friend and a Chicago lawyer who advised the American Medical Association, came to my office for lunch. We ate tuna fish with an early and tasteless version of diet mayonnaise. Morrie said nothing during the lunch, but two days later I received this note:

Dear Joe:
    Thanks for lunch. But the shit you've taken for the chef—it wasn't worth it.
    Best, Morrie

Chef or no chef, I did get on with it, because I was acutely conscious of how short tenure in office was. Even if I had been there for the full four years of Carter's term, instead of thirty months, that would have been too little time to get things done. I made a decision to reorganize the department from top to bottom within the first three months, then to select priorities and hold to them whatever crises erupted. I was determined to revitalize the department, to energize its career civil servants, and to move aggressively on discrimination, health care, and welfare reform.

For all my Washington experience, I was not prepared for the cultural chasm between me and President Carter and his closest Oval Office aides.

Jimmy Carter saw me as a Washington insider and was proud of himself as an outsider. He felt isolated in the capital, and his experience in the White House sharpened his sense that cynical, gotcha obsession motivated the press and that selfish political ambition and need for campaign money drove members of Congress. He saw the capital city as corrupted and one of his missions as cleaning it up; and failing that, he seemed determined not to get any Washington political dirt under his fingernails. On one occasion when he asked me to review what he considered actions in his early months in office that he might have taken out of "appalling ignorance" about Washington, the meeting quickly deteriorated into another presidential recitation of complaints that the *Washington Post*, other major papers, and the White House press corps were determined to make it impossible for him to govern.

Carter saw even small items as calculated efforts by the press to embarrass him. He had ordered all of us to travel economy class. He didn't want public servants in the cabinet travelling first class and he had no sense of humor about it. When a reporter spotted Bob Strauss, then U.S. special trade representative, in an airport and asked, "Mr. Ambassador, are you going to travel first class?" the irreverent Strauss snapped back, "You bet, until a better one comes along." I thought Strauss's retort was hilarious, that the reporter had a bit of fun, and the President should ignore it. Carter saw it as the press ridiculing him. Carter sounded like every president I had known or watched—Kennedy canceling his subscription to the *New York Herald Tribune*, LBJ with his furious tirades about leaks, Nixon's hatred of the Washington press corps, Ford's annoyance with the way reporters demeaned his intelligence.

President Carter hoped I could turn the *Washington Post* into his ally. Hadn't I represented the paper and written op-eds for it? What Carter did not understand was that the reporters I knew best at the *Washington Post* flexed their journalistic muscles being tough on me. In March 1978, the

Chicago Tribune quoted *Post* editor (and my friend) Ben Bradlee, "We give Califano more shit than anybody else. We are tough on him. You should see some of the pictures we run of him. They're almost always the worst ones, and then they are cropped out there by *Post* staffers to make him look like an idiot."

In the summer of 1978, the President and Rosalynn Carter had Kay Graham and top *Post* and *Newsweek* editors for dinner, one of a series of informal meetings the White House hoped would soften key media. At one point during the dinner, Mrs. Graham turned to Carter on her left and said, "Mr. President, we hear that Joe Califano is taking a bum rap in your administration. Because he worked so closely with us, he's blamed for many leaks. Actually, he bends over backward with us and if anything he takes a beating from us because we are all the harder on him."

The President replied, "I'm very high on Joe, I like Joe a lot. My staff is beginning to appreciate how good he is and even Charlie Kirbo [Carter's personal attorney and close Georgia confidant] now likes him."

Mrs. Graham asked, "Why wouldn't Charlie Kirbo like Joe?"

"Kirbo had problems with Joe. First, because he was so liberal coming out of the liberal Johnson administration with the Great Society. Then because he was Catholic, Italian, and a Northerner. But Kirbo has come to respect him."[3] The President spoke so matter-of-factly it stunned Graham and Howard Simons, who was sitting to next to Kay. When Simons called me the next morning to recount this exchange blow by blow, I was surprised but not concerned or inhibited from pursuing my goals for HEW.

.   .   .

With my background in government, I was prepared for monumental policy disputes over welfare reform and national health insurance. But I was not prepared for the way in which President Carter tried to negotiate the political rapids of the disputes that arose over these issues. From the first meeting of his cabinet at Sea Island, Georgia, over the Christmas holidays in 1976, I had sensed a naïveté among the President and his key staffers about the Washington world. I had cut my political and domestic policy teeth formulating and pushing to passage Great Society programs under a president who was the twentieth-century virtuoso in moving legislation and manipulating power elites in politics, business, and labor—and loved every minute of it. In the struggles over welfare reform and national health insurance I came to realize that I was point man for a president who did not understand the multicolored threads of power inside the beltway and neither liked nor respected legislators, newspeople, or lobbyists who enjoyed and found satisfaction weaving those threads.

I knew what a mess the welfare system had become. Enacted in the administration of Franklin Delano Roosevelt, the Aid for Dependent Children legislation had not only become for thousands a disincentive to work; with its requirement that there be no man in the house for the woman to receive payments for herself and her children, AFDC was breaking up two-parent families. In the Johnson administration we had repeatedly tried to eliminate that destructive requirement and reform the welfare system. We saw the frightful implications of savaging "the Negro family." In 1968, a generation ahead of his time, Johnson called "the welfare system in America . . . outmoded and in need of major change" and pressed Congress to create "a work incentive program, incentives for earning, day care for children, child and maternal health . . . and family planning services."[4]

Welfare reform required resources to provide incentives to work—funds to provide job training and day care for children and to schedule the loss of welfare payments and Medicaid entitlement in a way that permitted these mothers to make more money working than remaining on welfare. Faced with a conservative swing in the country, Carter pursued an impossible dream: welfare reform, with no draconian features to cut mothers off the rolls, at no additional cost.

In the course of putting our reform proposal together, Carter spent untold hours mastering minute details. Before final approval, he insisted on reviewing a lengthy single-spaced memorandum and making almost a hundred decisions about program details. What a contrast from LBJ, I thought at the time, who would have made one or two key decisions and spent his time trying to persuade key members of Congress to support his proposal. Once we sent the administration's proposal forward, Carter refused to compromise. He gave little time and consideration to members of Congress who had spent years on welfare reform, like Harlem's Charles Rangel and California's James Corman, dismissing their differences because he was convinced, as he told me several times, that we had "the right answer."

Our national health proposal went aground on different political shoals: Ted Kennedy's presidential ambitions and the labor movement's commitment to a government-controlled health care system. Disputes with Kennedy and party liberals over this and funding levels for new programs created serious strains for me with President Carter.

In November 1978, Office of Management and Budget Director James McIntyre proposed hundreds of individual cuts to the fiscal 1980 budget I had recommended. Funds for health maintenance organizations, immunization, other preventive health programs, medical schools, and research programs were to be sharply reduced or eliminated.

When I met with Ted Kennedy to discuss the 1979 hearing schedule for the Senate Subcommittee on Health, which he chaired, Kennedy asked what I was going to do about "cuts in the HEW budget." I told him I would fight them.

We were sitting at a coffee table in his office, he in a chair, I on the sofa to his left against the wall. In his shirtsleeves, thrusting his broad body forward, he said, "I think you have to resign over the health cuts."

I said nothing.

"If the cuts are anywhere near what OMB is proposing, you'll have to resign."

I started to disagree, but Kennedy was not about to be interrupted. "It'll be impossible for you to run the department."

"Ted, no decisions have been made," I protested.

"If the health care funds are not restored," Kennedy pressed on, "then you have an obligation to resign."

As soon as I got back to my office, I turned my attention to the Democratic Party national midterm convention that was scheduled to begin the next day in Memphis. The highlight was a discussion of national health insurance featuring Kennedy and me. Now I knew it would be grand political theater and I wanted to be prepared.

Delegate interest was so great that the session had to be moved to the largest theater available. The place was packed with liberal Kennedy partisans and press. The newly elected thirty-two-year-old governor of Arkansas, Bill Clinton, was moderator. He reveled in the excitement as he sat at the center of a long table; I was on his right, Kennedy on his left.

I insisted on speaking first. I stressed Carter's commitment to a national health plan and characterized our differences with Kennedy as largely tactical. Kennedy followed with the most electric speech I had ever heard him give (prior to his appearance at the 1980 Democratic convention). Half-rim glasses perched on the end of his nose, fist pounding the podium, fingers alternately jabbing at the colorful charts he held and the audience he faced, Kennedy attacked "the hypocrisy" of Congress, which had completely free health care but denied it to others. Emotionally he discussed the care "I can afford," for his son Teddy who had lost a leg to cancer, for his father after his stroke, and for himself when he broke his neck in a plane crash. He bellowed, "What about others, who cannot afford such care?" Kennedy had delegates cheering and stomping as he called for a Democratic Party "that will provide decent health care across this country, north and south, east and west, for all Americans as a matter or right and not of privilege."

Before he went to the next speaker, Bill Clinton asked if I had a comment. "I'm glad I spoke before Senator Kennedy," I quipped, and the audience broke into laughter.

White House aide Stuart Eizenstat spoke in support of President Carter. When he finished, Kennedy ostentatiously held the OMB budget sheet in his left hand and, peering down periodically through his half-glasses, he gestured, punching out with his right-hand and emotionally shouted, "Mr. Eizenstat talked of President Carter's support for HMOs. How much does the OMB budget mark provide for new starts for HMOs?" Kennedy asked. "Zero," he answered, and the audience cheered him on.

Hardball, I thought. But I was about to find out how hard.

"Joe Califano supports HMOs. I'm with Joe Califano, who's fighting for these programs," Kennedy roared, and my heart sank. He's going to try and make his suggestion that I resign happen, I thought. He may even suggest it publicly right now.

Kennedy belted out his lines. "For area health education centers, zero funds. For exceptionally needy medical students, zero. For financially distressed medical institutions, zero." His chorus following each item: "Joe Califano's fighting for these funds, and I'm with him."

I have to do something, I thought. It was bad enough that someone had leaked the OMB papers to Kennedy; but his use of them—and me—to embarrass Carter publicly destroys the chances of getting funds restored, and makes my position as HEW secretary politically untenable. I jumped in.

"These are not President Carter's decisions," I said. "OMB makes its recommendations and I make mine. But only the President decides. We should all hold our judgment until the President decides."

Mercifully, Clinton ended the session. The next morning, I called President Carter from Memphis rather than have him get his information solely from press reports and his aides.

"I think Kennedy wants very much to put me in a position adverse to the administration," I said. "Mr. President, I think he may be seeking to unravel your administration."

"I am glad you are concerned about this," the President responded. "I expect many arguments like this about the budget, but none from so formidable and powerful a person as Kennedy." Pausing for effect, he added, "And not from someone with such presidential ambitions."

At the cabinet meeting on the following Monday morning, Carter underscored his conviction that the midterm convention delegates were "far more liberal" than most Democrats and that the American people would support a tight budget. He thought Kennedy and liberals were politically on the wrong side of the issue. Vice President Mondale disagreed. "Some of our best people have doubts about us. We must work better with responsible liberals," he said, looking tired, almost grim. I was with Mondale on this, but I said nothing. I was worried that Carter already suspected that I was too close to Kennedy for his political comfort.

·   ·   ·

Carter's campaign commitments on welfare reform and national health insurance provided ample early warning that they would be high on my agenda. But I had no advance notice of the most controversial issues that would dominate my years as secretary: smoking, the handicapped, and vexing questions of science and public policy that stood me at the intersection of faith, morality, politics, and human nature.

During my years with LBJ, the nation's focus on discrimination had been centered on blacks. Now I would be at the cutting edge of efforts to extend concepts developed in those years to other populations. In 1973, Congress enacted the Rehabilitation Act; section 504 provided: "No otherwise qualified handicapped individual in the United States shall, solely by reason of his handicap, be excluded from the participation in, be denied the benefits of, or be subjected to discrimination under any program or activity receiving Federal financial assistance." The law gave the HEW secretary sweeping authority to issue regulations guiding all government agencies and all contractors and grantees who received federal funds. President Gerald Ford and my predecessor, David Matthews, had delayed promulgating any regulations, because such intense opposition had developed to the law, which had been passed without any public discussion.

In 1977 there were no accessible buses or trains and few sidewalks with curb ramps. A multitude of everyday-life barriers confronted people with difficulties walking, seeing, and hearing and with other disabilities. Universities, hospitals, transportation systems, libraries, corporations, and commercial establishments protested that they could not afford the costs of making their buildings and vehicles accessible to the disabled. The law, they argued, had been passed without any hearings and should be revisited by the Congress before any regulations were issued.

Soon after I became secretary, "Sign 504" buttons sprouted up. Handicapped groups announced that they would demonstrate at each of the ten HEW regional offices. I welcomed the prospect. Nothing is likelier to evoke sympathy, I thought, than the poignancy of a demonstration by the handicapped—people in wheelchairs, without sight or hearing, with bodies crippled by accidents or genetic defects beyond their control. I hoped the demonstrations would raise the public's awareness of the pending regulations. I asked HEW personnel to be "especially sensitive to these demonstrators and to respect their sincere exercise of fundamental First Amendment rights."

I was the first to be tested by my words. On Sunday, April 3, 1977, shortly before midnight, Trudy was awakened by a noise outside. "I think somebody's trying to break into one of the houses," she said anxiously. I looked out our second-floor bathroom window down the long driveway to the street. A Ryder rental truck had pulled up. People in wheelchairs were being lowered from the back. "I think it's a demonstration," I said.

Holding lit candles, they formed a cross in the round cul-de-sac at the entrance of the driveway. With television cameras whirring, the demonstrators prayed that I would sign 504 regulations. I heard my golden retriever, Cinnamon, bark outside. I raced down the stairs. All I needed was for Cinnamon to bite someone in a wheelchair. I didn't want to go out myself, so I called from the door, "Cinnamon, Cinnamon." There was no response.

"Cinnamon, Cinnamon," I called again.

The dog barked louder. I saw the television pictures and the newspaper headlines: CALIFANO DOG ATTACKS CRIPPLED WOMAN IN WHEEL-CHAIR . . . CALIFANO DOG BITES BLIND MAN. I called again as sweetly as I could, "Cinnamon, Cinnamon, come back here."

Though stopping occasionally for another bark along the way, the dog came back to the house. I hugged her and closed the door as soon as I got her inside.

The next day, three hundred disabled demonstrators occupied the lobby outside my office. They demanded that I issue section 504 regulations immediately. They were on crutches and in wheelchairs, speaking with their hands, accompanied by seeing-eye dogs. They sang, "We Want 504" to the tune of "We Shall Overcome." They shouted, "Why not now?" Protests and sit-ins broke out around the country. In San Francisco one hundred fifty disabled activists occupied that city's Old Federal Building for twenty-five days.

Though annoyed by their occupation of the HEW secretary's anteroom and nervous and sweating as I confronted my first set of demonstrators, to my surprise I found myself touched by their sincerity. As I stood before them, I couldn't help thinking of lessons that the nuns had drummed into us at St. Gregory's elementary school in Brooklyn: every individual is created in the image and likeness of God and entitled to the dignity appropriate for that image and likeness. It was the first time I'd been called upon to live that lesson, and under these circumstances it wasn't easy.

The draft regulations left unissued by the Ford administration proposed a cumbersome set of expensive and largely unworkable rules. Despite protests and bad press, we took time to simplify them. We decided to require, for example, that at universities every course must be made accessible rather than every building. We did insist on physical changes in transportation systems and buildings and public facilities like airports and rail stations where ramps and elevators were essential for accessibility.

Cost was not the only obstacle. There was also this politically sticky issue: Did the word "handicapped" in the law include alcoholics and drug addicts? At the cabinet meeting on March 21, 1977, President Carter made it clear that he did not want them classified as handicapped. California governor Jerry

Cover of *Time*, June 12, 1978.

The Washi

126th Year. No. 11

Copyright © 1978
The Evening Star Newspaper Co.

WASHINGTON, D.C., W

Califano Declares

INTERAGENCY COOPERATION PLEDGED, NEW RULES AT HEW

By Cristine Russell
Washington Star Staff Writer

Calling smoking a form of "slow-motion suicide," Health, Education and Welfare Secretary Joseph A. Califano Jr. today announced a "vigorous new program" of public education, regulation and research designed to discourage consumption of cigarettes.

The controversial campaign will be "backed by higher budgets, more energetic efforts and a renewed commitment from the government department that is charged with pro-

tecting the nation's health," pledged Califano, who proclaimed smoking "Public Health Enemy Number One in the United States."

His $23 million plan for combating cigarette smoking — the result of more than six months effort — includes new efforts within HEW itself as well as strategies for coordinating with other federal agencies, state governments, local school systems and voluntary health groups.

IT WAS OUTLINED in a speech prepared for delivery at a meeting of health organizations who belong to

the National Interagency Council Smoking and Health.

The anouncement came on the 14 anniversary of the famous surge general's report on smoking wh established the "causal link betwe cigarette smoking and lung cance and "suggested the strong connecti between smoking and heart diseas as well as other serious health pr lems, Califano recalled.

Since then, he said, research h found that "smoking is even m dangerous than we originally lieved." Yet, "in spite of all the
See SMOKING,

The start of the first national anti-smoking campaign in January 1978. It would spread across the nation, changing conversations from "Do you want a cigarette?" to "Do you mind if I smoke?" And encouraging Americans to say, "Yes, I do mind."

"NO, I'M NOT GOING TO TELL YOUR PARENTS! I'M GOING TO DO WORSE THAN THAT — I'M GOING TO TURN YOU IN TO JOE CALIFANO!"

gton Star

CAPITAL SPECIAL

DAY, JANUARY 11, 1978   Phone (202) 484-5000   CIRCULATION 484-3000   CLASSIFIED 484-6000   15 Cents

War on Smoking

TOBACCO INSTITUTE CHALLENGES ACTION BEFORE SPEECH

By Cristine Russell
Washington Star Staff Writer

Even before the Department of alth, Education and Welfare's conversial new campaign against arette smoking had been unveiled, opponents were already firing up ir crusade against it and the man ind the effort, HEW Secretary Joh A. Califano Jr.

n an unusual maneuver, the pacco Institute took the offensive d held a formal press conference heir headquarters here yesterday, day before Califano was sched-uled to deliver a major policy speech to a meeting of anti-smoking organizations concerned about the rise in teen-age smoking.

The senior vice president of the trade organization, William Kloepfer Jr., admitted that the action was "unusual," particularly since the tobacco group was apparently not privy to advance details about the new anti-smoking plan.

But it was clear that they were concerned about the prospect of any new government initiative whatsoever which would attempt to curb smoking, particularly since the tobacco manufacturers represented by the institute still do not acknowledge any of the health hazards attributed to cigarettes since the surgeon general's report was issued 14 years ago.

Horace R. Kornegay, president and executive director of the group (and a former congressman from the tobacco-growing state of North Carolina), said that the industry would be looking for the government campaign to be "above all, fair. . . . Fair means telling it like it is. It does not mean talking any more about 300,000

See TOBACCO, A-9

ETTA HULME   FORT WORTH STAR-TELEGRAM   N.E.A, 78

"RIGHT, JOE, O.K., JOE. ... 'SCUSE ME A MINUTE, JOE .... GO ON, JOE .... I'M LISTENING, JOE"

To Joe. Memphis lives! 15 years is long enough! Pass the Clinton Califano Kennedy health reform plan!

To Joe—Memphis started this long march in MA—Let's get it done after so many years! Bill Clinton 11-93

With Senator Ted Kennedy and Governor Bill Clinton, at the Democratic Mid-Term Convention in Memphis. Kennedy and I debated national health policy, with Clinton moderating before a boisterous overflow crowd. December 7, 1978.

Not seeing eye-to-eye: Discussing welfare reform with President Jimmy Carter and House Ways and Means Chairman Al Ullman over lunch at the White House in 1977.

In my office at HEW, Oscar-wining actress and recovering alcoholic Mercedes McCambridge urges me to mount an anti-alcoholism campaign, which I announced in May 1979.

With Vice President Walter (Fritz) Mondale at a symposium in Los Angeles in March 1979. Mondale encouraged President-elect Carter to name me secretary of Health, Education, and Welfare.

"REJOICE... WE HAVE COME TO OVERHAUL"

Washington pals at a party celebrating Edward Bennett Williams's sixty-sixth birthday. Left to right are: Art Buchwald, David Brinkley, Jack Valenti, Williams, me.

Ed Williams and I returned to our alma mater, College of the Holy Cross, for a commencement ceremony on May 27, 1988. With us (on either side) for a last hurrah on campus were Art Buchwald and Ben Bradlee. Ed passed away three months later.

LEFT: With former first lady Lady Bird Johnson, the best thing that ever happened to Lyndon Baines Johnson (who would be the first to agree).

BELOW: Bringing my daughter to work day. Seven-year-old Claudia helps me at HEW's twenty-fifth anniversary celebration on May 23, 1978.

With former first lady Betty Ford at a June 4, 1998, press conference to release *Under the Rug: Substance Abuse and the Mature Woman*, the first report addressing the impact of substance abuse on women over fifty-nine. It was prepared by the National Center on Addiction and Substance Abuse (CASA) at Columbia University, which I founded in 1992.

With Hilary on our honeymoon at her father Bill Paley's home at Lyford Cay in Nassau in 1983.

With Hilary and Rev. Walter Modrys, S.J., just after our Catholic wedding on June 14, 1993, at St. Ignatius Loyola Church in New York City.

The Califano family as of May 2003. Left to right: Margery, Olivia, Mark, Claudia, Evan, Brooke, Brian (below Brooke), Gene, Hilary, Russell (below Hilary), me, Pete (below me), Frick, Joe IV (Jack), Beth, Joe III. Missing: Nicholas James, six months at the time.

Brown had told him, Carter said, that a large proportion of the disabled in California were drug addicts and alcoholics.

I asked Attorney General Griffin Bell for his opinion. He concluded that the law provided protection for both alcoholics and drug addicts if they could otherwise meet the qualifications for admission to schools and employment. I signed the revised 504 regulations (reflecting Bell's conclusion) on April 28, deliberately beating my publicly announced May deadline to avoid another round of demonstrations.

A deluge of angry criticism followed. Universities balked at having to make accessible laboratories and auditoriums that couldn't be moved. Mayors protested that it would require millions of dollars to make buses and subway systems usable by people in wheelchairs. Rural libraries and the Postal Service complained about the cost of installing ramps, special toilets, and water fountains.

The press that had been so eager to cover the demonstrations hardly reported the issuance of these historic regulations. Unlike the protests and sit-ins opposing delay, signing the regulations offered no vivid pictures to television news producers. But these regulations set in motion a sea change across America; today handicapped parking spaces, ramps and graded corners at city street crossings, elevators that talk, and buses with hydraulic lifts for the wheelchair-bound are commonplace, and the disabled have access to mainstream education in elementary and high schools and on every college campus. For me, there was a practical lesson that influenced future public announcements: We had to provide picture stories if we hoped to get television coverage.

.   .   .

As the first secretary of Health, Education, and Welfare who had responsibility to enforce Title IX of the Education Amendments of 1972—prohibiting discrimination on the basis of sex in any education program or activity receiving federal financial assistance—I became a catalyst of another revolution. Colleges and universities that allocated millions of dollars for men's athletic programs spent only pennies (if that) for such women's programs. Academic administrators sat stonily silent when, speaking to the American Council on Education on December 13, 1977, I said, "Title IX is the law of the land. It's yours to obey and mine to enforce." A year later, I issued proposed guidelines requiring schools to provide athletic opportunities for women comparable to those for men. Expenditures on intercollegiate athletics, I ruled, must be proportionate to the number of men and women participating.

The controversy over my enforcement of Title IX became a pitched battle, with even my friend House Speaker Tip O'Neill asking me to back down, when Boston College claimed compliance would undermine its men's hockey and football programs. Notre Dame's athletic department, with its highly visible and highly profitable football program, declared war on the guidelines.

In May 1979 I delivered the commencement address at Notre Dame. Just before I spoke, the renowned actress Helen Hayes received the Laetare Medal, awarded each year to an outstanding Catholic. She gave a five-minute response so moving that many in the audience wept; she received a rousing, extended standing ovation. I was next to speak. How could I follow Helen Hayes? The earsplitting applause continued and Indiana Representative John Brademas (who supported Notre Dame's opposition to my guidelines and sat behind me on stage) whispered in my ear, "That'll teach you to take on one of my constituents." No matter, when I rose to speak, the women graduating raised high their black mortarboards with Roman IX's in white adhesive tape on the top.

I held fast on the Title IX guidelines, which are controversial to this day, with twenty-first-century opponents seeking to revoke them. I believe that colleges and universities—and the young women who attend them—have benefited from expanded athletic opportunities. Men's athletics have suffered none of the horrors predicted by opponents.

.   .   .

I sought to help lead the way in yet another expansion of civil rights in America in my waning days at HEW. Surgeon General Julius Richmond came by to see me, and he explained that for decades the Public Health Service had characterized homosexuality as "a mental disease or defect" under the immigration laws. As a result, homosexuals or suspected homosexuals were denied entry to the United States solely because of their sexual orientation. "There will probably be an explosive reaction," Richmond said, "but will you think about changing that?" To his surprise, I responded, "I don't have to think about it. Let's just order the Public Health Service to eliminate that characterization." I did—that day.[5]

.   .   .

Tense as some confrontations over civil rights were, the most vexing and challenging moments of my HEW years were spent in a riptide of issues swirling among science, law, religion, morality, and politics. My years there were marked by the dawn of the revolution in medical discovery that gave scientists powers that we once thought were reserved to God and that blurred the line between Madam Curie and Dr. Frankenstein. For me, those issues created a real tension between my faith and public policy, between my sense of obligation to my God and obligation to my country.

In grappling with those issues, I came to understand how much my Catholic faith had shaped me. I had been immersed in the Catholic religion, but my faith had never been tested until I became HEW secretary. I had not been forced to probe the depth of my commitment to it and its relevance to my public life. At HEW I went from the sidelines into the arena, from sitting in the pew at Mass on Sunday to living with my faith throughout the week.

In the Johnson White House, we were so confident that our Great Society programs were for the common good that I rarely reflected on the morality of our domestic agenda. My religious beliefs and moral values blended easily with public policies that promoted social justice, fought poverty, and aimed to end racial discrimination. At HEW eight years later determining what to give to God and what to Caesar was not easy. I often faced issues in which Caesar and God each claimed controlling jurisdiction and seemed to be facing off against each other: controversies over abortion and sterilization and scientific discoveries like cloning that threatened to outpace ethics and law.

I had worked for McNamara and LBJ as they made decisions involving life or death. Now, however, I was no longer a witness. A forty-five-year-old lawyer, I was the decision-maker. But I was so unsophisticated in medicine and science that I had difficulty figuring out the right questions to ask. I had never even taken a biology course.

Jimmy Carter openly campaigned as a born-again Christian. That was a little uncomfortable for a Brooklyn Catholic. I was skeptical about born-again Christians and public displays of fundamentalist religion, uneasy during the prayer breakfasts that Bert Lance conducted in the White House mess. Yet, ironically, I became, after the President, the most religiously identified figure of the Carter administration. That sometimes irritated me, but looking back, I realize that at HEW my Catholic faith and the philosophy courses taught by the Jesuits at Holy Cross gave me more support (and sometimes more angst) than at any other time of my life, as we confronted issues like abortion, in-vitro fertilization, and the use of extraordinary life-extending procedures. In a secular, pluralistic democracy these issues of life and death involve questions about the right of individual Americans to decide and the obligation of the federal government to finance their decisions. Such issues come freighted with religious beliefs and moral convictions, often further complicated by a lack of scientific certainty.

.   .   .

I first confronted the tension between my religious beliefs and public policy on the searing issue of whether Medicaid should fund abortions.

President Carter made his view clear in the campaign: he opposed federal funding for abortion unless the life of the mother was at stake. I agreed with him. When I realized that I was a leading candidate for the HEW cabinet post, I had to focus for the first time on the depth of my personal religious belief about abortion. As HEW Secretary, would I be able, in good conscience, to carry out the law of the land, even if that law provided for federal funding of all abortions? I asked that question of myself many times before others began asking it of me. I had no difficulty promoting family planning involving contraception, because I saw that not as taking a life but as preventing one from even being started.

With the Supreme Court's *Roe v. Wade* decision in 1973, by the time I became HEW secretary Medicaid was paying for 300,000 abortions a year. This federal financing set off a move in the House of Representatives, led by Republican representative Henry Hyde of Illinois, to prohibit the use of HEW funds "to perform abortions except where the life of the mother would be endangered if the fetus were carried to term."

I knew my obligation to enforce the law. But on the eve of my confirmation hearings—before becoming a public spokesman for myself and the administration—I felt a need to double-check my moral compass. I consulted a Jesuit priest, James English, my pastor at Holy Trinity Church in

Georgetown. He came by my law office on the Saturday morning before the Senate hearing. I wanted to make one final assessment of my ability to deal with the abortion issue. If I could not enforce whatever law the Congress passes, then I should not become secretary of Health, Education, and Welfare.

Father English spoke softly about our pluralistic society and the democratic system in which each of us has an opportunity to express our views. Most laws in our society, he noted, whether prohibiting stealing or slavery, promoting equal rights or civil rights, are founded in moral values. He said that my obligation to my personal conscience was satisfied if I expressed those views forcefully. If another view prevailed, however, I was free, indeed obliged, to enforce the law. "In a democratic society you are free to struggle to change the law even as you enforce the one on the books," he said. "So you can remain in office and enforce the law that's enacted as you work to change it. You wouldn't have that freedom—and you wouldn't be able to take the job—in a dictatorship." Father English suggested I speak to another Jesuit, Father Richard McCormick, a scholar in medical ethics at the Kennedy Institute of Bio-ethics at Georgetown University. I did, and Father McCormick gave me similar advice. I would fight for what I believed and I had no qualms about enforcing whatever law the Congress enacted.

At my confirmation hearing, I stated my position. Before I had departed the hearing room that afternoon the first of some 6,473 letters and telegrams and hundreds of phone calls, unyielding on one side or the other, arrived at my office. The next day, the *Washington Post* scolded me in an editorial:

> It is true that the opposition to abortion expressed by Health, Education and Welfare Secretary-designate Joseph Califano this week is consistent with the position taken by Jimmy Carter during the campaign. As Mr. Califano noted, he and the President-elect "come to it from different cultural and social and religious backgrounds, but we came to the same position. Abortion is wrong and federal funds should not be used. . . . But if the courts say that federal funds shall be provided, I'll enforce the law just like any other law."
>
> The fact that each man reached this conclusion as a matter of personal conviction makes the conclusion itself no less troubling. For, personal or not, the effect of their common position would be to deny to the poor what is available to the rich and not-so-rich. To argue, as they do, that the

emphasis should be on other medical services and/or pregnancy services does not address this inequity.[6]

As HEW secretary, I continued to espouse my view. To me, there was no issue of equity, because I considered abortion wrong for rich and poor. Congress then passed a law appropriating funds for abortions in wider circumstances than I considered appropriate. I had been given my say in our open, contentious, pluralistic society; now, like all other public parties to our freely arrived at social compact, my duty was to execute the law or get out. I decided to stay.

The law permitted federal funding of abortions in case of rape or incest when "promptly reported." I issued regulations giving women sixty days to make such reports, recognizing that in those days most women did not report such horrendous incidents unless they thought they were pregnant.

The Catholic hierarchy erupted. President Carter was not happy either. I told him that in my judgment sixty days were required by the law. The President thought the sixty-day period permitted too much opportunity for fraud and abuse and "would encourage women to lie."[7] At his insistence, I wrote Representative Daniel Flood, chairman of the Subcommittee on Labor, Health, Education, and Welfare, that the President thought "it may be advisable to reduce that period [of 60 days] to a shorter period of time." But the Congress did not change the law and I did not change the regulations.

.   .   .

In my first year at HEW I learned that, through Medicaid and the Public Health Service, the department was the largest single funder of sterilizations in the nation. We were financing some 100,000 a year. HEW had first adopted regulations attempting to limit funding for sterilizations in 1973 after two black sisters from Alabama, ages twelve and fourteen, alleged in a suit filed by their parents that they were sterilized without their consent. Other cases of forced sterilizations then came to light: a South Carolina doctor required sterilization after a patient on welfare delivered three children; social workers threatened clients with losing their welfare check if they did not get sterilized; prison officials were sterilizing inmates.

To end these abuses, I issued new rules to restrict federally funded sterilizations and to make certain that no sterilization was performed without informed consent. The new regulations prohibited federal funding for sterilization of anyone under twenty-one (on the ground that no minor could give informed consent to an irreversible procedure that goes to the essence of the life process) and of inmates of correctional facilities, mental hospitals, or other rehabilitative facilities. To reduce the chances of sterilization being chosen under duress, I prohibited soliciting consent from anyone in labor of childbirth, under the influence of alcohol or drugs, or seeking or obtaining an abortion.

The bishops of my church had pressed for a complete ban. The Catholic Church considers morally unacceptable any experimentation or action that threatens the sanctity of life, and that includes sterilization. Here again I had to weigh my personal beliefs against my obligation to issue regulations consistent with congressional policies and American pluralism. Despite the bishops' opposition, one devout Catholic who understood that obligation well, Eunice Shriver, sent me a handwritten note:

Back in Italy, four generations of your ancestors would have been proud of you as are millions of American citizens, of your motivation, actions and success in safeguarding the integrity of the mind, the will, and the human body. Keep up the good [work].

With many Catholic bishops questioning my decisions, Father English suggested that I sit down with William Cardinal Baum, archbishop of the Washington diocese. Father English hoped I could get Cardinal Baum and, through him, other members of the hierarchy to understand my position. In November 1977, upstairs in a private room at 1789, a favorite restaurant, I had dinner with Baum, Fathers English and McCormick, and Richard McCooey, owner of the restaurant and a thoughtful Catholic. Cardinal Baum insisted that I should further restrict abortion in cases of rape or incest. He chastised me for not banning all federal funding of sterilizations and for opposing tax credits for tuition paid to Catholic schools. In Baum's view carried to its logical conclusion, Catholics must adhere to the positions of the Church or resign from public office. I pointed out that such a position would disqualify all Catholics from the HEW post and thousands of other positions in local, state, and federal government. My arguments about serving in a pluralistic democracy fell on deaf ears.

Father McCormick weighed in on my side. He had been invaluable in helping me draw the lines between personal religious and moral conviction and sound public policy in our system of governing. His attempts to make these points with Baum were to no avail that evening.

It was a difficult, contentious discussion; our dinner ended with the archbishop and the secretary coolly agreeing to disagree. Our exchange didn't temper the assault of many Catholic bishops on me.

As I went home that evening, I thought with wry annoyance about the constant press references to me as "Secretary Califano, a Roman Catholic" when reporters covered the abortion issue. No such reference appeared next to my name in the stories reporting my opposition to tuition tax credits, which I feared would harm the nation's troubled public schools. If my reporter friends had been flies on the wall this evening, I mused, would they change their characterization of me?

The situation with the hierarchy became so antagonistic that Father Ted Hesburgh, president of Notre Dame, invited me to give the commencement speech in 1979 on the subject of being a Catholic in public life. "Maybe," he suggested, "we can get them to understand your position and that of other Catholics in public life." I accepted the invitation. I said I saw the resignation option as receding to a safe harbor rather than weathering the storm, a withdrawal from the arena, not an expression of principle. I was not about to retreat to my own Walden Pond or Vatican Hill. For me, there was too much to do in the public arena. Father Hesburgh sent a copy to every bishop in the United States.*

.   .   .

The year I took office, I faced another scientific controversy, this one over DNA—deoxyribonucleic acid—the genetic material that determines blueprints for all living cells. In the early 1970s, scientists discovered that genes from different species could be recombined in a laboratory. Recombinant DNA molecules contain segments of DNA from different organisms combined in a test tube or in an organism itself. The research held a remarkable

---

*Years later, I had a drink with Cardinal Baum and John Cardinal O'Connor of New York at the Vatican and spent a pleasant hour with them during which we did not discuss any HEW-related issues. I detected that both these conservative clerics had come to better appreciate the importance of having Catholics in public life in our pluralistic society.

potential for understanding fundamental biochemical processes and promised to revolutionize molecular biology. Scientists hoped, for example, that human insulin genes inserted into the DNA of a bacterium like E. coli could stimulate bacterial production of human insulin, thus revolutionizing the treatment of diabetes. Many worried, however, that recombinant DNA might unleash unknown and uncontrollable diseases into the world.*

In certain experiments, scientists took DNA from a virus that produced tumors and detectable antibodies in mice and inserted it into the DNA of another organism. They then cloned the result of that combination and reinserted it into mice. Concerns arose that even if the viral DNA was not infectious to human beings to start with, the genetic recombination might create a new virus that *was* infectious and that might escape from the laboratory and unleash uncontrollable epidemics.

Soon after National Institutes of Health director Donald Fredrickson introduced me to the recombinant DNA controversy, I received letters and calls from members of Congress and scientists fearful of the environmental impact of the research that NIH was funding and its threat to human life. A kind of panic began to spread on Capitol Hill. Members called me demanding immediate sharp limits on all public and private recombinant DNA research. Arkansas Democratic senator Dale Bumpers introduced a bill to curb such research. Others followed with even more restrictive legislative proposals. Senator Kennedy called for congressional hearings.

Fredrickson told me such measures could curtail important research and discovery. I agreed. We had to stop Congress from putting a straitjacket on DNA research. I convened the relevant government agencies and issued what I hoped would be a preemptive position paper proposing our own standards. Though I considered the standards "an unusual regulation of activities affecting basic science," I hoped they would permit research to go forward in "this vital scientific area." My goal was to keep such research out of the political pit stops on Capitol Hill. At the time, Fredrickson feared we would alienate powerful members of Congress. The NIH director wrote

---

*In 1974 a group of American academic molecular biologists called for a moratorium on experiments with recombinant DNA. In 1975, premier scientists from around the world gathered for three days at the Asilomar Conference to assess the risks involved and craft an approach for future research. Out of that conference came very tight *NIH Guidelines for Recombinant DNA Research* that were issued on June 23, 1976, and applied to recombinant DNA experiments conducted with any support from NIH.

twenty-five years later, however, that he appreciated my "understanding the chaos that could arise should regulation fall back into the hands of a congressional committee" and my determination "not to let this happen."[8]

We saw recombinant DNA as opening a new world of genetic engineering that could lead to spectacular medicines, such as the human growth hormone and insulin, to gene therapy, and to new prolific strains of agricultural crops. I worried then about how close scientists were getting to tampering with Mother Nature and knew that we could not at this early stage offer much more than a best guess in calculating the moral and ethical implications and the health costs and benefits of the new science of genomics.

In December 1978, I issued new national guidelines for recombinant DNA research, relaxing stringent rules and exempting a third of the research from the initial restrictions. I assured the public that I had been "guided by my responsibility to allow the maximum freedom of scientific inquiry consistent with the protection of the public health and the environment and with respect for the important ethical concerns surrounding genetic research in general." I took a deep breath and whispered a silent prayer, knowing that we were jumping into the scientific and ethical unknown.

.   .   .

Still acutely aware of my limitations in confronting such confounding scientific and ethical questions, I established an Ethics Advisory Board in the fall of 1977. I asked Jim Gaither to chair it and appointed members representing a wide spectrum of opinion and experience. Along with eminent experts in genetics and obstetrics, the board included Sissela Bok, a lecturer in medical ethics at Harvard who had written a book on lying; Father Richard McCormick, the Jesuit ethicist; and David Hamburg, president of the Institute of Medicine, National Academy of Sciences.

I asked this group for guidance in responding to the first grant application to HEW for funds to perform research on human in vitro fertilization—the union of sperm and ovum in a laboratory dish rather than within the female body and transplantation of the resulting embryo into a woman's womb. Soon afterward British scientists Robert Edwards and

Patrick Steptoe electrified the world by announcing the birth—on July 25, 1978, in London—of an apparently normal child following in vitro fertilization. The world had its first test-tube baby, and I had another thorny ethical problem to deal with.

I was asked for my views almost immediately, especially since the Catholic Church had come out strongly against the practice. As a public official and non-scientist, I said, my mind was open on the subject; that was why I had referred the issue to my Ethics Advisory Board. I made no reference to my personal experiences when Trudy and I had struggled to have children more than a decade before, but my memory of that wrenching emotional time tilted me toward funding in vitro fertilization research. In referring the matter to my Ethics Advisory Board, I wrote:

> From a medical perspective, advancing our knowledge of reproductive biology may contribute to reducing genetic diseases and infant mortality . . . [and to the] possibility that certain couples who cannot otherwise have children may now be able to have children of their own. On the other hand, these procedures raise serious moral and ethical questions. . . . Can techniques of *in vitro* fertilization . . . damage the resulting fetus and lead to abnormal children? Will this research lead to selective breeding, to attempts to control the genetic makeup of offspring or to the use of "surrogate parents," where, for example, rich women might pay poor women to carry their children?

I announced public hearings and called for a national debate. A few months later, on June 10, 1979, I released the Ethics Advisory Board's report. Its members, diverse in their backgrounds, concluded that under carefully circumscribed conditions, it was ethically acceptable for HEW to support research on human in vitro fertilization. But debate on federal funding of the next-generation issue—stem cell research—heated up twenty years later.

In vitro fertilization was not the only ethical and scientific issue that taught me the importance of locking individuals with clashing views in the same room. The controversy over fetal research was another. In one corner were Ford Foundation president McGeorge Bundy and the Guttmacher Institute; they favored unfettered fetal research. In the other, Sargent and

Eunice Shriver represented the opposing Roman Catholic viewpoint. Fetal research had been delayed for years because of disputes over the limits of scientific inquiry and what constitutes a human life. Fredrickson and I met with each side separately, then with both together. We reminded the Guttmacher group of the serious questions of morality and human dignity. We spoke to the Shriver group of the enormous potential benefits in the area of mental retardation and other birth defects. In the end, I told both sides that, in an effort to shed the political baggage of the past, I intended to call this "healthy baby research." I challenged them to recommend a budget sensitive to the considerations we had discussed and promised we would fight for it. They did, we did, and the research began—and the controversy persists a quarter century later.

.   .   .

The capacity of our scientific genius to keep hearts beating and lungs breathing delivered this tranche of ethical questions to my desk: When does death occur? What is the difference between murder, suicide, euthanasia, and natural death? With Medicare and Medicaid picking up the lion's share of health care costs, whose business is it to determine the difference? Who decides whether to use the miracles of modern technology and medicine to keep a person alive? The government? The patient? The physician? The family? The HMO or health insurer?

In philosophy courses at Holy Cross, I was taught that murder, suicide, and euthanasia were morally wrong. I learned that each individual had an obligation to take ordinary means to preserve his or her life, but as my ethics text stipulated, "one is not obliged to take extraordinary means."[9] Now, as HEW secretary, I had to make the vexing distinction between suicide, murder, and natural death, between ordinary and extraordinary means of maintaining life, as our scientists wrestled with the will of God and each day unveiled a new medical machine, miracle pharmaceutical, or surgical procedure.

In September 1978, between campaign stops with Connecticut governor Ella Grasso during her run for re-election, we discussed these issues and the way our society treated its elderly. She was appalled when I told her that a third of Medicare funds were spent on medical treatment for patients during their last year of life. "I want you to come back so I can show you something," she said as I left to fly to Washington.

When I returned, Ella Grasso introduced me to the hospice movement. The movement began in England, she explained, to ease the pain and fear of terminally ill patients, usually cancer victims, during their last days or months of life. Rather than tie people to machines and tubes, or subject them to savage long-shot chemotherapies, they are given a "hospice cocktail" of drugs to ease the pain sufficiently to permit the patient to live at home.

Grasso took me to the New Haven hospice team headed by Dr. Sylvia Lack in a small, three-room New Haven office. We then visited a man who was terminally ill with cancer in his home. Ella and I sat on the couch and talked with the man and his wife. This simple, unsophisticated man was more comfortable in the conversation than I was. He had come to terms with dying; I had not. I was forty-seven years old, my parents were alive, and I had never come close to someone who I knew was dying.

I asked Ella what I could do. "Medicare reimburses for all the expensive therapy, but it doesn't cover hospice as health care." I promised to look into it. Then she added, "I want to build a free-standing hospice in New Haven and I need a million dollars."

"You've got it," I said.

"We could also use a little encouragement from someone in high places," Dr. Lack added.

When I returned to HEW, I was told I had no authority to make a grant of one million dollars for a hospice. "I'll go to jail for giving Ella Grasso the money," I said, and personally signed an order to make the grant. Ella Grasso put up the first free-standing hospice in the United States, outside New Haven. At the first annual meeting of the hospice organizations from across the country, on October 5, 1978, I announced that HEW would begin funding hospice care.

Years after my time at HEW I had my own experience with medicine's ability to maintain life. In January 1986, my eighty-six-year-old father called me in Washington from his home in Spring Lake, New Jersey. He was crying. "They want to send your mother to the hospital. You told us you'd never let them send us to the hospital," he said through his sobs.

"What's wrong with Mother?" I asked.

"I don't know," my father said. "Here, talk to the doctor."

"She's going to be ninety-three this June. And she's demented. Why not leave her at home?" I asked.

"She must get kidney dialysis and other treatment in the hospital," the doctor responded. "If she stays here, she'll be dead in a matter of days."

"I'm leaving immediately for Spring Lake. Don't do anything till I get there."

When I arrived, it was almost three in the morning. My father's eyes were raw and red from crying as he sat next to my mother's bed, holding her hand.

"Don't let them send your mother to the hospital," he pleaded. In her own way, Mother made the same plea to me.

I turned to the doctor. "My mother's going to stay here," I said.

"I can't be responsible for what happens," he replied. "You realize that your mother will be dead in a few days."

"She's ready for God," I said softly.

The doctor left. I stayed for a few days and then returned to Washington. With my father at her side, holding her hand for the better part of each day, my mother lived for almost five months and died at peace in her own bed on May 27, 1986.

.   .   .

When Carter announced my selection for HEW in Georgia, an anti-smoking campaign was not on my radar screen. I had been a heavy smoker, on most days consuming four packs a day while I worked for Lyndon Johnson. I cut back to two packs a day during the years that I practiced law. I'd never thought much about quitting until the summer of 1975 when I was sitting on the beach at Cape Cod. Because my son Joe's birthday came right after Christmas and he never seemed to get a proper present, I asked him that August, "What do you want for your birthday? Tell me now and we'll get the present when we return to Washington in September."

"I want you to quit smoking," my eleven-year-old said.

"Seriously, what do you really want?"

"Dad, I really want you to quit smoking."

When I returned to Washington, Ben Bradlee was in a smoking-cessation program, because Sally Quinn wouldn't let him smoke at their apartment.

So was my law partner Vincent Fuller, because his doctor had diagnosed his early symptoms of emphysema. I went to the same cessation program on Monday nights for nine weeks and quit smoking on October 27, 1975. Shaking my nicotine addiction was as difficult as anything I'd ever done. Nevertheless, I didn't think much about it once I had stopped.

President Carter wanted me to mount a health promotion and disease-prevention program. I sought the opinion of every physician—more than a hundred—I was interviewing for HEW posts. Without exception, each said there could be no credible effort unless we went after cigarette smoking. We conducted a survey, which revealed that virtually every addicted adult smoker first lit up and was hooked as a teen, well before reaching age twenty-one, and that most had tried to quit within the last year. That set me on the course of an aggressive public information campaign.

I announced the anti-smoking campaign on January 11, 1978, the fourteenth anniversary of the first surgeon general's report, *Smoking and Health.* Thanks to my speechwriter, Ervin Duggan, I called smoking "slow-motion suicide" and designated it "Public Health Enemy Number One." I decreed that all HEW buildings must be smoke-free, and I pressed other government agencies to follow suit.

The *Washington Evening Star* banner-headlined "Califano Declares War On Smoking." The tobacco industry immediately counterattacked. The Kentucky legislature called for my impeachment. Red-and-white bumper stickers sprouted up across tobacco states proclaiming, "Califano Is Dangerous To Your Health," a play on the warning then printed on every cigarette pack. Southern politicians and close political advisors told Carter that he could not carry North Carolina, Virginia, and Kentucky, perhaps even Georgia, in 1980 unless I abandoned the anti-smoking campaign. Some, like North Carolina governor Jim Hunt, urged the President to fire me, noting that in addition to the anti-smoking campaign I was hurting the President's chances for reelection by pressing southern states to provide equal opportunity and comparable facilities at predominantly black universities and publicly embarrassing them by bringing attention to the enormous disparity compared with predominantly white colleges.

As the fury mounted, my sister-in-law, Barbara Bouvais, sent me a framed quotation by Teddy Roosevelt. I hung it in my office at HEW and in every place I've worked since:

It's not the critic who counts; not the man who points out how the strong man stumbles or where the doer of deeds could have done them better. The credit belongs to the man who is actually in the arena, whose face is marred by dust and sweat and blood; who strives valiantly; who errs, who comes short again and again . . . who knows great enthusiasms, the great devotions; who spends himself in a worthy cause; who at the best knows in the end the triumph of high achievement, and who at the worst, if he fails, at least fails while daring greatly, so that his place shall never be with those cold and timid souls who neither know victory nor defeat.

A year later, Dr. Julius Richmond and I issued a new surgeon general's report, also titled *Smoking and Health,* to celebrate the fifteenth anniversary of the original report by Dr. Luther Terry. It was a powerful compilation of years of research linking smoking to a host of deadly cancers and crippling and killing heart and respiratory diseases. Tobacco executives denounced our 1979 report and called me "Ayatollah* Califano." All the while, they hid in their files their own overwhelming evidence that their product caused the very cancers, heart ailments, and respiratory diseases that we had listed.

I had wanted the 1979 surgeon general's report to declare smoking addictive, but Dr. Richmond demurred, saying we lacked the scientific data to draw that conclusion beyond all doubt. Twenty years later, I learned that at the time the tobacco companies already had proof positive in their own research that their product was addictive. They had lied to us and to the American people.[†]

Though I scoured HEW for ideas to promote the anti-smoking effort, I missed one extraordinary opportunity. Unknown to me at the time, Postmaster General William Bolger had a no-smoking stamp designed. He sent it over to HEW, where it got lost in the department's vast bureaucracy; his idea never reached my desk. Hearing nothing from us and aware of the political maelstrom the campaign had ignited, Bolger concluded that we did

---

*A reference to Ayatollah Khomeini of Iran.
[†]When the tobacco litigation in the 1990s exposed the companies' knowledge, I talked to President Carter and Dr. Richmond. They agreed that had we known what the industry was hiding, we would have declared nicotine addictive and would have moved, as Food and Drug administrator David Kessler did in 1994, to have cigarettes declared a drug-delivery device. Measured in terms of the ravages of Big Tobacco's products over the intervening twenty years, concealing that evidence contributed to more than 6 million premature deaths and devastated families.

not want the stamp issued—and it never was. Years later he told me about this stamp and gave me the original design.

As the tobacco companies stepped up their pressure on the President to rein me in, Supreme Court Chief Justice Warren Burger visited me in my HEW office on January 23, 1979. He recounted his own efforts that had produced non-smoking cars on AMTRAK and a smoke-free cafeteria at the Supreme Court. He urged me to hang tough.

House Speaker Tip O'Neill, who'd become like a father to me, called me to his office. He warned me, quite seriously, that he thought the industry was capable of hiring a hit man to kill me. "You have got these tobacco guys so mad at you. These guys hate you! Be careful. These guys are capable of killing you," he cautioned. I passed his warnings off as the exaggerated foreboding of a dramatic Irishman. In later years, when I saw the threats to Jeffrey Wigand's life portrayed in the movie *The Insider*—including a bullet found in his mailbox—I gave more credence to the Speaker's assessment.

On Good Friday 1979 I joined Ted Kennedy for lunch at his home in McLean, Virginia. He urged me to leave the administration before Carter fired me. "Joe," Kennedy warned, "with you at HEW, Carter has no chance to carry North Carolina, Virginia, or Kentucky—and maybe even Connecticut, where they make cigars. That anti-smoking campaign will kill him." I discounted his comments, however, because he was planning to run against Carter for the Democratic nomination. With a campaign of his own brewing, Kennedy would relish my resignation over this and other liberal issues.*

President Carter was feeling the heat from my anti-smoking campaign. He spoke in the South about making a safer cigarette. Members of Congress and governors from tobacco-producing states asked him to curb my efforts. Fritz Mondale, Carter's vice president and a close colleague of mine, had me to lunch in his office. As soon as Mondale started to broach the subject, I interrupted, "Fritz, please don't put me in a position where I have to say you or the President tried to stop the anti-smoking campaign." He didn't.

Our anti-smoking campaign had an impact. Per capita cigarette consumption in the United States in 1979 dropped to its lowest level in twenty-two years. C. Everett Koop, surgeon general in the conservative Reagan

---

*I was so identified as the only liberal in the Carter cabinet that when I closed my remarks at the winter Gridiron dinner by saying that despite all the controversy, "I enjoy being the only Democrat in the Carter administration," it brought down the house of reporters.

administration, picked up the cudgel and added energy to the effort. Non-smoking policies are now common on aircraft and trains, in restaurants and other public enclosed spaces. Children encourage their parents not to smoke. As people have come to understand how the nicotine pushers had manipulated them for years, grassroots efforts have sprouted in towns and cities across America. Big Tobacco executives have been able to kill effective federal anti-smoking legislation, but they have not been able to hold back a surge of public disgust at their conduct and positive actions by an informed public.

·   ·   ·

The year 1979 was a traumatic one for me. In January, Trudy, my wife of twenty-three years, and I separated. In July, President Carter fired me as secretary of Health, Education, and Welfare. These events—both inconceivable to me before they occurred—were a double emotional whammy that went to the marrow of my life.

In October 1978, Ben Bradlee and Sally Quinn had been married and celebrated with a party at Sally's apartment off DuPont Circle. In her toast, Sally said, "The press will call this her first and his third. I know it as her only and his last." We all applauded, and I was struck by what a wonderful relationship they had. Soon afterward, I took a long official trip to Warsaw, Rome, Jerusalem, Cairo, and the Temple of Luxor, built in the thirteenth century B.C. Experiencing these civilizations left me with a profound sense of how fleeting life is and how unhappy Trudy and I were.

From our days in New York, when Trudy and I read the same books, worked together at the *cuartito* in Spanish Harlem, and campaigned for our friends, we had grown so far apart that we pursued distinctly different lives. After twenty-three years, we now disagreed on many religious and political issues. We had divergent social interests. We preferred the company of different friends. As work took me from a Wall Street law practice to the Pentagon and the White House and then to a highly visible Washington law practice, Trudy withdrew into her own life—becoming as uninvolved in mine as I became in hers. After my first few months on LBJ's staff, Trudy rarely attended White House functions. She found little satisfaction and enjoyment in the social glitter of Washington. As my professional and political life intensified, especially at HEW, the moral theology of the Catholic Church became more interesting and important to me, just as it was becoming less so to her as she searched elsewhere for her own spiritual satisfaction. I had valued the excitement of my career, but I had never appreciated what marriage meant in terms of commitment and personal sacrifice.

When Jimmy Carter was elected 1976, rumors circulated that I was being considered for a number of cabinet posts, including Defense, Justice, and HEW. Trudy called Vice President-elect Fritz Mondale, a friend whom she knew and liked, to tell him that if I went to the Defense Department, she would be no part of it. (I did not know of this conversation at the time—and when Carter asked if I had any interest in Defense, I told him that Harold Brown was the man for that job.)

During my years as secretary of HEW, she preferred privacy; I chose the limelight, determined to use it to shape public attitudes and policy. I went alone to public events at the White House and social and charitable functions like Ethel Kennedy's RFK tennis tournament. Our sons, Mark and Joe, were in the Jesuit high school at Georgetown Prep and Claudia was in elementary school at Stoneridge Country Day School of the Sacred Heart during my years at HEW. Trudy rarely accompanied us on Sunday mornings when we went to the 9:30 A.M. family Mass at Holy Trinity Church in Georgetown (and afterwards to the Georgetown drugstore of Doc Dalinsky, a fatherly pharmacist who listened to his customers like a friendly bartender, for a Sunday morning ritual of coffee, danish, and chatter with Buchwald, Geyelin, and Bradlee).

Like many women in the 1970s, Trudy went back to school for her master's degree to help develop an independent life and interests. I was too consumed with my work to give her much companionship. We had married young, just out of school, at a time when neither of us—or at least not I—understood what marriage was all about. Together we thought we had the recipe for a lasting marriage: like our parents, we were both Catholics and believed in raising and educating our children and contributing to society. In our early years in New York, it was Trudy who introduced me to social justice issues like the *cuartito* and to *Jubilee* magazine, through her own participation. Once in Washington, however, we grew almost imperceptibly into two separate lives—separated as much in interest as by time apart. Little was left between us except a profound love for our children and our ambition for their happiness and success. Try as we might, we had not—and I was convinced could not—provide each other the love and support essential for a real marriage.

In January 1979, we separated. Eileen Shanahan, the public affairs chief at HEW, announced it to the press on Friday, January 19, 1979. She refused to elaborate beyond the one-sentence statement: "Secretary Califano and Mrs. Califano, by mutual agreement, are temporarily living apart." The *Washington Star* carried this headline, "Califano, Wife Separate After 23 Years" with photographs of both of us. The story called me a "legendary workaholic" and cited Trudy's disappointment with my decision to take the HEW job because of its long hours.

Growing up Catholic and marrying when *Leave It to Beaver* epitomized American family culture, I had never in my life contemplated separation or divorce. My greatest concern (and Trudy's) was our children. Nothing written about family breakup can capture the torment it causes for children, even with the best efforts of parents.

To prepare for a formal separation, I retained Sidney Sachs as my lawyer. Ed Williams, Paul Connolly, and I had customarily referred our clients to Sachs for domestic-relations problems. But until he represented me I hadn't realized what a wise and compassionate counselor he was. For more than three years Sidney Sachs did as much as anyone to help me through this painful experience and quell the demons that so easily erupt during post-marital negotiations.

At our first meeting in my conference room at HEW, Sachs said he wanted to bring a psychologist to our next session. I saw no need for one, but he insisted, "I want you to understand some of the feelings you're going to experience. This is going to be different from anything you've been through."

"Like what?" I asked. "I've been through a helluva lot."

"Like your sense of failure," Sachs replied. "You're not used to failing at anything. And anger—at yourself as well as Trudy. And doubts as to whether you're capable of loving anyone."

"I loved Trudy when I proposed and we married," I said. "I love my parents."

"Let me bring the psychologist," Sachs said. "You don't have to listen to him."

I gave in to his persistence, with no idea of how precisely he was nailing what I'd feel over the next couple of years.

At our next meeting, the psychologist reviewed many of the emotions I would experience. Together with Sachs, he assured me that most of what I would feel was quite common. I was plagued by a sense of failure: why had I failed to make it work? Had I become so self-engrossed and consumed with work that I was unable to love anyone with the commitment, selflessness, and generosity required for a real marriage?

Fortuitously, during this time my high school sweetheart, Joan Hembrooke, called my office; she was coming to Washington with her husband, Dr. Lawrence Livornese, a thoracic surgeon. Could we get together? I had not seen or spoken to her for twenty years. I invited them to come by and have breakfast while they were in town. As soon as she walked into my office, I remembered that I had loved her deeply when we were in high school in Brooklyn in the 1940s. At that moment, I realized I was capable of love. Later, as we were going through the divorce negotiations, Sidney Sachs's psychologist told me that some of the most intense caring relationships in life are first loves between teenagers.

.   .   .

The second blow of 1979 came in July. After a couple of weeks meditating and deliberating outside Washington and at Camp David, as lines grew at gas stations across the country, President Jimmy Carter gave his famous "Malaise" speech, in which he described

a crisis of confidence that strikes at the very heart and soul and spirit of our national will. We can see this crisis in the growing doubt about the meaning of our own lives and in the loss of a unity of purpose for our nation. The erosion of our confidence in the future is threatening to destroy the social and the political fabric of America. . . .

After the President's public soul-searching, Washington became a hornet's nest of rumors about Carter lopping off some cabinet members. I was so high on the list I had to leave for my office through the basement and back alley of my hotel in order to avoid the television cameramen hunting me at 7 A.M. On the Tuesday after the speech, Carter announced that he had asked all cabinet officers for their resignations and would decide whose to accept. At lunch earlier that day House Speaker Tip O'Neill had tried to cheer me up. "Hell, Joe, I can't believe he would ever get rid of you."

I found some comfort in those words—until late afternoon, when my son

Mark, working that summer as a seventeen-year-old copy aide at the *Washington Post*, called me. He nervously kidded me as much to deal with his own concern as to allay mine. Mark said that he was distributing around the newsroom the "budget" listing the next day's stories. "Do you still have a job, Dad? We're running a story tomorrow that says you're going to be fired."

"Whose story?" I asked.

"David Broder and Ed Walsh," he said.

Broder was the leading political reporter in Washington; Walsh was the *Post* White House correspondent. I knew I was in trouble.

The next morning, I had a quiet breakfast with Ed Williams at the Metropolitan Club. Sitting virtually alone in its vast dining room on the fourth floor, we talked about the possibility that Carter might fire me.

"I can't believe it," Williams said. "It doesn't make any sense."

"No president would let his staff put this stuff out if he hadn't blessed it."

Williams leaned across the table. "It would be the best damn thing that could happen to you. The guy is through, and it will give you a way to get out. You ought to hope he fires you. You may not be that lucky."

I thought about calling Fritz Mondale but decided not to. I assumed he would not have wanted Carter to fire me and had said so to the President, but like every vice president, he was at bottom a creature of the president who selected him as a running mate. This, I now believed, was a decision made and Fritz would have to fall in line.

Late that afternoon, Carter called me to his office. As soon as we sat down, he said, "I have decided to accept your resignation."

"Mr. President, you are entitled to the cabinet people you want. I will work for an orderly transition." I recited the words I had rehearsed in my mind as the rumors had swelled up. I was surprised at how nervous my voice sounded as I spoke them.

Then the President astonishingly added, "Your performance as secretary has been outstanding. You have put the department in better shape than it has ever been in before. You've been the best secretary of HEW. The department has never been better managed."

I thanked him for his comments.

"I have never said a bad word about you or your performance and I never will," the President continued. "If anyone does around here, I will fire him."

As Carter spoke those words, I thought of the leaks criticizing me over past months coming from anonymous White House sources. I remembered the time President Johnson directed me to leak to the press that government officials considered Bethlehem Steel Company executives who raised prices to be "profiteering from the war in Vietnam." The papers ran with the story; editorials castigated the steel executives, and they were outraged. Weeks later at a meeting with businessmen, one of them complained to the President about the profiteering charge. I was standing next to Johnson, who feigned surprise. He said he considered the statement reprehensible. He assured the businessman, "If I find out some damn fool aide did it, I'll fire the sonuvabitch."

Carter spoke about my not getting along with some members of his staff—particularly Hamilton Jordan and Jody Powell—and the need to "get the cabinet and administration in shape for the 1980 election." He then urged me to come to Camp David for the weekend, alone or with my children. I told him that with all the attention and trauma this would bring in the press, I should spend the weekend with my kids alone.

I handed my letter of resignation to the President in the Oval Office the next morning at 7:30 A.M. Carter read it, called it a "beautiful letter," and promised to respond in kind well before my noon staff meeting.

Later that morning, I could not keep my composure in saying farewell to my staff. I got out a few words about how being secretary was "the greatest honor of my life," but then left abruptly as my eyes filled with tears and I began crying. I rushed to my bathroom, sobbing uncontrollably, wiping my eyes with cold water to hide the redness. I needed to get control of myself for the press conference about to begin.

The HEW auditorium was overflowing and hundreds of employees were packed outside in the hall. A dozen television cameras were squeezed where ordinarily three or four were set up. National political reporters and columnists were there, in addition to the usual HEW beat correspondents. The lights seemed harsh as I stood behind the lectern on the stage. I was sure they exposed my red eyes. I tried to find space to put my notes down in the forest of microphones to the podium. I took a sip of water to steady myself, breathed deeply, and began speaking, hoping I sounded firmer than I felt. I knew it would be a major effort not to break down and cry again:

> I remember reading, a few years ago, a wise admonition for those who
> would understand our politics: Try to tell the difference between the tides,
> waves, and ripples. By that measure, the matter of which individual runs
> a government department—or for how long—is surely little more than a

ripple; the matter of who wins next year's election, a wave. Certain issues, however, are truly tidal in their magnitude and meaning. Civil rights is one such issue. The issue of guaranteeing a fair share of this nation's plenty to poor, old, and helpless people is another. The issue of enhancing health and education for millions of people is yet another.

I was getting a sense of self-control. My voice was regaining its natural timbre. I began to think I might make it.

These great tidal issues describe the mandate of this department. And in the past thirty months, as secretary of Health, Education, and Welfare, I have found myself immersed in all of them. That experience has brought some frustrations. But I find myself thinking now only of the satisfactions. . . .

Inevitably, there will be those who will say, in trying to explain this event, that I made waves. I hope I did—but I will leave that judgment to you and to the passage of time.

On that afternoon, *Post* managing editor Howard Simons called and left this message at my office: "Stay on the high ground. It is going to get very bad."

Carter had forced several cabinet resignations and the reaction was furiously negative. As criticism mounted, White House press secretary Jody Powell, top political aide Hamilton Jordan, and the President himself had a background meeting with reporters and contradicted my press-conference statements recounting what the President had said to me about my performance as secretary when he asked for my resignation. Fortunately for me, however, the President had said the same things he said to me to members of Congress when he told them about my departure. New York congressman Charles Rangel told reporters that when he called Carter to urge him to keep me on (a call I knew nothing about), Carter's praise was so effusive, "I almost thought the President was going to name Califano chief of staff."

According to reporters present, the President questioned the accuracy of my report about his statements at our private meeting together, but refused to go on the record or permit direct quotation. Still, the Saturday and Sunday papers made it clear the President was seeking to portray me as a liar.

I was shocked and angry as I went to be interviewed on ABC's *Issues and Answers*, then the network's Sunday morning show. I took my children, Mark, Joe, and Claudia, to the studio with me. It is not pleasant to have your children see you accused of twisting the facts by the President of the United States and his aides; I wanted my sons and daughter to see and hear me respond.

ABC reporter Bob Clark put the question to me right away: "I don't really know how to bring this matter up delicately, so I will begin by quoting these words from the front page of yesterday's *Washington Post*: 'The President put out the word that Califano was lying about the reasons given for his being fired as Secretary of Health, Education, and Welfare.' Would you begin by telling us just what the President did say to you as he accepted your resignation?"

After I repeated what I had said at my press conference, Clark said that Carter and Powell had "denied almost every element specifically of what you said. . . . Who is right about this?"

"There were two people at that meeting, the President and me, and I know what he said to me," I replied. "It was one of the most attentive and searing moments of my entire life. But I would also like to say something else that I think is important. The President is not well served by this kind of a who-said-what or this kind of a personality discussion. The country is not well served by this, and I, myself, to the extent I have the power to do anything about it, intend to put an end to it." Throughout the interview, I underscored the importance of dealing with the real issues—poverty, health care, education.

Calls and messages came in from across the country. Some were light like the reference of Dave Bell, executive vice president of the Ford Foundation, to my earlier experience upon leaving the Johnson administration, "Congratulations on a superb job. . . . Could we interest you in a trip around the world?"

Katharine Graham wrote, "This is a sad day for the country—and even an ominous one—I just want to take this opportunity to say you have done a super job at the toughest time under the hardest circumstances. . . . Welcome back. Love, Kay."

Leon Jaworski and Judge John Sirica sent notes. Arkansas governor Bill Clinton called: "That is a hell of a job that you are in and you are the only person I have seen who has ever had a hold on it. You are the first person who ever did anything besides mouth about people who are on welfare. A lot of people down here [Arkansas] feel this way. I am a big fan of yours. . . ."

Even a nemesis from the LBJ years wrote. "Dear Joe: If I were the President and had you in my Cabinet, although we wouldn't agree much past non-smoking, I'll be darned if I would let you go. I am sorry we are losing you but I think you will live longer and happier. . . . *Barry Goldwater*".

A letter from Lady Bird Johnson was the most moving. "If public service sometimes rears the head of Hydra, Joe, I hope the countless frustrations will be overshadowed by a feeling of deep satisfaction in your many contributions to this country, and that your sense of achievement will be heightened in knowing that there are many, many of us who recognize and salute them."

Buchwald called. "Joey, I want you to know I feel better about the hands the country's in. The President has the greatest energy crisis in the nation's history—and so he consults Jesse Jackson and fires his secretary of Health, Education, and Welfare." I laughed, and my old friend said, "Good. I want you to remember that you laughed at least once today."

Milos Forman phoned from Czechoslovakia. I had represented Forman in his effort to become an American citizen so that he could safely visit his children, who were being held behind the Iron Curtain. He wanted to know if I needed any help.

"A bit part in one of your films," I said.

"You're a star to me," Forman replied.

"What are you doing in Czechoslovakia?" I said.

"Making a movie. There's a part for you if you come over here," he said, chuckling.

I declined, missing one of the great opportunities of my life: the movie was *Amadeus,* which in 1985 was nominated for eleven Oscars, including Best Director, which Forman won.

Mother and Dad wrote, "We were prouder of you than ever when we watched and listened to you on TV. . . . May you be guided in whatever you decide to do with the gifts God has given you."

Minutes before her swearing-in ceremony, President Carter pressed me to attend the induction of Patricia Harris, his choice to succeed me, but I was simply not up to it. Later that last day in office I got an abrupt reminder of what life would be like without the perks of a cabinet officer. I went to lunch with close members of my staff at Tiberio's. We ate pasta and veal, had drinks and wine. They went back to work. I drove my own car to the Jefferson Hotel, parked on M Street, and went to my room and fell asleep. When I awakened about 6 P.M. and went down to get into my car, it was gone. I had parked in a tow-away zone during rush hour. I went to the Indiana Avenue police station, waited in line, paid my fine, and then went to an impoundment lot under the K Street Freeway, where I handed my receipt to a clerk and picked up my car. None of the police knew who I was—or had been.

Licking my wounds that summer and fall of 1979 was not easy, but the salt water around Cape Cod helped. Kay Graham invited me to spend a week at her home on Martha's Vineyard. I was alone and she reached out to me as she had to so many people in pain. After that week, I went over to Wellfleet to work on a book about many of the public-policy controversies of my HEW years. For all the wonderful letters and calls I had received, I still missed being secretary of Health, Education, and Welfare.

The next May President Carter asked me to come to the unveiling of the new seal of the Department of Health and Human Services. (At his recommendation, Congress had created a separate Department of Education, a change I had opposed.) Carter ignored me at the ceremony, though he used terms I had coined as secretary and cited programs I had mounted, such as childhood immunization. As I returned to my law office that afternoon, the memories rushed through my mind, of my life there, and of this extraordinary department that was now coming to an end, of commitments kept and opportunities grasped and missed. Being secretary of the Department of Health, Education, and Welfare had been the greatest opportunity of my lifetime. It had given me a chance to show that the Great Society programs I had worked so hard to design and enact could be executed with competence and compassion. On longer-term reflection, I had the satisfaction of doing what I believed, of using whatever talents and experience I had acquired to help the most vulnerable citizens in our society.

The next day I received this handwritten note:

To Joe Califano:
    I really appreciated your being at the ceremony this morning. You did an outstanding job as Secretary. On occasion, I would like to call on you to help me again.
    Best wishes,
    Jimmy Carter
    P.S. The C David invitation stands.

In early 1991, David Hamburg, then president of the Carnegie Corporation foundation, invited me to his annual dinner at the Museum of Natural History in New York. Carter was to be the speaker before dinner. I accepted. When I arrived, David said, "I've put you at the same table with the President. You two should be working together now. I want to heal any remaining rift."

As I reached our table, President Carter asked me to step away with him for a private conversation. He shook my hand and said, "Joe, about smoking. You were right and I was wrong. If I can ever do something on that with you, let me know."

Moved by such a gracious act, all I could say was, "Thank you, Mr. President."

.   .   .

Was my firing by President Carter a self-inflicted wound? I was the most visible of his cabinet officers on a wide array of matters that touched just about every American. Early in the administration I realized that Congress was unlikely to act on our legislative initiatives. That set my sights on what I could get done administratively with departmental policies and regulations and what I could do through the media to arouse public opinion and spark action. I wanted to shake up—and wake up—the department to get those Great Society programs operating efficiently and effectively.

There was plenty of fire in my belly. I was angry when I learned that tobacco companies intentionally hook kids in their teens. I was appalled at the second-class status of black colleges and universities in the South and at how the Nixon administration had subverted civil rights enforcement. I was proud to be the secretary who opened up access for the handicapped and opportunity for female athletes in colleges and lower schools. I mounted a war on escalating hospital costs and unnecessary medical procedures. Presented with the dangers of excessive use of x-rays, I started an aggressive campaign to change the conduct of dentists and doctors. When I learned of the cancer-causing dangers of asbestos from Dr. Irving Selikoff, I struggled with how to alert hundreds of thousands of older workers who had already been unknowingly exposed, many while serving their country in naval shipyards in World War II. In April 1978, I ordered that a notice go along with every Social Security check to urge those whose jobs might have exposed them to asbestos to see a doctor. In 1979, in my last act as secretary of Health, Education, and Welfare, I published *Healthy People,* the first surgeon general's report devoted to health promotion and disease prevention, and the first to set goals for our people, such as reduction in infant mortality and improvements in teenage health. I was acutely conscious of how short the time to exercise public power is and I tried to use every minute in office to get things done.

Many of these actions were taken with little, often last-minute, notice to the White House, or none at all. This was because in some cases, like mounting the anti-smoking campaign, I feared politically driven staffers would have toned me down or tried to stop me from acting. In this sense, I suppose it can be concluded that I brought my firing on myself.

There was also the cultural chasm between President Carter and me. He was not comfortable in Washington. He had little regard for the national press corps or for the members of Congress, whose care and feeding, however necessary for legislative achievements, he nevertheless considered a waste of precious and limited presidential time. He had no use for the lawyers and lobbyists who lived off the federal establishment, seeking to inject their clients' interests in congressional and executive actions. But this was my world. It was the world in which I had found such excitement, satisfaction, and success. It was the world from which I had come, of which I was a significant part, and to which I would return. My friends while I was HEW secretary were the same as they were when I was practicing law—Ed Williams, Ben Bradlee, Phil Geyelin, Meg Greenfield, Kay Graham, Art Buchwald, Jack Valenti—and we continued to go to the same dinners, parties, and football games. So, too, I continued to eat, drink, and play with a host of reporters like Walter Pincus and Elizabeth Drew and senators and representatives I'd gotten to know over the fifteen years I had spent in Washington. And I saw no reason to change.

This was a world that had little respect for Carter as a president, and he knew that. He also must have sensed my reservations about his performance in the White House. I was completely loyal to him and I worked hard to carry out his policies and develop programs like welfare reform and national health insurance that met his criteria and served his objectives. But as I argued with him over issues, he likely suspected that I harbored doubts about his effectiveness as a president.

I had worked for a president who knew how to get things done in Washington. Jimmy Carter didn't bring those skills to the White House and I didn't see in him any inclination or ability to learn them. I knew that I could get important policies established and implemented whether or not I was one of his favored cabinet secretaries. I didn't want to usurp his powers as president; I did want the power to put in place policies in HEW's sphere of responsibility and influence—and I exercised it. I'll never know for sure whether I could have remained in office for the final eighteen months of his term if I had acted differently. But the price of doing so at the time would have been muting the HEW secretary's bully pulpit and limiting my ability to speak out on such matters as the anti-smoking campaign, soaring health care costs, unnecessary medical procedures, excessive use of x-rays, and aggressive civil rights and Title IX enforcement. That price was so high that it would have turned the cabinet post into another job, not the one I wanted when Carter was elected and not one in which I would have been comfortable.

I share the judgment of many historians and journalists that Carter will never rank among the best presidents. Indeed he may well go down as among the weakest. He never seemed to like Washington politics and he was perpetually ill at ease in the nation's capital. I was not surprised when, in his comments on receiving the Nobel Peace Prize in 2002, he indicated that he found more satisfaction in the twenty years after leaving office than during his presidency. He has been much more at ease and far more effective in his post-presidential years, during which he has used the stature of the presidency brilliantly.

What haunted me more than any economic or political controversy in my years at HEW was the department's deepening involvement in the most profound personal, moral, ethical, and religious questions. The problems I faced could not be resolved by a bend—or jerk—of the knee. I found no automatic answers in Christian theology and the teachings of my church, or in the Democratic Party position or the administration's, or in the science of medicine, to the perplexing questions of public policy on abortion, sterilization, recombinant DNA, aging, in vitro fertilization, fetal research, extending the final days of terminally ill patients. I was grateful for my entire life experience, from the streets of Brooklyn to the West Wing of the White House, the law firms, and the newsroom of the *Washington Post*. I brought it all—my religious traditions, education, American culture, friends, family, and experiences in public and private life—to the decisions at HEW, and I needed every bit.

The greatest hurdles I faced to pursuing policies I believed in were not within the Carter administration. They were in the growing power of special interests. While secretary of HEW, I appreciated for the first time how locked into special interests the Democratic congressmen and Democratic Party were. I also saw how distrustful of the White House Congress had become as a result of Nixon's failure to enforce civil rights and other laws, and his efforts to interpret statutes in ways that skirted legislative intent. As a result, the House and Senate had taken to writing laws in the kind of meticulous detail that had once been left to nitpicking executive branch bureaucrats. I came to understand that it made little difference to the barons on the Hill whether the occupant of the White House was a Democrat or Republican; the congressional Lilliputians were determined to tie the president in legislative strings. I left HEW disturbed by the power of special interests, especially those with big political bucks. There are many of them—corporate, racial, labor, and single-issue interests like the pro- and anti-abortion groups; the gun, education, and senior-citizen lobbies; and the alcohol and tobacco interests—and they exact undue control over congressional committees and subcommittees. At the very least, they have the power to checkmate laws adverse to their narrow interests. Washington is changing, I thought as I left HEW, and not necessarily for the better.

CHAPTER 26

What's Next?

O N THE MORNING after President Carter announced my forced resignation, Harlem congressman Charlie Rangel burst into my office unannounced, shouting, "Senator, Senator, how are you?"

The publicity about my firing, along with the media coverage that
marked my time at HEW, put me in the sights of the press and some politicians as a potential candidate for elective office. In February 1980, Republican New York senator Jacob Javits announced that he would seek a fifth term,
and disclosed that he had a motor-neuron condition commonly known as
Lou Gehrig's disease. His challenger, Alfonse D'Amato, an unknown Long
Island municipal politico, had already made Javits's health a campaign issue.
Liberal in a state Republican Party that was rapidly veering right, Javits was
in trouble. A small army of Democrats—former Miss America Bess Myerson, John Lindsay, Brooklyn congresswoman Elizabeth Holtzman, Queens
District Attorney John Santucci—lined up for the Democratic nomination.
Rangel told me, "It's yours for the taking. You got to go for it. It's made for
you!"

Rangel thought Lindsay had been indelibly tarnished as mayor of New
York City and that Liz Holtzman was unpopular within the Democratic
Party. The others, he said, were "lightweights."

Rangel had little respect and no love for Lindsay, often recounting a
meeting with the mayor when Lindsay was thinking of an experiment to
legalize heroin. Disgusted, Rangel, who knew firsthand the drug's savagery
in his Harlem district, asked Lindsay, "Under your plan can anyone get
heroin?"

"No, you'd have to be an adult, eighteen years old."

"So if a sixteen-year-old comes in and asks for it, you'll tell him he has to
wait two years?" Rangel cracked, and then asked, "Can any adult get it?"

"No," Lindsay replied. "You'd have to be addicted."

"Oh," Charlie said retelling the story, "so when the sixteen-year-old is eighteen and he wants it, you'd tell him you can't have it till you get hooked?"

As Charlie described it, Lindsay was getting angry and uncomfortable, faced as he was with governing a city that had become the heroin capital of the United States. "We'd just try this in a couple of places," Lindsay responded defensively. "To test it."

"Well," said Charlie, "we got plenty of heroin in my district. We don't need any more. So I suggest you try it in Queens and Staten Island. They don't have very much there."

"Can you believe that guy?" Rangel said to me. "With cockamamie ideas like that, you'll kill him in a primary."

New York governor Hugh Carey also urged me to run. "You'll be my candidate," he said. "You'll beat the Republican candidate whether it's Javits or someone else."

Carey told me that I would have to raise six to eight million dollars. "That's the most distasteful part," he said, "But you'll get it because I'll help and you'll be perceived as a winner." He also said I would have to return to New York to work the state.

This same winter of 1979–80, New Jersey governor Brendan Byrne, who was barred by term limits from running for re-election, urged me to seek the Garden State's Democratic nomination for governor. I had campaigned with Byrne when he ran for his second term in 1977. "Your parents have lived in Spring Lake for fifteen years," he said (impressing me with his homework). "You can use their house as your residence."

I gave both propositions serious thought. I promptly came to the conclusion that I did not want to be governor of New Jersey. I was interested in national policy and national politics.

Rangel's and Carey's idea intrigued me, however. I thought it would be exciting to run in the New York senate race. I talked to *Washington Post* managing editor Howard Simons. He was enthusiastic about my running. When I pointed out that I would probably have to win three times and wait twelve to eighteen years before getting to chair a senate committee, Simons's retort took me aback. "It's a fantastic bully pulpit," he said. "That's what you'd use it for, and you could run for president. Italian-American. Big state. Catholic but liberal."

I talked to Phil Geyelin and told him what Howard had said. "That's not for you, Joe," Geyelin told me. "You have to do too much pandering for money and lying and corrupt deal-making to be president."

Like many Democrats who had been in Carter's cabinet and seen this Georgia governor rise to the White House, I was presumptuous enough to think I had a chance of getting there, but Geyelin's comments stuck. And like so many who had served in top White House staff positions, I believed I could do the job if I were appointed president. But I knew I didn't have the consuming ambition essential to stomach the sacrifices to run for election to the nation's highest office. I remembered LBJ's crack, "Every senator sees a president when he looks in the mirror each morning," and I wondered if that was not happening to me.

The more I thought about it, the less appeal a run for the Senate held. I did not want to go through the grubby business of raising several million dollars. I had seen how demeaning it was when I watched LBJ raise money for the Democratic Party and its candidates. Johnson often complained about going "hat in hand," as he put it, "begging for money from people whose only interest is getting something from the president."

I had strong personal reasons not to run, and they were the tipping point. Since my separation from Trudy, I was concerned about my children: Mark was eighteen and at Princeton; Joe would be graduating from Georgetown Prep in the spring of 1980 and going to Amherst; Claudia was only ten. I could see that our separation had affected them; a political race for an office like the U.S. senator in New York would be all-consuming. I decided not to run and told Rangel and Carey in late 1979.

Later that year, Carey pronounced the vacant post the "Jewish seat," which got him in a little hot water with Lindsay and other non-Jewish aspirants. I called the governor to tease him. "How could you want me to run for the Jewish seat?"

"If you had run, it would have been the Italian seat," Carey said, laughing. "But now I'm supporting Bess Myerson and she doesn't have any Italian blood."

When D'Amato defeated Democrat Liz Holtzman to win the seat, Carey called. "See?" he said. "It was the Italian seat and you threw it away!"

The most unexpected opportunity to run for elective office came from Republican congressman John Anderson, who was expressing his disappointment with the increasingly conservative Republican Party that would nominate Ronald Reagan, and who considered Carter inept. In 1980, described as the most cerebral presidential candidate since Adlai Stevenson, Anderson declared himself a third party "unity" candidate.

On Sunday afternoon, June 1, 1980, Anderson and his wife Keke came to my house in Georgetown. We spent well over an hour together. Anderson described his views and quizzed me about mine. We were in the same policy ballpark, but I considered more rosy than realistic his view of his own chances and the impact he might have on national policy.

On August 15, Mitchell Rogovin, Anderson's campaign counsel and close advisor, visited me in my office. "How do you feel about being John Anderson's running mate?" he asked. "Anderson will make the selection quite soon on the basis of advice from David Garth and me."

I told him I had not given it any serious thought, but had my doubts whether I was the right person. "Are there any other possibilities?" I asked.

"Pat Lucey, the former Democratic governor of Wisconsin is interested," Rogovin responded. "Garth thinks you will be strong in states like New York, Massachusetts, and Connecticut. He gives Anderson 52 percent of the Jewish vote in New York and says he will get the Liberal Party line there. He also thinks you'll be helpful with Italians and blacks."

"I'm flattered, obviously. But it's not in me to be a vice presidential running mate. I've watched Humphrey and Mondale wilt in that job." When Humphrey had wanted me to leave the White House in 1968 and join his campaign to lead substantive policy development, I told him he had to ask LBJ. Humphrey went over to the mansion to do that. Johnson, cagey as he was, told Humphrey how beleaguered he was in those lame-duck days and needed everyone including me. Humphrey could not even bring himself to ask.

I recounted the story to Mitch. "Vice presidents are candidates for political castration," I said (speaking of the history of the office before Dick Cheney). "In any case, this is not the time—if ever—for me to run for any office."

Finally, I told Rogovin that from Anderson's point of view, I had a special liability. "I'll be subject to the charge of sour grapes, trying to mess up things for Carter because I'm angry that he rolled me out."[1]

·   ·   ·

While writing in Wellfleet that fall of 1979, I came down to Washington twice. On September 24, Ted Kennedy talked to me about joining his campaign to wrest the Democratic nomination for the presidency from Jimmy Carter. I wished him well, but said I could not become publicly involved. "It would confirm all the unwarranted Carter suspicions that I'd been disloyal and a secret ally of yours."

I did not say to Kennedy, though I felt it at the time, that I was still shaken by my firing and how the tobacco interests had been able to shove me out of my post. I had second thoughts about anyone's ability to achieve significant change in Washington. I had gagged on the overpowering odor of special-interest organizations and money and experienced the swelling nastiness of partisanship. I kept to myself my doubts about his ability to win in the wake of the Chappaquiddick tragedy. Tip O'Neill's comment stuck in my head: "At least 25 percent of the electorate will never vote for Ted Kennedy. That means he has to get more than two-thirds of the remaining 75 percent, and even he can't do that."

Another meeting a week later was harder. I had a sad dinner with Ed Williams at the Palm to tell him I was not returning to his law firm.

Ed had called me early on a July morning in 1978 to tell me that Paul Connolly had been rushed during the night to Georgetown Hospital. Half an hour later, Ed called to say that Paul had died of a heart attack. I immediately left my office at HEW and picked up Ed. We went to Paul's house and waited a good hour before his wife, Mary, arrived. During that hour, Ed had talked about how impossible it would be for him to run the firm alone. In the weeks that followed, Ed told me how lonely he was; he had no one to talk to at the office. He wanted me to leave HEW and return to the firm.

Now, knowing Ed wanted me to rejoin his firm, I told him of my decision to start my own. "I need to prove that I can do it on my own," I explained. It was a difficult decision for me and a heart-breaking evening for both of us; we wept.

We wept not only because we would not again be law partners, but because we knew that we could never recapture those six years of Williams, Connolly & Califano. The law firm had changed, as had the practice of law. The firm now housed more than seventy lawyers and was growing rapidly, with the conflicting ambitions, written partnership agreement, and bureaucratic jousting that this number of very bright attorneys under one roof brings. It was sad that, great as the firm was, it would never be the same place that we had started. Even sadder, for two such strong characters as Ed and me, we knew we would never have the power to reproduce the world we had created in 1971. I was tempted when great young lawyers like Brendan Sullivan and Jack Vardaman wanted to come up to Cape Cod to urge me to return. But I also remembered the young partners at Arnold & Porter who feared that the return of Abe Fortas would trim their sails if he took control of his old clients. Many lawyers we had trained now wanted to run their own show. I had taken some lawyers from the firm with me to HEW; others who wanted to go were disappointed when I didn't recruit them because I felt it would not have been fair to Ed and Paul to drain all the best young talent from the firm. Much as Ed wanted me to wrestle with this burgeoning behemoth (and much as I loved and admired him), that's not how I wanted to spend my time and energy.

I aspired to be the next Clark Clifford. Clifford, after serving as counsel to Harry Truman, set the standard for practicing law as an ultimate Washington insider. He dispensed wisdom, advised clients in deep trouble in Washington, saved their skins, or won for them laws or regulations worth enormous sums of money. In the process, Clifford amassed a personal fortune and advised Democratic presidents and House and Senate leaders. I had learned that no legal fee can be too high for a large corporation with billions at stake on a phrase in a law or the timing of a regulation. Corporate CEOs, with their jobs, their perks, and the value of their stock options dependent on solving some Washington problem, were eager for the sort of help I could provide. I wanted to be my own boss, to husband my resources and time in order to play a role in public policy and politics.

Previously, I had always been part of someone else's team—first Paul Porter's at Arnold & Porter, later Ed Williams's at Williams, Connolly & Califano. This time I wanted to go it alone. But Ed remained the brother I never had.

I started my own firm—Califano, Ross & Heineman—in 1981 with two colleagues: Stanford Ross, an international tax lawyer whom I had named Social Security commissioner, and Ben Heineman, who had been my executive assistant and later assistant secretary for planning and evaluation at HEW. I moved into a house on R Street in Georgetown next to Meg Greenfield's. Meg and I had grown up together in Washington. We both arrived in

1961. She came via Seattle, Smith College, and a job as a researcher in Adlai Stevenson's 1960 try for the Democratic presidential nomination (where she worked for Dorothy Hirshon, who would years later be my mother-in-law). I arrived via Brooklyn, Holy Cross, Harvard Law School, and a brief stint as a doorbell ringer in John Kennedy's presidential campaign. As neighbors now, we laughed about our new digs in the capital's most fashionable section. Meg had a lovely garden, "dominated by shade flowers," she constantly reminded me, "because of the high trees on your property that you refuse to chop down." (Years later, just as Meg had perfected her shade garden, I sold the house and the new owner cut down the trees. She called me that evening to ask if I needed any shade flowers and shrubs because she now had to redo her entire garden.)

With my own law firm and my new house in Georgetown, free of the daily pressures of HEW, I was prepared to become the capital's newest wise counselor and perhaps do one more tour in government if and when the Democrats recaptured the White House.

CHAPTER 27

My Own Law Firm

I N THE FALL OF 1980, New York governor Hugh Carey called. "We have a helluva mess up here with heroin," he said. "I'd like you to look at the problem and tell us what we can do about it."

Heroin was the nation's most terrifying drug and New York City was riddled with it. The drug's hammerlock addiction and the crime it spawned were spilling out of Harlem and Bedford-Stuyvesant into affluent white neighborhoods, including the Upper East Side and Brooklyn Heights. Word on the street was that there were as many heroin addicts in New York City as in the rest of the country. Heroin could doom Carey's chances for the third term he planned to seek.

I told Carey he should get a New Yorker. "I've been in Washington since 1961."

"You were born in Brooklyn," he said, laughing. "You were brought up here. You wouldn't run for the Senate and now we're gonna get a Republican. Do something for your hometown."

"I don't know anything about heroin."

"You'll learn fast."

I went up to New York and over steaks at Christ Cella on East 46th Street, I said to Carey, "I have no idea what to do about heroin. But I did put together a program for alcohol just before I left HEW."

"You've got a deal," Carey said. "You're special counsel to the governor on drug and alcohol abuse."

With that I embarked on one of the defining experiences of my life. I came to understand the terrifying savagery of addiction.

Repeatedly, during testimony and unsolicited conversations with New Yorkers, I was urged to examine the destructive force of heroin on a neighborhood and its people. Again and again I was told that certain neighborhoods in Harlem were among the hardest hit. President Johnson had once told me, "The way to reduce pollution in Detroit is to make automobile company executives drive in non-air-conditioned cars during summer rush hours. The way to get business to join the war on poverty is to make corporate executives drive through Harlem every day instead of going home on air-conditioned trains drinking martinis." Now it was my turn to open the windows and get out on the street.

On a hot and humid late afternoon in July and then again on a cool evening in October, I went on Harlem drug busts with the Street Enforcement Unit of the New York City Police Department's Narcotics Division—the cops who slog, day after day, through the human wreckage of New York's drug-infested mean streets. On my second visit I took my friend Diana Walker, the *Time* photographer covering the White House. Without pictures I doubted anyone would believe me.

Some sections of Harlem and the South Bronx looked worse than 1945 Fox Movietone newsreels of German cities carpet-bombed during World War II. In some neighborhoods, no life was left to destroy: block after block, no buildings left to tear down or spray paint with angry obscenities. I talked to Monsignor Emerson Moore, pastor of St. Charles Borromeo Roman Catholic Church on West 141st Street. "After Mass street pushers try to sell heroin to children on the steps of my church," the monsignor said. Sensing my disbelief, a Harlem businessmen nearby shouted, "Do you hear him? After Mass! On the steps of his church!"*

On the way to shooting galleries and drug busts, I drove through the streets of Harlem with Phil Sheridan, commanding officer of the city's Street Enforcement Unit. He identified loiterers on street corners. "Most of them are pushers or users or both."

As we drove along 116th Street, Sheridan pointed at a grungy hotel on the south side, its torn, filthy awning hanging still in the summer heat. "That's the hotel the Kennedy kid went into," Sheridan said sadly, referring to Robert Kennedy's son David, who was mugged in the hotel and a few years later died of a drug overdose in a Palm Beach hotel. "Imagine how desperate that kid had to be to go in there at two in the morning." Several women slouched around the hotel entrance, obviously prostitutes. As we drew close to the curb, I could see the punctures and scab tracks along their arms. One

*Years later Bishop Moore became an addict to alcohol, cocaine, and crack, and in 1995 at age fifty-seven died of AIDS.

grabbed the inside of her left arm with her right hand and jerked her left arm up sharply in a "Fuck you!" signal of defiance and despair.

The final bust that early evening was curdling. Diana Walker and I entered the brownstone at 360 West 166th Street behind a dozen police officers. The place was crowded with addicts, as many as fifty of them. The first floor was even filthier than the 103rd street shooting gallery where I had witnessed a drug bust in July and which, by our return in October, was back in business: rotting wood, torn and smashed plaster, the nauseating stench of urine, excrement, and vomit, visible in some corners and on the floor near an overflowed toilet.

On the second floor, I saw the ravages of heroin as I had never imagined them. In one room, two addicts were sitting, one to the right of the door, the other in the far left-hand corner.

"Pull up your pants legs," one of the narcotics squad members said. Neither addict moved. The cop turned to the addict slumped beside the door. "Pull 'em up," he repeated, gesturing at the pants.

The addict slowly pulled at his cuffs and rolled them up. His legs were eaten—there is no more accurate word—with open sores, dripping pus and encrusted with dried blood.

Why in the name of God? How? I thought.

A policeman near me said, "He has no veins left in his arms that he can shoot heroin into. They've all collapsed. So he shoots veins in his legs."

I couldn't take my eyes off his rancid sores. The policeman continued, "Look at the guy in the corner. He's even further advanced."

I turned. He looked like he had elephantiasis. His ankles were swollen to the circumference of thighs, his skin so crusted with infection and so dried-out that its dark color seemed faded to washed-out tan.

"Take off your shoes," a cop yelled from behind me. The addict shook his head, embarrassed.

"Mr. Califano's trying to help people stay off this stuff. Help kids. That's why he's got a photographer." The cop nodded in Diana Walker's direction. "Let her take a picture of your feet."

"To help kids?" the addict asked thickly. "For kids to see?"

"That's right," the cop responded.

The addict took off his shoes and frayed socks. His toes were so swollen they had merged together. Like an elephant's foot, I thought.

"The veins collapse, the feet and legs swell because blood can't circulate," Captain Sheridan said. "Water collects. Infection sets in. Eventually, they can't even walk. Ask him what caused all this."

I did.

"The needle," the addict answered.

"What about the heroin?" I asked.

"No, no. The mix was dirty," he said, referring to the quinine or whatever white powder had been mixed with the heroin to cut its strength.

"Addicts'll never blame the heroin," Sheridan said. "That's always good."

"Can you stand another floor?" Sheridan asked. "You might as well see it all."

We went up the stairs. A young man sat in a chair, nodding dumbly, his legs scarred with sores.

"He can't walk," one of the cops said. "How do you get your heroin?" I asked.

"Neck," he said, "neck," again pointing to the veins there.

The cop interpreted. "He's telling you he shoots people in the neck. It's hard to shoot yourself in the neck. He's become good at it. He shoots other people in the neck and in return they bring him heroin."

I turned, nearly tripping over a body crouched on the floor, then looked down. There on the floor, crouched, eyes rolling in a heroin high and utter despair, was an addict with hypodermic needles stuck through the hair on his head. I shuddered.

"They're not stuck in his veins," the cop next to me said. "He just wears them. He loves them like a broad loves jewelry."

Diana Walker, pale and breathing deeply through her mouth to avoid the stench, took her photographs.

Back downstairs, we were both quiet for a few moments. I was drained by the experience. The cruelest despots couldn't victimize people more brutally than this, I thought.

How did we get here? I asked myself. I'd been told that these addicts were the worst, that most heroin addicts are not so far gone. But I couldn't get the question out of my head: how in the name of God did the richest nation in the history of the world let any of its people get here? Seeing the horror of addiction, I silently vowed to try to do something to prevent it—for there I saw little chance of curing it.

In those years, despair was leading some public officials to suggest legal-ization. Not Harlem congressman Charlie Rangel. And not Julio Martinez, the street-smart official who headed New York's division of Substance Abuse Services. "I oppose legalization because the addict is a bad mathe-matician," he told me. "Addicts know only how to add. They add drugs into their veins, but they never know how to subtract. I don't want the govern-ment in the business of pushing drugs." I was solidly in the Rangel and Mar-tinez camp.

From this New York State study, I came to understand the monumental burden that all addiction—to alcohol, nicotine, and illegal drugs—imposed on the health care system. For the first time, we interviewed doctors who had admitted patients to hospitals as a result of accidents, violence, broken backs, cancer, heart disease, cirrhosis of the liver, kidney problems, and other ailments. We asked what their admitting papers never revealed: Did the patient drink? Was he drunk? Did he smoke? Did he use drugs? Was he high on alcohol or drugs when he fell down the stairs and broke his neck?

Their answers revealed a startling fact: most of the beds in New York hos-pitals—in New York City, Schenectady, Rochester, Albany, Binghamton, Syracuse—were filled because of substance abuse and addiction. How could I have been secretary of health for thirty months and not known this?

I gave our report to Governor Carey on June 14, 1982. My recommenda-tions included proposals for a saturation public information campaign to prevent all substance abuse; comprehensive health insurance coverage for alcoholism and other drug abuse treatment on the same basis as other dis-eases; and upping to twenty-one the age for the purchase of alcohol.[1]

The final lesson was one I learned in retrospect. Looking through the report, it's hard to find the word "cocaine."* As that drug became widely used later in the 1980s, I saw that the problem wasn't heroin, or alcohol, or nicotine, or cocaine. The problem was addiction.

.   .   .

On December 16, 1980, President Reagan nominated Alexander Haig to be secretary of state. Haig shared Reagan's hard-line determination to make

---

*It appears only in passing on page 268 of the 300-page report.

it clear to the Soviets that we would continue to commit resources (and blood) to prevail over communism.

As soon as Haig's nomination was announced, Democrats and liberal Republicans on the Senate Foreign Relations Committee promised a searching examination of his role in the Vietnam War, in the bombing of Cambodia, and as Nixon's chief of staff during the end game of that administration. Though the presidencies of Ford and Carter had intervened, Nixon continued to be the Republican that Democrats most loved to hate; suspicions ran high that Haig had been involved in last-ditch efforts to cover up Watergate and that he had engineered a deal with Gerald Ford to pardon the disgraced president.

Along with Reagan's victory, Republicans for the first time in twenty-six years took control of the Senate. Charles Percy, a liberal Republican from Illinois, replaced Idaho Democrat Frank Church as chair of the Senate Foreign Relations Committee; Tennessee Republican Howard Baker, a member of that committee, became majority leader.

Haig asked me to represent him during the confirmation process. We met privately with Howard Baker at the majority leader's home. Haig was not Baker's preferred candidate for the post, but Baker believed the Senate would confirm him, after a blistering hearing and by a close margin.

As an Army lieutenant colonel, Haig had served with me in the Pentagon. When I left for the Johnson White House, Haig pressed for a combat assignment in Vietnam, where he served for two years and then returned to the Pentagon. Henry Kissinger called me in January of 1969. As President Nixon's national security advisor, he had two candidates for his deputy— Elmo (Bud) Zumwalt, who would later become chief of naval operations, and Haig. I recommended Haig as someone who was familiar with both military and civilian politics and who would speak his mind without being intimidated. Haig got the job. Having sent him into one Republican administration, I agreed to try once again.

Ben Heineman and I examined every clipping about Haig and all his files from the Nixon years. We spent hours preparing him for every conceivable question. I drained him of everything he could remember about his days and nights with Nixon and confronted him with every news story accusing him of improper conduct. By the time of the hearing we had taken Haig through more than fifty thick binders of information about his actions, from the Cambodian bombing to the Saturday Night Massacre.

I interviewed Henry Kissinger about several sensitive subjects: wiretaps, the Cambodian bombing, the Vietnam Christmas bombing of 1972, the overthrow of Allende in Chile, and Haig's duties as national security staff aide from the summer of 1969 until he became vice chief of staff of the Army in 1973. Kissinger described Haig as his "alter ego."

On Christmas Eve, I wrote Senator Claiborne Pell, the lame-duck chair of the Foreign Relations Committee, expressing Haig's willingness to answer any questions. I also inquired about particular areas of interest. Pell's response was brief and blunt: "General Haig should expect to be questioned closely on his activities as a member of the National Security Council staff and as White House Chief of Staff."

I had known the patrician Pell since my days in the Johnson White House.* As secretary of HEW, I had campaigned with Pell in Rhode Island in 1978. A main issue in that campaign was Pell's age; he asked me to jog with him to start our day of campaigning. Since I had just begun jogging, I cautioned Pell that I could not go more than half a mile. Pell promised to keep it to that. After spending Sunday night at his home, we rose early to begin our jog along the magnificent rock ledges on the Rhode Island coast. By the time we reached the television cameras waiting for us at the end, we had jogged at least a mile. Thirteen years younger than Pell, I was panting like a hot puppy when we reached the cameras. Too late, I realized that he had deliberately exceeded my capacity, to show how much more vigorous he was than this younger secretary of health.

Pell and I lived near each other in Georgetown when the Haig nomination came up. We often jogged around the same track off R Street. Shortly after our exchange of letters, we found ourselves trotting around the track (I was now doing two miles at his pace). In the winter Pell jogged in gray

---

*When he got angry at Pell, LBJ would refer to him as "Stillborn." When Johnson, at Lady Bird's urging, pressed Congress to establish the Hirshhorn Museum to house the magnificent sculpture collection of Joseph Hirshhorn, Pell, who chaired the Senate subcommittee considering the legislation, objected to naming the museum after Hirshhorn, an Iranian Jew. Johnson had Pell to the White House, where the senator argued that it should be called the Smithsonian Sculpture Museum. Impatient, LBJ finally faced down Pell. "Now, the only way this man will give all his sculpture to the U.S. government so millions of people can see it is if we name this after him, if we call it the Hirshhorn Musuem. Clai, I don't care if he wants to call it the Horseshit Museum. If that's what it takes to let all our people see this sculpture, that's what we should do." Leaving Johnson's office shaking his head, Pell went along with the Hirshhorn name.

flannels, button-down striped Brooks Brothers shirt, cashmere sweater, and blue blazer. I was in gray sweats. On this morning we talked about the upcoming Haig hearings. "We are deeply concerned about Haig's involvement in Watergate," he said. "You can certainly expect a number of questions on that subject." He told me that the committee staff had reviewed all sorts of Watergate materials. Ominously, he indicated that not only Democrats, but several committee Republicans, including Chuck Percy, the new chair, had serious doubts about the nomination.

By the turn of the new year, word was out that Haig and I had teamed up once again. The Sunday *New York Times* reported that our friendship was eighteen years old and intertwined through five administrations. The paper saw us as "Washington's odd couple: Mr. Califano the backslapping, sometimes abrasive political operator serving Democratic administrations, and Mr. Haig the cool, smooth military man under President Nixon."[2] Two days before the hearing Haig asked if his brother, a Catholic priest, could attend. "I want him right behind you, alongside your wife, in every television and still picture we can get him in," I said.

When the hearings opened on Friday, January 9, Haig sat alone at the green-felt-covered table, facing the full committee. In addition to me and Tom Korologos, a Republican lobbyist helping White House nominees, in camera view sat Haig's wife, Patricia, and his brother Frank, the Jesuit priest, in full Roman collar.

That first day, seven hours of interrogation went well; a composed Haig displayed his mastery of foreign affairs. There were a few tense moments, especially when Democratic senator Paul Sarbanes of Maryland harshly questioned Haig. Seeing the back of Haig's neck turn red, I quickly scribbled a note and slipped it to him. As Sarbanes spoke, Haig opened it and read my words, "Keep cool in Kabul," an expression we had both used in moments of tension when working together in the Pentagon. The red color dissipated to pink.

As Haig cooled off, Chuck Percy's body language and tone made it clear that he was cool to the nomination. Percy had hoped Reagan would name him secretary of state, but his views were too liberal for the new president. Percy never forgot that I had marched in the Chicago Columbus Day parade in 1966 with Paul Douglas, his Democratic opponent for the Senate. We start with at least two strikes against us, I thought, as I watched Percy stare at Haig. The Illinois senator lived around the corner from me in George-town. He and I, and *Washington Post* editorial page editor Meg Greenfield, had joined forces in an effort to stop Christine Stevens, the animal rights zealot and wife of Kennedy Center president Roger Stevens, from putting out food for raccoons that the three of us wanted poisoned.

We could not risk having the chairman signaling that he was at best a reluctant supporter and a potential negative vote. I wanted Haig to go into office with an overwhelming vote, not by a narrow margin. So I called Percy that evening and set up a lunch for the three of us that Saturday. The lunch went well and I left believing Haig had Percy's support, lukewarm though it might be. Percy was not impressed with Haig and didn't share his views of the world, but he didn't want to clash with the new Senate majority leader or president.

The hearings resumed on Monday morning with the Democrats in an even tougher mood. At lunchtime, I met with Republican Senator Jesse Helms. Helms's pound of flesh for supporting Haig was the appointment of one of his aides to an assistant secretaryship in the State Department. The aide was too extreme for Haig; and in any case if we negotiated a deal with any one member of the committee, others would set their own price for supporting the nomination. Helms pressed me hard during our meeting. I said I had to advise Haig not to agree to any appointments or even consider them until he was confirmed and in office. "It would be inappropriate and arrogant of him to do so." Helms didn't like it, but after some grousing, he agreed on condition that I interview his candidate that evening, which I did. The aide was even more extreme than I expected.

That afternoon, Haig and I paid a courtesy call on Connecticut senator Lowell Weicker. The media ambushed us. Cameras rolling, Weicker, feisty and theatrical, attacked Haig in the hallway for his involvement in the Cambodian bombing and Watergate. He ended by saying he had no intention of meeting privately with Haig. It was a setup. I had arranged the meeting with Weicker's staff; Haig was outraged. I took him by the arm, whispered that Weicker looked bad—like a bully—and we could turn it to our advantage with other Republicans and even some Democrats. "We'll have the last laugh about this incident," I whispered. Haig nodded grimly.

On Tuesday, January 13, Senator Sarbanes launched an assault on Haig's values. He started with questions on the Cambodian bombing and the

Chilean coup in which President Allende had been killed, then quickly moved to Watergate. Regarding the issue of abuses of power by Nixon, Sarbanes pressed Haig to attack Nixon and Kissinger and disown them: "What I am asking you for is some indication of your value judgment of what took place."

With that Haig lost his cool. "I have not ever indulged in something that was wrong or illegal. I did not during that period. Others did. That is clear. . . . What is my observation going to contribute to this? Do you think I am going to endorse what was done? In no way, on either side. I want to be sure that balance is kept because there were tremendous abuses on both sides. . . . Nobody has a monopoly on virtue, not even you, Senator."

However outrageous, overbearing, and pompous the behavior of senators may be, witnesses—especially those who will have to work with them as cabinet officers—must hunker down and take it. Haig's final swipe at Sarbanes put every committee member on the Maryland senator's side. With a nudge from Baker, Percy adjourned the hearing for lunch. Haig and I retired to an adjoining committee room where we could find some quiet. Barry Goldwater and Howard Baker stopped by, eager to calm Haig. Haig, we knew, had to make a statement when the hearings resumed to put an end to what would become an endless stream of Watergate questions. He made it clear to me that he was not going to condemn either Kissinger or Nixon. "That's what they want me to do and I'm not going to do it!" he said, adding an ample supply of expletives about Sarbanes.

"Then say that it's not in you or for you, it's not your place to render judgments," I said.

When the hearings resumed, Haig read a statement we had drafted together:

> I would like to use this time to stress one point . . . about abuses of power and my views on the subject. . . . I cannot bring myself to render judgment on Richard Nixon, or, for that matter, Henry Kissinger. I worked intimately for both men. It is not for me, it is not in me, to render moral judgments on them. I must leave that to others, to history and to God.

I had alerted Percy to the statement and he immediately said, "That responds so forthrightly and directly to questions put to you," and vowed to

MY OWN LAW FIRM 389

distribute copies to absent senators "because I think it is a profound statement and a very helpful statement, and I think comes right from both the heart and the mind."

On January 15, after five days and thirty-two hours of testimony, the Senate Foreign Relations Committee confirmed Haig's nomination by a vote of 15–2 with only Sarbanes and Tsongas objecting. On January 21, the Senate confirmed Haig as the fifty-ninth secretary of state by a vote of 93 to 6.

Buchwald teased me relentlessly about representing Haig and took advantage of Haig's most memorable moment in office. When Ronald Reagan was shot two months later,[3] Vice President George Bush was in Texas. Haig rushed to the White House Press room and told reporters, "Constitutionally, gentlemen. . . . As of now I am in control here in the White House, pending return of the vice president and in close touch with him." (Haig was in error. The actual line of succession after the president is the vice president, Speaker of the House, president pro tempore of the Senate, and then secretary of state.)

A few months later, Buchwald introduced me at a Heart Association fundraiser: "Most of you remember Joe as the Secretary of Health. Well, I remember him as one of the great Washington constitutional lawyers. He represented Al Haig. When President Reagan was shot, Haig called Joe and Joe said to him, 'Al, get over to the White House right away. You're in charge.'"

Haig resigned on July 5, 1982. Two years later, the *Washington Post* revealed the payments made by two special funds that President Reagan had set up in 1980 to finance his transition into office. The largest expense paid out of the funds was $86,047.93—to my law firm for our representation of Haig.[4] Howard Baker had arranged for the transition fund to pay the bill, which was less than half our usual rates. Buchwald called me when the story broke. "I always knew you were a dedicated lawyer. You'll represent anybody, no matter where the money comes from."

CHAPTER 28

Hilary Paley Byers

O N THE EVENING of Reagan's Inauguration, January 20, 1981, Governor Hugh Carey and I were scheduled to have dinner in Washington to go over the report on alcohol and drug abuse I had prepared for him. Carey suggested dinner because, as he put it, "I've got to march in Reagan's parade, but I don't have to celebrate that night."

I met him, attaché case bulging with papers in hand; to my consternation Carey was accompanied by several people. We all went off to dinner at Mel Krupin's.

At dinner, Carey said, "I'm going to make a thousand dollars because of you. I've gotten ten-to-one odds that Al Haig will not get ninety votes for confirmation."

"You'll win," I said. "I believe we'll get at least ninety-one."

Carey smiled. "Anyone who can save Daniel Schorr from contempt in the House can get Haig ninety votes!"

Hilary Byers, a friend of Carey's sitting at my left, said, "Did you represent Daniel Schorr?"

"Yes," I responded.

"For an enormous fee," she added.

"You must be talking to Bill Paley," I said. "Even though he didn't help Schorr, we made Paley a First Amendment hero and he's been dining out on that fee for years."

"He's a complicated man, but I love him," she pointedly said.

Hilary Byers, I then learned, was Hilary Paley Byers. I was sitting next to Bill Paley's daughter.

After dinner, she went off to one of the inaugural balls. Carey and I joined House Speaker Tip O'Neill and went off to F. Scott's, where we shared political stories into the night.

A few weeks later, Dan Hofgren, a former Nixon aide and Goldman Sachs banker handling commercial paper for Fannie Mae,[1] asked if I was going to that company's annual dinner. As its Washington lawyer at the time, I was. He asked if I'd like to join him and his wife, Joan, and accompany Hilary Byers. I said I'd be delighted and took her phone number.

Later that morning, I received an urgent call from Tommy Viola, president of the nation's third-largest waste management company, SCA Services, Inc. Waste Management, Inc. was interested in acquiring SCA Services and wanted Viola out as soon as possible. Though Viola denied any ties to organized crime, an SCA manager had been shot and killed a few months earlier and the garbage-collection business in New Jersey was suspected of being infiltrated by the mob. I was negotiating Viola's exit. He wanted me to meet him that afternoon in New York at the offices of Rogers & Wells, which had been retained to do an independent investigation of allegations of mob involvement in SCA. I flew to New York for negotiations, which dragged on into the early evening. Rogers & Wells had found that Viola had no mob connections, had cleaned up SCA, and had removed any employees responsible for misconduct; I wanted the severance agreement to reflect their finding. When it appeared that we would not finish until the next morning, we broke so I could get a hotel room and buy underwear, a shirt, and toiletries. During the break, I called Hilary Byers on the off chance she might be free that evening. She was and I asked her to dinner, noting that it must be on the late side.

The negotiations concluded shortly before 9 P.M. Lawyers from Rogers & Wells were charged with drafting the agreement and sending it to the St. Regis Hotel, where I was staying. I planned to review it later that night so we could close the deal the next morning.

I rushed off to pick Hilary up at her Park Avenue apartment. I told her we would be going to Christ Cella. "I've heard of it, but I've never been there," she said, so politely that I knew I'd blown it again—a steakhouse was not this sophisticated woman's style.

As it turned out, we were so consumed in conversation at Christ Cella's that we were the last to leave the restaurant. In the cab on the way uptown to her apartment, she asked if I wanted to stop for a nightcap at Mortimer's, a place I'd never heard of. We closed that restaurant and piano bar at almost 4 A.M. By the time I dropped her home and got back to my hotel, I was too sleepy to plow through the lengthy legal draft. The next morning, to the discontent of the other attorneys, I told them I would have to read the draft on my way back to Washington and call them with any changes.

I was content in my Georgetown house, convinced I would never remarry. My social hours were taken up with my friends at the *Washington Post* and on the Hill and Ed Williams. As a single, I was in demand as an extra man at dinners. I could never have predicted that from that evening in New York on, Hilary and I would talk to each other every day.

.   .   .

Hilary met most of my Washington pals at a fiftieth birthday party Ben Bradlee and Sally Quinn gave for me at their apartment off DuPont circle in May. Hilary came down from Manhattan to be there. I was in New York that afternoon, taping a segment of *Firing Line* with William Buckley to publicize my new book, *Governing America*. When a brace of thunderstorms broke out between New York and Washington, I was unable to get back on time. My hosts were frustrated. Hilary and the other guests were annoyed. At ten o'clock, Art Buchwald put candles on the cake, cut it, and walked around the living room offering pieces to the guests. "Joe would have wanted it this way," he crowed.

I arrived at almost eleven, just as Kay Graham was coming down the stairs. It was one of the most embarrassing moments of my life; my chums Buchwald, Bradlee, Williams, and Valenti never let me forget it.

For the occasion, Buchwald had produced a video with his son Joel, who was then a cameraman for ABC News. It began with Buchwald on the steps of the Capitol holding two books—*Governing America* and *The Private Sex Lives of Public People*. He stopped three macho young men, briefly described both books, and asked which one they would pay twenty-five dollars for. As each selected *Private Sex Lives*, Buchwald turned to the camera and said, "Sorry, Joe."

In August, Hilary Paley Byers and I drove down from my house on Cape Cod for Ben Bradlee's sixtieth-birthday party in Easthampton. It was a grand evening, with warm and humorous toasts, enhanced by the surprise present that television producer Norman Lear gave Ben: a small army of violin players who serenaded us throughout the evening. For me, nothing compared to the moment we arrived.

Betty (Lauren) Bacall came across the room, threw her arms around me, and gave me a deep wet kiss. Then she pulled away, her arms outstretched as she held mine just above the elbows. "Well?" she said.

I stood there, flabbergasted. Hilary was stunned.

"Well?" she repeated. "Did you notice anything different?"

I just smiled and said, "It was great."

"How could you not notice?" she said. "I quit smoking!"

When I was at HEW, I had repeatedly urged Bacall to quit, once telling her, "Kissing a smoker is like licking a dirty ashtray." She loved embarrassing me.

That Wednesday, September 2, I appeared on NBC's *Today* show, then hosted by Tom Brokaw, to discuss the Reagan presidency. At the end of the interview, Brokaw closed with this: "Joe Califano. For all his success as a lawyer and all of his exalted positions in government, his friends say he still knows how to save a buck when he's getting back and forth between Massachusetts and New York. We'll be back in just a few moments. This is *Today* on NBC." Buchwald had called Brokaw and told him that I had driven Hilary to Bradlee's party from Cape Cod instead of chartering a plane because I was so cheap.

It wasn't Buchwald's only shot on this topic. Once Hilary and I were standing in line at Logan Airport in Boston waiting for a flight back to Washington. Buchwald was on the same plane. Hilary and I were travelling economy. He was travelling first class. After the plane took off, the stewardess came to our seats with a glass of wine for Hilary. "Mrs. Califano, Mr. Buchwald asked me to bring this to you because he did not think that Mr. Califano would purchase any from the trolley in economy."

By now, Hilary and I were seeing each other frequently. Polly Fritchey, a social major domo in the capital, told me that Bill Paley had called her and others checking me out. We laughed about it and I went on enjoying my single life.

In April 1982, Hilary and I traveled to Italy—our first trip together, during which we visited the writer Bill Pepper and his wife, Beverly, a sculptor, at their castle in Todi, in Umbria. On Sunday, April 25, Hilary went with the artist Milton Gendel to an antique-furniture show in town. Bill and I were driving to meet them for lunch. As we approached the cupola at the foot of the hill on which Todi is situated, we could see smoke rising from the middle of town. *Polizia* told us a fire was raging out of control at the antique show. "People are dying," an officer said, waving us away. "You cannot go up into town!" I was frantic. I told Bill we had to go. Bill just drove past three shouting *polizia* officers. As we came close to the square, I saw Hilary and felt a rush of relief. This was the moment when I realized how much I loved her. Bill saw it immediately. "Boy," he said. "That woman means a lot to you."

.   .   .

I had shut out any idea of remarrying. I thought remarriage would isolate me from my church and prevent me from receiving the Eucharist at Mass. Throughout my life, I had always gone to Mass on Sunday unless I was too sick to climb out of bed. To me, receiving Holy Communion, the Body and Blood of Christ, was as essential to my soul as food was to my body. I couldn't imagine living without it. I had been through so many jobs and the personal turmoil of a failed marriage. I had seen so many people rise and fall. I had enjoyed many successes, but I had also made many mistakes. My law practice and government service had immersed me in a world where compromise and relativism ruled the nest, a universe in which many powerful people believed that the end justified the means. My weekdays and weekends were crowded with activity; there was never enough time to get everything done. In this hectic life, Sunday Mass was a spiritual necessity for me, a time to reflect and remind myself that I was responsible to God. In a world of roiling social, legal, financial, and political sand, the Catholic Church was my spiritual rock.

I was deeply in love with Hilary, and I had to talk to someone about my dilemma. Over lunch at the Metropolitan Club, at a table for two against a window, where our conversation could be private, I spoke to Father Jim English, my pastor at Holy Trinity Church. Because I had no idea how he would react and even less what I was going to do, I told him hesitatingly that Hilary and I had begun talking about marriage after my civil divorce. I did not want to do something that would deny me the Eucharist.

Father English told me that remarriage did not necessarily put me in that position. "You know, some theologians now say that marriages can die. Love between a man and woman and the promises they make in marriage have always been a symbol of God's unbreakable love for his people. That's why the Church says these promises are unbreakable."

As I listened intently, he continued. "But in fact, the human experience is that a marriage can die despite best efforts to the contrary. It can be destructive to the couple and the family to continue once the marriage is dead."

"I understand."

Father English then added that the Church and priests struggle to confront this reality. "Today with the benefit of advances in psychology, some Catholic theologians question whether a dead marriage should be maintained as a symbol of Christ's love for his people."

Then he asked, "Do you think your marriage is dead?"

"I loved Trudy very much when we married. But yes, now, a quarter century later, my marriage is dead."

"As you face that reality in good conscience, you can remarry—though not in the Catholic Church—and continue to receive the Eucharist."

Over time, with Father English's counsel, I became convinced that marrying Hilary would not be sinful. There were, in Washington and numerous dioceses around the country, many priests who offered the "internal forum" or "good conscience" solution to permit remarried divorced Catholics to continue receiving Communion. Vatican II had stated in its "Declaration on Religious Freedom" that Catholics must follow their consciences: "On his part, man perceives and acknowledges the imperatives of the divine law through the mediation of conscience. In all his activity a man is bound to follow his conscience in order that he may come to God, the end and purpose of life. It follows that he is not to be forced to act in a manner contrary to his conscience. Nor, on the other hand, is he to be restrained from acting in accordance with his conscience, especially in matters religious."

Father English held that if, after consultation with a priest and through personal discernment, I had a clear conscience about my divorce and reconciled my relationship with God, I could receive Communion. I felt a good deal of guilt about my divorce. But I also considered myself a faithful Catholic; my conversations with Father English persuaded me that I could in good conscience present myself for Communion if I remarried. I could not believe that there was something morally or spiritually wrong with my love for Hilary, or hers for me.

Nevertheless, it was emotionally wrenching to experience a relationship die. I knew I should take care of Trudy in settling our divorce; but meeting that responsibility had its rocky moments. I was fortunate to have wise personal as well as legal advice from Sidney Sachs. Whenever anger and irritation erupted, Sachs counseled patience, silence, and a focus on the future. "There is light at the end of this tunnel," he reminded me a hundred times. The most crucial decision was made sitting around Ed Williams's conference table. We were in the final stages of property negotiations. Agreement had been reached on giving the family house in Washington to Trudy, my keeping the R Street house I had recently bought, sharing the summer house at Wellfleet until I sold it, and my taking care of all the financial, health, and educational needs of the children. The remaining issues were over financial support for Trudy. Sachs urged me to give her all my savings, at the time-some $750,000 in securities. I was resisting. "The other alternative is alimony," Sachs said. "Don't do that. Cut it clean. This will make it easier for you and Trudy to come to peace with each other. It will be better for the kids. You won't be writing a check every month. Over time it will be as irritating for her to receive that monthly check as it is for you to write it."

I continued to resist. "I'll have nothing left," I protested.

Then Ed Williams chimed in, "Look at it this way, Joe. It's only paper. You'll make plenty of paper if that's what you want to do."

"Paper for peace," I mused aloud.

"Do it," Ed said, as Sidney nodded.

I did. It turned out to be one of the wisest decisions of my life.

When the final decree was entered, I thanked Sidney, "not just for representing me, but far more importantly for keeping me a gentleman throughout. It wasn't easy. But you kept me in line and for that I'll be forever grateful." As the years have gone by I realize that Sidney Sachs fostered a settlement that made it easier to regain equilibrium emotionally for both Trudy and me, and hence for our children.

·   ·   ·

An item soon appeared in Liz Smith's column about Hilary and me. Her mother, Dorothy Hirshon, was curious; she wanted to meet me. I went to her apartment at 911 Park Avenue with a miserable cold. Dorothy perpetually puffed on cigarettes, unleashing a steady stream of smoke in my face, as New School president Jonathan Fanton, whom I had recruited to work with me at HEW, struggled to keep from laughing. Her first question to me was: "How could you ever have justified waging that disastrous war in Vietnam?"

This, I knew, was going to be interesting. Unlike most of her social set, Dorothy was a Roosevelt liberal before Roosevelt was a liberal. She cheered the New Deal battles for social justice. She was a fighter for equal justice for blacks decades before Lyndon Johnson took up the cause. In 1943, Dorothy encouraged her second husband,[2] Bill Paley, to have CBS radio broadcast a program entitled *An Open Letter on Race Hatred.*

Dorothy did not share my Catholic faith—or any belief in God. Indeed, when a year later Hilary told her we were going to be married, her first words were, "Oh my God. Not another Catholic!" (Hilary's first husband, Jeff Byers, who had died in 1977, was baptized a Catholic.) In the years that followed, Dorothy and I had many candid conversations, often at China Regency, a restaurant next to Carnegie Deli on Seventh Avenue that served what she considered Manhattan's finest Chinese food. We agreed almost all the time on politics, sometimes on people, never on religion. When she expressed a wish that Hilary, a devoted Republican, might some day come around to our political point of view, I said, "Dorothy, even you [then over eighty and healthy] can't live that long."

On September 3, 1982, I introduced Hilary to my extended family at a luncheon at an Italian restaurant on East 53rd Street in Manhattan that my father and I liked. Along with my father and mother, my cousin John Scotto, his wife, Joan, and my three aunts on my father's side—Rose, Jess, and Constance—were there. The three sisters were living together, since their husbands had died. I was nervous because all of them were devout Catholics and I had no idea how they would react. My family were simple people; Hilary moved in privileged circles. I needn't have worried. It turned out to be a marvelous long lunch at which everyone got along beautifully.

.   .   .

When Hilary and I decided to get married, she suggested I meet with her father and ask for her hand. On December 10, 1982, I went to Bill Paley's apartment at 820 Fifth Avenue for an 8 A.M. breakfast. Entering the apartment, I was greeted by his magnificent Picasso, *Boy Leading A Horse.* We had breakfast from mahogany trays in a room filled with paintings by impressionist masters. I told Bill that Hilary and I wanted to marry; he was delighted. Then he mused about his own life and the love he still had for his second wife, Babe Paley, who had died of lung cancer from smoking. "A man needs a woman who cares for him," Paley said. "Someone to be with when he's alone at night, to talk to, to get advice and ideas from." As he spoke, I realized how much he missed Babe Paley. She was the love of his life, I thought, as Hilary is the love of mine.

With the civil divorce, I was legally free to remarry—but not in the Catholic Church unless I got an annulment. How could there be any chance of that after twenty-three years of marriage? Again I sought advice from Father English. He suggested that I remarry in the Episcopal Church: "Because your Christian faith and God are central to your life and because you are marrying in good conscience, you should marry before God. What the Catholic Church can't do now, the Episcopal Church can."

Father English was prepared to take part in a ceremony in Washington at Christ Church, the Episcopal church in Georgetown. Hilary preferred to marry in New York, but she knew how important it was to me to have Father English participate, so she agreed to Christ Church in Washington. When Father English introduced us to the Reverend Sanford Garner, pastor of Christ Church, I discovered that Hilary had never been baptized. On February 17, 1983, Sanford Garner baptized Hilary with one of her oldest friends, Diana Walker, Diana's husband, Mallory, and me as her sponsors.

Two weeks later, on March 5, 1983, Father English said Mass early in the morning at Georgetown Chapel for Hilary, my children, and me. Later that morning Hilary and I were married at Christ Church by Sanford Garner with Jim English praying and speaking at the ceremony. Sally Quinn remarked later that it was "a most marvelous blend of two cultures: on the bride's side of the church, social New York; on the groom's, an assemblage of self-made Washington political and media ruffians."

At our reception, Bill Paley sat at the table with Hilary and me, my parents, and Ben Bradlee, among others. At the time, Bill Paley was jousting with Kay Graham and *New York Times* publisher Punch Sulzberger to become chairman of the *International Herald Tribune*. Jock Whitney, the prior chair, had died a year earlier and left his third of the *Tribune* to the care of Paley. The *Washington Post* owned another third, as did the *New York Times*. Shortly after we sat down to lunch, Paley started lobbying Bradlee, a *Tribune* board member, to vote for him as chair. Ben gave a snappy response: "Bill, you forget who butters my bread!" Less than a week later, the paper announced its new co-equal co-chairs: William Paley, Katharine Graham, and Arthur Ochs Sulzberger.

The toasts were lighthearted, from Governor Carey and others. Ed Williams lifted his glass. "Hilary, I've struggled with what to give you as a wedding present. You are about to enter into a great partnership. I am the only other person in this room who has been a partner of Joe's. I know what it's like. So, I've decided to give you an 800 number that you can call for support at any hour of the day or night." My cousin John Scotto read a poem that I had recited at his wedding almost forty years earlier.[3]

Bill Paley had rarely been in the same room with Dorothy Hirshon since their divorce in 1947. He bolstered himself with a few drinks. He began his toast by needling me about the fee I had billed him for representing Daniel Schorr. He concluded graciously:

> I feel very happy for Hilary today and very happy that she brings Joe into our family—you never know when you're going to need a good lawyer. A father wants his daughter to have a husband who's good at handling domestic affairs; one who can look after the children's education, keep them healthy, and provide for their welfare. Well, who could be better equipped for these important responsibilities than a former chief policy advisor to the president of the United States and later the secretary of Health, Education, and Welfare?

I toasted my new wife: "When I met Hilary, I knew how man felt when he discovered fire."

I had found material peace in my knowledge that Trudy was taken care of for the rest of her life, that I could earn the wherewithal to educate my children and to live comfortably in Washington. Now with Hilary I had also found an intimacy and loving relationship I had never before known. Thanks to Father English, I was comfortable receiving Communion each Sunday. He fully accepted Hilary, as did Father Dick McCormick and my old friend from the Vatican, Monsignor Paul Marcinkus, when the two of us visited him in Rome. But I was not fully at peace with my church.

CHAPTER 29

Lawyer in the House

I GOT TO KNOW how nasty and unfair the "gotcha" politics—which congressional partisans practice to intimidate presidential appointees whose policies they oppose—had become in 1981 when I represented John Shad, Ronald Reagan's chairman of the Securities and Exchange Commission.

Shad was the first Wall Street executive to lead the commission in half a century. To avoid conflicts of interest, Shad put his holdings in blind trusts and agreed to sell his 250,000 shares of E.F. Hutton, the brokerage house that he had headed. Because his stake in Hutton was so large, Shad gave the stock to Morgan Stanley in return for a $7.8 million note that permitted Morgan Stanley to sell the stock over several months, with the proceeds reducing the amount of the note. This arrangement was designed to maintain the value of Hutton stock by not dumping it all at one time and to reduce Shad's taxes on his gains from the sale.

The Senate Commerce Committee, which passed on Shad's nomination, found the arrangement appropriate. So did Reagan administration ethics lawyers. But Shad's policies—seen as pro–Wall Street—rankled John Dingell, the pugnacious Democrat who chaired the House Energy and Commerce Committee as well as its Subcommittee on Oversight and Investigations. To distract Shad and put him on the defensive, Dingell mounted a personal assault on the new chairman's ethics. Shad was an inviting target for the overbearing Dingell; the SEC chairman was extremely conservative and had raised big bucks for Ronald Reagan in New York State.

Based on suspicions but with no evidence, Dingell accused Shad of secretly controlling sale of his E.F. Hutton shares instead of leaving that to his blind trustee, Barton Biggs, a managing director at Morgan Stanley who had been Shad's personal investment adviser since 1965.

Shad tried to deal with Dingell in a straightforward way. He soon realized, however, that he was mud wrestling with a congressional bully determined to destroy him or at least disrupt his policy initiatives. At the suggestion of Nicholas Brady, a Republican who had been appointed to fill a U.S. Senate vacancy for New Jersey, Shad asked me to represent him.

Shad, a chain-smoking Mormon, sat uncomfortably across the desk in my office, which had a sign on it, "This Is A Smoke-Free Workplace." He had expected resistance from Democrats who disagreed with his policies, but he was not prepared for political kickboxing. As a Mormon, Shad was following his grandmother's adage to spend, as he put it, "a third of my life learning, a third earning, and now, a third serving." Despite our vastly different political philosophies, I liked him immediately. I readily agreed to represent him.

I reviewed Shad's arrangements to comply with conflict-of-interest laws with his personal lawyer, Irwin Schneiderman, a partner at the Wall Street firm of Cahill, Gordon & Reindel. Then I met with Dingell, who demanded that we reconstruct every sale of E.F. Hutton stock and every phone call or contact that Shad had with Schneiderman or his blind trustee, a massive and expensive job that kept Shad complaining about my legal bills and the costs of responding to Dingell and his staff.

The meetings with Shad were held in my office, and since he knew of my views on smoking, he never even asked if he could light up. (I would have said no.) Struggling in my office with all the discomfort of a deeply addicted smoker—constantly reaching in his pocket, forming his fingers as though they were holding a cigarette, playing with his lighter—Shad repeatedly suggested that we meet at the SEC, but I considered that inadvisable, since Dingell would be informed of every such meeting and would demand to know if any government property was being used for Shad's personal defense. Shad disagreed and we met once or twice in his office. But when Dingell insisted on knowing whether Shad was making personal calls on the SEC phones in connection with the committee's investigation, or otherwise using government facilities to deal with issues related to potential personal conflicts of interest, Shad reluctantly returned to meeting in my office.

It was clear to me that the Michigan congressman would use any tool at his disposal to discredit Shad. So I called Schneiderman and asked him if he had billed for the work he had done in helping his client comply with the conflict-of-interest requirements. "No," Schneiderman replied.

"Does your firm have any matters before the SEC?" I asked.

"Of course," he answered.

"Then bill Shad immediately, and at your regular rates," I said.

It had been common for lawyers and accountants to help friends going into public office in such circumstances. But in the superheated situation Shad faced, I feared Dingell would find some matter involving a client of Cahill that Shad had ruled on favorably. If that happened, Dingell would crucify Shad.

When Shad received Schneiderman's bill for $25,000, he exploded. He telephoned the New York lawyer, who told Shad that I had insisted he send the bill. Shad called me. "Not only are you sending me a big bill every month," he said furiously. "Now you tell Irwin he has to send me a bill! What kind of advocate are you? Are you on my side?"

Holding back a chuckle, I responded, "Sorry, John. But you've got to pay this, since Cahill has matters pending before the SEC." I could hear the deep drag Shad took on his cigarette before he grunted, "All right."

Despite my complaints and Shad's, Dingell and his staff continued to feed the press charges and tidbits from their investigation. Outraged, Shad wrote to newspapers complaining, but to no effect.

Dingell and his counsel demanded that Shad come up to the Hill for an in-depth interview. On June 24, I accompanied Shad to Room 2323 of the House Rayburn Building. I set a tape recorder on the table and announced that we intended to record the interrogation. Dingell objected. I insisted, knowing that he or his staff would leak a distorted version of the meeting. With a verbatim tape of what was asked and answered, we would be armed to respond. Dingell refused to participate unless I removed the tape recorder. When I refused, he stormed out and left his aide, Mike Barrett, to conduct the interrogation.[1] Shad handled himself well, and with the tape in our possession, there was never a press leak about our meeting.

As it became clear that Shad had complied fully with conflict-of-interest laws, Dingell began to question the tax treatment of the sale of Shad's Hutton holdings. He asked Shad if he had signed his tax return. Shad responded that he had not even seen the return; his blind trustee had prepared and submitted it.

In a letter of July 16, 1982, Dingell requested, without any reason, that Shad provide "all records, logs, billings, notations, or any other indications of telephone conversations that either you or your secretary have been party to, following assumption of your duties on the Commission. This includes the period prior to your confirmation by the Senate." The request was without limitation as to subject matter.

I refused to comply with the unreasonable demands absent a committee subpoena, which Dingell was unable to obtain. I suggested that if Dingell wanted to delve into tax aspects of Shad's disposition of Hutton shares, he refer the matter to the Internal Revenue Service, which had the professional staff and jurisdiction to investigate such matters.

I argued to Dingell that his fishing expedition illustrated why the government has difficulty recruiting responsible executives—even those with unblemished reputations. "They receive a fraction of their prior compensation. They're required to make detailed disclosures of their personal affairs; to forgo any knowledge of how their lifetime savings are being administered under blind trusts; and as in my client's case, they are required to liquidate certain investments." Dingell, much as he enjoyed being the House bully, knew if I made a public issue of it, I would win on "enough already" grounds in the press.

In early August, the *Washington Post* reported that a congressional subcommittee had asked John Fedders, the SEC enforcement chief, to testify "about [Shad's] role in a case involving a questionable corporate payment and possible cover-up." The article was another example of hostile leaks from Dingell's subcommittee. Shad was livid. He sent me a handwritten note: "Mike Barrett admitted in the presence of Ed Greene, SEC general counsel, Dingell and me that he leaked the story. . . . The time has come to fight back. It is outrageous to subject a presidential appointee to escalating harassment and press leaks of unfounded charges without a scintilla of evidence of wrongdoing. The more we accede to fishing expedition demands, the more they will demand."[2]

The investigation had become a witch-hunt. We ended all cooperation. As it became clear that Shad had done nothing wrong, I pressed Dingell for a letter clearing him of any wrongdoing. Dingell resisted, but finally agreed, "if we find nothing improper."

Then, without notice, on a Friday afternoon in November, Dingell sent a letter to Shad through the mail without even the courtesy of a phone call to Shad or me. "It is the staff's conclusion," the letter said, "that there was no wrongdoing in the method of disposition of Hutton securities or in the transfer of the proceeds thereof to your trust. While the transactions were complex, they appeared to satisfy all existing statutory and regulatory requirements. I concur in this conclusion." The letter was timed to get minimum notice in the press.

Shad received the letter on November 9. It took numerous phone calls from me to get it printed in newspapers that had run so many front- and front-business-page stories on Dingell's original charges. The *New York Times* finally printed a story on page one in its business section on November 23. The *Washington Post* printed its story on page nine of its business section on November 24. "After a long inquiry," the *Times* reported, "House investigators have found no impropriety in the way the chairman of the Securities and Exchange Commission disposed of shares in a major brokerage house upon his nomination last year to head the Commission."

Without consulting me, Shad issued a companion statement, which the *Times* quoted: "It has taken seven months and $70,000 in personal legal fees, but I am glad to get it over with."

Shad hadn't gotten my final bill, which took his fees even higher. He paid it.

.   .   .

On June 30 and July 1, 1982, more than 13 million Americans tuned in to the *CBS Evening News with Dan Rather* and watched two former pages of the House of Representatives, their teenage faces silhouetted to hide their identity, say that they had been victims of sexual misconduct by members of Congress. One described "homosexual advances" by congressmen and Capitol Hill staffers. CBS correspondent John Ferrugia reported that the page had been "homosexually harassed." The other page shocked the nation when he said that he had engaged in homosexual relations with three members of the House and had procured male prostitutes for House staffers.

CBS broke this story amid press reports and rumors of widespread illegal drug use and distribution by members, officers, and employees of the House and Senate.

Hilary and I were spending the Fourth of July at her father's estate in Southampton. Like most Americans, we were disgusted with the sexual exploitation of minors that CBS had reported. The story was a topic of conversation at parties throughout the long weekend. No one seemed to care much about the reports of drug use; pot smoking and cocaine snorting were too common in the Hamptons then for such use in Washington to raise any Long Island eyebrows.

In 1970 Congress had relaxed penalties for marijuana possession. In 1971, NORML—the National Organization for Reform of Marijuana Laws—was formed to press for legalization of marijuana. A presidential commission under Richard Nixon had recommended decriminalizing marijuana possession for personal use. In 1977 President Jimmy Carter had asked Congress to eliminate criminal penalties for possession of less than one ounce of marijuana and replace them with a $100 civil fine. As secretary of Health, Education, and Welfare, I had been more concerned—as were the department's top health officials—with herbicides used to kill marijuana plants than with marijuana itself. I opposed the use of paraquat to kill marijuana plants; the Centers for Disease Control and the National Institute of Environmental Health Sciences indicated "that the smoke of paraquat-contaminated marijuana is likely to cause damage when inhaled in sufficient quantities by marijuana users." By the time of the 1982 CBS broadcast, more than 60 million Americans had used illegal drugs, including 50 million who had smoked pot and 22 million who had tried cocaine. Several physicians, scientists, and sophisticates at the time touted cocaine as a non-addictive recreational drug. Earlier in the year, three former House aides had been arrested and claimed that they had provided cocaine to members of Congress. The Justice Department had convened a federal grand jury to investigate the charges. California Republican congressman Robert Dornan, the unguided right-wing missile, claimed that a Washington policeman, working undercover, had confirmed to him that members of Congress were using and distributing drugs. In this lurid climate, the CBS report of sexual abuse of Capitol Hill pages was gasoline thrown on a five-alarm political fire.

Now, over the Fourth of July weekend, Louis Stokes, chair of the House Ethics Committee, called me. "The Speaker wants our committee to look into these charges of sexual abuse and drug use. We want you to be special counsel and conduct the investigation."

I told Lou to look for someone else. "This is not my cup of tea." Ever so gently, Stokes suggested, "Just think about it. Don't slam all the doors shut."

Bill Paley urged me not to take the job. The last thing he wanted was a future son-in-law investigating charges made over his network.

A week later, the House authorized its ethics committee to "conduct a full and complete inquiry and investigation" into allegations of "sexual misconduct, illicit drug distribution and use, and offers of preferential treatment in exchange for sexual favors or drugs by Members, officers or employees of the House."

House Speaker Tip O'Neill summoned me to his office. He wanted to talk about my conducting the investigation. "Tip, if I go to your office, you'll rope me in," I said.

"At least talk to Lou Stokes," he said.

Next came a phone call from the Senate majority leader, Howard Baker, with an invitation to lunch with him on July 15. Baker urged me to take on the investigation in the House. "The way you'd do it, we might be able to avoid one in the Senate."

Again I expressed my reluctance. "Califano," Baker said, "you've been drafted by the Speaker and me. You make your life and living in this town, and this is one you've got to do."

If I had any doubt that the Speaker and Baker were in cahoots, it disappeared when I returned to my office. I learned that the Speaker expected to see me the following Tuesday. That weekend, based on a leak from House sources, the *Washington Post* reported that the House would ask me to head the probe.

Resigned to the task, I insisted that the entire House leadership, Democrat and Republican, and both Stokes and ranking Republican Ethics Committee member Floyd Spence, let me conduct the investigation with my own staff and that all of them be present at the press announcement of my appointment. They agreed, and on July 27, flanked by the bipartisan House leadership and facing a battery of microphones, I accepted the position "with the greatest reluctance." I knew I would win no popularity contest with this investigation and that the press would scrutinize my own private life.

A sense of what lay ahead came when *New York Times* reporter Martin Tolchin shouted the question, "Have you ever tried cocaine?"

"No, I never have," I responded. Then, after a second's hesitation—in which my irritation at the press's free ride sprouted—I shot back, "Have you, Marty?"

I got no response.

The *New York Times* story on my appointment, under Tolchin's byline, reported that as secretary of HEW I had shown "an independence that antagonized members of the White House staff. It ultimately led Mr. Carter to seek his resignation." Tip O'Neill called to say the *Times* story confirmed his judgment that my report, whatever it found, would have the credibility the House needed.

There were only two light moments to follow in the months ahead. Tom Brokaw penned a note: "Joe—re: your new assignment. In show biz we call that typecasting. Cheers, Tom." My sons, Mark and Joe, gave me a T-shirt with "Sex and Drugs and Rock and Roll" printed across the chest.

On the serious side, friends approached me quietly and asked, "Are you investigating all employees for drug use?" When I asked why, they said, "My son [daughter] works for a congressman. I hope you aren't going to name employees." These expressions of concern signaled how widespread drug use had become in our town—and how naïve I had been about it.

Assistant Deputy Attorney General Rudolph Giuliani was point man for the Justice Department and its grand jury investigation. We agreed to exchange all relevant information and that there would be no leaks. Rudy was true to his word. Despite rumors and fragments of information about numerous members of Congress that we each came across and shared, there were no leaks from him or me.

Sexual misconduct and drug use were raw meat for a voracious, scandal-hungry Washington press corps starved for news in the capital's summer doldrums. Concerned that Hill staffers could not resist the pressures and temptations to leak information, I set up offices in a separate building and employed two partners in my law firm, Rick Cotton and Hamilton P. (Phil) Fox. As chief investigator I hired Gerry McQueen, a New York City police officer.[3] We had Capitol Police guard our offices around the clock. Secrecy was paramount. I insisted that only my staff and I attend meetings of the Ethics Committee and that members be required to attend alone, without any personal staff accompanying them.

This was uncharted territory—an investigation of sexual escapades and drug use at a time where sexual freedom was growing and drug use was common. I wanted to think through the scope of our investigative activities—to draw a line carefully to distinguish purely personal from publicly relevant sexual activity and drug use. I secretly consulted Richard McCormick, the Jesuit ethicist who had advised me at HEW, asking him to help me set parameters for my investigation. After studying the enabling House resolution, he sent me a confidential letter:

> Official conduct—it seems to me that this will be determined by what society *expects* of officials. It will be based on and judged by community standards. Therefore, I believe your commission should be based on and controlled by *what society tolerates and does not tolerate* in elected officials. *That* is determined by the relation of character and conduct to the *ability to serve*. Whatever compromises the ability to serve is intolerable.
>
> I believe that our society would view the following as affecting the ability to serve, therefore as intolerable in public officials: (a) *illegal* sex (with minors); (b) immoral acts *publicly* done; (c) *use of office* (or connection of office) with such acts; (d) acts or relations which *expose to pressure or blackmail;* (e) illegal use of drugs; (f) preferential treatment surrounding any of the above. . . .
>
> the . . . important thing is the criterion which generates the listing. . . . It should be (for your purposes) not some religious body's moral code, but what society does or does not tolerate in public officials. And that roots in the ability to carry out one's duties. In this respect, society is likely to be more demanding of public officials than others. That is, it might tolerate certain things between consenting adults as "human weakness" or "peccadillos" in the general population, but not in public officials.[4]

Without letting anyone know of the letter, I adopted Father McCormick's suggestions to set the scope of our investigation. I also decided to restrict our investigation to allegations involving pages. Any effort to investigate sexual activities (and at the time drug use) among all employees in the House would have required a lifetime.

The first surprise came when both pages who had disclosed their allegations on the *CBS Evening News,* Leroy Williams and Jeffrey Opp, recanted when questioned under oath by our investigators. Under oath, Williams testified that, when interviewed by the CBS News reporter, he had lied about having sexual relations with members of the House and about procuring prostitutes. Opp testified that he no longer believed his conversations with certain congressmen were homosexual approaches or had any sexual over-tones. Each claimed that CBS reporter Ferrugia kept putting words into their mouths and ideas into their heads.[5]

I promptly held a press conference at which Leroy Williams admitted: "These allegations are not true. I have lied and I regret that. Words cannot express the remorse I feel."

Appalled by such careless and reckless reporting, we castigated it in our report, which concluded that "the allegations made by the two former pages to the press in June 1982 appear to have been stimulated more by their own resentment, egos and immaturity, and by contact with one reporter, than by any events involving actions by Members of Congress." Dan Rather was embarrassed, and CBS played down its mistakes. The reporter, John Ferru-gia, was dropped from the *Evening News* and shifted to a short-lived TV show, *West 57*, before leaving the network.

Unfortunately, uncovering the lies of the pages and exposing the reckless reporting of CBS didn't end our investigation. We had received a host of accusations about sexual activity and the use and sale of drugs by other pages and members of Congress. We interviewed, under oath, some two thousand past and present congressional pages, adults who supervised and taught those pages, and congressional staffers, as well as several House members. We issued scores of subpoenas. Our investigators traveled more than 100,000 miles to more than fifty cities, devoting more than seventy thousand hours of staff time to the investigation.[6]

Questioning teenage pages about their sexual activity and drug use was distasteful. We found no evidence of widespread improper or illicit sexual conduct by members of the House with pages or of preferential treatment in exchange for sexual favors during the period covered by the original charges. We did, however, find evidence of two cases of improper sexual conduct involving pages and congressmen that occurred earlier. We discov-ered that Representative Daniel Crane, an Illinois Republican, had a sexual relationship with a seventeen-year-old female page in 1980. We found that Representative Gerry Studds, a Democrat from Cape Cod, had a sexual rela-tionship in 1973 with a seventeen-year-old male page (who may have been sixteen when the relationship began). Studds, we learned, had made sexual advances in 1973 to two other male pages, one sixteen, the other seventeen.

Both Crane and Studds admitted this conduct.[7]

When I privately reported our findings to Tip O'Neill, the dishonor both members had brought on his beloved House of Representatives made him tremble with rage. Then, displaying that tough sense of humor common to most effective politicians, he said, "I always knew you got the luck of the Irish from your mother. Only someone with a shamrock could end a House sex investigation by nailing a conservative Republican with a girl and a liberal Democrat with boys!"

When Crane was censured on the House floor, he turned and faced the Speaker, as required by long-standing custom. Studds, however, was defiant. He first demanded that I leave the House floor, then turned his back on the Speaker as his censure was read. Studds then said, "It is not a simple task for any of us to meet adequately the obligations of either public or private life, let alone both, but these challenges are made substantially more complex when one is, as I am, both an elected public official and gay." Unlike his colleague, he exhibited no shame about having sexual relations with teenage pages.

Our investigation of drug use involved a significant number of House members and staffers. We believed that drug use and distribution were widespread on Capitol Hill, but we were unable to establish conclusively that any members had distributed drugs.[8] We did uncover convincing evidence that three House members had used drugs: Barry Goldwater, Jr., a Republican from Arizona and son of the 1964 presidential candidate; John Burton, a Democrat from San Francisco; and Frederick Richmond, a Brooklyn Democrat.[9] Goldwater refused to cooperate with the investigation, claiming we had no jurisdiction over former members. Burton ended his congressional career in 1982 to enter treatment for cocaine and alcohol addiction; he became a recovering addict with a productive political career on the state level. Granted immunity from prosecution, Richmond admitted buying and using illegal drugs. Pleading guilty to tax evasion and two misdemeanor charges, including possession of marijuana supplied by staff members, he resigned from the House in August 1982.

We concluded that between 1978 and 1982 illicit use or distribution of drugs involved a number of House and Senate employees. Marijuana and alcohol use was rampant among pages and a number of them used cocaine or mood-altering pills at work and private parties. Teenage pages were footloose and free. They were permitted to live anywhere they wished, with no supervision at night or when the House was not in session. We recommended a complete overhaul of the page program, which Speaker O'Neill immediately ordered. A page dormitory was established and all pages were required to stay there unless they lived at home with a parent or legal guardian residing in the Washington area. The House created a new separate school for its pages, independently accredited and staffed by teachers hired by the House, and established a Page Board that included three members of Congress.

Along with my study in New York State, this investigation was a bracing exposure to how pervasive alcohol and drug abuse was in our culture, especially among our young. The House of Representatives, which prided itself on being the nation's most representative body, was a mirror reflecting the widespread drug and alcohol abuse (and often consequent sexual exploitation of minors) in the nation. So in concluding the investigation, I said:

> . . . this investigation should be understood in the context of American society, in which addiction is the number one health problem of the nation. Every institution in the nation—corporations, unions, schools, the press—has problems resulting from the abuse of drugs and alcohol. Every American has a friend or family member who has suffered from drug or alcohol abuse. When all the sound and fury of . . . this report have died down, perhaps its most important contribution will be . . . that each of us [will be] more conscious of the extent and dangers of drug abuse.

House Ethics Committee rules prohibited destruction of its records. After releasing the final report, I went to see Stokes and Spence. Our files contained allegations against some fifty House members and many more staffers. We had found these allegations to be without merit, but I feared that, in the rough and tumble of political ambition, leaving records of unproven allegations lying around might subject members to charges in later years—charges that, though false, could be nonetheless damaging.

I discussed my concerns with Stokes and Spence. "We can't destroy these files," Spence said.

"What do you suggest we do?" Stokes asked me.

"What can't be destroyed can be lost. The rules say nothing about losing records."

Stokes smiled for a minute. Then, looking at his Republican co-chair, said, "You know, Floyd, records get lost all the time around here."

Spense nodded. "Yup."

Five years later, in the summer of 1987, in the revamped program, my daughter Claudia, age seventeen and a junior in high school, worked as a page in the Democratic Party cloakroom under the sponsorship of Represesntative Jack Brooks of Texas and the watchful eye of Massachusetts congressman Joe Moakley, chairman of the Committee on Rules.

CHAPTER 30

From Washington to Wall Street

BY LATE 1982, Stan Ross, Ben Heineman, Jr., and I decided to part ways. Our practice was highly profitable and growing, but I missed the adrenalin of public life, of being at the center of the action, and I was distracted and irritated by the drawn-out divorce negotiations. I found myself unable to muster the single-minded concentration essential to shape a law firm from scratch into a powerful Washington institution. I could not bring to this task the commitment and energy that came so easily when I was engaged in combat for a public cause in which I believed. I was wearing my personal and professional situation like a scratchy hair shirt, and it showed. Stan Ross decided to join Arnold & Porter and Ben Heineman took over the Washington office of Sidley & Austin. I had to decide what to do with myself and the dozen attorneys and staff who made up the remainder of the law firm.

As word of the split circulated, I was approached by several Wall Street law firms that were scouring Washington to establish their own powerful presence there. Fortune 1000 corporations were finding their profits increasingly sensitive to government regulation and legislation, and the big New York firms sought their own foothold in the nation's capital to protect client relationships and reap their share of the hefty fees ripe for harvesting. Remarkably, I ended up at the firm where I had first started as an associate—Dewey, Ballantine, Bushby, Palmer & Wood. The firm had gathered dust, losing ground among the Wall Street pack, unwilling or unprepared to play in the aggressive new Darwinian world of corporate law. I saw an opportunity to revitalize the firm (and replenish my resources after the divorce settlement) if the good partners would chop off dead wood and use the prestigious name to attract hard-charging young attorneys from lesser-known firms. I trusted senior partners like Charles MacLean, C. Gorham (Doc) Phillips, and Robert Fullem to keep their word when they said they would support my efforts to do just that.

In the first half of the twentieth century, only White Anglo-Saxon Protestants could hope to become partners at Dewey or similar firms. Catholics, Italians, Jews, and Irish could work there for a few years and then split off to found their own firms. The WASP curtain was just beginning to lift when I was a summer associate in 1954. Now, in November 1982 during our negotiations, I had dinner with Leonard Joseph, the chairman of the firm's management committee and the firm's first Jewish partner, in a private room at the Union Club, among the nation's stuffiest. "Len, do you realize how remarkable this is?" I asked. "You, the first Jewish partner in this firm, and I, an Italian-American kid from Brooklyn, are trying to put together a deal to save this WASP institution." Joseph, who was steeped in high-button-shoe Dewey tradition, saw no humor or irony in the situation; he was so taken aback by my candor that he immediately reverted to a dry, meticulous repetition of the firm's billings and the solid-gold clients it still served.

I was concerned that the firm had only one black associate and no black partners. I attributed this not to calculated discrimination but to a lack of interest in recruiting of minorities and a failure to make it clear that the firm offered a hospitable and welcoming environment for them. Myles Lynk, one of the bright young attorneys of my own firm and a black, was reluctant to come to Dewey. I told Joseph I wanted Lynk with me as part of any arrangement and Joseph said, "I'll take care of that."

Lynk had graduated from Harvard Law School, clerked for Judge Damon Keith on the Sixth Circuit U.S. Court of Appeals, and come to HEW as one of my special assistants. Later he had been a member of the White House domestic policy staff before joining our law firm. Myles had done his homework on the firm's history: its early years of anti-Semitism and anti-feminism. (When the firm finally hired women lawyers, it caged them in the estates and real estate departments and, until 1970, did not allow them to attend the firm's annual dinner for attorneys.)

When Myles returned to Washington after his meeting with Joseph, he was disconcerted. He had laid out his concerns about discrimination, to which Joseph had responded, "I know what it's like to be black."

"You have no idea what it's like to be black," Lynk snapped back.

When Myles related this exchange and his fears, I assured him that he had no need to worry, that the remark had been made by a Jew, the first to become a partner in the firm and one who surely felt he knew a lot about overcoming discrimination.

Lynk eventually decided to come with me to the firm—largely because Damon Keith, the black judge for whom he had clerked, told him that I would never go or take him to a place that practiced any discrimination. I had interviewed Keith for a slot on the federal district court when I was in the Johnson White House. At that time our litmus test for federal district judges in border and southern states was their support of racial desegregation, voting rights, and affirmative action, and I questioned all candidates I interviewed on those subjects.[1]

.   .   .

Myles Lynk proved an invaluable ally in my efforts to open membership to women in the Metropolitan Club, the capital's oldest (1863) and most prestigious, two blocks from the White House. Ed Williams had insisted I join when we were partners. "With so many clients on the edge of the law, we need to belong to this club," Ed said.

In 1977, when I was secretary of Health, Education, and Welfare, Clark Clifford had invited me to become a member of the Alfalfa Club, a bastion of the Washington establishment that met once a year to have dinner and listen to humorous mock presidential nominating and acceptance speeches. "You'll be returning to law practice here. It can help you." Alfalfa was then an all-male event, more prestigious than the Gridiron, a similar dinner-a-year club for prominent journalists. I told Clifford I couldn't accept because Alfalfa kept women out. He considered that an unreasonable position and warned, "No one turns down the Alfalfa Club."

"That's exactly why the club should admit women."

"If you turn this down, you will never again be asked to join."

"I'll have to live with that," I said. I'd rather do that, I thought not entirely altruistically, than live with all the hell I'd get from women, many of whom were already attacking me for my stand on abortion.*

In the early 1980s, the Metropolitan Club remained a male-only enclave, but the pressure was building. In 1985, Senator Paul Simon, an Illinois Democrat, blocked confirmation of Reagan's nominee Laurence Silberman to the U.S. Court of Appeals until he resigned from the club.

I was a member of the Century Association, in New York, which had

*The Alfalfa club inducted its first women members in 1994: Katharine Graham, Supreme Court justice Sandra Day O'Connor, and Elizabeth Dole.

experienced a bruising internal battle over the issue of female members. That club had finally admitted women when faced with a 1984 city ordinance prohibiting discrimination by clubs that derived significant income from non-members.

After leaving HEW, I and a number of others tried to persuade the Metropolitan Club to admit women, all unsuccessfully. I then adapted a copy of New York's law prohibiting discrimination against women by such clubs and asked Myles Lynk, who was active in District of Columbia affairs, to persuade a member on the D.C. City Council, Jim Nathanson, to introduce it. Nathanson did.

The City Council, against the opposition of the Metropolitan Club, unanimously passed the statute requiring all-male clubs with more than 350 members to admit women.[2] The next day I sent a letter to the club's president, Admiral John Kane, prodding it "to do what it should have done many years ago: open its membership to women."

The following June, the Metropolitan Club opened its doors to women.

.   .   .

What remained of my firm merged into Dewey Ballantine in January 1983. I became head of the Washington office and co-chair of the management committee. Over the next eight years, the firm prospered. As we recruited new partners, the Washington office grew rapidly from a dozen in early 1983 to almost one hundred when I left in 1992. We opened offices in London and Los Angeles, retired unproductive partners, and recruited some twenty-five new ones, including Morton Pierce, who would co-chair the firm's management committee in 2003, and Sanford Litvack, who had been managing partner at Donovan Leisure Newton & Irvine. Because I considered Litvack a potential candidate to lead the firm, I checked him out extensively. Frank Wells, then president of the Walt Disney Company, told me that when his company had faced a potentially catastrophic attack from environmentalists against a theme park complex, he had checked all over the country to get the best litigator. Litvack ended up on every list. The day Litvack's move to Dewey appeared in the *Wall Street Journal*, Wells sent me this cable: "Joe—You'll believe anything, won't you."[3]

Despite our financial and legal successes and the expansion of the firm, I was finding far less satisfaction than I had expected in the practice of law. It hit me when Lee Iacocca, chairman and CEO of Chrysler, wanted to block (or at least delay) the merger of General Motors and Toyota manufacturing plants in California. I told him that suing General Motors was a major undertaking. "You'll feel great the day we file and make the announcement, but you may come to regret it down the road." Iacocca was insistent; he felt disrupting the merger was of utmost importance for Chrysler. So in January 1984 we filed the suit in federal district court in Washington, D.C.

General Motors unleashed an army of attorneys to take testimony of Chrysler employees and executives, scheduling three depositions at the same time in different cities across the nation. What the giant automaker couldn't win on the merits, it was determined to win by exhausting Chrysler's resources and distracting its executives. It didn't affect Iacocca until he had to prepare for his own deposition. On one of the days of preparation, he sat in my office in Washington for several hours. I couldn't tell which annoyed him more, the fact that GM lawyers were going to depose him for at least a full day, or the "This Is A Smoke-Free Workplace" sign on my conference table. At the end of the afternoon, Lee was hoarse. Then, with a mischievous smile, he asked, "Is that all?" When I nodded, he rasped, "You know you're Goddamn lucky I've got a lousy cold. Because I'm paying the bills for you guys to sit around here, and I'd damn well fill this room with cigar smoke if I weren't so sick."

The first hurdle was defeating General Motors' motions for dismissal of the Chrysler claim and for a summary judgment. To prepare for a day of arguments, I had to go into the tank for two months—master all the relevant cases, review thousands of pages of depositions, craft the arguments why our suit should go forward, and get ready for questions from the bench and surprises from the GM lawyers. The oral argument was on April 18; six weeks later, on May 29, Judge Thomas Hogan denied General Motors motions and let our case go forward.[4]

In the course of preparing for our victory, I learned I had lost any stomach for litigation. No longer was I willing to turn off the rest of my life for weeks in order to appear in court. My experience at HEW—working on so many different matters at the same time—had rendered me incapable of such isolation and narrow concentration. I would never argue another matter in a courtroom.

.   .   .

I was also becoming disillusioned with Washington. In an article published in the Sunday *New York Times* in December 1980, I had written, "There's a new smoke-filled room in the Democratic Party and its doors lock out too many people that represent the broad interests of their urban areas, farm districts, and suburban counties. Those inside the room represent the National Education Association, and [single-issue] organizations that got them elected as convention delegates. The habit of making deals remains; only the brand of tobacco has changed. It is as important to air out these smoke-filled rooms as it was to clean out the big-city bosses." But the party's need for money was keeping the windows closed and blocking any political fresh air from getting in.

By the mid-1980s, the practice of lobbying law in Washington was changing. Members of the Congress were increasingly influenced more by money than policy, and I sensed a metastasizing corruption and pandering to special interests on Capitol Hill and in both political parties. Partners coming off the Hill were pressing the firm to have a political action committee, because money was now the only sure ticket to access. As one said to me when I expressed opposition to a law-firm PAC, "Campaign contributions are now the price of admission, more and more essential to get an appointment on the Hill." In prior years, when I took a corporate executive to see a senator about a problem, he was likely to receive a request to purchase tickets to a fund-raising event. But now, the very next day, I would often get a call from the senator: "Joe, I'd like to learn more about the problem. Perhaps your client could set something up at his corporate headquarters and have some of his executives brief me. At the same time, we might be able to have a little fund-raiser."

In 1988, I visited Maine senator George Mitchell with executives of a corporation that provided cardiac rehabilitation for heart attack patients and with an expert consultant, Dr. Antonio Gotto, who later became dean of the Weill Medical College at Cornell University. Medicare was paying for fewer rehab days a month than best medical practice and my for-profit client considered appropriate. We proposed that Medicare reimburse patients for additional days either by changing the regulations or amending the law. Mitchell heard us out. As we were leaving, he asked me to step back in his office alone for a minute. "Joe, you know I'm running for majority leader. I need some financial help." Mitchell said he needed political contributions to demonstrate to other senators that he could raise substantial sums despite hailing from a small state. He had to be able to make contributions to campaigns of fellow senators in order to attract their votes for majority leader. Mitchell closed with a suggestion. "Perhaps you can get some of your clients to kick in."

I had known and admired George Mitchell for years, since his days as state chairman of the Maine Democratic Party and a federal judge. He was a man of high integrity. As I left his office all I could think of was how demeaning and appalling it must have been for him to make such an appeal. I never mentioned his conversation to my clients.*

When I complained to another respected senator about the intense pressure for money on Capitol Hill, he said, "Five or ten grand can buy a veto vote in committee from many of my colleagues." Once the greatest deliberative body in the world, the U.S. Senate, I feared, was being corrupted by money. Much as I had relished it in the past, I was losing my desire to be part of this world.

My small protest came when I contributed to the 1986 Senate races of Tim Wirth in Colorado and Jim Jones in Oklahoma. Wirth was a longstanding friend; he and my wife, Hilary, were pals. Jim Jones and I had served together on the LBJ White House staff. Along with each check, I sent a letter telling the candidates that this was the last political contribution I would make for any candidate for Congress. It was a little way of practicing my preaching for public financing of campaigns.

·   ·   ·

As my disenchantment with the practice of law deepened, I devoted more time to pro bono matters. In 1986, New York City mayor Ed Koch asked me to head a mayoral committee on smoking and health. I accepted eagerly. Our committee recommended that restaurants, closed sports arenas, and convention halls reserve up to half their seats for nonsmokers, and that smoking be banned outright in retail stores, hearing rooms, taxis, restrooms, and theaters. When I reported to Koch, I said I realized that passing such an ordinance was hopeless; the tobacco interests would spend millions to kill the bill in the City Council.

*In November 1988, Mitchell was elected majority leader, succeeding Senator Robert Byrd of West Virginia, who had decided to relinquish the post.

"Nonsense," Koch said. "You propose the toughest law that makes sense. I'll get it passed."

I expressed skepticism about his nonchalance. "But they'll take the tobacco money," I responded.

"This is New York," Koch agreed. "Of course they'll take the tobacco money. Then they'll vote for your bill."

City Council members did take the money. Then, led by Peter Vallone, who at the time chaired the council's health committee, they voted unanimously for the bill. Koch signed it into law in January 1988, restricting smoking in public places, retail stores, restaurants, businesses, and other workplaces. (In 1995 and again in 2002, the law was strengthened to prohibit smoking in virtually all public places, making it one of the toughest anti-smoking laws in the nation.)

·   ·   ·

In January 1986, *Daily News* columnist Jimmy Breslin exposed a bribery ring involving top political appointees in New York City's Parking Violations Bureau. Several public officials, including Mayor Koch's transportation commissioner, Anthony Ameruso, resigned. Bronx Democratic leader Stanley Friedman and Michael Lazar, a major contributor to Koch and Governor Mario Cuomo, were convicted of bribery and racketeering in connection with the scandal.

The parking bureau scandal led to revelations of corruption in the courts. A key figure in the mess, Queens Democratic Party chairman and borough president Donald Manes, committed suicide. State and local prosecutors and the U.S. attorney for New York's southern district, Rudolph Giuliani, mounted more than a dozen investigations that uncovered corruption, including bribery, forgery, mail fraud, conspiracy, racketeering, and tampering with public records, in the office of Mayor Koch (though the mayor was never involved), the city's municipal hospital system, the Taxi and Limousine Commission, the Department of General Services, the Housing Authority, courthouses, and county political organizations.

In early December 1986, Columbia University president Michael Sovern and Giuliani called for a special commission with subpoena power to investigate unethical behavior by New York public officials. On the morning of

December 19, as I arrived at my law office, Governor Cuomo was on the phone. He wanted to establish "a Moreland Act Commission"[5] to investigate government corruption in New York City and State. "Would you be willing to chair it?" he asked.

I reminded Cuomo that I was a resident of Washington, not New York. "I know that," he said. "That's a plus. And you come from Brooklyn." I said I would want complete freedom to pick the staff, notably including the commission's counsel. I also wanted to work out the commission membership with him. Cuomo wanted to think about that; he would have his counsel, Evan Davis, call me.

When Davis called, I expressed concerns about two of Cuomo's suggested commission members: Ronnie Eldridge, wife of *Daily News* columnist Breslin, and federal district judge Constance Baker Motley. Eldridge was close to Cuomo; she and her husband, Breslin, were virulently anti-Koch (and Koch was virulently anti-Breslin). "I'm worried that she'll want to stick it to Koch and protect Cuomo," I said. "And Constance Baker Motley is difficult to work with." President Johnson had nominated Motley to be the first black woman to sit on the federal bench and I had known her since 1966; she was able, but prickly.

"Let me talk to the governor," Davis said, and added, "He's also extremely reluctant to let you choose the counsel for the commission." The counsel was a powerful position of some independence.

Over the next several days Cuomo and I went back and forth about commission members and staff. I found our discussions like trying to settle a lawsuit with a tough adversary. More than once, I wondered whether Cuomo wanted the kind of independent investigation I would give him. When we finally came to agreement on members, I was a little more assured. Among the other six commission members, at my insistence, would be Howard Simons, curator of the Nieman Foundation at Harvard University, who had been managing editor of the *Washington Post* throughout Watergate.[6] But Cuomo remained reluctant to let me select the counsel.

As I learned about the various allegations of corruption, I suggested that Cuomo think hard about establishing the commission at all. "It will be essential, in terms of credibility, for the commission to look hard at the Javits Convention Center and milk pricing in New York City," I said, "and from the news reports it appears these issues could involve your son Andrew."

On December 26, Cuomo called to say he was willing to have me choose the commission's counsel and he wanted to go forward. We set January 15 for an announcement.

On the morning of the press conference, the *New York Times* reported, "Though the counsel to the Governor, Evan Davis, has said the commission will not investigate the state legislature in general, it is expected that individual legislators may come under scrutiny if evidence of a conflict of interest between their private and public endeavors emerges." Just before the press conference, I raised this item with Cuomo. The governor had warned me that we should stay away from any public hint that legislators might be investigated; he feared jeopardizing the legislature's willingness to appropriate the five million dollars needed to fund the commission. The *Times* story made me uneasy; Evan Davis would not have spoken to the *Times* without Cuomo's approval. Some savvy observers had already suggested to me that deep in his political heart, Cuomo might want credit for establishing the commission, but not a commission with too independent a chair. Cuomo said again that it was important to avoid any mention in our announcement of state legislators being investigated.

We went out to meet the press, and the governor announced the establishment of a Commission on Government Integrity "to investigate instances of corruption in the administration of government and to determine the adequacy of laws, regulations, and procedures relating to government integrity."

I made a brief statement and we then invited questions. To my astonishment Cuomo went out of his way to say that no one would be immune from investigation. He said our commission would go beyond an earlier one that had recommended tough conflict-of-interest laws for legislators and would conduct "a thorough and searching inquiry, following every lead no matter where it takes them. . . ."[7]

After the press conference, I raised the comments with Cuomo, pointing out that state legislators would see us as targeting them. Cuomo said he had no choice but to say what he did; I shouldn't worry about it. I left his office wondering if I had been sandbagged.

Soon afterward, I spoke at a *Daily News* "Newsmakers" luncheon and said I would work with the prosecutors and hold public hearings. The next day, the *Daily News* ran this story line: "Jumpin' Joe Califano: He's eager to beard lyin' in their dens." I was quoted as saying, "We'll be tough. We'll be fair. We'll be persistent and tenacious, and you'll just have to watch us as we go."

By March 4, I had filled several top slots on the commission staff. The two top positions (chief counsel and staff director) were filled by Gerald Lynch and Benito Romano. Lynch was a criminal law professor at Columbia Law School. Romano was chief of the public corruption unit in the U.S. attorney's office and Giuliani's right hand there. Phil Fox, my law partner in Washington and an experienced criminal prosecutor, joined the staff as special counsel. Peg Breen was our director of communications; she had been the spokesperson at the New York City Department of Investigation.

Melvin Miller, speaker of the assembly in the New York State Legislature and a Brooklyn Democrat, expressed skepticism about the need for the commission and opposed its funding.[8] That spelled trouble. My concern shot up at the Inner Circle dinner, an annual New York City charity event where the media spoofs local politicians and newsmakers. A state legislator came over to shake hands and said, "Miller will never let you be chairman because you took on the tobacco industry and there was no control over you and nobody will ever have any control over you and they'd be crazy to let you do this." The *Times* story on the annual event headlined: "Politicians Laugh At Lampoon But Gusto Is Muffled," a reference to the cloud created by the corruption scandal.

Despite my repeated requests, there was no apparent help from Cuomo in getting our funding. Jack MacKenzie, an editorial page writer for the *New York Times* and a friend from my days representing the *Washington Post,* where he had been a reporter, urged me to go to Albany and negotiate with legislators. I told him I couldn't do that without compromising the integrity of the commission.

The state legislative leaders then indicated that they would not provide public funds for the commission unless all of its members were residents of New York State, a requirement that would disqualify both me and Howard Simons.

The governor called, suggesting that we consider private funding for the commission. I expressed serious reservations. "A commission with the enormous power to subpoena individual citizens, review all their financial and other personal records, and subject them to contempt for failure to obey, should be publicly funded," I told Cuomo. I said that the commission would get tied up in litigation for at least a year over the propriety of private funding.

I now had the sensation that Cuomo was stringing me along; that he was no longer enthusiastic about the commission. On April 7, Jeffrey Sachs, whom I had consulted before taking the job and who was close to Andrew Cuomo, phoned to say he thought I should abandon the chairmanship. "Get out," he put it. After that call, I trusted neither Cuomo nor the New York State Legislature.

As matters heated up, I pressed Cuomo to fix his own bottom line and find out where the legislators in Albany stood. His response was a Delphic parable: "All of them are like the guy who came home about eight in the morning with lipstick all over his face and blonde hairs all over his shoulders. He said to his wife, 'I had to take my friend John home. He got sick at dinner and I had to spend the night comforting him. When I got home it was about three in the morning, all the lights were out, you were sound asleep. I didn't want to wake you up so I slept in the hammock in the yard.' She said, 'You lying bastard. I took that hammock down and threw it away three weeks ago.' He said, 'That's my story and I'm sticking with it.'"

I held a press conference on April 9, making it clear that I would not negotiate with either the governor or the legislature to chair the commission. "When I agreed to chair the commission—without any compensation—I promised Governor Cuomo and the people of New York that I would pursue the investigation with the relentless energy, persistence, and determination that it demands. Nothing has shaken my resolve." I closed by saying, "I have been in public service long enough to know that no one is indispensable. It is the independent commission that is important, not who chairs it."

Immediately following my press conference, Cuomo released a statement supporting me as chairman: "I asked Joe Califano to chair the Commission on Government Integrity because he had the experience, intelligence, commitment and, most importantly, the enormous personal integrity required to restore public confidence in government in this state. His statement today confirms that judgment. . . . We await the action of the Legislature."

After the press conference I flew to Atlanta to deliver a speech to a national conference on health promotion. From there, I flew to Gainesville,

Florida, arriving around midnight. That night the legislature appropriated public funds for the commission but with a requirement that all commission members be New York residents. At midnight, Cuomo held a press conference to say that the decision whether to remain as chairman was mine. The governor was prepared to veto the bill if I asked him, but the legislative leaders had warned that they would file suit if the commission were privately funded. The entire state budget, already overdue, was hung up on this issue.

I arose the following morning, delivered a breakfast speech to the Business Coalition on Health for North Central Florida, and rushed to the airport to get a plane back to Atlanta with a tight connection to Boston, where I landed at 4 P.M.

Meanwhile, the phone was ringing off the hook in my office. By mid-afternoon the governor himself was calling. My secretary explained that I was on a plane from Atlanta to Boston, but he was frustrated and furious at his inability to reach me. "For the record," he said, "I want him to know that this is embarrassing to him and to the firm."

At 5 P.M., I placed a call to Governor Cuomo from my room at the Ritz Carlton Hotel in Boston, where my wife and I were staying. Cuomo explained the legislature's bill with the requirements that all members of the commission be New York State residents and that the investigation be limited to executive agencies of the state and to local government. There was a specific prohibition against using any funds to investigate any legislators. The governor wanted my opinion on whether he should veto or sign it. "I am willing to veto their bill at your request and take a lawsuit on privately funding the commission. The other alternative is for me to sign the legislation."

I told the governor that I wasn't qualified to make a judgment on what was going on in Albany. "The decision is yours. You're the governor and I'll support whatever you decide."

"That's not good enough, Joe!" Cuomo was shouting into the phone. "I want your recommendation! I don't want any stories written that I've made a deal with the legislature!"

"Governor, I said all I have to say in my press conference yesterday."

Cuomo was screaming: "That's not good enough! What I have to say is that I am signing legislation *at your request,* so that no one can say I made a deal with the legislature!"

I suspected Cuomo was protesting too much. I now believed he had cut a deal with the legislature and wanted to use me as a sort of beard. I was not about to provide cover for what I considered a corrupt deal in which the legislature would get a pass and Cuomo would get a new chair who would not investigate whether his son was involved in matters involving milk pricing and the Javits Center.

"My recommendation is not informed," I repeated. "I don't know what the voting situation is up there, what all the other considerations and conversations are that you have with the legislature."

"You certainly have plenty of opinions about private funding! And you had plenty of Goddamn opinions about the legislature at your press conference!" Cuomo was shouting so loudly I had to hold the phone away from my ear.

"It's your call, not mine."

Cuomo then said, "Look, if I set out all the mess that's going to compromise the commission, if I take the language and take the five million, I'll commend you, say what a great guy you are, and you can wrap it up. But I must be able to say that I'm doing this *at your request.*"

"Governor, I really have no opinion on what's going on in Albany," I repeated.

"Well, will you serve or won't you serve if I have private funding?" Cuomo bellowed.

"Governor, I told you that I don't think the commission is a viable instrument with private funding. I've been telling you that for weeks."

"Well, then, if you won't request that I sign the legislation, I'll strike the legislative language [restricting the commission membership and scope of investigation], and take the five million and the lawsuits. I'll say you're willing to spend months on lawsuits. But I want you to hold hearings next Wednesday."

"Governor, this is no way to deal with this problem."

"I'm ordering you to hold hearings Wednesday! Will you hold hearings Wednesday?" He shouted.

"Governor, this is no way to deal with the problem."

"Answer me yes or no! Yes or no!! Will you hold hearings on Wednesday? Yes or no!! I want the commission to hold hearings on Wednesday and start functioning!"

"Governor, this makes no sense."

"Answer me yes or no!! If you don't answer me then I'll assume it's a no."

"Governor, don't assume anything," I said. "We are an independent commission, you should not be ordering us when and whether to hold hearings."

"If you don't answer me, I'll say that I asked you to hold hearings Wednesday and you stood mute, and therefore I had no choice but to sign the legislation!" Cuomo screeched into the phone.

"Governor, let me please repeat, whatever you decide to do, I will support you. I'm exhausted from travelling. You are under a lot of stress and exhausted."

"I'm not tired," Cuomo snapped back. "I'm rarin' to go. If you won't answer me, I'll say that I tried to make you show up and function and you wouldn't answer me."

At that point, he slammed the receiver down.

I said to Hilary, "Let me tell you what the governor said." She replied, "You don't need to. I could hear every word."

Ten minutes later, Cuomo called back and read me a statement saying his judgment was to sign the legislation. It had a sentence in it that read, "Mr. Califano *concurs* in my judgment." Governor Cuomo said, "Will you agree with that statement?"

"Governor, I do not agree with the sentence that says, I *concur*. I am *not concurring* in any judgment you are making. I will support whatever judgment you make. You make the decision, it's yours to make."

Cuomo exploded once again, this time complaining about my spokesperson Peg Breen's response to reporters that I had no opinions on anything in Albany and that the ball was in the governor's court.

"Governor, look, I tried to set this up for you. I had a press conference, I tried to move the ball forward for you so you'd get the money and be able to conduct an investigation. You decide what you want to do and I'll support you."

He insisted, "You concur in my judgment or you hold hearings on Wednesday!"

"Governor, we've been through this."

"Will you or will you not hold hearings on Wednesday?" Cuomo shouted.

"Governor, please," I said.

He said, "I'm going to go out to the press and say I ordered you to hold hearings on Wednesday and you refused to answer me, that I mentioned that to you and you laughed. If you stand mute and don't say yes, then I'm going to consider it a no and I'm going to tell the press that."

"Governor, you tell the press whatever you want to tell the press. I'm telling you that you make a decision and I will support it. I tried to do everything I could yesterday to help you in my press conference," I said.

Cuomo said, "I don't agree with your views on private funding but I respect them. Now I need you to *concur* in this decision."

"Governor, I cannot do that," I said. Now I was certain in my own mind that he had made a deal with the legislature to protect them, wanted a new chair who would not investigate his son, and was looking to me for political cover.

"Joe. You used to be smart. You're not being smart now. Why are you doing this? Just concur in my judgment."

"Governor, whatever you decide, I'll support it."

There was a pause.

Finally, Cuomo said, "Suppose I say, Mr. Califano *accepted* my judgment."

I thought for a moment, then said, "All right, that's OK with me. Because what I'm telling you is that *whatever* you decide, I will support *your* judgment.

" OK, Joe," the governor said, "I'm sorry it had to end this way. It's been a difficult time. I appreciate everything you've done. I don't have a new chairman for the commission. Do you have any ideas for chairman?"

I didn't. The phone call ended.[9]

Later Governor Cuomo issued a statement. "I have spoken with Mr. Califano. . . . We discussed the legislature's action, the difficulties that would be presented by attempting to ignore or veto it, especially the effect it might have on the Commission's work. At the conclusion of my conversation, Mr. Califano stated that he accepted my judgment. I will accept the $5 million in the budget as provided and proceed with the important work of the commission, by having a new Chairperson as soon as possible. . . . I believe Mr. Califano would have made a great Chairman and that the legislature was wrong to eliminate him and Mr. Simons."

I now wondered whether Cuomo had ever contemplated letting me go forward with the commission once I told him that I would have to investigate the Javits Center and milk-pricing decisions in which his son was reported to be involved. At the time, he said "Fine," but at this point I suspected that at that moment Cuomo decided to let me go. He wanted credit for an independent commission, but not the kind of investigation I would conduct.

The day after Cuomo acted, the *New York Times* ran an editorial, "The Legislature Humiliates Itself:"

> Legislative leaders portrayed Mr. Califano as a fiercely partisan Democrat intent on embarrassing them. Yet he is widely respected for his intelligence and evenhandedness. Mr. Califano hardly singled out the Legislature. He told the Governor that the commission should, among other things, look at the representation of the milk industry by the law firm to which his son, Andrew Cuomo, belongs.
>
> To his credit Mr. Califano refused to fight for the job, much less grovel by hinting that he would spare anyone whose wrongdoing might come to light. He rightly said no one was indispensable. Now that Mr. Califano has been removed, the Governor will have to work hard to find a replacement of equal caliber and fresh perspective on ingrown Albany.

I called Jack MacKenzie to thank him for the editorial. He said he now knew that the commission would have been compromised if I had gone to Albany to negotiate with the legislature.

The next morning, on *Gabe Pressman News 4ORUM*, Giuliani called the legislature's decision a "terrible mistake." He said, "[Joe] gave every indication that he was going to investigate all of the institutions of the state, all of the political figures that may be involved in unethical or criminal behavior, and that he wasn't going to be stopped by political interference. That's precisely the kind of person that you want to do a job like that. So, I thought the action in getting rid of him, with some of the most spurious reasons that I've ever heard . . . was pretty harmful to the reputation of the state legislature."

Cuomo sent me a nice letter calling the restrictions on the commission's membership "senseless . . . but not surprising." On April 16, he announced his decision to appoint John Feerick, dean of Fordham University Law

School, as commission chairman. Feerick conducted an honest but low-key investigation that did not look into legislators or the milk-pricing activities of the law firm in which Andrew Cuomo was a partner.*

Some good came out of this incident. With the press keeping the spotlight on, Cuomo shamed the legislature into passing an ethics bill in July. It provided for independent audits of the legislature, executive, and judiciary, and imposed financial disclosure and conflict-of-interest requirements on state and local officials. I wrote Cuomo congratulating him on "bearding the lion in his own den." Cuomo thanked me "for the energy and sacrifice you brought to this effort. . . ."

.   .   .

That summer, Justice Lewis Powell stepped down after fifteen and a half years on the Supreme Court. President Reagan nominated U.S. appellate court judge Robert Bork to replace him. Bork's staunch opposition to *Roe v. Wade* and his conservative positions on affirmative action, federal aid to parochial schools, homosexuality, and antitrust laws sparked fierce opposition to his nomination. Lingering resentment over Bork's decision to execute Nixon's order to fire Special Prosecutor Archibald Cox in the Saturday Night Massacre fueled the opposition.

Senator Ted Kennedy was leading the effort to kill Bork's nomination. With Bork scheduled to appear before the Senate Judiciary Committee beginning on September 15, Kennedy asked me to write an op-ed for the *New York Times*. On September 14, the day before Bork testified, my op-ed on the nomination appeared. The article reflected on Lyndon Johnson's blocked nomination of Justice Abe Fortas to be chief justice in 1968 and on Nixon's failed nominations of Harrold Carswell and Clement Haynsworth. Responding to the central issue—whether Bork's personal views were relevant—I wrote: "The issue is not whether Robert Bork is a brilliant lawyer and judge, which he is, nor even whether his views are extreme, which they

---

*The press revealed that the milk industry in New York contributed more than $58,000 to the governor's campaign and the Urban Dairy Political Action Committee paid $39,000 in fees to the law firm in which Andrew Cuomo was then a partner. Milk prices in New York were among the highest in the nation as a result of the powerful group of milk distributors that dominated the market until 1987, when a federal judge declared it unconstitutional for the state to prohibit New Jersey dairy farms from selling milk in the city. The ensuing burst of competition lowered prices.

are. The issue is simply what his views are. Each Senator has a duty to assess Judge Bork's social, political and legal philosophy and then to vote his or her conscience. Senators who conclude that his views are incompatible with their vision of the Court have the same obligation in 1987 as Senators Thurmond, Baker and others [who had expressed opposition to Fortas because of his liberal positions] had in 1968: to oppose the nomination, by filibuster if necessary."

On October 6, the Judiciary Committee voted 9 to 5 (with Republican senator Arlen Specter of Pennsylvania joining eight Democrats) to recommend that the Senate reject Bork, which it did, by a 58-to-42 margin.

I am more convinced than ever that professional qualification alone should not be considered a ticket to any seat on the federal bench. For years partisan gridlock and political hustling for campaign dollars have led to failures of the Congress and the White House, whether Democrat or Republican, to legislate and execute laws on a variety of matters of urgent concern to our citizens. As a result, the federal courts have become increasingly powerful architects of public policy, and those who seek such power must be judged in the spotlight of that reality. As the legislature and executive increasingly fail to act, citizens have turned to courts for policies regarding tobacco company advertising to minors, a patient's bill of rights, a remedy to Microsoft's monopoly position, restrictions on handgun sales, environmental protection, and prison reform. The battle over who fills judicial vacancies has taken on an importance unimaginable just a generation ago. Who sits in federal district and appellate courts is more significant than struggles over the federal budget, the level of defense spending, second-guessing tax policy, and whose fingers are poised to dip into the Social Security and Medicare cookie jars.

.   .   .

I had learned a lot about the importance of federal judges who sit in lower courts from Ed Williams. Now, I watched my friend Ed fight cancer the way he jousted in a courtroom. He had been operated on for colon cancer in 1977 and was cancer-free for five years. The disease then spread to his liver. He started surgery and treatment at the Lombardi Cancer Center at Georgetown Hospital. When the doctors there exhausted their medical arsenal, he went to Memorial Sloan-Kettering, determined to lick this disease. Paul Marks, then president of the hospital, told me that the chances were slim. When I asked Marks what people do in those circumstances, he said, "One of three things. They get depressed and die quickly. They try to do the things they always wanted to do, like travel and take it easy. Or they work even harder at their jobs." I had no doubt what Ed would do. He'd go back to work.

While Ed was at Sloan-Kettering in the summer of 1983, I visited him. I was coming from my first meeting of Dewey Ballantine's management committee to set the rates for distributing profits among partners. It had been an exhausting and discouraging experience. For decades, the firm had functioned in a lock-step system where partners marched together based on seniority, regardless of business produced or billable hours logged. My objective, essential to raising productivity and profits, was a system of financial rewards based on clients collared and hours worked.

I reached Williams's hospital room at ten that evening. He was lying in bed, pallid, tied to multiple tubes, his blood running through a clear plastic box next to his bed. His arms were limp by his side. He appeared to be asleep. Ed's wife, Agnes, was there. As I entered, she said, "Joe, you look exhausted."

"I am." I described to her the meeting I had just left. At that point, Ed rose up and roared, "You deserve it. You put together that partnership agreement for our firm and then you left for HEW. Now you know what you've put me through all these years!"

I couldn't help smiling. "Agnes, he's going to be fine. He hasn't lost a beat. He's still pissed about my leaving to go into government."

But Ed wasn't fine. When the Sloan-Kettering doctors exhausted all their ideas, he persisted, moving next to Dana Farber in Boston. When that institution ran out of options, Ed went to the National Cancer Institute, where he received experimental interleukin treatment. After the first round, he and I had lunch at the Metropolitan Club. His skin was burned and peeling as though he had been out in the sun too long. As he sipped a martini, he told me that he could not go back for a second round. "The hallucinations. The pain. I just can't do it."

My last dinner at the Palm with Ed came in the spring of 1988. Over drinks and steak, since we both knew he was dying, we were in a valedictory mood. I asked, "What's the most important thing you've ever learned?"

"Always leave a light in the window. For the kids. So they know they always have a home to come to whatever happens to them, whatever they've done."

I took my last trip with Ed Williams that May, back to our alma mater, Holy Cross. We flew up to Worcester in Ed's private jet with Ben Bradlee and Art Buchwald, for commencement exercises. Ed was so weak he had to leave early from a small dinner that the college president, Father John Brooks, hosted the evening before. Ed barely made it through the graduation ceremonies the next day.

On a Saturday morning in August, I visited Ed at Georgetown Hospital. He was no longer a six-foot-one-inch massive tower of energy; this powerful man's once thick legs and arms were now down to the bones. He had to muster his energy even to whisper. I left his room briefly and was standing at the nurse's station. When a nurse entered his room and asked Agnes who the man by the nurse's station was, I heard Ed say, "That's not just some man. That's my friend." Those were the last words I heard him utter.

He was alive when I left him to go to 5:30 Mass at Holy Trinity Church. When I returned home, Hilary was outside on the steps crying. I knew Ed was dead. Hilary told me that Agnes wanted me at the hospital. I went immediately. I called the newspapers to report the death of a giant. To a *Washington Post* reporter's question, I answered, "He was the best—the best father, the best husband, the best lawyer, the best partner, the best friend . . . and he was extraordinarily brave."

That evening, Hilary and I went to the Palm for dinner. I recalled how Ed was the brother I'd never had. He was always there when I needed him, at every critical moment of my life, from the time we became partners. He stood up for my son Joe at his confirmation, and I chuckled as I remembered the Bible he gave him, with this inscription, "If you read this every day—and listen to your Mom and Dad—you will never have to call me for advice."

Vice President George Bush and his family were seated at the next table. When we told him that Ed Williams had just died, he came over, sat with us, and said that Ed had been of great help to one of his children. He asked me where the wake would be. He stopped there quietly the following evening for a private visit with Agnes and the children. He was on his way to New Orleans to be nominated as his party's presidential candidate.

At Ed's funeral, where I served as a pallbearer with Bradlee, Buchwald, Valenti, Vince Fuller, Brendan Sullivan, and others, I thought of how much fun Ed Williams had made lawyering and how different my life would be without him.

With the death of Ed Williams I found myself thinking more about how I was spending my own life as a Washington lawyer. I reflected on the experiences of Abe Fortas and Clark Clifford. Clifford and Fortas knew the secrets of Washington, who was between the sheets and what was under the bed, and how to press the hot buttons of almost any legislator or regulator. They began to believe that they could achieve just about any goal for a client. Clifford could not abide being a marginal player as he lost touch with the new breed of politicians in power, so he was easily seduced by a slick Arab group to front for a bank (which lent money to politicians), in an arrangement that ended his career in scandal. A sense of ethical invulnerability and greed brought down Fortas.

I did not consider myself any better able to resist the temptations of power and money than those men, each of whom had given years of commendable service to his country in Washington. Lawyering at its finest is a noble profession, one to which I devoted a good part of my life (and made money doing so). I subscribed wholeheartedly to Ed Williams's commitment to the proposition that in our society everyone is entitled to representation, but I was no longer prepared to represent every interest, regardless of my personal views. I began to feel that in my lawyering I was devoting much of my time and talent to proving (to borrow from Cole Porter) that anything goes: "good's bad today and black's white today and day's night today."

.   .   .

In September 1978 the Carter administration had its finest hour. The President held Israeli Prime Minister Menachem Begin and Egyptian President Anwar Sadat at Camp David for thirteen days, until they reached an agreement on governing Sinai, the West Bank, and the Gaza Strip. The two leaders signed on September 17. The following day I penned this note to President Carter:

Dear Mr. President,
    Whatever achievements lie ahead for you—and they are many—last evening will rank as one of the greatest of the century. I have long believed

that it is one thing to be elected President and quite another for a man to become President. Yesterday, you decisively became President of this great nation.

Two months later, I traveled to Egypt and Israel and met with ministers of health, education, and social services. My purpose was to do my part to help bring peace to this troubled region, the place where my religion was born. We signed agreements designed to engage the United States as catalyst in order to get Egyptian and Israeli professionals in those fields to work together on common problems. The ministers in both countries were enthusiastic about having health care professionals, educators, and social service providers join forces on matters of common concern, such as schistosomiasis (a parasitic disease that plagues Middle Eastern peoples), medical education, and social service delivery. Subsequent secretaries did not share my interest in the Middle East; they were frustrated by the difficulty of getting Arabs and Israelis together. So the agreements I negotiated were not carried out.

Early in 1982 Leonard Hausman, then a professor at Brandeis University, visited me to promote the idea that we could do through the private sector what I had tried to do in the government. "Why not found an academically based institute, a private not-for-profit, that can bring Israelis and Arabs together the way you wanted to at HEW?" he asked.

My initial reaction was that no such an undertaking could succeed. Hausman argued that academics in Israel and Egypt tended to be more open-minded and liberal; "by Middle Eastern standards even peacenik," he added. This, he said, made an academic base even better than the government. I doubted it could work. Hausman was at Brandeis, a predominantly Jewish university that would have little credibility in Egypt or the Arab world. I kept saying no. Hausman refused to accept my answer. He came by my office a half dozen times over the rest of the year, repeatedly insisting that I, "especially as a non-Jew," could do it.

I told Hausman that I had no experience in Middle East politics. My only exposure to Arab culture was when Aga Kahn retained me to persuade CBS to edit its portrayal of his father, Aly Kahn, in the network's 1983 docudrama on Aly's ex-wife, *Rita Hayworth: the Love Goddess*. Aga Kahn found two scenes offensive. In one, when Rita Hayworth discovered her husband, Aly

Kahn, with a mistress, he was portrayed as saying that Ismaili Muslims were entitled to a wife and all the mistresses they wanted. In the other, he said that as an Ismaili Muslim, he inherited from God his father's position as religious leader of his people. Both statements were incorrect. I asked CBS president Gene Jankowski to delete the scenes, a matter of less than two minutes in the film. He initially refused. I then wrote him, noting that if a Catholic or a Jew were depicted as making statements that were as blatantly incorrect about their religious tenets, CBS would make the changes, but because it was a Muslim and an Arab they were refusing to do so. I set out the accurate beliefs of Ismaili Muslims (they could have four wives; Aly Kahn did not receive from God the mantle of religious leader). I warned that my client and I were ready to go public with the issue if the network did not act. On his own, Jankowski made the changes over the objection of creative types on the West Coast, who leaked to a newspaper gossip columnist that he had caved under pressure because I was Bill Paley's son-in-law.

Hausman persisted. Moved by his commitment, intelligence, and tenacity—and flattered by the way he fed my ego—I agreed to found with Hausman the Institute for Social and Economic Policy in the Middle East. The institute would be based at Brandeis; it would pursue the same objectives—getting Arab and Israeli professionals to meet and work together—and be founded on the same principle as the aborted HEW agreements: politicians make pacts; people make peace. I agreed to chair such an institute with Hausman as its director. At its founding, the institute had no money, no staff, and no board, and there was not even the glimmer of a Middle East peace process.

Our first foray brought to Brandeis five Israeli and five Egyptian physicians to identify areas of common concern in the field of health care and medical research. The Israelis were easily persuaded to join this effort. The Egyptians were harder to persuade. Finally, remembering my 1978 meetings with the health minister of Egypt in the wake of the Camp David accords, they eventually signed on. We held a conference at Brandeis in March 1983. By mid-1985 we had professional health-training courses ready to go in Boston and Texas for groups of Arabs and Israelis.

Then in October, Palestinian Liberation Organization (PLO) terrorists hijacked the *Achille Lauro,* an Italian cruise ship in the Mediterranean. They fatally shot and flung overboard an American passenger, a wheelchair-bound retired Jewish businessman, Leon Klinghoffer. Our fledgling program fell apart.

Shaken, disappointed, but undeterred by this and the deterioration of the Arab-Israeli situation, in early 1987 Hausman and I visited the Middle East to try again to start our institute. During our visit it became apparent that we had no credibility in Jordan or with Palestinians.

Back in America Hausman and I shared our problem with Henry Taub, founding chair of the data processing company ADP. Taub, one of our early contributors and a successful businessman, said, "I suggest you talk to Cardinal O'Connor. He's head of Catholic Near East and he might be willing to help you." Catholic Near East, the American Church's effort to help the poor in the Middle East, had credibility and contacts with the Jordanians and Palestinians through its charitable work and through Bethlehem University, a Catholic college on the West Bank.

Looking at me, a Catholic visible in public life, Taub, a Jewish leader, said. "Just call the cardinal."

"I don't know him," I said, embarrassed.

"He's a good friend of mine," Taub said, with a twinkle in his eye. "I'll introduce you."

Taub arranged a breakfast at the cardinal's residence on Madison Avenue in May 1987. Over scrambled eggs and bacon, this remarkable prelate listened to our idea and promised to help. As I listened to Taub and O'Connor talk, I thought, only in New York City could a successful Jewish businessman put together the nation's top cardinal and a lay Catholic in such a high-risk enterprise.

Hausman and I then embarked on a fifteen-day trip to the Middle East in June. We visited Israel, Egypt, and Jordan in an effort to set up seminars on economic, political, and social issues and to launch a fellowship program that would bring Arab and Israeli health professionals in mid-career to Boston to live under the same roof, study together, and earn advanced degrees at Brandeis University. Cardinal O'Connor had provided us with contacts at Bethlehem University and other institutions on the West Bank. In Jordan, a Jesuit priest gave us access to King Hussein. We gained commitments from local leaders, as well as the Israeli prime minister and King Hussein, to recruit fellows into our program.

When we returned, we reported to O'Connor. On the spot the cardinal agreed to chair the fellowship program and volunteered to contribute one million dollars to get it off the ground. He set only one condition: he did not want any credit or publicity. Brandeis president Evelyn Handler and I announced the program, and the cardinal's leadership, to a small group of supporters at Brandeis House in Manhattan on August 27, 1987. She was such a reluctant participant and so personally antagonistic—I thought rude—to the cardinal that I decided to get the institute out of Brandeis.

Remembering how committed Harvard President Derek Bok was to making the Kennedy School of Government at Harvard a launching pad for innovative programs, I called him. He was intrigued and urged me to talk to Graham Allison, then dean of the Kennedy School. Allison reacted with enthusiasm. By the fall of 1988, the Institute for Social and Economic Policy in the Middle East at the Kennedy School of Government at Harvard University was formed. Our board became a board of advisors, which I chaired. Cardinal O'Connor and Alexander Haig became vice chairs; Hausman gave up tenure at Brandeis for a non-tenured position at the Kennedy School.

The institute fellowship program was designed to enable mid-career health professionals—hospital administrators, public health officials, physicians, nurses, clinic directors—to come to Harvard, study at the Kennedy School or the School of Public Health, or both, and after a year receive a master's degree in public administration or public health. The program required students—Arab and Jewish Israelis, Palestinians, Jordanians, and Egyptians—to live together. In the early days, some Palestinians and Jordanians feared for their lives if, upon their return home, some of their colleagues found out that they had lived with a Jew. Many risked their lives and reputations by committing to such an enterprise.

In September 1993, Israeli Prime Minister Yitzhak Rabin and PLO leader Yasser Arafat signed a new peace accord in Washington granting limited self-rule to Palestinians living in Gaza and the West Bank. In 1994, shortly after the Palestinian Authority was established, Kenneth Lipper, Wall Street money manager and producer of Oliver Stone's *Wall Street,* and his wife, Evelyn, donated one million dollars to our institute with a mandate that we help Arafat organize his government. Hausman and I (and my wife, Hilary) visited Arafat in Gaza in September 1994.

We arrived in Jerusalem on a Thursday. On Sunday afternoon, we had tea with Leah Rabin, the Israeli prime minister's wife. Then we drove in two

Israeli taxis to the border of the Palestinian Authority on the Gaza Strip. It was dark, about nine in the evening, when we arrived. Cars from the Palestinian Authority were supposed to meet us at the border, but only a pickup truck—with several teenagers with AK-47s and other automatic weapons slung over their shoulders—was there. We followed the trucks to Arafat's headquarters on the beachfront. Hilary was extremely nervous. Our driver, Rafi, remarked that, because we were in an Israeli cab, we had to stay close behind the truck in order to avoid being stoned by angry Palestinians.

We raced through Gaza and its abject poverty. Rafi told us that most of the young were unemployed; men were fortunate to make a dollar a day. We arrived at Arafat's headquarters just before 10 P.M. We waited an hour before he saw us. In the anteroom were young English and American Palestinians, well educated, who had come to help put this government together. Everyone carried a gun either in a shoulder holster or tucked into his waist.

Arafat had a rectangular table extending from the middle of his desk. He sat behind his desk; we sat around the table. He apologized for being late. "You see, I had to mediate a dispute between two tribes. A member of one killed a member of another. These matters take much time."

I wondered whether Arafat was one of those revolutionaries who can do battle but are incapable of governing. It's the next generation, I thought, those young men from the United States and England that we saw while waiting, who offer hope of putting a governing system together, not this warrior with the stubble beard. We discussed the institute's providing help for his new government and sending experts from Harvard to Gaza.

That December, Arafat and Rabin jointly received the Nobel Peace Prize. On October 24, 1995, Arafat made his first speech on an American campus at Harvard University, funded through the Lipper grant. Less than two weeks later, on November 5, Yitzhak Rabin was assassinated by a right-wing Israeli and the world's hope for peace was set back.

Tragically, Arafat had no ability (or desire) to govern. Government, economic, and public policy experts from Harvard were unable to organize a tax system, labor department, or health care or social service system because of the corruption, ineptitude, and personal politics with which the Palestinian National Authority was riddled. The well-educated young Palestinians from abroad grew frustrated and returned to England and the United States.

Nevertheless, there were small steps forward. Almost one hundred fellows have been trained at Harvard's Kennedy School, School of Public Health, and Graduate School of Education and received master's degrees from those institutions. These fellows are hospital and health clinic directors, public health professionals, journalists, medical researchers, social workers, educators, economists, and businessmen—the kind of professional leaders whose working together is the stuff of lasting peace.[10] From Egypt, Israel (Arab and Jew), Jordan, Lebanon, Morocco, the Palestinian Authority, Saudi Arabia, Syria, and Tunisia, they formed an Alumni Society to meet in Jerusalem and in a different Middle Eastern capital alternatively each year.

Along with the fellowship program, we assembled working groups of experts from Israel, the Palestinian Authority, Jordan, Egypt, and other Islamic countries to develop plans for economic development, trade, water policy, and Palestinian refugees. These groups enriched the peace process, often providing basic concepts and data in specific areas of negotiation like the Israeli-Palestinian trade agreement signed in Paris in April 1994.[11]

Over two years, we held a series of extraordinary meetings of Egyptians, Israelis, Jordanians, Lebanese, Palestinians, and Syrians to discuss and develop economic plans for the Middle East. We also held conferences on the water problems and were beginning meetings on the status of Jerusalem, topics that intellectuals and experts could discuss in ways politicians dared not.

For thirteen years, I served as chairman of the institute's unique board of Arabs and Jews, Muslims and Christians, from the United States, the United Kingdom, and the Middle East. In 1997 we realized a dream: that an Arab and a Jew would co-chair the board. Mahmoud Abdel Aziz and Poju Zabludowicz took over. I stepped down to become founding chair, while Cardinal O'Connor and General Haig became founding vice chairs.

In 1998 the institute was scrapped by Harvard Kennedy School dean Joseph Nye, who had little interest in the endeavor. My disappointment was profound. Nevertheless, the alumni association of Israelis and Arabs continued their annual get-together until the crisis between Ariel Sharon and Arafat in 2001.

I took home a lesson of great importance from developing the institute: the non-political professional elites are fed up with conflict and killing and yearn for peace. Despite heartbreaking setbacks—and the end of our institute was one—I believe that these elites will see that peace will come to the Middle East.

.   .   .

In addition to pro bono activities, I sought to cushion my dwindling interest and fermenting disenchantment with the private practice of law by joining several corporate boards of directors, beginning with Chrysler.

I had first met Lee Iacocca at 11 A.M. on February 4, 1966, when he accompanied Henry Ford to my office in the White House West Wing. They came to express opposition to the auto safety bill President Johnson had proposed.

Ford had earlier complained to the President, who sent him to me. Ford did almost all the talking, flashing his support for the President personally and as a big-time donor and fundraiser. He was polite but angry. The red of resentment and impatience rose in his face at having to explain to a thirty-four-year-old White House aide how the bill would undermine confidence in the auto industry.

He claimed that the proposed requirements for seat belts and other safety measures would break the Big Three car companies and sharply jack up prices for buyers. "They could not have been thought of by anyone who knows a damn thing about the industry," he concluded, to put me in my place and imply that I had misled the President.

"We consider this one of the President's major proposals," I said. Though buried in the State of the Union message amid scores of more sweeping measures, auto safety had acquired a life of its own. Johnson's proposal, coming soon after Ralph Nader's book *Unsafe at Any Speed*, had pushed auto safety near the top of virtually every news story the morning after the State of the Union.

Ford responded with his line in the sand. "If there's going to be a bill, the President should not include any criminal penalties for failure to comply." On this point, Iacocca chimed in. While they opposed even civil fines, both men thought it "outrageous that criminal penalties were even under consideration." I promised Ford and Iacocca to discuss their concerns with the President.

When I reported the conversation to LBJ, he told me to eliminate the criminal penalties in the bill. I argued that, with 50,000 deaths on the road every year, our liberal allies in Congress would demand criminal sanctions. "We'll be accused of having a weak bill if we don't include them in what we send up," I said.

Johnson cut me off. "We don't have to antagonize Henry Ford. You call him and tell him that just for him I'm taking the criminal penalties out of the bill we send forward."

I tried once more. "Congress will never enact your criminal penalties," LBJ snapped impatiently. "We might as well get credit for dropping them."

On June 21 the Senate Commerce Committee approved the proposal for an auto safety bill with civil penalties of $1,000 for each violation, but struck down a motion to include criminal penalties. The House passed the Senate bill, and on September 9 Johnson signed the Traffic Safety and Highway Safety Acts.

I never saw Iacocca again while I was in government, but our paths crossed when Ed Williams and I were law partners during the seventies. Our firm did some legal work for Iacocca, and Ed and I occasionally joined up with him and his pal Bill Fugazy at P.J. Clarke's, one of our favorite late-night stops in Manhattan.

On July 14, 1978, while I was secretary of Health, Education, and Welfare, I read that Henry Ford had abruptly fired Iacocca. The black-and-white photo of Iacocca was striking; it revealed a hurt so deep that I called him. "Lee, don't be so down. This could be one of the best things that ever happened to you."

One year later, the morning after President Jimmy Carter announced that he had asked for and accepted my resignation, Iacocca called.

"Joe," he said. "You told me that being fired by Henry Ford *could* turn out to be *one* of the best things that ever happened to me. Well, let me tell you this. Getting fired by this guy Carter *is the* best thing that ever happened to you."

Iacocca had taken over Chrysler in September 1978. With the company on the brink of bankruptcy, joined by United Automobile Workers (UAW) president Douglas Fraser, Iacocca persuaded Congress and President Carter to provide $1.5 billion dollars in loan guarantees to keep the automaker afloat. As part of the deal, Iacocca agreed to put the union leader on the Chrysler board, a first for a Fortune 500 company.

I watched from the sidelines as Chrysler struggled. In early 1981, Iacocca invited me to join the Chrysler board of directors. "I've got a weak board," he said. I asked him what the time commitment was. "A couple of days a month and an emergency meeting now and then. This company's a God-damn disaster!"

I was flattered, but declined. I had just started my own law firm and could not devote that much time to another enterprise.

A few weeks later, Iacocca called again. "Meet me in New York," he said. "I want you on this board; you can really help me and Chrysler."

On March 23, 1981, we met at 2:30 P.M. in Iacocca's Waldorf Towers suite. Our talks continued through dinner at Romeo Salta on West 56th Street. Iacocca was aghast at Chrysler's health care costs. "They'll break this company if we don't do something."

My efforts at HEW to alert American businesses to the dangers of rising health care costs had been like twigs snapping in an abandoned forest. No one heard. But now the noise was deafening to Iacocca.

"Look," Lee said. "We'll set up a board health care committee. You, Doug Fraser, me. The three of us did more to create this mess than any three people in America. You with your Great Society programs. Fraser with his crazy demands for health care benefits in union contacts. And me—I agreed to damn near every one of them."

I couldn't help smiling.

Between forkfuls of pasta spiked with tomato sauce and sautéed red peppers, Iacocca added, "You say you want to do something about health care costs. Well, you chair the committee. All those ideas you couldn't do in Washington because of the politicians, we'll do every one of them."

I was tempted. I wanted a chance to test the potential of the private sector to contain costs and push health promotion and disease prevention. I promised to get back to Lee within a few days. Back in Washington, I visited Bob McNamara, who had worked with Iacocca at Ford. McNamara urged me to accept. "The company can't possibly survive. It'll go under in six months. But do it. You'll learn more about business from Lee in this situation in six months than you'll learn anywhere else in six years."

On June 4, 1981, I was elected to the Chrysler board of directors. Lee established the Health Care Committee the same day. No other corporate board had such a committee. After the meeting, Lee took me aside. "Buy a ton of stock," he said, "and you'll make a lot of money." Unfortunately, reacting to McNamara's comments, I bought only a few shares, even though the stock was selling at about two dollars a share.

At the second board meeting I attended, Iacocca opened by scrapping the prepared agenda. "We have to decide today whether to sell the headquarters at Highland Park in order to meet the payroll. Gerry Greenwald [Chrysler's number two in command and top financial officer] will take us through the pros and cons." As Greenwald spoke, I feared that McNamara's six months was optimistic.

As I dug into Chrysler's health care costs, I found the company was paying more for health care than for steel. If Chrysler was to defy the *Wall Street Journal*'s injunction to "die with dignity," we had to wrestle them to the mat. The Chrysler plan paid it all: no deductibles or copayments, giving employees and retirees and their families the greatest free lunch since saloons gave away food with five-cent beer. To top it off, Chrysler, with only 61,000 active workers, was paying health care expenses for 107,000 retirees and employees who had been laid off. The bill was gushing toward half a billion dollars a year.

Chrysler's system was not only profligate; there were no controls to prevent outright corruption. Doctors were charging for performing two appendicitis operations on the same patient. Podiatrists were treating foot problems one toe at a time to ratchet up their fees. Prescription drugs were overused and abused. In a twelve-month period, one Chrysler employee obtained fifty-one prescriptions for 6,030 ten-milligram Valium pills; another had eighty-eight prescriptions filled for 2,376 five-milligram Dilaudids. Both drugs had high street value for sale to addicts.[12]

Our first committee meeting with Doug Fraser did not go well. I suggested that we institute a gatekeeper system under which employees would be required to go though a primary care physician before they could see a specialist and that we put all employees in health maintenance organizations. Fraser balked.

"This would take away their free choice," Fraser argued.

I reminded him: "When you visited me at HEW to press for a national health plan, and I said Americans would not stand for denial of their choice of a physician, you called it 'nonsense.' You said, 'They'll get used to it.'"

Fraser smiled. "Today I'm representing my union members."[13]

We put in place for non-union employees all the controls and incentives that I tried unsuccessfully to institute under Medicare and Medicaid: second opinions for non-emergency surgery; use of generic drugs whenever available; screens on physicians, procedures, and prescriptions; health promotion and disease prevention incentives. We launched an anti-smoking campaign (the cost of health care for Chrysler employees who smoked averaged 75 percent higher than for non-smokers). We imposed limits on hospitalizations and lengths of stays. In 1984, the first full year of our plan, we saved $58 million.[14]

We expected another big reduction two years later when the UAW agreed to similar provisions in its health plan. To our surprise, that further reduction never materialized. When we interviewed doctors to find out why, we discovered that as physicians changed the way they practiced medicine to accommodate the new Chrysler rules for non-union employees, they put the same changes in place for all their other patients. As a result, we were already realizing the savings.

Business, I started thinking, was key to changing our national health care system. It was uninhibited by the political interests that knotted up government. Within a couple of years at Chrysler, we had reduced costs but also had a notable failure. Costs of treating substance abuse and addiction (largely involving alcohol, marijuana, and cocaine) continued to rise at a double-digit rate at Chrysler and throughout the auto industry. Some progress was later made by improving prevention programs, and by training supervisors to spot substance abusers, get them into treatment, and deal with recovering workers after treatment.

As Chrysler prospered and paid off its government loan years ahead of time, the bold, outspoken Iacocca became a national folk hero. He was even being mentioned as a presidential candidate to succeed Ronald Reagan. Iacoccamania erupted. His memoir, *Iacocca*, moved out of bookstores at a rate of 15,000 copies a day and hit the top of the bestseller list. Lee headed the foundation to restore Ellis Island and the Statue of Liberty for its Fourth of July centennial celebration.*

Chrysler publicists positioned Iacocca as a national hero who turned a

---

*Interior Secretary Donald Hodel fired Iacocca from the Statue of Liberty-Ellis Island Centennial Commission in February 1986. Many charged that the George H.W. Bush campaign feared Iacocca's publicity would overshadow the vice president, who was intent on succeeding Reagan.

major corporation around and took a stand about buying American rather than Japanese. They had him claim he did not intend to enter the race, but I knew that deep down Lee harbored a desire to run for the presidency. Lee loved the attention. He began to believe all the glorious things that were written about him. His poll numbers topped those of presidential candidates like Mario Cuomo, Jack Kemp, and Bob Dole. There were even (ridiculous) rumors that I would be his running mate.

To keep him in the Washington limelight and expose him to the capital's power elite, Hilary and I gave a party for him in the spring of 1985. With publicity about Iacocca at a fever pitch, an invitation became one of the season's hottest tickets. Guests included political columnist David Broder, Ben Bradlee and Sally Quinn, Meg Greenfield, Kay Graham, Democratic National Committee chairman Paul Kirk, Dick Gephardt, and others. After I delivered a brief toast, Lee rose and unfortunately delivered an endless tirade about trade and the Japanese.

Time White House photographer Diana Walker wrote, in thanking my wife for the party, "I thought that Lee Baby talked too long about nothing." George Stevens, head of the American Film Institute and a committed liberal Democrat, said, "Lee really blew it. He lost his chance to be president at your dinner party." I had the same feeling. Within a few weeks, word of Iacocca's talk that evening made the gossip circuit; all too soon the Chrysler chairman was seen among the press corps and in the thin air of the capital's high political altitude as someone who lacked the political pitch to be a serious presidential candidate.

There is a difference, however, between Washington and the rest of the country. Two years after Washington's beltway establishment had written Iacocca off, he was the subject of a wave of draft movements. By now, Lee had concluded that he did not have the stomach or sufficiently thick skin for a presidential run. So at his request I assigned my partner Myles Lynk to monitor the Federal Elections Commission and take action to remove Iacocca's name from state primary ballots.

National publicity and widespread adulation changed Lee. He came to believe that by his stature alone, he could realize his dream: Global Motors, a worldwide auto company. His first effort to this end was to unite Chrysler and Fiat. In October 1990, Iacocca was in secret talks with Gianni Agnelli, the Italian tycoon who controlled Fiat, about a possible combination with

Chrysler. When my father in-law, Bill Paley, died that month, Agnelli came over to pay his respects to the family of his deceased friend. Sitting in a corner of Paley's Fifth Avenue apartment the day before the memorial service, Agnelli began probing me about Iacocca: Had Lee stopped working hard? Was he so full of himself that he would be impossible to work with? Did Lee still have the fire to knuckle down and put two companies together? Would he devote sufficient time and energy to put Fiat on the map in the United States, alongside Chrysler?

Agnelli feared that Iacocca would not exhaust himself in the trenches to meld together these two proud and independent companies, continents apart. I surmised as I listened to him that the Fiat deal would never go forward. Though I deflected Agnelli's questions and kept changing the subject, I heard enough of his doubts at the start of our conversation to signal the announcement that came a few days later, after six months of talks, that Chrysler and Fiat had abandoned any joint venture or merger.

As Iacocca neared Chrysler's retirement age of sixty-five, he worked less and became something of a caricature of his own public persona. Starring in the widely seen television commercials had given him a celebrity status equal to that of a Hollywood actor or rock star. Leo Kelmenson, a top Iacocca advisor and chairman of the agency that designed Chrysler's ad campaigns, told me he thought that the commercials, and the celebrity, had changed Lee from a hungry, ambitious worker to someone decidedly different. Knowing how Iacocca treasured the notoriety and perks of corporate power—private jet, bodyguards, constant attention—the board expected him to resist stepping down. The Chrysler directors conducted their own search and selected Robert Eaton to succeed Lee. The issue came to a head over the press release announcing the shift.

The board had designated me to work out the final version with Lee. We met over a lunch at the new Chrysler headquarters. Iacocca came with a draft about Eaton and his own retirement, but with no mention of a firm date for stepping down as chairman. I raised this issue. Lee admitted that he and the board had agreed that the date should be December 31, 1992. I asked Lee to make the correction, which he did in his own hand. When we issued the press release, Iacocca exploded, claiming that he had never agreed to the date. We were able to show him the date in his own writing, and Eaton assumed the posts of chairman and CEO on January 1, 1993. When Iacocca later sided with Kirk Kerkorian in the corporate raider's attempt to take over Chrysler, the board reversed its decision to name the new headquarters building after Lee, the retired chairman who had saved the company.

It was a sad ending for Lee, an icon genuinely regarded an American folk hero. He could have built on his success at Chrysler to have a great impact on almost any subject he chose. But, he never really committed to anything. What led to this and to Lee's bumpy exit? An extraordinary leader, he became too focused on accumulating wealth and fame. For me, his tragedy was captured in his remarks to me after spending an afternoon on Kirk Kerkorian's yacht at the 1992 Olympics in Spain. Lee returned talking about the kind of money it must take to live like Kerkorian. Like too many CEOs, it seemed to me, Lee had come to measure his own worth by comparing his income with that of other chief executives. In valuing his stature by money and celebrity, Lee belittled himself, what he had accomplished, and what he was capable of doing.

.   .   .

As I lost interest in practicing law, I joined several other corporate boards, including ADP (Automatic Data Processing), Kmart, and Northrop Grumman. When William Woodside asked me to join the American Can Company board, life has come full circle, I thought. As a young associate my work on the American Can tax case was such a dreary experience that it hastened my exit from the world of Wall Street corporate law. Now I would be on the company's board. (American Can evolved into Primerica, Travelers Group, and finally Citigroup). These boards, and others, gave me an extraordinary education about American business at its best and worst, a ringside seat to troublesome issues of corporate governance and the extent to which profits—and greed—drive too many corporate executives.

I got a snapshot of the excessive exuberance of corporate America. When Woodside retired in January 1987, he was succeeded by his hand-picked choice, Gerald Tsai. The retirement party Tsai gave for Woodside was a giddy event at the Tivoli Hotel in Manhattan. In courting his wife, Migs, Woodside had driven recklessly fast to and from Connecticut on so many evenings that he amassed a record number of speeding tickets. Eventually Woodside required some heavy legal lifting to maintain his driver's license.

The highlight of the evening came when Tsai rolled in Woodside's retirement present—a red Ferrari. Everyone cheered. It was a high-altitude event even for the high-flying 1980s.

My experience on these boards—and a number of others—confirmed my instinct that I would not find in business any greater satisfaction than I was finding in the private practice of law. I came to appreciate and understand the pride that a Sandy Weill experiences in building a great financial-services company like Citigroup, that Iacocca knew in saving Chrysler, and that a Henry Taub found in starting ADP and Frank Lautenberg, Josh Weston, and Art Weinbach felt in taking the company to premier stature. I enjoyed the sense of being a small part of building these private enterprises, but my energies would have to be spent on a different kind of building.

CHAPTER 31

A New Life

B Y THE CLOSE of the 1980s, I knew that practicing law in New York and Washington was not for me. I missed the sense of purpose and excitement of government service. Nothing in my current practice matched the thrill of representing the *Washington Post* during the Watergate era. Dewey Ballantine was becoming a mega-firm with rising profits. For most hard-driving partners this was an ultimate measure of success. For me, the firm had become another way station. I felt fungible—the corporate counseling, lawyering, and Washington lobbying that I provided clients was available from a host of similarly situated attorneys. I experienced a frustration in representing narrow interests of clients, in being the agent rather than the actor.

The world of mergers and acquisitions that kept partners and associates awake and alert for endless hours put me to sleep. I found the perpetual hustle for corporate clients as demeaning as LBJ had found pandering for political contributions. I found myself wondering how much better our nation would be if the monumental concentration of brain power, energy, and creativity assembled at the law firm were devoted to revitalizing public schools, fashioning effective incentives for environmental protection and corporate responsibility, reducing poverty, or reforming cumbersome civil and criminal court systems. My partners, men like Harvey Kurzweil and Fred Kanner, were talented, hardworking professionals and fine people. But Dewey Ballantine was a suit that did not fit me.

I had none of the satisfaction of trying to make the world, or some part of it, a little better. I did not believe that I was putting the talents God had given me, my experience, and my good fortune to best use. I was itching to take on another task in life but had no idea where I could make a difference. I got a spark of encouragement at a dinner with Lady Bird Johnson at the LBJ Library. As we got up from the table, she put her hands on my arms and looked at me. "Joe, you were so young when you worked for Lyndon. How old are you now?"

"I'm sixty, Mrs. Johnson," I answered.

"Well, let me give you some advice," she said. "Between now and seventy-five you work very hard and play very hard. Because after that it gets a little difficult."

I began to reflect on my experience in search of clues for the best way to commit my energies.

Much of my Navy time in the Office of the Judge Advocate General had been spent defending, on appeal, sailors and marines convicted at courts martial of illegal drug- (usually marijuana) and alcohol-related offenses—either for possession or drunkenness, or for assaults and rapes committed while high on such substances.

While on President Johnson's staff, I helped push through Congress the Drug Rehabilitation Act of 1966, authorizing the first federal funds to treat addicts. We requested $15 million; in our wildest estimates we never thought the annual appropriation would exceed $50 million. By the 1990s, federal spending for treatment topped $2 billion.

In preparing President Johnson's message on crime, we recommended (a first for any national leader) that, in the absence of disorderly conduct or some other offense, states treat drunkenness—then the nation's number one crime—as a disease requiring detoxification and treatment.

In the 1960s I had tried to consolidate law enforcement responsibilities to deal more effectively with the nation's burgeoning drug problem. Responsibility was fragmented among three agencies: the Department of Justice, the Bureau of Drug Abuse Control in the Department of Health, Education, and Welfare, and the Federal Bureau of Narcotics in the Treasury Department. I wanted to fold all these law enforcement responsibilities into the Federal Bureau of Investigation, and LBJ agreed, "If you can work it out with the cabinet officers and [FBI director J. Edgar] Hoover." There was little resistance from the cabinet officers, but Hoover opposed placing drug enforcement in the FBI. "These drug enforcement agents do not meet the Bureau's standards," he insisted, noting that all FBI agents had to be either attorneys or certified public accountants. In meetings with the FBI director, I learned his rock-bottom fear: drug money might corrupt his own agents. As Hoover and I tussled over this issue, Drew Pearson, then Washington's top exposé columnist, began writing about corruption in the drug enforcement bureaus in Treasury and HEW. I assumed Hoover was leaking these stories. When President Johnson read the second Pearson column, he called me. "You'd better make peace with Hoover on this reorganization."

"I'm trying to get him to take these bureaus into the FBI."

"He doesn't want it. He won't have it. He's already making his case to the Hill that they don't belong in the FBI. If you don't make a deal with him, you'll soon see Pearson asking whether you're covering up corrupt drug enforcement."

With that, the President hung up. I settled for Hoover's acceptance of a plan to create in the Justice Department an independent Bureau of Narcotics and Dangerous Drugs that would report directly to the attorney general and not be part of the FBI. The news stories and Pearson columns on corruption in drug enforcement agencies ended.[1]

After I left the White House in 1969, I served as a member of the Special Committee on Crime Prevention and Control in the District of Columbia. We tried to focus public attention on the district's epidemic of heroin addiction and the related rise in crime.

As secretary of Health, Education, and Welfare in 1977, as I pressed the anti-smoking campaign, people interested in fighting alcoholism and alcohol abuse asked me to take up their cause. Mercedes McCambridge, the movie actress who had won an Oscar for her portrayal of the tough political hatchet in *All The King's Men*, the 1949 film classic inspired by Louisiana governor Huey P. Long, visited me. "You talk about tobacco all the time, but you never talk about alcoholism. That's an even worse problem. I know. I've been through it. I struggle with it every day." We went to work preparing a program on alcoholism that I announced in May of 1979. When President Carter asked for my resignation in July, the program fizzled.

In the early 1980s at Governor Hugh Carey's request, I had studied substance abuse in New York. On Chrysler's board of directors, I confronted the difficulty in reducing alcohol, marijuana, and cocaine abuse and its impact on productivity and health care costs. In 1982 and 1983, as special counsel to the House Ethics Committee, I had found the widespread pill popping, illegal drug use, and abuse of alcohol among teen pages and Capitol Hill employees.

In the mid-1980s, as counsel for Johnson & Johnson, I got to know Jim Burke, chairman and CEO of the pharmaceutical company, who had brilliantly handled the crisis in the 1980s when some Tylenol capsules were laced with cyanide. Burke planned to retire and chair the Partnership for a Drug-Free America. "You could really do something about this and you ought to," he said. "There's no good public policy research out there. You could make a helluva contribution." Burke confronted me with articles I had written attacking the war on drugs as too narrowly focused on criminal punishment, interdiction, and illegal drugs and calling for more research and for the creation of a National Institute on Addiction. "Don't just write about this," he challenged. "Do something!"

I began discussing the problem of substance abuse with people around the nation—doctors, businessmen, lawyers, film and television artists and producers, editors and reporters, government officials, frontline experts in voluntary agencies, recovering alcoholics and drug addicts. I saw the problem as addiction—regardless whether the substance was alcohol, nicotine, or illegal or prescription drugs. To me, substance abuse was among the most pernicious threats to our society, and our political leaders were not facing up to it. I wasn't sure what I could do about that, but as I struggled with what role, if any, I might be able to play, it came together as I witnessed Bill Paley's desperate struggle to stay alive.

.   .   .

If I had to choose the time when I came to a new understanding of what a precious gift my faith was and that God would hold me accountable for how I used the talents He had given me, it would be the moment when my wife's father, William Paley, died.

Bill Paley's was a life of extraordinary power and affluence. He founded and dominated CBS for half a century, making it the nation's most influential broadcast network, shaping world news and American culture. He was capable of making or breaking entertainment stars and corporate executives. He was an American pasha, living amid spectacular settings in Manhasset and Southampton, Long Island, Lyford Cay in Nassau, and a Manhattan apartment filled with priceless works by Picasso, Matisse, Lautrec, and Degas. He lived to the fullest, his every desire—for food, women, and fun—satisfied. At the end he fought tenaciously to hang on.

Bill Paley had conquered emphysema in the 1950s and had quit smoking. In 1990 his eighty-nine-year-old body was losing its long struggle with that respiratory killer. He also suffered from a bone marrow disease and internal bleeding that doctors couldn't stem.

Hilary and I were at the Gritti Palace Hotel in Venice when Harvey Klein, her father's internist, summoned us home. We booked on the first plane available and went directly to his Fifth Avenue apartment.

Bill's master bedroom suite had been transformed into a high-tech hospital. This man of enormous charm, energy, intelligence, presence, wealth, and independence was locked in a self-imposed prison of modern medical technology. He was shackled to plastic and stainless-steel tubes for oxygen to help him breathe, dialysis equipment to do the work of his failed kidneys, machines to pump his blood and keep his heart beating. Tubes fed him intravenously, drained his waste, and vented blood from the internal bleeding.

That evening his team of doctors assembled, the most talented medical superstars that money and power could command. Gravely, they told Bill's six children that the end would come at most within weeks, more likely days. Five of the six initially preferred to end their father's mechanistic misery that evening, but one child, his daughter Kate, reminded them how desperately their father wanted to live. One of the doctors remarked then how terrified Bill was of dying; he wouldn't even let the nurses lower the hospital bed they'd installed from a sitting to a lying position for fear he wouldn't wake up. Bill Paley's children decided that their father would want to hang on as long as the machinery and his powerful determination to live would permit.

Two weeks later, on October 26, 1990, Hilary and I at the last minute cancelled a long-planned dinner at Primavera with Migs and Bill Woodside and Patty and John Rosenwald. Hilary felt a powerful premonition that her father was on the brink of death. We went to Bill's apartment in the late afternoon. Over the course of the evening, five of the six children gathered, along with a handful of friends, among them Ford Foundation president and CBS board member Franklin Thomas and his constant companion Kate Whitney, who was Paley's niece. Frank and I, who were not close, ended up in an extended intimate conversation about the meaning of life and death, and how much Bill Paley had achieved publicly—and missed personally—during his own life.

At 9 P.M. the doctors assembled the Paley children to tell them the situation was hopeless. So much blood had accumulated in Bill Paley's lower abdomen that it was rock hard from the pressure. The doctors said the time had come to release his body from the tubes and machinery. A few minutes later, the children went into their father's bedroom. I stood with Hilary at the foot of the bed as Bill Paley breathed his final breath. I watched as his jaw and tongue slackened, and then his shoulders, arms, and entire body collapsed into death.

It was heartbreaking for Hilary.

It was the first time I had ever watched someone die.

All that night, I lay awake next to my wife, reflecting with awe on all that this gargantuan man had built. All his money and power, I thought, had offered him little comfort as he lay dying. As I tossed, I thanked God for enriching much of my own life by His gift of faith, and I rued the fact that I had spent so much time and energy in selfish pursuits. By dawn, I had silently determined to live the rest of my life getting to know, love, and serve God better.

Bill's memorial service at Temple Emmanuel on Fifth Avenue was one he had put together a few weeks earlier in a rare visit there. After the service, on November 12, the lawyers read the will to the children. After generous gifts to the Museum of Modern Art to preserve the William S. Paley Collection, and to support the Museum of Television and Radio and his own foundation, most of the remainder of the estate was given in trust to his children.

That afternoon Hilary and I walked uptown along the Central Park side of Fifth Avenue. We talked about what had happened and what it meant to us. With instincts as perceptive and a heart as loving as any I've ever encountered, Hilary volunteered before I even had a chance to tell her what was on my mind. "You know you can do whatever you want now, what you believe in. I have enough to take care of my children and myself. You don't have to keep making so much money."

With God making it this easy, I thought, I had better deliver on the promise I made to Him last night.

.   .   .

Buoyed by the support of family and friends, I decided to put together a new organization, a think/action tank that would assemble all the professional skills needed to research and combat abuse of all substances in all sectors of society. My initial thought was to reduce practicing law to half time and become "of counsel" to Dewey Ballantine.

Where should I base this unique enterprise? Should it be independent, part of a large think tank like the Urban Institute or Heritage Foundation, or affiliated with some university? In short order—and at the particular urging of David Mahoney, then chairman of the Dana Foundation—I decided to affiliate with a university. I talked to several, including Harvard, Yale, Columbia, and New York University. Once I made it clear that we would aggressively go after tobacco as well as alcohol and illegal drug abuse, NYU president John Brademas suggested that such a center would not be comfortable (or even welcome) at NYU: It would create too much tension with Larry Tisch, chairman of the university trustees and of Loews Corporation, which owned the Lorillard Tobacco Company. Harvard had little interest. Both Yale and Columbia were enthusiastic. I had several conversations with Yale president Benno Schmidt, but I was uncertain that he understood the concept and I was uneasy about his long-term commitment to Yale.

On March 5, 1991, I had breakfast with Herb Pardes, the brilliant psychiatrist whom I had recruited to head the National Institute of Mental Health when I was HEW secretary and who was now vice president for medical affairs at Columbia University and dean of the medical school there. Pardes urged me to talk to Columbia president Michael Sovern, with whom I had a passing acquaintance as a fellow member of the legal profession when Mike had been dean of Columbia Law School.

The big break came on March 18, 1991, when I met with Dr. Steven Schroeder, newly installed president of the Robert Wood Johnson Foundation. Before our meeting, I had sketched my concept on eleven pages of a large yellow legal pad. I took Schroeder through my basic idea: to approach the problem as addiction, regardless of substance; to go after abuse of all drugs—nicotine, alcohol, and illegal, prescription, and performance-enhancing drugs. We would examine the problem in every sector of society, not simply criminal justice and health, but business, sports, schools, cities, welfare. We would bring to bear all the skills needed to combat substance abuse—not simply medicine and law enforcement, but anthropology, communications, economics, epidemiology, law, psychology, public health, religion, statistics, social services. As I made my presentation, I detected a sense of excitement in this academic from San Francisco who had been named to vitalize the world's largest foundation devoted to health.

I found out why when he said, "I've just concluded a six-month assessment of where to take the foundation. I am going to my board soon with a proposal to concentrate in three areas: health care costs, access to health care—especially for those with chronic ailments—and substance abuse."

I was overjoyed. Like me, Schroeder saw the problem as addiction, not as separate problems linked to one or another substance. He asked me to put together a complete proposal. As an academic, and for reasons of scientific credibility, he thought it important to affiliate with a university.

Mike Sovern, Herb Pardes, and I met in Sovern's apartment on the East Side at 5 P.M. on April 26. Mike was leaving the next day for Italy with his wife, who was seriously ill, but we talked for more than two hours. Sovern and Pardes understood the concept and were prepared to support the creation of a center within the Columbia family. Such a center would demonstrate Columbia's determination to tackle an area of serious concern for New York's Harlem and Washington Heights communities, where the university and its medical school were situated.

Since the university could not provide financial support, the center must have its own board and raise its funds independently. While the center would be closely aligned with Columbia's schools of medicine and public health, it would stand alone at the university. That would make it easier to work with all the graduate schools (such as business, law, and the renowned Teachers College), a key attraction of Columbia, because none of them would look at the center as being part of another graduate school. I also hoped to engage nearby Barnard, John Jay College of Criminal Justice, and Union and Jewish Theological Seminaries. This array offered a unique concentration of professional disciplines. The stand-alone characteristic was also important, since we planned to be more proactive than a typical university graduate school.

After this meeting, I asked Hale Champion and Fred Bohen, who had served with me at HEW, to negotiate the details with Jonathan Cole, Columbia's provost. Hale and Fred had the academic experience to put together an arrangement that would benefit the university and help me build the center into a national asset.

In addition to seeking funds from Schroeder, I approached David Hamburg of the Carnegie Corporation, Margaret Mahoney of the Commonwealth Fund, David Mahoney of the Dana Foundation, Frank Thomas of the Ford Foundation, and Drew Altman of the Kaiser Family Foundation. They were willing to commit the necessary core funding to get the center off the ground, if I was willing to give it my all. As Steve Schroeder put it, "You commit and we'll commit." I decided to retire completely from the practice of law and devote full time to this new enterprise.

Following a weekend during which my wife and I made that decision, we had dinner with John and Patty Rosenwald. John, along with Ace Greenberg, had built Bear Sterns into a Wall Street powerhouse; he was then the firm's vice chairman. Upon hearing my idea, John's immediate response was "If you're going to give your life to this, I'm going to be your first supporter. I'm committing a hundred thousand dollars to help get you started."

John's vote of personal confidence was even more important than the generous donation. I went home that night elated, convinced that I was moving in the right direction.

Another vote of support came from Sandy Weill, then chairman of Primerica Corporation (en route to building the financial behemoth Citigroup), on whose corporate board I served. "We'll have a lot of battles with tobacco, alcohol, and beer companies," I told Sandy, "so I should resign. I know there'll be financial opportunities in those industries for you."

"Joe," Weill said instantly, "I want you more than ever as a board member. And I'll help you raise money."

Weill suggested that I ask for five-year commitments from corporations to show continuing support. "In what amounts?" I asked.

"Ask for $50,000 a year," he said. "Most CEOs can easily do that, and it isn't likely to inhibit their ability to take care of all their pet projects."

I decided on the spot to adopt that strategy. Before I could even ask Weill if he would get the ball rolling, he said, "You've got my commitment, now use it to get others."

Not everyone was so supportive. Mitchell Rosenthal, president of the treatment center Phoenix House, invited me to lunch at the University Club on May 17, 1991. He pressed me not to start the center, because he feared it would hurt his fundraising efforts for Phoenix House. "If the center succeeds," I said, "there will be more funds for all treatment as well as research." Rosenthal was also concerned that I would redirect some of my mother-in-law's planned contributions away from Phoenix House. Dorothy Hirshon had been on his board; she had contributed generously and planned to leave much of her estate to Phoenix House and to the New School. I never discussed Rosenthal's conversation with her, and I never asked her for any assistance beyond attending our annual dinners.

Schroeder and I talked about the need for me to enlist a drug expert with impeccable credentials to be my right arm. In calls around the country, the name of Dr. Herbert Kleber repeatedly came up. Kleber had established the largest drug-treatment research clinic in the nation at Yale, where he had been a professor at the medical school. Now he was serving as deputy for demand reduction in the White House Office of National Drug Control Policy. Recruited to Washington by William Bennett, Kleber had the added asset of being a conservative Republican. His presence would provide instant non-partisanship to the center and balance the liberals who were likely to be attracted to any institution focused on prevention and treatment. Kleber was being courted by every major university in the nation that had any interest in drug abuse. I tracked him down in Italy and pitched him on my idea over the phone for more than an hour. When he returned, we met for the first time in my Washington office. I knew immediately that he was the right partner for this undertaking. Moreover, Kleber after his divorce had found a true love, Marian Fischman, a drug researcher at Johns Hopkins, who preferred living in New York. Excited by the concept and nudged by Marian, Kleber signed on.

Schroeder recommended to his board a grant of $8 million over five years. The board, however, dominated by business-oriented conservatives, raised questions about the appropriateness of including tobacco and alcohol in a substance-abuse program: Weren't they legal products? Some board members also questioned the nature of my commitment: Would Califano stay the course? Would he be able to raise other funds? Was he too liberal? Would he use the center as a political launching pad?

After the board meeting, Schroeder told me that the foundation trustees needed to hear directly from me before making any decision. Could I make a personal presentation to the board at its April meeting? Never before had a grant applicant been called to appear before the board, but I was eager. I took with me Herb Kleber, and his scientific and political credentials proved priceless. I asked Columbia provost Jonathan Cole to join our presentation to make clear the university's commitment to this undertaking. We made our case; after polite but pointed questions, we left. I couldn't tell what impression we had made. I was concerned that all the other support I had mustered, all the individuals I had recruited, might be for naught.

We were victorious. After a spirited discussion the board voted to include tobacco and alcohol in the foundation's substance-abuse program, and it agreed to fund the center.

I decided on a name, the Center on Addiction and Substance Abuse at Columbia University. The name lent itself to the acronym CASA, the Italian and Spanish word for house. In my mind, it symbolized our bringing under one roof all the skills needed to attack all substance abuse in all corners of society. Ivan Chermayeff, a brilliant illustrator and designer, captured the concept in a striking logo, shaped like a house. In October 1995, Leo Kelmenson (then chairman of Bozell International and later a CASA board member) suggested we add "National" in front of CASA to make it clear we were not limited to New York.

.   .   .

I worked hard to recruit a committed board of directors. Jim Burke, chair of the Partnership for a Drug-Free America, agreed to serve. In search of someone from a national icon company interested in youngsters, I asked Don Keough, the president of Coca-Cola, to join the board and commit Coca-Cola to be a founding supporter. I had seen Keough's marketing genius in action and knew that if he committed he would deliver. He committed in one phone conversation.

Seeking a representative of the labor movement, I asked Lane Kirkland, president of the AFL-CIO, to suggest a member of the organization's executive committee. "What is your position on drug testing employees?" Kirkland asked. I responded that we had none, but would look at the issue and eventually come to a conclusion. Kirkland said that if anyone from his executive committee went on the board we would have to oppose all testing of employees. "CASA can't take a predisposed view," I said. "But I do need someone who will have the respect of the labor movement and express their view vigorously."

"What about Doug Fraser?" Kirkland asked. "He's retired from the United Auto Workers, but he arbitrates disputes among our unions and he sure as hell is respected." I called Fraser that very day. He immediately agreed to serve.*

My next call was to LaSalle Leffall, who chaired the Department of Surgery at Howard University's medical school and hospital. He had been president of the American Cancer Society when I was HEW secretary and I knew of his interest in smoking cessation. LaSalle, who considered smoking the most deadly threat to the health of blacks, agreed immediately to serve.

I called Frank Wells, president of Disney and a colleague from his days as a practicing attorney in New York. When Wells invited me to his home to talk it over, I flew to Los Angeles and met with him at 6:30 one morning. He came downstairs, freshly showered after his morning jog. The meeting lasted almost three hours. As we talked, Frank worked over my draft mission statement, insisting that we make it "simple, like a Disney movie, so everyone can understand what you're about."

By the end of the meeting, we had crafted CASA's missions: to inform Americans of the cost of substance abuse and the impact on their lives, to find out what works in treatment and prevention, and to encourage every individual and institution to take responsibility for combating substance abuse and addiction. Then Frank said, "I'm on board. This is an enormous problem for the nation and God knows, there's plenty of it in the entertainment industry." Smiling, he added, "I'll give you $50,000 a year for five years out of my own funds. When you're soliciting corporations, say it's from Disney. When you're soliciting individuals, tell them it's personal."

I had planned on four board meetings a year. "If you do that," Wells said, "as a charitable board, you'll only get about 50 percent attendance at each meeting. Do only two a year and tell members you expect them to be at all meetings when you invite them on the board. They'll come." Frank was an attentive board member. On one occasion he left Houston after the premiere of The Lion King and flew all night to make the CASA board meeting the next day.[2]

I considered it important to have a Hispanic on the board, but I wanted no mere token. I needed someone who cared about this problem and who would make an excellent founding board member. I called friends in Texas, California, New York, and Washington. Thus I discovered Manuel Pacheco,

*In 2002, AFL-CIO president John Sweeney joined the board, succeeding Fraser, who retired in 2003.

then the president of the University of Arizona. Pacheco had been president of the University of Houston-Downtown and among the first academic leaders to ask business leaders what they wanted their college graduates to learn. I called Pacheco and introduced myself, and we spoke at length. He agreed to go on the board.

Mike Sovern joined the board as president of Columbia and established the precedent that the president of the university would always serve as a member.[3]

My call to Barbara Jordan brought back a flood of memories. I had gotten to know her during my years on the Johnson staff. Johnson was peacock-proud of his discovery of Barbara, the first black elected to the Texas senate. When we were setting up a presidential task force on income maintenance, I sent a list of names into LBJ, including Northwest Industries chairman Ben Heineman as chair and, as members, the financier Andre Mayer, Bob McNamara, and several top-flight economists. Johnson approved the list and wrote, "Add Barbara Jordan." Never having heard of her, I checked with White House aide Marvin Watson, who told me, "She's a Negro Texas state senator, a friend of the President's." I assumed that as a local Texas politician she would be over her head. Since she was a friend of LBJ's, I waited for an appropriate moment, over dinner alone one evening, to raise the issue. "You know, Mr. President, this income maintenance group is high powered and the subject is complex as hell. You suggested I add Barbara Jordan. If you want to do something for her, I can find another task force to put her on."

LBJ exploded. "Let me tell you something. She didn't go to Harvard and she never worked on Wall Street, but she's got more brains and common sense in her pinky fingernail than all those other members put together. She's going to be the first Negro governor or United States senator from the state of Texas. Put her on your Goddamn task force."

I did and she dominated its deliberations. Barbara Jordan later became the first black woman elected to Congress from the South. Now, years later, she was teaching at the LBJ School of Public Affairs in Austin. I knew she was interested in the impact of alcohol on African-Americans; she had written the introduction to a pamphlet on the subject.

Barbara was reluctant to join the CASA board because of her declining health. She never spoke about it, but she was suffering from multiple sclerosis, which confined her to a wheelchair, and leukemia. I asked her to serve for a couple of years to get us off the ground. She agreed and was such a powerful board member that John Rosenwald once remarked, "Barbara Jordan is the most interesting and compelling board member I've ever served with."[4]

When the health trade press reported that I was launching CASA, Betty Ford sent me a wonderful letter of support: "Your early awareness of the dangers of smoking helped change the habits of an entire nation. Your warnings about a serious health hazard saved thousands of lives. Substance abuse and addiction may well be the most harmful component of today's society. I was delighted that you are including alcohol and prescription drugs in your studies."

I called to thank her. "This nation has needed an organization like this for so long," she said. "I'm so glad you're doing this. If there's anything I can do to help, let me know."

I jumped at the opening. "You can come on the board as a founding member. We have no recovering individual on the board and you'd add enormous prestige."

There was a pause of five or ten seconds which seemed like five or ten minutes to me. Then Betty said, "If I can work out my schedule to do the meetings, I will.'"

"We'll work out the schedule," I said.

"Okay, Joe," she said. "You can be mighty persuasive."[5]

On May 18, 1992, at a press conference at the St. Regis Hotel, I announced the formation of the National Center on Addiction and Substance Abuse at Columbia University.

I abandoned the practice of law completely and devoted myself totally to building CASA into a national asset. We scheduled our first fund-raising event for June 1, 1993—a black-tie dinner to introduce CASA to New York's leading citizens and to get the problem of abuse and addiction on their agendas. A board meeting was scheduled for the following day to put the finishing touches on our mission statement and set the agenda for the first few years.

As was the case when I went to HEW, I had no sense of making a sacrifice in leaving a lucrative law practice. I was riding a great wave, convinced that I was putting whatever talent, celebrity, energy, and contacts God had given me to right use.

CHAPTER 32

The Annulment

HOWEVER CORNY it might seem to sophisticates, I now felt a genuine sense of vocation, of religious mission. As worldly and experienced as I had become, until age sixty I don't think I appreciated how indelibly branded I had been by the water and oil of Roman Catholic baptism. For me, establishing and building CASA and committing myself to this battle against substance abuse was doing the Lord's work.

At about this same time, the indelibility of that baptismal branding was firing a desire to have the Catholic Church consecrate my marriage to Hilary. Seven years into our life together, I knew we had that rare relationship, a marriage of beauty and strength, two people supportive of each other, growing closer each day, bringing out the best in each other, there for each other in times of difficulty. For a Catholic marriage, I would need an annulment. I looked down on the Church's annulment process, viewing it as cover for Catholic divorce, a process tinged with hypocrisy, reserved for the rich and powerful. Anyone brought up in a devout Catholic family, with sixteen years of education by nuns and priests, has a lingering sense of guilt about divorce and remarriage outside the Church, but for years I had pretty much relegated that to a level of irrelevance in my personal and spiritual life. Now, I was experiencing a nagging feeling of incompleteness in my marriage and twinges of Catholic guilt.

My first wife, Trudy, and I were married on July 4, 1952, during High Mass at St. Mary's Church in Taunton, Massachusetts. I had graduated from Harvard Law School that June, sweated through a cram course in New York state law sitting in the balcony of the Brooklyn Academy of Music, taken the bar exam on the last day of June and the first of July, and rushed to Taunton for the wedding. Trudy and I had dated for three years, mostly while I was at law school in Cambridge and she was at the College of New Rochelle in New York. Immature as we may have been at the time of our wedding, over the next twenty-three years, we had three wonderful children—Mark, Joe III, and Claudia—and an annulment seemed out of the question.

Occasionally I had talked to Catholic friends about my simmering uneasiness. Phyllis Wagner, wife of the New York City mayor, at a dinner party at their home urged me to seek an annulment. "It's meant a lot to Bob," she said. "Being married in the Church has brought him peace and joy." Richard McCooey, a devout Catholic and friend, suggested that I talk to a Jesuit psychiatrist in New York about an annulment, so I went to see Father Louis Padovano at his Park Avenue office. He suggested that I visit the Church Tribunal in Long Island City. I did. It was a depressing experience. The person I talked to made the process sound like a courtroom drama in which Trudy and I would be expected to appear for a hearing, face off, and lay out all the problems of our marriage. The visit soured me against seeking an annulment.

I talked to Dick McCormick, the Jesuit moral theologian, after he'd sent me galleys of his book *The Critical Calling: Reflections on Moral Dilemmas Since Vatican II*, which had a chapter on "Divorce, Remarriage and the Sacraments." McCormick tried to soothe my uneasiness.

I listened to him as intently as I had to Father English years earlier in deciding whether I could continue receiving Communion if I married Hilary. For me, the most important of McCormick's points was that "viewing all irregular [outside the Catholic Church] second marriages as involving a state of sin makes the rupture of the first marriage an unforgivable sin. The Church does this with no other failures," McCormick said, "even when, as in the case of murder, the objective effects of the sin are irreparable."

"There's no unforgivable sin," I mused aloud.

"That's right," he said quietly.

McCormick did not encourage me to seek an annulment. He offered me comfort in my existing situation. But another Jesuit did. When in Manhattan, I usually attended Mass at St. Ignatius Loyola on Park Avenue and 84th Street. After Hilary and I moved to Roxbury, Connecticut, in 1991 and spent more time in New York, I saw more of the Jesuit pastor, Father Walter Modrys, and he replaced Jim English as my spiritual advisor and confessor.

On one occasion in 1993, Father Modrys said to me, "You know, you've mentioned several times you were not married in the Catholic Church. It obviously bothers you. Why don't you seek an annulment?"

"How can I do that? " I said. "I was married for more than twenty years before we separated. I've got three children."

"Don't be so sure. The Church is understanding—especially if you were married young and didn't fully understand at the time what marriage was all about. How old were you and your wife when you got married?"

"I was twenty-four, she was twenty-two."

"Think about it," he said.

I very much wanted to be married in the Catholic Church, even though I was attending parish churches in Roxbury and New York that allowed me to receive Communion. I was troubled by the occasional but persistent gnawing of my Catholic conscience. I was imbued with the traditional Catholic motivations instilled from my earliest years at St. Gregory's: love of God and fear of Hell. They were as much a part of me as the blood running through my veins. I needed the security and blessing of having my church officially consecrate my union with Hilary.

With each year and the onrushing changes in American society, the Church had become more important to me. As a Catholic I was finding little support and reinforcement for my faith and values in our society, particularly in my milieu, the New York Upper East Side and Ivy League academia. Popular films, television, books, and the nation's style-setting institutions, it seemed to me, were becoming more aggressively secular. Our culture was materialistic and hedonistic. In politically liberal elites, it was acceptable, sometimes politically correct, to ridicule Catholicism. Like many other Catholics, I found the Church to be my most solid and reassuring rock. As the culture seemed to me to drift further from faith-based values, I found myself embracing that rock more tightly.

Getting an annulment would end any remaining estrangement from the Church. But how could there be a determination that there never was a marriage after twenty-three years? How would my three children, Mark, Joe, and Claudia, react to any attempt by me to have their parents' marriage annulled? Our divorce had not been easy for them. They were still puzzled, hurt, and suffering emotionally from our breakup. Annulment would raise another issue for them—were they legitimate? My wife, Hilary, had two children, one of whom, her daughter, Brooke, had become a devout Catholic. How would she react? I was concerned that my getting an annulment would in some way undermine their faith and commitment to the Church, which I considered the most important legacy I could bestow upon them. And Hilary's son, Frick, who was still searching for his place in the sun and who I hoped would someday receive the gift of faith—how would he take it? I had no idea how Trudy would react to such a proceeding. Would she choose to contest or ignore it?

I talked to Hilary. She understood how much it meant to me to marry her in the Catholic Church. For my own peace of mind, I needed to sanctify my marriage this way.

Father Modrys suggested that I talk to Sister Amadeus McKevitt at the Metropolitan Tribunal of the New York Archdiocese. In late 1992, I visited Sister Amadeus in her office at the archdiocese building on First Avenue. Uneasy all the way up to the thirteenth floor, I sheepishly asked for her when I stepped off the elevator. Sister Amadeus rose from behind her desk with bounce in her step and a twinkle in her eyes that belied her seventy-five years and snow-white hair. Within minutes of settling in her small office I knew I was in the presence of a compassionate, kind person. Sister Amadeus, I learned, was an Ursuline nun living at the Convent of St. Teresa at the College of New Rochelle in New York. Small world, I thought—this was the college that my great aunts had founded, and where I had met Trudy on a blind date (with one of her classmates) long ago.

As I told Sister Amadeus my doubts and explained how long I had been married, she gently interrupted. "The Church seeks ways to have divorced and remarried Catholics fully integrated and permit them to marry within the Church. That's what I am here for."

"What's important," she continued, "is whether you fully understood the nature and obligations of marriage at the time you wed. What we want to look at is how well you understood—or were capable of understanding—all the rights and obligations of married life at the time you married."

I was skeptical, but she was so reassuring that I began to feel some hope. She explained the Catholic tenet that the bond of marriage should contain "an efficacious grace"—which attaches to all sacraments. "That grace enables the couple to raise children and love one another through good times and bad," Sister Amadeus said. "That grace is essential. The annulment process tries to determine if that sacramental grace was there at the beginning of a marriage and seeks to restore the possibility of that grace occurring in another marriage."

She urged me to think about my state of maturity and mind at the time of the wedding; to see if there were any friends or relatives who could give testimony about that and about my marriage in the early years. She explained that I would have to respond in writing to a rigorous series of questions. If the grounds for annulment were based on psychological factors, which she believed mine would be, then I would have to be examined by a psychologist, who would report to the tribunal. Based on my application, the testimony of any witnesses, and the psychologist's assessment, a determination would be made whether there was sufficient reason to hold a formal hearing. If so, I would receive a petition to sign and submit to the tribunal. That would set the stage for the hearing.

I would next be asked to give sworn testimony before a canon law judge. The judge would contact any witnesses. "Remember," Sister Amadeus said, "the point is to determine the conditions that existed at the time your marriage was contracted. Your maturity and understanding of the nature of the relationship you were entering."

"Would Trudy and I face off against each other?" I asked.

"The annulment process is not adversarial," Sister Amadeus insisted. "What we seek here is healing. An effort is always made to contact the other spouse. If your wife wants to testify, the judge will hear her privately but she is not obligated." Sister Amadeus knew I was a lawyer and had been through a civil divorce—a precondition to getting an annulment. But she stressed that the annulment process is of an entirely different character. "Although many call an annulment a 'Catholic divorce,'" she said, "it is not. It is differentiated from the civil process because the judges look only at the person you were, your maturity and understanding at the time of the wedding, your previous dating experience, and your courtship. They do not focus on what went wrong during your marriage—though these facts often support the allegation of invalidity."

My mind was opening to a world of hope as I listened to this caring nun. "In fact, the annulment process can heal the scars of divorce," she added.

After testimony was taken, she said, the tribunal would consider the matter and make a decision. She explained that the tribunal consisted of the judge; a defender of the bond, who was responsible for marshalling and presenting the arguments against annulment; an advocate, to present my case for annulment; and an advocate for my former spouse, if Trudy wished to participate.

Sister Amadeus then said, "Normally there is a charge, $600, to cover the costs of the tribunal."

I was surprised that the amount was so low, having heard stories that obtaining a Catholic annulment could involve a significant contribution to the Church.

Seeing the surprise on my face, Sister Amadeus said, "For those who cannot pay all at once, we can work out installment payments. And if the parish priest tells us that an individual—say a single parent—cannot afford to pay anything, there is no charge."

This caring nun had misread my expression. "Sister," I said, "I am more than able to pay the $600. I was just surprised that it was so little."

Sister Amadeus suggested that I read a book *Annulment: Your Chance To Remarry Within the Catholic Church,* by Joseph Zwack. I promised to do that. Now sensing the skepticism I continued to harbor, she insisted, "You read that book and then come back and talk to me, and I'll help you respond to the questions and prepare your statement. Don't you worry. I'm going to help you."

I bought the book at a small Catholic bookstore. I learned that for years, the American Catholic Church had examined annulment applications from the perspective of marriage as a covenant and considered psychological factors in determinations of the validity of the bond (and granted many thousands of annulments on these grounds). Out of Pope John XXIII's Vatican II Council came a new code of Canon Law in 1983. Section 1095 included among those considered incapable of "matrimonial consent" men and women who "suffer from a grave lack of discretionary judgment concerning the essential matrimonial rights and obligations to be mutually given and accepted. . . ." The ability to grasp fully—not just intellectually, but emotionally and spiritually—and to understand and assume the real obligations of a mature, lifelong commitment was a necessary prerequisite to valid matrimonial consent. In the absence of such full understanding, the Church could find that no valid marriage ever existed.

I was encouraged by what I read. I remained quite dubious, however, when I conferred again with Father Modrys. "You just go see Sister Amadeus," he said as we ended our meeting.

When I returned to see her in November 1992, Sister Amadeus was upbeat, comforting, and committed to helping me. She instructed me to assemble all the basic papers—baptismal and marriage certificates, final order of civil divorce—and prepare statements responding to the questionnaire for submission to her. "I'll review it with you before we finally submit it," she said. "Then you send it in through Father Modrys and he can write something about you."

She said I needed a witness who could testify about my level of maturity and understanding at the time of my marriage and during the early years that Trudy and I were together.

During this time, Sister Amadeus sent me clippings and messages, each with a cheery note in red ink on light-blue paper. The first one she penned was "Notes distributed at one of my annulment talks. Any questions?" Among her talking points enclosed was this passage: "An annulment implies no moral judgment one way or another about either of the parties. . . . An annulment has no effect on the legitimacy of the children." A week or two later, Sister Amadeus sent along an *America* magazine article of personal reflections by someone who had been through the annulment process, with this handwritten note: "This emphasizes the spiritual and healing aspects. I hope it helps." That Christmas, she sent me a card with angels and the printing *Gloria In Excelsis Deo* on the cover and this note: "Joe. My best wishes for a happy Christmas-time and a blessed 1993 for you and your family. I hope the enclosed will speed you along the way. Optimistically, Sister Amadeus."

Once I decided to start the annulment process, I faced the prospect of telling Trudy and the children. Sister Amadeus offered to speak to them to explain the process. I had no idea how Trudy would react. When I called, she expressed no surprise. I think she expected me to pursue this course at some point. She was no longer deeply engaged as I was in the Catholic Church. I told her that at some point the tribunal would give her a chance to respond and participate. She expressed little interest and when formally contacted by the tribunal, never responded.

Next I had to tell my children. I explained to each individually how important it was to me to be married in the Catholic Church, to share the sacrament of matrimony with Hilary. Mark and Joe simply listened, as did Brooke.* Claudia was concerned: Would this mean she was an illegitimate child? I explained that the ecclesiastical annulment had nothing to do with the fact that she was the legitimate and much-loved child of Trudy and me. I suggested that she see Father Modrys, which she did. He put her at ease. "Claudia is a special young lady," he told me later. "I think she understands. You should be proud of her." In the end, I suspect all the children considered

---

*I did not tell Hilary's son, Frick—who, though baptized Catholic, had not practiced any religion—until the proceedings were at an end.

this the Catholic Church's cover for divorce—that Mark, Joe, and Claudia didn't like it, but they were willing to accept whatever would make me happy.

With the help of Sister Amadeus, I worked on my statement—a short biographical account of my background, upbringing, courtship, and marriage, including my relationship with my parents as well as with Trudy when we were dating and engaged. I noted that neither Trudy nor I had gone through any pre-Cana preparation, to discuss and gain an appreciation of the rights and obligations of marriage. Today pre-Cana preparation is required for all marriages in the Church.

For a witness, I called upon Larry Levinson. Larry and I had been classmates at Harvard Law School, and we became soul mates working together at the Pentagon and especially during our three and a half years in daily contact as colleagues at the White House. Larry was privy to the marital problems that Trudy and I faced; he had observed me closely on a daily basis for eight early years of my marriage. He was the only person to whom I had confided my difficulties at the time. Larry was Jewish, not Catholic; I had not seen him for several years. I gingerly called and asked whether he would be a witness—*the* witness—in my case before the tribunal. He immediately agreed.

Sister Amadeus questioned Larry by phone and then sent him documents and many written questions. I never saw them, nor was I privy to any of her conversations with him. Sister Amadeus arranged for him to be interviewed under oath.

In early February, I went to the West 61st Street office of C. Edward Robins, a psychologist, for an interview and psychological assessment. I entered nervously, uncomfortable going to be analyzed by a psychologist. It was a quiet time, focused entirely on my upbringing, parental relationships, courtship with Trudy, and early years of our married life. At the end, he expressed the view that there might be a good case for an annulment.

On March 1, I received and signed the petition, which set forth the critical dates of our courtship and marriage, as well as my baptismal date, and listed the documents (which I never saw) that were part of the record (the psychologist's report and statements of Levinson and Father Modrys) and the concluding petition. It requested that "according to the laws of the Catholic Church on the ground of lack of due discretion on my part, in accordance with Canon 1095 . . . my marriage . . . be declared null and void."

The petition was accompanied by a "mandate," by which I appointed Rosemary Doherty of the Metropolitan Tribunal to be my "procurator-advocate" and authorized her to represent me and make my case before the tribunal and before the Court of Second Instance, the ecclesiastical court that would review any decision of the tribunal. If the tribunal ruled in my favor and the ecclesiastical court agreed, the annulment would be granted. I never met Rosemary Doherty, but Sister Amadeus said she was an excellent advocate. I had wanted Sister Amadeus to represent me, but she couldn't at the time.

My petition was promptly accepted and a formal meeting was scheduled with Monsignor Desmond Vella, J.C.D. (juris canonici doctor), who would take my sworn testimony. Monsignor Vella placed me under oath and tape-recorded my testimony. His questions were similar to those I had answered in my final statement. They focused on my understanding of the covenant of marriage, at the time I entered into it, the lack of any preparation for marriage and the extent to which I appreciated—or failed to appreciate—the rights and obligations of marriage at the time. He asked pointed questions about my courtship and engagement and the early years of my marriage to Trudy. He spoke in a firm, sometimes insistent, but invariably courteous way. He seemed genuinely determined to grasp my understanding of the rights and obligations of the covenant of marriage at the time I entered into it. I had entered his office on edge and nervous, but left feeling gratitude for his thoroughness and courtesy.

Sister Amadeus called me afterwards. She said it would be a while before I would hear anything, but she would be praying for my petition and me.

On May 5, 1993, I received word that the tribunal had acted and the ecclesiastical second court had reviewed its action. An annulment had been granted on April 20, 1993. I was free now to marry Hilary in the Church.

Rarely had the world looked better or the future brighter. Hilary and I set June 14 for our marriage at St. Ignatius. We also prepared to christen CASA at its first dinner, a black-tie gala at the Pierre Hotel on June 1. I was as high as I'd ever been in my life. And then suddenly I learned that I might not have long to live.

CHAPTER 33

Confronting Cancer

Two days after receiving news about the annulment, I gave a morning speech in Washington, D.C., to the National Summit on Drug Policy. After lunch with Ben Bradlee, I went to the bathroom. I found my stool saturated with blood. My next stop was Roanoke, Virginia; I was scheduled to deliver a commencement address the next day at Roanoke College, where my niece Dana Parkinson was graduating.

Nervous, I told Hilary what had happened. She urged me to call my physician, Dr. Thomas Nash, in New York. Lucinda Harris, a gastroenterologist, was covering for him. Dr. Harris told me that if I passed blood again, I should either immediately go to the hospital in Roanoke or return to New York. That evening I saw blood again.

I didn't want to spoil my niece's graduation. Dr. Harris said it was okay to give the commencement address if I was up to it, but to return to New York immediately afterward. Hilary and I said nothing to her sister, Joy Ingham, Dana's mother. We went to the dinner party for Dana that evening, and the following afternoon I delivered the commencement address.

We chartered a small plane to fly back to the city and went directly to New York Hospital. That same Saturday night Dr. Harris performed a battery of tests. She released me the next morning, telling me to prepare for a colonoscopy on Tuesday. On Monday, May 10, Hilary and I met with Father Modrys to prepare for our Catholic wedding at St. Ignatius, and at noon Hilary went to the Pierre Hotel to complete plans for the inaugural CASA dinner.

On Tuesday, Dr. Harris performed the colonoscopy. After it was done, as I lay resting she told me that it would take a couple of days to get the biopsy results. I pressed her. "You've done a lot of these, Doctor, what's your best guess?" She refused to respond, but she couldn't disguise the concern on her face. For the first time it hit me: I might have cancer.

Hilary, who for twenty years had been serving on the board at Memorial Sloan-Kettering, was reassuring. "Let's face what we have to do when we know what we have to do," she said, holding my hand as she stood alongside my bed. Privately, I was crazily confident that I could dodge the cancer bullet. After all, I thought, neither my mother nor father had suffered from that awful disease; it simply couldn't happen to me.

Nevertheless, I was forced to come to terms with my own mortality. I went to see Father Walter Modrys that Thursday, and asked him to hear my confession. The Catholic Church now called it the sacrament of reconciliation, a more accurate designation reflecting its purpose: to make peace with God by atoning for sin. But I continued to think of it as penance.

On Friday Hilary and I went to our home in Roxbury, Connecticut. The call came not from Dr. Harris but Tom Nash. "The test is positive," he said. "You must have surgery to remove a malignant tumor." What couldn't happen to me had just happened to me. How could God do this? I thought. And just as I was starting CASA! Nash, Hilary, and I got on the phone together to talk about surgeons and where I would have the surgery. Nash, a brilliant, thoughtful, and sensitive physician, took us through various options.

Hilary suggested Dr. John Whitsell, who had operated on her father and performed minor surgery on her. Nash agreed: Whitsell was a top surgeon. For me, Whitsell had another critical advantage: he practiced at New York Hospital, not Memorial Sloan-Kettering.

We discussed Memorial Sloan-Kettering. I didn't want to go there; I didn't want anyone to know I had cancer. At this critical juncture for CASA, I feared that if potential contributors knew I had a life-threatening disease they would not donate. Moreover, it would be virtually impossible to recruit top talent if the professionals being interviewed thought that I might not be around very long.

I had come to believe that building this asset for the nation—to research and combat all substance abuse and awaken Americans to addiction's threat to our society—was the most important work I would do in all my life. I had never considered retiring, or even slowing down. What kind of God would cut me off just as I was starting out on such a crucial mission?

CASA's inaugural dinner was just two weeks away. Nash said there was no guarantee that I would be able to go to the dinner if the operation took place beforehand. Should I wait until after the dinner? I asked. "That's a reasonable option," he replied.

Then I remembered that my son Joe was graduating from Harvard Medical School on June 10. "Tom, if I have the operation after the dinner, will I be able to get to my son's graduation?"

"Not likely," he answered.

I told Nash that I was determined to be there.

"If that's the case," Nash said, "then it makes the most sense to have the surgery as soon as possible."

"Would that increase the likelihood that I would be able to attend the CASA dinner?"

"Yes, but there are no guarantees."

Hilary could see my head was spinning. She suggested that we think about the timing and call back. In the meantime, Nash would call Dr. Whitsell and see what his operating schedule was.

On Saturday, as Hilary and I struggled with these decisions, I played tennis on our court with a foursome; my partner was Dr. Paul Marks, then president of Memorial Sloan-Kettering. How eerie, I thought, having this partner as I was contemplating this decision. Both of us were hyper-competitive on the tennis court; that Saturday morning I played with a damn-the-torpedoes ferocity to win, and we did.

That afternoon I told Hilary that in order to avoid the possibility of anyone finding out I had cancer, I would not even tell our children. I also didn't want to put a damper on Joe's graduation, another reason for secrecy. Hilary disagreed. Bill and Dorothy Paley had adopted Hilary at birth. She felt strongly that I should tell my three biological children the truth about my condition. She was particularly conscious of this because she knew little about her biological parents and nothing of their medical histories. I promised that I would tell Mark, Joe, and Claudia in due course, in plenty of time for them to take care of themselves, but not right away. Hilary also urged me to tell her two children, Brooke and Frick, to whom I had become so close over the years. Their knowing, I felt, would have no impact on their health practices. And both bore permanent scars from the suicide of their father; they shouldn't have to worry about losing me. I persuaded my reluctant wife to honor my desire for secrecy.

We talked to Nash on Sunday. I would schedule the operation as soon as possible with Dr. Whitsell at New York Hospital. Understanding my desire for secrecy, Nash suggested we could talk about it as "stomach surgery," for a clogging of the intestinal tract.

We returned to the city on Monday and I met with Dr. Whitsell, a slight man with gray hair and glasses. I found myself staring at his hands and fingers. I had not yet come to terms with the fact that I might die from this cancer, but my conversation with Dr. Whitsell changed that. With clinical detachment, Dr. Whitsell said that until he "got inside" he would not know the full extent of the cancer and could not predict whether I would have to have a colostomy inserted.

"A what?"

"A colostomy, a tube coming out from your lower stomach to replace your lower intestine and bowel." He explained that many patients live with those attachments for years: "You get used to them." I was shaken by the thought that I might have to spend the rest of my life, however long or short, with a tube coming out of my lower stomach and a bag tied to my leg.

From my days at HEW I knew that the more often a doctor performed a procedure, the greater the likelihood of success. I asked Whitsell about his experience. He spent at least two or three days a week in surgery at the hospital, he answered, much of it involving intestinal cancer.

I then rushed over to the radiology clinic on East 60th Street to have my stomach scanned. I drank liquid barium, waited the hour it took to penetrate my system, and then went under a CAT scanner. Whitsell wanted these pictures to look for any evidence of metastatic spread of the tumor and any enlarged lymph nodes around the area of the tumor, and to give him a road map of my system. They would enable him to be more precise with his entering incision and throughout the operation, since the images identified the exact location of all organs in my belly. To ease the claustrophobic sensation of undergoing the scan, the nurse gave me earphones and asked me what kind of music I preferred. I picked old Sinatra classics. "It's in stereo," she said, but one earphone wasn't working, so I heard the music only in my left ear. I felt claustrophobic for the first time in my life, and I have never been able to go into tight spaces since.

The next morning, the day I was to enter the hospital, I went on my treadmill at my maximum speed and incline. I wanted to be in the best cardiovascular shape possible going into the surgery. I remembered that Ed Williams, when he was undergoing surgery and chemotherapy for his cancer, worked out at Washington's Metropolitan Club playing squash furiously in order to build up his strength and resistance. I thought of all the people in hospitals who got pneumonia, or couldn't keep their lungs clear, lying in bed after serious surgery. I hoped this strenuous exercise would help me recover more rapidly so that I could preside at the CASA dinner.

I entered the hospital on May 18, under an assumed name—Mr. Joseph Anthony. I was desperate to minimize the possibility of any leaks about my cancer.

That evening, Father Modrys came by. Again I received the sacrament of reconciliation. This time he also gave me the Sacrament of the Sick, which I had studied years ago in St. Gregory's elementary school as the Sacrament of Extreme Unction, the last rites. Floored that this was happening to me, all I could think was how these rites were portrayed by Hollywood in the forties in World War II movies, with the priest leaning over a dying (or dead) soldier on the battlefield.

As he took out the vial of oil to anoint me, Father Modrys said gently, "Remember, Jesus restored the sick to health. Think of the sacrament in the words of the apostle James, who said, 'Is there anyone sick among you? Let him call for the elders of the Church, and let them pray over him and anoint him. . . . The Lord will restore his health, and if he has committed any sins, they will be forgiven.'"

I sat on the edge of the bed as Father Modrys recited the litany of the sacrament. "Lord, through this holy anointing, come and comfort Joseph with your love and mercy; free him from all harm. . . ." I responded, "Lord, hear our prayer." Father Modrys then laid his hands on my head in a moment of silence. Finally, he anointed me with the oil, making a small sign of the Cross with his right thumb and praying, "Lord God, loving Father, . . . may your blessing come upon all who are anointed with this oil, that they may be freed from pain and illness and made well again in body, mind and soul."

"Amen," I responded.

"May the Lord who frees you from sin save you and raise you up."

"Amen."

Father Modrys concluded with a prayer: "Lord Jesus Christ, our Redeemer, by the power of the Holy Spirit, ease the sufferings of our sick brother Joseph and make him well again in mind and body. In your loving kindness, forgive his sins and grant him full health so that he may be restored to your service."

I raised my head. For the first time since my visit with Dr. Whitsell, I believed that whatever the nature of the cancer, God would get me sufficiently back on my feet to continue my work and at least get CASA off the ground.

As he was leaving, Father Modrys said, "Understand, Joe, this is to help heal you. It's not a sacrament for the dying. It's for the living and it has healing power."

With a sense of peace and with Hilary holding my hand, I fell right to sleep that evening. I didn't need the pill that the nurse suggested I take.

The surgery lasted more than four hours. After an overnight stay in the intensive care unit, I was moved to Room 1219 the following morning. Hilary had insisted that I have private-duty nurses, attentive Irish nurses who often held my hand during the long, empty hours of late night and early morning.

I found myself reflecting on the importance of touching to recovery. In November 1978, I had met with the heroic Polish prelate Stefan Cardinal Wyszynski at his residence in Warsaw. The cardinal's presence was powerful. He seemed to fill the cavernous room, despite his slight frame, his illness, and the weakness of his voice. He had just returned from Rome, where he had undergone medical treatment. "There are too many machines and tubes and wires," he said. "Even with the best machines, people often die or remain sick because they have no human contact, because they do not touch other people. People need contact to be cured."

The cardinal asked if doctors I'd met in Poland or the United States understood "the need for one person to touch another."

"Some," I replied.

"You are the minister of health," he said. "When you go back home I hope you will urge doctors in the United States to recognize how important human contact is."

Now I knew. Human touching did help enormously, when Hilary and those devoted nurses held my hand or put a cool washcloth on my forehead.

I was told the operation had gone well. There should be no need for a colostomy. Soon we would have biopsy and other reports. "We got it all," Dr. Whitsell said. "You're going to be fine." Dr. Nash explained to Hilary and me that mine was a "C class tumor." I saw an ashen tone creep into Hilary's face. This was not good news.

I learned that the severity of colon cancer is measured through Duke's Systems, which has four categories: "A" is a malignant tumor only within the lining of the intestine—it has not penetrated the intestinal wall and there is no lymph node involvement. "B" is a malignant tumor that has penetrated the intestinal wall to the muscle or fat of the intestine but there is still no lymph node involvement. "C" has the characteristics of a "B" tumor, but with the dreaded lymph node involvement. "D" has the characteristics of a "C" tumor and the cancer has spread to a remote organ such as the liver.

Dr. Whitsell had removed a section of my intestine comprising the tumor plus ten centimeters in either direction. He also removed a few circles of lymph nodes. Lymph nodes act like lines of soldiers surrounding and protecting a building; they circle the intestine to protect and battle tumors and infections. The first circle of lymph nodes that Dr. Whitsell removed was hard and enlarged, white instead of pink—a signal that they were malignant. The next couple of circles he removed, however, were not malignant. As a result, Dr. Whitsell was confident that he had removed all the cancerous cells.

Dr. Nash was encouraging, but not as optimistic as Whitsell, with his assurances of a clean sweep.

My children came to see me in the hospital. Later, Claudia told me what a difficult experience it had been for her. "Daddy," she said, "I'd never seen you so weak."

Hilary was with me every day, and Dr. Nash visited every evening. Dr. Whitsell assured me that I'd get out of the hospital in time for the CASA dinner.

On Sunday morning, May 30, Dr. Whitsell released me. With Irish nurse Anne Kelly in tow, Hilary took me to our apartment. The CASA dinner was one night away.

Hilary and I walked a little the next day and sat on the steps of St. Ignatius Loyola Church on Park Avenue to get a touch of sun on my face. On the afternoon of the dinner, I worked on my remarks, rehearsed aloud, and tried to rest. I was interrupted, however, with the last-minute questions that arise in connection with big black-tie dinners in New York. Barbara Walters, our master of ceremonies for the dinner, wanted to sit next to Henry Kravis, one of New York's richest financiers. "Sit her wherever she wants," I said. Mayor Dinkins wanted to stop by and say a few words, which would increase the length of the dinner. We needed to keep the event as brief as possible, so that I could get through it. Jaded New Yorkers, moreover, tend to get up and leave fund-raising dinners that last beyond 10 P.M. We had to accommodate the mayor, however. "Just tell him it's more important to be short than sweet," I said.

There was great concern about my ability to get through the dinner. I was still exhausted from the surgery. My system was still not under full control, so I wore adult diapers to avoid any embarrassing accident. Dr. Nash, with his wife, Elizabeth, would be seated at my table. Marguerita McGonnell-Guerin, one of my favorite nurses, would be at an adjacent table ready to take care of any crises. For me, there would be only some broth and water to sip, nothing else.

Hilary, Marguerita, and I arrived at the dinner (in the limo of Michael and Zena Wiener,[1] our New York and Connecticut friends and neighbors, who insisted on taking me to save my energy) near the end of the cocktail hour, because I was unable to stand up for very long. Thanks to its chairman, Tom Murphy, ABC had done a video about CASA and Charlie Gibson and Joan Lunden had done a film about the Burke brothers, Jim and Dan, whom we honored. Barbara Walters opened the dinner with some wonderful remarks, good-humored and expressing high hopes for CASA. I had told people that I had been in the hospital for abdominal surgery, so when Barbara introduced me, she said, "Stand up here, Joe, and show us your scar!"

My friend Art Buchwald performed at his best, putting the crowd in the aisles as he teased me. "There are many legends about Joe's fund-raising," he said, and continued:

The one I like the best concerns a New York couple named Rappaport. They were on a cruise ship in the South Pacific. The boat hit a rock and sank. Rappaport and his wife swam to shore; crawled up on a bit of sand unmarked by any map.

Rappaport said, "Is the will in order?"

Mrs. Rappaport said, "Yes."

Rappaport asked, "Are the children taken care of?"

And she said, "Yes, they are."

Then Rappaport asked, "What about the CASA dinner?"

Mrs. Rappaport said, "We took a table."

Mr. Rappaport asked, "Did you pledge or pay cash?"

And she said, "We pledged."

"Thank God!" Mr. Rappaport cried. "Joe Califano will find us!"

The dinner was a success. On the way out, Peter Jennings said, "I don't know what they're talking about. You've never looked better."

My loving wife, never to miss a chance, hugged my arm and, smiling with a sparkle in her eye, said, "See. It's because you've lost twenty pounds."

The next morning, I chaired the CASA board meeting. Immediately afterwards, Hilary and I went to our home in Connecticut. We spent an invigorating five days walking and sitting in the sun. We came back to the city on June 7. The following day we went to City Hall to get our marriage license for the ceremony at St. Ignatius. Later that day Dr. Whitsell removed the staples he had used, along with dissolving surgical string, to seal up my stomach.

The next issue was whether to have chemotherapy. Hilary and I met with Dr. David Wolf, one of the world's great hematologist oncologists, in his office on East 61st Street. Hilary and I sat in two maroon, high-backed chairs with wooden arms, facing his desk. I was struck that the inset bookshelves behind him were filled with red-leather bound volumes with the title *Blood* on each.

A short, gray-haired man with glasses and a bow tie, Dr. Wolf looked like a genius and was one. He had treated Bill Paley during the last few years of his life, which was when I first came in contact with him. He had asked me to intercede with the Food and Drug Administration to obtain a compassionate exemption to make erythropoietin available for Bill, an action that gave his patient another year of life.

Dr. Wolf was now testing a new chemotherapy protocol for patients with stage III (letter C in Duke's classification) colon cancer, and I fit the profile. The issue was whether I should go through this course of treatment, called adjuvant chemotherapy—a combination of three drugs: 5-fluorouracil (an anti-metabolite), the vitamin leucovorin (folinic acid), and levamisole.[2]

Dr. Whitsell thought it unnecessary. "I got it all," he had said. "You don't need to do anything." He was of a time and generation that believed the way to cure cancer was to cut it out.

Dr. Nash had given me his medical opinion in years past, but always said it was up for me to decide. This time he told me firmly: "You must see Dr. Wolf." I thought Nash viewed it as an insurance policy that could do no harm. What I did not know until years later was that the recurrence rate for my stage colon cancer was 60 to 70 percent and such recurrence is usually fatal. Dr. Nash knew the odds; he knew Wolf's treatment might reduce significantly the chance of recurrence.

Dr. Wolf explained to Hilary and me what would be involved in adjuvant chemotherapy: a dose of chemo once a week for a year. "The fluid is injected through a vein in the arm. It takes half an hour." At each session, blood would be taken to keep track of my white and red blood-cell counts and platelet count. There would be a bitter metallic taste in my mouth during the chemo treatment "which you can alleviate by sucking on some candy." He said I might feel tired after the treatment. I could not have any alcohol on the day of chemotherapy and for two days thereafter.

Dr. Wolf urged me to take the course of treatment. At the end of our hour-long discussion, Hilary agreed.

Again I insisted on complete secrecy. Dr. Wolf arranged to get me in and out of his office with no waiting (a monumental achievement with top New York physicians) in order to minimize the chance of identification. I saw Dr. Wolf every day that first week; for the next year I went once a week to his office for treatment. To deal with the terrible taste I sucked on Lifesavers and Jujyfruit candies. It was five years before I could look at another Jujyfruit, and to this day I cannot stand peppermint or spearmint Lifesavers. I stepped up the frequency of exercise on my treadmill to avoid getting tired so I could continue working at full tempo.

Nash wanted me to change my diet substantially: more fiber, far less fat. I asked him how often I could eat steak.

"Where?" he asked.

"The Palm or Christ Cella," I responded, mentioning two New York restaurants noted for their mouthwatering, hefty portions.

"Not more than once a month," he said with a twinkle. "If you eat a small steak, once a week."

He was even stricter when I asked about corned beef or pastrami sandwiches. "Twice a year," he said, smiling but serious.

Nash suggested I see Dr. Richard Rivlin at Memorial Sloan-Kettering, an expert in nutrition. Dr. Rivlin told me what pills to take (vitamin E and Caltrate D, among others), gave me materials on diet, and told me to say away from fats in all shapes and forms—little meat, no cheese, no ice cream, no butter. I stressed to him how important it was that he keep our visit secret. He asked me if "that is absolutely necessary." I said, "Absolutely."

Throughout this experience, I was determined to come out of it. I kept praying, asking God not to let me drop everything to start CASA and then take my life away. I had the best doctors—in the last decade, clinical trials have proved that adjuvant chemotherapy reduces recurrence in patients with stage III colon cancer and prolongs their survival—and a mighty determination to stay alive and healthy, in order to build CASA into a national asset for a country that had been very good to me and for a people that did not seem to understand the threat that drug, alcohol, and nicotine abuse and addiction posed to their society and their children.

.   .   .

On June 14, 1993, at 7 P.M., two weeks after I was released from the hospital, Hilary and I were married in St. Ignatius Loyola Catholic Church with Father Modrys officiating. Larry Levinson and his wife, Dee, were our witnesses. The only other person in that spectacular Baroque Church was the music director and organist, Kent Tritle.

It was a beautiful ceremony. Father Modrys was in white vestments. I was in a dark-blue suit, white shirt, and tie with small polka dots. Hilary was in a cornflower-blue silk dress, with a small bouquet of roses and freizas and wearing strands of pearls. One string had been given her by my father on the first Christmas after my mother died, in 1986: Hilary came down the stairs at our Georgetown home, and when she reached the bottom, my father took this string of pearls that he had given my mother—her favorite jewelry—and placed it around Hilary's neck. "If Katherine [my mother] could see what a beautiful person you are and how wonderful you are with my son, she would want you to have these." Led by Hilary, we each shed some tears.

At the end of the ceremony, Father Modrys asked Hilary if she wanted anything. "Yes," she said with a mischievous smile. "I want to march back down this long aisle with that marvelous organ playing Mendelssohn." Thanks to an anonymous donor, a million-dollar organ—the best in New York, if not the United States—had recently been installed at St. Ignatius.

Kent Tritle, the organist, pumped the organ, and Hilary and I walked down the aisle to the most beautiful wedding march that I ever heard fill a church.

I have rarely known such peace as I experienced that evening. There was a sense of integration with my church and within myself, a letting go of guilt and failure. The bond with Hilary has been immeasurably strengthened with sacramental grace.

I had often thought about the stigma that annulments were granted only to the biggest donors or most famous members of the Church. In reality, in 1991, when I took my first steps toward the annulment process, Roman Catholic marriage tribunals in the United States heard nearly forty thousand cases and approved more than 90 percent of them. Still, I took notice in 1997 when Sheila Rauch Kennedy published a scalding book, *Shattered Faith,* about the annulment of her marriage to Massachusetts congressman Joseph P. Kennedy, II. She recounts a conversation in which she says she will oppose the annulment and Joe Kennedy responds, "I don't believe this stuff. Nobody actually believes it. It's just Catholic gobbledygook, Sheila. But you just have to say it this way because, well, because that's the way the Church is." It may be impossible for those outside the Catholic tradition—and for many within it—to understand, but my experience could not be more different.

Most of my friends, and many if not most Catholics, think of the Church's annulment process as some kind of mumbo jumbo, a sop to the large number of Catholics who have divorced and remarried, especially those with money or contacts in the Church hierarchy. Trudy and my own children in all likelihood share that sort of perception, as did I until I experienced the process. To be sure, the Catholic Marriage Tribunals and the annulment process they adjudicate are institutions of man, not God, with the limitations and imperfections that attend any institution that seeks to accommodate human frailty. But they fill a very real need of divorced and remarried Catholics committed to their faith.

Going through the spiritual, psychological, and emotional process of reflection on my marriage to Trudy and why it did not work out, and then entering into a sacramental marriage with Hilary within my church, gave me a peace of mind and soul I had never before known. It is a peace that was so foreign to me I didn't even realize it was missing from my life. I have since felt peace with my first wife. Though my children were not at the ceremony,

I believe that the spiritual peace of that event has spilled over into their lives and their relationship with Hilary and me. As Sister Amadeus promised, my marriage has been enriched by a penetrating infusion of sacramental grace that has deepened our commitment and love and touched all of our children, hers as well as mine.

I told Sister Amadeus a decade later, "Sister, I still don't understand what motivated me to get an annulment in the first place and what's happened to me since."

"Maybe you'll never understand it," she said softly. "The fact is, you experienced it."

.   .   .

CASA was moving rapidly to center stage as the nation's premier think/action tank on alcohol, tobacco, and prescription, illegal, and performance-enhancing drug abuse and addiction. The center's seminal reports identifying the relationship of substance abuse and addiction to the nation's domestic problems—crime, bulging prisons, teen pregnancy, the spread of AIDS and other sexually transmitted diseases, child abuse, family breakup, domestic violence, health-care costs—were influencing schools, parents, and governments. So were its demonstration projects, which gave hope to high-risk children and their families and to welfare mothers with drug and alcohol problems struggling to become economically self-sufficient and responsible parents. Scientific discoveries validated CASA's concept that use of tobacco, use of alcohol, and use of drugs like marijuana, cocaine, and heroin are related. To CASA's statistical evidence, bench scientists have added their findings that these substances have similar impacts on the brain.

With CASA's rise in influence came counterpressures from government officials, politicians, and alcohol and tobacco executives who balked when the Center's findings did not support their policy, political, or economic interests. I came to realize that it was imperative to assure CASA's independence; our nation needed an independent institution that has no drug war to defend or attack; that is not subject to pressures through campaign contributions or personal political ambitions; that is driven to solutions pragmatically, not ideologically. I wanted to make certain that CASA would be free to look objectively at this pervasive and devastating problem and figure out what works and is cost effective, how best to prevent kids from experimenting and abusing substances, and how to motivate those who get hooked to enter treatment, stay the course, and maintain sobriety—no matter what institution or individual might be gored.

To guarantee CASA's independence and integrity would require a financial bedrock. We decided to raise a Program Concentration Fund of $35 million. In the first phase completed, in early 1999, we raised $15 million, with the final $147 coming spontaneously from the CASA staff when they saw we were within a nose of the finish line. Just as I was beginning the second phase in the winter of 1999–2000 to raise the remaining $20 million, I faced another critical hurdle. In my annual physical with Dr. Nash, he noticed that my PSA (prostate-specific antigen) had risen. "It's at 3.5, and 4 or below is a normal level for your age," he said, "but the jump from 1.1 a year ago is big enough for me to want to take another test in a couple of months." Dr. Nash put me on antibiotics to determine whether the increase was due to a low-grade prostate infection. That next PSA, three months later, showed another increase, to 3.9, and heightened his concern.

In May 2000, when Dr. Harris completed my annual colonoscopy, she told me my colon was fine, but she thought I should have a prostate biopsy. Nash agreed and set it up with Dr. Menachem Shemtov at New York-Presbyterian Hospital. In a prostate biopsy, the physician inserts what looks like a little gun in the rectum and fires what sounds like twelve shots, each of which cuts a small core of the prostate for testing. Dr. Shemtov thought things looked fine, but he warned that it was impossible to know for sure without the biopsy results.

Several days later, I was told I had prostate cancer.

Another cancer! Hilary told me that prostate cancer was something that could be handled and that I should not be so concerned. But this time I was concerned, especially when my PSA jumped to 5.5. Yet, whether out of arrogance or wishful thinking, I again thought that my work on this earth was not yet finished, and I was determined to complete it. My daughter, Claudia, had started medical school at age thirty and I wanted to be around to call her Doctor. My son Mark and his wife, Margery, were to have their first baby in July of 2000 and my stepdaughter, Brooke, and her husband, Gene, were to have their third child in December; I wanted to be there for all of them.

I prayed as I never had before. My first stop was to see Father Modrys, who, this time in his rectory office, again gave me the Sacrament of the Sick.

My son Joe was a fellow at Memorial Sloan-Kettering Hospital honing his head-and-neck-cancer surgery skills. With him and Hilary, at Dr. Nash's suggestion, I visited Dr. Darracott Vaughan, New York Hospital's top prostate cancer surgeon. Vaughan, a courtly southerner who completed his medical school and residency at the University of Virginia and had lost none of his southern accent or charm, recommended surgery. He explained that the intensity of prostate cancer is measured by Gleason scores. My scores were 7 and 8, Dr. Vaughn said, and he thought the 8 was sufficiently high to suggest surgery as the best shot to eliminate all the malignancy. He was explicit about the risks: impotence and incontinence. The plus of surgery was the "certainty of getting it all if that is possible," an outcome, Vaughan said, that could not be guaranteed with radiation. He expected I'd be out of the hospital within a few days after surgery and would be able to return to work at the end of a week or two.

I was so impressed with him that I made immediate arrangements to give blood so it would be available if needed during the surgery. I stressed with Dr. Vaughan the need for secrecy, because once again I did not want to inhibit my fundraising capacity and ability to recruit the best talent as CASA expanded. So we resurrected Mr. Joseph Anthony, which was how I would be admitted to the hospital for surgery, and I gave a pint of blood in his name.

Hilary, my son Joe, and Nash urged me to talk to Dr. Steven Leibel at Memorial Sloan-Kettering. Joe believed Memorial had the world's most advanced radiation therapy for prostate cancer. Hilary, Joe, and I met with Dr. Leibel on June 6. Leibel is a forceful, forthright, efficient, fast-thinking, fast-speaking radiation oncologist; he was in his early fifties, in excellent physical shape, with flecking gray hair and a winning smile. He explained that with "3-D conformal radiation therapy you do not run the same risk of incontinence or impotence as with surgery, but there is the risk of rectal bleeding." He had developed a technology that could deliver much higher doses of radiation to the cancerous prostate cells without harming normal tissue cells. Leibel admitted that he did not have experience beyond five years in terms of remission, since the procedure was relatively new. But his five-year rate of remission was about the same as with surgery.

Leibel said he wanted to have his own pathologist review the biopsy findings. When he saw the expression on my face, he smiled. "I want our guy to read the slides, not do another biopsy on you." Using his pathologist would assure consistency of interpretation. Leaving Leibel, I was now leaning toward radiation instead of surgery because of the lower risk of impotence or incontinence, and I had no desire to undergo surgery again.

Leibel's pathologist came up with a Gleason score of 7, not 8, which was not high enough to require hormone therapy, and there was no indication that a tumor had escaped the prostate. "You're an ideal candidate for radiation therapy because of your age." As I nodded, he added, "Even if there is relapse, you're not likely to die of it. Many older men who die have prostate cancer that isn't detected until the autopsy."

If I took the radiation route, Leibel wanted to begin on July 6. I would receive radiation five times a week for nine consecutive weeks. There could be no interruption. To reduce the danger of discovery, the times could be set early in the morning or late in the afternoon. After consulting with Dr. Nash, Hilary, my son Joe, and again with Drs. Vaughan and Leibel, I selected radiation therapy.

The first step was to be fitted for a thermoplastic mold, a strong, tight, inflexible plastic molding that would fit over my back, from just below my shoulders to the middle of my buttocks. It had to be skintight to prevent any movement while the radiation was aimed at my prostate. The fitting session of a few hours occurred while my stomach was distended with gas. Unbelievably, I learned two days later that my intestine had twisted and become blocked. Nash informed me, "This can occasionally happen with intestinal surgery. Unfortunately, it can be serious."

When I asked how serious, he responded, "If your intestine doesn't open up in a couple of days, you will have to have surgery." Thankfully, when I followed Nash's instructions meticulously—liquids only and lots of walking—my intestine untangled and opened up. But with the distension of my stomach eliminated, the mold was a little loose. The technicians at one of the radiation sessions said, "Mr. Califano, it's important that you not lose any more weight or we will have to make a new mold." It was the first time in my life anyone had told me not to lose any weight!

I went to Memorial at 7 A.M. each weekday morning for nine weeks. As my son Joe put it, "There is no cancer on weekends." I would arrive most mornings in jogging shorts and sneakers. I wanted to be as well conditioned as possible during the treatments, so I jogged back from Memorial at 67th Street and York Avenue to our apartment on 85th and Park Avenue.

In *The Gift of Peace*, written as he was dying, Joseph Cardinal Bernardin said that he had for years gotten up early and devoted the first hour of each day to praying the rosary, "because it brings into vivid images some of the high points in the Lord's life and ministry as well as that of his Blessed Mother. It's a real help. Some people think it may be repetitious, and in a sense it is. But it keeps you focused on the mysteries of the Lord, Joyful Mysteries, Sorrowful Mysteries, Glorious Mysteries."[3]

As a result, I prayed the rosary as I jogged or went on my treadmill and found it enhanced my spiritual life. I hoped the jogging would help reduce any side effects of the treatment, which Leibel warned could include being tired, being too weak for a full work schedule, and experiencing some changes in urinary and bowel functions. I hoped that the prayers would get me through this ordeal. Whatever my good fortune was due to, I never suffered severely any of those side effects and did not miss a day of work. Since the treatment, tests have shown that my PSA has gone down and, despite some normal bounces, has remained below 1.0.

Reviewing the results over a few years, Dr. Nash said, "Let's hope this is the last big bump before you hit ninety-four. You've got a lot of work to do."

A Final Reflection

THE JESUIT PHILOSOPHER Teilhard de Chardin wrote in his book *The Phenomenon of Man*, "I doubt whether there is a more decisive moment for a thinking being than when the scales fall from his eyes and he discovers that he is not an isolated unit lost in the cosmic solitudes, and realizes that a universal will to live converges and is hominised in him."

Writing this memoir has shaken the scales from my own eyes and reminded me of how the threads of my life have been woven by those who taught me by example, gave me opportunities that have enriched my life, recognized my successes and tolerated my mistakes, helped me get up when I fell, and instilled values that focused my energies.

I have been caught up in some of the great tides of the twentieth century: the revolutions in race relations, the Catholic Church, and biomedical science, the political upheaval in the Democratic Party, the Great Society's recasting the federal government into an active participant in every corner of American life (health, education, environment, consumer protection, the arts), the rise of relentless skepticism among the media (especially in the nation's capital), Watergate, the corrosive influence of money in politics, and the unprecedented spread of substance abuse and addiction.

I have come to value courage as the most precious asset anyone can bring to the public arena. Lyndon Johnson had the courage of his conviction to insist on racial justice and equal opportunity for blacks even though he knew he and his party would pay a fearful price. Katharine Graham had the courage to put her entire fortune and the *Washington Post* on the line during the Watergate battle with President Nixon. Both these leaders were an inspiration as in 1978 I took on the tobacco industry, risking the job I loved as secretary of Health, Education, and Welfare.

Courage is the bedrock of two other characteristics essential for success in the public arena. First is insistence on determining the right course and refusing to limit the horizon of public policy to what appears to be politically or fiscally feasible. It's not doing what is right, as so many presidents have said, but finding out what is right that is their toughest problem. The lesser options are always available.

Second is the tenacity to stay the course. Tenacity is key to achievement in the public arena. The struggle for Medicare and Medicaid and for civil rights began in 1948 with Harry Truman and Hubert Humphrey and didn't succeed until Lyndon Johnson pushed legislation through Congress in 1964 and 1965. The *Washington Post* hung in on Watergate for months before the rest of the media and Congress showed any serious interest. I kicked off the anti-smoking campaign in 1978 to a doubting press that reported it as all smoke and no fire. It took years before the culture changed from "Would you like a cigarette" to "Do you mind if I smoke," and Americans became comfortable in answering, "Yes, I do mind."

I have come to understand why the First Amendment is first. A free, rambunctious, skeptical, and uninhibited press is essential to preserving our democracy. In a nation of powerful federal, state, and local governments (and their curbs on civil and privacy rights in the name of security), wealthy multi-national corporations, and strong unions, a free press is the citizenry's best hope of preserving individual liberty and of getting a fair shake in the marketplace, in the workplace, and, as we have sadly seen in the early 2000s, in the churches.

I have broken more than my share of china along the way, driving myself to the limit and demanding from those around me all they had to give and then some. I found government (and private institutional) bureaucracy to be, as Jack Valenti once said, "Like a huge shaggy bear sitting in the middle of the road who needs a good kick in the ass to get moving." I did plenty of kicking—perhaps too much on occasion—but by and large I believe kicking is essential in order to effect significant change in our society.

Among the most precious inheritances my parents passed on to me was their faith in God. They gave me a sense of not just who I was, but also of Whose I was. Growing up Catholic has had its wrenching moments—personally, as I struggled to have children, and with divorce and remarriage; publicly, as a cabinet officer when I sought to render to Caesar and God what each was due. Faith in God and the Catholic religion have provided spiritual adrenaline for my life in public policy and government. To some in the public arena, just the word "God" sends shivers of secularism down the spine, but faith is a big part of who I am and what I've done. It has given me strength and passion for public service and enabled me to stand firm by my choices no matter how loud the criticism and whether it came from the Catholic bishops, those favoring federal funding for abortion, the tobacco industry, universities complaining about Title IX enforcement, hospitals about cost containment, whites about fair housing and school integration, or Jimmy Carter's White House staff about the anti-smoking campaign. That faith has given me the ability to understand that the Church is strong enough to weather the sins of pedophile priests and the bishops who protected them. As Cardinal Consalvi is said to have reminded Napoleon when in a fit of anger the French general threatened to destroy the Church, "Cardinals and archbishops have been trying to do that for centuries with no success."

For the first two decades of my life, most of the people who formed my thoughts and shared my experiences were Catholics, many of them Jesuits. The rest of my life I have been exposed to people and ideas of all faiths and beliefs, and all manner of agnostics and non-believers. The values I have treasured are Jesuitical in the best sense of the word: the belief that we should study, debate, discuss, and act for social justice.

Some experiences I chose intentionally and others came upon me unexpectedly. They piled one on another, forcing me as I confronted them to dig deep into my whole life—what I picked up on the streets of Brooklyn; the education and training from the nuns at St. Gregory's, the Jesuits at Brooklyn Prep and at Holy Cross, and the professors at Harvard Law School; and the loving example of my parents and relatives. We are what we have experienced. What I learned in private practice was invaluable in government—and vice versa. Bradlee and Simons showed me that flexing the muscle of the First Amendment is essential to preserve human freedom and our democracy. What Vance and McNamara taught me was an essential part of what I did for President Johnson, and what I garnered from the three of them informed my actions at HEW. I tried to use all that, and my experiences as a corporate board member and Washington and Wall Street lawyer, in putting together CASA, to give this nation a national asset that would combat substance abuse and addiction in America. My parents often reminded me that God would hold me accountable for how I used the talents He gave me.

That's a big part of the reason why I have tried to use them to help the most vulnerable in our society.

I was born and brought up in a nation of unlimited opportunity. It gave a kid from Brooklyn with no connections a chance to make national policy at the highest levels of government, law, and business. Nothing approaches the excitement of unlimited opportunity and the satisfaction of trying to make this society a better place. I have tried to leave each place I've worked a little better than I found it. I have always received more than I have given in public life. I believe that the American dream is nourished by the openness of our society—the reality that anyone can do anything, anyone can grow up to be president. That dream has survived civil war, two world wars, a depression, racial strife, half a century of cold war with communist nations, and the terrorist attack of September 11, 2001.

As for myself, when people ask how would I like to be remembered—as a McNamara whiz kid, an LBJ assistant, an architect of the Great Society, the *Washington Post* lawyer during Watergate, the originator of the anti-smoking campaign, the founder of The National Center on Addiction and Substance Abuse at Columbia University, I answer: The same way Supreme Court Justice Thurgood Marshall wanted to be remembered, "as someone who did the best he could with what God gave him."

And, I would add, someone who tried to make a few waves.

Acknowledgments

THIS MEMOIR has been more than seventy years in the making and more than four in the writing.

Several people read all or parts of the manuscript: Sue Brown, Marcel Bryar, Ervin Duggan, Jim English, Mort Janklow, Walter Modrys, Gerry Rosberg, and Jeanne Reid. I'm especially grateful to Ervin Duggan and Gerry Rosberg for their thoughtful suggestions over the past year.

Peggy Collins was my research assistant throughout the writing of this book. Her care, intelligence, and energy have been invaluable. She is a young woman of extraordinary talent, mature and incisive beyond her twenty-eight years, and a delight to work with. This book is far better for her painstaking research and insights and for her insistence that I "get it right" and "tell it like it was." She has a brilliant career ahead in her chosen profession of journalism and as a committed citizen and thoughtful Catholic.

Many colleagues, friends, and relatives helped refresh my memory. I can't list all those I interviewed for this book, but I do want to thank Robert McNamara, Alexander Haig, Brendan Sullivan, Joan Hembrooke Livornese, Robert Gillespie, and my cousins Jane Gill McDonald and John Scotto.

The Lyndon Baines Johnson Library in Texas, the finest of the presidential libraries thanks to Harry Middleton, was unfailingly cooperative. Archivist Linda Seelke was particularly helpful. So were librarian David Man and his colleagues Barbara Kurzweil and Ivy Truong-Tom at The National Center on Addiction and Substance Abuse at Columbia University. Marcia Lee, senior advisor for drug policy and research for the Senate Judiciary Subcommittee on Crime, helped track down a variety of House and Senate hearings and documents. For years, the law firm of Dewey Ballantine stored my papers, all 525 boxes of them, in a Brooklyn warehouse, and provided working space for more than a year so Peggy Collins and I could go through them.

My assistant Jane Nealy provided yeowoman service as interminable drafts made their way through the word processor and in helping keep the extensive files in order. JoAnn McCauley somehow kept my schedule going through all these years (as she has for so many before).

Peter Osnos offered penetrating and wise insights when he read the manuscript, and this memoir is richer and more intimate thanks to the profound questions he insisted I try to answer. I had heard of William Whitworth when he was associate editor of the *The New Yorker* and editor of *The Atlantic Monthly,* but I never expected to have the benefit of his talent. His meticulous and thoughtful editing has been exceptional. The entire team at PublicAffairs has been a pleasure to work with: David Patterson, Robert Kimzey, Kasey Pfaff, Gene Taft, and Matthew Goldberg, and Nina D'Amario and Craig Winkelman, who designed the cover.

Robert Barnett, whom years ago I recruited to Williams, Connolly & Califano as a young associate, was my lawyer and supportive and encouraging agent.

I owe a special thanks to my wife, Hilary, who read various versions of this manuscript. She has lived through years of weekends, and a number of weeks, as I locked myself in the wonderful study she created for me in Roxbury, Connecticut, to write this book. Most importantly, she has given me so much love—and taught me so much about how to love.

In this, my book about my life, I must thank Trudy Kendrew, mother of my children, for the extraordinary job she did in raising them over so many years when I was consumed with work. She is such a large part of the reason why Mark, a United States attorney in Connecticut; Joe III, a head and neck cancer surgeon and researcher at Johns Hopkins in Baltimore; and Claudia, completing medical school and soon to be a physician, have become such caring and committed adults. And finally, a word of appreciation to Mark, Joe, and Claudia, and to my wonderful stepchildren, Brooke, a lawyer and mother of three, and Frick, a photographer, all of whom missed many weekends and holidays with me as I worked to make this book something special for them.

With eternal gratitude to all who helped, as always the responsibility for what is on these pages is mine alone.

JAC, Jr.

March 2004

Photo Permissions

Mother and Dad/Courtesy of the Author.
A sassy, six-month-old/Courtesy of the Author.
Seven-years-old/Courtesy of the Author.
1955 Navy Officer Candidate/Courtesy of the Author.
The "guns and butter team"/Photo courtesy of LBJ Library/Yoichi Okamoto.
Making a point/Photo courtesy of LBJ Library/Yoichi Okamoto.
Whispering in the President's ear/Photo courtesy of LBJ Library/Yoichi Okamoto.
For LBJ's ear only/Photo courtesy of LBJ Library/Yoichi Okamoto.
LBJ loved parading me/Photo courtesy of LBJ Library/Yoichi Okamoto.
LBJ never stopped working/Photo courtesy of LBJ Library/Yoichi Okamoto.
Four-year-old Joe/Photo courtesy of LBJ Library/Yoichi Okamoto.
Late on the evening/Photo courtesy of LBJ Library/Yoichi Okamoto.
After 3:00 A.M./Photo courtesy of LBJ Library/Yoichi Okamoto.
Three days after the Watergate break-in/Photo courtesy of the *Washington Post*.
As a lawyer/Courtesy of the Author.
Counseling CBS correspondent Daniel Schorr/Courtesy of the Author.
With Alexander Haig/Photo courtesy of UPI.
Cover of Time/Courtesy of *Time* Magazine.
The start of the first national anti-smoking campaign/Courtesy of the Author.
Cartoon/Courtesy of Pat Oliphant.
Cartoon/Courtesy of Etta Hulme.
With Sen. Ted Kennedy/Courtesy of the Author.
Not seeing eye-to-eye/Courtesy of the Author.
In my office at HEW/Courtesy of the Author.
With Vice President Walter (Fritz) Mondale/Courtesy of the Author.
Cartoon/Courtesy of Gene Basset.
Washington pals/Courtesy of the Author.
Ed Williams/Courtesy of the Author.
With former first lady Lady Bird Johnson/Courtesy of the Author.
Bringing my daughter to work day/Courtesy of the Author.
With former first lady Betty Ford/Courtesy of the Author.
With Hilary/Courtesy of the Author.
With Hilary and Rev. Walter Modrys/Courtesy of the Author.
The Califano family/Courtesy of Frick Byers.

Notes

D URING THE FOUR years spent writing this memoir, Peggy Collins, my
research assistant, and I first sifted through some 525 two-foot-long
boxes, stored in a warehouse in Brooklyn, filled with personal and professional papers I had kept throughout my life. We read thousands of pages of
memoranda, reports, speeches, clippings, briefing books, court cases, minutes of cabinet and other meetings, and personal correspondence contained
in those boxes.

We dug through cartons of family papers and scrapbooks my father and
mother had kept. To deal with the early family history, my daughter Claudia went to Italy to search records of our ancestors in Meta Sorrento; I trav-
elled to Eyrecourt, Ireland, to trace my maternal grandparents; we obtained
the manifest of the ship on which my Grandfather Califano came to America. We did research in New York Public Library branches and also the the
archives of the Brooklyn diocese, of Brooklyn Preparatory High School
(now kept at Xavier High School in New York City), and of St. Joseph's Convent in Brentwood, New York. I obtained records from all the schools I
attended.

Peggy Collins and I interviewed scores of people, in person and by telephone, to check my recollection of conversations and events. I visited the
sites of my childhood, the schools I attended, and offices where I worked.

For the chapters regarding my various positions at the Pentagon, we
reviewed, in addition to my personal papers, fourteen boxes of my files,
totaling some 15,000 pages now included among the JFK Assassination
Papers at the National Archives in College Park, Maryland; another ten
boxes, 30,000 pages of material, at the National Archives; and six boxes of
papers of the Joint Chiefs of Staff.

In connection with chapter 13, "Getting Fidel," I submitted numerous
requests to the Department of Defense, the Central Intelligence Agency, and

the National Archives to declassify documents I had prepared or read during the Kennedy administration. We examined eleven boxes of classified papers at a facility in Suitland, Maryland, and four more boxes, classified as top secret, held at the Pentagon. Most (but not all) of the documents we requested were declassified, and information from them is revealed for the first time in this book.

I requested copies of files on me that are held by the Federal Bureau of Investigation, the Central Intelligence Agency, and the Internal Revenue Service. The FBI files I was able to obtain were heavily redacted.

In order to give the reader perspective and to set out the impact on me of events during my years as President Johnson's chief domestic aide and President Jimmy Carter's secretary of Health, Education, and Welfare, a few incidents that appear in *The Triumph and Tragedy of Lyndon Johnson* and *Governing America* will be found here, particularly in chapters 17 and 25, but from a different and more personal perspective.

We reviewed dozens of folios of newspaper and magazine clippings and did extensive library research to help refresh my recollection and set the historical context of the times I lived in and have written about. I reviewed relevant congressional hearings, court files, federal and corporate archives, oral histories, and other materials available at the LBJ and other libraries. I read scores of books and hundreds of articles, listened to many audio tapes, and viewed numerous video tapes. Of particular help were the *Washington Post*, the *New York Times*, *Newsweek*, *Time*, *Congressional Quarterly*, *National Journal*, and *Facts on File*.

I have not cluttered the memoir with endless citations where information used is easily obtained from public documents like newspapers and encyclopedias or is from my personal files. At a few points, I have cited memoranda or letters to support incidents of special significance. Over the course of my public service and private life, I often wrote a memorandum to record important conversations and events immediately after they occurred, and those have been invaluable in writing this memoir.

For historians, I have compiled source materials chapter by chapter, and they, along with all information used for this book and my papers, will be available at the LBJ Library in Austin, Texas.

Chapter 1: The Family

1. Opened in 1899, it was the world's first museum for children.
2. By the end of the twentieth century, St. Joseph's (co-ed since 1970) had added a campus in Suffolk County, Long Island.
3. Today, the College of New Rochelle has three additional schools, which are co-ed: the Graduate School (1969), the School of Nursing (1976), and an extraordinary adult-education program called the School of New Resources, founded in 1972 with campuses in Brooklyn, the Bronx, lower Manhattan, and Harlem, and at a theological seminary in midtown Manhattan.
4. The Feast of the Epiphany, in the Western tradition, commemorates the arrival of the Three Wise Men, who followed a star to the newborn Messiah, Jesus. In the Eastern Christian tradition, the Epiphany celebrates Christ's Baptism.

Chapter 2: The Early Years

1. On May 19, 1979, as secretary of Health, Education, and Welfare, I announced an alcoholism program at the National Council on Alcoholism Conference in Washington, D.C. Among the invited celebrities was Don Newcombe, a recovering alcoholic. I was just as much in awe of him as when I had seen him pitch at Ebbets Field, and I still have the Brooklyn Dodgers jacket he gave me that day.
2. Reiser's career-stunting head-on collision with the concrete center field wall at Sportsman's Park in St. Louis led to the padding of outfield walls and the laying of warning tracks at the outer edge of every major league outfield.

Chapter 3: Born, Bred, and Branded Catholic

1. At college, law school, and later when I worked in the government, I periodically received notes from the Carmelite nuns expressing their appreciation for my mother's support and offering their prayers for me.
2. They were: the Circumcision of Jesus—later called The Solemnity of Mary—(January 1); Ascension Thursday (forty days after Easter, when Christ went to heaven); The Assumption (August 15 to celebrate when Mary was assumed, body and spirit, to heaven); All Saints' Day (November 1); Immaculate Conception (December 8 to celebrate Mary's conception without original sin); Christmas (December 25). In 1991, the National Conference of Catholic bishops stipulated that whenever January 1 or August 15 fell on a Saturday or a Monday, the precept to attend Mass was abrogated.
3. Mite boxes come from the gospel story of the "Widow's mite," about the widow who gave up her two pennies, which was "all she had, her whole livelihood." (Mark 12:42–44).
4. Brooklyn Prep closed in 1972 and became Medgar Evers Community College.

Chapter 4: A Jesuit Education

1. Skinner, J. *The Cross and the Cinema: Legion of Decency and the National Catholic Office for Motion Pictures 1933–1970.* Praeger: Westport, CT: 1993, p. 37.
2. Walsh, F. *Sin and Censorship: The Catholic Church and the Motion Picture Industry.* Yale University: New Haven, CT: 1996, pp. 149, 195.
3. Six years later, in 1949, the Legion of Decency would raise its rating of *The Outlaw* to a B after the film bombed and Hughes agreed to many suggested changes.

4. In 1968 the new head of the Motion Picture Association, Jack Valenti, said that Hollywood's obligation was only to provide parents with information to make decisions for their children, and in 1970 the Legion was dissolved for its lack of influence.

5. Dulles, Avery. *A Testimonial to Grace and Reflections on a Theological Journey, 1946.* Sheed and Ward, Kansas City: 1996, p. 115. (50th Anniversary Edition.) In February 2001, Pope John Paul II made Jesuit priest Avery Dulles a cardinal, the first American theologian so elevated.

6. Green, J. *The Encyclopedia of Censorship.* Facts on File, New York: 1990, pp. 136–141.

7. In 1966, the Vatican formally abolished the Index because it was no longer being enforced. The volume of publications—which had reached 4,126 books—coupled with the "increasing maturity and sophistication of Catholic laymen," rendered the Index obsolete.

8. Sullivan, J. F. *General Ethics.* Holy Cross College, Worcester, MA: 1931, p. 181.

9. Sullivan, J. F. *Special Ethics.* Holy Cross College, Worcester, MA: 1931, p. 219.

10. Ibid, pp. 205–206.

Chapter 5: A Harvard Law School Education

1. "Harvard's President Pusey." *Time.* 1 March 1954, p. 60.

2. Casner, J. and Leach, W. B. *Cases and Text on Property.* Little, Brown, Boston: 1951, p. 483.

3. Smith, D. *Zechariah Chafee, Jr.: Defender of Liberty and Law.* Harvard University, Cambridge, MA: 1986, p. 153.

Chapter 6: Landlubber in the Navy

1. Califano, J. A. "In Retirement, Limitations on the Employment of Retired Naval Officers," 1957.

2. Section 201 of the Reserve Officer Personnel Act of 1954.

Chapter 7: A Bite of the Big Apple

1. Born in 1726 in Muro in southern Italy, Saint Gerard, a tailor, joined the Redemptorists as a lay brother and became known for his extraordinary supernatural gifts, such as bilocation, prophecy, visions, and infused knowledge. In 1754 he was accused of lechery by one Neria Caggiano, a charge she later admitted was false. He spent his final years in Caposele in southern Italy ministering to the poor, and died of consumption in 1775. His feast day is celebrated on October 16.

Chapter 9: Comfortable and Catholic in New York

1. Ruddy, J. *The Apostolic Constitution Christus Dominus.* Catholic University, Washington, DC: 1957, p. 117.

2. *Ad Petri Cathedram: Encyclical of Pope John XXIII on Truth, Unity and Peace in a Spirit of Charity.* 29 June 1959.

3. Califano, J. A. "Review: The House of Intellect, by Jacques Barzun." *Jubilee.* Vol 7. No. 10. 1960, p. 53.

4. Whyte, W. *The Organization Man.* Simon and Schuster, New York: 1956, p. 3.

5. Galbraith, J. K. *The Affluent Society.* Houghton Mifflin, New York: 1958, p. 1.

6. Mills, C. W. *The Power Elite.* Oxford University, New York: 1959, p. 11.

7. Ibid, p. 324.

8. Merton, T. *The Seven Storey Mountain.* Harcourt Brace, New York: 1948, p. 57.
9. Murray was the architect of Vatican II's Declaration on Religious Freedom. He played a liberalizing role at the Second Vatican Council along with other Jesuit thinkers, like Karl Rahner of Germany and Cardinal Jean Danielou of France. He died suddenly in 1967.
10. Mary and Ellen Lukas wrote the definitive biography, *Teilhard,* published by Doubleday in 1977.
11. Harrington, M. *The Other America: Poverty in the United States.* Macmillan, New York: 1962, p. 2.

Chapter 10: Ringing Doorbells for Kennedy

1. Burns, J. M. *John Kennedy: A Political Profile.* Harcourt & Brace, New York: 1961, p. 275.
2. Secretary of Labor Frances Perkins was the only woman.
3. Schlesinger, A. *Age of Roosevelt: II. Coming of the New Deal.* Houghton Mifflin, Boston: 1959, p. 22.
4. Kennedy, J. F. *Strategy of Peace.* Harper & Row, New York: 1960, p. 66.
5. Wilson, J. *The Amateur Democrat: Club Politics in Three Cities.* University of Chicago, Chicago: 1962, p. 34.
6. An extraordinary builder and businessman, Richard Ravitch would help Governor Hugh Carey save New York City during its fiscal crisis in the 1970s and as chair of the Metropolitan Transit Authority revitalize the city's subways in the early 1980s. Arnold Fein became an associate justice of the Appellate Division of the New York State Supreme Court.
7. In one of the earliest examples of spinning the press, Kennedy forces emphasized this anti-Catholicism, dampening expectations and setting the stage for dramatic coverage of a win that they hoped would propel their candidate to the front of the pack and thus persuade hard-nosed professional politicians to support his candidacy, or at least not oppose it on grounds of unelectability.

Chapter 11: A Whiz Kid in McNamara's Pentagon

1. The term originated when a group of brilliant young Air Force officers, including McNamara, Tex Thornton (who later founded Litton Industries), and Arjay Miller (who later headed Ford Motor Company), sold themselves as a package to Ford at the end of World War II.
2. The Soviets launched the first satellite into space in 1957.
3. The RAND Corporation was a nonprofit research organization formed in 1948 to promote "scientific, educational and charitable purposes for the public welfare and security of the United States." RAND was the source of several McNamara whiz kids.
4. Kahn, H. *On Thermonuclear War.* Princeton University, Princeton, NJ: 1961, p. 22.
5. Sullivan, J. F. *Special Ethics.* Holy Cross College, Worcester, MA: 1931, pp. 222–227.
6. Testimony of Robert McNamara. 26 July 1961. *Congressional Record–House.* 10 August 1961, pp. 15326–15327.
7. Kennedy, J. F. Memorandum to Secretary of Defense McNamara. "National Security Action Memorandum No. 2." Retrieved from John F. Kennedy Library. National Security files, Meeting and Memoranda Series, Box 331. Folder: "National Security Action Memorandum 72."
8. McNamara, R. *In Retrospect.* Times Books, New York: 1995, pp. 33–34.
9. Mundt presided over the House Un-American Activities Committee hearings in the Alger Hiss case and served as chairman of the Senate Permanent Investigating Subcommittee during the McCarthy hearings.
10. Goldwater's book *Conscience of a Conservative,* a bestseller in 1960, set the stage for his presidential nomination in 1964.

11. *POW, the Fight Continues after the Battle: The Report of the Secretary of Defense's Advisory Committee on Prisoners of War*. GPO, Washington, DC: 1955, p. 14.

12. *Communist Interrogation, Indoctrination and Exploitation of American Military and Civilian Prisoners*. GPO, Washington, DC: 1957, pp. 1–16.

13. *POW, the Fight Continues after the Battle: The Report of the Secretary of Defense's Advisory Committee on Prisoners of War*. GPO, Washington, DC: 1955, p. 12.

14. Fulbright, W. Memorandum submitted to the Department of Defense on propaganda activities of military personnel. *Congressional Record–Senate*. 2 August 1961, pp. 14433–14439.

15. Department of Defense Directive No. 5122.5 of 10 July 1961. *Congressional Record–Senate*. 26 July 1961.

16. "McNamara faces quiz on policy on military anti-red activities." *Washington Post*. 1 September 1961, p. A2.

17. In 1972, after Senator Richard Russell's death, the building was renamed the Russell Senate Office Building.

18. In years to come, that Caucus Room would continue its tradition as the scene of major public hearings: Watergate in 1973, Iran-Contra in 1987, and the Supreme Court nomination of Clarence Thomas in 1991.

19. Soft-spoken and hard-working, Lawrence was the inconspicuous son of a Nebraska barber, an Army private in World War II, married with two children. Thurmond called him the "wielder of a red pen," a phrase the *New York Times* headlined the next morning. As a result, Lawrence, who had devoted twenty-two years to government service, received mail calling him a pro-communist traitor.

20. Letter from President Kennedy to Secretary of Defense McNamara. 8 February 1962.

Chapter 12: In the Army on the Home Front

1. Branch, T. *Parting the Waters: America in the King Years 1954–63*. Simon and Schuster, New York: 1988, p. 663.

2. "John F. Kennedy tapes: Federal intervention in 'Ole Miss' crisis takes shape in phone call." *Washington Post*. 24 June 1983, p. A12.

3. Branch, T. *Parting the Waters*, p. 670.

4. Six months later, on April 10, 1963, a gunman shot at, and barely missed, General Walker outside his home in Dallas. The gunman was Lee Harvey Oswald. Report of the Warren Commission on the Kennedy Assassination.

5. Branch, T. *Parting the Waters*, p. 660.

6. Meredith went to summer school and graduated from the University of Mississippi in August, 1963. He was shot by a sniper during a civil rights march in 1966, but recovered. He shocked the civil rights movement when he later campaigned for Governor Barnett, worked for North Carolina Senator Jesse Helms, and endorsed former Ku Klux Klansman David Duke in his run for governor of Louisiana. At the turn of the century he lived in Jackson, Mississippi, sporting an Ole Miss cap and bumper sticker while developing an institute to teach black males standard English. The campus of Ole Miss now counts some 1,800 blacks among its 14,500 students.

7. The first black student, Autherine Lucy, was admitted to the University of Alabama in 1956, but she left after three days, when university officials expelled her, saying they could not provide protection in the face of threats by Tuscaloosa townspeople and Ku Klux Klansmen.

8. General Abrams was then director of operations at the Pentagon. He would serve as U.S. commander in the Vietnam War from 1968 to 1972.

9. Medgar Evers's assassin, Byron De La Beckwith, escaped prosecution until 1990, when he was convicted of murder. Beckwith died in 2001 while serving a life sentence.

10. Hood became a social worker, a minister, and the first black deputy police chief in Detroit. When in

1997 Hood received from the University of Alabama his doctorate in interdisciplinary studies, he was one of six hundred blacks to receive degrees and 12 percent of the student body was black. Hood invited George Wallace, who had renounced his segregationist views, to attend.

11. Malone became the first black to graduate from the University of Alabama. She worked in Washington, D.C., for the Justice Department, the Veterans Administration, and the President's Council on Youth Opportunity before settling in Atlanta, where she headed the Atlanta-based Voter Education Project and worked at the Environmental Protection Agency.

12. In 1941, Randolph threatened a march on wartime Washington to demand more jobs for blacks in defense plants. FDR responded with an executive order banning employment discrimination in defense industries.

13. In 1947, Rustin was arrested for participating in the first freedom ride, then called a Journey of Reconciliation. His account of his twenty-two days on the chain gang led to its abolition in North Carolina.

14. Fauntroy was pastor of New Bethel Baptist Church in Washington, D.C. In 1971, he became the district's first elected congressional representative, serving in that post until 1990.

15. Devinney, J. and Crossley, C. *Eyes on the Prize*. Blackside, Boston: 1987, videorecording.

16. Ibid.

Chapter 13: Getting Fidel

1. Each Brigade member had a serial number with the numbers starting at 2501 to give the impression that the contingent was much larger. The name Brigade 2506 was in honor of the number of Carlos Rodriguez Santana, who died during training for the invasion.

2. "National Security Memorandum No. 213." To the Secretary of State on the subject of Interdepartmental Organization for Cuban Affairs. 8 January 1963.

3. Lansdale had gone to South Vietnam in 1954 as head of the Saigon Military Mission, a group of American CIA agents specializing in covert actions and dirty tricks. He returned to Vietnam as an adviser to U.S. Ambassador Henry Cabot Lodge and the South Vietnamese government from 1965 to 1968. He is considered the prototype for Colonel Hillandale in the William Lederer and Eugene Burdick novel *The Ugly American*.

4. Memorandum from Brig. Gen. Lansdale on the subject of Task 33, Cuba Project. 19 January 1962. Retrieved from the National Archives, JFK Assassination Records, JCS Papers, Box 1, Doc. 184, 202–10001–10183.

5. Memorandum for the record, minutes of the Caribbean Survey Group. 21 March 1962. Retrieved from the National Archives, JFK Assassination Records, JCS Papers, Doc. 174, 202–1001–10173.

6. Memorandum for the Special Assistant to the Secretary of the Army from W. Wendt. 28 March 1963. Califano papers.

7. Memorandum on "U.S. Training for Cubans." 18 January 1963. Retrieved from the National Archives, JFK Assassination Records, Califano Papers, Box III, Doc. 198–100004–10200.

8. Handwritten note to Joseph A. Califano, Jr., from James Patchell. 22 June 1963.

9. Memorandum to Joseph Califano from V. P. Mock. "Review of U.S. Policy with respect to Cuba." 1 April 1963. Retrieved from the National Archives, JFK Assassination Records, Califano Papers, Box III, Doc. 198–10004–10156.

10. Memorandum prepared by Col. J. K. Patchell on "U.S. Policy concerning clandestine and covert actions directed against Cuba." 18 April 1963. Califano papers.

11. Memorandum to Joseph Califano from Office of the Chief of Naval Operations. "Measures to restrict travel to Cuba for subversive training." 14 February 1963. Retrieved from the National Archives, JFK Assassination Records, Califano Papers, Box IV, Folder 18, 198–10007–10050.

12. Memorandum from Joseph F. Dolan. "Special White House Task Force on United States Problems, Re: Cuba." 29 May 1975. Joseph A. Califano, Jr., files.

13. Memorandum from Cyrus Vance. 18 February 1963. "Cuban Based Communist Subversion in Latin America." JFK Assassination Records, Califano Papers, Box III, 198–10007–10232.

14. In 1980, as secretary of state, Vance would object to a military rescue of American hostages in Iran and become one of three secretaries of state to resign over principle. The other two were William Jennings Bryan, who resigned as secretary of state in 1915 over President Woodrow Wilson's policies toward Germany, which he thought might lead to war, and Lewis Cass, who in 1860 resigned over President James Buchanan's refusal to block the secessionists from taking over forts in Charleston, South Carolina.

15. King's December 11, 1959, memo to CIA director Allen Dulles contained the first known proposal to assassinate Castro. Weiner, T. "Word for Word: The Bay of Pigs." *New York Times*. 25 March 2001, p. 7.

16. Memorandum for the record. "Meeting with the President on 18 February 1963." By Joseph Califano on 22 February 1963. Retrieved from the National Archives, JFK Assassination Records, Califano Papers, Box III, 198–10007–10232.

17. Memorandum from Cyrus Vance. "Cuban based communist subversion in Latin America." 18 February 1963. Retrieved from the National Archives, JFK Assassination Records, Califano Papers, Box III, 198–10007–10232.

18. "Memorandum from Gordon Chase to McGeorge Bundy on the Cuban Coordinating Committee, 3 April 1963." White, M. J., ed., *The Kennedys and Cuba: The Declassified Documentary History.* Ivan R. Dee, Chicago: 1999, p. 309.

19. White House Daily Calendar retrieved from the John F. Kennedy Library.

20. "Memorandum from Joseph Califano to Cyrus Vance. Presidential Action on special Group Items Concerning Cuba, 9 April 1963." White, M. J., ed., *The Kennedys and Cuba: The Declassified Documentary History.* Ivan R. Dee, Chicago: 1999, p. 313.

21. Ibid.

22. Ibid.

23. Memorandum on "Department of Defense Support to CIA Covert Activities." 29 July 1963. Retrieved from the National Archives, JFK Assassination Records, JCS Papers, J–3, Doc. 1, 202–10001–10000.

24. Memorandum on "Summary and Conclusions of U.S. Policy toward Cuba." 19 July 1963. Retrieved from the National Archives, JFK Assassination Records, Califano Papers, Box VI, Folder 5, 198–10004–10005.

25. Ibid.

26. "Talking paper for the JCS for CIA Briefing, 25 September 1963." 25 September 1963. Prepared by Col. Wyman, USA. Retrieved from the National Archives, JFK Association Records, JCS Papers, J–3, Doc. 77, 202–10001–10076.

27. CIA memorandum for Joseph A. Califano on the subject of "The Cuban Military Establishment." 21 August 1963. Retrieved from the Office of the Secretary of Defense, Califano Papers, Box I, 74–0041. Folder: Cuban military personalities.

28. Memorandum for Cyrus Vance from A. M. Haig on the subject of "Talking paper for use by JCS." 3 September 1963. Retrieved from the National Archives, JFK Assassination Records, Califano Papers, 198–10004–10203.

29. Memorandum for the secretary of the Army from Curtis LeMay on the subject of "Department of Defense Support of Covert Operations conducted by the Central Intelligence Agency against Cuba." 24 September 1963. Retrieved from the National Archives, JFK Assassination Records, JCS Papers, J–3, Doc. 11, 202–10001–10010.

30. Memorandum to the director, Joint Staff, from Walter Higgins on the subject of a "Briefing by Mr. Fitzgerald." 25 September 1963. Retrieved from the National Archives, JFK Assassination Papers, JCS Papers, J–3, Doc. 28, 202–10001–10027.

31. Memorandum for the record from Walter Higgins on the subject of "Briefing by Mr. Desmond Fitzgerald on CIA Cuban Operations and Planning." 25 September 1963. Retrieved from the National Archives, JFK Assassination Records, JCS Papers, J–3, Doc. 29, 202–10001–10028.

32. "Alleged Assassination Plots Involving Foreign Leaders." An Interim Report of the Select Committee to Study Governmental Operations with Respect to Intelligence Activities. United States Senate. GPO, Washington, DC: 20 November 1975, p. 5.

33. Ibid, pp. 71–73.

34. Holland, M. "After thirty years: making sense of the assassination." *Reviews in American History.* Vol. 22, n2, p. 191.

35. Memorandum for the record prepared by Earle Wheeler. "Meeting with the President on Cuba, 1100 hours. 19 December 1963." 19 December 1963. Retrieved from the National Archives, JFK Assassination Records, JCS Papers, 202–10002–10010.

36. Press release, 25 February 1964. Statement made by Joseph A. Califano, Jr.

37. Erneido Oliva became deputy commanding general of the District of Columbia National Guard. Other Brigade members went into Wall Street banking firms, the Florida legislature, teaching at universities, and careers in medicine, law, and business. Several had successful careers as officers in the U.S. military; some went to work for the CIA. Most became American citizens.

Chapter 15: Isthmus Insurrection

1. Baxter, R. and Carroll, D. *Panama Canal: Background Papers and Proceedings of the Sixth Hammarskjöld Forum.* Oceana, Dobbs Ferry, New York: 1965, p. 50. *Report of the Events in Panama January 9–12, 1964.* Prepared by the Investigating Committee appointed by the International Commission of Jurists, p. 12.

2. Ibid, p. 54.

3. Thomas Mann's appointment as assistant secretary of state for Latin American affairs was Lyndon Johnson's first, made just three weeks after Kennedy's assassination. Johnson also named Mann a special assistant to the president. Though a career foreign service officer, Mann took a harder anti-communist line than most of his State Department colleagues. By naming Mann, LBJ pleased conservatives and hoped to get negotiating room to come to some agreement acceptable to Panama on the future of the Canal Zone.

4. *Report of the Events in Panama January 9–12, 1964.* Prepared by the Investigating Committee appointed by the International Commission of Jurists, p. 28.

5. Hearings of the Committee of the International Commission of Jurists in Panama. Transcript of Proceedings. March 1964.

6. Poor, Peggy. "Drop gag on Panama; A shift in U.S. policy." *New York Journal-American.* 7 March 1964.

7. *Report of the Events in Panama January 9–12, 1964.* Prepared by the Investigating Committee appointed by the International Commission of Jurists, p. 18.

8. Ibid, p. 28.

Chapter 16: Troubleshooting for McNamara

1. McNamara used his deputy secretary of defense as an alter ego. They shared the same staff (mine), and McNamara had breakfast or lunch almost every day with his deputy, initially Roswell Gilpatric and after January 28, 1964, Cy Vance. As the special assistant, I joined those meals at least weekly.

2. The committee was composed of the secretaries of the Treasury (Douglas Dillon) and commerce (Luther Hodges), the administrators of the National Aeronautics and Space Administration (James

Webb) and the Federal Aviation Agency (Najeeb Halaby and later William McKee, who succeeded him in July 1965), CIA Director John McCone, and civilians Eugene Black (former president of the World Bank) and Stanley Osborne (chairman of the board of Olin Mathieson).

3. The politics involved forced LBJ to accept congressional appropriations for research on the SST, but in 1971, during the Nixon administration, Congress took note of McNamara's arguments and ended government funding.

4. Johnson had appointed this native Puerto Rican an admiral and deputy chief on July 10, 1964. President Nixon named Rivero ambassador to Spain in 1972.

5. LBJ Library. Recordings of conversations and meetings. Tape WH6411.03. 4 November 1964, 9:56 A.M.

6. Beschloss, M. *Reaching for Glory: Lyndon Johnson's Secret White House Tapes, 1964–1965*. Simon and Schuster, New York: 2001, p. 123.

7. Scotto had given about $20,000 to Kennedy's 1964 campaign. In 1979, Scotto was convicted of labor racketeering and related felonies. Edward Bennett Williams represented him on appeal but was unable to persuade the court to overturn the conviction. Scotto was released from prison in 1984.

8. After I did join the White House staff, Walter's wife, Ann Pincus, wrote a column about me in the *New York Post* on April 26, 1967: "Since he first entered government service in 1961, Califano has consistently filled the role of troubleshooter in delicate areas. . . ."

9. Memorandum for the record on the subject of "Communist Participation in the current Dominican rebellion." 30 April 1965. Retrieved from Office of the Secretary of Defense, Califano Papers, 74–0041, Box 1, no folder title.

10. "Forces in Dominican Republic." Undated. Retrieved from Office of the Secretary of Defense, Califano Papers, 74–0041, Box 1. No folder title.

11. McNamara, R. *In Retrospect*. Times Books, New York: 1995, p. 183.

12. Memorandum for Secretary McNamara from Joseph Califano. 11 May 1965. Retrieved from Office of the Secretary of Defense, Califano Papers, 68A5770, Box 4, Folder: Peace Demonstrations 1965.

13. Memorandum for Joseph Califano from William Sullivan on the subject of "Interreligious Committee on Vietnam and Its Members." 12 May 1965. Retrieved from Office of the Secretary of Defense, Califano Papers, 68A5770, Box 4, Folder: Peace Demonstrations 1965.

Chapter 17: The LBJ Years

1. Recordings of conversations and meetings. From LBJ Library. Tape WH6508.04. 14 August 1965, 8:09 P.M.

2. Recordings of conversations and meetings. From the LBJ Library. Tape WH6509.02. 8 September 1965, 6 P.M.

3. President's Daily Diary from LBJ Library. 9 November 1965.

4. Ibid.

5. President's Daily Diary from LBJ Library. 9 November 1965.

6. Eventually we learned that the problem began when a shoebox-size relay at a Canadian plant was activated but could not handle the power flows expected of it, thus sparking the failure that cascaded throughout New England and southeastern New York. The report of the Federal Power Commission ruled out sabotage.

7. Also, McGeorge Bundy (later president of the Ford Foundation); Jim Jones (later chair of the House Budget Committee and ambassador to Mexico); Clifford Alexander (secretary of the Army in the Carter administration); Stuart Eizenstat (ambassador to the European Union in the Clinton administration); Major Hugh Robinson (the first black presidential military aide, who became a major general in the U.S. Army and a successful businessman); Barefoot Sanders (later a distinguished federal district judge); and Marvin Watson (later president of Occidental Petroleum and then Dallas Baptist College).

8. "Remarks at the Federal Woman's Award Ceremony, March 14, 1968." *Public Papers of the Presidents, Lyndon B. Johnson 1968.* GPO, Washington, DC: p. 399.

9. It included: Fred Bohen, Jim Gaither, Larry Levinson, Matthew Nimetz, John Robson, and Stanford Ross. All except Fred Bohen, who had graduated from the Woodrow Wilson School of Public and International Affairs at Princeton University, were lawyers. Gaither and Nimetz had clerked for Supreme Court justices. Robson later served in the administrations of Gerald Ford and both George Bushes.

10. Drew, Elizabeth. "Pools . . . Last Summer and Next," *Washington Post Potomac Magazine,* October 2, 1966.

11. Caro, Robert A., *Master of the Senate,* p. 624.

12. Unfortunately, one person later died as a result of action by regular forces.

13. LBJ did the same thing when he met with Italians, hauling Valenti and me before them as his "closest advisors." Once, he overstepped at a meeting with the American Bar Association, then dominated by Republican lawyers. He made a big deal of the fact that I had come from Tom Dewey's law firm, suggesting that I was as conservative a Republican as that party's former presidential candidate. One of the lawyers present was Cloyd Laporte, the Democratic partner at Dewey's firm, who knew the truth about my politics.

14. Beschloss, M. *Reaching for Glory.* Simon and Schuster, New York: 2001, p. 419.

15. *Griswold v. Connecticut* (1965).

16. Peace and social activists Daniel and Philip Berrigan, a Jesuit and Josephite priest respectively, were arrested in 1968 and jailed as part of the Catonsville 9, who burnt draft records to protest the Vietnam War. Both brothers repeatedly served prison time for pacifist actions.

17. The liberal community ostracized staffers like Walt Rostow for his part in the Vietnam War. Rostow and his wife Elspeth went to the University of Texas in Austin, where he taught and wrote and she became dean of the LBJ School of Public Affairs.

18. LBJ assigned Lady Bird to select the architect and me to conceptualize both institutions. Mrs. Johnson looked at libraries across the country. The Beinecke Rare Book and Manuscript Library, which Gordon Bunshaft had designed for Yale University in New Haven, impressed her, and she selected him to design the LBJ library and museum. Jim Gaither of my staff traveled around the country, visiting schools of public policy. Together we developed the concept for the LBJ School of Public Affairs. We then put together a dog-and-pony presentation for prospective funders. Johnson wanted to get the library built within two years of his leaving the White House (the library was dedicated on May 22, 1971), and he wanted the school to be part of the University of Texas so that it would receive state funding.

19. James Gaither returned to San Francisco and built Cooley Godward LLP, a premier law firm on the West Coast. John Robson became undersecretary of the Treasury in the administration of Bush I and chairman of the Export-Import Bank under Bush II. Lawrence Levinson became top vice president and right hand of Charles Bludhorn as they built Gulf and Western. Fred Bohen became chief operating officer of the Rockefeller Institute in New York. Matthew Nimetz became undersecretary of state for security, science, and technology in 1980 and President Clinton's special envoy to Greece and the former Yugoslav republic of Macedonia. Stan Ross became commissioner of Social Security.

20. LBJ vetoed the bill on November 13, 1966.

21. McGovern, G. "Discovering greatness in Lyndon Johnson." *New York Times.* 5 December 1999, p. 17. Galbraith, K., speech delivered at LBJ Library, 23 November 1999.

Chapter 18: Recharging Batteries

1. In February 1968, President Johnson instituted a lottery for the draft and ended most graduate school deferments (except for medical, dental, and divinity students), beginning with those who had

entered graduate school in the fall of 1967, because he considered it unfair for the poor to bear the burden of the war while the affluent avoided service by enrolling in graduate schools.

2. Horne, A. "House panel queries Bundy on Ford Foundation's status." *International Herald Tribune.* 22 February 1969, p. 5.

3. Those hearings, fueled in no small measure by Bundy's testimony, provided the momentum to pass legislation tightening the rules on foundations, requiring them to spend at least 5 percent of their capital each year and prohibiting grants such as the one I had received.

4. Califano, J. A. *The Student Revolution: A Global Confrontation.* W. W. Norton & Co., New York: 1970.

Chapter 19: Washington Lawyer: Arnold & Porter

1. Haynsworth continued on the Fourth Circuit Court of Appeals until retiring in 1981. He died in 1989.

2. Herb Block cartoon. *Washington Post.* 18 March 1970, p. A18.

3. After an unsuccessful run for the Republican senate nomination in Florida, Carswell practiced law in Tallahassee. In 1976 he was convicted of battery and fined $100 for making sexual advances to an undercover male police officer in a men's room. He died in 1992 at age seventy-two.

4. In 2002, the ABA's fifteen-member Standing Committee on the Judiciary included three African-Americans , one Asian-American, and seven women.

5. Joseph A. Califano, Jr., Memorandum to the President, December 6, 1968.

6. Joseph A. Califano, Jr., Daily Calendar, November 13, 1969.

7. Joseph A. Califano, Jr., Daily Calendar, November 21, 1969.

8. A year later Joplin and Hendrix died of drug overdoses.

9. *Comprehensive Drug Abuse Prevention and Control Act of 1970.* P.L. 91–513.

10. Memorandum for Ellis Anderson. May 24, 1973.

11. Colen, B. "Adventurous chemist and his pill: Valium, the most popular most abused prescription pill." *Washington Post.* January 20, 1980, p. A1.

12. "Chronology of events leading to demonstration." *Washington Post.* 10 May 1970, p. A4.

13. "Tragedy at Kent: Cambodia and dissent, crisis of Presidential leadership." *Life.* 15 May 1970.

14. "Chronology of events leading to demonstration." *Washington Post.* 10 May 1970, p. A4.

15. "You've done more for your country than most of your countrymen will realize in your lifetime," Gardner told Johnson when he resigned. "But at this point in time, I don't believe you can lead the country . . . pull it together."

16. Joseph A. Califano, Jr., personal papers.

17. Upon his graduation from Yale Law School in 1971, I brought Greg Craig with me to Williams, Connolly & Califano. He went on to represent John Hinckley, who attempted to assassinate President Ronald Reagan; President Clinton during his impeachment; and the father of Elian Gonzales, the child returned to Cuba in June 2000.

18. Joseph A. Califano, Jr., Daily Calendar.

19. *Migrant and Seasonal Farmworker Powerlessness: Hearings Before the Subcommittee on Migratory Labor of the Committee on Labor and Public Welfare United States Ninety-first Congress.* July 24, 1970, pp. 5884–5886.

Chapter 20: Washington Lawyer: Williams, Connolly & Califano

1. Ungar, S. J. "Former LBJ aide switches law jobs." *Washington Post.* 29 April 1971, p. B1.

2. Levey, R. "Father's Court Plea: Show her any mercy." *Washington Post.* 29 May 1971, p. A1.

3. Joseph A. Califano, Jr., personal correspondence. June 4, 1971.

4. Timm and Caldwell were convicted of murder and robbery in March 1972 and sentenced to life imprisonment.

5. Graham, K. *Personal History*. Vintage Books, New York: 1997.

6. In 1964, Harry Sonneborn settled his divorce case with his wife, June, with a property settlement based on valuing their jointly held McDonald's stock at $2.50 a share. In April 1965, McDonald's went public and the stock was worth $22.50 a share. June sued her ex in February 1969 for $20 million, arguing that he knew he was going to take the company public at the time of their settlement.

7. Erwin Griswold, Johnson's appointee as solicitor general, who stayed on in the Nixon administration, argued the case for the government (he later said he didn't think he had a chance of winning). Yale University professor Alexander Bickel, a constitutional law expert, argued for the *Times*. William Glendon argued for the *Post*.

8. On April 3, Nixon announced plans to review the case. Aubrey Daniel III, then a twenty-nine-year-old Army JAG captain, had persuaded a military court of six officers, including five Vietnam veterans, to convict Calley. Daniel wrote to Nixon, lambasting the President's intervention, and his letter became public. Impressed by the conviction and the letter, Williams hired Daniel over the phone. Calley's conviction was eventually overturned and he was released after three years of house arrest.

9. Hackworth, D. *About Face*. Pan Books, London: 1989.

10. Hackworth left the country soon after and settled in Australia for a number of years. He resurfaced in the 1979 movie *Apocalypse Now*, as the inspiration for Francis Ford Coppola's character Colonel Kurtz. In 1990, *Newsweek* hired him to cover Operation Desert Storm, and he has been a television military analyst.

11. Joseph A. Califano, Jr., personal papers. Heineman had attended Northwestern University law school with Kerner and served as first chairman of the Illinois Board of Higher Education when Kerner was governor. I got to know Heineman when he chaired our presidential task force on income maintenance and when I unsuccessfully tried to recruit him as undersecretary of commerce with a promise that he would eventually be moved to the cabinet post. He knew never to take one government job in anticipation of another.

12. In April 1973, Kerner was sentenced to three years in prison. After the case was affirmed on appeal, in a letter to Richard Nixon, Kerner finally resigned his seat on the Court of Appeals and entered a minimum-security prison in Kentucky. Kerner, a heavy smoker, was released on parole March 6, 1975, for lung cancer surgery. He died of that cancer a year later.

13. In August 2000 a federal judge awarded $8 million to 502 former inmates and their families to settle a twenty-five-year-old lawsuit. As of 2003, families of former prison guards were still waiting for a task force appointed by New York governor George Pataki in 2001 to decide on their demands for restitution.

14. "The Shame of the Prisons," Ben H. Bagdikian. *Washington Post*. 30 January 1972 through 6 February 1972.

15. *Saxbe, Attorney General et al. v. Washington Post Co. et al.,* U.S. Supreme Court (June 24, 1974).

Chapter 21: The Democratic Party's Cultural Revolution

1. *Mandate for Reform: Report of the Commission on Party Structure and Delegate Selection to the Democratic National Committee.* April 1970. Washington, DC.

2. Committee members included Kenneth Clark, professor of psychology at City College in New York; Philip Lee, chancellor of the University of California Medical Center; Richard Lee, mayor of New Haven, Connecticut; former Federal Communications chairman Newton Minow; Merton (Joe)

Peck, chairman of the Yale University Department of Economics; and Gus Tyler, of the International Ladies Garment Workers Union.

3. Mink, P. "Equal rights for women: A national priority." *Congressional Record*, 1 June 1970.

4. Transcript of a meeting of the Democratic Policy Council. 30 April 1970. Califano Papers.

5. Letter to Humphrey from Mink, 23 June 1970. Califano Papers.

6. Letter from Berman to Mink, 14 July 1970. Califano Papers.

7. Califano Papers.

8. Ross, N. "Democrat Hits Views of Berman." *Washington Post.* 30 July 1970.

9. Bender, M. "Doctors deny woman's hormones affect her as an executive." *New York Times.* 31 July 1970, C-33.

10. Califano personal papers. Oral argument 1972.

11. For example, where half the state's population was female and half the state's Democratic Party strength was female, half the delegates had to be female; where 5 percent of the population was black and 25 percent of the party strength was black, 15 percent of the delegation had to be black. In 1970, the voting age was lowered from twenty-one to eighteen under a constitutional amendment proposed by Lyndon Johnson in 1968.

12. In 1965, LBJ had named Harris as the first black woman ambassador (to Luxembourg). She became dean of Howard University Law School in 1969.

13. To Daley, the Chicago 7 were a sleazy crew out to subvert our government and party: David Dellinger, chairman of the National Mobilization Committee to End the War in Vietnam; Rennie Davis and Tom Hayden, leaders of the Students for a Democratic Society; Abbie Hoffman and Jerry Rubin, leaders of the Youth International Party (Yippies); Lee Weiner, a research assistant at Northwestern University; and John Froines, a professor at the University of Oregon. On February 18, 1970, the jury acquitted Froines and Weiner of all charges. The other five were convicted and sentenced to five years in prison. Bobby Seale, the Black Panther founder, whose trial was severed from the rest, was sentenced to four years in prison for contempt of court. All convictions were later overturned by the U.S. Seventh Circuit Court of Appeals because of procedural errors.

14. Among the young attorneys assisting me was a summer associate who expressed excitement at working on a case headed for the Supreme Court within a week of the time it was argued in federal district court. I told him that this had never happened in my experience and wasn't likely to happen again. He joined our firm upon graduation from law school, but soon decided that politics offered a more satisfying life. The associate, Chuck Robb, went on to become governor of Virginia and for two terms U.S. senator from that state.

15. Berman, E. *Hubert: The Triumph and Tragedy of the Humphrey I Knew.* G. P. Putnam's Sons, New York: 1979. For a measure of the man Humphrey, consider this. In late 1977 when I was secretary of Health, Education, and Welfare, he called me from the hospital bed where he was dying of cancer. Humphrey had seen Jesse Jackson on CBS's *60 Minutes* talking about Operation Push to help black teens; he called to ask me to provide funds to help the civil rights leader, which I did.

16. Only the 1924 Democratic convention held a longer session, during the debate that Catholics and liberals mounted there to have the party platform condemn the Ku Klux Klan. That plank was defeated. The convention, the first ever broadcast live on radio, lasted seventeen days and 103 ballots before the party nominated John W. Davis, as Catholic candidate Al Smith failed in his first attempt to gain the party's presidential nomination.

17. "Introducing . . . the McGovern machine." *Time.* 24 July 1972. Vol. 100, No. 4, pp. 18–28.

18. Hixon, S. and Rose, R., eds. *Official Proceedings of the Democratic National Convention, 1972.*

19. Ibid.

20. Ibid.

21. Ibid.

22. Hixon, S. and Rose, R., eds. *Official Proceedings of the Democratic National Convention, 1972*, was an

invaluable aid in refreshing my memory about the 1972 convention and the source of statements by participants.

23. McGovern launched his national campaign with little money and party support. He had mobilized many young stars: Bill Clinton ran his campaign in Texas along with fellow Yale Law classmate Hillary Rodham; Sandy Berger wrote speeches. All three would one day work in the White House, but not McGovern.

24. Eagleton was reelected to the Senate in 1974 and 1980. He retired from public life in 1986.

25. Hixon, S. and Rose, R., eds. *Official Proceedings of the Democratic National Convention, 1972.*

Chapter 22: Watergate

1. Bernard Barker, Virgilio Gonzalez, Eugenio Martinez, James McCord, and Frank Sturgis.

2. On the day of our press conference, Woodward and Bernstein had a story linking Howard Hunt, a $100-a-day consultant to White House special counsel Chuck Colson, to two Watergate burglars. Unknown to me, that same day presidential aide John Dean purged Hunt's office safe.

3. Kutler, S. ed. *Abuse of Power: New Nixon Tapes.* Touchstone, New York: 1997, p. 56.

4. Bernstein, C. and Woodward, B. *All the President's Men.* Warner Books, New York: 1974, p. 50.

5. Califano personal papers. Memorandum of interview with Al Baldwin, 28 August 1972.

6. On February 28, 1973, it was again increased to $6.4 million.

7. John Dean reported this to Nixon on September 15, 1972. Watergate tapes, National Archives, Cassette E–3 Segment 1.

8. Kenneth Parkinson, Thomas Jackson, Jr., and Paul O'Brien appeared for defendant Stans and CREEP. James Stoner appeared for defendant Sloan; Henry Rothblatt for the Watergate burglars; William Bittman for Hunt; and Peter Maroulis for Liddy. Assistant U. S. Attorney Earl Silbert represented the Department of Justice.

9. Lawrence F. O'Brien et al. v. James W. McCord et al., Francis Dale et al. v. Lawrence F. O'Brien, Maurice Stans v. Lawrence F. O'Brien. C.A. 1233–72; CA. 1847–72; CA 1854–72. September 21, 1972. United States District Court for the District of Columbia.

10. Watergate Tapes, National Archives, Cassette E–3, Segment 1.

11. Roseboom, E. *History of Presidential Elections from George Washington to Jimmy Carter.* Macmillan, New York: 1979, p. 313.

12. Bernstein, C. and Woodward, B. *All the President's Men.* Warner Books, New York: 1974, p. 254.

13. Kutler, S. ed. *Abuse of Power: New Nixon Tapes.* Touchstone, New York: 1997, p. 202.

14. North Carolina Democrat Sam Ervin, a conservative and a constitutional expert, was named chair; Tennessee Republican Howard Baker, Jr. (son-in-law of the late minority leader Sen. Everett Dirksen of Illinois), vice chair and ranking minority member. A mild-mannered criminal law professor from Georgetown University Law School, Samuel Dash, was appointed majority counsel. Baker selected a Nashville lawyer, Fred Thompson, as minority counsel. Thompson would become an actor and then U.S. senator succeeding to Al Gore's seat in 1994 and would return to acting in 2002.

15. In March 1974, Parkinson was charged with conspiracy to obstruct justice (he was acquitted a year later). During Senate Watergate hearings, John Dean testified that Parkinson had told him that Judge Richey "was going to be helpful whenever he could."

16. Had I known, as John Dean later revealed, that Roemer McPhee met with Richey in his Rose Garden over the March 2 weekend in the middle of the pending subpoena battle, I would have been certain the judge would rule against us.

17. Simons, H. and Califano, J. eds. *Media and the Law.* Praeger, New York: 1976, p. 17.

18. Larry O'Brien and I had a difficult time finding another Washington law firm willing to represent

him and the DNC and risk antagonizing the Nixon administration. Finally, Edward Morgan of Welch & Morgan volunteered.

19. Kutler, S. ed. *Abuse of Power: New Nixon Tapes.* Touchstone, New York: 1997.

20. Kissinger, H. *Years of Upheaval.* Little Brown, Boston: 1982, p. 77.

21. Haig, A. *Inner Circles: How America Changed the World.* Warner, New York: 1992, pp. 339–340.

22. In May 1973, the Pentagon Papers trial proceedings in Los Angeles revealed that the Nixon administration, as early as 1969, had tapped the phones of reporters and government officials suspected of leaking information.

23. Bernstein, C. and Woodward, B. *All the President's Men.* Warner Books, New York: 1974, p. 151.

24. As an Army JAG captain, Sullivan had defended the Presidio 27, white soldiers in San Francisco who in 1968 staged a sit-in to protest the Vietnam War, linking their arms and singing "We Shall Overcome." They were charged with mutiny, a capital offense. Soon after his successful defense of the protestors, Sullivan became the only Army captain ever ordered over to Vietnam with only six months left to serve. A San Francisco paper picked up the story, as did Walter Cronkite, who ran several "Where is Captain Sullivan Now?" pieces on the *CBS Evening News.* Sullivan said, "If you send me, I'll go." Bowing to public outrage, on the eve of Sullivan's departure Army Secretary Stanly Resor canceled his orders. Wowed by Sullivan's handling of the case and its aftermath, Ed Williams hired him immediately upon his release from the Army. Sullivan would represent Oliver North during the Senate's Iran-Contra investigation.

25. Cohen would become one of the *Post*'s top columnists; he wrote about the Agnew situation in his book *A Heartbeat Away.* Viking, New York: 1974.

26. Califano personal papers, letter to John Bradenas, 25 September 1973.

27. Graham, K. *Personal History.* Vintage Books, New York: 1997.

28. Over my years in the White House, the President received more vitriolic mail for his pursuit of racial justice than for his Vietnam policies. When Johnson sent his fair-housing bill to Congress in 1966, it prompted some of the most vicious mail he received on any subject.

29. Charles Colson, John Ehrlichman, H. R. Haldeman, Robert Mardian, John Mitchell, Kenneth Parkinson, and Gordon Strachan.

30. Califano personal papers, memorandum for the record. July 17, 1974.

31. Califano personal papers, letter to FBI Director Clarence Kelly. July 24, 1974.

Chapter 23: Putting the First Amendment First

1. Califano personal papers, letter to Geyelin. May 17, 1974.

2. Califano personal papers, letter from Geyelin. May 20, 1974.

3. Califano personal papers, letter to Colby, May 1, 1975.

4. Califano personal papers, May 24, 1976.

5. Letter of July 27, 1976.

Chapter 25: The Last Secretary of Health, Education, and Welfare

1. Sullivan, J. F. *Special Ethics.* Holy Cross College, Worcester: 1931, pp. 280–281.

2. Haas, R. *Power to Persuade.* Houghton Mifflin, New York: 1994, p. 120.

3. Califano personal papers, memorandum for the record, August 3, 1978.

4. Public papers of the President, Lyndon Johnson, 1968–69, vol. 1, p. 14, January 2, 1968.

5. In August 1979 the Immigration and Naturalization Service followed with a temporary order to cease denying homosexuals entry to the U.S. It was not until 1990 that this policy was enacted as federal law in the Immigration Reform Act.

6. "Mr. Califano on abortion." *Washington Post.* 15 January 1977, p. A18.
7. Califano personal correspondence with President Carter, February 25, 1978.
8. Frederickson, D. *The Recombinant DNA Controversy: A Memoir.* ASM, Washington, DC: 2001, p. 154.
9. Sullivan, J. F. *Special Ethics.* Holy Cross College, Worcester: 1931, p. 42.

Chapter 26: What's Next?

1. Califano personal papers, memorandum for the record, August 15, 1980.

Chapter 27: My Own Law Firm

1. Califano, J. A. *1982 Report on Drug Abuse and Alcoholism.* Warner Books, New York: 1982.
2. Rosellini, L. "Haig and Califano team up again for hearings in Senate." *New York Times.* 4 January 1981, p. 10.
3. On March 30, 1981, by John W. Hinckley, who would be represented by my former colleagues Vince Fuller and Greg Craig of Williams & Connolly.
4. Hoffman, D. "Fund paid for Haig legal aid." *Washington Post.* 9 June 1984, p. A1.

Chapter 28: Hilary Paley Byers

1. The Federal National Mortgage Association, privatized by President Johnson in 1968.
2. Her first was John Hearst, one of five sons of the newspaper mogul William Randolph Hearst; her third was Walter Hirshon, a Wall Street stockbroker, who had died by the time I met her.
3. The poem:
Good wishes on your wedding day, a shower of them too.
Like blossoms in the bride's bouquet,
I'm wishing to you two.
May health and fortune richly blessed provide life's kindly weather.
And always may true happiness attend your lives together.

Chapter 29: Lawyer in the House

1. Califano personal papers, memorandum for the record, June 24, 1982.
2. Califano personal papers, letter to Califano from John Shad, 18 August 1982.
3. McQueen later would clean up corruption in the Javits Center as its inspector general. In 1997 he became the center's president.
4. Califano personal papers, letter to Califano from Richard McCormick, 17 August 1982.
5. Report by the committee on standards of official conduct pursuant to H. Res. 518. (Rep. No. 97–965). GPO, Washington, DC: 1983.
6. Ibid.
7. Ibid.
8. Ibid.
9. Ibid.
10. Ibid.

Chapter 30: From Washington to Wall Street

1. Lynk became Dewey's first black partner and was president of the D.C. Bar Association in 1996. He left the firm in 1999 to become the Kiewit Foundation Professor of Law and the Legal Profession at Arizona State University College of Law.
2. Council of the District of Columbia. *Human Rights Act of 1977 Amendment Act of 1987*. D.C. Law 7–50. December 10, 1987.
3. In 1991 Michael Eisner and Wells lured Litvack to Disney as its senior vice president and general counsel.
4. The suit was eventually settled.
5. In 1907 New York governor Charles Evans Hughes signed into law a bill sponsored by Assemblyman Sherman Moreland that gave the governor power to investigate departments or agencies and to develop legislative proposals. In 1963 Governor Nelson Rockefeller invoked it to investigate alcoholic-beverage control; in 1976 Governor Carey to investigate nursing-home corruption; in 1985 Cuomo to investigate police violence.
6. The others were Richard Emery, staff counsel to the New York Civil Liberties Union; Patricia Hynes, former executive assistant and chief of the Official Corruption and Special Prosecutions Unit of the Office of the United States Attorney of the Southern District of New York; James Magavern, former counsel to the state comptroller and head of that office's Division of Legal Services; Bernard Meyer, former associate judge of the New York Court of Appeals; Bishop Emerson Moore.
7. Califano personal papers. Press release from Governor Cuomo's office. 15 January 1987.
8. Five years later, on December 13, 1991, while he was still speaker of the Assembly, a federal jury convicted Miller of cheating law clients in a real-estate deal and he was expelled from the legislature. The fraud conviction was overturned on appeal in June 1993.
9. Califano personal papers, memorandum for the record, April 11, 1987.
10. "A history: 15 years of the Institute on Social and Economic Policy in the Middle East." Harvard University, October 1998.
11. Ibid.
12. Califano, J. A. *America's Health Care Revolution: Who Lives? Who Dies? Who Pays?* Random House, New York: 1987.
13. Having a union leader on the board proved a short-lived experiment. Because so many elements of company strategy affected workers or union negotiations, Iacocca created a finance committee that did not include Doug Fraser. That committee (of which I was a member) became the de facto board for discussing and deciding all serious issues; directors not on the finance committee became second-class board members. After Owen Bieber succeeded Fraser as UAW president in 1984, and as board members not on the finance committee increasingly resented their diminished status, Iacocca moved Bieber off in 1991.
14. Califano, J. A. *America's Health Care Revolution: Who Lives? Who Dies? Who Pays?* Random House, New York: 1987.

Chapter 31: A New Life

1. The President sent the reorganization plan to Congress in 1968 and it went into effect without controversy. On July 1, 1973, the Bureau of Narcotics became the Drug Enforcement Agency, still independent of the FBI.
2. Wells died in a helicopter crash in April 1994.
3. As George Rupp and then Lee Bollinger succeeded to the Columbia presidency, each joined the CASA board.

4. Barbara died from complications of her leukemia in January 1996.

5. Over the years, several other committed Americans became CASA board members: Columba Bush, First Lady of Florida; Kenneth Chenault, chairman and CEO of the American Express Company; actress Jamie Lee Curtis; James Dimon, chairman and CEO of Bank One Corporation, president and CEO-designate of J. P. Morgan Chase; Peter Dolan, chairman and CEO of the Bristol-Myers Squibb Company; Mary Fisher; Victor Ganzi, president and CEO of the Hearst Corporation; Leo Kelmenson, chairman of the board of FCB Worldwide; David Kessler, dean of the medical school and vice chancellor for medical affairs at the University of California, San Francisco; Joseph Plumeri, chairman and CEO of the Willis Group Limited; former first lady Nancy Reagan; Shari Redstone, president of National Amusements Inc.; Linda Johnson Rice, president and CEO of Johnson Publishing Inc.; Michael Schulhof; Louis Sullivan, president emeritus of Morehouse School of Medicine; John Sweeney, president of the AFL-CIO; and Michael Wiener, founder and chairman emeritus of Infinity Broadcasting Corporation.

Chapter 33: Confronting Cancer

1. Mike Wiener would become a CASA board member and he and his wife would donate the CASA conference center.

2. The drug levamisole had originally been used by veterinarians who treat worms in animals. Once the FDA approved it as an anticancer drug for humans, the price shot up manyfold.

3. The rosary has five decades of prayers, each comprising one Our Father, ten Hail Marys, and one Glory Be to the Father. While saying each decade, a meditation is made upon a specific mystery: Joyful (Annunciation of Gabriel to Mary, Visitation of Mary to Elizabeth, Birth of Jesus, Presentation of Jesus in the Temple, Finding of Jesus in the Temple); Sorrowful (Agony in the Garden, Scourging at the Pillar, Crowning with Thorns, Carrying of the Cross, Crucifixion); and Glorious (Resurrection of Our Lord, Ascension of Our Lord, Descent of the Holy Spirit, Assumption of Mary, Coronation of Mary). In 2002, the Pope added Luminous mysteries (Baptism of Jesus, Wedding at Cana, Proclamation of Kingdom of God, Transfiguration, Institution of Eucharist).

Index

PUBLICAFFAIRS is a publishing house founded in 1997. It is a tribute to the standards, values, and flair of three persons who have served as mentors to countless reporters, writers, editors, and book people of all kinds, including me.

I. F. STONE, proprietor of *I. F. Stone's Weekly,* combined a commitment to the First Amendment with entrepreneurial zeal and reporting skill and became one of the great independent journalists in American history. At the age of eighty, Izzy published *The Trial of Socrates,* which was a national bestseller. He wrote the book after he taught himself ancient Greek.

BENJAMIN C. BRADLEE was for nearly thirty years the charismatic editorial leader of *The Washington Post.* It was Ben who gave the *Post* the range and courage to pursue such historic issues as Watergate. He supported his reporters with a tenacity that made them fearless, and it is no accident that so many became authors of influential, best-selling books.

ROBERT L. BERNSTEIN, the chief executive of Random House for more than a quarter century, guided one of the nation's premier publishing houses. Bob was personally responsible for many books of political dissent and argument that challenged tyranny around the globe. He is also the founder and was the longtime chair of Human Rights Watch, one of the most respected human rights organizations in the world.

·   ·   ·

For fifty years, the banner of Public Affairs Press was carried by its owner Morris B. Schnapper, who published Gandhi, Nasser, Toynbee, Truman, and about 1,500 other authors. In 1983 Schnapper was described by *The Washington Post* as "a redoubtable gadfly." His legacy will endure in the books to come.

Peter Osnos, *Publisher*